HEINLE & HEINLE'S

COMPLETE GUIDE to the TOEFL® TEST

CBT EDITION

BRUCE ROGERS

ECONOMICS INSTITUTE

HEINLE & HEINLE

THOMSON LEARNING

United States • Australia • Canada • Mexico • Singapore • Spain • United Kingdom

HEINLE & HEINLE ™

THOMSON LEARNING

Editorial Director/ESL:
Nancy Leonhardt

Acquisitions Editor/ESL
Eric Bredenberg

Marketing Manager/Academic ESL
Charlotte Sturdy

Marketing Manager/Global ESL:
Amy Mabley

Production Editor:
Sarah Cogliano

Print Buyer:
Mary Beth Hennebury

Interior Designer:
Rollins Design and Production

Cover Designer:
ColourMark

Illustrator:
Markus Maxim Dubrowski—Mdesigns

Cover Image:
© Paul A. Souders/CORBIS

Compositor:
PRD Group

Text Printer/Binder:
Von Hoffmann Graphics

Library of Congress Cataloging-in-Publication Data
Rogers, Bruce
Heinle & Heinle's complete guide to the TOEFL test, CBT ed. / Bruce Rogers.
p. cm.
ISBN 0-8384-0226-7
1. English language—Textbooks for foreign speakers. 2. Test of English as a foreign language—Study guides.
3. English language—Examinations—Study guides. I. Title: Complete guide to the TOEFL test, CBT ed. II. Title.
PE1128 .R63443 2000
428'.0076—dc21   00-044845

ASIA (including India):
Thomson Learning
60 Albert Street #15-01
Albert Complex
Singapore 189969
Tel 65 336-6411
Fax 65 336-7411

AUSTRALIA/NEW ZEALAND:
Nelson
102 Dodds Street
South Melbourne
Victoria 3205
Australia
Tel 61 (0)3 9685-4111
Fax 61 (0)3 9685-4199

LATIN AMERICA:
Thomson Learning
Seneca, 53
Colonia Polanco
11560 México D.F. México
Tel (525) 281-2906
Fax (525) 281-2656

CANADA:
Nelson
1120 Birchmount Road
Toronto, Ontario
Canada M1K 5G4
Tel (416) 752-9100
Fax (416) 752-8102

UK/EUROPE/MIDDLE EAST:
Thomson Learning
Berkshire House
168-173 High Holborn
London, WC1V 7AA
United Kingdom
Tel 44 (0)020 497-1422
Fax 44 (0)020 497-1426

SPAIN (includes Portugual):
Paraninfo
Calle Magallanes, 25
28015 Madrid
España
Tel 34 (0)91 446-3350
Fax 34 (0)91 445-6218

ISBN: 0-8384-0226-7

Contents

SECTION 3: Guide to Reading

SECTION 4: Guide to Essay Writing

Two Complete Practice Tests

Preface
About this Book

If you are preparing for the TOEFL® test, you are not alone. Almost a million people all over the world took the test last year. A high score on this test is an essential step in being admitted to graduate or undergraduate programs at almost all colleges and universities in North America. But preparing for this test can be a difficult, frustrating experience. Perhaps you haven't taken many standardized, multiple choice tests such as the TOEFL® test. Perhaps you are not familiar with the format for the TOEFL® test. Maybe you've taken the TOEFL® test once but were not satisfied with your score, or maybe you've taken it several times but can't seem to improve your score beyond a certain point.

And now that the TOEFL® test is computer-based, you may be even more confused. What computer skills are required? What specialized tactics are needed to get the top scores? How can you best practice for the test?

More than ever, you need a guide. That's why this book was written—to guide those people preparing for this important exam to maximum scores.

Heinle & Heinle's Complete Guide to the TOEFL® Test, CBT Edition is the most complete, accurate, and up-to-date TOEFL preparation book available. It is based on years of research and on years of classroom experience teaching preparation classes for the TOEFL® test in the United States and abroad. It is simply written and clearly organized and is suitable for any intermediate or advanced student of English as a second or foreign language, no matter what computer background he or she may have.

Heinle & Heinle's Complete Guide to the TOEFL® Test, CBT Edition offers a step-by-step program designed to make you feel confident and well prepared when you sit down in front of the computer on testing day. It teaches you the test-taking techniques needed to do well on the new version of the test. It helps you polish both the language skills and computer skills needed for the exam. It generally makes you a smarter test-taker. And the *Guide* is an efficient way to prepare for the TOEFL® test; by concentrating only on the points that are actually tested on the TOEFL® test, it lets you make the most of your preparation period and never wastes your time.

About this Edition: What's New?

Heinle & Heinle's Complete Guide to the TOEFL® Test, CBT Edition contains many of the same explanations and exercises as the second edition of this text. However, the text has been completely updated to reflect the new, computer-based format of the TOEFL® test.

In the Listening section, visual cues (photographs) now accompany the Preview and Review Tests to give them the same feel as the Listening section on the actual computer-based test. Questions are now written out as they are on the actual test. New lessons about computer-unique Listening items have been added.

In the Structure section of the computer-based test, Sentence Completion and Error Identification items are no longer presented in separate sections. To reflect this change, lessons about both types of items have been combined in this edition of the book.

There are several types of computer-unique items new to the Reading section. To prepare you for these, new lessons have been added.

Because of the increased importance of the Essay Writing section of the test (it now counts for about half of the grade in Section 2), Section 4 of the book has been expanded and there are more topics for practice.

The two practice tests have also been revised and reformatted to simulate taking the exam on computer.

The TOEFL® Mastery™ CD-ROM that accompanies the text features exercises involving every type of item found on the computer-based test.

Not all changes were made in response to the changes in the format of the TOEFL® test. Teachers and students who have used this text have offered valuable insights and comments through letters and e-mail messages. My own students in preparation classes for the TOEFL® test have also been a great source of feedback.

Organization of this Book

- **Getting Started** This section serves as an introduction to the exam.

    - **Questions and Answers about the TOEFL® Test** This provides you with basic information about the format of the computer-based test, guides you through the process of registering for the exam, and helps you understand the revised scoring system.
    - **Twelve Keys to High Scores** This presents the "secrets" of being a good test-taker: arranging your preparation time, using the process of elimination to make the best guess, coping with test anxiety, pacing yourself during the test, and other important techniques.
    - **What It's Like to Take the Computer-Based TOEFL® Test** This provides a preview of the testing experience and lets you know what it will feel like to take the test at a typical center.
    - **Guide to Testing on Computer** This provides an overview of the skills you will need to take the test on computer.

The main section of the book is divided into four parts, reflecting the Listening, Structure, Reading, and Essay Writing sections of the test. Each of these parts consists of the following components:

- An introduction to each test section with basic strategies
- A full-length preview test to give you a feel for each part of the test and to provide a basis for understanding the lessons.
- Lessons that break down the knowledge and skills needed for each part of the test into comprehensible "bites" of information. Each of the 42 lessons in the book contains sample items that illustrate exactly how the point brought up in that lesson is tested on the TOEFL® test. Furthermore, each lesson contains one or more exercises that practice the relevant points.
- Review Tests that go over the points brought up in the lessons. These tests put together the points practiced in isolation in the lessons.
- Mini-Lessons (found at the end of each section) covering important testing points which require more time to master than points brought up in the lessons. You should begin studying and working the exercises in the Mini-Lessons as soon as you begin each section of the *Guide*.

- **Guide to Listening** This section is divided into two parts: Part A: Dialogues and Part B: Longer Talks. The exercises are intended to be used with the audio program that accompanies the *Guide*. The Mini-Lessons for this section teach common idioms that are often heard in Part A.
- **Guide to Structure** This section categorizes common grammatical points tested in Sentence Completion items and typical errors found in Error Identification items. The Mini-Lessons for this section cover preposition usage.
- **Guide to Reading** This section prepares you for the third section of the test by suggesting reading skills and presenting the various types of items you will encounter in the third section of the TOEFL® test. The Mini-Lessons for this section provide exercises for vocabulary development.

- **Guide to Essay Writing** This section presents the best methods to plan your essay, write the introduction, body, and conclusion, and edit and improve your essay. There are student-written essays that illustrate what an essay at each of the six levels looks like. The Mini-Lessons for this section consist of additional essay topics for further practice.
- **Two Complete Practice Tests** Taking practice tests is one of the best ways to get ready for the TOEFL® test. The practice tests in this book simulate the computer-based test in format and content.

The text is also accompanied by a listening program on cassette tapes or audio CD-ROMs.*

Tapescripts and Answer Keys are also available as a separate text, or online at www.heinle.com. They contain a script (written version) of all the spoken material in the listening program and provide answers and in some cases explanations for the exercises and tests.

Suggestions for Using this Book

Heinle & Herinle's Complete Guide to the TOEFL® Test, CBT Edition is designed to be used either as a textbook for preparation classes for the TOEFL® test or as a tool for individuals preparing for the exam by themselves. Whether working alone or in a group, you should begin your preparation for the TOEFL® test by reading the introductory chapters in the section of the book titled **Getting Started.** You can then work through the book in the order in which it is written or begin with the section in which you are weakest. You can determine which area is your weakest by looking at the scores from a previous test or by using one of the practice tests as a diagnostic tool.

The CD-ROM is meant to provide hands-on experience in answering all types of computer questions. The material on the CD-ROM has been divided, like the book, into Listening, Structure, Reading, and Writing sections. Each of these sections is meant to supplement the corresponding part of the text. Because of the randomization of items, you can use these computerized exercises over and over—at home, in class, or in a computer lab.

Although it is certainly important to get exposure to computers, the computer skills required to take the test are relatively basic and the focus should be on learning language skills, not developing computer proficiency.

Following are the amounts of time required to cover each segment of the *Guide.* Keep in mind that these times are very approximate and do not include review sessions.

Getting Started	1–3 hours
Guide to Listening	12–16 hours
Guide to Structure	20–25 hours
Guide to Reading	15–20 hours
Guide to Essay Writing	3–8 hours
Two Complete Practice Tests	6–8 hours

I welcome your comments, questions, and suggestions. Please feel free to contact me at the addresses below.

Bruce Rogers

c/o Heinle & Heinle Publishers
20 Park Plaza
Boston, MA 02116
E-mail Address: brogers@colorado.edu

*Audio tapes and audio CD-ROMs are sold separately.

About the Author

Bruce Rogers has taught English as a Second Language and test-preparation courses at the Economics Institute in Boulder, Colorado since 1979. He has also taught in special programs in Indonesia, Vietnam, South Korea, and the Czech Republic. He is the author of *The Complete Guide to TOEFL: Practice Tests* (Heinle & Heinle Publishers), *The Complete Guide to the TOEIC Test* (International Thompson Publishing), and *TOEFL Success* (Peterson's, Princeton, New Jersey). He has also helped develop the software programs *TOEFL Mastery* and *TOEIC Mastery* (American Language Academy).

Acknowledgments

I would like to thank the following professionals for their comments and suggestions during the development of this text:

Steven A. Stupak	Korea International Human Resources Development Center
Virginia Hamori	American Language Institute, American University of Paris
Jim Price	International Language Center, Bangkok
Stephen Thewlis	San Francisco State University
Connie Monroe	Queens College
Steven Horowitz	Central Washington University
Dan Douglas	Iowa State University
Frederick O'Connor	Washington State University
Claire Bradin	Michigan State University
Karen Avila-John	University of Dayton
James Beaton	Boston University
Debra Dean	University of Akron
Glenn Hawkes	University of Georgia
Thomas Leverett	Southern Illinois University
John Levis	North Carolina State University
Maryann O'Brien	Interlink Language Center, Colorado School of Mines
Ian Palmer	LASPAU, Harvard University
Ellen Polsky	University of Colorado
Mary Kay Purcell	University of Evansville
Antonina N. Rodgers	Northern Virginia Community College
Seth Sicroff	University of California at Davis
Ayse Gursel Stromsdorfer	St. Louis University
Ted Tucker	China Institute of Technology, Taiwan
Nelleke Van Deusen-Scholl	University of California, Berkeley

And again, special thanks to the students in my preparation courses for the TOEFL® test at the Economics Institute.

Photo Credits

Photos on the following pages are the exclusive property of Heinle & Heinle publishers: 2, 3, 10, 11, 12, 13, 14, 15, 16, 18, 27, 32, 33, 37, 48, 49, 50, 51, 53, 57, 61, 62, 63, 69, 70, 73, 76, 77, 82, 83, 84, 86, 87, 88, 90, 91, 109, 111, 114, 508, 509, 510, 511, 512, 513, 515, 516, 517, 541, 542, 543, 544, 545, 546, 547, 548, 549, 551.

Cover © Paul A. Souders/CORBIS
Page xi © Paul A. Souders/CORBIS
Page 1 © Robert Holmes/CORBIS
Page 9 Digital Imagery© copyright 2000 PhotoDisc, Inc.
Page 10 **Top and Bottom:** Digital Imagery© copyright 2000 PhotoDisc, Inc.
Page 14 **Top:** PDigital Imagery© copyright 2000 PhotoDisc, Inc.
Page 16 **Right:** Digital Imagery© copyright 2000 PhotoDisc, Inc.
Page 18 Digital Imagery© copyright 2000 PhotoDisc, Inc.
Page 22 Digital Imagery© copyright 2000 PhotoDisc, Inc.
Page 44 Digital Imagery© copyright 2000 PhotoDisc, Inc.
Page 49 Digital Imagery© copyright 2000 PhotoDisc, Inc.
Page 50 **Top:** Digital Imagery© copyright 2000 PhotoDisc, Inc.
Page 51 **Middle:** © Pablo Corral V/CORBIS
Page 54 Digital Imagery© copyright 2000 PhotoDisc, Inc.
Page 56 Digital Imagery© copyright 2000 PhotoDisc, Inc.
Page 65 Digital Imagery© copyright 2000 PhotoDisc, Inc.
Page 71 Digital Imagery© copyright 2000 PhotoDisc, Inc.
Page 78 Digital Imagery© copyright 2000 PhotoDisc, Inc.
Page 86 © TSM/Charles Gupton/1999
Page 89 Digital Imagery© copyright 2000 PhotoDisc, Inc.
Page 90 Digital Imagery© copyright 2000 PhotoDisc, Inc.
Page 91 Digital Imagery© copyright 2000 PhotoDisc, Inc.
Page 108 Digital Imagery© copyright 2000 PhotoDisc, Inc.

Page 113 Digital Imagery© copyright 2000 PhotoDisc, Inc.
Page 135 © Danny Lehman/CORBIS
Page 319 © Joel W. Rogers/CORBIS
Page 455 © The Purcell Team/CORBIS
Page 500 © Kelly-Mooney Photography/CORBIS
Page 507 Digital Imagery© copyright 2000 PhotoDisc, Inc.
Page 508 **Top:** Digital Imagery© copyright 2000 PhotoDisc, Inc.
Page 510 **Top:** Digital Imagery© copyright 2000 PhotoDisc, Inc.
Page 512 **Bottom:** Digital Imagery© copyright 2000 PhotoDisc, Inc.
Page 514 © Archive Photos
Page 543 **Bottom:** Digital Imagery© copyright 2000 PhotoDisc, Inc.
Page 544 **Top:** Digital Imagery© copyright 2000 PhotoDisc, Inc.
Bottom: © TSM/Charles Gupton/1999
Page 547 **Right:** Digital Imagery© copyright 2000 PhotoDisc, Inc.
Page 550 Digital Imagery© copyright 2000 PhotoDisc, Inc.

Getting Started

University of Maryland

Questions and Answers about the Computer-Based TOEFL® Test

Q: What is the TOEFL® test?

A: TOEFL stands for *Test of English as a Foreign Language.* The TOEFL® test is designed to measure the English-language ability of people who do not speak English as their first language and who plan to study at colleges and universities in North America.

Educational Testing Service (ETS) of Princeton, New Jersey prepares and administers the TOEFL® test. This organization produces many other standardized tests.

Although there are other standardized tests of English, the TOEFL® test is by far the most important in North America. ETS has offered this exam since 1965. Each year, almost a million people take the TOEFL® test at testing centers all over the world.

Q: And what is the computer-based TOEFL® test?

A: Up until July, 1998 the TOEFL® test was given as a paper-and-pencil based multiple-choice test. However, at that time, ETS introduced the computer-based version of the test in the United States, Canada, Latin America, the Middle East, Africa, and certain countries in Asia. The Listening and Structure sections are computer adaptive, while the Reading Section of the test is a "linear" computerized test.

Q: Computer adaptive? What does that mean?

A: A computer adaptive test adapts to individual test-takers. Each time you answer a question, the computer program adjusts to your responses when determining which question to present to you next. The program chooses questions from a large pool of items that are classified according to difficulty. The first question in each section will be of medium difficulty. If you answer that question correctly, then the next question tends to be more difficult. If you answer it incorrectly, then the next question tends to be easier. The program continues presenting questions based on your answers, with the goal of determining your exact level of ability. In the computer adaptive sections, you may not skip any items, and once you have confirmed an answer, you cannot change it. However, in the Reading section, which is "linear" you may change your answers and work on items in any order.

Here is a simplified diagram of part of a computer adaptive test section:

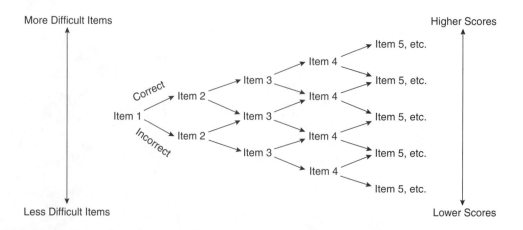

Q: What format does the computer-based test follow? How long does it take to complete?

A: The computer-based test is divided into four sections: Listening, Structure, Reading, and Essay Writing, each with its own time limit. The four sections are always given in the same order.

Before the actual test, you must take a tutorial that demonstrates the computer skills needed to take the test. This part is ungraded, of course, and untimed. Most test-takers take about 40 minutes to complete this section. The first three sections consist mainly of multiple-choice questions while Essay Writing is a single essay-writing item.

Computer-Based Format for the TOEFL® Test			
Tutorial Untimed—Average 40 minutes			
1. Listening 40-60 minutes	30-50 questions	**(Computer adaptive)**	
Part A: Dialogues	11-17 items		
Part B: Longer Talks	4-6 talks/conversations 3-6 questions per talk		
2. Structure 15-20 minutes	20-25 questions	**(Computer adaptive)**	
Sentence Completion and Error Recognition			
Mandatory break	10 minutes		
3. Reading 70-90 minutes	4-5 readings	44-70 questions	**(Linear)**
4. Essay Writing 1 essay prompt	30 minutes		
Total Time: Approximately 4 hours			

Q: What are the main differences between the paper-based test and the computer-based test?

A: The first three sections of the computer-based test generally have fewer items. For example, on the most recent version of the paper-based test, there were 40 Structure items, while on the computer-based version there are 20 to 25. Another difference is the use of visuals in the Listening section. There are also some new "computer-unique" item-types in Listening and in Reading. And there is a new scoring system.

Q: How does the new scoring system work?

A: On the paper-based test, overall scores ranged from a high of 677 to a low of 200. On the computer-based test, the overall range of scores is from 0 to 300. The scores in each section range from 0 to 30. To calculate the overall score, these scores are added, multiplied by ten, then divided by three. Half of the score for the second section is based on your score on the Essay Writing section. ETS has published a *concordance*—a table that converts scores on the new test to scores on the paper-based version. Here are some equivalencies taken from that concordance:

Paper-Based Score	Computer-Based Score
677	300
650	280
600	250
550	213
500	173
450	133
400	97
350	63

You can download the complete concordance from the TOEFL® Web site.

Q: Are the computer-based test scores simply based on the number of correct answers?

A: No. Test-takers A and B may get the same number of correct answers on one section but test-taker A may get a higher score because he or she answered more difficult items correctly.

Q: When will I receive my test scores?

A: You will receive unofficial on-screen scores right after you take the test. The scores for Listening and Reading will be final scores, but the score for Structure and your overall score will be reported as a range of scores.

Here is an example of what these on-screen scores look like:

Listening	20
Structure	6-25
Reading	24
Overall	167-230

What your final scores will be depends on the score you receive on the Essay Writing section (which cannot be instantly graded). The Essay Writing score ranges from 0-6. Here are some examples of scores you might receive, depending on your essay score:

Essay Score	Structure Score	Overall Score
0	6-7	167-170
1	9-10	177-180
3	15-16	198-201
5	22-23	220-223
6	24-35	227-230

You, and the schools that you designate should receive final scores within two weeks if you word-process the essay. If you handwrite the essay, you should receive scores in 4-6 weeks.

Q: How are universities notified of my scores?

A: After the test is over, you will be able to choose up to four universities from a pull-down menu. You may also request that your score be sent to additional schools for an additional fee.

Q: What is a passing score on the TOEFL® test?

A: There isn't any. Each university has its own standards for admission, so you should check the catalogues of universities you are interested in or contact their admission offices. Most undergraduate programs require scores between 173 and 213 (between 500 and 550 on the paper-based test) and most graduate programs ask for scores between 195 and 250 (between 525 and 600 on the paper-based test). Recently, there has a been a tendency for universities to raise their minimum requirements for the TOEFL® test.

Q: If I feel I haven't done well on the TOEFL® test can I cancel my scores?

A: Yes. Right after the test, you may either cancel your scores or view them. You may NOT cancel your scores once you have looked at them. However, if you are not satisfied with your unofficial scores, you can direct ETS to NOT send them on to any universities. Keep in mind that, even if you cancel your scores, you cannot take the test again until the next calendar month. It is generally NOT a good idea to cancel scores. You may have done better on the test than you thought you did.

Q: Can I get my scores by phone?

A: Yes. Call 1-888-TOEFL-44 in North America and 1-609-771-7267 elsewhere 14 days after the test (4-5 weeks after the test if you handwrite the essay). ETS charges a fee for this service.

Q: How many times may I take the computer-based TOEFL® test?

A: There is no limit; you may take it as often as you like. However, you may not take the test more than once in any calendar month.

Q: How do I register for the computer-based TOEFL® test?

A: There are a number of ways to register. You can register for the computer-based test by telephone if you have a credit card (VISA, MasterCard, or American Express). In North America, you can call Prometric TOEFL® Test Registration Center at 800-GO-TOEFL (1-800-468-6335) or you may call your local test center. There is a complete list of these in the *TOEFL® Information Bulletin*. Outside North America, call the Regional Registration Center for the country where you live. These are listed in the *Bulletin*. You'll be given a confirmation number and be told when and where to report.

You can also register by mail. If you are in North America, you can use the CBT Voucher Test Request Form found in the *Bulletin*. You can pay with credit card, check, or money order. You will receive a CBT voucher in several weeks. After that, you can call a center to schedule an appointment. If you live outside North America, you need to fill out the International Test Scheduling Form and mail it to your Regional Registration Center. Payment may be in the form of check, credit card, money order, bank draft, or UNESCO coupons.

Outside North America, you may also register by faxing the International Test Scheduling Form to the Regional Registration Center for your country. Fax numbers for these centers are listed in the *Bulletin*.

You can register in person by visiting the nearest testing site, and in the near future, you will probably be able to register on-line by going to the TOEFL® Web site.

Q: What computer skills do I need to take the computer-based TOEFL® test?

A: The computer skills required are fairly basic. You really only need to know how to point to and click on a choice with a mouse, how to scroll up and down through a document, and how to access help if you need it. If you choose to type your essay on the computer (rather than write it by hand) you will also need basic word-processing skills. Before you take the test at the center, you must complete a tutorial to make sure you have mastered the skills you need.

Q: Where is the computer-based test offered?

A: It is given at designated test centers, universities, bi-national institutes, and ETS field offices all over the world. There are two types of test centers, permanent and mobile. Tests are given at mobile centers only during certain months. A complete list of testing centers is given in the *Bulletin*.

The computer-based test is not offered at nearly as many centers as the paper-based test was. Depending where you live, you may have to travel a rather long distance to take the test.

Q: Can I choose whether to take the computer-based test or the paper-based test?

A: No. Once the computer-based test has been phased in, you will no longer have the option of taking the paper-based test.

Q: How much will the computer-based test cost?

A: It will cost US$110. (The paper-based version of the test had cost US$45.) If you need to reschedule the test, you will have to pay a US$40 rescheduling fee.

Q: What should I bring with me to the exam site?

A: You should bring the following:

- Your passport
- Your appointment confirmation number
- Your CBT voucher, if you are using one
- A list of the universities that you want your scores sent to

Don't bring any reference books, such as dictionaries or textbooks, or any electronic devices, such as translators, cellular phones, or calculators. You are not permitted to smoke, eat, or drink in the test center. You do not have to bring pencils or paper.

Q: Has the format of the Institutional TOEFL® test also changed?

A: No, the Institutional TOEFL® test (a form of the test given by English language schools and other institutions) is still a paper-based test.

Q: Will there be other changes to the TOEFL® test in the near future?

A: Quite possibly. ETS has been working on a project called "TOEFL 2000" that could change the test even more dramatically within the next few years. For example, in the future, the test may routinely include a test of your speaking ability.

Q: How can I get more information about the TOEFL® test?

A: You can contact ETS via e-mail or get updated information about the test from their home page on the World Wide Web:

E-mail: toefl@ets.org
Web site: http://www.toefl.org

Twelve Keys to High Scores

 Key #1: Increase your general knowledge of English.

There are two types of knowledge that will lead to high scores on the TOEFL® test:

- A knowledge of the tactics used by good test takers and the "tricks" of the test (which you will learn by using this *Guide*)
- A general command of English (which must be built up over a long period of study)

Following a step-by-step preparation program for the TOEFL® test such as this one will familiarize you with the tactics you need to raise your scores. The practice tests that are part of this program will help you polish these techniques.

But no matter how many test-taking tips you learn, you won't do well on the test without a solid foundation of English language study. The best way to increase your general knowledge of English is simply to use English as much as possible. Other classes in English will be useful, as will opportunities to speak, read, write, or listen to English.

Some people who are preparing for the TOEFL® test think that conversation classes and practice are a waste of time because speaking skills are not tested on the exam. In fact, one of the best ways to get ready for the exam is to speak English whenever you can. Not only will you improve your ability to listen to everyday English, but you'll also learn to think in English. You can improve your listening comprehension skills by going to English language lectures and movies. Listening to news and informational broadcasts on the radio is especially useful.

Reading books, magazines, and newspapers in English can help you prepare for the Reading section of the test.

One of your most important jobs is to systematically improve your vocabulary. Vocabulary building will help you, not just in the Reading section, but throughout the exam. You may want to keep a personal vocabulary list. When you come across an unfamiliar word, look it up in a dictionary and write the word and its definition in a notebook.

 Key #2: Get as much information about the test as possible.

It's important to have up-to-date information about the test. This is especially true now that the test is computer-based. The first step is to obtain the current edition of the *TOEFL® Information Bulletin for Computer-Based Testing*. A new edition is published for each "testing year" (July to July). These are widely available in North America at English language schools, international student programs, or university admission offices. Outside North America, they can be obtained at many U.S. cultural or educational facilities, bi-national centers and libraries, U.S. Information Service offices, and many other locations. You may also order them directly from ETS:

Address: TOEFL/ETS Services
             P.O. Box 6151
             Princeton, NJ 08541-6151

Telephone: (609) 771-7100
Fax: (609) 771-7500
E-mail: toefl@ets.org

If you have Internet access, you can download a bulletin from the ETS Web site: http://www.toefl.org

It's also a good idea for you to get a copy of the CD-ROM put out by ETS, called *TOEFL Sampler.* This CD-ROM contains basically the same tutorial that you will take on testing day. There are also examples of all the item-types you will see on the test.

 Key #3:   Make the most of your preparation time.

You need to train for the TOEFL® test just as you would train for any important competitive event. Obviously, the sooner you can start training, the better, but no matter when you begin, you need to get the most out of your preparation time.

Make a time management chart. Draw up an hour-by-hour schedule of your week's activities. Block out those hours when you are busy with classes, work, social activities, and other responsibilities. Then pencil in times for preparation for the TOEFL® test. You will remember more of what you study if you schedule a few hours every day or several times weekly than if you schedule all your study time in large blocks on weekends. During that last week before the testing date, reduce your study time and begin to relax.

If possible, reserve a special place where you do nothing but work on preparation for the TOEFL® test separate from where you do your regular homework or other work.

One good method of studying for the TOEFL® test is the "30-5-5" method:

■ Study for thirty minutes.
■ Take a five-minute break—leave your desk and do something completely different.
■ When you return, take five minutes to review what you studied before the break and preview what you are going to study next.

Incidentally, it's a great idea to meet regularly with a small group of people who are also preparing for the TOEFL® test. Research has shown that this study group approach to test preparation is very effective.

 Key #4:   Be in good physical condition when you take the exam.

The most important physical concern is to not become exhausted during your preparation time. If you aren't getting enough sleep, you'll need to reduce your study time or another activity. This is especially important in the last few days before the exam.

 Key #5:   Get some computer practice.

According to research done by ETS, the level of computer skill and experience that a person has before taking the computer-based test does not influence his or her scores.

You should use the enclosed TOEFL® Mastery™ CD-ROM. It closely simulates the experience of taking a computer-adaptive test.

The most difficult skill to master is the ability to word-process an essay. Although you have the choice of handwriting the essay or word-processing it, you are better off word-processing it.

As mentioned in the *Preface,* however, your focus in preparing for the TOEFL® test should not be on learning how to use a computer but on learning English. No more than 15–20% of your preparation time should involve working at a computer.

 Key #6: Be familiar with the format and directions.

You should have a clear "map" of the TOEFL® test in your mind. Then as you're taking the exam, you'll know exactly where you are and what's coming next. You can familiarize yourself with the basic format of the TOEFL® test by looking over the chart on page xi.

The directions for each part of the computer-based TOEFL® test will always be the same. If you're familiar with the directions, you won't have to waste time reading them during the test. You can become familiar with these directions by studying the directions for the practice tests in this book.

 Key #7: Organize the last few days before the exam carefully.

You shouldn't try to "cram" (study intensively) during the last few days before the exam. Last-minute studying can leave you exhausted and you need to be alert for the test. The night before the exam, don't study at all. Find your passport, confirmation number, CBT voucher (if you have one), and anything else you'll need; then go to a movie, take a long walk, or do something else to take your mind off the test. Go to bed when you usually do.

If you are testing in the morning, have breakfast before you leave. Wear comfortable clothes because you'll be sitting in the same position for a long time. Give yourself plenty of time to get to the testing center, keeping in mind traffic, weather, and parking problems. If you have to rush, that will only add to your stress.

 Key #8: Use time wisely during the test.

The TOEFL® test would be far easier if you could spend an unlimited amount of time working on it. There is no time limit on individual items—you can take as long as you want to answer, even in the Listening section—but each section has a strict overall time limit. Although you will receive a score even if you do not complete all of the items in a section, you'll need to answer nearly every question to obtain top scores.

Doing well on the TOEFL® test means that you must find a balance between speed and accuracy. Although the time limits on the computerized test are more generous than those on the paper-based test, time management during the test is still crucial.

In the two computer adaptive sections (Listening and Structure), the first items that you see may seem fairly easy. You may be tempted to rush through the easy items to save time for the difficult ones at the end of each part. This is not a good strategy. As explained in Key #9, the first half of these sections is extremely important.

Work steadily. Never let yourself get stuck on any one problem. If you are unable to decide on an answer, guess and go on.

The most important tools for timing yourself are on the upper display bar. The time clock on the left side tells you how much time remains and the information displayed on the right side tells you how many items you have completed as well as the total number of items in that section. You activate the clock by clicking on the clock icon on the left side of the lower toolbar. (The "time-remaining" function automatically comes on in the last five minutes of each section.) It is probably best to leave the clock on during the entire test, but only glance at it now and then. Don't become obsessed with checking it.

Key #9:   Remember the special nature of the computer adaptive sections.

When taking the Listening and Structure sections of the test, you should be as confident as possible of an answer before confirming it because you must answer the questions in these sections as they are presented. You can't skip a difficult item and come back to it later as you can on paper-based test (or in the Reading section). You cannot review items that you have already answered but weren't sure of.

In the computer adaptive sections, the first half of each section has more "weight" than the second half. The first half determines your general ability level—whether you will receive a high score, middle score, or low score. Once the computer program determines this, it presents questions designed to pinpoint your specific level. As you progress further into a section, it becomes more difficult to raise your score dramatically even if you answer most items correctly. Therefore, you need to invest as much time and effort as you can to answer the early questions correctly.

Remember that your score is not determined entirely by the number of questions that you answer correctly, but also by the difficulty of those questions.

Key #10:   Improve your concentration.

The ability to focus your attention on each item is an important factor in achieving a high score. The test may take four hours or more, and that is a long time to spend in deep concentration. However, if your concentration is broken, it could cost you points. When an outside concern comes into your mind, just say to yourself, "I'll think about this after the test."

Some people suffer from eyestrain from staring at a computer monitor for an extended time, especially if they have to read long passages such as in the Reading section. If you find this true for you, rest your eyes occasionally during the test and bring some eye drops.

Key #11:   Use the process of elimination to make the best guess possible.

Unlike some standardized exams, the TOEFL® test has no penalty for guessing. In other words, incorrect answers aren't subtracted from your total score. Even if you are not sure which answer is correct, you should guess. In the computer adaptive sections, you will have to guess in order to proceed. But you want to make an educated guess. To do this, use the process of elimination.

To understand the process of elimination, it may be helpful to look at the basic structure of a multiple choice item. On the TOEFL® test multiple choice items consist of a **stem** and four (usually) **answer choices.** One answer choice, called the **key,** is correct. (In a few Listening items, there are two keys.) The incorrect choices are called **distractors** because their function is to distract your attention from the right answer.

STEM. . . . .

        O distractor
        O key

○ distractor
○ distractor

The distractors, however, are usually not equally attractive. One is usually "almost correct." This choice is called the **main distractor.** Most people who answer an item incorrectly will pick this answer-choice.

STEM. . . . .

○ distractor
○ key
○ distractor
○ main distractor

To see how this works in practice, look at this Structure item:

Winter wheat _____ planted in the fall.

○ because
○ is
○ which
○ has

If you are sure of the answer, you should mark your choice immediately and go on. If not, you should use the process of elimination. In this item, the first and third choices are fairly easy to eliminate. Because this sentence consists of a single clause, connecting words such as *because* and *which* are not needed. It may be a little more difficult to choose between the second and fourth choices because both form verb phrases. Even if you are unable to decide between these two choices, you have a 50% chance of guessing correctly. (The second choice is the key; a passive verb, not a present perfect verb, is required to complete the sentence correctly.)

What if you eliminate one or two answers but can't decide which of the remaining choices is correct? If you have a "hunch" (an intuitive feeling) that one choice is better than the others, choose it. If not, just pick any remaining answer and go on.

In the Reading section, you should NEVER leave any items unanswered. If you are unable to finish this section, you should answer all the remaining questions in the last few minutes of the test. In the two computer adaptive sections, however, you should not guess blindly at questions you have not had time to work on. That technique will probably not improve your score and can actually lower it.

 Key #12: Learn to control test anxiety.

A little nervousness before an important test is normal. After all, these tests can greatly influence your plans for your education and career. If you were going to participate in a big athletic contest or give an important business presentation, you would feel the same way. There is an expression in English that describes this feeling quite well: "butterflies in the stomach." These "butterflies" will mostly fly away once the test starts. And a little nervousness can actually help by making you more alert and focused. However, too much nervousness can slow you down and cause you to make mistakes.

If you begin to feel extremely anxious during the test, try taking a short break—a "ten-second vacation." Close your eyes or look away from the monitor, take your hand off the mouse, and lean back in your chair. Take a few deep breaths, shake out your hands, roll your head on your neck, relax—then get back to work. A positive, confident attitude towards the exam can help you overcome anxiety. Think of the TOEFL® test not as a test of your knowledge or of you as a person but as an intellectual challenge, a puzzle to be solved.

What It's Like to Take the Computer-Based TOEFL® Test

(Note: The testing experience may differ somewhat from center to center.)

1. The first step is to call the closest testing center. You should call at least a month before you need to take the test. There is typically a three-week waiting time, but this may vary by time of year and center. The waiting time for certain days—especially Saturdays—will be longer than for other days. If you have a credit card or have already purchased a CBT voucher, you can make an appointment over the phone to take the test. Otherwise, make arrangements to stop by the center. If you do make an appointment when you call, you will receive a confirmation number. Write this number down and keep it in a safe place.

2. A week after registering, you'll receive directions to the center in the mail (including public transportation routes). Put this card with your confirmation number. On the day before the test, get this card, your confirmation number, and your passport ready to take with you the following day.

3. Arrive at least a half hour early for your appointment. At the time you arrive, you will be given a form to fill out.

4. At the time of your appointment, or whenever a computer is free, you will be taken into a room near the testing room and given a paragraph to copy and sign. This paragraph says that you really are who you say you are and that you promise not to tell anyone what is on the test. At this time you will also have to show your passport and you will be photographed. Before you actually go into the testing room, you will have to sign a register. Center officials will then take you into the testing room and seat you at a computer. There may be a number of other people in the room taking tests—not only the TOEFL®. Your testing space will resemble a study carrel at a library.

5. Your computer will prompt you to answer some questions about yourself, your plans, and your reason for taking the test. After that, the tutorial will begin. This tutorial teaches you the basic computer skills required to take the test.

6. After you have finished the tutorial (which is not timed) you may begin the Listening section. You will have a chance to adjust the volume, read the directions, and answer a few practice items. Remember, you are NOT allowed to take notes during the Listening section.

7. After the Listening section, you may take a one-minute break or go directly on to the Structure section.

8. After completing the Structure section, there is a mandatory 10-minute break. You'll have to sign out before you leave the testing area.

9. After the break, you will again have to sign in. You will be given six sheets of scrap paper and will be shown back to your computer. The next section of the test is Reading. Remember that this section of the test is NOT computer adaptive, and that you can move forwards and backwards through the readings. You can skip questions (although this is seldom a good idea) and go back and change your answers any time you want.

10. After you finish the Reading section of the test, you may take a one-minute break or proceed with the Essay Writing section. If you choose to word-process the essay, you will see a brief tutorial explaining *cut, paste, delete,* and other commands you need to write the essay on the computer. You may use the scrap paper you have been given to write a quick outline for your essay.

11. After you have written your essay, you will receive an unofficial grade report. You will then have a chance to choose from a pull-down menu the universities which

will receive your scores. You may then be asked a number of questions about your experience taking the test. After that, you must hand in your scrap paper. You will then sign out.

12. If you word-process your essay, you will receive your final test scores in 2 weeks. If you handwrite your essay, you will receive your final scores in 4-5 weeks.

Guide to Testing on Computer

The Computer

The computer that you will use to take the computer-based TOEFL® test is a standard personal computer, consisting of these components:

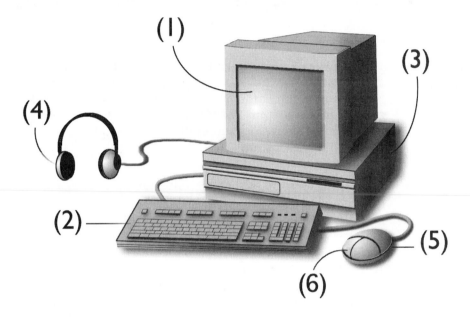

(1) **Monitor or screen.** All the text and visual information will be displayed here.

(2) **Keyboard.** You will use this to word-process your essay.

(3) **Central Processing Unit,** or **CPU.** Because the testing program is loaded by the Center personnel, you won't need to do anything with this part of the computer.

(4) **Headphones.** You will hear all the recorded material for the Listening section through the headphones. At the beginning of the Listening section you may change volume on the screen with your mouse.

(5) **Mouse.** This is the primary tool for computerized testing. You will use the mouse to answer questions, move the pointer around the screen, scroll through Reading passages, click on icons, and cut and paste in the Essay Writing section. As you move the mouse on its pad, the pointer (arrow) on the screen will move in corresponding directions. With only a few minutes of practice, you will be able to move the pointer wherever you want on the screen. To click on answers and icons, press once with your forefinger on the left front button of the mouse (6), then release it.

The Screen

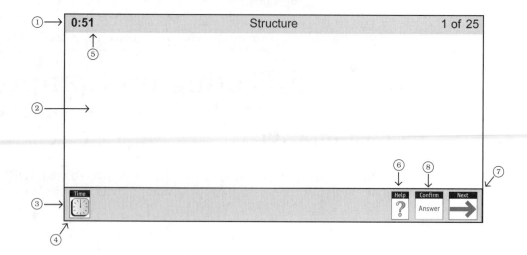

(1) **Title bar** The name of the section that you are working on will appear in the center of this strip. On the left side is the time-remaining indicator. This is activated when you click on the clock icon at the bottom left side. During the last five minutes of each section it comes on automatically. The right side of the title bar indicates the number of the item you are working on and the total number of items in this section.

(2) **Display screen** The questions and answer choices will appear in this part of the screen. During the Listening and Reading sections, graphics may also appear here. During the Reading section, the passage will appear in the left half of this screen and questions will appear on the right side.

(3) **Tool bar** There are generally four icons (symbols or words in boxes) visible here. An icon can only be used when it appears black; a grey icon cannot be activated. The **clock icon** on the left side (4) activates the **time remaining** function (5) up on the title bar. The **Help icon** (6) provides you with directions for the section you are working on and a menu of other information that may be helpful. It does NOT provide any help in answering a specific question. The use of the two other icons—**Next** (7) and **Confirm Answer** (8)—is explained in the following section.

Choosing an Answer

For most of the multiple-choice questions, there will be four answer choices with empty ovals to their left. To choose an answer, you can either position the pointer over the oval and click on it OR you can simply click on the answer itself. You will probably find it easier and faster to click on the answer rather than the oval because it is a larger target!

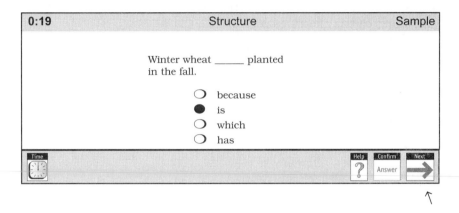

The answer is the second choice, *is*, so you can either move the pointer to the oval next to *is* and click on it or click on the word *is* itself. The oval will turn black.

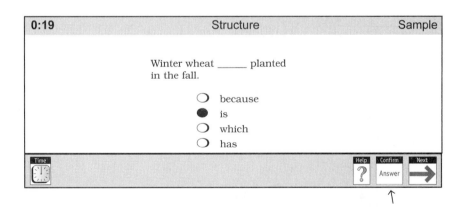

After answering a question, you will have to move the pointer to the lower right-hand section of the screen and click on the **Next** icon. This icon will appear black until you click on it, and then it will turn grey.

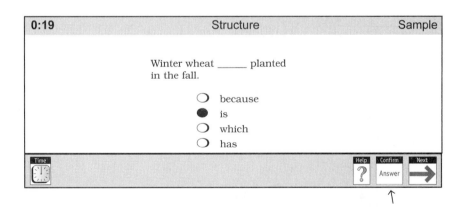

The **Confirm Answer** icon will turn black. Click on this icon and you will automatically go to the next item. (The process of answering questions in the Reading section is somewhat different. It will be explained in the introduction to the Reading section.)

What if you want to change an answer? Let's say that you first chose the fourth answer choice, *has*, and that you decide to change your answer to *is*.

The easiest way to change your answer is to click on the answer that you now think is correct. The blackened oval next to your first choice will then appear empty, and the oval next to your new answer will appear black. Remember, you can change your answer until you click on the Confirm Answer icon

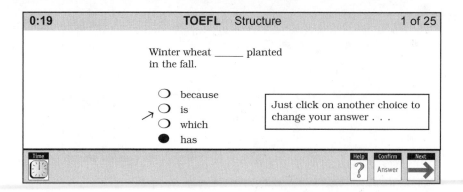

There are special directions for answering certain kinds of questions. You may have to click on a picture or part of a picture (in Listening and Reading), click on two answers (in Listening), click on part of a sentence (in Structure), or click on words or sentences in a passage (in Reading). These techniques will be demonstrated in the Computer Skills section of each introduction, and you will get a chance to practice these techniques in the exercises and on the CD-ROM.

Guide to Listening

University of California at Berkeley

About Listening

The Listening section of the TOEFL® test is always given first. The purpose of this section is to test your understanding of spoken English. On the computer-based test, you will hear the Listening material through headphones, so the sound quality will be better than it was through loudspeakers. You will be able to control the rate at which you hear items and the volume. (NOTE: The *TOEFL Sampler* says that you can only change the volume before the test starts, but in fact, you can make volume changes by adjusting the on-screen volume icon at any time during the Listening section.)

Section I is divided into two parts. Part A consists of short dialogues with one question about each one. Part B consists of three types of longer listening stimuli with sets of multiple questions following them.

Here's what to expect during the Listening section:

1. As you listen to the dialogues and the longer talks and discussions, you will see photographs of the people involved or of things related to the discussion. There are two types of photographs. Most are *context* photos that merely set the scene for you.

A few are *content* photos that clarify points made in the lectures or academic discussions.

2. Immediately after you hear the material, the photograph will disappear and a question will appear on the screen. At the same time, another speaker will read the question.

3. Immediately after hearing the question, the four answer choices will appear. (Unfortunately, you cannot preview the answer choices as you listen to the

dialogues or longer talks.) At this point you may click on the oval beside the answer choice that you think is correct.

4. After you have chosen an answer and are sure of it, you will click on the "Next" icon and then the "Confirm Answer" icon.

The directions for this section are spoken as well as visible on the screen. There are four speakers, two male and two female. All the speakers have standard North American accents and they read the items at a normal speed. The tone of the items is conversational, less formal than the items in the other test sections.

Listening Format		
Part A: Dialogues		11–17 questions
Part B: Longer Talks		
	2–3 Conversations	2–3 questions
	2–3 Mini-Lectures	3–6 questions
	1–2 Academic Discussions	3–6 questions
Total Listening Section		30–50 questions
		40–60 minutes

Questions about Dialogues and Conversations are all multiple-choice problems. Mini-Lectures and Academic Discussions include both standard multiple-choice items and a number of other types of questions. These will be practiced in the lessons for Part B.

The Listening section actually tests both your listening ability and your reading skills since you must understand both the spoken material you hear through the headphones and the answer choices on the screen.

Many test-takers find the Listening section to be the most difficult. Because it is given first, you may be more nervous during this part of the test, and you may find voices in a headphone more difficult to understand than "live" voices. And some test-takers find the questions asked about the dialogues and talks somewhat tricky.

The exercises and tests in the Listening section of this text are designed to help you overcome these difficulties. You will become more comfortable listening to materials on tape or computer. You'll also become alert to many of the test writers' "tricks."

When you are taking the practice tests in the book, listen on headphones if they are available. Look only at the photo while you listen to the dialogue or talk. Then, when questions are being read, look only at those questions. Don't preview the answer choices (because you won't be able to do this during the actual test). Don't go back and change an answer once you have finished an item.

On the computer-based test, you control the speed at which you hear items. However, in the listening material for this book, items are separated by twelve-second pauses, as they were on the paper-based test.

You should spend some time working with the Listening sections of the CD-ROM in order to get used to controlling the speed at which you hear items and choosing answers with a mouse rather than with a pencil.

Computer Skills for the Listening Section

Before the beginning of this section, you will hear a voice that will be at the same volume level as the voices you hear in the Listening section. At this time you can adjust the volume up or down on the screen. If you want the volume to be louder, click on the arrow pointing up, and if you want the volume lower, click on the arrow pointing down.

Volume

Remember, you can also adjust the volume during the test by using the slide-switch on the headphone cord.

After adjusting the volume, you will see the directions for Part A on the screen. To begin working on this section, click on the Dismiss Directions icon on the Directions screen.

Because all of the questions in Part A are one-answer multiple-choice questions, no special computer skills are required. After you have heard the dialogue and the question about it, you simply use your mouse to point to the arrow at the oval next to the answer choice you think is correct, or at the answer itself, and click on it. The oval will then darken.

If you are sure this is correct, or it's your best guess, you will then click on the "Next" icon and then on the "Confirm Answer" icon at the bottom of the screen. If you decide to change your answer before you confirm your answer, click on a second oval or answer. The oval next to that choice will then darken, and the first one you clicked on will appear blank again.

Most of the questions in Part B are also one-answer multiple-choice questions, but there are a few other types of questions.

To answer two-answer multiple-choice items, click on two of the squares next to the answer choices, or on the answers themselves, and an *X* will appear in each square. To change an answer, click on the answer again and the *X* will disappear.

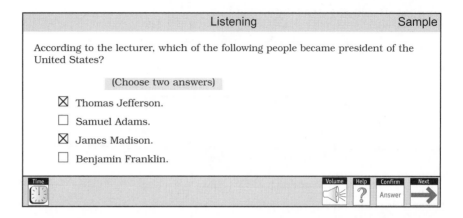

To answer questions involving graphics (maps, charts, photographs, drawings, and so on) you will either click on one of four graphics or on one of four letters on a single graphic. The letter will then darken, or a box will be drawn around the picture to indicate that this is your choice. If you change your mind, just click on another choice.

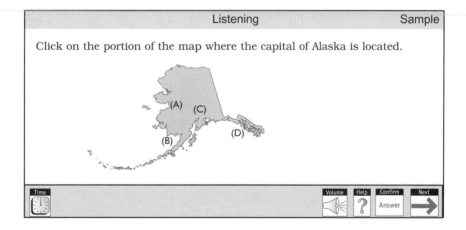

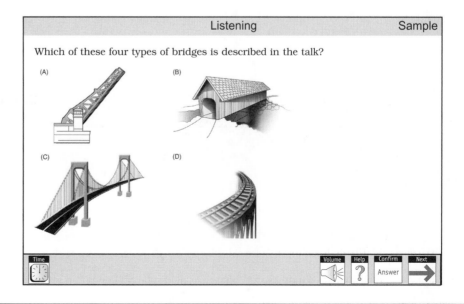

Two other computer-unique question types that you will see in the Listening section are *matching* and *ordering* questions.

To answer matching questions, first click anywhere on one of the three choices at the top of the screen. That answer will then be highlighted. Then click in the appropriate box, and the choice will appear inside the box. Do this for all three choices. To change an answer, just click on the box again, and your first choice will disappear.

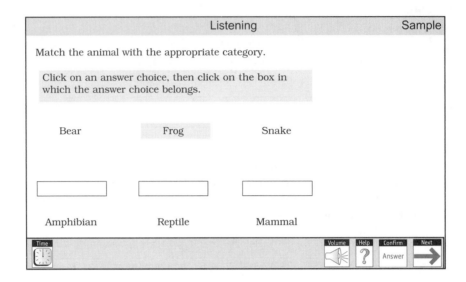

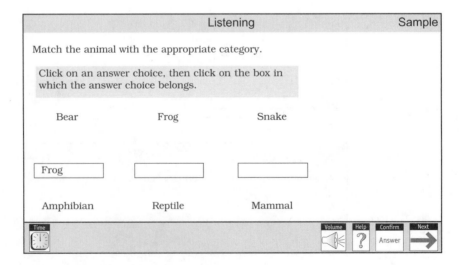

To answer ordering questions, click anywhere on one of the four answer choices. This will highlight the choice.

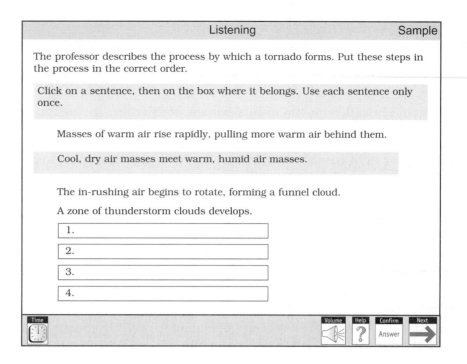

Next, click on the position in which you think that choice belongs. The choice will then appear in that position.

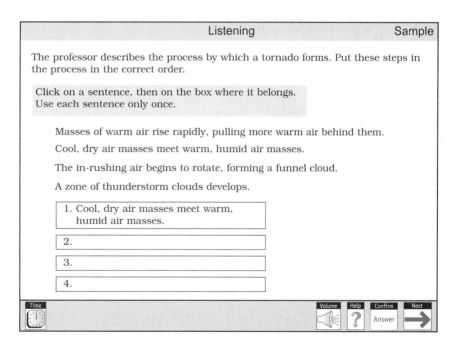

To change your answer, simply click on that position again. Do this for each of the choices. The program will not allow you to place the same choice in more than one position at one time. It will not allow you to go on until you have placed all four of the choices in one of the positions.

■ Familiarize yourself with the directions for each part before the exam. Then, as soon as you begin this section, click on the Dismiss Directions icon and begin.

■ Time management is crucial in this section. Remember, the computer will let you take as long as you like to answer each question, but there is a fairly tight time limit for the entire section (40–60 minutes). Keep your eye on both the clock icon and item number in the upper right corner of the screen that tells you how many items you have completed and how many items there are in the section. Simple subtraction gives you the number of items you still have to complete.

■ Always answer promptly after the answer choices appear, not only to save time but also to keep the listening material fresh in your mind.

■ Use your "power of prediction." While you are looking at the photo and listening to the spoken material, try to guess what the question or questions will be. Then, while you are listening to and reading the question, try to guess what the correct answer will be. Look for your predicted answer or something similar to it among the four choices.

■ If you are not sure of an answer, try to eliminate unlikely choices and make your guess. If you have no idea which answer is correct, click on your guess answer and go on.

■ Never spend too long on any one problem.

■ Concentration is very important in this part of the test. Once you have confirmed an answer, don't think about that item—start thinking about the next one. Focus your attention on the voices in the headphones and the words on the screen.

Begin your preparation for Section 1 by taking the Preview Test 1: Listening. This will familiarize you with the first section of the exam.

PREVIEW TEST 1: Listening

This section tests your ability to comprehend spoken English. It is divided into two parts, each with its own set of directions. There are 40 questions. The material that you hear and the questions about it are presented only once.

Part A

Directions: Each item in this part consists of a brief dialogue involving two speakers. Following each dialogue, a third voice asks a question about it.

When you have heard each dialogue and question, read the four answer choices and select the *one* that best answers the question based on what is directly stated or on what can be inferred. Don't look at the questions until they are read on the tape.

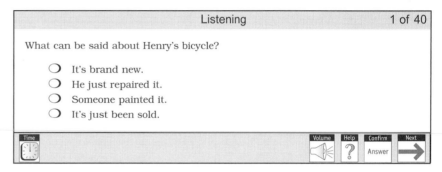

What can be said about Henry's bicycle?

- ○ It's brand new.
- ○ He just repaired it.
- ○ Someone painted it.
- ○ It's just been sold.

Time | Volume | Help | Confirm Answer | Next →

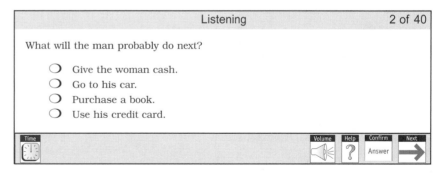

What will the man probably do next?

- ○ Give the woman cash.
- ○ Go to his car.
- ○ Purchase a book.
- ○ Use his credit card.

Time | Volume | Help | Confirm Answer | Next →

What does the woman tell Mark?

- ◯ He should have listened to Professor Bryant's suggestions.
- ◯ He doesn't have to read all the books.
- ◯ All of the books on the list are important.
- ◯ Some of the books are unavailable now.

Time | Volume | Help ? | Confirm Answer | Next →

What does the man mean?

- ◯ The software isn't convenient to use.
- ◯ He's not familiar with the software.
- ◯ Using the software is simple.
- ◯ He wishes he'd bought that software.

Time | Volume | Help ? | Confirm Answer | Next →

What does the man want to know?

- ◯ What time his brother called.
- ◯ Where to meet his brother.
- ◯ Why his brother called.
- ◯ When to meet his brother.

Time | Volume | Help ? | Confirm Answer | Next →

What does the man say about Howard?

- ◯   He left on a long trip yesterday.
- ◯   His letter arrived unexpectedly.
- ◯   He seemed to be sad yesterday.
- ◯   The letter he sent was very funny.

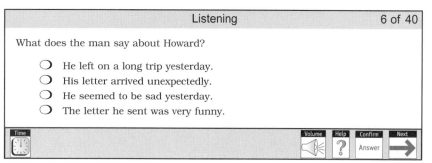

What can be inferred about Professor Welch from this conversation?

- ◯   He'll probably give the man another grade.
- ◯   He doesn't teach chemistry anymore.
- ◯   He rarely changes his grades.
- ◯   He'll probably retire soon.

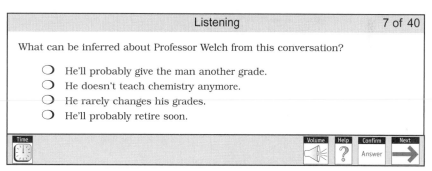

What is the woman really saying to Allen?

- ◯   His class has been canceled.
- ◯   He shouldn't drop the class.
- ◯   An earlier class would be better for him.
- ◯   He doesn't need to study political science.

What does the man say about Professor Porter?

○ She mailed the grades to her students.
○ She left the students' tests in her office.
○ She can't get into her office.
○ She put a list of grades on the door.

Time | Volume | Help | Confirm Answer | Next

What do the speakers imply about William?

○ He has a good excuse for being late.
○ No one has heard from him for a week.
○ He's still waiting to be contacted.
○ He doesn't take responsibility for errors.

Time | Volume | Help | Confirm Answer | Next

What did the man think he had lost?

○ His wallet.
○ An identification card.
○ His job at the bookstore.
○ A check.

Time | Volume | Help | Confirm Answer | Next

What can be inferred about the man?

- ○ He got on the wrong bus.
- ○ He's afraid he'll be late for his flight.
- ○ He's sorry he took a bus instead of flying.
- ○ He had to wait for the bus a long time.

Time | Volume | Help ? | Confirm Answer | Next →

What does the woman imply?

- ○ The meeting will have to be rescheduled.
- ○ She doesn't care whom the board picks as dean.
- ○ She's not sure where the meeting will be.
- ○ The board will not choose a dean this month.

Time | Volume | Help ? | Confirm Answer | Next →

What do they mean?

- ○ They wish they hadn't paid attention to Harvey.
- ○ They asked for some information about Harvey.
- ○ Harvey told them not to ignore him.
- ○ Only Harvey could give them any assistance.

Time | Volume | Help ? | Confirm Answer | Next →

What are the men probably discussing?

- ◯ A hotel room.
- ◯ The man's family.
- ◯ A reasonable offer.
- ◯ The man's schedule.

Time		Volume	Help	Confirm	Next

What can be inferred from Professor White's remark?

- ◯ He must change his syllabus.
- ◯ The woman cannot take his class.
- ◯ He has extra copies of the syllabus.
- ◯ Some students are not on his list.

Time		Volume	Help	Confirm	Next

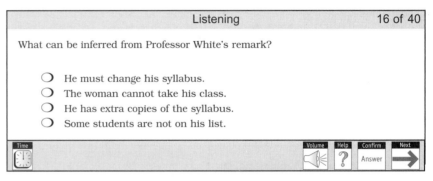

What had the man *originally* assumed?

- ◯ Peter wouldn't be favored in the match.
- ◯ The match had already been played.
- ◯ The match wouldn't be played.
- ◯ Peter would win the match.

Time		Volume	Help	Confirm	Next

Part B

Directions: Part B involves conversations, discussions, and lectures. After each talk, there are a number of questions. You will hear the talks only once.

When you have read and heard the questions, read the answer choices and select the best answer or answers based on what is directly stated or can be inferred.

Don't forget: During actual exams, taking notes during the Listening section is not permitted.

Listening	18 of 40

What course does Scott want to drop?

○ Biochemistry.
○ Mathematics.
○ Language.
○ Music.

Listening	19 of 40

What does Professor Lamont suggest that Scott do?

○ Change majors.
○ Study music.
○ Get a tutor.
○ Drop the class.

Listening	20 of 40

Which of the following best describes Professor Lamont's attitude towards Scott?

○ Condescending.
○ Angry.
○ Encouraging.
○ Disappointed.

ASTRONOMY CLASS

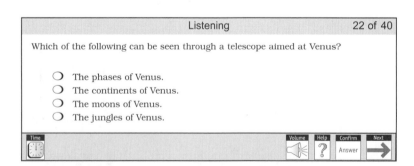

According to the speaker, in what ways are Earth and Venus twins?

Choose two.

☐ They have similar surface conditions.
☐ They are about the same size.
☐ They spin in the same direction.
☐ They are relatively close together.

Time   Volume   Help   Confirm   Next
?   Answer

Which of the following can be seen through a telescope aimed at Venus?

○ The phases of Venus.
○ The continents of Venus.
○ The moons of Venus.
○ The jungles of Venus.

Time   Volume   Help   Confirm   Next
?   Answer

According to the speaker, which of the following were once common beliefs about the planet Venus?

Choose two.

☐ That it was not a single object but two objects.
☐ That its surface temperatures were much colder than those on Earth.
☐ That it had two moons: Phosphorous and Hesperus.
☐ That there was life beneath its cloud cover.

Time   Volume   Help   Confirm   Next
?   Answer

Which of the following does the speaker say about the length of a day on Venus?

   ○   It is shorter than an Earth day.
   ○   It is longer than an Earth year.
   ○   It is longer than a Venus year.
   ○   It is the longest of any known planet.

| Time | | Volume | Help ? | Confirm Answer | Next → |

In what order were these space probes sent to Venus?

Place the letter of the choice in the proper box. Use each choice only once.

(A)   Mariner 2
(B)   Venus Pioneer 2
(C)   Magellan
(D)   Venera 4

1. _____
2. _____
3. _____
4. _____

| Time | | Volume | Help ? | Confirm Answer | Next → |

It can be inferred that the topic of the next student's presentation will be which of the following?

   ○   The Moon.
   ○   The Sun.
   ○   The Earth.
   ○   The planet Mars.

| Time | | Volume | Help ? | Confirm Answer | Next → |

Why does Dana want to find a job?

○ To pay for everyday expenses.
○ To pay for tuition.
○ To pay back a bank loan.
○ To pay for room and board.

Time   Volume   Help   Confirm   Next
     ?   Answer   →

What job is Dana probably going to apply for?

○ Selling gifts at a museum.
○ Directing an art gallery.
○ Working as a receptionist.
○ Working in a cafeteria.

Time   Volume   Help   Confirm   Next
     ?   Answer   →

What must Dana do first to apply for the job she is interested in?

○ Go to an interview with Dr. Ferrarra.
○ Mail her application to the Financial Aid Office.
○ Fill out some forms.
○ Call the personnel office.

Time   Volume   Help   Confirm   Next
     ?   Answer   →

MUSIC HISTORY CLASS

What is the main topic of this lecture?

○ The role of religious music in Europe.
○ Books of the colonial period.
○ Domestic life in the nineteenth century in the United States.
○ Eighteenth and nineteenth century music in the United States.

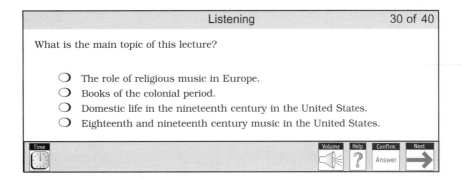

What does the speaker indicate about the song "Old Hundred"?

Choose two.

☐ It has a long history.
☐ It appeared in the *Bay Psalm Book*.
☐ It was extremely unusual.
☐ It was composed by Steven Foster.

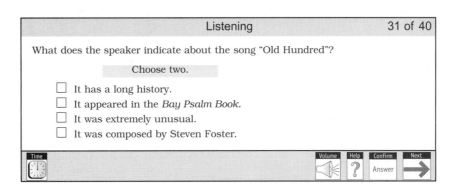

Which of these is the best representation of the notational system used for Southern revival hymns?

(A) *Babbus*

(B) ◆ ✛ ▲ ● ▼

(C) A-B♭-C-G-F♯

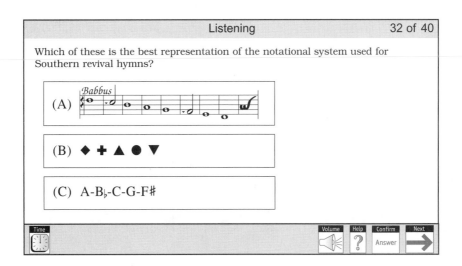

Which of these instruments was typically used to play minstrel songs?

(A)

(B)

(C)

(D)

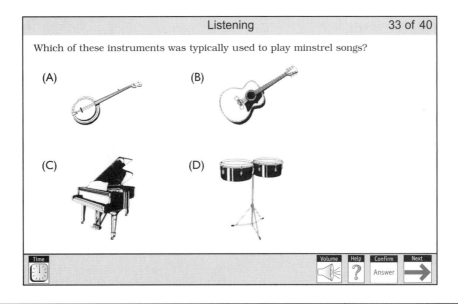

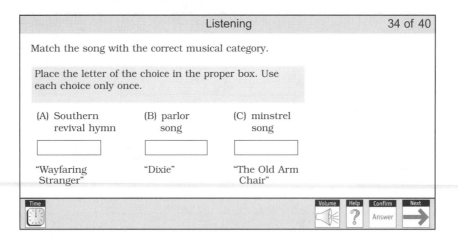

Match the song with the correct musical category.

Place the letter of the choice in the proper box. Use each choice only once.

(A) Southern revival hymn	(B) parlor song	(C) minstrel song
"Wayfaring Stranger"	"Dixie"	"The Old Arm Chair"

Time   Volume   Help   Confirm   Next
Answer

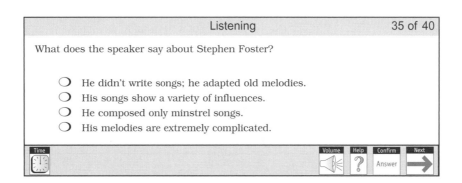

What does the speaker say about Stephen Foster?

- ○ He didn't write songs; he adapted old melodies.
- ○ His songs show a variety of influences.
- ○ He composed only minstrel songs.
- ○ His melodies are extremely complicated.

Time   Volume   Help   Confirm   Next
Answer

	GROUP	INDEPENDENT VARIABLE	DEPENDENT VARIABLE
1)	EXPERIMENTAL	EXERCISE	GRADE PERFORMANCE
2)	CONTROL	NO EXERCISE	GRADE PERFORMANCE

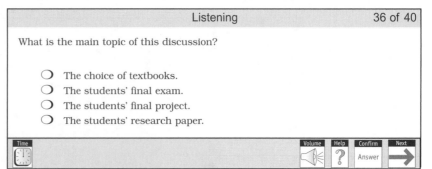

What is the main topic of this discussion?

- ○ The choice of textbooks.
- ○ The students' final exam.
- ○ The students' final project.
- ○ The students' research paper.

Time   Volume   Help   Confirm   Next
Answer

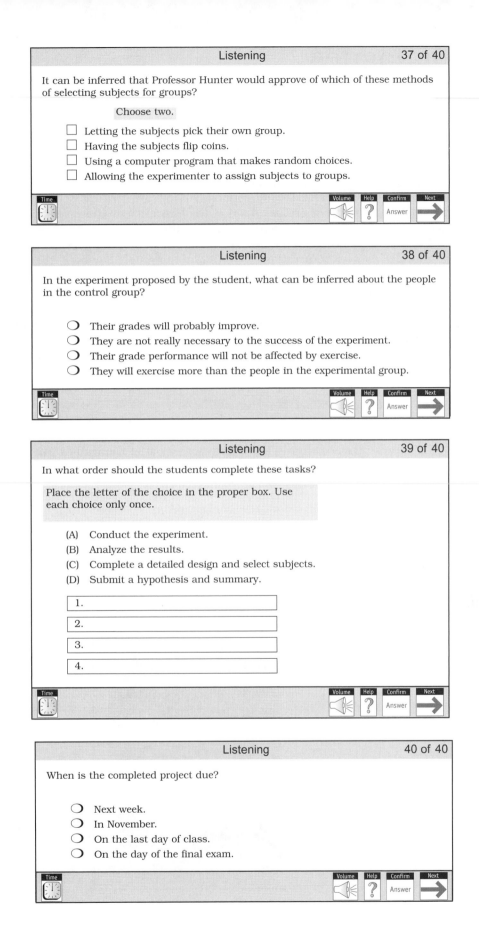

It can be inferred that Professor Hunter would approve of which of these methods of selecting subjects for groups?

Choose two.

☐ Letting the subjects pick their own group.
☐ Having the subjects flip coins.
☐ Using a computer program that makes random choices.
☐ Allowing the experimenter to assign subjects to groups.

Time   Volume   Help   Confirm   Next
Answer

In the experiment proposed by the student, what can be inferred about the people in the control group?

○ Their grades will probably improve.
○ They are not really necessary to the success of the experiment.
○ Their grade performance will not be affected by exercise.
○ They will exercise more than the people in the experimental group.

Time   Volume   Help   Confirm   Next
Answer

In what order should the students complete these tasks?

Place the letter of the choice in the proper box. Use each choice only once.

(A) Conduct the experiment.
(B) Analyze the results.
(C) Complete a detailed design and select subjects.
(D) Submit a hypothesis and summary.

1.
2.
3.
4.

Time   Volume   Help   Confirm   Next
Answer

When is the completed project due?

○ Next week.
○ In November.
○ On the last day of class.
○ On the day of the final exam.

Time   Volume   Help   Confirm   Next
Answer

This is the end of Preview Test 1: Listening.

ABOUT DIALOGUES

The first part of the Listening Comprehension section consists of 11–17 dialogues (short conversations) between two speakers. These are read while a photograph appears on your screen. A third speaker—the narrator—then asks a question about what was said or implied in the conversation. This question also appears on your screen along with four answer choices. You must decide which of the four choices that appears on the screen is the best answer for the question you hear, and then click on that choice.

The questions about dialogues are generally easier for most test-takers to answer correctly than those about the longer talks. Remember, however, that this part of the test is computer adaptive, and if you are doing well, the last few dialogues you hear may be quite difficult.

Timing is important. Answer each item as soon as it appears. Sitting and thinking about the best answer will not help your score in this part. Don't forget: On the computer-based test, there is no time limit per item, but there is an overall time limit for the Listening section. To get a top score, you must answer most of the Listening questions.

SAMPLE ITEM

You will hear a dialogue in your headphones:

    M1: Do you think I should leave this chair against the wall or put it somewhere else?

    F1:   Over by the window, I'd say.

                Note: M1 = first male voice
                             M2 = second male voice
                             F1   = first female voice
                             F2   = second female voice

At the same time, you will see a photograph:

Immediately after the dialogue is spoken, the photograph will disappear, and you will hear and read a question about the dialogue:

    M2: What does the woman think the man should do?

The question about the dialogue will appear on your screen, and right after it is spoken, the four answer choices will also appear.

What does the woman think the man should do?

○   Open the window.
○   Move the chair.
○   Leave the room.
○   Take a seat.

Time   Volume   Help   Confirm   Next   Answer

The woman indicates that she thinks the man should put the chair over by the window rather than leave it where it is. In other words, he should move it. Therefore, the best answer is the second choice. You should click on the oval next to it.

THE PHOTOGRAPHS

The photographs depict the two speakers at the moment the conversation is taking place. Most involve a male and a female student in a campus setting: standing in the hallway of a classroom building, sitting in a classroom or lab, walking across campus, eating in a cafeteria, and so on. The photographs shown with the dialogues are always "context" photographs rather than "content" photographs. In other words, they only serve to set the scene of the dialogue rather than to provide information you need to answer the question. You could answer the question just as easily without the photograph.

THE DIALOGUES

Most of the dialogues involve a man and a woman. A few involve two men or two women. Most dialogues are two-part exchanges, following this pattern:

> Speaker 1 says something.
> Speaker 2 responds.
> Narrator asks question.

Some are three- or four-part exchanges, following these patterns:

> Speaker 1 says something.
> Speaker 2 responds.
> Speaker 1 responds.
> Narrator asks question.

> Speaker 1 says something.
> Speaker 2 responds.
> Speaker 1 responds.
> Speaker 2 responds.
> Narrator asks question.

Most dialogues are about life at North American universities: attending classes, talking to professors, writing research papers, taking tests. Some dialogues are about more general activities students may engage in: shopping in grocery stores, looking for housing, taking vacations, going to meetings and parties. The tone of the dialogues is informal. Idioms, first names, contractions (*I'm, doesn't, can't*) are often heard. Some of the items test your ability to understand various language functions. For example, you must be able to determine if one speaker is agreeing or disagreeing with the other speaker, or if one speaker is accepting or rejecting the other speaker's offer.

The Questions Unlike the questions in the Listening section of the paper-based test, the questions about the dialogues ARE written out, and will remain on the screen along with the four answer choices. Most questions about dialogues focus on the last line of the dialogue. However, it is usually necessary to understand the entire dialogue in order to choose the correct answer. For example, in the Sample Item, it is not clear what the woman means when she says, "Over by the window" unless you understand what the man says first.

Common Part A Question Types	Examples
1. **Meaning questions** These are the most common questions. They ask for a restatement of what the last speaker or both speakers say. They may be general questions or ask what the speakers say about some specific topic. They often follow dialogues that contain idioms.	"What does the man/woman mean?" "What do the speakers say about ____?"
2. **Inference questions** These are the second most common type of questions about dialogues. The answer for these questions are not directly stated in the dialogue, but they can be inferred (concluded) from what the speakers say.	"What does the man/woman imply?" "What can be inferred about ____?" "What can be concluded from the conversation about ____?"
3. **Questions about suggestions** One speaker talks about a problem or asks for advice. The other speaker makes a suggestion for solving the problem.	"What does the woman suggest the man do?" "What does the man suggest they do?" "What does the man suggest?" "What does the woman think the man should do?"
4. **Questions about future actions** These ask what one or both of the speakers will do next or in the near future, or what one or both are planning to do.	"What will the woman do?" "What will they probably do next?" "What are the speakers planning to do?"
5. **Topic questions** These ask about the subject of the dialogue.	"What are they talking about?" "What are they discussing?"
6. **Questions about opinions** These ask how one or both of the speakers feel about some topic.	"How does the man/woman feel about ____?" "What is their opinion of ____?"
7. **Questions about assumptions** These ask what one speaker thought (assumed) before he or she spoke to the other speaker.	"What had the man assumed about ____?" "What had the woman previously assumed?"
8. **Questions about questions** One speaker makes a statement; the other speaker asks a question to get more information.	"What does the man want to know?" "What does the woman ask the man?"
9. **Questions about reasons** These ask why one or both of the speakers did something.	"Why did the man/woman ____?"
10. **Questions about problems** These ask about some trouble one or both of the speakers are having.	"What problem is the man/woman having?" "What is the problem with ____?"

THE ANSWER CHOICES

All four of the answer choices are logical answers for the question, but of course only one—the key—is correct according to the dialogue. However, as in all parts of the TOEFL® test, not all of the answer choices are equally attractive. You can often eliminate one or two choices easily even if you are not sure which answer is correct, and so make a better guess.

Correct answers are seldom stated word for word by either of the speakers. Correct answers often contain synonyms (words with the same meaning) for words in the dialogues and use different sentence structures.

Grammatically, there are three types of answer choices, depending on the type of question asked:

1.   Complete sentences

     What does the man mean?

     ○   He prefers coffee to tea.
     ○   He'd like some lemon in his tea.
     ○   He doesn't want anything to drink.
     ○   He likes his coffee black.

2.   Incomplete sentences, usually beginning with verb forms

     What will the woman do next?

     ○   Call her cousin.
     ○   Take her cousin home.
     ○   Park the car.
     ○   Get some gasoline.

3.   Short noun or prepositional phrases

     What are the speakers discussing?

     ○   A text book.
     ○   An essay exam.
     ○   A new schedule.
     ○   A magazine article.

The test writers sometimes use various techniques in this part to make it more difficult to pick the correct answer. These techniques include the use of sound-alike words, homonyms, words with multiple meaning, idioms, and others. You'll practice avoiding these traps in this part of the *Guide*.

Tactics for Dialogues

- Answer each question promptly and go on to the next dialogue as soon as you can.

- Be familiar with the directions for answering dialogue questions.

- Focus on listening to the dialogue, not looking at the photograph.

- As you listen to the dialogue, try to predict what the question and answer will be. (The more practice you get before the test, the easier you will find this!)

- Remember that the answer for the question is most often contained in the last line of the dialogue.

- If you are not sure of an answer, eliminate as many answer choices as you can.

- If you don't understand all or part of a conversation, guess and go on.

- As soon as you click on the "Confirm Answer" icon, the next dialogue will begin automatically, so be ready.

LESSON 1: Dialogues with Sound Confusion

Some of the items in Part A involve confusion between words that have similar sounds. Here's how they work: one of the speakers uses a word or phrase that sounds like a word or phrase in one or more of the answer choices. If you don't hear the word clearly, you might incorrectly choose an option with a sound-alike word or phrase.

SAMPLE ITEM

You will hear:

M1: So how often do you have to take that medicine?

F1: The doctor told me to take three pills a day. And he said to always take them after meals.

M2: What did the doctor tell the woman?

You will see on your screen:

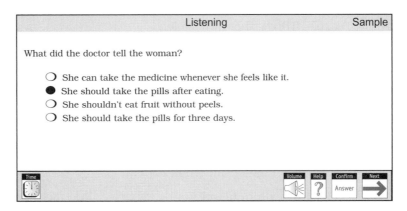

What did the doctor tell the woman?

○ She can take the medicine whenever she feels like it.
● She should take the pills after eating.
○ She shouldn't eat fruit without peels.
○ She should take the pills for three days.

The word *feels* in the first choice sounds a little like the word *pills* in the dialogue. In a different way, the word *peels* in the third choice also sounds like the word *pills*. Notice that the second choice—the correct answer—and the fourth do not contain sound-alike words.

Many sound-alike expressions in dialogues are **minimal pairs**. Minimal pairs are two words that are pronounced alike except for one vowel sound (*peels* and *pills*, *lack* and *lake*, *point* and *paint*) or one consonant sound (*peels* and *feels*, *vine* and *wine*, *mop* and *mob*).

Another sound problem involves two words that sound like one word, such as *mark it* and *market*, *sent her* and *center*, *in tents* and *intense*.

A third type of sound problem involves one word that sounds like part of a longer word, such as *give* and *forgive*, *mind* and *remind*.

Hint: If an answer choice contains a word that sounds like a word in the dialogue, that choice is usually wrong. For example, if you clearly hear the word *spell* and you read the word *spill* in one of the answer choices, you can usually eliminate that choice.

When you're taking Part A during an actual exam, you can use the **context** of the dialogues to help you solve problems with sound confusion. If you hear and understand all of the dialogue, you won't have much trouble eliminating choices involving sound-alike words. However, if you understand only part of a dialogue, or if you "mis-hear" one or two words, you may easily choose an incorrect answer.

EXERCISE 1.1

Focus: Discriminating between sound-alike words in dialogues and in answer choices.

Directions: Listen to the dialogues. Decide which of the two choices, (A) or (B), best answers the question, and mark the appropriate blank.

 Now start the listening program.

1. What does the woman suggest the man do?

 ____ (A) Get in a different lane.

 ____ (B) Stand in another line.

2. What did the children do?

 ____ (A) Go down the slide.

 ____ (B) Play on the sled.

3. What does the woman tell the man to do with the letters?

 ____ (A) Put them in a file.

 ____ (B) Throw them in a pile.

4. What is the man's problem?

 ____ (A) He can't shut his suitcase.

 ____ (B) His suitcase doesn't fit in the closet.

5. What is learned about Annie's bread?

 ____ (A) It's made from whole wheat.

 ____ (B) It's white bread.

6. What does the man say about the story?

_____ (A) Brenda is typing it.

_____ (B) It's being taped.

7. What is learned about Emily?

_____ (A) She recently moved.

_____ (B She bought a new dress.

8. What does Dennis say about the coffee?

_____ (A) Its taste has improved.

_____ (B) It tastes slightly bitter.

9. What does the man ask Ellen?

_____ (A) How much the ticket cost.

_____ (B) What she might win.

10. What does the woman say about the bottle?

_____ (A) It's been chipped.

_____ (B) There's a ship inside it.

11. What happened to Jerry?

_____ (A) He tripped in the aisle.

_____ (B) He slipped in some oil.

12. Why is this area well known?

_____ (A) For its fast horses.

_____ (B) For its natural resources.

13. How did the Student Council spend the afternoon?

_____ (A) Thinking about the decision.

_____ (B) Arguing about the issue.

14. What is the problem with the shirt?

_____ (A) It doesn't fit around the neck.

_____ (B) The color is too bright.

15. What did Professor Maguire do?

_____ (A) Wrote his name on the paper.

_____ (B) Told his students to write a paper.

EXERCISE 1.2

Focus: Practicing answering questions about dialogues that involve sound confusion.

Directions: Listen to the dialogues. Each dialogue contains a word or phrase that sounds like a word or phrase in one or more of the answer choices. Blacken the oval next to the correct answer.

Now start the listening program.

1. What is learned about Steven and Gloria?
   - ○ He went to the shopping mall with her.
   - ○ He wrote her an e-mail.
   - ○ He lent her some money.
   - ○ He plans to contact her later.

2. What does the woman say about Stuart?
   - ○ He has an appointment with the president.
   - ○ He was just appointed vice-president.
   - ○ He's unhappy because he lost the election.
   - ○ He's going to serve as president.

3. What does the woman say about the class she is going to take?
   - ○ It is the study of living plants.
   - ○ It is about life on other planets.
   - ○ It concerns the breeding of cattle.
   - ○ It deals with life on Earth.

4. What does Janet tell the man?
   - ○ She won't leave until the rain is over.
   - ○ Their drain has stopped up.
   - ○ They shouldn't board the train until it completely stops.
   - ○ She's been under a lot of strain lately.

5. What does the woman say about Sam?
   - ○ He offered his help to Darlene.
   - ○ He made an offer to Darlene's sister.
   - ○ When Darlene was gone, he missed her.
   - ○ He spoke to Darlene's assistant.

6. What does the man suggest the woman do?
   - ○ Get a job at the hotel.
   - ○ Buy some cough drops.
   - ○ Get some copies made.
   - ○ Eat in the coffee shop.

7. What does the woman say about Gus?
   - ○ He has a pain behind his ear.
   - ○ He didn't hear what the woman said.
   - ○ He can lend the man a pen.
   - ○ He has fallen behind in class.

8. What does the woman imply?
   - ○ The food in her dormitory isn't very good.
   - ○ She didn't need boots when she left the dorm.
   - ○ The students decided to take a vote.
   - ○ The flooding in the east part of campus was severe.

9. What does Jane help Professor Ramsay do?
   - ○ Evaluate the texts.
   - ○ Correct the exams.
   - ○ Inspect the desks.
   - ○ Collect the tests.

10. What does Bonnie mean?
   - ○ She's not pleased with her lawyer.
   - ○ Her name is not on the list.
   - ○ The lease is difficult to read.
   - ○ The lawyer told her to call the police.

LESSON 2: Dialogues with Homonyms and Words with Multiple Meanings

Two words are **homonyms** if they have the same pronunciation but are spelled differently and have different meanings. The words *flour* and *flower, bare* and *bear* are homonyms. In some dialogues, one or more incorrect answer choices refer to a homonym of a word that you hear, as in the example below.

SAMPLE ITEM

You will hear:

    M1: Eugene missed a lot of classes last week.

    F1: That's because he was sick. I think he had the flu.

    M2: What is learned about Eugene?

You will see on the screen:

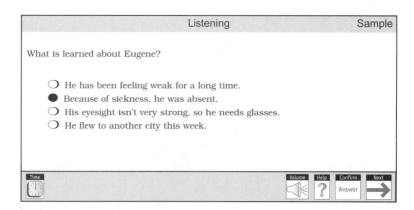

Listening	Sample

What is learned about Eugene?

    ○ He has been feeling weak for a long time.

    ● Because of sickness, he was absent.

    ○ His eyesight isn't very strong, so he needs glasses.

    ○ He flew to another city this week.

The dialogue contains the word *week*, meaning a seven-day period. The first and third choices refer to a homonym of that word, *weak*, which means *not strong*. The dialogue also contains the word *flu*, an illness similar to a bad cold. The fourth choice refers to a homonym of that word, *flew* (took a trip by plane).

Dialogues may also contain **words with multiple meanings.** In these items, one or two of the answer choices refer to another definition of a word used in the dialogue.

SAMPLE ITEM

You will hear:

F1:   Are you sure this is how Lois spells her last name?

M1:   It doesn't look right, does it? In fact, I'm not even sure it starts with that letter.

M2:   What does the man mean?

You will see on the screen:

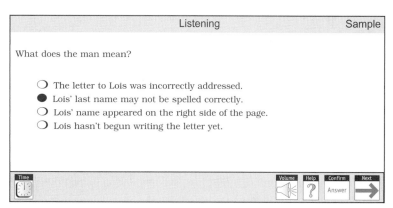

The dialogue contains the word *right*, meaning *correct*, and the word *letter*, meaning a character in the alphabet. The first and last choices also contain the word *letter*, but in those choices the word has another definition—a message sent through the mail. The third choice also contains the word *right,* but in that choice, it refers to a direction—the opposite of left.

You won't be confused by these items if you understand the entire dialogue. Again, the **context** of the dialogues can help you choose the correct answer. But if you focus only on single words, like *week* and *flu* or *letter* and *right* in the two samples, you can easily make mistakes.

EXERCISE 2.1

Focus: Using the context of dialogues to identify homonyms.

Directions: Listen to the dialogues. Decide which of the pair of homonyms appears in the dialogues and mark the appropriate answer, (A) or (B).

 Now start the listening program.

1. ____ (A) presents
   ____ (B) presence

2. ____ (A) overdue
   ____ (B) overdo

3. ____ (A) pains
   ____ (B) panes

4. ____ (A) where
   ____ (B) wear

5. ____ (A) find
   ____ (B) fined

6. ____ (A) right
   ____ (B) write

7. ____ (A) board
   ____ (B) bored

8. ____ (A) brakes
   ____ (B) breaks

9. ____ (A) sail
   ____ (B) sale

10. ____ (A) site
    ____ (B) sight

11. ____ (A) rose
    ____ (B) rows

12. ____ (A) aloud
    ____ (B) allowed

EXERCISE 2.2

Focus: Using the context of the dialogues to identify the definitions of words with multiple meanings.

Directions: Listen to the dialogues. One word from the dialogue is given, along with two possible definitions of the word. Choose the definition of the word as it is used in the dialogue and mark the appropriate answer, (A) or (B).

 Now start the listening program.

1. cold
   ____ (A) minor illness
   ____ (B) chilly weather

2. kind
   ____ (A) type
   ____ (B) considerate

3. light
   ____ (A) not heavy
   ____ (B) not dark

4. wing
   ____ (A) part of an airplane
   ____ (B) part of a building

5. tables
   ____ (A) charts
   ____ (B) furniture

6. coat
   ____ (A) layer
   ____ (B) warm clothing

7. field

    ____ (A) outside the classroom

    ____ (B) area of study

8. playing

    ____ (A) having fun with a game

    ____ (B) appearing as

9. party

    ____ (A) celebration

    ____ (B) group

10. period

    ____ (A) punctuation mark

    ____ (B) class time

EXERCISE 2.3

Focus: Using the context of dialogues to answer questions involving both homonyms and words with multiple meanings.

Directions: Listen to the statements. Decide which of the choices best answers the question and mark the appropriate answer.

 Now start the listening program.

1. What does the woman suggest Tom do?

    ◯ Look for mistakes.
    ◯ Complete his research.
    ◯ Write a check.
    ◯ Read the newspaper.

2. What are they discussing?

    ◯ Events in the historic past.
    ◯ The man's performance in class.
    ◯ A physical exam.
    ◯ A historical study.

3. What does the man mean?

    ◯ He'd never heard of that park before.
    ◯ That was the first herd he'd ever seen.
    ◯ He'd never heard buffaloes before.
    ◯ He wanted to go to the park but he couldn't.

4. What does the woman tell the man to do?

    ◯ Sign his name on this line.
    ◯ Follow the directions on the sign.
    ◯ Sign up for another class.
    ◯ Stand in another line.

5. What does the man mean?

    ◯ He can't carry the luggage by himself.
    ◯ The handle on one of the suitcases is broken.
    ◯ He bought his luggage in that store.
    ◯ There isn't enough room for his luggage there.

6. What does the woman think John should do?

   ○ Close the window right away.
   ○ Take a quick shower.
   ○ Go for a swim.
   ○ Put on some other clothes.

7. What does Patrick mean?

   ○ The class had a better opinion of him.
   ○ He had to stand in front of the class.
   ○ No one in the class understands him.
   ○ He wasn't hurt in the accident.

8. What does the woman mean?

   ○ The seminar meets in the room above them.
   ○ She was often absent from the seminar.
   ○ The seminar lasted longer than usual.
   ○ She's sorry that the seminar is over.

9. What does the woman tell the man?

   ○ They can park their car at the zoo.
   ○ The picnic will be held at the zoo.
   ○ The park is across the street from the zoo.
   ○ The zoo is on the right side of the park.

10. What is the problem?

   ○ The phone is out of order.
   ○ He doesn't have enough coins.
   ○ Cindy's phone number has changed.
   ○ He hasn't been paid this week.

LESSON 3: Dialogues with Idioms

On some exams for the TOEFL® test, up to half the dialogues contain idiomatic expressions.

Many of the idiomatic expressions are two- or three-word verbs, such as *call off* and *look out for*.

SAMPLE ITEM

You will hear:

> M1: I wonder where Mike is.
>
> F1: He'll show up as soon as the work is done, I bet.
>
> M2: What does the woman say about Mike?

You will see on your screen:

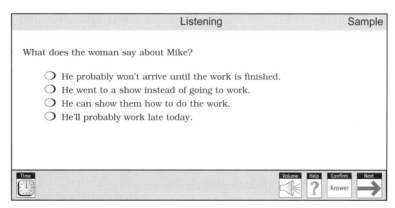

The idiom *show up* means "arrive." The second and third choices contain the word *show* but it is not used in the idiomatic sense.

In most dialogues, the last person to speak uses the idiomatic expression. Most questions about this type of dialogue are questions about meaning ("What does the woman mean?"), but some are inference questions or other types of questions. The correct answer often contains a synonym for the idiom (*arrive* for *show up* in the first choice of the Sample Item.) Incorrect choices often contain references to the literal meaning of idioms, as in the second and third choices above.

The Mini-Lessons for Section 1, at the end of the Listening section (pages 116–134), are intended to familiarize you with a large number of idioms. You should work on these lessons and study these expressions as often as possible.

However, memorizing these phrases does not guarantee that you will recognize all the idiomatic expressions in the Listening section. There are, after all, thousands of these expressions in English. You must develop "a good ear" for guessing the meaning of idioms. The context of the sentence will help you understand the expression even if you're unfamiliar with it.

EXERCISE 3.1

Focus: Recognizing synonyms for idiomatic expressions.

Directions: Listen to the spoken statements. Each contains an idiomatic expression that is also written out. First decide which of the two choices best answers the question and mark the appropriate answer, (A) or (B). Then underline the phrase in the correct answer that has the same meaning as the idiom. (This has been done for you in item 1.) If necessary, rewind the tape or replay this exercise on the CD-ROM and listen to the exercise again.

 Now start the listening program.

1. bumped into

   What does the man mean?

   ____ (A) He <u>met</u> Caroline <u>unexpectedly</u> at the cafeteria.

   ____ (B) He and Caroline had an accident.

2. got into hot water

   What does Rita mean?

   ____ (A) She was in trouble.

   ____ (B) She took a warm bath.

3. hit it off

   What does the man mean?

   ____ (A) He and Chuck argued as soon as they met.

   ____ (B) He and Chuck quickly became friends.

4. piece of cake

   What does the woman mean?

   ____ (A) The exam was simple.

   ____ (B) She had a snack after the test.

5. at the drop of a hat

   What does Robert imply?

   ____ (A) He can't leave until he finds his hat.

   ____ (B) He's ready to leave immediately.

6. under the weather

What does the man imply about Julie?

____ (A) She didn't want to practice because of the bad weather.

____ (B) She wasn't there because she felt a little sick.

7. takes after

What does the man say about Albert?

____ (A) He looks like his grandfather.

____ (B) He takes care of his grandfather.

8. give me a hand with

What does Paula ask the man to do?

____ (A) Hand her the suitcase.

____ (B) Help her carry the suitcase.

9. a stone's throw away

What does the man mean?

____ (A) His new apartment isn't very comfortable.

____ (B) His new apartment isn't far from campus.

10. didn't think much of

What does the woman say about Graham's proposal?

____ (A) She didn't consider it.

____ (B) She didn't like it.

EXERCISE 3.2

Focus: Understanding dialogues involving idiomatic and figurative expressions.

Directions: Look over the idiomatic expressions listed alphabetically before each set of items. If you are unfamiliar with any of the idioms, you may want to look them up in the "Mini-Lessons for Section 1" that follow the Listening portion of this book (pages 116–134). The dialogues each contain one of the listed expressions. Listen to the dialogues and mark the one answer choice, (A) or (B), that best answers the question.

 Now start the listening program.

Set A

believe one's eyes	push one's luck
get off the ground	run of the mill
lend a hand	short for
music to one's ears	turn in
over one's head	what the doctor ordered

1. What does the man mean?

   ____ (A) He's not sure Max's business will succeed.

   ____ (B) He doesn't know if Max is on the plane.

2. What does the woman imply?

   ____ (A) Gary shouldn't drive his car much further.

   ____ (B) It's time for Gary to get some new tires.

3. What will the man do next?

   ____ (A) Go to bed.

   ____ (B) Turn on the television.

4. What does Alice mean?

   ____ (A) She didn't understand all the jokes.

   ____ (B) She left before the performance was over.

5. What does the woman mean?

   ____ (A) Ice water sounds perfect.

   ____ (B) The doctor told her to drink a lot of water.

6. What is learned from this conversation?

   ____ (A) Elizabeth is taller than Liz.

   ____ (B) Elizabeth's nickname is "Liz."

7. What does the man say about the restaurant?

   ____ (A) The service is very fast there.

   ____ (B) It's just an average restaurant.

8. What does the woman mean?

   ____ (A) She enjoys the sound of nature.

   ____ (B) She wishes she'd brought a radio.

9. What does the woman offer to do?

   ____ (A) Lend the man some books.

   ____ (B) Help the man with the boxes.

10. What does the woman mean?

   ____ (A) She doesn't think the man is telling the truth.

   ____ (B) She was surprised to see the snow.

Set B

by heart	go without saying
call it a day	look who's talking
chip in	ring a bell
come around	slowly but surely
get in one's blood	take a lot of nerve

11. What does Karen mean?

    ____ (A) Skiing can be a dangerous sport.

    ____ (B) It's easy to get into the habit of skiing.

12. What does the woman imply about Norman?

    ____ (A) She has to look for him.

    ____ (B) He doesn't study much himself.

13. What does the man mean?

    ____ (A) They'll all pay for the gasoline.

    ____ (B) There will be plenty of room in the van.

14. What does the man say about Donna?

    ____ (A) She seemed too nervous.

    ____ (B) She took a bold approach.

15. What does Dan mean?

    ____ (A) He doesn't want to do any more painting today.

    ____ (B) He'll phone the woman later today.

16. What does the woman mean?

    ____ (A) She is going to speak the lines in an emotional way.

    ____ (B) She's already memorized the scene.

17. What does Marina think her parents will do?

    ____ (A) Agree to let her go.

    ____ (B) Go with her to Alaska.

18. What does the man imply?

    ____ (A) Rob Martin hasn't called him yet.

    ____ (B) The name Rob Martin doesn't sound familiar.

19. What does Arlene mean?

    ____ (A) She's making steady progress.

    ____ (B) She thinks the work is going too slowly.

20. What does the man imply about Molly?

    ____ (A) Of course he was sorry that she left.

    ____ (B) She went to San Francisco without saying goodbye.

EXERCISE 3.3

Focus: Using the context of dialogues to understand the meaning of idioms.

Directions: Listen to the following dialogues. Decide which of the choices best answers the question about the dialogue and mark the appropriate answer.

 Now start the listening program.

1. What is the woman going to do next?

   ○ Go to work with Jim.
   ○ Go out for coffee.
   ○ Get some exercise.
   ○ Study for a test.

2. What does the man want to know?

   ○ If the woman will go to the party with him.
   ○ If the red tie looks good with his shirt.
   ○ If he should wear a tie to the party.
   ○ If the party is already over.

3. What does the woman imply?

   ○ They both missed class because they were sailing.
   ○ The man should take better notes during Professor Morrison's class.
   ○ She missed Friday's class, too.
   ○ She dropped Professor Morrison's class.

4. What can be concluded about Ron?

   ○ He cut himself while he was preparing food.
   ○ He doesn't want to work in a restaurant.
   ○ He's planning to open up his own restaurant.
   ○ He's not going to eat at a restaurant tonight.

5. What does the man mean?

   ○ He wants to know if the woman is joking.
   ○ He wants the woman to leave him alone.
   ○ He'd like to know what the quiz will be about.
   ○ He needs a doctor to look at his injured leg.

6. What does Brian mean?
   ○ The program was canceled.
   ○ The shuttle was launched yesterday.
   ○ The weather was better than expected.
   ○ The launch was delayed.

7. What does the man say about Jennifer?
   ○ She stood up and left the lecture.
   ○ It was too warm for her to wear a sweater in the lecture hall.
   ○ Her sweater made her easy to spot.
   ○ Her notes on the lecture were easy to read.

8. What does the woman say about Phil?
   ○ He deserved to get a speeding ticket.
   ○ He was going to a good restaurant.
   ○ He probably wasn't speeding.
   ○ His ticket was no longer valid.

9. What does the woman imply about George?
   - ○ He's out of breath.
   - ○ He'll be glad to help.
   - ○ If he helps, it will save the man some money.
   - ○ He won't be very co-operative.

10. What is learned about Jill from this conversation?
   - ○ The man didn't get her a watch.
   - ○ The weather won't be warm when she graduates.
   - ○ She won't be graduating.
   - ○ She isn't going to watch the graduation.

11. What does the man say about Dora?
   - ○ She ordinarily works in a florist's shop.
   - ○ In the end, she won't have a problem.
   - ○ She wears too much perfume to work.
   - ○ She can always anticipate problems at work.

12. What does Roy tell the woman?
   - ○ He doesn't have any questions for her.
   - ○ He won't be able to take a trip.
   - ○ He can't study during spring break.
   - ○ He hasn't decided if he can take a trip.

13. What is learned about Mick from this conversation?
   - ○ His father told him to go to medical school.
   - ○ His father studied medicine.
   - ○ He and his father walked to the school.
   - ○ He surprised his father with his decision.

14. What does the woman imply about Fred?
   - ○ He would be upset if he had lost money.
   - ○ He shouldn't be paid for singing.
   - ○ He is generally very sympathetic.
   - ○ He doesn't know the words to the song.

15. What does the woman want to know about Wally?
   - ○ If he has been injured.
   - ○ If his trip has been canceled.
   - ○ If he has told anyone the news.
   - ○ If he has been informed.

16. What does Deborah mean?
   - ○ The lake is not very scenic.
   - ○ Her parents won't let them use the cabin.
   - ○ The cabin is not luxurious.
   - ○ The trip will be a long one.

LESSON 4: Answering Inference Questions about Dialogues

Sometimes the answer to a question about a dialogue is not directly stated in the dialogue. How can you answer this type of question? You must be able to draw an **inference** about the dialogue. In other words, there will be enough information in the dialogue to indirectly provide you with the answer to the question.

This type of question can be phrased in two ways:

■ What does the man/woman imply?

■ What can be inferred from the conversation?

Some inference items involve **overstatement**, or exaggeration.

     F: Are you interested in selling your car?

     M: Sure—if someone has a million dollars!

Because of the exaggeration, we can infer that the man doesn't want to sell his car at all.

SAMPLE ITEM

You will hear:

     M1: Can I take this bus to the art museum?

     F1: No, this bus goes north to Bank Street. You want a bus that goes the opposite way.

     M2: What can be inferred from this conversation?

You will see on the screen:

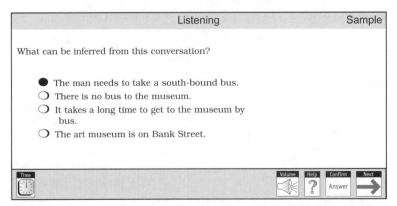

Listening   Sample

What can be inferred from this conversation?

    ● The man needs to take a south-bound bus.
    ○ There is no bus to the museum.
    ○ It takes a long time to get to the museum by bus.
    ○ The art museum is on Bank Street.

Time   Volume Help Confirm Next
                                    ?   Answer

The answer can be inferred because the first bus is going north, but the man must take a bus going in the opposite direction, south, to get to the art museum. The second choice is incorrect; it IS possible to get to the museum by bus. There is no information about the third choice. The fourth choice can't be true because the first bus—which is not the right bus—is going to Bank Street.

EXERCISE 4

Focus: Listening to dialogues that are followed by inference questions and identifying the best answers.

Directions: Listen to the following dialogues. Decide which of the four choices best answers the question and mark the appropriate answer.

Now start the listening program.

1. What can be inferred about the man?

    ○ He's not related to Larry.
    ○ He doesn't think Larry won the contest.
    ○ He's not a very good dancer.
    ○ He has never believed Larry.

2. What can be inferred from this conversation?

    ○ The man doesn't like the way the suit looks.
    ○ The suit costs a lot of money.
    ○ The man dresses as if he were very wealthy.
    ○ The man already owns an expensive suit.

3. What does the man imply?

    ○ There is just enough food.
    ○ Many uninvited guests will come.
    ○ The woman has prepared too much food.
    ○ The party will be moved to another location.

4. What can be inferred about the man?

    ○ He took a physics test tonight.
    ○ He has a class every evening.
    ○ He was studying by himself tonight.
    ○ He's concerned about his grade.

5. What does the woman imply about Greg?

    ○ He's changed his major often.
    ○ He hasn't really changed his major.
    ○ He won't do well in his new major.
    ○ He was changed by his experience.

6. What can be inferred from this conversation about Professor Sutton?

○ His lectures put his students to sleep.
○ He's a middle-aged man.
○ He lectures about history.
○ His lectures are very difficult to follow.

7. What does the woman imply?

○ She hasn't been to the dentist for years.
○ She wasn't able to see the dentist yesterday.
○ She had a long wait before she saw the dentist.
○ She was quite late for her dental appointment.

8. What does the man imply about the experts and the plan?

○ They have agreed on it.
○ They have different opinions about it.
○ It depends on their cooperation.
○ It doesn't require their attention.

9. What does the woman imply about Louis?

○ His new boss shouldn't have been promoted.
○ He and his old boss argued.
○ He should get a better job.
○ His boss has helped him a lot.

10. What does the woman imply?

○ There's not enough snow to cause a cancellation yet.
○ It will probably snow all night.
○ The university has already decided to cancel classes.
○ It has already stopped snowing.

11. What does the man imply?

○ He has been interested in folk dancing for a long time.
○ He's interested in making new friends.
○ He wants to form a new folk dancing club.
○ He'll never learn how to dance.

12. What can be inferred from the woman's remark?

○ She didn't enjoy the music.
○ She couldn't see the concert very well.
○ She had a good seat near the stage.
○ She found her seat uncomfortable.

13. What does the man imply?

○ Last summer was even hotter.
○ This is the hottest summer he can remember.
○ He didn't live here last year.
○ The weather is cooler than usual.

14. What can be inferred from this conversation?

  ○ Students must pay a fee to swim in the pool.
  ○ The public cannot use the pool on campus.
  ○ The swimming pool is temporarily closed.
  ○ The pool can be used by students for free.

15. What can be inferred about the speakers?

  ○ They can't see the stars clearly.
  ○ They're not in the city tonight.
  ○ They are looking at the lights of the city.
  ○ They've never seen each other before tonight.

16. What does Mike imply?

  ○ He generally works on Saturday.
  ○ He doesn't know many people at work.
  ○ He isn't allowed to get phone calls at work.
  ○ He wasn't expecting a phone call.

17. What can be inferred about the man?

  ○ He didn't solve any of the problems.
  ○ Only one of the problems was assigned.
  ○ He solved more problems than the woman did.
  ○ The calculus problems were easy to solve.

18. What can be inferred about Fran?

  ○ The scarf looks great on her.
  ○ She wears that scarf too often.
  ○ In this weather, she needs a scarf.
  ○ She should never wear a blue scarf.

19. What can be inferred from this conversation about Milly?

  ○ She doesn't have an accent.
  ○ Her parents have very strong accents.
  ○ Her accent is stronger than her parents'.
  ○ Everyone likes her parents' accent.

20. What does the woman imply about Robert?

  ○ He usually has a hard time skiing.
  ○ He didn't find the slope difficult.
  ○ He is in a lot of trouble.
  ○ He is an excellent skier.

Directions: Each item in this part consists of a brief dialogue involving two speakers. After each dialogue, a third voice asks a question.

When you have heard each dialogue and question, read the four answer choices and select the one that best answers the question based on what is directly stated or on what can be inferred. Don't look at the questions until they are read on the tape.

Now start the listening program.

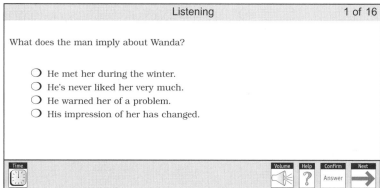

Listening   1 of 16

What does the man imply about Wanda?

○ He met her during the winter.
○ He's never liked her very much.
○ He warned her of a problem.
○ His impression of her has changed.

Time   Volume   Help   Confirm Answer   Next

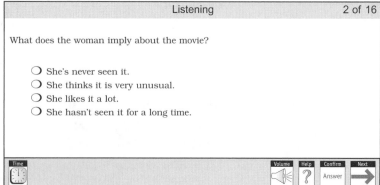

Listening   2 of 16

What does the woman imply about the movie?

○ She's never seen it.
○ She thinks it is very unusual.
○ She likes it a lot.
○ She hasn't seen it for a long time.

Time   Volume   Help   Confirm Answer   Next

What does the woman mean?

○ The glasses are stacked on the shelf.
○ The juice is no worse than the other brands.
○ The new glasses are quite attractive.
○ She plans to stock up on this juice.

Time   Volume   Help   Confirm   Next
                             ?   Answer

What does Adam imply?

○ He hasn't finished working on the bookshelves.
○ The tools have been misplaced.
○ He hates working with tools.
○ The tools have already been returned.

Time   Volume   Help   Confirm   Next
                             ?   Answer

What can be inferred from this conversation?

○ There is no charge for drinks here.
○ The first woman wants some ice water.
○ The man is not the woman's waiter.
○ The iced tea isn't very good here.

Time | Volume | Help | Confirm Answer | Next

What does the man want to do?

○ Review the last point.
○ Go on to the next chapter.
○ Leave the classroom.
○ Point out the teacher's mistake.

Time | Volume | Help | Confirm Answer | Next

What does the woman think the man should do?

○ Meet a friend of hers.
○ Keep a budget.
○ Increase his income.
○ Get some exercise.

Time | Volume | Help | Confirm Answer | Next

What can be inferred from the man's comment?

○ The woman should clean out her closet.
○ The lamp will look better in a small space.
○ He doesn't like the lamp very much.
○ The living room is the best place for the lamp.

Time | Volume | Help | Confirm Answer | Next

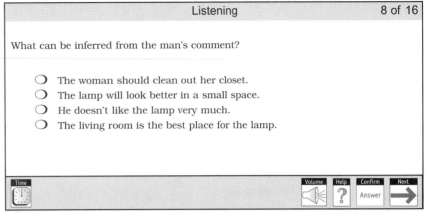

What does the man mean?

○ He certainly likes Ernie's red car.
○ The man in the red car resembles Ernie.
○ Ernie has a car just like that red one.
○ He can't see the man in the red car.

Time | Volume | Help | Confirm Answer | Next

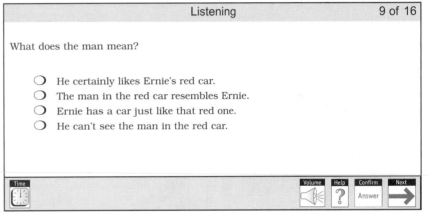

What does the man say about John?

○ He hurt his hand when he was scuba diving.
○ He hasn't gone scuba diving in a long time.
○ He's not too old to go scuba diving.
○ He's an experienced scuba diver.

Time | Volume | Help | Confirm Answer | Next

What can be inferred from this conversation?

○ The man would like to use Becky's computer.
○ Becky will need the computer for a long time.
○ The computers in the library are already in use.
○ Becky wants the man to go to the library.

Time | Volume | Help ? | Confirm Answer | Next →

What do the speakers mean?

○ The ring is quite attractive.
○ Laura got a bargain on the ring.
○ The ring was probably expensive.
○ Laura had to sell her ring.

Time | Volume | Help ? | Confirm Answer | Next →

What does the man imply by his remark?

○ Professor Clayburn is going to speak some other night.
○ He's never heard of Professor Clayburn.
○ He didn't realize Professor Clayburn was speaking tonight.
○ Professor Clayburn is giving his speech in this room.

Time | Volume | Help ? | Confirm Answer | Next →

What can be concluded from this conversation?

○ Joe has been making too much noise.
○ Dogs are not allowed in the dorm.
○ No one understands the parking regulations.
○ Joe is not allowed to leave his room.

Time   Volume   Help   Confirm   Next
        ?   Answer

What can be inferred from this conversation?

○ The woman didn't realize Bill had to work.
○ Bill has not finished his work.
○ The break has not lasted long enough.
○ The work didn't take long to complete.

Time   Volume   Help   Confirm   Next
        ?   Answer

What can be inferred from this conversation?

○ The woman has just begun to collect rocks.
○ Paul is unwilling to help.
○ The box is very heavy.
○ There's nothing in the box.

Time   Volume   Help   Confirm   Next
        ?   Answer

This is the end of Review Test A.

LESSON 5: Dialogues Involving Agreement and Disagreement

To answer questions about some of the dialogues, it is necessary to understand if one speaker agrees or disagrees with the other speaker's ideas or proposals.

There are many ways to express agreement and disagreement:

Agreement

So do I.	I'll say!
Me too.	You can say that again.
Neither do I.*	Is/Has/Was it ever!
I don't either.*	You bet!
Who wouldn't?	I couldn't agree with
Isn't he/she/it though!	you more.
(Didn't he/wasn't she/	I feel the same way you do
hasn't it though!)	about it.
I'll second that.	You took the words right out
You're absolutely	of my mouth.
right.	Of course.

*These two expressions show agreement with a negative statement:

I don't really like my schedule this term.

I don't either.   *OR*   Neither do I.

Disagreement

I don't think so.	I'm afraid I don't agree.
That's not what I think.	Probably not.
That's not the way I	Not necessarily.
see it.	Not really.
I can't say I agree.	I'm afraid not.
I couldn't agree with	I'm not so sure.
you less.	Of course not.
Yes, but . . .	Of course, but . . .

There are, of course, other expressions that show agreement and disagreement. Some are practiced in the exercises.

SAMPLE ITEM

You will hear:

    M1: Howard certainly is a talented journalist.

    F1: Isn't he though!

    M2: What does the woman mean?

You will see on the screen:

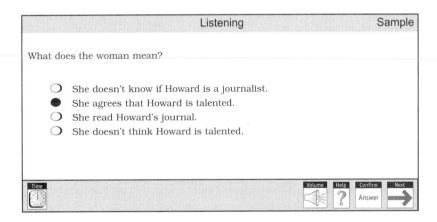

Although the woman's reply seems negative in form, it actually signals agreement. Therefore, the second answer choice is the best one.

SAMPLE ITEM

You will hear:

      F1: I thought Cheryl's photographs were the best at the exhibit.

      F2: I didn't really see it that way.

      M1: What does the second woman mean?

You will see on the screen:

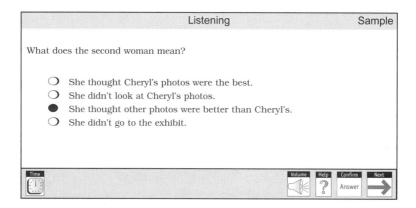

The second woman's response, "I didn't really see it that way" means that she disagreed with the first woman's opinion that Cheryl's photographs were the best. The best answer is therefore the third one.

EXERCISE 5.1

Focus: Determining if one speaker agrees or disagrees with the other speaker.

Directions: Listen to the following dialogues. Decide if the second speaker agrees or disagrees with the first speaker, and mark the appropriate blank.

 Now start the listening program.

1. ____ (A) Agrees   3. ____ (A) Agrees
   ____ (B) Disagrees   ____ (B) Disagrees

2. ____ (A) Agrees   4. ____ (A) Agrees
   ____ (B) Disagrees   ____ (B) Disagrees

5.   ___ (A) Agrees   9.   ___ (A) Agrees
     ___ (B) Disagrees   ___ (B) Disagrees

6.   ___ (A) Agrees   10. ___ (A) Agrees
     ___ (B) Disagrees   ___ (B) Disagrees

7.   ___ (A) Agrees   11. ___ (A) Agrees
     ___ (B) Disagrees   ___ (B) Disagrees

8.   ___ (A) Agrees   12. ___ (A) Agrees
     ___ (B) Disagrees   ___ (B) Disagrees

EXERCISE 5.2

Focus: Listening to dialogues that involve agreement and disagreement and answering questions about them.

Directions: Listen to the following dialogues. Decide which of the four choices best answers the question and mark the appropriate answer.

 Now start the listening program.

1. What does the man mean?

    ○   He prefers taking a final exam.
    ○   He thinks an exam takes too much time.
    ○   He'd rather write a research paper.
    ○   He has plenty of time to work.

2. How does the woman feel about the first chapter?

    ○   It was difficult, but she understood it.
    ○   She hasn't had a chance to read it yet.
    ○   She doesn't think it is as useful as some chapters.
    ○   It's probably easier than the other chapters.

3. How does the man feel about the woman's idea?

    ○   He completely disagrees with it.
    ○   He doesn't believe the university will accept it.
    ○   He thinks it's a good one.
    ○   He wants more information about it.

4. What was the woman's opinion of Jack's story?

    ○   She doesn't think that Jack wrote it.
    ○   She thought it was quite funny.
    ○   She thinks it had too many details.
    ○   She found it well-written.

5. What does the man mean?

    ○ He has the perfect bicycle.
    ○ He thinks it's a good day for bike riding, too.
    ○ He doesn't agree with the woman's opinion of the weather.
    ○ He didn't hear what the woman said.

6. What does the woman mean?

    ○ She thinks Arthur wasn't doing well in the class.
    ○ She's not sure why Arthur dropped the class either.
    ○ She believes Arthur dropped the class for no reason.
    ○ She's decided to drop the class too.

7. What does the woman say about Tom's plan?

    ○ It's very impractical.
    ○ It's never been tried before.
    ○ It's unnecessary.
    ○ It might work.

8. What was the man's *initial* reaction to the editorial?

    ○ He didn't understand it.
    ○ It made him angry.
    ○ He agreed with it.
    ○ He thought it was depressing.

9. What does the woman say about the library?

    ○ She's never been there during final exam week.
    ○ It's not crowded now, but it soon will be.
    ○ It's crowded because students will be taking exams soon.
    ○ It will be closed right after the final exams.

10. What does the man mean?

    ○ He likes the costumes Madeleine made.
    ○ He's not sure who designed the costumes.
    ○ He recommends the play.
    ○ He doesn't think the costumes are attractive.

11. How does the man feel about the ending of the movie?

    ○ It was very happy.
    ○ It was very exciting.
    ○ It was unhappy.
    ○ It was unexpected.

12. What does the woman mean?

    ○ She thinks Pamela is right.
    ○ She thinks the regulations are fair.
    ○ She disagrees with the man's opinion.
    ○ She has no opinion about the regulations.

LESSON 6: Dialogues Involving Suggestions, Invitations, Offers, and Requests

A number of dialogues involve a speaker making and/or responding to **suggestions, invitations, offers,** and **requests.** There are many ways to express these language functions. Some ways are listed in the charts in this lesson, while others are practiced in the exercises.

A) SUGGESTIONS

These are pieces of advice that one speaker gives another. In most of these dialogues, one speaker poses a problem and the other speaker suggests a possible solution to that problem. In some dialogues, one speaker makes a suggestion, and the other speaker responds to that suggestion positively or negatively.

Making Suggestions	
Why don't you/we . . .	If I were you . . .
Why not . . .	If I were in your shoes . . .
Have you ever thought of . . .	You/We should . . .
Have you considered . . .	Shouldn't you/we . . .
You/We could always . . .	What about . . .
Maybe you/we could . . .	What if you/we . . .
Try . . .	How about . . .

Positive Responses	Negative Responses
Why not!	I don't think so.
Good idea!	I don't believe so.
That's an idea.	I already thought of that.
Sounds good to me.	I don't think that will work.
By all means!	Don't look at me!
Why didn't I think of that?	
That's worth a try.	
Thanks, I'll give that a try.	
That sounds pretty good.	

SAMPLE ITEM

You will hear:

M1: I'm doing so poorly in physics class, I think I'm going to have to drop it.

F1: You know, Frank, you should talk to Professor de Marco before you do anything. He's given special help to lots of students who were having trouble.

M2: What does the woman suggest Frank do?

You will see on the screen:

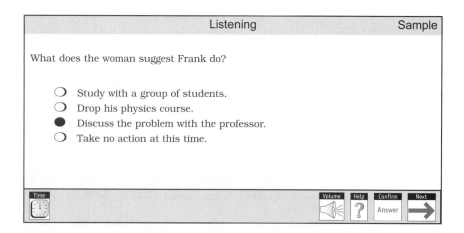

The woman suggests that the man talk to Professor de Marco because the professor has helped many students in the past.

B) INVITATIONS

These are requests for someone to come somewhere or to take part in some activity.

Making Invitations	
Shall we . . .	Let's . . .
Would you like to . . .	Do you want to . . .
Would you care to . . .	Could you . . .
Would you be able to . . .	Can you . . .
Want to . . .	

Positive Responses	Negative Responses
Yes, let's.	I'm sorry, but . . .
Sure, thanks.	I'd like to, but . . .
Sounds good.	I'd love to, but . . .
All right, I'd love to.	Thanks a lot, but . . .
I'd like that.	That sounds nice, but . . .
What a great idea!	I'll pass.
Sure. Thanks for inviting me.	Thanks for the invitation, but . . .
	I don't think I'll be able to make it this time.
	Can I take a rain check?*

*This means, "Could we do this some other time?"

SAMPLE ITEM

You will hear:

    M1: Would you like to join us on Sunday? We're going to go on a picnic at the lake.

    F1: I'd love to, but I have a test Monday, and I have to get ready for it.

    M2: What will the woman probably do on Sunday?

You will see on the screen:

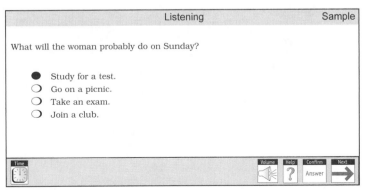

What will the woman probably do on Sunday?

- ● Study for a test.
- ○ Go on a picnic.
- ○ Take an exam.
- ○ Join a club.

The man invites the woman to come to a picnic. The woman says that she'd love to go, but that she must study for a test she is taking Monday. (If the woman had accepted the man's invitation, the second choice would have been correct.)

C) OFFERS

These are proposals to help someone or to allow someone to do something. Either speaker in the dialogue may make an offer.

Making Offers	
Let me . . .	Can I . . .
Shall I . . .	May I . . .
Would you like me to . . .	Should I . . .
Do you want me to . . .	I could . . .
How does . . . sound?	

Positive Responses	Negative Responses
That would be nice.	I don't think so.
Yes, please.	I'm afraid not.
Please do.	That won't be necessary.
Sure, thanks.	Thanks anyway.
Be my guest.	Please don't.
If you wouldn't mind.	Don't bother.
	Not on my account.

SAMPLE ITEM

You will hear:
    F1: Should I make reservations for dinner Friday night?
    M1: Thanks anyway, but I've already made them.
    M2: What does the man mean?
You will see on the screen:

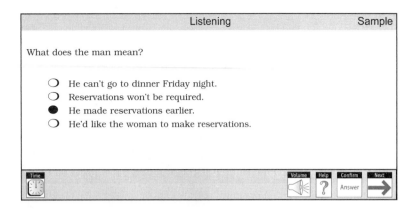

What does the man mean?

○   He can't go to dinner Friday night.
○   Reservations won't be required.
●   He made reservations earlier.
○   He'd like the woman to make reservations.

The woman offers to make reservations. The man replies that he's already made them.

D) Requests

To make a request is to ask someone to do something, or to ask for help or information.

Making Requests	
Would you . . .	Will you . . .
Could you/I . . .	May I . . .
Do you mind if . . .	Can you/I . . .
Would you mind if . . .	

Positive Responses	Negative Responses
I'd be glad to.	Sorry, but . . .
I'd be delighted.	I'm afraid not.
Sure thing.	I'd like to, but . . .
Certainly.	I wish I could, but . . .
Why not?	*Actually, I do/would.
If you want to.	*I'm afraid I do/would.
If you'd like.	*As a matter of fact, I do/would.
You bet.	
*Not at all.	
*Of course not.	
*Responses for "Do you mind if . . ." or "Would you mind if. . . ."	

SAMPLE ITEM

You will hear:

     M1:   I have to make one more phone call before I go.

     F2:   Take your time. Would you just lock up the office when you finish?

     M2:   What does the woman want the man to do?

You will see on the screen:

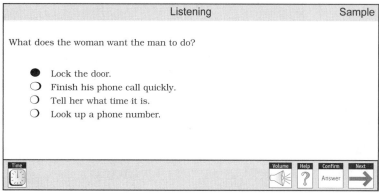

The woman requests that the man lock up the office.

EXERCISE 6.1

Focus: Identifying suggestions, invitations, offers, and requests and responses to them.

Directions: Listen to the following dialogues. Decide which of the two choices best completes the sentence and mark the appropriate space.

 Now start the listening program.

1. The man is

   ____ (A) Declining an offer.

   ____ (B) Making a suggestion.

2. The woman is

   ____ (A) Accepting an invitation.

   ____ (B) Making an offer.

3. The woman is

   ____ (A) Declining an offer.

   ____ (B) Making a suggestion.

4. Mark is

   ____ (A) Rejecting a request

   ____ (B) Agreeing to a request.

5. The woman is

    ____ (A) Giving an invitation.

    ____ (B) Making a suggestion.

6. The man is

    ____ (A) Agreeing to a request.

    ____ (B) Turning down an offer.

7. Ed is probably going to

    ____ (A) Receive a suggestion.

    ____ (B) Make an offer.

8. The woman is

    ____ (A) Suggesting a solution.

    ____ (B) Offering help.

9. Cynthia is

    ____ (A) Giving an invitation.

    ____ (B) Accepting an offer.

10. The woman is

    ____ (A) Declining an offer.

    ____ (B) Making a request.

11. The man will probably

    ____ (A) Do what the woman suggests.

    ____ (B) Turn down the woman's invitation.

12. Bob is

    ____ (A) Agreeing to an offer.

    ____ (B) Refusing a request.

13. The man is

    ____ (A) Making a suggestion.

    ____ (B) Accepting an invitation.

14. The man is

    ____ (A) Requesting that Jacquelyn do something.

    ____ (B) Giving Jacquelyn a suggestion.

15. Matt is

    ____ (A) Rejecting a suggestion.

    ____ (B) Agreeing with a suggestion.

16. James tells the woman that

    ____ (A) He can't accept her invitation.

    ____ (B) He'd enjoy another sandwich.

EXERCISE 6.2

Focus: Listening to dialogues involving suggestions, invitations, offers, and requests, and answering questions about them.

Directions: Listen to the following dialogues. Decide which of the four choices best answers the question and mark the appropriate answer.

 Now start the listening program.

1. What does the man mean?
   - ○ He would like a cigarette.
   - ○ The woman can smoke if she likes.
   - ○ He doesn't want the woman to smoke.
   - ○ He thinks he smells smoke.

2. What does the woman say about the gray suit?
   - ○ The man wears it too often.
   - ○ It needs to be cleaned.
   - ○ It's not as nice as the blue one.
   - ○ The man could wear it tonight.

3. What does the man say about Cathy?
   - ○ She could plan the trip.
   - ○ She may not feel well.
   - ○ She can go on the class trip.
   - ○ She has some other plans.

4. What does the man mean?
   - ○ He doesn't want more coffee.
   - ○ He doesn't want to use his credit card.
   - ○ He hasn't had enough coffee.
   - ○ He doesn't want to make coffee.

5. What does the woman mean?
   - ○ She doesn't think it's warm.
   - ○ She'll open the window herself.
   - ○ She wants the window closed.
   - ○ She's going to turn down the heat.

6. What will the man probably do?
   - ○ Go somewhere else for lunch.
   - ○ Order another type of sandwich.
   - ○ Skip lunch today.
   - ○ Have some soup for lunch.

7. What does the woman imply?
   - ○ The kitchen also needs cleaning.
   - ○ The living room doesn't have to be cleaned.
   - ○ The man shouldn't do the cleaning.
   - ○ There's not enough time to clean both rooms.

8. What does the man offer to do for the woman?

   ○ Give her some information about classes.
   ○ Go with her to the registrar's office.
   ○ Help her find her way to the registrar's office.
   ○ Tell her where to get her own map.

9. What does the woman suggest they do?

   ○ Work on their statistics homework.
   ○ Have breakfast.
   ○ Stop studying for a little while.
   ○ Go to work on the math problems.

10. What does the man suggest that Lisa do?

    ○ Buy a new toaster.
    ○ Replace her old shoes.
    ○ Have repairs done.
    ○ Make another piece of toast.

11. What does the man tell the woman?

    ○ It's time for her to go now.
    ○ She can read his magazine if she wants.
    ○ He hasn't finished reading the magazine.
    ○ She should finish writing the article.

12. What does the woman think the man should do?

    ○ Buy an antique desk.
    ○ Get a new computer.
    ○ Sit down and get to work.
    ○ Use another computer disk.

13. What does Christopher tell the woman?

    ○ He'd rather study alone tonight.
    ○ He doesn't like to study at the library.
    ○ He doesn't have to take the test.
    ○ He doesn't plan to study tonight.

14. What does the man mean?

    ○ He hasn't seen the letters yet.
    ○ He doesn't know the right answers.
    ○ He doesn't want to respond to the letters.
    ○ He can't find the letters anywhere.

15. What does the woman mean?

    ○ She wants to go even though it's raining.
    ○ She can't come to lunch today.
    ○ She'll pay for lunch with a check.
    ○ She won't have time to make lunch today.

LESSON 7: Dialogues Involving Contradictions, Assumptions, and Questions

A) CONTRADICTIONS

These involve one speaker correcting what the other speaker says, as in the samples below:

SAMPLE ITEMS

You will hear:

      F2: Amy didn't work overtime last week.

      M1: As a matter of fact, she *did*!

      M2: What does the man say about Amy?

You will see on the screen:

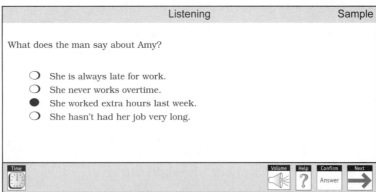

The man's emphatic use of the auxiliary verb *did* shows that he is contradicting what the woman said.

You will hear:

      M1: Martin always talks about how he loves to dance.

      F1: Yes, but you don't see him out on the dance floor very often, do you?

      M2: What does the woman say about Martin?

You will see on the screen:

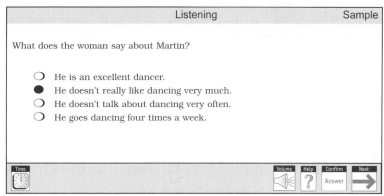

What does the woman say about Martin?

○ He is an excellent dancer.
● He doesn't really like dancing very much.
○ He doesn't talk about dancing very often.
○ He goes dancing four times a week.

The woman's use of the word *but* and the tag question (. . . *do you?*) suggests that she doesn't believe that Martin really loves to dance even though he says he does.

You will hear:

F1: All of the students voted for the proposal to expand the Student Council.

M1: Well, most of them did, anyway.

M2: What does the man mean?

You will see on the screen:

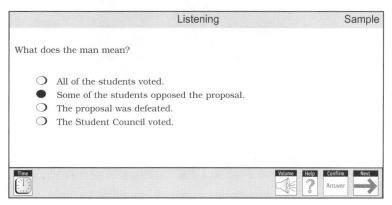

What does the man mean?

○ All of the students voted.
● Some of the students opposed the proposal.
○ The proposal was defeated.
○ The Student Council voted.

The man says that most of the students voted for the proposal, contradicting the idea that all of them did. Therefore, some of the students must have opposed the proposal.

In some dialogues, such as the third Sample Item above, the second speaker does not completely contradict what the first speaker says but rather limits the first speaker's idea.

B) ASSUMPTIONS

These are beliefs that one speaker has until he or she receives information from another speaker. These items are considered difficult, but once you understand how they work and practice answering them, you should find them no more difficult than any other type of item. In this type of dialogue, the first speaker makes a statement. The second speaker is surprised because the first statement contradicts what he or she believes to be true. The second speaker's response often begins with the word "Oh" and ends with the phrase " . . . after all." Remember: The answer to assumption questions is what the second speaker *initially* believes, and the opposite of what he says.

SAMPLE ITEM

You will hear:

F1: No, Judy's not here right now. She's at her economics class.

F2: Oh, so she decided to take that course after all.

M2: What had the second woman assumed about Judy?

You will see on the screen:

What had the second woman assumed about Judy?

● She wouldn't take the course.
○ She had already completed that course.
○ She was busy studying economics.
○ She wouldn't find economics difficult.

Time   Volume Help Confirm Next
                                      Answer

The second woman is surprised that Judy is at an economics class because she had thought that Judy had decided not to take the course. Therefore, before she spoke to Judy's roommate she had obviously assumed that Judy was not going to take the course.

C) QUESTIONS

One of the speakers questions the other. The narrator then asks what the meaning of the question is. The first speaker makes a statement and the second speaker questions that statement.

SAMPLE ITEM

You will hear:

F1: Professor Petrakis said that Mark Twain was his favorite writer.

M1: When did he say that?

M2: What does the man want to know?

You will see on the screen:

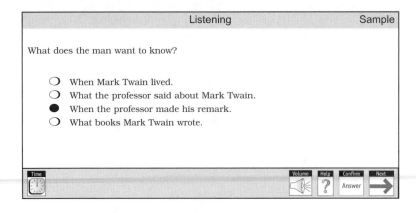

What does the man want to know?

○   When Mark Twain lived.
○   What the professor said about Mark Twain.
●   When the professor made his remark.
○   What books Mark Twain wrote.

Time   Volume   Help   Confirm   Next

Answer

The man asks when Professor Petrakis called Mark Twain his favorite author.

EXERCISE 7

Focus: Answering questions about dialogues involving contradictions, assumptions, and questions.

Directions: Listen to the following dialogues. Decide which one of the four choices best answers the question, and mark the appropriate answer.

1. What does the man say about Ginny?

   ○   She is definitely coming to dinner.
   ○   She likes fish more than chicken.
   ○   She may invite them to dinner.
   ○   She doesn't mind eating chicken.

2. What had the man assumed about Mona?

   ○   She had already moved.
   ○   She hadn't found a new apartment yet.
   ○   She'd already made an appointment.
   ○   She was no longer planning to move.

3. What does the woman want to know?

   ○   What the man's name is.
   ○   Who told the man to see the dean.
   ○   Where the dean's office is.
   ○   Who the dean is.

4. What does the man mean?

   ○   He wants to take part in the election.
   ○   He's not interested in being president.
   ○   He wants to get more facts from the president.
   ○   He'll have to run to get to class on time.

5. What had the man assumed about Carol?

   ◯ She didn't need to do any research for this paper.
   ◯ She wasn't going to word-process the paper.
   ◯ She hadn't completed all the research.
   ◯ She had finished the final draft a long time ago.

6. What does the woman imply about Bert?

   ◯ He doesn't really like horseback riding.
   ◯ He rides horses whenever possible.
   ◯ He doesn't talk about riding very much.
   ◯ He loves to watch people ride horses.

7. What does the woman want to know?

   ◯ When her travel agent called.
   ◯ What time her flight will leave.
   ◯ How far she will be flying.
   ◯ If her flight has been canceled.

8. What had the woman assumed about Cliff?

   ◯ He was working full time.
   ◯ He was eating in the cafeteria.
   ◯ He couldn't make a decision.
   ◯ He didn't want a job.

9. What does the woman want to know?

   ◯ When they returned.
   ◯ Who went hiking.
   ◯ Where they hiked.
   ◯ How long their hike was.

10. What does the man mean?

    ◯ He thinks the clothes at that store are expensive.
    ◯ He doesn't think the clothes at that store are very nice.
    ◯ He thinks the woman is being unreasonable.
    ◯ He's never been to the store on Collins Street.

11. What does the woman ask the man?

    ◯ Where the meeting will be held.
    ◯ When the meeting will start.
    ◯ Where the recreation center will be built.
    ◯ What has been proposed.

12. What had the woman assumed?

   ○ Joy did not want to study abroad.
   ○ The overseas program had been canceled.
   ○ Joy was already living overseas.
   ○ Joy would study overseas this year.

13. What does the woman ask the man?

   ○ If the party was at Ben's house.
   ○ What time the party ended.
   ○ If the man enjoyed the party.
   ○ Who attended the party.

14. What does the man mean?

   ○ All of Ted's answers were incorrect.
   ○ Most of the problems were done correctly.
   ○ Ted doesn't have to solve the problems.
   ○ Ted has had a few good jobs.

15. What does the man ask the woman?

   ○ How she got to the grocery store.
   ○ Why she went to the grocery store.
   ○ How much she paid for groceries.
   ○ What street the grocery store is on.

16. What had the woman assumed about the flashlight?

   ○ It had needed batteries.
   ○ There had been some other problem with it.
   ○ The man hadn't changed the batteries in it.
   ○ It couldn't be repaired.

17. What does the woman want to know about Steve?

   ○ Why he is in the Pacific Northwest.
   ○ Where he will go next.
   ○ When he will return from his trip.
   ○ How long he has been traveling.

18. What had Beverly originally assumed about the movie?

   ○ It hadn't been released yet.
   ○ It wouldn't be very good.
   ○ Calvin Pierce would not be starring in it.
   ○ The man had already seen it.

LESSON 8: Answering Questions about Plans, Topics, and Problems

A) QUESTIONS ABOUT PLANS

These questions follow dialogues in which two speakers discuss what one or both of them are going to do in the future.

SAMPLE ITEM

You will hear:

F2: Are you going to go to Boston with Michael this summer?

M1: Wish I could, but if I want to graduate next year, I've got to stay here and take a couple classes.

M2: What does the man plan to do this summer?

You will see on the screen:

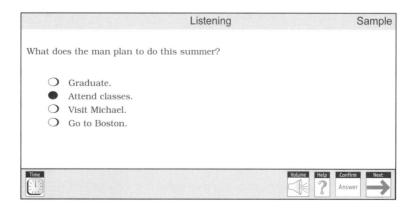

The man indicates that he must stay where he is and take classes in order to graduate next year.

B) QUESTIONS ABOUT TOPICS

In this type of item, the narrator asks what the other two speakers are talking about. The topic is not usually mentioned directly; it must be inferred from a general understanding of the dialogue. The topic can be a person, a thing, or an activity.

SAMPLE ITEM

You will hear:

M1: Have you seen this letter from the bursar's office?

F1: Oh, no, not another increase! If you ask me, we're already spending too much to go to school here.

M2: What are these speakers talking about?

You will see on the screen:

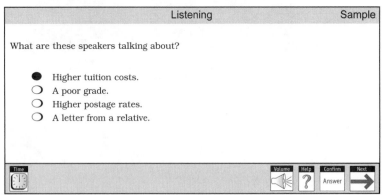

| Listening | Sample |

What are these speakers talking about?

- ● Higher tuition costs.
- ○ A poor grade.
- ○ Higher postage rates.
- ○ A letter from a relative.

From the facts that the letter comes from the bursar's office (a bursar is a financial officer at a university) and that the woman is upset about an increase and feels they are spending too much to go to school, it is clear that they are talking about an increase in tuition.

C) QUESTIONS ABOUT PROBLEMS

These questions follow dialogues in which the speakers are discussing some trouble one or both of them are having. The third speaker asks what the problem is.

SAMPLE ITEM

You will hear:

    F1: Gordon, what happened to your window?

    M1: When I was painting the house yesterday, I hit it with the ladder.

    M2: What problem does Gordon probably have?

You will see on the screen:

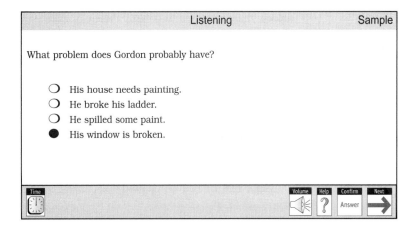

Gordon, the second speaker, says that he hit the window with the ladder when he was painting the house. The logical result—a broken window!

EXERCISE 8

Focus: Answering questions about plans, topics, and problems.

Directions: Listen to the dialogues and the questions about them. Decide which of the four choices best answers the question and mark the appropriate blank.

 Now start the listening program.

1. What are they talking about?

   ○ Road conditions.
   ○ A weather report.
   ○ A motel reservation.
   ○ Highway repairs.

2. What are they probably going to do this afternoon?

   ○ Go to a party.
   ○ Move Beth's belongings.
   ○ Get ready to have a party.
   ○ Clean up Beth's apartment.

3. What is the problem?

   ○ The man's car is not running.
   ○ The man isn't going to the party.
   ○ No one knows where the party will be.
   ○ The car isn't big enough for four people.

4. What are they probably talking about?

   ○ A shopping center.
   ○ A bridge.
   ○ A street.
   ○ An office.

5. What are the speakers probably planning to do tomorrow?

   ○ Shop for groceries.
   ○ Go on a camping trip.
   ○ Go to a circus.
   ○ Leave on a business trip.

6. What does Brian intend to do?

   ○ Get some medicine for his headaches.
   ○ Buy some new frames for his eyeglasses.
   ○ Find another doctor.
   ○ Get different lenses for his glasses.

7. What are these people discussing?

   ○ Clothing.
   ○ Hair styling.
   ○ Painting.
   ○ Cooking.

8. What is the man going to do next?

   ○ Take a trip.
   ○ Watch television.
   ○ Examine some documents.
   ○ Go to sleep.

9. What problem did the man have with the book?

   ○ He lent it to someone else.
   ○ It was ruined in the rain.
   ○ He forgot where he left it.
   ○ One of the pages was torn.

10. What are the speakers probably discussing?

    ○ A car.
    ○ A magazine.
    ○ A computer.
    ○ A piano.

11. What will Shirley probably do right after she finishes her undergraduate program?

    ○ Go to business school.
    ○ Look for a job with a big company.
    ○ Start her own business.
    ○ Take a trip around the world.

12. What is Dave's problem?

    ○ He doesn't have Phyllis' address.
    ○ He doesn't like any of the post cards.
    ○ He can't find the post office.
    ○ He doesn't have a stamp.

13. What will the woman probably do?

    ○ Order a salad.
    ○ Go to another restaurant.
    ○ Put some salt in her soup.
    ○ Go home for lunch.

14. Where does Gilbert probably plan to go today?

    ○ To a bookstore.
    ○ To a travel agency.
    ○ To a bank.
    ○ To an airport.

15. What was the man's problem?

    ○ The chair wasn't big enough.
    ○ He has gained a lot of weight recently.
    ○ The light bulb was broken.
    ○ The chair broke as he was standing on it.

LESSON 9: Dialogues with Special Verbs

A) CAUSATIVE VERBS

These verbs indicate that someone caused someone else to do something. When a dialogue contains a causative verb, you must understand who performs the action. The verbs *have, get, make,* and *let* are the most common causative verbs.
They are used in the following patterns:

Have

have someone do something ➻ Dave had the mechanic fix his car.
have something done ➻ Dave had his car fixed.

The causative verb *have* indicates that one person asks or pays another to do something. The subject of these sentences, *Dave*, does not perform the action. In the first sentence, the mechanic does. In the second sentence, an unnamed person does.

Get

get someone to do something ➻ Jerry got his cousin Sarah to cut his hair.
get something done ➻ Jerry got his hair cut.

The causative verb *get* usually means to persuade someone to do something. Again note that the subject, *Jerry*, does not perform the action.

Make

make someone do something ➻ She made her son do his homework.

The causative verb *make* means to force someone or compel someone to do something.

Let

let someone do something ➻ The boss let us go home from work early.

The verb *let* means *permit* or *allow*.

SAMPLE ITEM

You will hear:
F1: Did you speak to the head of the department?
M1: No, she was too busy, so she had her assistant meet with me.
M2: What does the man mean?
You will see on the screen:

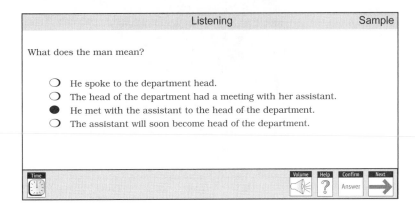

According to the dialogue, the head of the department directed her assistant to meet with the man.

B) *USED TO*

The expression **used to** has two functions:

used to + simple form

I used to live in New York.	**means** ➤→	I once lived in New York (but now I don't).

+ gerund (-*ing* verb)

be/get + *used to*

+ noun phrase

I'm not used to driving on the left side of the road.	**means** ➤→	I'm not accustomed to driving on the left side.
I've finally gotten used to my new job.	**means** ➤→	I've finally become accustomed to my new job.

The dialogues sometimes take advantage of these two functions of *used to*.

SAMPLE ITEMS

You will hear:

F2: What does Hank's father do for a living?

M1: He's a salesman now, but he used to be a truck driver.

M2: What does the man say about Hank's father?

You will see on the screen:

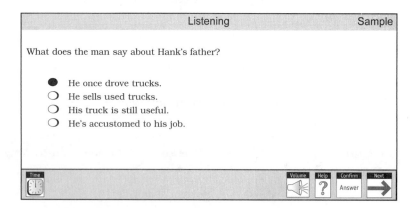

The man says that Hank's father used to be a truck driver. In other words, Hank's father once drove trucks, but he no longer does so.

You will hear:

F1: Nancy is working late again today?

M1: Yeah, she must be getting used to it by now.

M2: What does the man say about Nancy?

You will see on the screen:

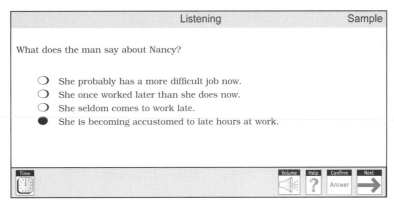

The second speaker indicates that Nancy has probably adjusted to working late.

EXERCISE 9

Focus: Listening to dialogues that contain causative verbs or expressions with *used to*.

Directions: Listen to the dialogues and the questions about them. Then decide which of the two answer choices—(A) or (B)—best answers the question and mark the appropriate blank.

 Now start the listening program.

1. What does the man say?

    ____ (A) Doug is happy to be Rose's friend.

    ____ (B) Doug and Rose are no longer good friends.

2. What does the woman tell Roger?

    ____ (A) He can do the job as well as a professional.

    ____ (B) He should hire an electrician to do the job.

3. What does the man say about the radio station?

_____ (A) It now plays classical music.

_____ (B) It doesn't broadcast anything but news.

4. What can be inferred from Lynn's remark?

_____ (A) Changing the oil was easy for her.

_____ (B) The oil didn't need to be changed.

5. What does the man mean?

_____ (A) He's not accustomed to early classes yet.

_____ (B) His classes are difficult, too.

6. What does Peggy mean?

_____ (A) She's finally accustomed to skating.

_____ (B) She doesn't go skating as often as she once did.

7. What does Kenny mean?

_____ (A) He's going to clean his tie.

_____ (B) He's going to take his tie to the cleaner's.

8. What does the man mean?

_____ (A) He moved the poster.

_____ (B) He no longer likes the sofa and desk.

9. What does the woman mean?

_____ (A) She will take a vacation in August no matter what her boss says.

_____ (B) She'll probably be too busy to go on vacation in August.

10. What did Greg's teacher do?

_____ (A) She asked Greg to explain the point.

_____ (B) She explained the point to Greg.

11. What do the speakers say about Carter?

_____ (A) He isn't accustomed to his glasses.

_____ (B) He looks quite different without glasses.

12. What does Nick tell the woman?

_____ (A) This type of weather is not new to him.

_____ (B) He once lived in a very different climate.

13. What does Sally mean?

_____ (A) She's going to take a picture of the members of her club.

_____ (B) Someone is going to photograph her club.

14. What does the woman say about the microwave oven?

    ____ (A) The man uses it too often.

    ____ (B) The man will cook with it a lot.

15. What does Jan ask the man?

    ____ (A) If the deer will come near them.

    ____ (B) If they can approach the deer.

16. What does the woman tell the man?

    ____ (A) After a few minutes, the water didn't feel too cold.

    ____ (B) She could swim in the lake for only a few minutes.

Directions: Each item in this part consists of a brief dialogue involving two speakers. After each dialogue, a third voice asks a question.

   When you have heard each dialogue and question, read the four answer choices and select the one that best answers the question based on what is directly stated or on what can be inferred.

 Now start the listening program.

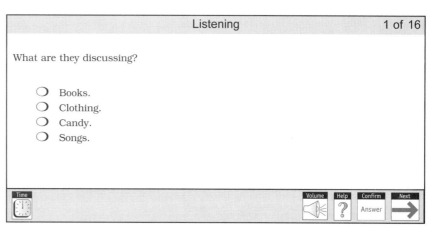

Listening	1 of 16

What are they discussing?

- ○ Books.
- ○ Clothing.
- ○ Candy.
- ○ Songs.

Time | Volume | Help | Confirm Answer | Next

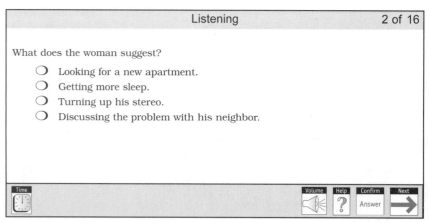

Listening	2 of 16

What does the woman suggest?

- ○ Looking for a new apartment.
- ○ Getting more sleep.
- ○ Turning up his stereo.
- ○ Discussing the problem with his neighbor.

Time | Volume | Help | Confirm Answer | Next

What does the man tell Sonya about the seminar?

- ○ Professor Osborne probably won't lead it.
- ○ It is not a required course for her.
- ○ It is being offered now, not next semester.
- ○ She doesn't need Professor Osborne's permission to take it.

Time   Volume   Help   Confirm   Next
                    ?   Answer

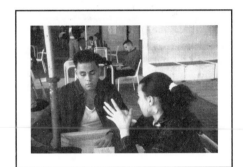

What does Adam imply?

- ○ He hasn't finished working on the bookshelves.
- ○ The tools have been misplaced.
- ○ He can't work with his hands very well.
- ○ He didn't really need the tools to build the bookshelf.

Time   Volume   Help   Confirm   Next
                    ?   Answer

What does the man imply?

- ○ He doesn't like the woman's suggestion very much.
- ○ His sister needs several new roommates.
- ○ He didn't really want the woman to give him advice.
- ○ Grace is the perfect roommate for his sister.

Time   Volume   Help   Confirm   Next
                    ?   Answer

What does the woman ask Mark?

○   What he is writing.
○   Where he is living now.
○   Why he doesn't want to go.
○   Why he is in a hurry.

Time   Volume   Help   Confirm   Next
                       ?   Answer

What does the woman mean?

○   She doesn't know where his hat is.
○   It's not very cold today.
○   She likes the way the hat looks.
○   The man ought to wear his hat.

Time   Volume   Help   Confirm   Next
                       ?   Answer

What does the man mean?

○   He doesn't believe what his friend told him.
○   He thinks the team was unprepared, too.
○   He disagrees with his friend's idea.
○   He isn't ready to go to the game either.

Time   Volume   Help   Confirm   Next
                       ?   Answer

What problem is Richard having?

- ○ His shoes hurt his feet.
- ○ He was injured in a skiing accident.
- ○ His shoes are old and in bad shape.
- ○ He walked so far that his legs hurt.

Time   Volume   Help   Confirm   Next
                              ?   Answer

What are these people discussing?

- ○ A television commercial.
- ○ A history class.
- ○ The woman's field of study.
- ○ Some famous artists.

Time   Volume   Help   Confirm   Next
                              ?   Answer

What does the woman mean?

- ○ She was about to suggest the same thing.
- ○ She doesn't feel like giving a party.
- ○ She's completely surprised by the man's suggestion.
- ○ She isn't hungry right now.

Time   Volume   Help   Confirm   Next
                              ?   Answer

What do the speakers imply about Victor?

○ He doesn't go out as often as he once did.
○ He doesn't always tell the truth.
○ He isn't as friendly as he once was.
○ He hasn't always been so sociable.

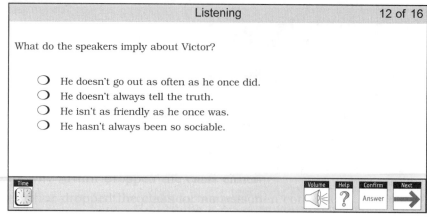

Time   Volume Help Confirm Next
               ?   Answer   →

What does the man mean?

○ The woman may see his painting.
○ He'd like the woman to visit him.
○ The woman should draw a picture herself.
○ He's going to take a guess.

Time   Volume Help Confirm Next
               ?   Answer   →

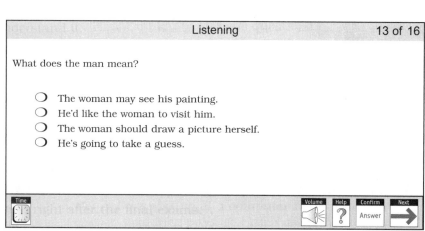

What does the woman tell the man?

○ The weather will probably improve by tomorrow.
○ She doesn't listen to the news on the radio anymore.
○ Tomorrow probably won't be such a nice day.
○ She heard about a big new store on the radio.

Time   Volume Help Confirm Next
               ?   Answer   →

What does the second woman want to know?

○ Where the medical center is located.
○ Which office Dr. Norton is in.
○ What Dr. Norton told the first woman.
○ Why the first woman went to see Dr. Norton.

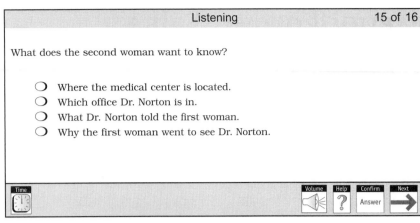

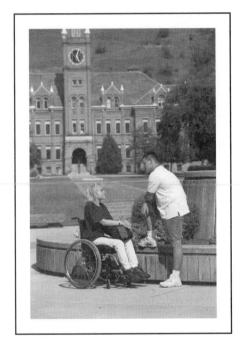

What had the man assumed about Angela?

○ She liked chemistry.
○ She would graduate in May.
○ She didn't have to repeat a course.
○ She hadn't completed the required courses.

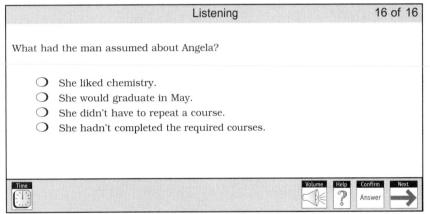

This is the end of Review Test B.

PART B: Longer Talks

ABOUT LONGER TALKS

The second part of the Listening section consists of three types of longer talks: Conversations, Mini-Lectures, and Academic Discussions.

THE INTRODUCTIONS

The introductions for Conversations are quite simple. A speaker will say something like the following:

"Listen to a conversation between a student and a professor."

"Listen to a conversation between two students."

Introductions for the Mini-Lectures and Academic Discussions may be more elaborate. A screen will generally identify the type of class in which the talk is taking place and a narrator's voice will announce the general topic and sometimes provide other information as well.

"You will now hear part of a lecture given in biology class. The class has been discussing parts of the cell, and is now focusing on the nucleus."

"You will listen to part of a discussion that takes place in a seminar in sociology. Today's topic is social interaction, the way in which members of a group respond to one another and to other groups."

THE VISUALS

The photographs that accompany the conversations are very similar to those that go with the dialogues in Part A. You will see a photograph of the two speakers. One part of the photograph may lighten, the other darken to indicate which of the two is speaking.

A series of up to five photos will appear as you are listening to the Mini-Lectures and Academic Discussions. Some of the pictures are **context pictures**, showing a lecturing professor or a group of students sitting at a seminar table, but others are **content pictures.** These provide information that can help you answer the questions. Besides photographs, you may see screens that present difficult terms from the lecture. You may also see drawings, charts, maps, or other types of visual information.

Some people prefer to close their eyes or look away from the screen while listening to Part B talks. In fact, it is better to look at the visuals shown on the screen, but you should concentrate on the talk, not on the visuals.

THE TALKS

Conversations are similar to the Part A dialogues in style, but are longer—from 30 to 90 seconds long. They frequently take place in a campus setting between two students or between a professor and a student, but are not necessarily academic. There will be two to four Conversations per test.

Mini-Lectures resemble parts of classroom lectures given in a university course in classes such as history, literature, psychology, or biology. There is a single speaker, usually a professor. There will be two to three Mini-Lectures per test.

Academic Discussions involve three or four speakers, most often a professor and several students. They resemble the kind of discussion that would take place in a university seminar or class. You will hear one or two Academic Discussions per test.

Both Mini-Lectures and Academic Discussions are longer than the Conversations. They may be up to two and a half minutes in length. They are usually more formal in tone than the Conversations and always deal with academic topics.

THE QUESTIONS

There are two or three questions about the Conversations and three to six questions about the Mini-Lectures and Academic Discussions.

Only standard multiple-choice questions are asked about the longer Conversations. Most of the questions asked about Mini-Lectures and Academic Discussions are also standard multiple-choice questions, but some are "computer-unique" questions.

There are three main types of standard multiple-choice questions:

Main Idea/Main Topic Questions ask what the conversation, lecture, or discussion is primarily about. These require a broad understanding of the entire talk.

Detail Questions ask about specific points in the talk. Many detail questions begin with phrases such as these:

> According to the professor, . . .
> According to the man, . . .
> According to the woman, . . .
> According to the lecturer, . . .
> According to the conversation, . . .
> According to the speakers, . . .
> According to the lecture, . . .

Inference Questions ask about information that is not directly given by the speakers, but can be concluded from the information that IS stated. These are typical inference questions:

> What can be inferred from the woman's comment about . . . ?
> What does the man imply about . . . ?
> What can be inferred from the lecture?

There are a number of computer-unique questions:

Click on a Picture items involve visual answer choices. You may have to click on one of four (sometimes three) different visuals or on part of a single visual labeled A, B, C, and D. This item type is actually a type of detail question.

Multiple-Choice Questions with Two Answers may be main idea, detail, or inference questions. You must choose two answers instead of one. (The program will not allow you to go on until you have chosen two.) There are empty squares next to the choices rather than ovals.

Matching Questions require you to match three items with three related items—usually three examples with three categories.

Ordering Questions require you to arrange four items in the proper order. The order is usually based on chronology or on the order of steps in a process.

THE ANSWER CHOICES

The four choices for the multiple-choice questions are all plausible answers for the questions. Usually the answer choices are mentioned in some way in the conversation; however, only the key (or keys, in a two-answer question) answers that particular question correctly.

In the next section of this *Guide,* you will practice listening to all three types of Part B talks and answering all types of questions about them.

Tactics for Part B

- Be familiar with the directions for Part B. As soon as the directions appear, you can click on the "Dismiss Directions" icon.

- Be certain you understand how to answer the computer-unique questions for Part B: questions with two answers, click on a picture items, matching questions, and ordering questions.

- Answer each question promptly and go on to the next one as quickly as possible.

- Pay attention to the introductions for each talk. These will help "set the scene" for you and may give you a general idea of what the talk will be about.

- As you listen to the talk, try to guess what the questions and answers will be.

- Pay attention to the visuals, especially the "content" visuals. However, you should concentrate your attention on listening to the talks, not on looking at the visuals.

- Listen for main ideas: What is the talk generally about? The answers to main idea/main topic questions are often suggested in the first few lines of the talks, but you must understand the entire talk to answer these questions correctly.

- Matching and ordering questions usually require you to understand a large portion of the talk.

- You are not permitted to take written notes, but try to take "mental notes" on specific details: facts, figures, dates, places, and so on. You can sometimes check the information you think you hear against information you see in the visuals on the screen.

- If you are not sure of an answer, eliminate as many answer choices as you can and then guess.

- Even if you have no idea which answer choice is correct, guess and go on.

LESSON 10: Answering Main Idea/Main Topic Questions about Longer Talks

After each talk in Part B, there are sets of three to six questions. Often the first question in any set is a **main idea** or a **main topic question**. To answer these questions, you need an understanding of the whole lecture or conversation. There are a number of ways that these questions can be phrased:

> What is the main idea of this lecture?
> What is the main point of this lecture?
> What is the main topic of this discussion?
> What is this conversation primarily about?
> What is the purpose of this talk?

Most main idea/main topic questions are standard one-answer questions, but some about Mini-Lectures and Academic Discussions may be two-answer questions.

Main idea/main topic questions must correctly summarize the talk. Incorrect answers are either too general, too specific, or incorrect according to the lecture.

Although these questions require an overall understanding of the talks, the first few sentences often "set the scene" and give you a general idea what the topic of the lecture is about. Read the opening lines of the conversation given below:

M1: (Answering phone) Hello?

F1: Hi, Rod, this Rita—I'm in your nine o'clock class. I missed class because of a cold, and I was wondering if I could borrow your notes.

M1: Sure, I can tell you what happened. Professor Phillips went over the material in Chapter 4, about different types of stars in our galaxy. And she talked about what the mid-term exam is going to be like.

F1: Uh-oh, you better tell me all about the mid-term. I really need to do well on it.

From this portion of a conversation, we learn that the speakers are students in the same astronomy class, and you can guess that the main topic of the conversation will be the content of the mid-term exam.

EXERCISE 10

Focus: Listening to the opening portions of Conversations, Mini-Lectures, and Academic Discussions and answering main idea/main topic questions about them. (NOTE: These practice talks are shorter than the ones you will typically hear on actual exams.) Remember: don't look at the questions until they are read on the tape.

Directions: Listen to the talks and the questions about them. Then mark the answer choice that correctly answers the question.

 Now start the listening program.

1. What will the main topic of this conversation probably be?

- ○ Methods of predicting earthquakes.
- ○ Ways to improve the man's presentation.
- ○ The many new uses of computer graphics.
- ○ The role of statistics in geology.

2. What are the main purposes of this discussion?

Choose two.

- ❑ To explain the reason for higher rents.
- ❑ To review a reading assignment.
- ❑ To contrast two forms of taxation.
- ❑ To discuss the need for sales taxes.

3. What will the main subject of this conversation probably be?

   ○ Professor Quinn's approach to teaching.
   ○ The process of getting a student identification card.
   ○ Procedures for checking out reserve materials.
   ○ Several recent articles in sociology journals.

4. What will the rest of this talk mainly be about?

   Choose two.

   ❑ The disadvantages of being in the program.
   ❑ The physical rewards of dancing.
   ❑ The importance of the program to the university.
   ❑ The procedures for arranging a tryout.

5. What will the two speakers probably discuss?

   ○ Their plans for the coming school year.
   ○ Tina's volunteer position.
   ○ Tina's trip to Europe.
   ○ An archaeology class that they both took.

6. What are the speakers mainly discussing?

   ○ Reading experiments at Duke University.
   ○ Reasons why scientists don't believe ESP is valid.
   ○ The accomplishments of Professor Rhine.
   ○ The failure of recent experiments in parapsychology.

7. What is this lecture primarily going to concern?

   ○ The historical record contained in shipwrecks.
   ○ The role of the State Historical Society.
   ○ The history of New England.
   ○ The leading causes of shipwrecks.

8. What will the rest of the lecture probably concern?

   ○ Problems of the tobacco industry in the United States.
   ○ Government regulation of advertisers.
   ○ Tactics involved in deceptive advertisements.
   ○ Self-regulation of the advertising industry.

9. Why does the woman want to talk to Dr. Marshall?

   ○ To ask for a job.
   ○ To get some career advice.
   ○ To discuss a medical problem.
   ○ To ask permission to take a class.

10. What will the rest of the conversation probably deal with?

   ○ The location of Nicholson Hall.
   ○ Requirements for graduation.
   ○ Directions to another office.
   ○ The woman's need for a scholarship.

LESSON 11: Answering Detail and Inference Questions about Longer Talks

Most of the questions in Part B are **detail questions** that require an understanding of specific points in the talks. These questions ask what, where, when, why, how much, and other questions about the conversation. To answer these questions, you need to listen quite carefully.

Other questions are **inference questions**. As previously explained, the answers to inference questions are not directly stated, but are suggested by information in the talk.

If anything in the conversation is emphasized, it will probably be asked about. In other words, if something one speaker says is repeated by the second speaker, or if one speaker talks about something in an emphatic tone of voice, there will probably be a question about that information, as in this section of a conversation:

> M1: My project for my film-making class took me six weeks to finish.
>
> F1: Six weeks! I can hardly believe it. Doesn't the teacher realize you have other classes too?

You can be fairly sure that there will be a question like this; "How long did the man's project take to complete?"

Some of the detail and inference questions may be two-answer questions. Some detail questions will involve clicking on a picture.

EXERCISE 11

Focus: Answering detail and inference questions based on specific points in Conversations, Mini-Lectures, and Academic Discussions.

Directions: You will hear a number of longer talks. After each, there will be a set of detail and inference questions based on the talk. Mark the best answer choice. (Note: To give you more practice, there are more questions after most of these talks than there are after the talks on the actual exam.)

 Now start the listening program.

1. Why is Steve tired?

    ○ He stayed up most of the night.
    ○ He had to take a test last night.
    ○ He's been studying all morning.
    ○ He's been too nervous to sleep well lately.

2. How did Steve feel about the grade he received?

    ○ It was an improvement.
    ○ It was disappointing.
    ○ It was unfair.
    ○ It was a surprise.

3. Who teaches the seminars at the Study Skills Center?

    Choose two.

    ❏ Undergraduate students.
    ❏ Professors.
    ❏ Graduate students.
    ❏ Librarians.

4. What seminar will Steve probably take?

   ○ Basic scientific research.
   ○ Business management.
   ○ Test-taking skills.
   ○ Chemistry.

5. Where is the main office of the Study Skills Center?

   ○ In the library.
   ○ In the Physics Tower.
   ○ In a dormitory.
   ○ In Staunton Hall.

6. What does the woman think Steve should do next?

   ○ Study for his next exam.
   ○ Go to the Study Skills Center.
   ○ Talk to his chemistry professor.
   ○ Get some sleep.

7. When did orbital debris first appear?

   ○ In the 1950s.
   ○ In the 1960s.
   ○ In the 1980s.
   ○ In the 1990s.

8. What happens to most pieces of orbital debris?

   ○ They fly off into deep space.
   ○ They remain in orbit forever.
   ○ They collide with other pieces.
   ○ They burn up in the atmosphere.

9. How many orbital bodies are being monitored today?

   ○ Three to four hundred.
   ○ Three to four thousand.
   ○ About eight thousand.
   ○ Half a million.

10. Why is it impossible to monitor most pieces of orbital debris?

    ○ They are too small.
    ○ They are too far away.
    ○ They are moving too fast.
    ○ They are made of reflective material.

11. Which of the following types of orbital debris are probably most dangerous to astronauts on a spacecraft?

    Choose two.

    ❏ A large booster rocket.
    ❏ A piece of metal the size of an aspirin.
    ❏ A lost tool.
    ❏ A tiny fleck of paint.

12. What makes orbital debris such a danger to spacecraft?

- ○ Its high speed.
- ○ Its jagged shape.
- ○ Its gigantic size.
- ○ Its unusual composition.

13. Assume that this is a representation of a satellite equipped with a collector. Where would the space debris be stored? Circle the letter of the correct response.

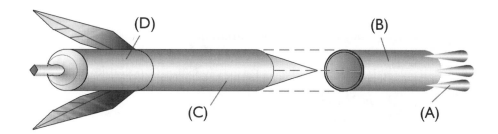

14. In which ways could the collector be used to solve the problem of orbital debris?

Choose two.

- ❑ It could be used to track even very small pieces of orbital debris.
- ❑ It could serve as a protective device for manned spacecraft.
- ❑ It could be mounted on unmanned spacecraft to find and trap pieces of debris.
- ❑ It could burn up large pieces of orbital debris.

15. What can be inferred about the collector described in the talk?

- ○ It has already been tested on Earth.
- ○ It is no longer in common use.
- ○ It has already been installed on spacecraft.
- ○ It has not been built yet.

16. Where is the town of San Juan Capistrano located? (Circle the letter of the correct response.)

17. What were the professor's main reasons for going to San Juan Capistrano?
    Choose two.

    ❑ To visit a friend.
    ❑ To see the swallows arrive.
    ❑ To help a colleague.
    ❑ To see a parade.

18. What can be inferred about the swallows?

    ◯ They are a type of insect.
    ◯ They are a kind of fish.
    ◯ They are a type of bird.
    ◯ They are a type of mammal.

19. When do the swallows return to San Juan Capistrano?

    ◯ In March.
    ◯ In early summer.
    ◯ In October.
    ◯ In mid-winter.

20. How far do the swallows migrate?

    ◯ About 200 miles.
    ◯ About 1,000 miles.
    ◯ About 3,000 miles.
    ◯ About 7,000 miles.

21. According to the professor, how was the mission church in San Juan Capistrano damaged?

    ◯ By a storm.
    ◯ By a fire.
    ◯ By an earthquake.
    ◯ By the swallows.

22. According to the professor, why are the swallows popular with the people of San Juan Capistrano?

    Choose two.

    ❑ They eliminate insect pests.
    ❑ They help bring money into the community.
    ❑ They are believed to bring good luck.
    ❑ They are extremely beautiful creatures.

23. When is the guided tour of the campus given?

    ◯ Before the semester begins.
    ◯ Only during the first week of the semester.
    ◯ Whenever students ask for them.
    ◯ Only in the afternoon.

24. What did the man have trouble locating the week before?

   ○ A tour guide.
   ○ A classroom.
   ○ A map.
   ○ A pamphlet.

25. Where does the self-guided tour start?

   ○ In the Science Building.
   ○ In the Student Center Building.
   ○ In the University Recreation Center.
   ○ In the planetarium.

26. According to the lecturer, why did the ancient Greeks think that the Earth was the center of the universe?

                    Choose two.

   ❑ Because the Earth did not seem to move.
   ❑ Because the objects in the sky seemed to revolve around the Earth.
   ❑ Because this idea was part of their religious beliefs.
   ❑ Because the movement of the planets was unpredictable.

27. What did the ancient Greeks believe the spheres circling the Earth were made of?

   ○ Gas.
   ○ Metal.
   ○ Light.
   ○ Crystal.

28. This is a simple representation of the geocentric model. Which letter represents the Earth's moon? (Circle the letter of the correct response.)

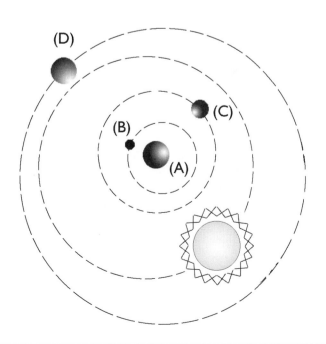

29. This is a simple representation of the heliocentric model. Which letter represents the Earth's moon? (Circle the letter of the correct response.)

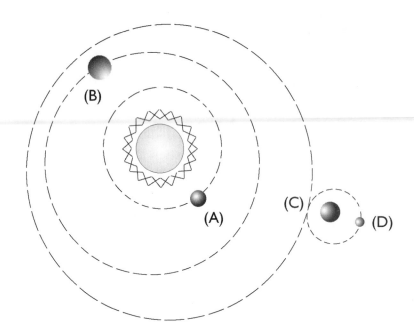

30. When was the heliocentric model proposed?

   ○ In the second century.
   ○ In the fourteenth century.
   ○ In the sixteenth century.
   ○ In the twentieth century.

31. Which of these phrases is a synonym for *heliocentric model*?

   ○ Ptolemaic model.
   ○ Geocentric model.
   ○ Clockwork model.
   ○ Copernican model.

32. What does the lecturer imply about the heliocentric model?

   ○ It was immediately accepted.
   ○ It was ignored because no one was interested in astronomy.
   ○ It is much more logical than the geocentric model.
   ○ It is no longer considered accurate.

33. Which of the following did Copernicus believe about the stars?

   ○ They were very far away.
   ○ They were similar to the Sun.
   ○ They made up billions of galaxies.
   ○ They revolved around the Earth.

LESSON 12: Answering Matching and Ordering Questions about Longer Talks

These two types of items are unique to the computer-based TOEFL® test. They did not appear on the paper-based form of the test. They require understanding not just single details but a large portion of the talk. It would be much easier to answer these questions if you could take notes on paper, but this is not permitted. You'll have to try to take "mental notes" to remember what you hear.

For most test-takers, matching and ordering items are probably the most difficult parts of the Listening section.

Ordering questions require you to put four events or four steps of a process in the correct order. Any time you hear the lecturer or speakers discussing a sequence of events, a biography of a person, the steps of a process, or a ranking of things according to their importance, there will probably be an ordering question. Listen for words that signal a sequence, such as next, then, after that, later, or before that, previously, earlier. Try to keep track of the events or steps. They may not be given in the talk in the order in which they are listed in the questions.

To answer these questions on the computer, you must first click on one of the four words, phrases, or sentences in the top half of the screen and then click on the appropriate box (labeled 1, 2, 3, and 4) in the lower half of the screen. The expression from the top will then appear in the box that you clicked on. Do this for all four boxes.

You really have to put only three answers in their proper positions because the fourth answer must of course go in the remaining position.

Matching questions require you to connect three words, phrases, or sentences with three other words or phrases somehow related to them. If the lecturer or speaker lists three or more concepts and then gives definitions, examples, characteristics, or uses of those concepts, you can expect to hear a matching question.

To answer a matching question, you must click on one of the three expressions in the top half of the screen and then on the box above the expression that you think is related to it. That word or phrase will then appear in the box. Do this for all three boxes.

You really have to correctly match two pairs of answers because obviously the one remaining pair of answers must be matched.

EXERCISE 12

Focus: Listening to portions of Mini-Lectures and Academic Discussions and answering matching and ordering questions about them.

Directions: Write the letters of the words or phrases in the appropriate boxes. (Note: There are no letters by the choices in the computer version. You simply click on the choice and then on the box where you think it belongs.)

 Now start the listening program.

CHEMISTRY CLASS

The lecturer discusses the steps involved in the creation of coal.
Summarize this process by putting the events in the proper order.

Place the letters in the proper boxes.

(A) During the process of decomposition, plants lose oxygen and hydrogen.

(B) Layers of sand and mud put pressure on the peat.

(C) Plants grow in swampy areas.

(D) Plants die and fall into swampy waters.

1.
2.
3.
4.

Time   Volume   Help   Confirm   Next
                     ?   Answer

Match the form of coal with the type of industry which primarily uses it.

Place the letters in the proper boxes.

(A) coal tar   (B) bituminous coal   (C) coke

Electric   Plastic   Steelmakers
utilities   manufacturers

Time   Volume   Help   Confirm   Next
                     ?   Answer

ACCOUNTING SEMINAR

GAAP

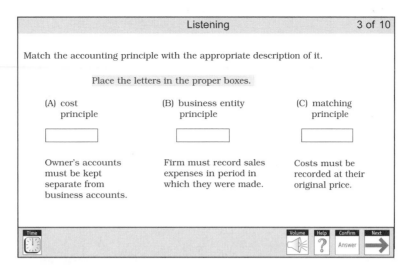

Match the accounting principle with the appropriate description of it.

Place the letters in the proper boxes.

(A) cost
     principle

(B) business entity
     principle

(C) matching
     principle

Owner's accounts
must be kept
separate from
business accounts.

Firm must record sales
expenses in period in
which they were made.

Costs must be
recorded at their
original price.

Time   Volume   Help   Confirm   Next
                  ?   Answer

The lecturer mentions four types of crops that are grown in Harrison County.
Rank these four crops in their order of economic importance, beginning with the
MOST important.

Place the letters in the proper boxes.

(A) Wheat.
(B) Organic fruit.
(C) Corn.
(D) Soy beans.

1.

2.

3.

4.

Time   Volume   Help   Confirm   Next
                  ?   Answer

Match the type of wheat with the product that is most often made from it.

Place the letters in the proper boxes.

(A) Hard red
     wheat

(B) Soft white
     wheat

(C) Durum wheat

Pasta

Bread flour

Breakfast cereals

Time   Volume   Help   Confirm   Next
                  ?   Answer

HISTORY
CLASS

The professor discusses some of the history of Antarctic exploration. Summarize this history by putting these expeditions in the order in which they began.

Place the letters in the proper boxes.

(A) Amundson's.
(B) Scott's.
(C) Byrd's.
(D) Shackleton's.

1. _____
2. _____
3. _____
4. _____

Time   Volume Help Confirm Next
                      Answer

Match these Antarctic explorers with the countries from which they came.

Place the letters in the proper boxes.

(A) Scott   (B) Amundson   (C) Byrd

[ ]   [ ]   [ ]

United States   Norway   Britain

Time   Volume Help Confirm Next
                      Answer

MUSICAL ACOUSTICS CLASS

Match the performance with its maximum decibel level.

Place the letters in the proper boxes.

(A) The first   (B) The   (C) The Creatures'
    violin's   Metropolitan   concert
    solo   Philharmonic
                      Symphony
                      concert

[ ]   [ ]   [ ]

60 decibels   90 decibels   115 decibels

Time   Volume Help Confirm Next
                      Answer

The professor gives a brief biography of the writer Edgar Allen Poe. List the events from his life in the order in which they occurred.

Place the letters in the proper boxes.

(A) Wrote his first book of poems.
(B) Entered West Point, the U.S. military academy.
(C) Worked as a clerk.
(D) Went to England.

1.
2.
3.
4.

Time   Volume   Help   Confirm   Next
                   ?   Answer

Match these works by Edgar Allen Poe with the type of writing that they represent.

Place the letters in the proper boxes.

(A) "The Gold Bug"   (B) "The Raven"   (C) "The Fall of the House ofUsher"

Poem   Horror story   Detective story

Time   Volume   Help   Confirm   Next
                   ?   Answer

REVIEW TEST C: Longer Talks

Directions: This part involves longer talks: conversations, discussions, and lectures. You will hear the talks only once. After each of these talks, there are a number of questions.

When you have read and heard the questions, read the answer choices and select the best answer or answers based on what is directly stated or on what can be inferred.

Don't forget: During actual exams, taking notes during the Listening section is not permitted.

 Now start the listening program.

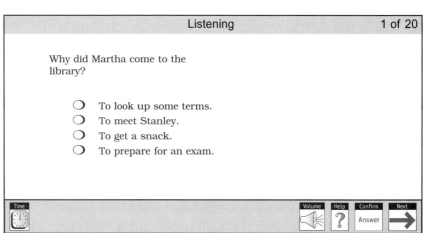

Listening	1 of 20

Why did Martha come to the library?

- ○ To look up some terms.
- ○ To meet Stanley.
- ○ To get a snack.
- ○ To prepare for an exam.

Time Volume Help Confirm Answer Next

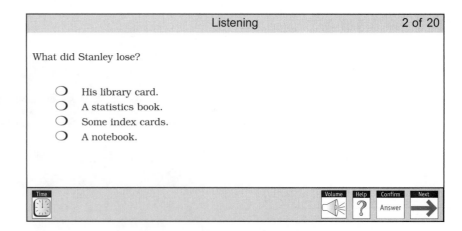

Listening	2 of 20

What did Stanley lose?

- ○ His library card.
- ○ A statistics book.
- ○ Some index cards.
- ○ A notebook.

Time Volume Help Confirm Answer Next

According to Stanley, what does the term "stacks" refer to?

- ○ The part of the library where journals are stored.
- ○ Piles of note cards.
- ○ The part of the library where books are shelved.
- ○ A place to get something to eat in the library.

Time   Volume   Help   Confirm Answer   Next

ANTHROPOLOGY CLASS

What are the main purposes of the lecture?

Choose two.

- ☐ To talk about the hunter-gatherer stage of humankind.
- ☐ To outline the process of domestication in general.
- ☐ To discuss the domestication of dogs.
- ☐ To describe the various tasks dogs have been given.

Time   Volume   Help   Confirm Answer   Next

According to the lecturer, how did early humans adapt dogs to different tasks?

○ By crossing wolves with other animals.
○ By careful training.
○ By selective breeding.
○ By rewarding dogs with pieces of food.

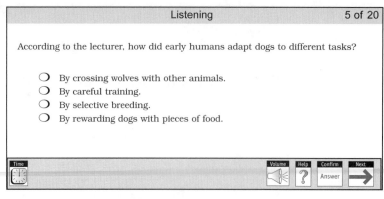

Why does the lecturer mention Idaho?

○ The first dogs were domesticated there.
○ A famous mural of a dog was painted there.
○ The remains of an early specimen of domesticated dog were found there.
○ It was there that dogs first learned how to help humans to hunt.

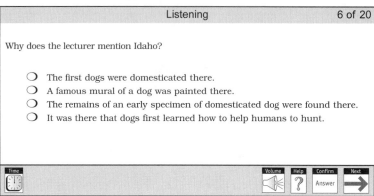

The lecturer mentions a number of roles that dogs have played since they were first domesticated. List these roles in the correct chronological order.

Place the letters in the proper boxes.

(A) Hunter.
(B) Herder.
(C) Companion.
(D) Guard.

1.
2.
3.
4.

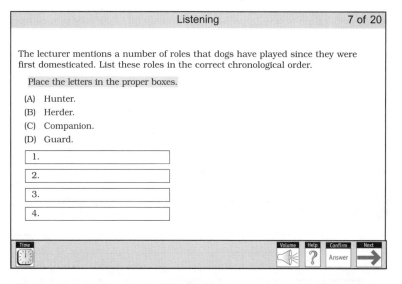

Click on the part of the picture that represents the herders' "best friend."

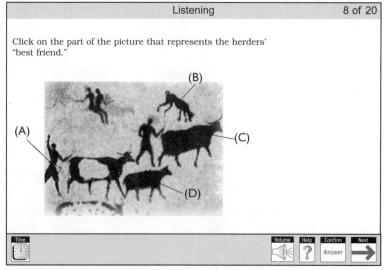

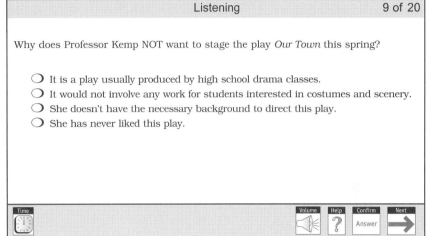

Why does Professor Kemp NOT want to stage the play *Our Town* this spring?

○ It is a play usually produced by high school drama classes.
○ It would not involve any work for students interested in costumes and scenery.
○ She doesn't have the necessary background to direct this play.
○ She has never liked this play.

Time   Volume Help Confirm Next
                  ?   Answer

Professor Kemp and her students discuss a number of plays. Match the characteristics of the play with the title of the play.

Place the letters in the proper boxes.

(A) A Shakespearean comedy.
(B) A play about the Salem witch trials.
(C) A musical.

The Tempest   *A Chorus Line*   *The Crucible*

Time   Volume Help Confirm Next
                  ?   Answer

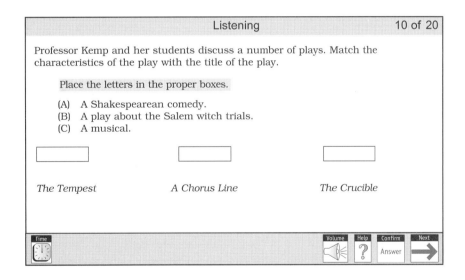

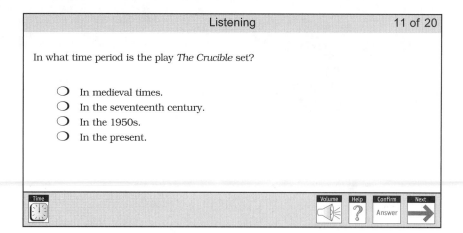

In what time period is the play *The Crucible* set?

- ○ In medieval times.
- ○ In the seventeenth century.
- ○ In the 1950s.
- ○ In the present.

Time Volume Help Confirm Next
Answer

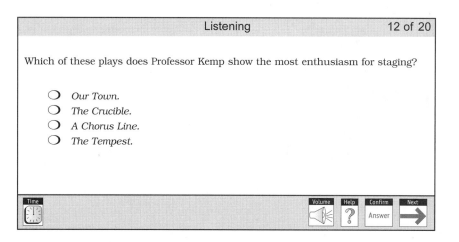

Which of these plays does Professor Kemp show the most enthusiasm for staging?

- ○ *Our Town.*
- ○ *The Crucible.*
- ○ *A Chorus Line.*
- ○ *The Tempest.*

Time Volume Help Confirm Next
Answer

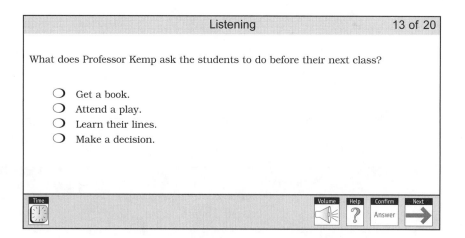

What does Professor Kemp ask the students to do before their next class?

- ○ Get a book.
- ○ Attend a play.
- ○ Learn their lines.
- ○ Make a decision.

Time Volume Help Confirm Next
Answer

What does the article that Nicole is reading say about Hambleton College?

○   Its tuition rates are going up faster than the ones at Babcock University.
○   It has the highest tuition rates in the state.
○   Its tuition rates are still lower than those at Babcock University.
○   It has actually lowered its tuition rates recently.

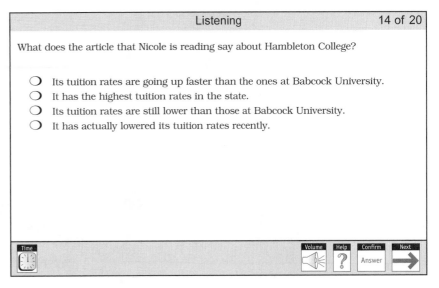

Time		Volume	Help	Confirm	Next
			?	Answer	→

Who is Penny Chang?

○   The president of the Student Council.
○   A member of the Board of Regents.
○   A spokesperson for the administration.
○   A journalist for the campus newspaper.

Time		Volume	Help	Confirm	Next
			?	Answer	→

What can be inferred from the remark made by the spokesperson for the administration?

○   The new dormitory will not be built.
○   The proposal to increase student services will not be adopted.
○   The tuition will not be raised.
○   New computers will be bought.

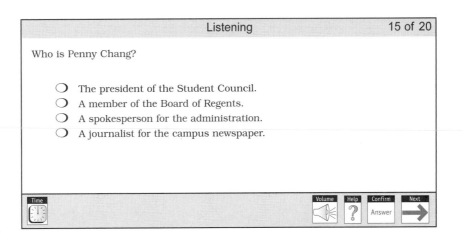

Time		Volume	Help	Confirm	Next
			?	Answer	→

LINGUISTICS
CLASS

CENTER   COLOR
CENTRE   COLOUR

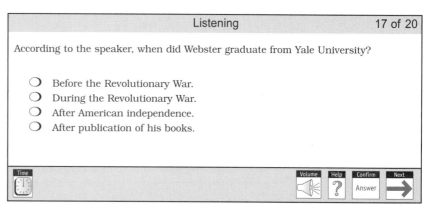

According to the speaker, when did Webster graduate from Yale University?

○ Before the Revolutionary War.
○ During the Revolutionary War.
○ After American independence.
○ After publication of his books.

Time   Volume Help Confirm Next
                      ?   Answer   →

What is Noah Webster mainly remembered for today?

○ His military service.
○ His political philosophy.
○ His dictionary.
○ His unusual spellings.

Time | Volume | Help ? | Confirm Answer | Next →

According to the speaker, what kind of book was the "blue-backed book"?

○ A history book.
○ A dictionary.
○ An autobiography.
○ A spelling book.

Time | Volume | Help ? | Confirm Answer | Next →

Which of the following are spellings that Benjamin Franklin would probably have approved of?

Choose two.

☐ T-H-E-A-T-R-E instead of T-H-E-A-T-E-R.
☐ F-O-T-O-G-R-A-F instead of P-H-O-T-O-G-R-A-P-H.
☐ L-A-B-O-U-R instead of L-A-B-O-R.
☐ N-I-F instead of K-N-I-F-E.

Time | Volume | Help ? | Confirm Answer | Next →

This is the end of Review Test C.

A knowledge of idioms is important for the Listening section, especially Part A. These Mini-Lessons contain alphabetical lists of some 300 expressions and their definitions as well as exercises to familiarize you with these expressions. Many of the expressions listed here have appeared on the Listening sections of the TOEFL® test in the past, some of them several times.

NOTES

1. If a phrase contains a word in parentheses, that word is used only if the verb is followed by a noun or pronoun.

   Example:

   catch up (with)

   You go ahead. I'll catch up later. (no noun or pronoun)

   I'll catch up *with* you later. (pronoun)

2. The words *one* and *someone* are used to indicate that any personal pronoun (or sometimes a noun) can be used in this expression.

   Example:

   on one's own

   How long have you been on *your* own?

   Tom's been on *his* own for several years.

MINI-LESSON 1.1

about to almost ready to

add up make sense; be logical

all at once suddenly; without warning

as a rule generally; customarily

at ease not nervous; calm

at the drop of a hat quickly; without any preparation time

back out (of) withdraw (an offer)

bank on depend on; count on

be my guest do what you want; feel free; help yourself

be rusty need practice or review

beats me I don't know; I have no idea (often used in response to a question)

better off an improved condition

bite off more than one can chew take on more responsibility than one can handle

bound to certain to; sure to

break down stop functioning (a machine, for example)

break in (on someone) interrupt

break the ice break through social barriers (as at a party)

break the news (to someone) inform; give bad news

break up end (a meeting, for example)

break up (with someone) stop being a couple (a boyfriend and girlfriend, for example)

a breeze something very simple and easy to do

bring about cause to happen

bring up (1) raise (a child) (2) introduce (a topic, for example)

brush up on review; study; practice

bump into meet unexpectedly; run into

by and large mostly; generally; on the whole

by heart by memory; learned word for word

by no means in no way

Directions: Fill in the blanks in the sentences or dialogues with idioms from the list. There will be one word per blank. It may be necessary to change the verb form in order for the sentence to be grammatically correct. The first one is done as an example.

1. "Can you talk now?"

   "No, I'm _about_ _to_ go to the grocery store, but I'll call you as soon as I get back."

2. "You're all packed and ready to go, I see."

   "I could leave ———— ———— ———— ———— ———— ————."

3. "Do you know what the name of this street is?"

   "———— ————. This is the first time I've ever been in this town."

4. I was talking to my aunt when suddenly my cousin Georgia ———— ———— ———— our conversation.

5. "I understand Audrey lost her job."

   "Yes, but she's actually ———— ————. She found a more interesting job with a higher salary."

6. ———— ———— ————, Carlos is very punctual, but he sure was late tonight.

7. My car ———— ———— last week and I had to take the bus to work until it was repaired.

8. "How's that biology class you're taking?"

   "So far, it's been ———— ————. We've just been going over things I studied last semester."

9. Kent is ———— ———— fail that class if he doesn't start studying.

10. They ———— ———— their children to be honest.

11. There were a few things I didn't like about Professor Wong's class, but ———— ———— ———— I enjoyed it.

12. "I think Matthew was cheating on that quiz."

   "That doesn't ———— ————. Why should the best student in the class cheat?"

13. "Can I have another sandwich?"

   "Sure, ———— ———— ————. I made plenty."

14. Actors and actresses must know their lines ———— ————.

15. If you don't want to talk about this problem, why did you ———— it ————?

16. "What time did the party ———— ———— last night?"

   "I don't know. It was still going on when I went home."

17. "I was awfully nervous when I gave that speech."

   "Really? You hid it well. I thought you were completely _____ _____."

18. "What a boring party. No one is talking to one another."

   "Maybe we should put on some music and start dancing. That might _____ _____ _____."

19. "Have you studied Spanish before?"

   "Yes, but it's been years since I took a Spanish class, so I'll need to _____ _____ _____ it before I go to Venezuela."

20. "You're taking five classes this term?"

   "Yes, and I'm having trouble getting caught up. I'm afraid I _____ _____ _____ _____ I _____ _____ this time."

MINI-LESSON 1.2

call it a day stop working for the day; go home

call off cancel

call on visit

calm down relax

care for (1) take care of (2) like; feel affection for

catch on become popular

catch on (to) understand, learn

catch up (with) go as fast as; catch

check in (or into) register (at a hotel)

check out (of) (1) leave (a hotel) (2) take material (from a library, for example)

cheer up become cheerful; be happy

chip in (on/for) contribute

clear up (1) clarify; make understandable (2) become nice and sunny (used to talk about the weather)

come across find; meet; encounter

come around (to) begin to change one's opinion; begin to agree with

come down with become sick with (an illness)

come up with think of (an idea)

cost an arm and a leg be very expensive

count on depend on; rely on

count out eliminate; no longer consider as a factor

cut off stop; discontinue (a service, for example)

cut out for have an aptitude for; be qualified for

Directions: Fill in the blanks in the sentences or dialogues with idioms from the list. There will be one word per blank. It may be necessary to change the verb form in order for the sentence to be grammatically correct.

1. The reception in the garden had to be _____ _____ because of rain.

2. Don't get so excited. Just _____ _____ and tell us what happened.

3. I was looking up some information in the almanac when I _____ _____ an interesting fact.

4. I can _____ _____ my car. It's very dependable and never breaks down.

5. How did you _____ _____ _____ such a strange idea?

6. I arrived in town last night at seven-thirty and _____ _____ my hotel at around eight. This morning I plan to _____ _____ at about nine.

7. "Did you rent this videotape?"

   "No, I _____ it _____ _____ the library."

8. You look tired. Why don't we _____ _____ _____ _____ and finish up tomorrow?

9. It won't be too expensive to buy Professor Macmillan a present if we all _____ _____.

10. If Jim doesn't pay his electric bill soon, the utilities company might _____ _____ his electricity.

11. "I don't understand this theorem at all."

    "Talk to Professor Adler. I'll bet she can _____ _____ your confusion."

12. "Your friend is still planning to vote for Smithson for president of the Student Council?"

    "Yes, but I'm going to keep talking to him. I think eventually he'll _____ _____ _____ our point of view and vote for Brannigan."

13. A good stereo system doesn't have to _____ _____ _____ _____ _____ _____. You can find one for a reasonable price.

14. Cauliflower isn't my favorite vegetable. In fact, I don't _____ _____ it at all.

15. "I'm depressed. I didn't do very well on the first quiz."

    "_____ _____! That quiz only counted for 10% of the total grade, and I'm sure you'll do better on the other tests."

16. "How did Eric do in the cross-country ski race?"

    "He got off to a bad start, so he never _____ _____ _____ the leaders."

17. "Why did Brenda drop out of business school?"

    "She decided she wasn't _____ _____ _____ a career in business. She's going to study art instead."

18. This song wasn't very popular when it was first recorded, but now it's starting to _____ _____.

MINI-LESSON 1.3

day in and day out constantly; for a long time

die down become less severe; quiet down

do over do again; repeat

do without not have

down the drain wasted; done for no reason (work, for example)

dream up invent; think of; come up with

drop in (on) visit informally

drop (someone) a line send someone a letter

drop off (1) leave something (a package, for example) (2) take (someone) home; let someone out of a car

drop out (of) stop attending (classes, for example)

dwell on focus on; think about too much

easy as pie very simple

eyes bigger than one's stomach said of people who take more food than they can eat

fall behind not move as quickly as; lag behind

fall through fail to happen

a far cry from not similar to; not as good as

fed up (with) not able to tolerate; disgusted with; annoyed by

feel free do something if one wants

feel like be inclined to

feel like a million dollars feel very good

few and far between uncommon and infrequent

figure out understand; solve

Directions: Fill in the blanks in the sentences or dialogues with idioms from the list. There will be one word per blank. It may be necessary to change the verb form in order for the sentence to be grammatically correct.

1. It took me hours to _____ _____ how to record programs on my VCR.

2. "Ralph really loaded up his tray with food."

   "He'll never eat it all. Ralph's _____ are _____ _____ his _____."

3. "What a wonderful masquerade party!"

   "People certainly _____ _____ some delightful costumes, didn't they?"

4. "Do you _____ _____ going out tonight?"

   "No, I'd rather stay home and read."

5. "Why have you _____ _____ in your French class?"

   "I was sick and I missed a few classes. But I'm studying hard to catch up."

6. "Why do we need to get gas now? We have quite a bit left."

   "This highway goes through some very empty country, and gas stations are _____ _____ _____ _____."

7. "I really need to use a computer for a few hours."

   "_____ _____ to use my laptop computer. I don't need it this morning."

8. I'm _____ _____ _____ my roommate's lack of responsibility. He never pays his bills or his share of the rent on time.

9. "I've missed James since he moved to Seattle."

   "You should _____ him _____ _____ and let him know how you're doing. I'm sure he'd love to get a letter from you."

10. "The food at that new restaurant isn't bad."

    "It's all right, but it's _____ _____ _____ _____ the food at Mario's. Now *that* is a great restaurant!"

11. Adrian had to _____ _____ _____ the university because of financial problems.

12. After blowing furiously all day, the wind finally _____ _____.

13. "Do you telephone friends before you visit, or just _____ _____ _____ them?"

    "It depends. If they're close friends, I just visit them. If they're acquaintances, I generally call first."

14. "I'm tired of the same old routine."

    "I know how you feel. I get tired of doing the same things _____ _____ _____ _____ _____ too."

15. "I keep thinking about that mistake I made last night."

    "If I were you, I wouldn't _____ _____ it another minute. Don't give it another thought."

MINI-LESSON 1.4

fill in write in a blank (on an application form, for example)

fill in (for someone) substitute for

fill (someone) in provide someone missing information

fill out complete (an application form, for example)

find out learn; discover

a fish out of water someone not in his or her normal surroundings

follow in one's footsteps do what someone else did (especially an older relative)

for good permanently; forever

for the time being temporarily; for now

get a kick out of (doing something) enjoy; have fun doing something

get along with have good relations with

get carried away go too far; do too much; buy too much

get the hang of something learn how to do something

get in one's blood become a habit; become customary

get in over one's head take on too much responsibility

get in the way block; obstruct

get in touch with contact

get off leave (a vehicle)

get off the ground start to be successful

get on board (a vehicle)

get over recover from (an illness)

get rid of discard; no longer have

get under way begin; start

give away distribute (for free)

give (someone) the cold shoulder act unfriendly toward someone; ignore

---

Directions: Fill in the blanks in the sentences or dialogues with idioms from the list. There will be one word per blank. It may be necessary to change the verb form in order for the sentence to be grammatically correct.

1. "Has Edward _____ _____ _____ _____ you lately?"

   "No, he hasn't. I don't think he has my new telephone number."

2. "I'm interested in the job that was advertised in the newspaper."

   "Fine. Just _____ _____ this application form."

3. Don't forget to _____ _____ the date on your check.

4. "Is Agnes still mad at you?"

   "I suppose so. I saw her at a party last weekend, and she just _____ me _____ _____ _____."

5. "Are you moving to Baltimore _____ _____?"

   "No, just _____ _____ _____ _____. I'll be back here in a month or two."

6. "That old paint that you have stored in your garage is a fire hazard."

   "You're right. I should _____ _____ _____ it."

7. Some companies _____ _____ free samples of new products in order to familiarize consumers with them.

8. "How's that advanced computer science class you're taking, Polly?"

   "Not so good. I can't understand a word that the teacher or any of the other students are saying. I really feel like _____ _____ _____ _____ _____."

9. "Don't you just hate all this graffiti?"

   "It *is* ugly, isn't it? I've never understood why people ———— ————

   ———— ———— ———— writing on walls. It doesn't seem like much fun

   to me."

10. When the train stopped, a mysterious looking woman in a black raincoat

    ———— ———— the train and found her seat.

11. "Maxwell's project will be very successful, don't you think?"

    "Oh, I don't know. I'm not sure it will ever ———— ———— ————

    ————."

12. Do you ———— ———— ———— your new roommate, or do you two

    argue?

13. Professor Dunbar came down with the flu, so her teaching assistant ————

    ———— ———— her for a few days.

14. "Will the concert start soon?"

    "It should ———— ———— ———— any minute now."

15. This is the last stop. Everyone has to ———— ———— the bus here.

MINI-LESSON 1.5

give a hand applaud; clap for

give a hand (with) assist

go easy on not punish severely

go on (with) continue

go overboard do too much; buy too much

go with (1) accompany (2) look good together; complement (for example, two articles of clothing)

go without saying be clear; be obvious

grow up mature; become an adult

hand in give back to; return

hand out distribute

hang on wait

hard to come by difficult to find

have a big mouth not be able to conceal secrets

have a chip on one's shoulder be easily angered; quarrelsome

have a heart be compassionate; show mercy

have a hunch have an intuitive feeling

have a word with (someone) talk to someone briefly

have on wear

have one's hands full be very busy; have a challenging job

have the time of one's life have fun; have a great time

hear first hand (from someone) get information directly from someone

hear from be contacted by; be in touch with

hear of know about; be familiar with

hit it off (with someone) become friendly (especially at a first meeting)

hit the road leave, go away

hold on wait

hold on (to) grasp

hold still not move

hold up delay

Directions: Fill in the blanks in the sentences or dialogues with idioms from the list. There will be one word per blank. It may be necessary to change the verb form in order for the sentence to be grammatically correct.

1. Everett was born in the South but he ———— ———— in Michigan.

2. At the beginning of the class, the instructor ———— ———— the quizzes and told the students they had ten minutes in which to finish. Then after ten minutes, the students ———— ———— their quizzes to the instructor.

3. It's getting late. I'd better ———— ———— ———— if I want to get home by midnight.

4. "Can I ———— ———— ———— ———— you now, Professor Rivera?"

   "I've got to go to class right now. Drop by my office later and we'll talk then."

5. "You're graduating next month, right?"

   "Yes, but I intend to ———— ———— ———— my studies in graduate school."

6. ———— ———— while I take your photograph. I don't want the picture to be blurry.

7. "I got stopped by the police for speeding. I have to pay a big fine."

   "Well, you could talk to the judge and ask him to reduce it. Since you've never been stopped for speeding before, maybe he'll ———— ———— ———— you."

8. Do you like this blouse?"

   "Yes, but I think the grey silk one would ———— better ———— your jacket."

9. "Why is Leonard in such a bad mood?"

   "I don't know. He's really ———— ———— ———— ———— his ———— all day."

10. "You sure bought a lot of groceries."

    "Yeah, I guess I ———— ————. I should never go grocery shopping when I'm hungry."

11. The audience ———— the cast a big ———— after their wonderful performance.

12. "Do you think Iris will pass the history test?"

    "That ———— ———— ————. In fact, she'll probably have the best grade in the class."

13. "What ———— ———— your flight?"

    "There was a big snowstorm in Denver that delayed a lot of flights."

14. "Have you ———— ———— Maureen since she went to Hawaii?"

    "Yeah, I got a post card from her yesterday. She said she's ———— ———— ———— ———— her ———— and never wants to come home."

15. Can you ———— me ———— ———— ———— this luggage? It's too heavy for me to carry myself.

16. "Oh, I see you bought that new book by Richard Stone."

    "Yes, but this book is ———— ———— ———— ————.

    I looked for it in three or four bookstores before I finally found a copy."

in a nutshell in summary; in brief

in hot water in trouble

in no time very soon; very quickly

in person face to face (not by telephone, letter, e-mail, etc.)

in store in the future; coming up

in the dark not knowing; confused

in the long run over a long period of time

in the same boat in the same situation; having the same problem

iron out solve (a problem)

join the club have the same problem as other people

jump to conclusions form opinions without sufficient evidence

keep an eye on watch; take care of; look after

keep an eye out (for) look for

keep on (with) continue

keep track of know where something or someone is

keep up (with) maintain the same pace as

kill time spend time doing unimportant things (before an appointment, for example)

know like the back of one's hand be very familiar with

learn the ropes become familiar with; get used to; get the hang of

leave out not include; omit

leave someone/something alone not disturb

let someone down disappoint

let up decline in intensity (rain, for example)

look after take care of; mind

look for try to locate

look forward to anticipate (with pleasure)

look into investigate

Directions: Fill in the blanks in the sentences or dialogues with idioms from the list. There will be one word per blank. It may be necessary to change the verb form in order for the sentence to be grammatically correct.

1. Will you _____ _____ _____ _____ my dog while I go in the drug store?

2. Kathy's daughter has such short legs that she has a hard time _____ _____ _____ the older children.

3. "Has Marilyn gotten used to her new job at the bank yet?"

   "It took her a while, but I think she has finally _____ _____ _____ there."

4. "What's that novel about?"

   "It has a very complicated plot. It would take a long time to explain."

   "Can't you just put it _____ _____ _____?"

5. Don't _____ _____ _____. Maybe your jewelry wasn't stolen after all.

6. "I need to find a new apartment."

   "There might be some vacancies in the building where I live. I'll _____ _____ _____ _____ _____ one."

7. The company may lose some money now, but _____ _____ _____ _____, this is a good investment.

8. Alex complained that no one invited him to any social events and that he felt _____ _____.

9. "Can you hurry over here? I need to see you right away."

   "Sure. I'll be there _____ _____ _____."

10. "May I help you, sir?"

"No, I'm just looking around and trying to _____ some _____ until my wife finishes shopping."

11. "Has it stopped raining yet?"

"No, but it's beginning to _____ _____ a little."

12. "I can't go to Darryl's party this weekend. I have to study."

"Guess we're _____ _____ _____ _____. I've got to study too."

13. "Should we stop and spend the night at this motel?"

"No, let's _____ _____ driving for a few more miles."

14. If you find a baby animal in the woods, don't touch it. Just _____ it _____ .

15. "Are you familiar with this neighborhood?"

"I grew up here, so I _____ it _____ _____ _____ _____ my _____ ."

16. "Is your roommate at home now?"

"I have no idea. I can never _____ _____ _____ his comings and goings."

17. "If you don't know how to use this software, why don't you ask Joanne to help?"

"I *did* ask her, but I'm still _____ _____ _____. I didn't understand a word she said."

18. "I understand that you have a new dean over at the Business School."

"Yes, his name is Dean Nishimura. He has a completely different philosophy of business education from the one Dean Woodford had, so I'm sure that some big changes are _____ _____ for us."

19. "Did Amanda ever complete her project?"

"She's almost finished. She just has a few minor problems left to _____ _____ ."

20. Alfred is _____ _____ _____ with his boss because he didn't finish an important project by the deadline.

MINI-LESSON 1.7

look like   resemble

look out (for)   be careful; try to avoid

look over   examine; read

look up   (1) find information (especially in a book) (2) try to locate someone

look up to   respect; admire

make a fool of oneself   act embarrassingly

make a point of   make a special effort

make ends meet   balance a budget

make sense (of)   be logical and clear; understand

make up   invent, create

make up one's mind   decide

make way for   allow space for

mean to   intend to

mixed up   confused

music to one's ears   something that sounds pleasant

a nervous wreck someone who is very nervous

next to nothing very little (money, for example); cheap

no doubt about it certainly; definitely

no harm done there was no damage done

not believe one's ears (or **eyes**) be unable to believe what one hears (or sees)

not think much of not like; not have a good opinion of

odds and ends small, miscellaneous items

off the cuff spontaneous; not practiced (remarks, for example)

an old hand (at) an experienced person

on edge nervous

on end consecutively, without a break (*days on end*, for example)

on hand easily available

on one's own independent

on pins and needles nervous; anxious

on second thought after reconsidering

on the go always busy; always moving

on the tip of one's tongue almost able to remember

on the whole in general

out of (something) not having something

out of one's mind insane; illogical; irrational

out of order broken; not functioning properly

out of the question definitely not; impossible

over and over again and again; repeatedly

over one's head not understandable (a joke, for example); obscure

---

Directions: Fill in the blanks in the sentences or dialogues with idioms from the list. There will be one word per blank. It may be necessary to change the verb form in order for the sentence to be grammatically correct.

1. "I didn't know you could play horseshoes so well."

   "Oh, I'm _____ _____ _____ _____ horseshoes. I've been playing since I was a kid."

2. "I think I'll have the prime rib, waiter."

   "All right, sir."

   "Wait, no— _____ _____ _____, I think I'll have the chicken."

3. Is this story true, or did you just _____ it _____?

4. You can't get a soda from that machine. There's a sign on it that says "_____ _____ _____."

5. Sherry _____ _____ _____ her father because of all the help and good advice he's given her.

6. I don't have much cash _____ _____, but I can get some from an automatic teller machine.

7. What a confusing movie! I couldn't _____ _____ _____ it.

8. "You did a fine job on this research paper, especially on the bibliography."

   "Thanks. I _____ _____ _____ _____ getting the bibliography exactly right. I did it _____ _____ _____ until it was perfect."

9. "What's Fritz's cousin's name?"

   "It's _____ _____ _____ _____ my _____, but I can't quite remember."

10. "Hello. I'd like to reserve a room for this weekend."

    "I'm afraid that's _____ _____ _____ _____, sir. The hotel is fully booked this weekend."

11. "Do you have any peaches?"

    "Sorry, I'm _____ _____ them. I just sold the last crate of peaches."

12. "Listen to the roar of the engines."

    "Yeah, it's _____ _____ my _____. I just love going to these car races."

13. The plane was delayed for hours _____ _____. I thought we'd never get off the ground.

14. "Have you finished moving into your new apartment?"

    "Almost. There are still a few _____ _____ _____ in my old apartment that I need to move today."

15. "Brad sure is busy, isn't he?"

    "Yeah, he's involved in so many activities that he's always _____ _____ _____."

16. There are so many interesting dishes on the menu that it's hard for me to _____ _____ my _____ which one to order.

17. You must be _____ _____. This isn't River Street; it's Laurel Avenue.

18. "When will you be informed of the test results?"

    "Not until Monday, so I'll be _____ _____ _____ _____ all weekend."

19. "Do you know what the capital of South Dakota is?"

    "I'm not sure. Let's _____ it _____ in this atlas."

20. They're going to tear down those old warehouses to _____ _____ _____ a big new hotel.

21. "I like that painting you bought. Did it cost much?"

    "No, the artist sold it to me for _____ _____ _____."

22. "How long have you been living alone?"

    "I've been _____ my _____ since I graduated from high school."

23. "I'm sorry I knocked that vase over. I didn't mean to."

    "_____ _____ _____. It wasn't damaged."

24. I must have been _____ _____ my _____ when I signed the lease on this apartment. I can't afford this much rent.

25. "Christine is so funny, she should be a stand-up comic."

    "I suppose, but a lot of her jokes go right _____ my _____. I just don't get them."

part with no longer have; get rid of

pass up not accept; not choose

pass with flying colors do very well (on a test)

pat oneself on the back congratulate oneself

pay attention (to) concentrate on; focus on

pick on be cruel to; torment

pick out choose; select

pick up (1) take something from a surface (for example, a floor) (2) go to a location and get someone or something (3) learn (especially without formal training)

pick up the tab (for) pay for

the picture of a perfect example of something

play by ear do something without a definite plan

play it safe choose a cautious plan

point out indicate

a pretty penny a lot of money

pull one's leg joke with someone; make up a story

push one's luck to continue doing something too long; to keep taking chances

put aside save for later; set aside

put away return something to its proper place

put off delay; postpone

put on begin to wear

put together assemble

put up with tolerate

Directions: Fill in the blanks in the sentences or dialogues with idioms from the list. There will be one word per blank. It may be necessary to change the verb form in order for the sentence to be grammatically correct.

1. Vanessa is allergic to tobacco smoke, so she can't _____ _____ _____ smoking.

2. "That conference you attended in San Diego must have cost _____ _____ _____ ."

   "You're right, it was quite expensive, but fortunately, the company I work for _____ _____ _____ _____ _____ it."

3. "I finally finished collecting all the materials I need to write my report."

   "Great, but don't be too quick to _____ yourself _____ _____ _____ . You still have to write the report."

4. "What do you want to do tomorrow?"

   "I don't know. Let's just _____ it _____ _____ ."

5. "You should get rid of that old leather jacket. It's in pretty bad shape."

   "I know, but I hate to _____ _____ it. I've had it for years."

6. "How did you learn to make such beautiful pottery? Did you take a class in ceramics?"

   "No, I just _____ it _____ on my own."

7. "Can you read that sign?"

   "Just a minute. Let me _____ my glasses _____ ."

8. It took Linda weeks to _____ _____ that thousand-piece jigsaw puzzle.

9. "How did you do on your final exams?"

   "Great! I _____ them all _____ _____ _____ ."

10. _____ _____ as I read the directions or you won't understand what to do.

11. I wouldn't believe a word Lynn told you. She's just _____ your _____ .

---

12. The child _____ _____ her toys from the floor and then _____ them _____ in her toy box.

13. Bert and Mary had to _____ _____ their dinner party until next weekend because Bert wasn't feeling well.

14. "Who _____ _____ that tie for you?"

    "No one. I chose it myself."

15. "Are you going to take that job?"

    "No, I decided to _____ it _____ because I don't want to relocate."

MINI-LESSON 1.9

right away   immediately

ring a bell (with)   sound familiar to

rough it   experience somewhat difficult or primitive conditions

rub someone the wrong way   irritate; annoy

rule out   say something is impossible; eliminate a possibility

run a temperature   have a fever

run for office   try to get elected

run into   (1) meet unexpectedly (2) collide with

run late   be late; be in a hurry

run of the mill   ordinary

run out (of something)   exhaust the supply

save one's breath   don't bother asking someone

search me   I don't know; I have no idea

see eye to eye (with someone) (on something)   have the same opinion; be in agreement

see (someone) off   accompany (to an airport or train station, for example)

see to   take care of; check on; fix

serve one right   receive the proper punishment; get the penalty one deserves

short for   a nickname for

show around   orient; give a tour

show off   try to attract attention by unusual behavior; display expertise

show up   arrive

shut down   close

sign up (for)   enroll (for a class, for example)

sing another tune   change one's opinion; feel differently

size up   measure; estimate

sleep on it   postpone a decision until the next day

slowly but surely   gradually; steadily but not quickly

snowed under   very busy

so far, so good   up until now, there are no problems

sooner or later   at some indefinite future time

speak one's mind   say what one is thinking

speak up   speak more loudly

speak up for   support

spell out (for)   make something very clear; explain in detail

Directions: Fill in the blanks in the sentences or dialogues with idioms from the list. There will be one word per blank. It may be necessary to change the verb form in order for the sentence to be grammatically correct.

1. "Has John gone back to Minneapolis yet?"

   "Yes, I just _____ him _____ at the airport."

2. "Your sister's name is Jessie?"

   "That's what everyone calls her—it's _____ _____ Jessica."

3. I was late because I _____ _____ _____ gasoline on the way over here.

4. Write down your ideas _____ _____. If you wait to write them down, you may forget them

5. "Did you have a busy night at the restaurant?"

   "We weren't just busy—we were _____ _____! I've never seen so many customers!"

6. "Did you _____ _____ _____ Professor Carmichael's class?"

   "No, I decided to take Professor Knudson's class instead."

7. "Vicki, how's that project you're working on coming along?"

   "_____ _____, _____ _____, but the tricky part will be next week."

8. "Have you ever heard of an actor named Anthony Reed?"

   "Hmm, I don't think so. The name doesn't _____ _____ _____

   _____ me at all."

9. "Frank doesn't take a hint very well, does he?"

   "No, you have to _____ things _____ _____ Frank. He likes

   everything crystal clear."

10. I'd heard that the clothes in this store were very nice, but I found them

    _____ _____ _____ _____.

11. "Bennett thought those stories Tina told about you were pretty funny."

    "They weren't funny, they were embarrassing. Bennett would be _____

    _____ _____ if Tina had told that kind of story about him."

12. Norman doesn't like to _____ _____ when he goes on vacation. He

    prefers to stay at luxury hotels.

13. I don't like to go to parties too early. I'd rather _____ _____ a little bit late.

14. It's expensive to _____ _____ _____ these days. Political campaigns

    cost a lot of money.

15. "So, do you plan to buy this motorcycle or not?"

    "I'm still not sure. Can I _____ _____ _____ and let you know

    tomorrow morning?"

16. "I feel awful. I have a terrible cold or maybe even the flu."

    "Are you _____ _____ _____? If you have a fever, then you probably

    have the flu."

17. "I'm collecting money for the Red Cross. I think I'll ask Pat to contribute."

    "_____ _____ _____. Pat never contributes to anything."

18. My brother and I agree on most issues, but I sure don't _____ _____

    _____ _____ _____ him _____ this proposal to build a new

    stadium.

19. I _____ _____ my old friend Leslie downtown yesterday. I hadn't seen her

    for months.

20. "I understand you're learning how to speak Russian."

    "Yes, and it was really hard for me, especially at first. Now, though, I'm _____

    _____ _____ getting the hang of it."

MINI-LESSON 1.10

spick-and-span extremely clean; spotless

stack up against compare with

stamp out eliminate; wipe out

stand for (1) tolerate; put up with (2) symbolize; represent

stand out be noticeable

stand up for support

stay out not come home

stay out (or **up**) **to all hours** come home (or go to bed) very late

stay up not go to bed

stick with not change; stay with

stock up on get a large supply of something

a stone's throw from not far away from; close to

stop by visit informally; go to see

straighten up clean up; make tidy

stuck with have something one cannot get rid of

take a break stop working (for a short time)

take a lot of nerve require a lot of courage

take a lot out of (someone) be hard on someone; drain energy from someone

take advantage of utilize; make use of; exploit

take after resemble; look like (especially an older relative)

take apart disassemble

take it easy relax; calm down

Directions: Fill in the blanks in the sentences or dialogues with idioms from the list. There will be one word per blank. It may be necessary to change the verb form in order for the sentence to be grammatically correct.

1. Vaccines have permitted doctors to virtually _____ _____ a number of diseases, including smallpox and polio.

2. "How late do you usually _____ _____?"
   "I'm normally in bed by eleven on weekdays."

3. "How late do you usually _____ _____ on weekends?"
   "I sometimes don't come home until two or three in the morning."

4. "Do you _____ _____ your mother or father?"
   "I don't think I look much like either one of them."

5. Earl had no trouble _____ _____ the engine on the lawn mower, but then he couldn't put it back together.

6. "Do you live near Cecilia?"
   "Oh, sure. My apartment building is just _____ _____ _____ _____ hers."

7. The teacher won't _____ _____ cheating. When she caught one student cheating on the mid-term exam, she gave him a zero on that test.

8. "I tried and tried to find a buyer for this old car."
   "Looks like you're _____ _____ it for now."

9. "My brother is going to invest all his savings in a new business venture."
   "That _____ _____ _____ _____ _____. I'd be afraid to take a risk like that."

10. "I give up. I can't solve this chemistry problem."
    "_____ _____ it. Eventually, you'll figure it out."

11. We have to leave the apartment _____–_____–_____. The landlord said that if it wasn't clean when we moved out, we'd lose part of our security deposit.

12. Don was wearing jeans and a T-shirt while all the other guests had on formal dinner wear. He really_____ _____.

13. "Tim, you've eaten at both these restaurants—how does Chez Michele _____ _____ _____ the Oak Room?"

    "Oh, they're both good. I think the Oak Room has slightly better food, but the service is better at Chez Michele."

14. The fifty stars on the American flag _____ _____ the fifty states.

15. "Do you _____ _____ your apartment before guests _____ _____?"

    "A little bit. I don't mind if it's a little messy, but I don't want it to look like a disaster area."

16. "My new roommate is from Italy."

    "You should _____ _____ _____ this opportunity to learn some Italian."

17. "I just heard on the news that the Florida orange crop was damaged by the hurricane last week, and that orange juice prices are going to go way up."

    "If we had a big freezer, we could _____ _____ _____ frozen orange juice now and we wouldn't have to pay those prices later."

MINI-LESSON 1.11

take off (1) remove (clothing, for example) (2) ascend (as a plane does) (3) become popular quickly

take over assume control or responsibility

take part in participate in

take the plunge finally take action; do something different

take a shortcut take a more direct or faster route than usual

take time off (from) take a vacation or a break (from work or school)

take up begin to study some topic or engage in some activity

talk down to speak to someone as if he or she were a child; patronize

talk into persuade; convince

talk out of dissuade; convince not to do something

talk over discuss

tear oneself away from something stop doing something interesting

tear up rip into small pieces

tell apart distinguish

things are looking up the situation is improving

think over consider

throw away discard; get rid of

throw the book at someone give someone the maximum punishment

throw cold water on discourage; force to cancel (a plan, for example)

try on test clothing before buying (for size, style, and so on)

try out test a product before buying

try out (for) audition for (a role in a play, for example); attempt to join (a team, for example)

Directions: Fill in the blanks in the sentences or dialogues with idioms from the list. There will be one word per blank. It may be necessary to change the verb form in order for the sentence to be grammatically correct.

1. You'd better _____ _____ these gloves before you buy them; they may not fit.

2. At first, I didn't want to go to the party, but I'm glad Annette _____ me _____ it. It was fun.

3. The spy _____ _____ the document so that no one else could read it.

4. The twins look so much alike that almost no one can _____ them _____.

5. "I need more excitement in my life."
   "Why don't you give up stamp collecting and _____ _____ sky diving instead?"

6. "How did you get home so quickly?"
   "I _____ _____ _____ through the woods."

7. Most air accidents take place when a plane is _____ _____ or landing.

8. "Will your friend Scott be coming to the reception?"
   "If he can _____ himself _____ _____ those computer games he's always playing."

9. Dan was afraid the judge would _____ _____ _____ _____ him because he had been charged with the same offense several times.

10. _____ _____ your muddy boots before you go into the house.

11. I wish I'd _____ _____ this calculator before I bought it. It doesn't seem to be working right.

12. Marvin was going to drop out of school, but his grandfather _____ him _____ _____ it.

13. "So, Louisa, you're going to _____ _____ _____ a part in the play?"
    "Yes, I've been interested in acting for quite a while, so I finally decided to _____ _____ _____."

14. "I'm going to _____ _____ those old newspapers."
    "Don't just put them in the trash—recycle them instead."

MINI-LESSON 1.12

turn around face in a different direction; change directions

turn down (1) reject an offer (2) decrease in intensity

turn in (1) return; give back; hand in (2) go to bed

turn into change to; transform into

turn off stop the operation (of an appliance, for example); shut off

turn on start the operation (of an appliance, for example)

turn out (1) result; end up; be the final product

(2) produce (3) arrive; gather (for a meeting, for example)

turn up (1) increase in intensity (2) arrive

under the weather slightly ill

use up use completely

wait on serve

walk on air be very happy

warm up (1) heat (2) practice; prepare for

warm up (to) become friendly with; start to enjoy

watch out (for) be alert; look out for

wear out become no longer useful because of wear

what the doctor ordered exactly what was needed; the perfect thing

wipe out eliminate

without a hitch without a problem

work out (1) exercise (2) bring to a successful conclusion; solve

Directions: Fill in the blanks in the sentences or dialogues with idioms from the list. There will be one word per blank. It may be necessary to change the verb form in order for the sentence to be grammatically correct.

1. The story of Dr. Jekyll and Mr. Hyde is about a scientist who _____ _____ a monster after drinking a chemical potion.

2. _____ _____ the water or the tub will overflow.

3. It's warm in here. Could you _____ _____ the heat a little?

4. I love that song. Could you _____ _____ the volume on the radio a little?

5. I can't see a thing. Please _____ _____ the light.

6. This sweater looked nice when it was new, but now it's _____ _____ .

7. "I'm hungry!"
   "Why don't you _____ _____ some of the leftovers from dinner last night? You can use the microwave oven."

8. Not many people _____ _____ for the meeting last night.

9. It's been a rough day. I'm going to _____ _____ early and get a good night's sleep.

10. "How about a nice cup of hot tea?"
    "That's exactly what I'm in the mood for. It's just _____ _____ _____ _____ ."

11. "How was your presentation?"
    Great. It went off _____ _____ _____ ."

12. I'm going to the gym to _____ _____ on the exercise machines.

13. If you're on a crowded bus or subway, you must _____ _____ for pickpockets.

14. "A bear! I don't see a bear! Where is it?"
    "_____ _____ slowly. It's right behind you."

15. Maria had quite a few problems last year, but she _____ them all _____ .

16. Don't ask me to _____ _____ you! I'm not your servant.

17. Brian was offered the manager's job but he _____ it _____ . He said he didn't want the responsibility.

18. Before the game starts, the players need to _____ _____ .

19. "You must be happy about getting that scholarship."
    "Are you kidding? I'm still _____ _____ _____ ."

20. "Mitchell looked pale and tired."
    "He told me he was feeling a little _____ _____ _____ ."

Guide to Structure

Texas Tech University

About Structure

The second section of the TOEFL® test examines your understanding of English grammar and usage. There are two types of questions in this section of the test: Sentence Completion and Error Identification. On the paper-based test, these two types of items were presented in separate parts of the section, but on the computer version, the two types of items are intermingled. Except for that fact, this section of the test has changed very little from the paper-based format.

There are 20 to 25 items in this section, and the time limit is from 15 to 20 minutes. On the average, you have about 45 seconds in which to answer each item. For most test-takers, this is plenty of time.

Remember that your grade on the fourth section of the test, Essay Writing, counts for about half of your grade in Structure. If you have problems with writing essays, it is especially important that you do well on this part of the test to pull up your Structure grade.

Although a wide range of grammar points are tested, there are certain points that appear again and again, and you can master these points with the information and practice this *Guide* provides.

Section 2 should be less stressful for you than Section 1 because you don't have to divide your attention between the spoken material and the information on the screen. It may also seem less stressful than Section 3 because it is easier to finish all the items in the amount of time allotted.

Like Listening, Structure is computer adaptive. The first items you see will be of medium difficulty. Don't rush through these items, however, because the first half of the section is very important to your score. If you keep answering the questions correctly, the items will become progressively more difficult.

Structure sentences are generally about academic subjects: the physical sciences (such as astronomy or geology), the social sciences (such as anthropology or economics), or the humanities (such as music or literature). You will NOT see sentences that deal with "controversial" subjects such as abortion, illegal drugs, or sensitive political issues.

Any cultural references in the sentences are to the culture of the United States or Canada. Many of the sentences contain references to people, places, and institutions that you will not be familiar with. (In fact, many North Americans are not familiar with these either!) It's not necessary to know these references; you should simply concentrate on the structure of the sentences. It's also not necessary to understand all the vocabulary in a sentence; you can often answer a question correctly without a complete understanding of the sentence.

There are two possible approaches to Section 2 problems: an analytical approach and an intuitive approach. A test-taker who uses the analytical approach quickly analyzes the grammar of a sentence to see what element is missing (in Sentence Completion items) or which element is incorrect (in Error Identification items). Someone who uses the second approach simply chooses the answer that "sounds right" (in Sentence Completion items) or the one that "sounds wrong" (in Error Identification items). Although this *Guide* emphasizes the first approach, the second can be useful too, especially for people who learned English primarily by speaking it and listening to it rather than by studying grammar and writing. You can also combine the two approaches: if you get "stuck" using one method, you can switch to another.

Sentence Completion

This type of item consists of an incomplete sentence. Some portion of the sentence has been replaced by a blank. Under the sentence, four words or phrases are listed. One of these completes the sentence grammatically and logically.

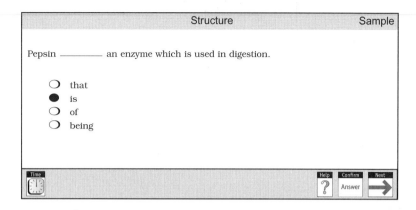

The sentence consists of an incomplete main clause (*Pepsin —————— an enzyme*) and an adjective clause (*which is used in digestion*). Each clause must contain a subject and a verb. There is a subject but no verb in the main clause. Only the second and fourth choices are verbal forms. However, an *-ing* verb can never be used alone as a sentence verb. Only the second choice, the verb *is*, supplies a verb for the main clause.

What is the best way to answer Sentence Completion items?

If the answer choices are fairly short, you should begin by taking a quick look at the answer choices to get an idea of what is missing from the sentence. A glance at the answer choices can often tell you that you are looking at a problem involving verb forms, word order, parallel structure, misplaced modifiers, and others.

If the answer choices are long or complicated, begin by reading the stem. Don't analyze it word for word, but as you are reading, try to form a picture of the sentence's overall structure. How many clauses will there be in the complete sentence? Does each clause have a complete subject and verb? Is there a connecting word to join clauses? Are any other elements obviously missing?

If you can't find the answer immediately, try to eliminate as many distractors as possible. Distractors for Sentence Completion items are generally incorrect for one of the following reasons:

- A necessary word or phrase is missing, so the sentence is still incomplete.

- An unnecessary word or phrase is included.

- Part of the answer choice is ungrammatical when put into the stem.

Don't click on an answer until you've read the sentence completely; sometimes an option seems to fit in the sentence unless you read every word.

After you have eliminated as many answer choices as possible, read the sentence quickly to yourself with the remaining choice or choices in place of the blank. If an answer doesn't "sound right," it probably isn't. If you still can't decide, guess and go on.

Error Identification

This type of item consists of a sentence in which four expressions—single words or two- or three-word phrases—are underlined. Your job is to identify which of these phrases must be rewritten (it can't simply be omitted) in order for the sentence to be correct. All the errors involve grammar or usage—never punctuation or spelling.

SAMPLE ITEMS

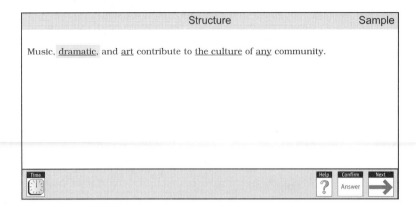

This sentence should correctly read, "Music, *drama*, and art contribute to the culture of any community." The first underlined expression would have to be rewritten to correct the sentence, and so that is the best answer.

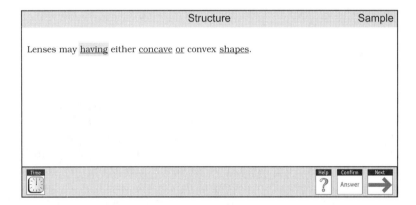

The correct verb form after a modal auxiliary is the simple form *have*. This sentence should read, "Lenses may have either concave or convex shapes" so the best answer is the first underlined expression, *having*.

What is the best way to answer Error Identification items?

You should begin with a quick reading of each sentence to find any obvious errors. **Don't** simply read the underlined portions, because in most items, the underlined expression is incorrect only in the context of the sentence. **Don't** answer the question until you've read the entire sentence.

Easy questions can be answered after the first reading; click on the answer and go on to the next problem. If you can't find the error immediately, reread the sentence, now concentrating on the underlined expressions. You can't use the same techniques for reading these items as you would to read other materials, such as newspapers or magazine articles. Usually, a person's eyes move very quickly over "little words" like articles and prepositions because these words don't contain much information. However, in this part of the test, these expressions may be used incorrectly. You should train your eyes to move slowly and pronounce the sentences in your mind as if you were speaking them.

If you haven't identified the error after a careful reading of the sentence, go through a mental checklist of the most common errors: word form, word choice, and verb error. Do the underlined expressions seem to fit into any of these categories?

If you still can't find an error, eliminate expressions that seem to be used correctly, then make the best guess you can from any items that remain.

Computer Skills for the Structure Section

Answering Structure items on the computer is easy. For Sentence Completion items, you simply click on either the oval by the choice that you think is the best answer, or on any part of the answer itself. As in all parts of the test, it is easier to click on the answer choice itself than on the oval.

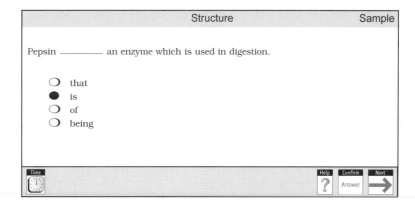

The oval will darken, indicating that this is your choice. After that, click on the *Next* icon, and then, to see the next item, click on the *Confirm Answer* icon. Until you click on the *Confirm Answer* icon, you may change your answer. The easiest way to change an answer is simply to click on the choice that you now think is correct. The oval that you first clicked on will automatically become blank when you do.

To answer an Error Identification item, you must click on some portion of the answer that you think is best. You can click anywhere within the underlined portion. (There are no ovals to click on when answering this type of item.)

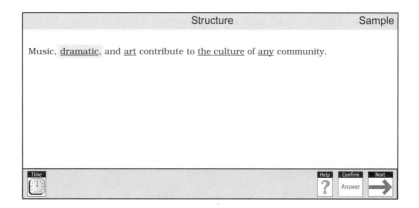

When you click on an underlined phrase, it will become highlighted, indicating that this is your choice. Again, you must click on the *Next* icon and the *Confirm Answer* icon to move to the next item.

The easiest way to change an answer is to click on another underlined word or phrase. That choice will then be highlighted, and the highlight will disappear from the first choice.

And that's all there is to it!

Strategies for Structure

In General

■ Be familiar with the directions for Structure. As soon as this section starts, click on *Dismiss Directions.*

■ You can spend an average of about forty-five seconds on each item. If an item seems difficult, eliminate unlikely items and make the best guess that you can. Don't spend too much time working on items you find difficult.

■ Never answer any item too quickly, even if it seems easy. Always consider all four answer choices. It is easy to make mistakes in Structure because of carelessness.

■ Pace yourself carefully through this section by keeping an eye on the *Time Remaining* indicator and the item number indicator. Don't work so slowly that there will still be unanswered problems when time expires, but don't work so quickly that you finish long before the time expires.

Sentence Completion

■ If the answer choices are short, look them over before you read the sentence. Try to get an idea of what type of problem you are working with.

■ Read the sentence, trying to determine which elements are missing. Never choose an answer until you have read the entire sentence; sometimes an answer will seem to fit until you have read the last few words of the sentence.

■ Mark your choice immediately if the answer is obvious. If you're not sure, try to eliminate incorrect answers.

■ Read the sentence with the remaining answer choices in place of the blank. Choose the option that sounds best.

■ Save yourself time by clicking on the answer itself rather than on the oval.

■ If you are still unable to decide on an answer, guess and go on.

Error Identification

■ Skim each sentence, looking for obvious errors.

■ If you haven't found the error, read the sentence again carefully, concentrating on the underlined parts. Go through a mental checklist of the most common types of errors (word form, word choice, verb error) to see if any of the underlined expressions seem to fall into those categories.

■ If you are still unable to find an error, try eliminating options that seem to be correct. If more than one option remains, take a guess and go on.

Now begin your preparation for Section 2 by taking the Preview Structure Test. Be sure to observe the 20-minute time limit.

Time: 20 minutes

Directions: This section tests your ability to recognize both correct and incorrect English structures. There are two types of items in this section.

One type involves a sentence that is missing a verb or phrase. Four words or phrases appear below the sentence. You must choose the one that best completes the sentence.

_____ large natural lakes are found in the state of South Carolina.

○ There are no
○ Not the
○ It is not
● No

This sentence should properly read, "No large natural lakes are found in the state of South Carolina." You should select the fourth choice, _No._

The other type of item involves a sentence in which four words or phrases have been underlined. You must identify the one underlined word or phrase that must be changed for the sentence to be considered correct.

<u>When</u> painting a fresco, an artist <u>is applied</u> paint <u>directly</u> to the damp plaster <u>of a wall</u>.

This sentence should read, "When painting a fresco, an artist applies paint directly to the damp plaster of a wall." You should therefore select the second underlined answer, _is applied._

As soon as you understand the directions, begin work on this Preview Test. There are 25 questions.

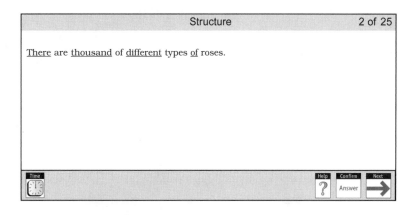

Structure   1 of 25

Martha Graham, _____ of the pioneers of modern dance, didn't begin dancing until she was twenty-one.

○ who, as one
○ she was
○ one
○ was one

Time | Help ? | Confirm Answer | Next →

Structure   2 of 25

There are <u>thousand</u> of <u>different</u> types <u>of</u> roses.

Time | Help ? | Confirm Answer | Next →

Sponges <u>have</u> neither <u>heads</u> <u>or</u> separate body <u>organs</u>.

Tiger moths ——————— wings marked with stripes or spots.

- ○ have
- ○ with
- ○ their
- ○ whose

The first <u>recorded</u> use of natural gas <u>to light</u> street lamps <u>it was</u> in <u>the town of</u> Frederick, New York in 1825.

Most of Annie Jump Cannon's career as an astronomer involved the observation, classification, and ——————.

- ○ she analyzed stars
- ○ the stars' analysis
- ○ stars were analyzed
- ○ analysis of stars

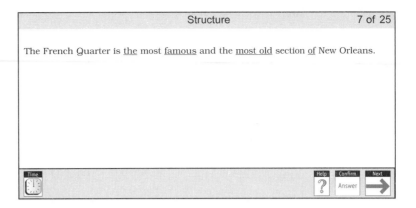

The French Quarter is <u>the</u> most <u>famous</u> and the <u>most old</u> section <u>of</u> New Orleans.

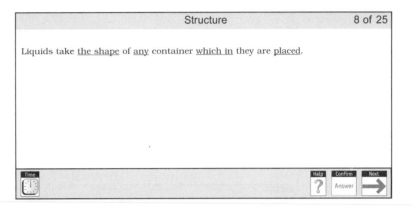

Liquids take <u>the shape</u> of <u>any</u> container <u>which in</u> they are <u>placed</u>.

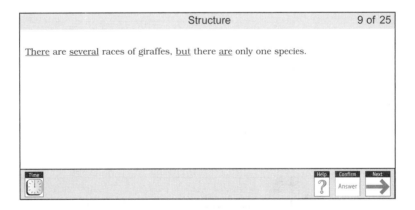

<u>There</u> are <u>several</u> races of giraffes, <u>but</u> there <u>are</u> only one species.

Platinum is harder than copper and is almost as pliable _____.

    ○ gold
    ○ than gold
    ○ as gold
    ○ gold is

Many communities are dependent on groundwater ———— from wells for their water supply.

- ◯ that obtained
- ◯ obtained
- ◯ is obtained
- ◯ obtain it

Boolean algebra is <u>most often</u> used <u>to solve</u> problems in <u>logic</u>, probability, and <u>engineer</u>.

There were ———— federal laws regulating mining practices until 1872.

- ◯ none
- ◯ not
- ◯ no
- ◯ nor

<u>A number of</u> the materials used in manufacturing paint <u>are</u> <u>potential</u> dangerous <u>if mishandled</u>.

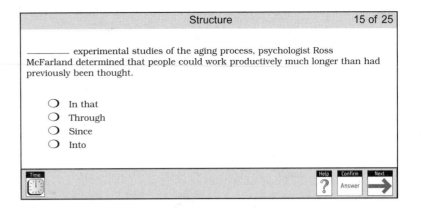

———— experimental studies of the aging process, psychologist Ross McFarland determined that people could work productively much longer than had previously been thought.

○ In that
○ Through
○ Since
○ Into

Time   Help ?   Confirm Answer   Next →

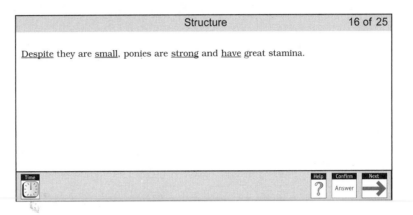

<u>Despite</u> they are <u>small</u>, ponies are <u>strong</u> and <u>have</u> great stamina.

Time   Help ?   Confirm Answer   Next →

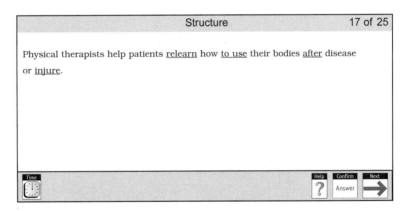

Physical therapists help patients <u>relearn</u> how <u>to use</u> their bodies <u>after</u> disease or <u>injure</u>.

Time   Help ?   Confirm Answer   Next →

Designed by Frederic Auguste Bartholdi, ————.

○ the United States was given the Statue of Liberty by the people of France
○ the people of France gave the Statue of Liberty to the United States
○ the Statue of Liberty was given to the United States by the people of France
○ the French people presented the United States with a gift, the Statue of Liberty

Time   Help ?   Confirm Answer   Next →

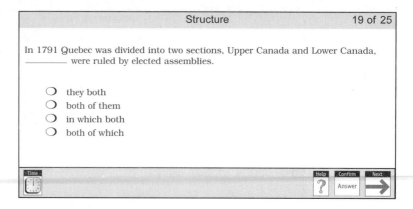

In 1791 Quebec was divided into two sections, Upper Canada and Lower Canada, _____ were ruled by elected assemblies.

- ○ they both
- ○ both of them
- ○ in which both
- ○ both of which

Time   Help ?   Confirm Answer   Next →

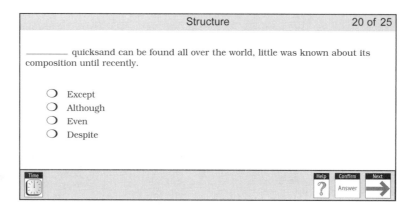

_____ quicksand can be found all over the world, little was known about its composition until recently.

- ○ Except
- ○ Although
- ○ Even
- ○ Despite

Time   Help ?   Confirm Answer   Next →

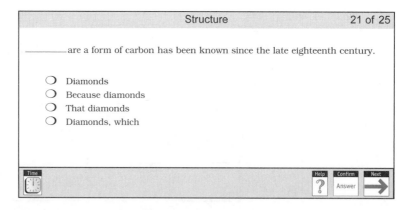

_____ are a form of carbon has been known since the late eighteenth century.

- ○ Diamonds
- ○ Because diamonds
- ○ That diamonds
- ○ Diamonds, which

Time   Help ?   Confirm Answer   Next →

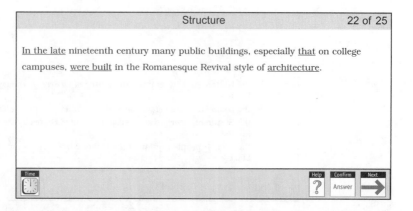

In the late nineteenth century many public buildings, especially that on college campuses, were built in the Romanesque Revival style of architecture.

Time   Help ?   Confirm Answer   Next →

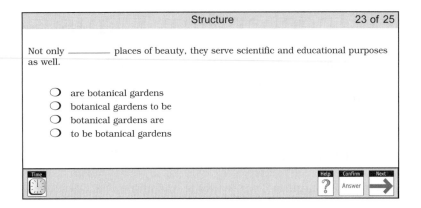

Not only _____ places of beauty, they serve scientific and educational purposes as well.

- ○ are botanical gardens
- ○ botanical gardens to be
- ○ botanical gardens are
- ○ to be botanical gardens

Time | Help ? | Confirm Answer | Next →

<u>Since</u> 1908 breeders <u>set out</u> to produce chickens that could <u>survive</u> Canada's <u>cold climate</u>.

Time | Help ? | Confirm Answer | Next →

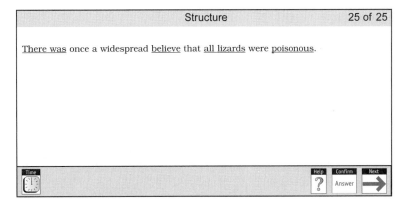

<u>There was</u> once a widespread <u>believe</u> that <u>all lizards</u> were <u>poisonous</u>.

Time | Help ? | Confirm Answer | Next →

This is the end of Preview Test 2: Structure

LESSON 13: Independent Clauses

Items involving **independent clauses** are tested only in Sentence Completion items. Independent clauses are not specifically tested in Error Identification items.

All sentences consist of one or more clauses. A **simple sentence** consists of one clause.

> People need vitamins.
> The man took a vitamin pill.
> Judy lives in northern California.
> In the summer Tom walks to his office.

A **compound sentence** consists of two independent clauses joined by a coordinate conjunction (such as *and* or *but*).

> The man took a vitamin pill and he drank a glass of orange juice.
> Judy lives in northern California now, but she was raised in Ohio.

A **complex sentence** consists of an independent clause (called the main clause) and a subordinate (dependent) clause. Subordinate clauses may be **adverb clauses, noun clauses**, or **adjective clauses.** In the sentences below, the independent clauses are italicized.

> *The man took a vitamin pill* because he had a cold.
> (independent clause + adverb clause)
> *I didn't realize* that Nancy was here. (noun clause)
> *Tom walks to his office,* which is located on Broadway, *every day during the summer.*
> (independent clause + adjective clause)

All three types of subordinate clauses are commonly seen in the Structure part of the test, and each is considered in separate lessons (Lessons 14, 15, and 16). The emphasis in this chapter, however, is on the basic components of independent clauses.

A) MISSING SUBJECTS, VERBS, OBJECTS, AND COMPLEMENTS

All clauses have a **subject** and a **verb.** Many clauses have a **direct object** as well.

Subject	Verb	Direct Object
People	need	vitamins.

In Sentence Completion items, it is common for any of these elements or a combination of them to be missing from the stem. The most common problem in Structure involves a missing verb. A missing subject and a missing subject-verb combination are common as well. The missing element may also be part of rather than all of the verb or noun phrase.

The verb missing from an independent clause may be a single-word verb (*need, was, took, had, walked*) or a verb phrase consisting of one or more auxiliary verbs and a main verb (*will need, has been, should take, would have had, had walked*). The verbs may be active (*need, take*) or passive (*was needed, is taken*).

The missing subject and direct object may be a noun (*people, vitamins, Tom*), a noun phrase (*some famous people, a vitamin pill, my friend Tom*), or a pronoun. (*He, she, it*, and *they* are subject pronouns; *him, her, it*, and *them* are object pronouns.)

After the verb *to be* and certain other non-action verbs, a **subject complement** is used rather than a direct object. (Subject complements are also known as predicate nominatives and predicate adjectives.)

Subject	Verb	Complement
She	is	an architect.
The teacher	seemed	upset.

SAMPLE ITEMS

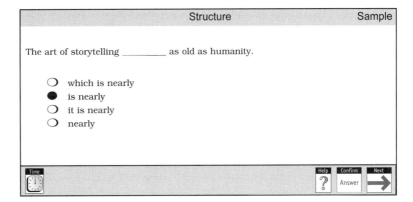

The correct answer supplies the missing verb. The first choice is incorrect because the word *which* is used to connect a relative clause to a main clause; in this sentence, there is only one verb, so there can be only one clause. The third choice is incorrect because there is an unnecessary repetition of the subject (*The art of storytelling it . . .*). The fourth choice is not correct because it does not supply a verb.

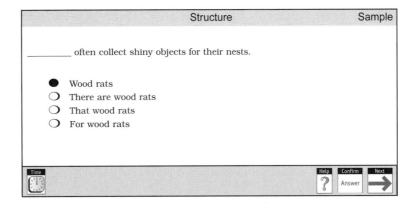

The correct answer supplies a noun phrase to serve as the subject of the sentence. The phrase *There are* in the second choice is incorrectly used; it provides two verbs (*are* and *collect*) for a single clause. In the third choice, the word *That* seems to create a noun clause, which cannot stand alone. The fourth choice is incorrect because a preposition may not be used directly before the subject.

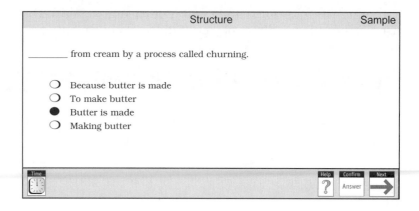

The best answer supplies a subject (*Butter*) and a verb (*is made*). The first choice is incorrect; the word *because* joins an adverb clause to a main clause, but there is only one verb in this sentence, so there can only be one clause. (*Called* is used as a participle, not a sentence verb.) The second and fourth choices are incorrect because there is no main verb in the independent clause; neither an infinitive (*To make*) nor an *-ing* form (*Making*) can be used as a sentence verb.

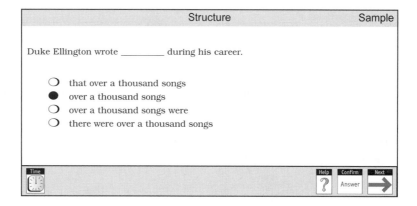

The direct object is missing from this sentence. In the first choice, the connecting word *that* is used unnecessarily. In the third choice, the verb *were* is used unnecessarily because there is only one clause and it has a verb (*wrote*). In the last choice the phrase *there were* is not needed between a verb and its direct object. Only the second choice correctly provides a noun phrase for a direct object.

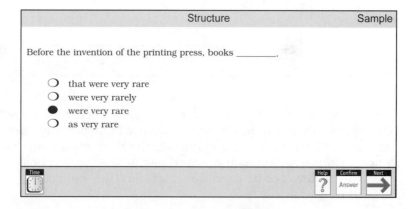

Because there is no verb in the stem, you must look for an answer choice that contains a verb. The first choice contains a verb but the connecting word *that* is not needed. The second choice contains an adverb; after the verb *to be*, an adjective is required. The fourth choice does not contain a verb. The third choice correctly supplies a verb and an adjective complement.

B) CLAUSES WITH *IT* AND *THERE*

Some clauses begin with the introductory words *it* or *there* rather than with the subject of the sentence. These introductory words are sometimes called **expletives.**

The introductory word *there* shows that someone or something exists, usually at a particular time or place. These sentences follow the pattern *there* + verb *to be* + subject.

> *There* are many skyscrapers in New York City.
> *There* was a good movie on television last night.

The introductory word *it* is used in a number of different situations and patterns:

> *It* is important to be punctual for appointments. (with the verb *to be* + adjective + infinitive)
> *It* was in 1959 that Alaska became a state. (with the verb *to be* + adverbial + noun clause)
> *It* takes a long time to learn a language. (with the verb *to take* + time phrase + infinitive)
> *It* was David who did most of the work. (with the verb *to be* + noun + adjective clause)

It and *there*, along with the verb and other sentence elements, may be missing from the stem.

SAMPLE ITEMS

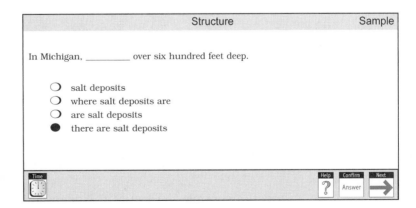

The first choice lacks a verb. The second choice contains a subordinator, used to introduce a clause; there is only one verb, however, so there can be only one clause. The third choice is missing the introductory word *there*. The fourth choice correctly supplies an introductory word (*there*), a verb, and a subject.

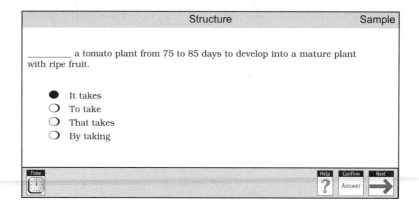

Structure   Sample

_____ a tomato plant from 75 to 85 days to develop into a mature plant
with ripe fruit.

● It takes
○ To take
○ That takes
○ By taking

The first choice correctly completes the sentence with the introductory word *It* and a
verb. The second and fourth choices lack a sentence verb; the third choice incorrectly
creates a noun clause.

EXERCISE 13

Focus: Structure problems involving incomplete independent clauses. (Note:
Several items in this exercise do NOT focus on missing subjects, verbs,
complements, or introductory words; these items are marked in the answer key with
asterisks.)

Directions: Choose the one option that correctly completes the sentences, then mark
the appropriate oval.

1. In the United States, _____ is generally the responsibility of municipal
   governments.

   ○ for water treatment
   ○ water treatment
   ○ where water treatment
   ○ in which water treatment

2. Crop rotation _____ of preserving soil fertility.

   ○ it is one method
   ○ one method
   ○ a method is one
   ○ is one method

3. _____ the dollar as its monetary unit in 1878.

   ○ Canada adopted
   ○ Adopted by Canada,
   ○ It was adopted by Canada
   ○ The Canadian adoption of

4. _____ almost impossible to capture the beauty of the aurora borealis in
   photographs.

   ○ Being
   ○ It is
   ○ There is
   ○ Is

5. _____ two major art museums, the Fogg and the Sackler.

   ○ Harvard University has
   ○ At Harvard University
   ○ Harvard University, with its
   ○ At Harvard University there

6. American actress and director Margaret Webster _____ for her production of Shakespearean plays.

   ○ who became famous
   ○ famous as she became
   ○ becoming famous
   ○ became famous

7. _____ gas tanks connected to welding equipment, one full of oxygen and the other full of acetylene.

   ○ It is two
   ○ Of the two
   ○ There are two
   ○ Two

8. _____ is more interested in rhythm than in melody is apparent from his compositions.

   ○ That Philip Glass
   ○ Philip Glass, who
   ○ Philip Glass
   ○ Because Philip Glass

9. _____ by cosmic rays.

   ○ The Earth is constantly bombarded
   ○ Bombarded constantly, the Earth
   ○ Bombarding the Earth constantly
   ○ The Earth's constant bombardment

10. _____ primary colors are red, blue, and yellow.

    ○ There are three
    ○ The three
    ○ Three of them
    ○ That the three

11. _____ who was elected the first woman mayor of Chicago in 1979.

    ○ It was Jane Byrne
    ○ Jane Byrne
    ○ That Jane Byrne
    ○ When Jane Byrne

12. Every computer consists of a number of systems _____ together.

    ○ by working
    ○ work
    ○ they work
    ○ that work

13. On the moon, _____ air because the Moon's gravitational field is too weak to retain an atmosphere.

   ○ there is no
   ○ where no
   ○ no
   ○ is no

14. The Glass Mountains of western Texas _____ with flecks of gypsum, which shine in the sunlight.

   ○ they are covered
   ○ covered them
   ○ that are covered
   ○ are covered

15. In some cases, _____ to decide if an organism is a plant or an animal.

   ○ difficult if
   ○ it is difficult
   ○ the difficulty
   ○ is difficult

16. The first American novelist to have a major impact on world literature _____.

   ○ who was James Fenimore Cooper
   ○ James Fenimore Cooper was
   ○ it was James Fenimore Cooper
   ○ was James Fenimore Cooper

17. _____ important railroad tunnel in the United States was cut through the Hoosac Mountains in Massachusetts.

   ○ At first
   ○ It was the first
   ○ The first
   ○ As the first of

18. Generally, _____ in the valleys and foothills of the Pacific Coast ranges.

   ○ the California poppy grown
   ○ the growth of the California poppy
   ○ the California poppy grows
   ○ growing the California poppy

19. When bats are at rest, _____ hang upside-down.

   ○ they
   ○ and
   ○ those
   ○ as

20. _____ that the capital of South Carolina was moved from Charleston to Columbia.

   ○ In 1790 was
   ○ There was in 1790
   ○ In 1790
   ○ It was in 1790

LESSON 14: Adjective Clauses

As mentioned in the previous lesson, there are three types of dependent clauses, all of which are tested in the Structure section. **Adjective clauses**—also called **relative clauses**—are the most commonly tested of the three. You will see one or two items involving adjective clauses on most tests.

Adjective clauses are a way of joining two sentences. In the joined sentence, the adjective clause modifies (describes) a noun (called the **head noun**) in another clause of the sentence. It begins with an **adjective clause marker.**

I wanted the book. The book was already checked out.
The book *which I wanted* was already checked out.

The adjective clause in this example begins with the marker *which* and modifies the head noun *book*.

Adjective clause markers are **relative pronouns** such as *who, that,* or *which* or the **relative adverbs** *when* or *where.*

Adjective Clause Marker	Use	Example
who	Subject (people)	A neurologist is a doctor *who* specializes in the nervous system.
whom	Object (people)	This is the patient *whom* the doctor treated.
whose	Possessive (people/things)	Mr. Collins is the man *whose* house I rented.
which	Subject/Object (things)	That is a topic *which* interests me. (*which* as subject) That is the topic *on which* I will write. (*which* as object of preposition)
that	Subject/Object (people/things)	Art *that* is in public places can be enjoyed by everyone. (*that* as subject) The painting *that* Ms. Wallace bought was very expensive. (*that* as object)
where	Adverb (place)	That is the site *where* the bank plans to build its new headquarters.
when	Adverb (time)	This is the hour *when* the children usually go to bed.

Like all clauses, adjective clauses must have a subject and a verb. In some cases the adjective clause marker itself is the subject; in some cases, there is another subject.

The painting was very expensive. Ms. Wallace bought it.
The painting *that Ms. Wallace bought* was very expensive.

The adjective clause marker in the joined sentence replaces *it*, the object of the verb *bought*. In the joined sentence, the adjective clause keeps the subject—*Ms. Wallace*—that it had in the original sentence.

> That is a topic. It interests me.
> That is a topic *which interests me.*

The adjective clause marker in the joined sentence replaces *it*, the subject of the second original sentence. In the joined sentence, the marker itself is the subject of the adjective clause.

> Notice that the inclusion of the pronoun *it* in the joined sentences below is an error.

> **Incorrect:** *The painting that Ms. Wallace bought *it* was very expensive.
> *This is a topic which *it* interests me.

When the markers *which*, *that*, and *whom* are used as objects in relative clauses, they can correctly be omitted.

> The painting Ms. Wallace bought is very expensive.   (*that* omitted)

In some adjective clauses, the relative pronoun *that* may be used in place of *which* or *who*. These sentences are called **identifying adjective clauses** (also called **restrictive adjective clauses**). The information in the clause is needed to identify the head noun. This type of clause is NOT set off by commas.

> The island that we visited was beautiful.
> The people that moved in next door are very friendly.

In other adjective clauses (called **non-identifying** or **non-restrictive**) the clause provides "extra" information. It's not needed to identify the head noun. These clauses are always set off with commas.

> Maui, which is one of the Hawaiian Islands, is quite beautiful.
> The Smiths, who are our new neighbors, are very friendly.

The word *that* can NOT be used to introduce this type of clause.
> **Incorrect:** *Maui, that is one of the Hawaiian Islands, is quite beautiful.
> *The Smiths, that are our new neighbors, are very friendly.

The adjective clause markers *which* and *whom* can also be used as objects of prepositions:

> That is the topic. I will write on it.
> That is the topic *on which I will write.*

Notice the word order: preposition + relative pronoun (*on which*), NOT relative pronoun + preposition (*which on*).

> You may also see sentences with adjective clauses used in this pattern:

> quantifier + *of* + relative clause

> He met with two advisors. He had known both of them for years.
> He met with two advisors, *both of whom* he had known for years.

> I read a number of articles. Most of them were very useful.
> I read a number of articles, *most of which* were very useful.

Quantifiers are words that show number or amount: *much, some, a few, both, many, most, all, each, one, two,* etc.

Sentence Completion

Any part of an adjective clause can be missing from the stem of Sentence Completion items, but most often, the marker and the subject (if there is one) and verb are missing.

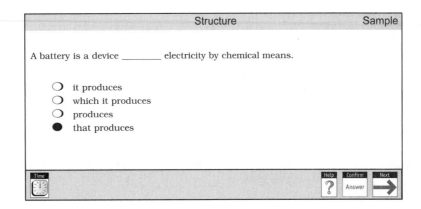

The first choice is incorrect because the pronoun *it* cannot be used to join two clauses. The second choice is not appropriate because the subject *it* is not needed in the adjective clause; the marker *which* serves as the subject of the clause. The third choice is incorrect because there is no marker to join the adjective clause to the main clause. The best answer is the fourth choice, which uses the marker *that* to join the two clauses.

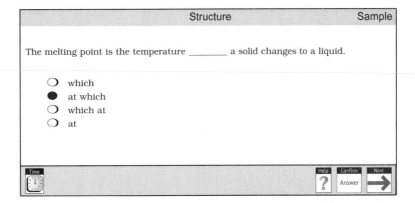

The first choice is incorrect because a preposition is needed before the adjective clause. The third choice is incorrect because the relative pronoun comes before the preposition. The fourth choice is incorrect because the relative pronoun has been omitted.

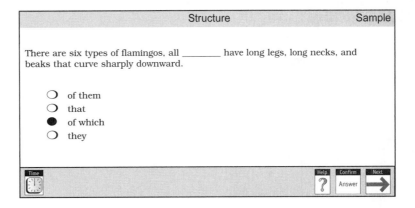

The first and last choices do not contain connecting words needed to join clauses. The second choice does not follow the correct pattern of relative clauses after a quantifier (*all*). The correct pattern needed to complete this sentence is quantifier + *of* + marker. Only the third choice follows this pattern.

Error Identification

A) INCORRECT CHOICE OF ADJECTIVE CLAUSE MARKER

The wrong relative pronoun is used, or a personal pronoun is used in place of the relative pronoun.

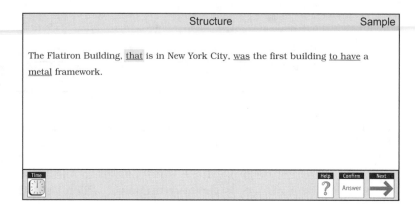

This is a non-identifying (non-restrictive) relative clause. The correct relative pronoun is *which*. (Remember: if the clause is set off by commas, the pronoun *that* cannot be used.)

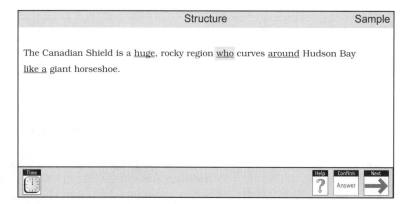

The relative pronoun *who* is only used to refer to persons. Either *that* or *which* should be used here.

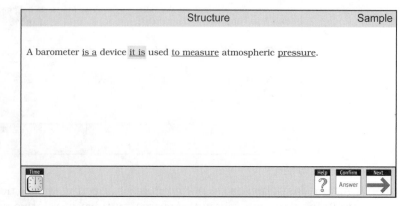

A personal pronoun (*it*) cannot be used to introduce an adjective clause.

B) INCORRECT INCLUSIONS

An adjective clause marker may be used unnecessarily in a sentence, or a personal pronoun may be used unnecessarily in an adjective clause.

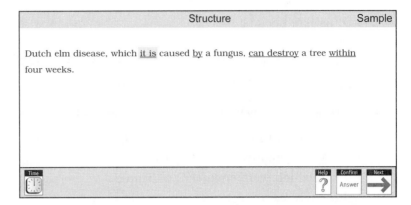

Structure	Sample

Dutch elm disease, which <u>it is</u> caused <u>by</u> a fungus, <u>can destroy</u> a tree <u>within</u> four weeks.

The relative pronoun *which* is the true subject of the adjective clause; the personal pronoun *it* is unnecessary.

C) INCORRECT WORD ORDER IN ADJECTIVE CLAUSES

The most common word order problem is adjective clause marker + preposition:

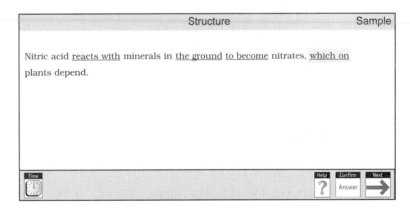

Structure	Sample

Nitric acid <u>reacts with</u> minerals in <u>the ground</u> <u>to become</u> nitrates, <u>which on</u> plants depend.

The correct word order is *on which.*

EXERCISE 14

Focus: Structure problems involving adjective clauses and adjective clause markers. (Note: Several items in this exercise do NOT focus on adjective clauses; these items are marked in the answer key with asterisks.)

Directions: For Sentence Completion items, mark the oval next to the answer choice that correctly completes the sentence. For Error Identification items, put an X under the underlined portion of the sentence that would not be considered correct.

1. Most folk songs are ballads _____ have simple words and tell simple stories.
   - ○ what
   - ○ although
   - ○ who
   - ○ that

2. After its introduction in 1969, the float process _____ the world's principal method of manufacturing flat sheets of glass.

   ○ by which it became
   ○ it became
   ○ became
   ○ which became

3. Dolphins <u>lack</u> vocal cords but they have a large, <u>oil-filled</u> organ called the "melon" <u>which with</u> <u>they can</u> produce a wide variety of sounds.

4. In 1850 Yale University established Sheffield Scientific School, _____ .

   ○ engineers were educated there
   ○ where engineers were educated
   ○ in which were engineers educated
   ○ where were engineers educated

5. There are <u>thousands</u> of kinds of bacteria, <u>many</u> of <u>whom</u> are <u>beneficial</u>.

6. The Ringling Brothers were five brothers <u>which</u> built a small group of <u>performers</u> into <u>the world's</u> <u>largest</u> circus.

7. Most beans _____ are a form of kidney bean.

   ○ that are cultivated in the United States
   ○ their cultivation in the United States
   ○ are cultivated in the United States they
   ○ they are cultivated in the United States

8. In addition to being a naturalist, Stewart E. White was a writer _____ the struggle for survival on the American frontier.

   ○ whose novels describe
   ○ he describes in his novels
   ○ his novels describe
   ○ who, describing in his novels

9. Diamonds are often found in rock formations called pipes, _____ the throats of extinct volcanoes.

   ○ in which they resemble
   ○ which resemble
   ○ they have a resemblance to
   ○ that resemble

10. William Samuel Johnson, <u>who</u> helped <u>write</u> the Constitution, <u>become</u> <u>the first</u> president of Columbia University in 1787.

11. Seals appear clumsy on the land, _____ are able to move short distances faster than most people can run.

    ○ but they
    ○ which they
    ○ they
    ○ which

12. The Pritzker Prize is given <u>every year</u> to architects <u>their</u> work <u>benefits</u> humanity and <u>the environment</u>.

13. The instrument panel of a light airplane has at least a dozen instruments _____ .
    - ◯ the pilot must watch
    - ◯ what the pilot must watch
    - ◯ which the pilot must watch them
    - ◯ such that the pilot must watch them

14. A keystone species is a species of plant or animal _____ absence has a major effect on an ecological system.
    - ◯ that its
    - ◯ its
    - ◯ whose
    - ◯ with its

15. Active stocks are <u>stocks</u> <u>they are</u> <u>frequently</u> bought and <u>sold.</u>

16. Pipettes are glass tubes, open <u>at both</u> ends, <u>which</u> chemists <u>use them</u> to transfer small <u>volumes</u> of liquid.

17. The size and shape of a nail depends primarily on the function _____ intended.
    - ◯ which it is
    - ◯ for which it is
    - ◯ which it is for
    - ◯ for which is

18. Gene Krupa had one of <u>the few</u> big <u>band</u> <u>that</u> was centered <u>around</u> a drummer.

19. In geometry, a tangent is a straight line _____ a curve at only one point.
    - ◯ it touches
    - ◯ whose touching
    - ◯ its touching
    - ◯ that touches

20. <u>There</u> are <u>many species of</u> plants and animals <u>that they</u> are <u>peculiar to</u> Hawaii.

21. It was the ragtime pianist Scott Joplin _____ the *Maple Leaf Rag*, perhaps the best known of all ragtime tunes.
    - ◯ wrote
    - ◯ the writer of
    - ◯ who wrote
    - ◯ writing

22. <u>Today</u> scientists obtain the <u>informations</u> <u>which they</u> use to make weather predictions <u>chiefly from</u> satellites.

23. Smoke jumpers are _____ descend into remote areas by parachute to fight forest fires.

○ firefighters
○ when firefighters
○ who, as firefighters
○ firefighters who

24. There are over 2,000 varieties of snakes, _____ are harmless to humans.

○ mostly they
○ most of them
○ most of which
○ which most

25. Charlotte Perkins Gilman's best known book _____ she urges women to become financially independent.

○ is *Women and Economics*, in which
○ *Women and Economics*, in which
○ is *Women and Economics*, which
○ which is *Women and Economics*

LESSON 15: Adverb Clauses

Sentence Completion

A) FULL ADVERB CLAUSES

An **adverb clause** consists of a connecting word, called an **adverb clause marker** (also called a **subordinate conjunction**), and at least a subject and a verb.

The demand for economical cars increases *when gasoline becomes more expensive*.

In this example, the adverb clause marker *when* joins the adverb clause to the main clause. The adverb clause contains a subject (*gasoline*) and a verb (*becomes*).

An adverb clause can precede the main clause or follow it. When the adverb clause comes first, it is separated from the main clause by a comma.

When gasoline becomes more expensive, the demand for economical cars increases.

The following markers are commonly seen in the Structure section:

Adverb Clause Marker	Use	Example
because	cause	*Because* the speaker was sick, the program was canceled.
since	cause	*Since* credit cards are so convenient, many people use them.
although	opposition	*Although* Mr. Crane earns a good salary, he never saves any money.
even though	opposition	*Even though* Rosa was tired, she stayed up late.
while	contrast	Some people arrived in taxis *while* others took the subway.
if	condition	*If* the automobile had not been invented, what would people use for basic transportation?
unless	negative condition	I won't go *unless* you do.
when	time	Your heart rate increases *when* you exercise.
while	time	Some people like to listen to music *while* they are studying.
as	time	One train was arriving *as* another was departing.
since	time	We haven't seen Professor Hill *since* she returned from her trip.
until	time	Don't put off going to the dentist *until* you have a problem.
once	time	*Once* the dean arrives, the meeting can begin.
before	time	*Before* he left the country, he bought some traveler's checks.
after	time	She will give a short speech *after* she is presented with the award.

In Sentence Completion items, any part of a full adverb clause—the marker, the subject, the verb, and so on—can be missing from the stem.

B) CLAUSE MARKERS WITH -EVER

Words that end with -ever are sometimes used as adverb clause markers. (In some sentences, these words are actually noun-clause markers.)

The -ever words that you are likely to see in the Structure section are given in the chart below:

Adverb Clause Marker with -ever	Meaning	Example
wherever	any place that . . .	Put that box *wherever* you can find room for it.
whenever	any time that . . .	They stay at that hotel *whenever* they're in Boston.
however	any way that . . .	*However* you solve the problem, you'll get the same answer.
whatever	any thing that . . .	We'll do *whatever* we can to help you.

C) REDUCED ADVERB CLAUSES

When the subject of the main clause and the subject of the adverb clause are the same person or thing, the adverb clause can be reduced (shortened). Reduced adverb clauses do not contain a verb or a subject. They consist of a marker and a participle (either a present or a past participle) or a marker and an adjective.

> *When astronauts are orbiting the earth*, they don't feel the force of gravity.
>   (full adverb clause)
> *When orbiting the earth*, astronauts don't feel the force of gravity.
>   (reduced clause with present participle)
> *Although it had been damaged*, the machine was still operational.
>   (full adverb clause)
> *Although damaged*, the machine was still operational.
>   (reduced clause with a past participle)
> *Although he was nervous*, he gave a wonderful speech.
>   (full adverb clause)
> *Although nervous*, he gave a wonderful speech.
>   (reduced clause with an adjective)

You will most often see reduced adverb clauses with the markers *although, while, if, when, before, after,* and *until*. Reduced adverb clauses are NEVER used after *because*.

D) PREPOSITIONAL PHRASES WITH THE SAME MEANING AS ADVERB CLAUSES

There are certain prepositions that have essentially the same meaning as adverb clause markers but are used with noun phrases or pronouns, not with clauses.

Preposition	Related Marker	Example
because of	because/since	Roberto chose that university *because of* its fine reputation.
due to	because/since	The accident was *due to* mechanical failure.
on account of	because/since	Visibility is poor today *on account of* air pollution.
in spite of	although/even though	He enjoys racing motorcycles *in spite of* the danger.
despite	although/even though	*Despite* its loss, the team is still in first place.
during	when/while	Her grandfather lived in England *during* the war.

SAMPLE ITEMS

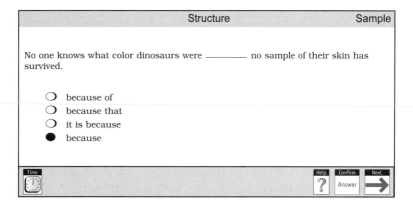

The first choice is incorrect; *because of* can only be used before nouns or pronouns. In the second choice, *that* is unnecessary. In the third choice, the phrase *it is* is used unnecessarily. The fourth choice correctly forms an adverb clause.

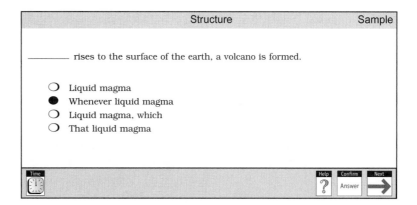

The first choice creates two clauses, but there is no connecting word to join them. The third choice creates a sentence with a main clause and an adjective clause, but the main clause has two subjects (*liquid magma* and *a volcano*). The fourth choice incorrectly creates a noun clause. The second choice correctly creates an adverb clause with *whenever*.

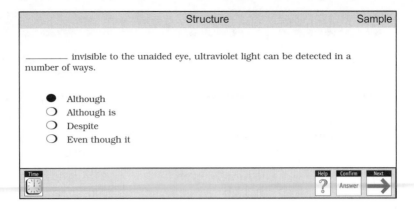

The first choice is best because it completes a reduced adverb clause. In the second choice, the adverb clause lacks a subject. In the third choice, *despite* cannot be used with an adjective (only with a noun phrase or pronoun). The fourth choice does not supply a verb for the adverb clause.

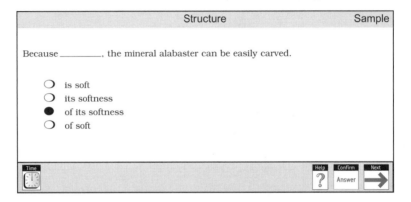

The first choice is incorrect because the adverb clause lacks a subject. The second choice is incorrect; the marker *because* must be used with a full clause. The third choice correctly uses *because of* with a noun phrase (*its softness*). The fourth choice is incorrect; the phrase *because of* cannot be used with an adjective such as *soft*.

Error Identification

Error Identification items usually involve the use of prepositions (discussed in Section D of this lesson) in place of adverb clause markers. Remember: adverb clause markers are only used before full or reduced adverb clauses while prepositions are used before noun phrases.

SAMPLE ITEMS

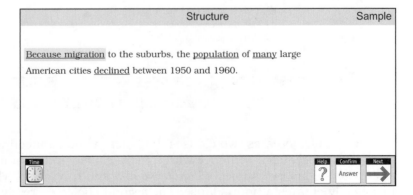

Before a noun phrase (*migration*), the preposition *because of* must be used.

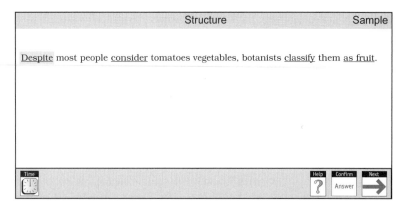

Structure	Sample

<u>Despite</u> most people <u>consider</u> tomatoes vegetables, botanists <u>classify</u> them <u>as fruit</u>.

Time | Help ? | Confirm Answer | Next →

Before a full clause (*most people consider tomatoes vegetables*) the adverb marker *although* must be used.

EXERCISE 15

Focus: Structure problems involving adverb clauses, reduced adverb clauses, and prepositional expressions. (Note: The focus for several items is NOT one of these structures. These items are marked in the answer key with asterisks.)

Directions: For Sentence Completion items, mark the oval next to the answer choice that correctly completes the sentence. For Error Identification items, put an *X* under the underlined portion of the sentence that would not be considered correct.

1. Small sailboats can easily capsize ———— they are not handled carefully.
    - ○ but
    - ○ which
    - ○ if
    - ○ so

2. ———— they are tropical birds, parrots can live in temperate or even cold climates.
    - ○ Despite
    - ○ Even though
    - ○ Nevertheless
    - ○ But

3. <u>Despite</u> cats cannot see in complete darkness, <u>their eyes</u> are <u>much more</u> sensitive <u>to light</u> than humans' eyes.

4. ———— added to a liquid, antifreeze lowers the freezing temperature of that liquid.
    - ○ That
    - ○ As is
    - ○ It is
    - ○ When

5. <u>Because of</u> cheese is <u>essentially</u> a <u>concentrated</u> form of milk, it contains <u>the same</u> nutrients as milk.

6. In spite of their frightening appearance, the squid is shy and completely harmless.

7. _____ advertising is so widespread in the United States, it has had an enormous effect on American life.
   - ○ Why
   - ○ The reason
   - ○ On account of
   - ○ Since

8. _____ towards shore, its shape is changed by its collision with the shallow sea bottom.
   - ○ During a wave rolls
   - ○ As a wave rolls
   - ○ A wave rolls
   - ○ A wave's rolling

9. Snakebirds were not given their name because they eat snakes, but because of their long, slender necks resemble snakes.

10. _____ people are increasingly linked over long distances by electronic communication, but many of them still prefer face-to-face encounters.
    - ○ Although
    - ○ Despite
    - ○ Today
    - ○ The fact that

11. _____ together in one place, they form a community.
    - ○ When people who live
    - ○ When people living
    - ○ Whenever people live
    - ○ Whenever living people

12. _____ managed by an independent governor and board of directors, the Bank of Canada is owned by the Canadian government.
    - ○ And yet
    - ○ In spite of it
    - ○ Although
    - ○ It is

13. In the sixteenth century, it was thought that a compass needle pointed north because some mysterious influence of the stars.

14. During lava cools exceptionally fast, it forms a natural glass called obsidian.

15. _____, the seeds of the Kentucky coffee plant are poisonous.
    - ○ Until they have been cooked
    - ○ Until their cooking
    - ○ They have been cooked until
    - ○ Cooked until

16. <u>Although</u> Adlai Stevenson was <u>never</u> elected president, he was one of the preeminent American <u>politics</u> of the mid-twentieth <u>century</u>.

17. Natural silk is still highly prized _____ similar artificial fabrics.
   - ○ although is available
   - ○ despite there are available
   - ○ in spite of the availability of
   - ○ even though an availability of

18. Cattle ranches are found almost _____ in Wyoming.
   - ○ wherever
   - ○ everywhere
   - ○ overall
   - ○ somewhere

19. <u>Since</u> its acute sense of <u>smell</u>, <u>the</u> bloodhound is often <u>used in</u> tracking.

20. _____ through a prism, a beam of white light breaks into all the colors of the rainbow.
   - ○ When shines
   - ○ It shines
   - ○ It is shone
   - ○ When shone

21. _____ the outer rings of a gyroscope are twisted or turned, the gyroscope itself continues to spin in exactly the same position.
   - ○ Somehow
   - ○ Otherwise
   - ○ However
   - ○ No matter

22. <u>Despite</u> their light <u>weigh</u>, aluminum alloys <u>can be</u> very <u>strong</u>.

23. _____ large bodies of water never freeze solid is that the sheet of ice on the surface protects the water below it from the cold air.
   - ○ Because
   - ○ Why do
   - ○ The reason that
   - ○ For the reason

24. _____ granted by the Patent Office, it becomes the inventor's property and he or she can keep it, sell it, or assign it.
   - ○ Once a patent is
   - ○ When a patent
   - ○ A patent, once
   - ○ A patent, whenever it is

25. _____ most bamboo blooms every year, there are some species that flower only two or three times a century.
   - ○ Whenever
   - ○ That
   - ○ While
   - ○ However

LESSON 16: Noun Clauses

Noun clauses are the third type of subordinate clause. They begin with **noun clause markers**. Noun clauses that are formed from statements begin with the noun clause marker *that*. Noun clauses formed from *yes/no* questions begin with the noun clause markers *whether* or *if*. Those formed from information questions begin with *wh-* words: *what, where, when,* and so on.

Dr. Hopkins' office is in this building. (statement)
I'm sure *that* Dr. Hopkins' office is in this building.

Is Dr. Hopkins' office on this floor? (yes/no question)
I don't know *if (whether)* Dr. Hopkins' office is on this floor.

Where is Dr. Hopkins' office? (information question)
Please tell me *where* Dr. Hopkins' office is.

Notice that the word order in direct questions is not the same as it is in noun clauses. The noun clause follows statement word order, not question word order.

*I don't know what *is her name.* (INCORRECT)
 I don't know what *her name is.* (CORRECT)

*She called him to ask what time *did his party start.* (INCORRECT)
 She called him to ask what time *his party started.* (CORRECT)

Noun clauses function exactly as nouns do: as subjects, as direct objects, as prepositional objects, or after the verb *to be.*

Noun clause as subject
When the meeting will be held has not been decided.
Noun clause as direct object
The weather announcer said *that there will be thunderstorms.*
Noun clause as prepositional object
Take pride in *what you do.*
Noun clause after *to be*
This is *what you need.*

Notice that when the noun clause is the subject of a sentence, the verb in the main clause does not have a noun or pronoun subject.

Sentence Completion

The noun clause marker, along with any other part of the noun clause—subject, verb, and so on—may be missing from the stem, or the whole noun clause may be missing.

SAMPLE ITEMS

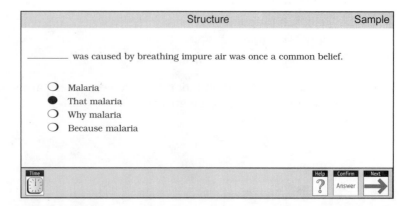

The first choice is incorrect because there are two verbs (*was caused* and *was*) but only one subject. The third choice is incorrect because *Why* is not the appropriate noun clause marker in this sentence; the noun clause is based on a statement, not on an information question. The fourth choice is incorrect because it forms an adverb clause, but the main clause lacks a subject. In the correct answer the noun clause itself (*That malaria was caused by breathing impure air*) is the subject of the verb *was* in the main clause.

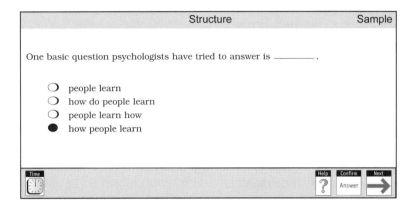

The first choice is incorrect; there is no connector between the two clauses. The second choice incorrectly follows question word order. The third choice is incorrect because *how* is in the wrong position. The fourth choice correctly completes the sentence with a noun clause.

Error Identification

Not many error identification problems involve noun clauses. You may see a few in which the incorrect word order is used in a noun clause.

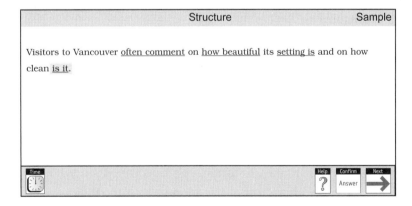

This is not a direct *wh-* question but a *wh-* noun clause. The correct word order is subject + verb (*it is*).

EXERCISE 16

Focus: Structure problems involving noun clauses. (Note: The focus for several items in this exercise is NOT noun clauses; these sentences are marked in the answer key with asterisks.)

Directions: For Sentence Completion items, mark the oval next to the answer choice that correctly completes the sentence. For Error Identification items, put an *X* under the underlined portion of the sentence that would not be considered correct.

1. _____ begin their existence as ice crystals over most of the Earth seems likely.

   ○ Raindrops
   ○ If raindrops
   ○ What if raindrops
   ○ That raindrops

2. Scientists cannot agree on _____ related to other orders of insects.

   ○ that fleas are
   ○ how fleas are
   ○ how are fleas
   ○ fleas that are

3. It was in 1875 _____ joined the staff of the astronomical observatory at Harvard University.

   ○ that Anna Winlock
   ○ Anna Winlock, who
   ○ as Anna Winlock
   ○ Anna Winlock then

4. A test pilot <u>tries out</u> new <u>kinds of</u> aircraft <u>to determine</u> if <u>are they</u> safe.

5. _____ is a narrow strip of woods along a stream in an open grassland.

   ○ Ecologists use the term "gallery forest"
   ○ What do ecologists call a "gallery forest"
   ○ "Gallery forest" is the term ecologists use
   ○ What ecologists call a "gallery forest"

6. _____ developed so rapidly in Alabama primarily because of its rich natural resources.

   ○ That heavy industry
   ○ Heavy industry
   ○ Heavy industry that was
   ○ When heavy industry

7. _____ so incredible is that these insects successfully migrate to places that they have never even seen.

   ○ That makes the monarch butterflies' migration
   ○ The migration of the monarch butterflies is
   ○ What makes the monarch butterflies' migration
   ○ The migration of the monarch butterflies, which is

8. Art critics <u>do not all</u> agree on what <u>are the qualities</u> that <u>make</u> a painting <u>great</u>.

9. In order to grow vegetables properly, gardeners must know _____.

   ○ what the requirements for each vegetable are
   ○ that the requirements for each vegetable
   ○ what are each vegetable's requirements
   ○ that is required by each vegetable

10. <u>Exactly</u> when <u>was the wheel</u> <u>invented</u> is <u>not</u> known.

11. For many years people have wondered ―――――― exists elsewhere in the universe.
    - ○ that life
    - ○ life which
    - ○ whether life
    - ○ life as it

12. <u>Although</u> geologists have a <u>clearly</u> understanding of why earthquakes <u>occur</u>, they cannot reliably predict when <u>they will</u> take place.

13. ―――――― of all modern domestic poultry is the red jungle fowl is widely believed.
    - ○ The ancestor
    - ○ The ancestor is
    - ○ How the ancestor
    - ○ That the ancestor

14. ―――――― the right side of a person's brain is dominant, that person is left-handed.
    - ○ That
    - ○ If
    - ○ Which
    - ○ For

15. Amerigo Vespucci, like Christopher Colombus, mistakenly believed ―――――― he had reached the shores of Asia.
    - ○ that
    - ○ if
    - ○ where
    - ○ in

LESSON 17: Parallelism

In both types of Structure items, the correct use of **parallelism** is sometimes tested. Parallel structures have the same grammatical form and function. Look at the following sentences:

> She spends her leisure time *playing* cards, *reading*, and *bicycling*.
> Henry *changed* the oil, *checked* the tire pressure, and *filled* the tank with gas.
> Amy plans to either *study* medicine or *major* in biology.
> Amy plans to study either *medicine* or *biology*.

All of the structures in italics are parallel. In the first, three gerunds are parallel; in the second, three main verbs; in the third, two simple forms; in the fourth, two nouns. Many other structures may be parallel in certain sentences: adjectives, adverbs, infinitives, prepositional phrases, noun clauses, and others.

The most common situation in which parallel structures are required is in a sequence (*A, B,* and *C*) as in the first two sentences above. Parallel structures are also required with correlative conjunctions such as *either . . . or* or *not only . . . but also.*

Sentence Completion

Many types of structures may be involved in this type of Sentence Completion item: adjectives, noun phrases, prepositional phrases, clauses, and others.

SAMPLE ITEM

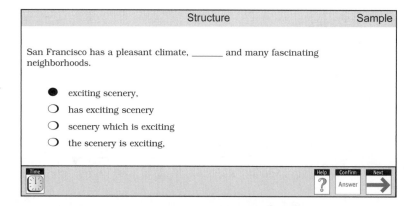

This sentence contains a series of three objects after the verb *has:* the first and third are noun phrases (*a pleasant climate* and *many fascinating neighborhoods*). To be parallel, the second object must also be a noun phrase. Therefore, the first choice is the correct answer; the second, third, and fourth choices are not parallel.

Error Identification

Error Identification items involving parallelism usually feature noun phrases, adjectives, verbs, prepositional phrases, gerunds, and infinitives.

Some problems with parallelism are actually word form problems similar to those in Lesson 18.

SAMPLE ITEM

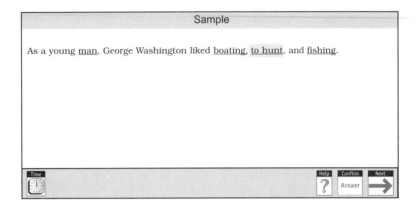

The second item in the series, *to hunt,* is not parallel with the other items in the series: *to hunt* is an infinitive, while the other items (*boating* and *fishing*) are gerunds.

EXERCISE 17.1

Focus: Identifying errors involving parallelism.

Directions: If the underlined form is parallel to other forms in the sentence, mark the sentence C. If the underlined form is not parallel, mark the sentence X and write a correction for the underlined form in the blank at the end of the sentence.

_____ 1. Steel is alloyed with manganese to increase its strength, hardness, and <u>resistance</u> to wear.

_____

_____ 2. The type of plant and animal life living in and around a pond depends on the soil of the pond, <u>what the quality of the water is</u>, and the pond's location.

_____

_____ 3. Philosophers are concerned with questions about nature, <u>human behavior,</u> society, and reality.

_____

_____ 4. When taking part in winter sports, one should wear clothing that is lightweight, <u>warmth</u>, and suitable for the activity.

_____

_____ 5. Folklore consists of the beliefs, customs, traditions, and <u>telling stories</u> that people pass from generation to generation.

_____

_____ 6. Major sources of noise pollution include automobiles and other vehicles, industrial plants, and <u>heavy construction equipment</u>.

_____

_____ 7. Because of their hardness, industrial diamonds can be used for cutting, <u>grind</u>, and drilling.

_____

_____ 8. Scholar John Fiske wrote on history, <u>religious</u>, and social issues.

_____

_____ 9. Electricity is used to light, <u>hot</u>, and cool buildings.

_____

_____ 10. T. S. Eliot was equally distinguished as a poet, <u>he wrote criticism</u>, and a dramatist.

_____

_____ 11. Jute is a glossy fiber that is strong, does not easily stretch, and <u>inexpensive</u>.

_____

_____ 12. Wetlands were once considered useless areas, but they have been found to purify water, nurture wildlife, and <u>flood control</u>.

_____

EXERCISE 17.2

Focus: Structure problems involving parallelism. (Note: The focus for several items in this exercise is NOT parallelism; these sentences are marked in the answer key with asterisks.)

Directions: For Sentence Completion items, mark the oval next to the answer choice that correctly completes the sentence. For Error Identification items, put an *X* under the underlined portion of the sentence that would not be considered correct.

1. The bellflower <u>is</u> a wildflower that <u>grows in</u> shady fields, in <u>marshes</u>, <u>and mountain</u> slopes.

2. Insects provide many beneficial services, such as _____, breaking down dead-wood, and pollinating plants.
   - ○ they condition soils
   - ○ to condition soil
   - ○ conditioning soil
   - ○ soil conditioned

3. Computers are <u>often used</u> to control, <u>adjustment</u>, and <u>correct</u> complex <u>industrial</u> operations.

4. Eggs may be <u>boiling</u> in <u>the shell</u>, scrambled, <u>fried</u>, and cooked in countless <u>other</u> ways.

5. Frozen orange juice must be packed, _____, and stored when the fruit is ripe.

   ○ be frozen
   ○ must be frozen
   ○ frozen
   ○ it must be frozen

6. In 1900 electrically powered cars were more popular than gasoline powered cars because they were quiet, operated smoothly, and _____.

   ○ handled easily
   ○ ease of handling
   ○ handling easily
   ○ easy to handle

7. Many places of <u>history</u>, scientific, <u>cultural</u>, or <u>scenic</u> importance have been designated <u>national</u> monuments.

8. Roger Williams was a clergyman, _____ the colony of Rhode Island, and an outspoken advocate of religious and political freedom.

   ○ founded
   ○ the founder of
   ○ was the founder of
   ○ he founded

9. <u>Modern</u> motorcycles are <u>lighter</u>, faster, <u>and specialized</u> than <u>motorcycles</u> of 25 years ago.

10. Paint can be applied to a surface with rollers, _____, or spray guns.

   ○ brushes
   ○ brushes can be used
   ○ with brushes
   ○ by brush

11. Many people who live near the ocean <u>depend on</u> it as a source of <u>food</u>, <u>recreation</u>, and <u>to have economic</u> opportunities.

12. The use of labor-saving devices at home, _____, and in factories added to the amount of leisure time people had.

   ○ the office
   ○ used in offices
   ○ offices
   ○ in offices

13. Throughout history, trade routes have increased contact between people, _____, and greatly affected the growth of civilization.

   ○ have resulted in an exchange of ideas
   ○ an exchange of ideas has resulted
   ○ resulted in an exchange of ideas
   ○ resulting in an exchange of ideas

14. Large commercial fishing vessels are <u>equipped</u> to clean, <u>packaging</u>, and <u>freeze</u> the fish that they catch <u>at sea</u>.

15. As a breed, golden retrievers are intelligent, loyally, and friendly dogs.

16. Mathematics can be considered a language, an art, a science, a tool or playing a game.

17. Photographers' choice of a camera depends on what kind of pictures they want to take, how much control they want over exposure, and _____ they want to spend.

    ○ the amount of money
    ○ what money
    ○ how much money
    ○ so much money that

18. Barbara Jordan was the first woman in the South to win an election to the House of Representatives, _____ as Congresswoman from Texas from 1973 to 1979.

    ○ to serve
    ○ served
    ○ serving
    ○ has served

19. Paper may contain mineral, vegetables, or man-made fibers.

20. R. Buckminster Fuller was a design, an architect, an inventor, and an engineer.

21. According to Susan Sontag, our concepts of art, beauty, and nature has been changed by photography.

22. Atlanta is the commercial, financial, and _____ of Georgia.

    ○ center of administration
    ○ administrative center
    ○ center for administering
    ○ administering center

23. The economist Kenneth Boulding proposed a single social science that would unify economic, political science, and sociology.

24. An ant's antennas provide it with the senses of hear, touch, smell, and taste.

25. Even after the Revolutionary War, American importers obtained merchandise from Britain because British merchants understood American tastes, offered attractive prices, and _____.

    ○ easy credit was provided
    ○ because of easy credit
    ○ easy credit
    ○ provided easy credit

Directions: For Sentence Completion items, mark the oval next to the answer choice that correctly completes the sentence. For Error Identification items, put an X under the underlined portion of the sentence that would not be considered correct.

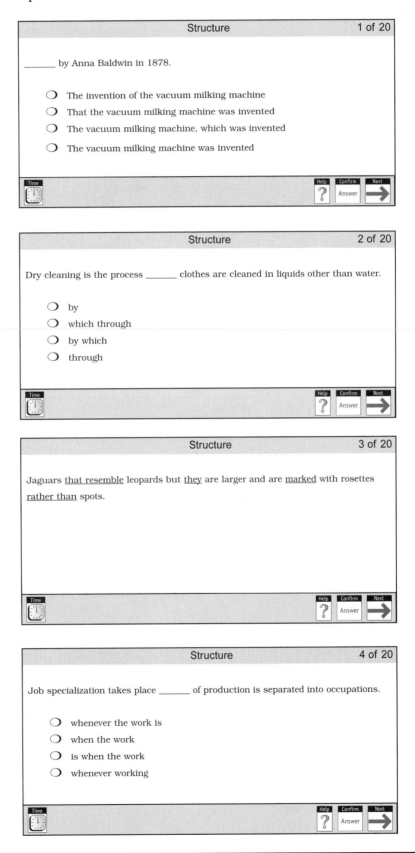

Structure   1 of 20

_____ by Anna Baldwin in 1878.

○ The invention of the vacuum milking machine
○ That the vacuum milking machine was invented
○ The vacuum milking machine, which was invented
○ The vacuum milking machine was invented

Time · Help ? · Confirm Answer · Next →

Structure   2 of 20

Dry cleaning is the process _____ clothes are cleaned in liquids other than water.

○ by
○ which through
○ by which
○ through

Time · Help ? · Confirm Answer · Next →

Structure   3 of 20

Jaguars that resemble leopards but they are larger and are marked with rosettes rather than spots.

Time · Help ? · Confirm Answer · Next →

Structure   4 of 20

Job specialization takes place _____ of production is separated into occupations.

○ whenever the work is
○ when the work
○ is when the work
○ whenever working

Time · Help ? · Confirm Answer · Next →

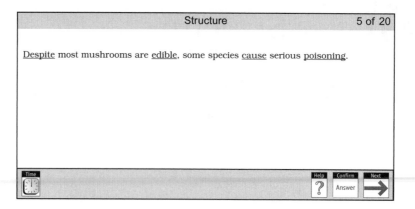

Despite most mushrooms are <u>edible</u>, some species <u>cause</u> serious <u>poisoning</u>.

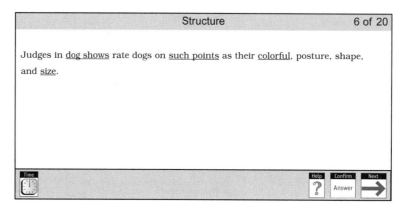

Judges in <u>dog shows</u> rate dogs on <u>such points</u> as their <u>colorful</u>, posture, shape, and <u>size</u>.

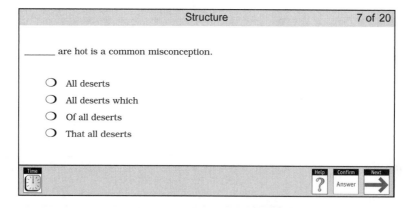

_____ are hot is a common misconception.

- ○ All deserts
- ○ All deserts which
- ○ Of all deserts
- ○ That all deserts

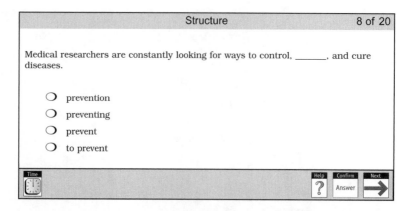

Medical researchers are constantly looking for ways to control, _____, and cure diseases.

- ○ prevention
- ○ preventing
- ○ prevent
- ○ to prevent

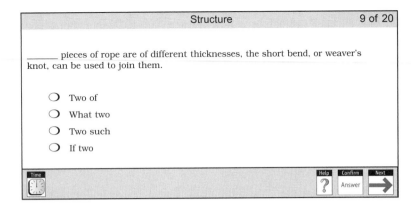

_____ pieces of rope are of different thicknesses, the short bend, or weaver's knot, can be used to join them.

○ Two of

○ What two

○ Two such

○ If two

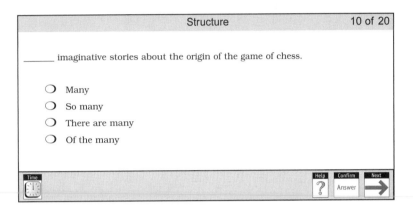

_____ imaginative stories about the origin of the game of chess.

○ Many

○ So many

○ There are many

○ Of the many

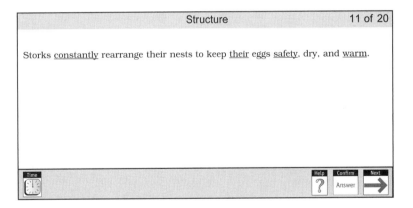

Storks <u>constantly</u> rearrange their nests to keep <u>their</u> eggs <u>safety</u>, dry, and <u>warm</u>.

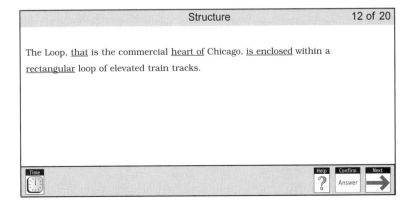

The Loop, <u>that</u> is the commercial <u>heart of</u> Chicago, <u>is enclosed</u> within a <u>rectangular</u> loop of elevated train tracks.

Judge Francis Hopkinson is probably best known as a signer of the Declaration of Independence, but he also excelled as a poet, _____, and an orator.

- ○ as a musician
- ○ by playing music
- ○ a musician
- ○ he played music

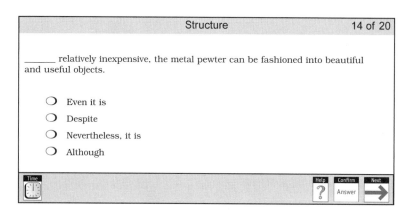

_____ relatively inexpensive, the metal pewter can be fashioned into beautiful and useful objects.

- ○ Even it is
- ○ Despite
- ○ Nevertheless, it is
- ○ Although

Owls can hunt in total darkness because their remarkably keen sense of smell.

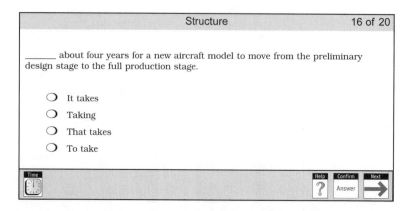

_____ about four years for a new aircraft model to move from the preliminary design stage to the full production stage.

- ○ It takes
- ○ Taking
- ○ That takes
- ○ To take

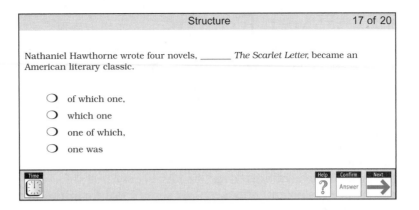

Nathaniel Hawthorne wrote four novels, _____ *The Scarlet Letter*, became an American literary classic.

- ○ of which one,
- ○ which one
- ○ one of which,
- ○ one was

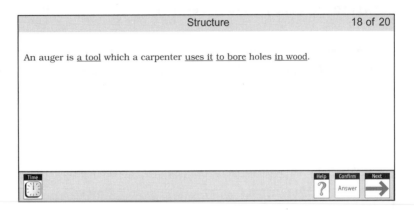

An auger is <u>a tool</u> which a carpenter <u>uses it</u> <u>to bore</u> holes <u>in wood</u>.

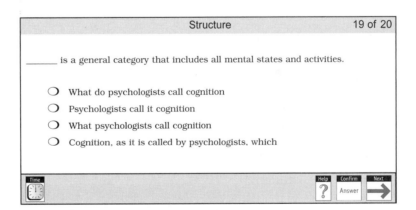

_____ is a general category that includes all mental states and activities.

- ○ What do psychologists call cognition
- ○ Psychologists call it cognition
- ○ What psychologists call cognition
- ○ Cognition, as it is called by psychologists, which

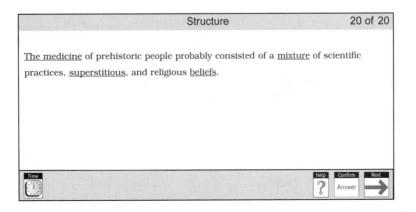

<u>The medicine</u> of prehistoric people probably consisted of a <u>mixture</u> of scientific practices, <u>superstitious</u>, and religious <u>beliefs</u>.

LESSON 18: Word Forms

Word form problems are tested only in Error Identification items.

By far the most common type of Error Identification problem involves word forms. Four or five items per test will probably be word form problems. Most errors of this type involve using one part of speech in place of another. Both the incorrect word and the correction come from the same root (*rapid* and *rapidly,* for example, or *inform* and *information*). The four parts of speech generally involved are verbs, nouns, adjectives, and adverbs. The most common problems are adjectives in place of adverbs and adverbs in place of adjectives. Nouns in place of adjectives and adjectives in place of nouns are also commonly seen. In some word form problems, different forms of the same part of speech may be involved. For example, a noun that refers to a person (*leader*) may be used in place of the field (*leadership*). A gerund (a verbal noun) may also be used in place of an ordinary noun (*judging* for *judgement,* for example).

Parts of speech can often be identified by their suffixes (word endings).

Common Noun Endings

-tion	information	-ery	recovery
-sion	provision	-ship	scholarship
-ence	existence	-tude	multitude
-ance	acceptance	-ism	capitalism
-ity	creativity	-cracy	democracy
-hood	childhood	-logy	biology
-dom	wisdom	-ness	happiness
-th	health	-ment	experiment
-age	marriage		

Endings for Nouns that Refer to Persons

-er	explorer	-ee	employee
-or	sailor	-ic	comic
-ist	psychologist	-ian	technician
-ent	student	-ant	attendant

Common Verb Endings

-ize	realize	-ify	satisfy
-en	shorten	-ate	incorporate
-er	discover		

Common Adjective Endings

-ate	moderate	-y	sunny
-ous	dangerous	-ic	economic
-al	normal	-ical	logical

Common Adjective Endings (continued)			
-ial	remedial	-ory	sensory
-able	comfortable	-less	hopeless
-ible	sensible	-ive	competitive
-ish	foolish	-ly	friendly
-ant	resistant	-ful	colorful
-ent	different	-ile	sterile
Adverb Endings			
-ly	quickly	-ally	historically

A) ADJECTIVE/ADVERB ERRORS

The most common type of word form problem involves the use of an adverb in place of an adjective or an adjective in place of an adverb. A few points to keep in mind:

■ **Adjectives** modify nouns, noun phrases, gerunds, and pronouns.

Hang up your *wet* clothes.
(adjective modifying the noun *clothes*)

The two children were *kind*.
(adjective modifying the noun phrase *the two children*)

We saw some *wonderful* acting in the play.
(adjective modifying the gerund *acting*)

They were very *brave*.
(adjective modifying the pronoun *they*)

● Adjectives often come before words they modify.

an *important* test   a *quiet* evening   a *long* letter

● Adjectives may also follow the verb *to be* and other linking verbs.

The glass was *empty*.

That song sounds *nice*.

They look *upset*.

● They often answer the question *What kind?*

She is a *brilliant* doctor. (What kind of a doctor is she? *A brilliant one.*)

■ **Adverbs** modify many types of words, inclucing verbs, participles, adjectives, other adverbs, prepositions, and some adverb clause markers.

Ann *eagerly* accepted the challenge.
(adverb modifying the verb *accepted*)

It was a *rapidly* changing situation.
(adverb modifying the present participle *changing*)

She wore a *brightly* colored scarf.
(adverb modifying the past participle *colored*)

Ted seemed *extremely* curious about that topic.
(adverb modifying the adjective *curious*)

The accident occurred *incredibly* quickly.
(adverb modifying the adverb *quickly*)

We arrived at the airport *shortly* before our flight left.
(adverb modifying the adverb clause marker *before*)

We arrived at the airport *shortly* before noon.
(adverb modifying the preposition *before*)

- Sometimes adverbs are used at the beginning of sentences, usually followed by a comma. These adverbs sometimes modify the entire sentence rather than one word in the sentence.

  Generally, I like my classes.

  Usually Professor Ingram's lectures are more interesting.

- Most adverbs tested in this section are adverbs of manner. They are formed by adding the suffix -*ly* or -*ally* to an adjective.

  quick   quickly   comic   comically

  comfortable   comfortably   historic   historically

- Adverbs of manner answer the question *How?*

  Ms. Lang treats her employees *honestly*. (How does she treat her employees? *Honestly*.)

- A few adverbs (*fast* and *hard*, for example) have the same form as adjectives.

  Charles bought a *fast* car. (adjective)

  He was driving so *fast* that he got a speeding ticket. (adverb)

- *Well* is the irregular adverb form of the adjective *good*.

  Juan is an exceptionally *good* student.

  He did very *well* on the last test.

- Some adjectives also end in -*ly*: *friendly*, *yearly*, *costly*, and *lively*, for example.

  That was a *costly* mistake.

  I found Houston a very *friendly* city.

SAMPLE ITEMS

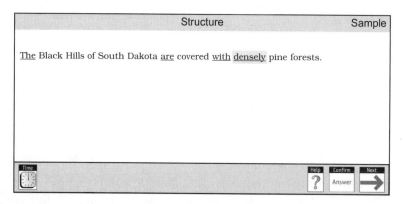

Densely is incorrect. An adjective, *dense*, not an adverb, is required to modify the noun phrase *pine forests*.

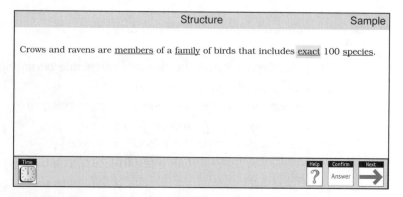

The adverb *exactly* is needed in place of the adjective *exact*.

B) INCORRECT FORMS OF WORDS CONNECTED WITH CERTAIN FIELDS

This error involves a confusion between the names of fields (*biology*, for example) and the name of a person who practices in that field (*biologist*) or between one of those terms and the adjective that describes the field (*biological*).

SAMPLE ITEM

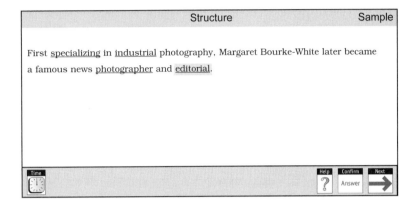

The adjective *editorial* is used to describe the field of editing. However, a noun referring to a person (*editor*) is needed in this sentence.

C) OTHER WORD FORM PROBLEMS

There are many other word form problems. Some examples are given here:

SAMPLE ITEMS

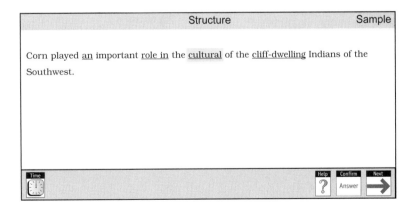

The noun *culture*, not the adjective *cultural*, is needed.

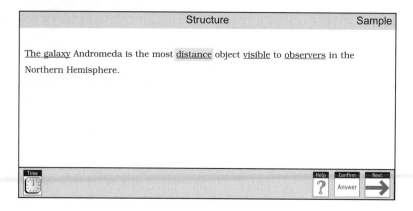

The galaxy Andromeda is the most distance object visible to observers in the Northern Hemisphere.

The adjective *distant* is needed in place of the noun *distance.*

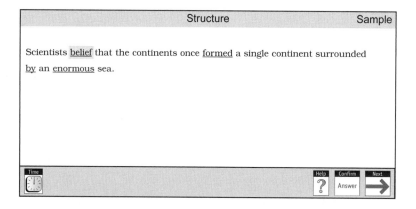

Scientists belief that the continents once formed a single continent surrounded by an enormous sea.

In this sentence, the verb *believe* is needed in place of the noun *belief.*

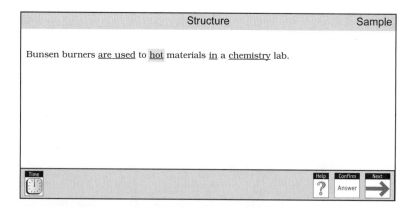

Bunsen burners are used to hot materials in a chemistry lab.

The verb *heat* is needed in place of the adjective *hot.*

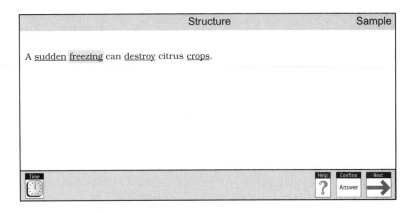

	Structure	Sample

A <u>sudden</u> <u>freezing</u> can <u>destroy</u> citrus <u>crops</u>.

Rather than the gerund (*-ing*) form, the noun *freeze* is required.

EXERCISE 18.1

Focus: Recognizing parts of speech of the type that are commonly confused in Error Identification items.

Directions: Fill in the lines in the blanks below with the appropriate word forms. In some cases, there may be more than one correct answer. The first one is done as an example.

	Verb	Noun	Adjective	Adverb
1.	*differ*	*difference*	different	*differently*
2.	compete			
3.				deeply
4.		decision		
5.	beautify			
6.	prohibit			
7.			emphatic	
8.			inconvenient	
9.		glory		
10.	mystify			
11.			general	
12.				simply
13.			pure	
14.	free			
15.	restrict			

EXERCISE 18.2

Focus: Recognizing word forms related to the names of fields, to adjectives describing those fields, and to people involved in those fields.

Directions: Fill in the blanks in the chart below with the appropriate form. The first one is done as an example.

Field	Person	Adjective
1. music	*musician*	*musical*
2. _____	surgeon	_____
3. _____	_____	poetic
4. _____	technician	_____
5. administration	_____	_____
6. _____	_____	financial
7. _____	photographer	_____
8. theory	_____	_____
9. _____	_____	athletic
10. grammar	_____	_____
11. _____	philosopher	_____
12. _____	criminal	_____
13. _____	_____	political
14. _____	lawyer	_____
15. humor	_____	_____

EXERCISE 18.3

Focus: Identifying errors and recognizing correct use of adjectives and adverbs.

Directions: Underline the form that correctly completes the sentence.

1. In any animal community, herbivores (great/greatly) outnumber carnivores.

2. Floods cause billions of dollars' worth of property damage (annual/annually).

3. (Regular/Regularly) airmail service in the United States began in 1918.

4. Writer Ernest Hemingway is known for his (simple/simply) language and his lively dialogue.

5. The tiny coral snake is (beautiful/beautifully) but deadly.

6. (General/Generally), bauxite is found near the surface, so it is relatively (simple/simply) to mine.

7. The colony of New Hampshire was (permanent/permanently) separated from the Massachusetts Bay Colony in 1692.

8. The most numerous and (wide/widely) distributed of all insectivorous animals are the shrews.

9. The endocrine system functions in (close/closely) relationship with the nervous system.

10. A gap in the Coast Range of California provides (easy/easily) access to the San Francisco Bay area.

11. Mushrooms are found in an (incredible/incredibly) range of sizes, colors, and shapes.

12. Some airplanes have an automatic pilot that is connected to the airplane's controls and (automatic/automatically) keeps the plane on course.

13. Winslow Homer, who had no (formal/formally) training in art, became famous for his paintings of the sea.

14. The nuclear-powered cargo ship *Savannah* proved (commercial/commercially) impractical.

15. In 1948 Stan Getz made a (masterful/masterfully) solo recording of the song *Early Autumn* which (deep/deeply) influenced younger musicians.

EXERCISE 18.4

Focus: Identifying which parts of speech are appropriate in sentences.

Directions: Underline the form that correctly completes the sentence. Then identify the part of speech of the correct word in the parentheses after the sentence. You can use these abbreviations for parts of speech:

N = noun   G = gerund (-*ing*) noun
V = verb   Adj = adjective
PN = "person" noun   Adv = adverb
Prep = preposition

The first one is done as an example.

1. Sinclair Lewis' novel *Babbitt* is set in the (fiction/<u>fictional</u>) town of Zenith. (___*Adj*___)

2. By-products from chicken eggs are used by (industry/industrial) in manufacturing such (produces/products) as soap and paint. (_____) (_____)

3. The daylily is an attractive plant having (fragrance/fragrant) yellow, orange, or red flowers shaped like funnels. (_____)

4. An equation is a (mathematics/mathematical) statement which says that two expressions are (equal/equality). (_____) (_____)

5. The Richter scale measures the (severely/severity) of earthquakes. (_____)

6. Justin Winsor promoted the (developing/development) of libraries throughout the United States in the nineteenth century. (_____)

7. Scientists (differ/different) in their opinions of how snow crystals (originate/origin). (_____) (_____)

8. Harry Blackstone was a famous (magic/magician). (_____)

9. Glass sponges are found in oceans at a (deep/depth) of 300 feet or more. (_____)

10. Colorado shares with Wyoming the (distinction/distinctly) of having four (perfect/perfectly) straight borders. (_____) (_____)

11. Rose Han Lee wrote a number of (scholar/scholarly) accounts about the effects of (immigrant/immigration) on mining towns in the western United States. (_____) (_____)

12. Most snails venture out to look for (feed/food) only after sunset or on (rain/rainy) days. (_____) (_____)

13. Hats may (symbolize/symbol) social status or (occupation/occupational) as well as being fashion items. (_____) (_____)

14. Analgesics are used to (relieve/relief) pain and reduce fever. (_____)

15. A (member/membership) of the Paiute tribe of Nevada, Sarah Winnemuca worked as a guide and (interpret/interpreter). (_____) (_____)

16. The Earth's (out/outer) shell is divided into sections called plates, which are (constant/constantly) in motion. (_____) (_____)

17. The Nassau grouper is a (tropics/tropical) fish that is noted for its (able/ability) to change color. (_____) (_____)

18. Alpha rays (loss/lose) energy (rapidity/rapidly) as they pass through matter. (_____) (_____)

19. The cherry is one of the only fruits that will not (ripe/ripen) if it is removed from the tree. (_____)

20. A good proofreader (painstaking/painstakingly) examines a manuscript for errors in spelling and (grammar/grammarian) as well as for (fact/factual) mistakes. (_____) (_____) (_____)

EXERCISE 18.5

Focus: Identifying errors involving word form problems. (Note: One or two items in this exercise do not focus on word form errors. These are marked in the answer key with an asterisk.)

Directions: Decide which of the four underlined words or phrases would not be considered correct and put an X under that expression.

1. Liberal arts colleges <u>cultivate</u> general <u>intellectually</u> <u>abilities</u> rather than technical or <u>professional</u> skills.

2. Goats are extremely <u>destruction</u> to <u>natural</u> <u>vegetation</u>, and are often <u>responsible</u> for soil erosion.

3. <u>Wild</u> plants were of <u>considerable</u> <u>important</u> to early settlers, and many are still used <u>medicinally</u> and as foods.

4. One important <u>branch</u> of <u>linguistics</u> is semantics, which <u>analysis</u> the <u>meaning</u> of words.

5. Unlike folk <u>dancers</u>, which are the <u>product</u> of a single <u>culture</u>, ballet is an <u>international</u> art form.

6. The <u>strong</u> of a rope is <u>directly</u> <u>proportional</u> to its <u>cross-sectional</u> area.

7. Black bears can move <u>rapidly</u> when <u>necessary</u> and are <u>skillful</u> tree-climbers for their size and <u>weigh</u>.

8. In an arboretum, trees are <u>cultivated</u> for <u>scientific</u> and <u>educational</u> <u>purpose</u>.

9. In most Western states, the first major <u>industry</u> was mining, which was <u>gradually</u> <u>supplemented</u> by <u>farms</u> and ranching.

10. Peach trees <u>grow</u> <u>good</u> in a <u>variety of</u> soil types, but do best in <u>sandy</u> loam.

11. The <u>unit</u> of <u>measuring</u> called the foot was <u>originally</u> based on the <u>length</u> of the human foot.

12. <u>Philosopher</u> Theodore A. Langerman was <u>interested</u> in the fields of <u>literary</u> and <u>music</u>.

13. A <u>chemical</u> <u>react</u> that <u>absorbs</u> <u>heat</u> is called endothermic.

14. One <u>characteristic</u> of the <u>poems</u> of Emily Dickinson is the <u>sharp</u> of her <u>images</u>.

15. Luther Gulick was a <u>teacher</u> and <u>physician</u> who spent much of his <u>live</u> promoting <u>physical fitness</u>.

16. A dog should be checked <u>regularly</u> by a veterinarian <u>to ensure</u> that it <u>remains</u> in good <u>healthy</u>.

17. <u>Southwestern</u> Boston is made up of Hyde Park, West Roxbury, and other <u>pleasant</u> <u>residential</u> <u>neighbors</u>.

18. <u>Pure</u> nitric acid is colorless, but it <u>acquires</u> a yellow <u>color</u> when it is <u>exposed of</u> air.

19. Hunting and fishing techniques were <u>highly</u> developed among the North American Indians, <u>particularly</u> in regions where <u>agriculture</u> was less <u>success</u>.

20. <u>Science</u> requires the <u>careful</u> <u>collect</u> and <u>organization</u> of data.

21. The Natchez Trace was <u>an important</u> <u>commercial</u> and <u>military</u> route between Nashville, Tennessee <u>to</u> Natchez, Mississippi.

22. Some games rely <u>mainly</u> on <u>skill</u> and practice while others <u>primarily</u> involve <u>lucky</u>.

23. In the <u>absent</u> of <u>natural</u> enemies, the gypsy moth has <u>become</u> a <u>serious</u> pest in North America.

24. Huey Long and his <u>brother</u> Earl were the two most <u>powerful</u> <u>politics</u> in the <u>history</u> of Louisiana.

25. To make candles, pioneers <u>twisted</u> string into wicks, dipped the wicks into <u>hot</u> fat, then <u>hung</u> the candles to cool and <u>hard</u>.

LESSON 19: Word Choice

Word choice is specifically tested only in Error Identification items. Word choice errors involve the incorrect use of one word in place of another. The two words may be related forms (*other* and *another*, for example) or they may be completely different (*do* and *make*, for example).

Descriptions of some of the most common word choice errors are given below.

A) WRONG CHOICE OF *MAKE* OR *DO*

The verb *to do* is often used in place of *to make*, and *to make* in place of *to do*. In its basic sense, *to make* means to produce, to create, to construct, while *to do* means to perform, to act, to accomplish. These verbs are also used in a number of set expressions:

Common Expressions with *make*	
make advances (in)	make a law
make an attempt	make a mistake
make a choice	make an offer
make a comparison	make a plan
make a contribution	make a point
make a decision	make a prediction
make a difference	make a profit
make a discovery	make a promise
make a distinction	make a suggestion
make a forecast	make a sound/noise
make an investment	

be made of (= be composed of)
make up (= compose)

To make is also used in this pattern: *make* + someone/something + adjective. (The gift *made* her happy.)

Common Expressions with *do*	
do an assignment	do someone a favor
do one's best	do harm to
do business (with)	do research
do damage (to)	do one's work
do an experiment	do wrong

The auxiliary verb *do* is used rather than repeating main verbs: My computer doesn't operate as fast as theirs *does*.

Any time you see the verb *make* or *do* underlined in an Error Identification item, suspect a word choice error.

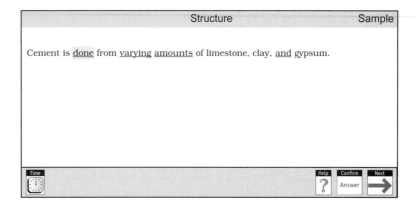

The verb *done* is incorrect in this sentence. The correct word choice is *made*.

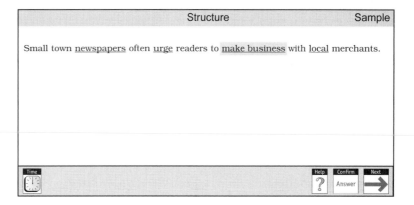

The phrase should read *do business with*.

B) WRONG CHOICE OF *SO, SUCH, TOO,* AND *AS*

The words *so, such,* and *too* are used in the following patterns:

so + adjective + *that* clause
These boxes are *so* heavy that we can't lift them.

So is also used with *many . . . that* and *much . . . that*:
There were *so* many people in the auditorium that we could barely get in the front door.

such + adjective + noun + *that* clause
It was *such* a pretty view that he took a photograph of it.

too + adjective + infinitive
It's *too* cold to go swimming today.

Notice that *so* and *such* are both followed by *that* clauses, but *too* is followed by an infinitive.

The words *as* and *so* are also sometimes confused:

*Jane did *so* well as I did on the economics exam. (INCORRECT)
*The coffee was *as* hot that I couldn't drink it. (INCORRECT)

In the first sentence, the word *as* should be used in place of *so;* in the second, *so* should be used in place of *as.*

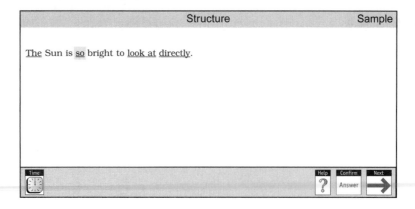

The correct pattern is *too* + adjective + infinitive.

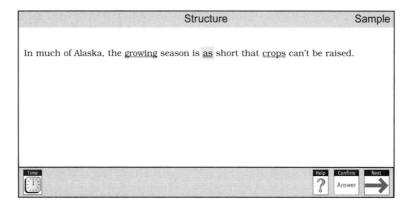

The correct pattern is *so* + adjective + *that* clause.

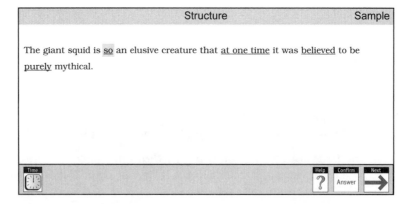

Before an adjective + noun + *that* clause, the word *such* should be used.

C) WRONG CHOICE OF *ANOTHER* OR *OTHER*

Another means "one more, an additional one." It can be used before singular nouns or alone.

> He needs *another* piece of paper.
> I have one class in that building, and *another* in the building across the quadrangle.

Other is used before a plural noun. *Other* is also used before a singular noun when preceded by a determiner such as *the, some, any, one, no,* and so on.

> There are *other* matters I'd like to discuss with you.
> One of the books was a novel; the *other* was a collection of essays.
> There's no *other* place I'd rather visit.

Other is also used in the expression *other than,* meaning *except for.*

> *Other* than Kim, no one signed up for the table tennis tournament.

SAMPLE ITEMS

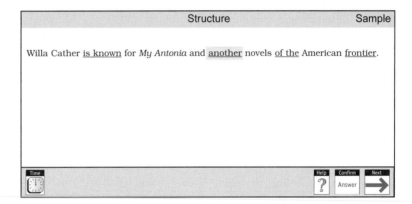

Before a plural noun, *other* must be used.

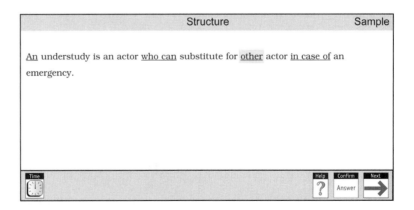

Other is used incorrectly in place of *another.*

D) WRONG CHOICE OF *MUCH* OR *MANY* AND SIMILAR EXPRESSIONS

Certain expressions can be used in phrases with plural nouns; others can be used only in phrases with uncountable nouns.

Used with Plural Nouns	Used with Uncountable Nouns
many	much
few, a few	little, a little
fewer, the fewest	less, the least
number	amount, amounts

SAMPLE ITEMS

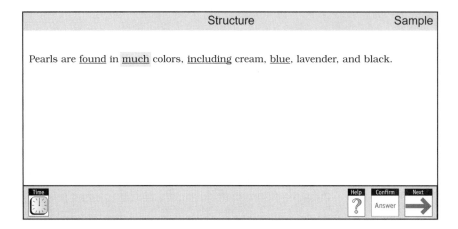

Many must be used with a plural noun (*colors*).

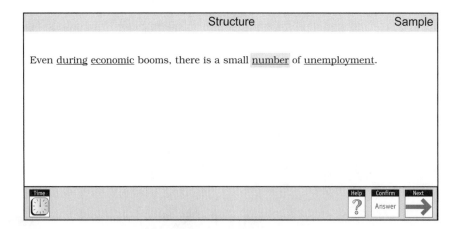

The word *amount* must be used to refer to an uncountable noun such as *unemployment*.

E) OTHER WORD CHOICE PROBLEMS

Other words are sometimes confused in Error Identification items, including the words listed below. Examples are given of the correct uses of these as well as of the types of errors you will most likely see on the test.

most Means "the majority." Also used in superlative adjective phrases.
almost Means "nearly." Incorrectly used in place of *most* or *almost all*.

I've read *most* of the chapters in the book. (CORRECT)
I've read *almost all* of the chapters in the book. (CORRECT)
*I've read *almost* of the chapters in the book. (INCORRECT)
The *most* important chapter is Chapter 4. (CORRECT)
Almost important chapter is Chapter 4. (INCORRECT)

twice Used as an adverb to mean "two times."
double Used as a verb to mean "make twice as large." Incorrectly used in place of *twice*.

Henry has *twice* as much money as he did before he invested it. (CORRECT)
*Henry has *double* as much money as he did before he invested it. (INCORRECT)

earliest Means "most distant in time," "first."
soonest Means "most promptly." Used incorrectly in place of *earliest*.

These are the *earliest* known examples of the artist's works. (CORRECT)
*These are the *soonest* known examples of the artist's works. (INCORRECT)

percent Used after a number. May be incorrectly used in place of *percentage*.
percentage Not used after a number. May be incorrectly used in place of *percent*.

Fifty *percent* of the people voted in favor of the initiative. (CORRECT)
*Fifty *percentage* of the people voted in favor of the initiative. (INCORRECT)
The *percentage* of people who approve of the initiative has been steadily growing. (CORRECT)
*The *percent* of people who approve of the initiative has been steadily growing. (INCORRECT)

somewhat Used as an adverb to mean "slightly."
some A determiner that means "an indefinite number, an indefinite amount. May be used incorrectly in place of *somewhat*.

There was *some* rain yesterday, but none today. (CORRECT)
Today was *somewhat* cooler than yesterday. (CORRECT)
*Today was *some* cooler than yesterday. (INCORRECT)

after Used as a preposition before a noun or as an adverb clause marker before a clause. May be confused with *afterwards*.
afterwards Used as an adverb; means "after that." May be confused with *after*.

We'll go to dinner *after* the play. (CORRECT)
*We'll go to dinner *afterwards* the play. (INCORRECT)
We went to the play and *afterwards* we had dinner. (CORRECT)
*We went to the play and *after* we had dinner. (INCORRECT)

ago Used to talk about a time earlier than the present. May be mistakenly used for *before*.
before Used to talk about a time earlier than some other point in time.

Harold won the golf tournament last year, and he came in second the year *before*. (CORRECT)
*Harold won the golf tournament last year, and he came in second the year *ago*. (INCORRECT)

tell Used with an object; also used in certain set expressions: *tell a story, tell the truth, tell a secret*. May be confused with *say*.
say Used without an object. May be confused with *tell*.

Dr. Hunter *told* us that he'd had a good trip. (CORRECT)
Dr. Hunter *said* that he'd had a good trip. (CORRECT)
*Dr. Hunter *said* us that he'd had a good trip. (INCORRECT)
*Dr. Hunter *told* that he'd had a good trip. (INCORRECT)

José *told* a wonderful story. (CORRECT)
*José *said* a wonderful story. (INCORRECT)

ever Used after a negative word (such as *not* or *hardly*). Also used in some set expressions such as *ever since*. May be incorrectly used for *never*.

never Not used with a negative word. May be incorrectly used for *ever*.

He hardly *ever* goes to that club. (CORRECT)
He *never* goes there anymore. (CORRECT)
*He hardly *never* goes there anymore. (INCORRECT)
Diane has *never* been to a hockey game. (CORRECT)
*Diane has *ever* been to a hockey game. (INCORRECT)

alive Used after a linking verb. May be confused with *live*.

live Used before a noun. May be confused with *alive*.

Akiko likes to have *live* plants in her apartment. (CORRECT)
*Akiko likes to have *alive* plants in her apartment. (INCORRECT)
Even though she forgot to water it for a week, the plant was still *alive*.
(CORRECT)
*Even though she forgot to water it for a week, the plant was still *live*.
(INCORRECT)

around A preposition meaning "in a circular path." May be mistakenly used for *round*.

round An adjective meaning "circular in shape."

The new office building will be a *round* glass tower. (CORRECT)
*The new office building will be an *around* glass tower. (INCORRECT)

age Used as a noun, often in these patterns:
at the age of twenty-one
thirty years of age
May be confused with *old*.

old Used as an adjective, often in this pattern:
thirty years old
May be confused with *age*.

Harriet will be twenty-three years *old* next week. (CORRECT)
*Harriet will be twenty-three years *age* next week. (INCORRECT)
You must be sixteen years *old* to get a driver's license in this state. (CORRECT)
*You must be sixteen years *age* to get a driver's license in this state. (INCORRECT)

near Used as an adjective; means "close to." May be incorrectly used in place of *nearly*.

nearly Used as an adverb; means "almost." May be incorrectly used in place of *near*.

Lynn is looking for an apartment *near* the Medical Center. (CORRECT)
*Lynn is looking for an apartment *nearly* the Medical Center. (INCORRECT)
The two-bedroom apartment she looked at costs *nearly* a thousand dollars a
month. (CORRECT)
*The two-bedroom apartment she looked at costs *near* a thousand dollars a
month. (INCORRECT)

NOTE: The distinctions between words such as *desert* and *dessert*, *stationary* and *stationery*, *capital* and *capitol*, which are really spelling problems, are NOT tested on the TOEFL® test.

EXERCISE 19.1

Focus: Word choice problems involving the distinction between *do* and *make*.

Directions: Underline the word that correctly completes each sentence below.

1. The tips of high-speed dental drills are (done/made) of tungsten steel and often contain diamonds.

2. A cottage industry is a form of manufacturing (done/made) at home.

3. Margaret Meade (did/made) fundamental contributions to both the theory and field work of anthropology.

4. Many universities receive grants to (do/make) research for the federal government.

5. Research in genetics in the early nineteenth century (did/made) much to improve agriculture.

6. Futurologists study current trends to (do/make) predictions about the future.

7. Filmmaker George Lucas has (done/made) many advances in the production of motion pictures, especially in the use of computer-generated special effects.

8. The distinction between wildflowers and weeds is one that is often difficult to (do/make).

9. The helicopter can (do/make) jobs that no other aircraft can.

10. Yeast is added to dough to (do/make) bread light and porous.

EXERCISE 19.2

Focus: Word choice problems involving the distinction between *so, such, too,* and *as.*

Directions: Underline the word or words that correctly complete each sentence below.

1. The mineral talc is (so/such) soft that it can be scratched with a fingernail.

2. Oceanographers use robots and unmanned submarines to explore parts of the ocean that are (so/too) deep for people to explore safely.

3. (So/As) much paper money was printed during the Revolutionary War that it became almost worthless.

4. The walking stick is an insect with (so/such a) close resemblance to a twig that it escapes the notice of its enemies.

5. At present, solar cells are (so/too) expensive and inefficient to be used in the commercial generation of electricity.

6. Acrylic plastics are very hard and are (so/as) clear as glass.

7. Founded in 1682, Norfolk developed (so/such a) prosperous sea trade that it quickly became the largest town in the colony of Virginia.

8. Continental islands are (so/as) close to continents that their plant and animal life are identical to life on the mainland.

9. Timberline is the elevation on a mountainside above which temperatures become (so/too) cold for most trees to grow.

10. A few people have (such/too) good eyesight that they can actually see the brightest stars during full daylight.

EXERCISE 19.3

Focus: Word choice problems involving the distinction between *other* and *another*.
Directions: Underline the word that correctly completes each sentence below.

1. Lightning is a rush of electrical current from a cloud to the ground or from one cloud to (another/other).

2. A ballet dancer's techniques and skills are very different from those of (another/other) dancers.

3. The commercial center of New York City, the island of Manhattan is joined to the (another/other) boroughs by bridges and tunnels.

4. The legal surrender of a criminal suspect from one state or country to (another/other) is called extradition.

5. Life expectancy for both males and females is higher in Hawaii than it is in any (another/other) state.

6. Rocky Mountain Spotted Fever is one type of disease that is carried by ticks, and Colorado tick fever is (another/other).

7. The art of photography has often been influenced by—and has influenced—(another/other) fine arts.

8. (Another/Other) than the cheetah, all cats have retractable claws.

9. Few (another/other) Supreme Court justices have had as much impact on American law as William O. Douglas did during his thirty-six years on the bench.

10. In physics, diffusion is the spread of one substance's molecules or atoms through those of (another/other).

11. A basketball player may advance the ball by dribbling it or passing it to (another/other) player.

12. Engineer Ed Patton was responsible for planning and building the Alaskan pipeline and many (another/other) large scale engineering projects.

EXERCISE 19.4

Focus: Word choice problems involving the distinction between *much* and *many* and similar words.

Directions: Underline the word that correctly completes each sentence below.

1. (Many/Much) industrial products can be made from soybeans.

2. Desert plants compete fiercely for the (few/little) available water.

3. The American designer Louis Comfort Tiffany took (many/much) of his inspiration from nature.

4. A (few/little) simple precautions can prevent accidents at home and on the job.

5. In a formal debate, the same (number/amount) of persons speak for each team, and both teams are granted an equal (number/amount) of time in which to make their arguments.

6. Bats do (few/little) damage to people, livestock, or crops.

7. Even small (numbers/amounts) of zinc can have a significant effect on the growth of plants.

8. The adrenal glands, one on top of each kidney, secrete (many/much) important hormones.

9. (Many/Much) of the stories in Mason Weems' biography of George Washington are difficult to believe.

10. Folk artists have (few/little) or no formal art training.

EXERCISE 19.5

Focus: Word choice problems involving other words that are commonly confused.
Directions: Underline the words that correctly complete each sentence below.

1. In 1941 nylon was first used to make stockings, and the year (ago/before), it was first used to make toothbrush bristles.

2. The Missouri River is about (double/twice) as long as the Colorado River.

3. Catherine Esther Beecher established schools in Connecticut and Ohio, and (after/afterwards) founded the American Women's Educational Association.

4. (Most/Almost) antibiotics are antibacterial agents, but some are effective against fungal, protozoal, or yeast infections.

5. At eight weeks of (age/old), red foxes begin to get their adult markings.

6. Chuck Berry was one of the (soonest/earliest) and most influential performers of rock music.

7. Long before Columbus, various thinkers believed that the Earth was (around/round).

8. Apricots are (some/somewhat) smaller than peaches.

9. Huge radio telescopes aimed into space may someday (say/tell) us whether intelligent life exists elsewhere in the universe.

10. Except for humans and apes, all mammals can produce vitamin C in their livers, so they (ever/never) suffer from a lack of it.

11. One of Canada's most beautiful botanical gardens is Butchardt Gardens (near/nearly) Victoria, British Columbia.

12. When the Hopi Indians perform the Snake Dance, the dancers handle (alive/live) rattlesnakes.

13. Around eighty-five (percentage/percent) of the bauxite produced in the United States is mined in Arkansas.

14. Artist Clementine Hunter continued to paint until she was over one hundred years (age/old).

15. The period immediately (after/afterwards) the Civil War is known as Reconstruction.

16. The (most/almost) familiar type of pump in use today is the piston pump.

17. (Most/Almost) every county in the United States has agricultural extension agents who provide help to farmers.

18. Murals (say/tell) narrative stories through visual images.

19. Forests cover (near/nearly) half the land area of Tennessee.

20. Giraffes hardly (ever/never) sleep more than twenty minutes at a time.

EXERCISE 19.6

Focus: Word choice problems in an Error Identification format involving a variety of word choice problems. (Note: One or two items in this exercise do not focus on word choice errors. These items are marked in the answer key with an asterisk.)

Directions: Decide which of the four underlined words or phrases would not be considered correct, and put an X under that expression.

1. One should never throw water on an alive electrical fire.

2. The University of Chicago is unlike most other U.S. universities in that it has emphasized graduate student programs so much as undergraduate programs ever since it opened.

3. The mass production of paper bags cut costs so much that a bag soon became a routine part of near every purchase.

4. A person must be at least thirty years age in order to serve as a U.S. senator.

5. No other state receives as few rainfall as the state of Nevada.

6. Because of refraction, the water in a tank ever looks as deep as it actually is.

7. The *lei*, which is made of flowers, shells, and other materials, is presented to visitors as a symbolize of Hawaiian hospitality.

8. The botanists Katherine Hunter and Emily Fose spent many difficult months making research in the Rocky Mountains.

9. Oysters are today grown and harvested much like any another crop.

10. Walter Hunt invented an enormous amount of devices, including the safety pin and a machine for making nails.

11. Connecticut, like the other New England states, are dotted with many little lakes.

12. The soonest parachutes were made of canvas, but later, silk and then nylon were used.

LESSON 20: Verbs

Verb use is tested in both types of Structure items. Some points about verbs to keep in mind:

- ■ An infinitive, gerund, or participle cannot be used alone as a sentence verb.

- ■ If the subject of the sentence *performs* the action, the verb must be in the active voice. If the subject of the sentence *receives* the action, the verb must in the passive voice.

    The architect *designed* the building. (active verb)

    The building *was designed* by the architect. (passive verb)

- ■ The verb must agree with its subject. Singular subjects require singular verbs; plural subjects require plural verbs.

- ■ The appropriate tense must be used according to the time words or ideas in the sentence.

- ■ The correct form of the main verb—simple form, *-ing* form, past tense, past participle—must be used as appropriate in the sentence (depending on context and on the auxiliary verbs used).

Sentence Completion

In Sentence Completion items involving verbs, the answer choices are all (or almost all) different forms of the same verb. You'll have to decide which form best fits into the sentences. Distractors are usually incorrect because they break one of the rules given above.

SAMPLE ITEM

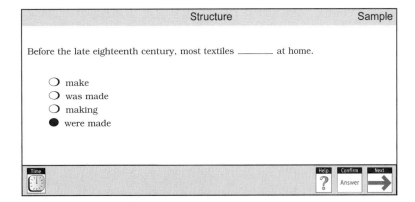

The fourth choice—a past tense passive verb—is the best answer. The first choice is a present tense active verb, and so it is wrong for two reasons: A past form is required because of the time phrase (*Before the late eighteenth century*) and a passive form is needed because the subject (*textiles*) does not perform the action. The second choice is incorrect because the plural subject *textiles* requires a plural verb, *were*. The third is incorrect because, by itself, an *-ing* form cannot be the sentence verb.

Error Identification

Whenever the verb is underlined in an Error Identification problem, you should check for the common verb errors of agreement, tense, and form.

A) ERRORS IN SUBJECT/VERB AGREEMENT

Most problems involving subject-verb agreement are simple, but a few are tricky.

SAMPLE ITEMS

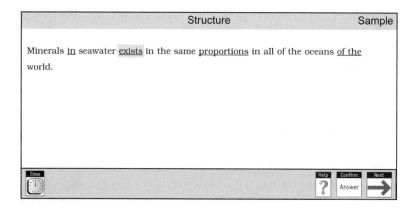

The plural subject *minerals* requires a plural verb, *exist*. You might have found this question tricky because the singular noun *seawater* comes between the subject and the verb, and you may have mistaken that word for the true subject.

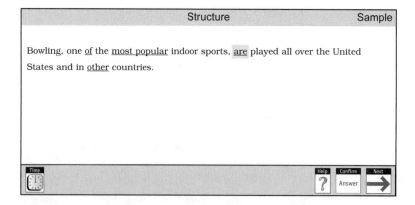

The subject of the sentence is *bowling*, not *sports*. The singular verb form *is* should therefore be used.

There are some specific rules about subject-verb agreement that you should be familiar with:

■   A sentence with two subjects joined by *and* takes a plural verb.

The chemistry lab and the physics lab *are* . . .

- Some words end in -s but are singular in form. Many of these words are the names of fields of study (*economics, physics,* and so on). *News* is another word of this kind.

  > Economics *is* . . .

  > The news *was* . . .

- Irregular plural nouns (*children, people, feet,* and so on) do not end in -s but take plural verbs.

  > The women *were* . . .

  > His feet *are* . . .

- When a clause begins with the expletive *there,* the verb may be singular or plural, depending on the grammatical subject.

  > There *was* a loud noise . . .

  > There *were* a few problems . . .

- Subjects with *each* and *every* take singular verbs. (This includes compound words like *everyone* and *everything.*)

  > Each state *has* . . .

  > Each of the representatives *was* . . .

  > Every person *was* . . .

  > Everyone *wants* . . .

- The verb in many adjective clauses depends on the head noun.

  > The house that *was* built . . .

  > The students who *were* selected . . .

  Other adjective clauses contain noun or pronoun subjects that determine the verb.

  > The houses that he *builds* . . .

  > The student whom the teachers *select* . . .

- The phrase *the number of* + plural noun takes a singular verb. The phrase *a number of* + plural noun takes a plural verb.

  > The number of trees *is* . . .

  > A number of important matters *have* . . .

- Singular subjects used with phrases such as *along with, accompanied by, together with, as well as,* and *in addition to* take singular verbs.

  > The mayor, along with the city council, *is* . . .

  > Together with his friends, Mark *has* . . .

- Quantities of time, money, distance, and so on usually take a singular verb.

  > Five hundred dollars *was* . . .

  > Two years *has* . . .

  > Ten miles *is* . . .

B) ERRORS INVOLVING TENSE

Most tense errors involve the simple present tense, the simple past tense, and the present perfect tense.

- The simple present tense is a general time tense.

  It usually indicates that a condition is always true or that an action always occurs. It may also indicate that an action regularly occurs.

  > The atmosphere *surrounds* the Earth.

  > Karen often *stays* at this hotel.

  > Generally, the lectures in this class *are* very interesting.

- The simple past tense indicates that an action took place at a specific time in the past.

  > They *moved* to Phoenix five years ago.

  > This house *was built* in the 1920s.

  > Dinosaurs *lived* millions of years ago.

- The present perfect tense usually indicates that an action began at some time in the past and continues to the present. It may also indicate that an action took place at an unspecified time in the past.

  > Mr. Graham *has worked* for this company since 1999.

  > She *hasn't been* to a doctor for a year.

  > Jennifer *has* recently *returned* from Europe.

SAMPLE ITEMS

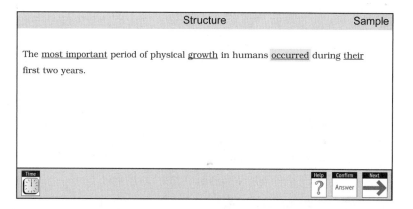

The third underlined expression is the correct answer. The simple present tense, not the past tense, should be used because the situation described in this sentence always occurs.

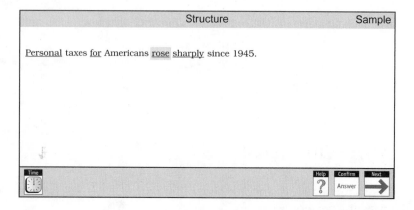

The third choice is again the best one. The time phrase *since 1945* means *from 1945 until now*. Therefore, the present perfect (*have risen*) is required in place of the past tense.

C) INCORRECT VERB FORMS

Some of the verb errors are errors in form. Most verb-form problems involve main verb forms: An *-ing* form may be used in place of a past participle, a past participle in place of a past tense form, a simple form in place of an *-ing* form, an infinitive in place of a simple form, and so on. Some involve irregular verbs that have different forms for the past tense and the past participle (*took* and *taken*, for example). The following information may help you chose the correct form of the main verb.

- The simple form follows all modal auxiliaries.

might be	can remember	should study
must know	could go	may follow

    Certain similar auxiliary verbs require infinitives:

    ought to attend   used to play   have to hurry

- The past participle is used after a form of *have* in all perfect forms of the verb.

has done	had called	should have said
have run	will have read	could have made

- The *-ing* form is used after a form of *be* in all progressive forms of the verb.

is sleeping	has been writing	should have been wearing
was working	had been painting	will be waiting

- The past participle is used after a form of *be* in all passive forms of the verb.

is worn	has been shown	would have been lost
is being considered	had been promised	might have been canceled
were told	will have been missed	

Verb-form problems may also involve auxiliary verbs: *has* may be used in place of *did*, *is* in place of *does*, and so on.

*I enjoyed the play, and so *does* my friend.   (INCORRECT)

I enjoyed the play, and so *did* my friend.   (CORRECT)

*They have a much nicer garden this year than they *have* last year. (INCORRECT)

They have a much nicer garden this year than they *did* last year. (CORRECT)

SAMPLE ITEMS

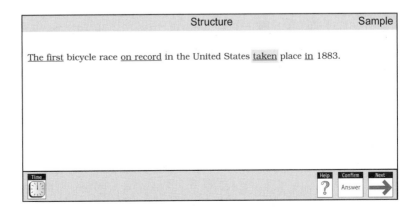

The first bicycle race on record in the United States taken place in 1883.

The correct verb is the past tense form (*took*), not a past participle.

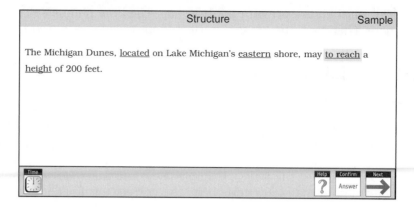

After a modal auxiliary, the simple form of the verb (*reach*) should be used in place of the full infinitive (*to reach*).

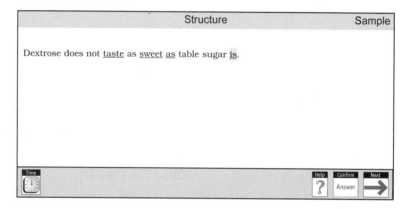

The correct auxiliary verb in this sentence is *does*, not *is*. The auxiliary *does* replaces the present tense verb *tastes*.

EXERCISE 20.1

Focus: Error Identification problems involving subject-verb agreement.

Directions: Underline the form that correctly completes each sentence.

1. Ethics (is/are) the study of moral duties, principles, and values.

2. The first bridge to be built with electric lights (was/were) the Brooklyn Bridge.

3. There (is/are) two types of calculus, differential and integral.

4. George Gershwin, together with his brother Ira, (was/were) the creator of the first musical comedy to win a Pulitzer Prize.

5. Unlike the game of chess, the game of checkers (is/are) not governed by an internationally recognized set of rules.

6. The Earth and Pluto (is/are) the only two planets believed to have a single moon.

7. A number of special conditions (is/are) necessary for the formation of a geyser.

8. Each of the Ice Ages (was/were) more than a million years long.

9. The battery, along with the alternator and starter, (makes/make) up the electrical system of a car.

10. Teeth (is/are) covered with a hard substance called enamel.

11. The more or less rhythmic succession of economic booms and busts (is/are) referred to as the business cycle.

12. The number of protons in the nucleus of an atom (varies/vary) from element to element.

13. All trees, except for the tree fern, (is/are) seed-bearing plants.

14. Fifteen hundred dollars a year (was/were) the per capita income in the United States in 1950.

15. Everyone who (goes/go) into the woods should recognize common poisonous plants such as poison ivy and poison oak.

EXERCISE 20.2

Focus: Written expression problems involving errors in verb tense and form.

Directions: If the underlined form is correct, mark the sentence C. If the underlined form is incorrect, mark the sentence X and write a correction for the underlined form in the blank at the end the sentence.

____ 1. Coal, grain, steel, and other products are often <u>shipping</u> by barge on inland waterways. _____

____ 2. The first cotton mill in Massachusetts <u>has built</u> in the town of Beverly in 1787. _____

____ 3. Physician Alice Hamilton <u>is knowing</u> for her research on industrial diseases. _____

____ 4. When scientists search a site for fossils, they begin by examining places where the soil has <u>wore</u> away from the rock. _____

____ 5. The popularity of recreational vehicles <u>has been grown</u> over the last few decades. _____

____ 6. Experts have estimated that termites cause as much property damage every year as fire <u>has</u>. _____

____ 7. In music, a chord is the sound of two or more notes that <u>are playing</u> together. _____

____ 8. The white pine <u>is</u> the most commercially important forest tree in North America until the beginning of the twentieth century. _____

____ 9. In 1846 the Swiss naturalist Louis Agassiz <u>come</u> to the United States to give a series of lectures. _____

____ 10. Parrots and crows <u>are considered</u> the most intelligent birds. _____

____ 11. The first experimental telegraph line in the United States <u>run</u> from Baltimore to Washington, a distance of forty miles. _____

____ 12. Portable fire extinguishers generally <u>contain</u> liquid carbon dioxide. _____

____ 13. The first seven American astronauts <u>were chose</u> in 1959. _____

____ 14. Since ancient times, farmers <u>used</u> scarecrows to protect their crops from hungry birds. _____

____ 15. In the late nineteenth century, many important theories in both the biological and the physical sciences <u>have been produced</u>. _____

EXERCISE 20.3

Focus: Structure problems involving verbs. (Note: Several items in this exercise do not focus on verbs. These sentences are marked in the answer key with asterisks.)

Directions: For Sentence Completion items, mark the oval next to the answer choice that correctly completes the sentence. For Error Identification items, put an *X* under the underlined portion of the sentence that would not be considered correct.

1. Medical students must <u>to study</u> <u>both</u> the <u>theory</u> and practice of <u>medicine</u>.

2. R. M. Bartlett of Philadelphia _____ the first private business college in the United States in 1843.
   - ○ founding
   - ○ founded
   - ○ was founded
   - ○ has founded

3. The seal, <u>like</u> the sea lion and the walrus, <u>is</u> a <u>descendant</u> of ancestors that once <u>have lived</u> on the land.

4. In 1989 the space probe Voyager 2 _____ by the planet Neptune.
   - ○ fly
   - ○ having flown
   - ○ flying
   - ○ flew

5. <u>The top</u> layer of the ocean <u>stores</u> as much <u>heat</u> as <u>does</u> all the gases in the atmosphere.

6. A cupful of stagnant water may _____ millions of microorganisms.

   ○ contains
   ○ to contain
   ○ contain
   ○ containing

7. Sarah Knight _____ a fascinating account of a journey she made from Boston to New York in 1704.

   ○ written
   ○ writes
   ○ wrote
   ○ writing

8. Every one of the body's <u>billions</u> of cells <u>require</u> a <u>constant</u> <u>supply</u> of food and oxygen.

9. <u>In</u> colonial times, flax and wool <u>required</u> months of preparation before they <u>could</u> be dyed and <u>spin</u> into cloth.

10. Although some people <u>find</u> bats terrifying, they <u>are</u> actually beneficial <u>because</u> they <u>ate</u> harmful insects.

11. All animals _____ on other animals or plants.

    ○ feed
    ○ feeds
    ○ fed
    ○ feeding

12. Chromium _____ in the manufacture of stainless steel.

    ○ using
    ○ is used
    ○ uses
    ○ is using

13. Each <u>of the</u> four types of human <u>tooth</u> <u>is suited</u> to a <u>specific</u> purpose.

14. The Masters, one of the most important of all golf tournaments, _____ every year in Augusta, Georgia since 1934.

    ○ has held
    ○ held
    ○ is held
    ○ has been held

15. Porous rocks such as chalk and sandstone allow water _____ through them.

    ○ soaks
    ○ is soaked
    ○ to soak
    ○ can soak

16. Electric <u>milking</u> machines <u>have made</u> dairy <u>farming</u> a much easier job than it once <u>did</u>.

17. <u>Playwright</u> and novelist Frank Chin has often <u>describes</u> the <u>lives</u> of Chinese Americans in his literary <u>works</u>.

18. Weavers are social birds that _____ complex nests housing hundreds of families.
    - ○ build
    - ○ are built
    - ○ are building
    - ○ built

19. Cans of paint must be <u>shaking</u> before <u>use</u> to <u>mix</u> the pigments with the medium in which they <u>are suspended</u>.

20. The American dancer Maria Tallchief first _____ prominent in Europe.
    - ○ to become
    - ○ become
    - ○ has become
    - ○ became

21. <u>It is estimated</u> that ninety <u>percent</u> of all scientists <u>who have</u> ever lived are <u>lived now</u>.

22. Sheep <u>are</u> often <u>dip</u> in liquid chemicals to <u>eliminate</u> ticks and <u>other</u> external parasites.

23. By 1790 rice _____ an important crop in the South.
    - ○ being
    - ○ has been
    - ○ was
    - ○ had been

24. Computers and new methods of communication _____ revolutionized the modern office.
    - ○ have
    - ○ having
    - ○ that have
    - ○ has

25. The Baltimore and Ohio Railroad _____ the first air conditioning system for trains in 1931.
    - ○ has installed
    - ○ installed
    - ○ was installed
    - ○ installing

LESSON 21: Participles

Participles are verbal adjectives. Two kinds of participles are tested: present participles and past participles. The present participle always ends in *-ing*. The past participle of regular verbs ends in *-ed*, but many verbs have irregular past participles. Participles are tested in both types of Structure problems.

Sentence Completion

Sentence Completion items usually test the use of **participial phrases** (a participle and related words) after nouns. Participial phrases used this way are actually **reduced** (shortened) **adjective clauses.** Present participles are used to reduce adjective clauses that contain active verbs.

> Minnesota, *which joined the Union in 1858*, became the thirty-second state.
> (full adjective clause with active verb)

> Minnesota, *joining the Union in 1858*, became the thirty-second state.
> (participial phrase with a present participle)

Past participles are used to reduce adjective clauses with passive verbs.

> The College of William and Mary, *which was founded in 1693*, is the second oldest college in the United States.   (full adjective clause with a passive verb)

> The College of William and Mary, *founded in 1693*, is the second oldest college in the United States.   (participial phrase with a past participle)

Participial phrases can also come before the subject of a sentence.

> *Joining the Union in 1858*, Minnesota became the thirty-second state.

> *Founded in 1693*, the College of William and Mary is the second oldest college in the United States.

Usually, the participle itself is missing from this type of Structure item, but any part of a participial phrase as well as parts of a main clause may be missing.

SAMPLE ITEM

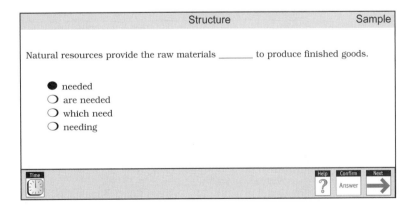

The first option correctly completes the sentence. The second choice is a passive verb; the sentence cannot contain two main verbs (*are needed* and *provide*) in the same clause. The third choice creates an adjective clause, but the verb in the clause is active and a passive verb is needed. (However, a relative clause with a passive verb—*which are needed*—would also be a correct answer.) The fourth choice is a present participle and has an active meaning; a past participle is needed.

Error Identification

Error Identification items most often test participles used before nouns as one-word adjectives. When used before a noun, present participles have an active meaning; past participles have a passive meaning.

>It was an *exhausting* ten-kilometer race.   (present participle)

>The *exhausted* runners were too tired to move after the race.   (past participle)

In the first sentence, the race exhausts the runners. The race "performs" the action. In the second sentence, the runners are exhausted by the race. They receive the action.

Error Identification items may also test the use of participles in phrases after nouns as reduced (shortened) relative clauses. Again, present participles imply an active idea, past participles a passive one.

>The man *stealing* the money was arrested.   (present participle; means "who stole")

>The money *stolen* from the bank was recovered.   (past participle; means "which was stolen")

In Error Identification items, you may see past participles used incorrectly for present participles or present participles used incorrectly for past participles.

You may also see a main verb used when a participle is required.

SAMPLE ITEMS

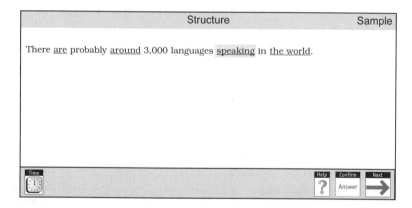

A past participle (*spoken*) is required because the idea is passive. The phrase means, " . . . 3,000 languages *which are spoken*. . . ."

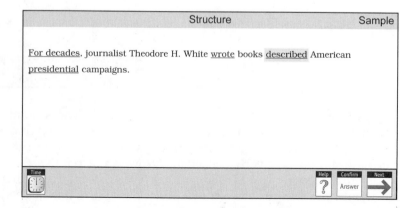

The present participle *describing* should be used. (A relative clause—*which described*—could also be used.) Because the verb in the relative clause is active, the present participle is required.

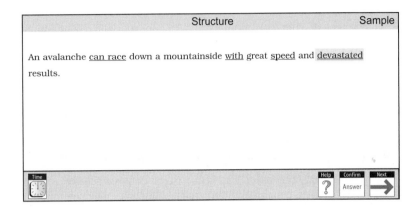

A present participle (*devastating*) is required here because the avalanche "performs" the action; it causes devastation. (The past participle implies that the avalanche itself is devastated rather than devastating other things.)

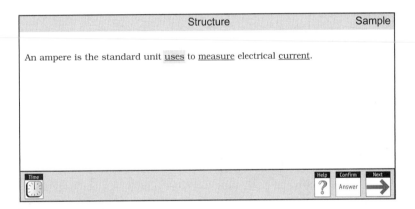

Rather than the main verb *uses*, a past participle (*used*) is required. (This sentence could also be corrected with a relative clause: *which is used*.)

EXERCISE 21.1

Focus: Identifying errors and correct forms of participles.

Directions: Underline the form that best completes each sentence.

1. The largest (knowing/known) insects are found in tropical rain forests.

2. A hummingbird's heart beats at the (astonished/astonishing) rate of 615 beats per minute.

3. A bill of lading is a (writing/written) receipt for goods that are sent by public transportation.

4. At the peak of his jump, a pole vaulter performs a series of (twisting/twisted) body motions to clear the bar.

5. Anyone (working/worked) under conditions that cause a heavy loss of perspiration can suffer heat exhaustion.

6. A mosquito (filled/is filled) with blood is carrying twice its own body weight.

7. The state of Wisconsin has seventy-two counties, many (naming/named) after Indian tribes.

8. Sun spots occur in cycles, with the greatest number generally (appearing/are appearing) every eleven years.

9. A delta is a more or less triangular area of sediments (depositing/deposited) at the mouth of a river.

10. William H. Kilpatrick was a philosopher and scholar now generally (regarding/regarded) as the father of progressive education.

EXERCISE 21.2

Focus: Structure problems involving participles. (Note: Several items in this exercise do NOT focus on participles or participial phrases; these structures are marked in the answer key with asterisks.)

Directions: For Sentence Completion items, mark the oval next to the answer choice that correctly completes the sentence. For Error Identification items, put an *X* under the underlined portion of the sentence that would not be considered correct.

1. Aerodynamics is the study of the forces _____ on an object as it moves through the atmosphere.
   - ○ acting
   - ○ act
   - ○ are acting
   - ○ acted

2. Most candles are <u>made of</u> paraffin wax <u>mixing</u> with compounds that have higher <u>melting</u> points <u>to keep</u> them from melting in hot weather.

3. _____ for their strong fiber include flax and hemp.
   - ○ Plants are grown
   - ○ Plants grown
   - ○ Plants that grow
   - ○ To grow plants

4. _____, methane can be used as a fuel.
   - ○ It's produced by the fermentation of organic matter
   - ○ Produced by the fermentation of organic matter
   - ○ The production by fermentation of organic matter
   - ○ The fermentation of organic matter is produced

5. Ralph Blakelock <u>specialized</u> in <u>painting</u> wild, lonely nighttime <u>landscapes</u>, usually with black trees <u>were silhouetted</u> against the Moon.

6. Elfreth's Alley in Philadelphia is the oldest residential street in the United States, with _____ from 1725.

   ○ houses are dated
   ○ the dates of the houses
   ○ the dating of houses
   ○ houses dating

7. The Farallon Islands are <u>a group of</u> <u>uninhabited</u> islands <u>lying</u> about <u>40 mile</u> west of San Francisco.

8. In 1821 the city of Indianapolis, Indiana was laid out in a design _____ after that of Washington, D.C.

   ○ patterned
   ○ was patterned
   ○ a pattern
   ○ that patterned

9. The <u>crushing</u> leaves of yarrow plants <u>can serve</u> as a <u>traditional</u> medicine for <u>cleansing</u> wounds.

10. _____ in front of a camera lens changes the color of the light that reaches the film.

   ○ Placed a filter
   ○ A filter is placed
   ○ A filter placed
   ○ When a filter placed

11. The Massachusetts State House, _____ in 1798, was the most distinguished building in the United States at that time.

   ○ completing
   ○ which was completed
   ○ was completed
   ○ to be completed

12. Checkerboard Mesa in Utah <u>features</u> a <u>strangely</u> <u>cracking</u> expanse of <u>stone</u>.

13. Barbara McClintock _____ for her discovery of the mobility of genetic elements.

   ○ known
   ○ who is known
   ○ knowing
   ○ is known

14. Throughout <u>the</u> long career, Pete Seeger <u>has been</u> a <u>leading</u> figure in <u>reviving</u> folk music.

15. The solitary scientist _____ by himself or herself has in many instances been replaced by a cooperative scientific team.
    ○ to make important discoveries
    ○ important discoveries were made
    ○ has made important discoveries
    ○ making important discoveries

16. Geometry is the branch of mathematics _____ the properties of lines, curves, shapes, and surfaces.
    ○ that concerned with
    ○ it is concerned with
    ○ concerned with
    ○ its concerns are

17. _____ an average of 460 inches of rain a year, Mount Waialeale in Hawaii is the wettest spot in the world.
    ○ It receives
    ○ Receiving
    ○ To receive
    ○ Received

18. It <u>has been known</u> <u>since</u> at least the third century <u>that</u> coffee has a <u>stimulated</u> effect.

19. A <u>wooden</u> barrel is made from <u>strips</u> of wood called staves <u>holding</u> together with <u>metal</u> hoops.

20. Usually political cartoons _____ on the editorial page of a newspaper.
    ○ appearing
    ○ whose appearance
    ○ that appear
    ○ appear

LESSON 22: Gerunds, Infinitives, and Simple Forms

The use of verbal forms—gerunds, infinitives, and (for the purposes of this lesson) simple forms—are tested in both types of Structure problems.

Gerunds are verbal nouns: *being, going, giving, building.* Like present participles, gerunds end in *-ing.* Gerunds are often followed by objects: *giving directions, building a house.* Together, a gerund and its object form a **gerund phrase.**

Gerunds are used as any other noun is used. You will see gerunds as subjects, as the objects of certain verbs (see the list on page 222), and as the objects of prepositions.

> *Dancing* is good exercise. (gerund as subject)

> He enjoys *going* to good restaurants. (gerund as object of a verb)

> You can solve this problem by *using* a calculator. (gerund as object of a preposition)

Gerunds are also used after verb + preposition combinations.

> Michael's father didn't approve of his *changing* his major from accounting to acting. (gerund after verb + preposition)

This is true even after phrases that contain the word *to.*

> Ruth is looking forward to *taking* a long vacation.

Infinitives consist of the word *to* and the simple form of the verb: *to be, to go, to give, to build.* Infinitives are often followed by an object: *to give directions, to build a house.* Together, an infinitive and its object form an **infinitive phrase.** Like gerunds, infinitives can be the subjects of verbs and the objects of certain verbs (see the list on page 222). Unlike gerunds, infinitives can NEVER be the objects of prepositions.

> *To help* others is rewarding. (infinitive as subject)

> He attempted *to swim* across the river. (infinitive as object of a verb)

Infinitives are used in several other ways:

■ *To* show purpose (to explain *why* an action takes place)

> He took lessons *to learn how to dance.* (Why did he take lessons? To learn how to dance.)

These infinitive phrases often come at the beginning of a sentence, and are set off by commas.

> *To learn how to dance,* he took lessons.

The phrase *in order* + infinitive also shows purpose.

> *In order to learn how to dance,* he took lessons.

■ After certain adjectives

> It's important *to change* the oil in your car frequently.

■ After nouns

> The first person *to walk* on the moon was Neil Armstrong.

You will often see this after noun phrases containing the word *first, last, only,* and other ranking words.

You may also see items that focus on **passive infinitives.** A passive infinitive consists of the words *to* + *be* + past participle.

> Nancy Hong was the only person *to be asked* to speak at the ceremony.

Simple forms are the base forms of verbs; they consist of the infinitive without the word *to*: *be, go, give, build.*

Simple forms are used after the causative verbs *have*, *make*, and *let* and after the phrase *would rather*.

Mark had the carpenter *repair* the door.

His father makes him *study* hard.

Penny let her son *go* on the trip.

She'd rather *go* jogging than *use* the exercise machines.

Common Verbs that Take Verbal Objects		
Verbs Used with Gerunds	**Verbs Used with Infinitives**	**Verbs Used with Simple Forms**
admit	agree	have
anticipate	aim	let
avoid	allow	make
consider	appear	would rather
deny	arrange	
delay	ask	
discuss	attempt	
dislike	cause	
enjoy	choose	
finish	claim	
justify	convince	
postpone	decide	
practice	deserve	
resist	enable	
resume	expect	
risk	hope	
quit	instruct	
recommend	know (how)	
suggest	learn (how)	
understand	need	
	permit	
	persuade	
	prepare	
	promise	
	require	
	seem	
	teach (how)	
	tell	
	tend	
	use	
	vote	
	warn	

Sentence Completion

Most often, the gerund or infinitive itself is missing from the sentence. In some cases a complete gerund or infinitive phrase or some other portion of the sentence phrase may be needed to correctly complete the sentence.

SAMPLE ITEMS

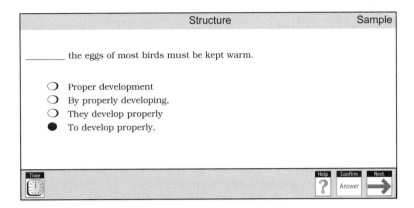

The only one of the four phrases listed here that can show purpose is the last choice, an infinitive. This expression means, *In order to develop properly.*

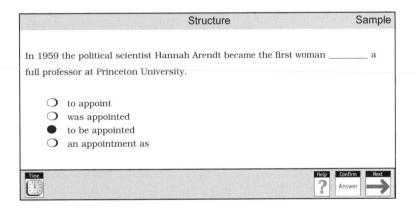

After a noun phrase such as *the first woman,* an infinitive is used as an adjective phrase. Because a passive form is needed (Hannah Arendt receives the action; she doesn't perform the action), the first choice is not the correct infinitive form. The third choice, a passive infinitive, is best.

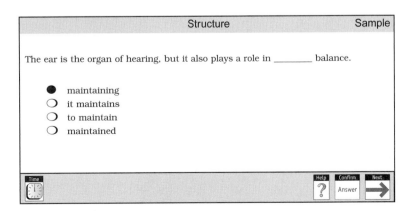

A gerund is correctly used after a preposition. The second, third, and fourth choices are not appropriate after a preposition.

Error Identification

Watch for the these two errors involving gerunds, infinitives, and simple forms:

A) INCORRECT CHOICE OF VERBAL FORMS

Any of these three forms—gerund, infinitive, or simple form—may be incorrectly used when another one of them is required.

SAMPLE ITEMS

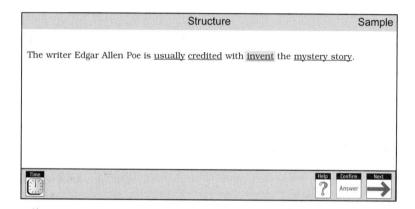

After a preposition (*with*), a simple form cannot be used. The correct form is a gerund (*inventing*).

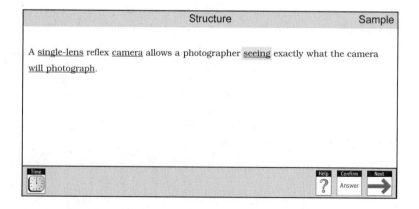

After the verb *allow*, a gerund (*seeing*) cannot be used. An infinitive (*to see*) is correct.

B) INCORRECT FORMS OF INFINITIVES

Incorrect infinitive forms such as *for go* or *to going* may be used in place of the correct form, *to go.*

SAMPLE ITEM

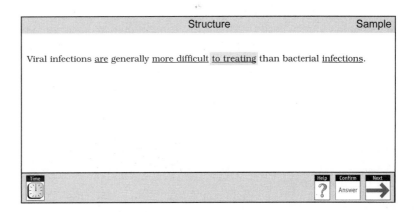

The correct form of the infinitive is *to treat.*

EXERCISE 22.1

Focus: Identifying errors and correct forms of gerunds, infinitives, and simple forms.

Directions: Underline the form that best completes each sentence.

1. Sports parachutes are relatively easy (controlling/to control).

2. Sleeve bearings let pistons (to move/move) back and forth.

3. One of the most important steps in (producing/to produce) a motion picture is film editing.

4. An opera singer is required (having/to have) a powerful and beautiful voice.

5. The Wampanoag Indians taught the Pilgrims how (growing/to grow) corn.

6. Frogs and certain kinds of birds use their tongues (to catch/catch) insects.

7. Modems permit computers (communicating/to communicate) with one another over telephone lines.

8. Smells can be more effective than any other sensory stimuli in vividly (bringing/bring) back memories.

9. Isadora Martinez invented a knee transplant that allows people with severe arthritis (to bend/bend) their knees easily.

10. A sudden sound can make a golfer (to miss/miss) a shot.

11. Heavy spring snows may cause the branches of trees (snap/to snap).

12. Modern race cars store fuel in rubber bladders that are almost impossible (rupturing/to rupture).

13. New words are constantly being invented (describe/to describe) new objects and concepts.

14. Dr. Mary Walker, a surgeon in the Union Army during the Civil War, was the first, and so far only, woman (to be awarded/awarding) the Congressional Medal of Honor.

15. In 1957 Ralph Abernathy founded an organization devoted to (achieve/achieving) racial equality for black Americans.

EXERCISE 22.2

Focus: Structure problems involving gerunds, infinitives, and simple forms. (Note: Several items do NOT focus on of these structures. These are marked with an asterisk in the answer key.)

Directions: For Sentence Completion items, mark the oval next to the answer choice that correctly completes the sentence. For Error Identification items, put an X under the underlined portion of the sentence that would not be considered correct.

1. The most widely used material for package consumer goods is cardboard.

2. _____ for a career in dance generally begins at an early age.
   - ○ People train
   - ○ That people train
   - ○ If training
   - ○ Training

3. A baby's first teeth _____ are generally the lower incisors.
   - ○ appearance
   - ○ appear
   - ○ to appear
   - ○ in appearing

4. One of the latest methods of quarrying stone is to cutting the stone with a jet torch.

5. In 1944 biologist Charles Michener devised a system for to classify the approximately 20,000 species of bees.

6. A climbing helmet _____ a rock climber's head from falling rocks and other hazards.
   - ○ to protect
   - ○ protects
   - ○ protecting
   - ○ that protect

7. Power tools require careful handling _____ injuries.

    ○ by avoiding

    ○ they avoid

    ○ to avoid

    ○ that avoid

8. Geothermal <u>energy</u> is energy <u>obtaining</u> by <u>using</u> heat from <u>the Earth's</u> interior.

9. An electromagnet is created _____ electrical current through a coil of wire.

    ○ by passing

    ○ passes by

    ○ to be passed

    ○ passed

10. _____ at home requires only three types of chemicals, several pieces of simple equipment, and running water.

    ○ For the development of film

    ○ To develop film

    ○ When film is developed

    ○ In developing film

11. Brown lung is a <u>respiratory</u> disease <u>caused</u> by <u>inhaling</u> dust from cotton or some <u>another</u> fiber.

12. The purpose of cost accounting is _____ involved in producing and selling a good or service.

    ○ as a determination of its costs

    ○ the costs determined

    ○ that determines the costs

    ○ to determine the costs

13. _____ was one of the most difficult tasks pioneers faced on their journeys west.

    ○ Crossing rivers

    ○ While crossing rivers

    ○ Rivers being crossed

    ○ By crossing rivers

14. It is <u>the facets</u> <u>cut</u> into a diamond <u>that</u> make it <u>to sparkle</u>.

15. <u>Bathe</u> in mineral water has <u>long been</u> believed <u>to have</u> beneficial <u>effects</u>.

16. Energy can be defined as the ability _____.

    ○ do working

    ○ to do work

    ○ doing work

    ○ work to be done

17. The process of _____ by hand has changed little since the fifteenth century.

    ○ to bind books

    ○ binding books

    ○ books are bound

    ○ bound books

18. Robert A. Moog <u>developed</u> an electronic device that could <u>be</u> used <u>for play</u> <u>synthesized</u> music.

19. _____ often obtain funds from the sale of stocks.

    ○ For corporations to operate

    ○ The operation of corporations

    ○ Corporations operate by

    ○ To operate, corporations

20. A crescent wrench has adjustable jaws for _____ a nut, bolt, or pipe.

    ○ to grip

    ○ they grip

    ○ gripping

    ○ gripped

21. Hypnosis <u>is sometimes</u> employed <u>as a</u> means of <u>helping</u> people to quit <u>to smoke</u>.

22. Compressed air is _____ air brakes, pneumatic tools, and other machinery.

    ○ used to powering

    ○ to use powering

    ○ used to power

    ○ in use by powering

23. Some people believe that the crystals of certain minerals _____ curative powers.

    ○ have

    ○ having

    ○ that have

    ○ to have

24. Fishing cats, <u>found</u> in Southeast Asia, are <u>distinguished</u> by their <u>webbed</u> feet, which enable them <u>catching</u> fish.

25. The first library _____ in the Nebraska Territory was in Fort Atkinson in 1870.

    ○ to be established

    ○ was established

    ○ could establish

    ○ to establish

Directions: For Sentence Completion items, mark the oval next to the answer choice that correctly completes the sentence. For Error Identification items, put an *X* under the underlined portion of the sentence that would not be considered correct.

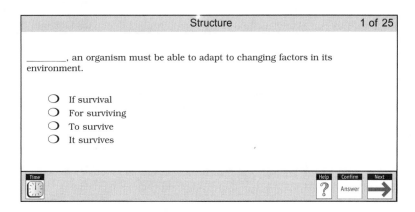

Structure   1 of 25

_____, an organism must be able to adapt to changing factors in its environment.

- ○ If survival
- ○ For surviving
- ○ To survive
- ○ It survives

Time   Help Confirm Next
              ?   Answer   →

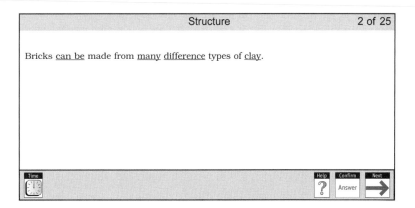

Structure   2 of 25

Bricks <u>can be</u> made from <u>many</u> <u>difference</u> types of <u>clay</u>.

Time   Help Confirm Next
              ?   Answer   →

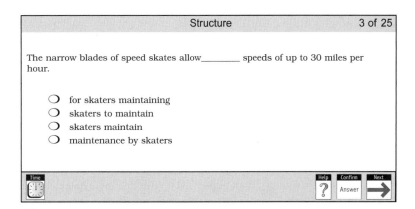

Structure   3 of 25

The narrow blades of speed skates allow_____ speeds of up to 30 miles per hour.

- ○ for skaters maintaining
- ○ skaters to maintain
- ○ skaters maintain
- ○ maintenance by skaters

Time   Help Confirm Next
              ?   Answer   →

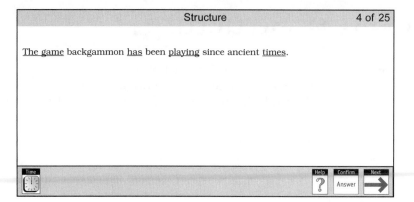

The game backgammon has been playing since ancient times.

Time | Help ? | Confirm Answer | Next →

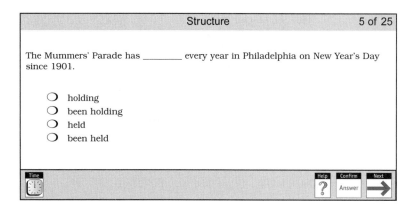

The Mummers' Parade has _____ every year in Philadelphia on New Year's Day since 1901.

- ○ holding
- ○ been holding
- ○ held
- ○ been held

Time | Help ? | Confirm Answer | Next →

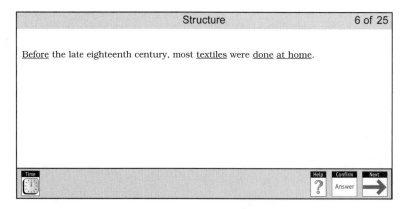

Before the late eighteenth century, most textiles were done at home.

Time | Help ? | Confirm Answer | Next →

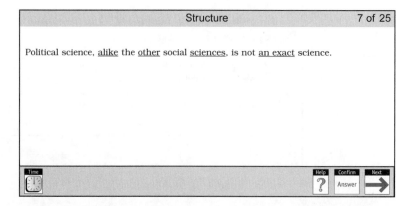

Political science, alike the other social sciences, is not an exact science.

Time | Help ? | Confirm Answer | Next →

_____ on barren slopes can help prevent erosion.

- ○ Planting trees
- ○ For trees to be planted
- ○ In order to plant trees
- ○ Trees are planted

Animals that hibernate usually eat large numbers of food in the autumn.

Lightly, sandy soil absorbs water more quickly than clay or loam.

In 1870 Hiram R. Revels _____ the first black to be elected to the U.S. Senate.

- ○ becoming
- ○ became
- ○ to have become
- ○ has become

<u>During</u> the Depression of the 1930s, <u>many</u> artists <u>were giving jobs</u> by the Federal Arts Project.

Time | Help ? | Confirm Answer | Next →

Sand dunes are made of loose sand _____ up by the action of the wind.

○ it builds
○ builds
○ is building
○ built

Time | Help ? | Confirm Answer | Next →

A <u>feeding</u> animal will usually permit competitors <u>approaching</u> only within a certain area, the boundaries <u>of which</u> are called <u>its</u> feeding territory.

Time | Help ? | Confirm Answer | Next →

It is a <u>chemical</u> called capsaicin <u>that gives</u> hot peppers <u>their</u> <u>spice</u> flavor.

Time | Help ? | Confirm Answer | Next →

Amber is a hard, yellowish-brown _____ from the resin of pine trees that lived millions of years ago.

- ○ substance formed
- ○ to form a substance
- ○ substance has formed
- ○ forming a substance

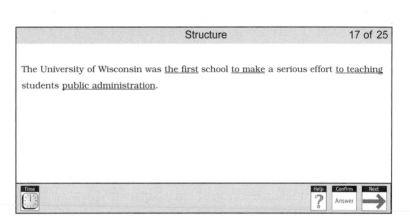

The University of Wisconsin was <u>the first</u> school <u>to make</u> a serious effort <u>to teaching</u> students <u>public administration</u>.

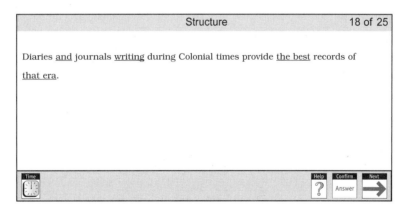

Diaries <u>and</u> journals <u>writing</u> during Colonial times provide <u>the best</u> records of <u>that era</u>.

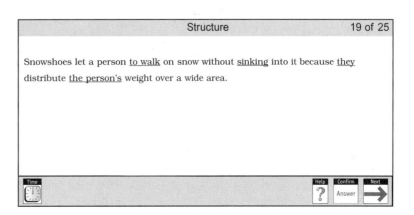

Snowshoes let a person <u>to walk</u> on snow without <u>sinking</u> into it because <u>they</u> distribute <u>the person's</u> weight over a wide area.

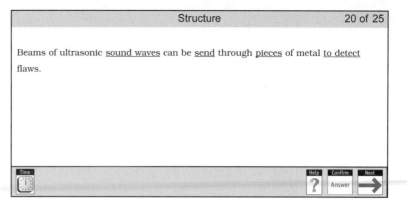

Beams of ultrasonic sound waves can be send through pieces of metal to detect flaws.

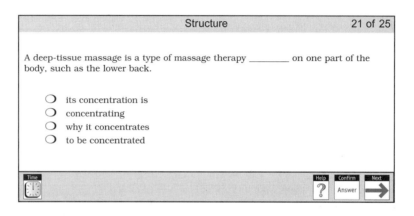

A deep-tissue massage is a type of massage therapy _____ on one part of the body, such as the lower back.

○ its concentration is
○ concentrating
○ why it concentrates
○ to be concentrated

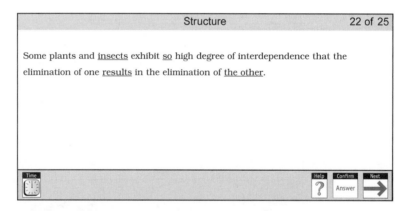

Some plants and insects exhibit so high degree of interdependence that the elimination of one results in the elimination of the other.

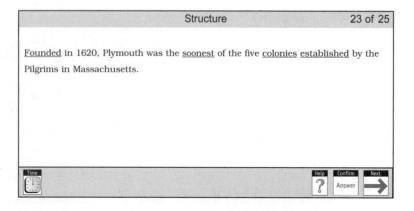

Founded in 1620, Plymouth was the soonest of the five colonies established by the Pilgrims in Massachusetts.

Trucks <u>can be</u> used <u>to transport</u> <u>a wide</u> <u>various</u> of cargoes.

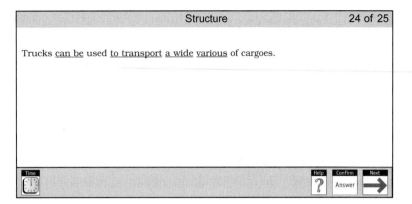

<u>The astronomer</u> George Hale was <u>a pioneer</u> in <u>the art</u> of <u>photograph</u> the sun.

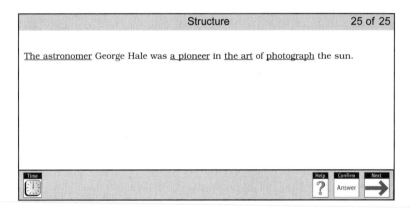

LESSON 23: Pronouns

Pronouns are specifically tested only in Error Identification items. These items feature several types of pronouns:

■ **Personal pronouns**

   (*he, she, it, they,* and so on)

■ **Reflexive pronouns**

   (*himself, herself, itself, themselves,* and so on)

■ **Demonstrative pronouns**

   (*this, that, these, those*)

For the purposes of this lesson, possessive adjectives (*his* house, *their* bicycles) are considered personal pronouns and demonstrative adjectives (*that* book, *those* horses) are considered demonstrative pronouns.

Errors with **relative pronouns** (*that, which, who,* etc.) are introduced in the lesson about adjective clauses (Lesson 14).

The greatest number of errors involve personal pronouns.

A) ERRORS IN PRONOUN/NOUN AGREEMENT

A pronoun must agree with the noun to which it refers (the pronoun's **referent**).

Most agreement errors with personal pronouns, reflexive pronouns, and demonstrative pronouns consist of a singular pronoun referring to a plural referent or a plural pronoun referring to a singular referent.

SAMPLE ITEMS

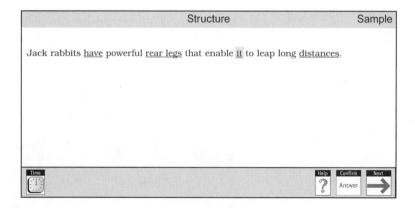

The pronoun referring to the plural noun *Jack rabbits* must be plural.

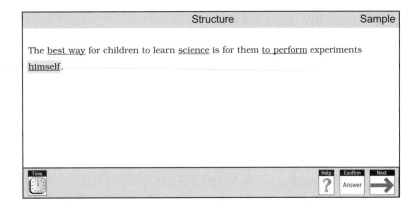

The referent is plural (*children*), so the reflexive pronoun must also be plural (*themselves*) to agree with it.

B) ERRORS IN PRONOUN FORM

These errors almost always involve personal pronouns. A subject form like *he* might be used in place of an object form like *him*, or a possessive pronoun like *hers* might be used in place of a possessive adjective like *her*. This type of pronoun error is usually easy to spot.

Another error involves the use of *this* or *these* in place of *that* and *those*. (*This* and *these* are used to refer to things that are close in time or space; *that* and *those* are used to refer to things that are distant in time or space.)

SAMPLE ITEMS

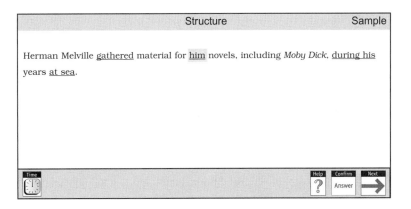

The possessive form *his*, not the object form *him*, is required.

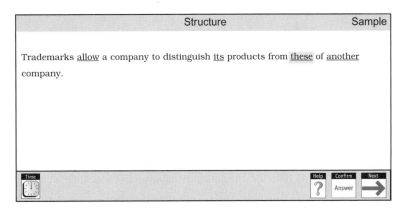

The demonstrative *these* cannot be used to refer to the products of another company. The demonstrative *those* should be used instead.

C) INCORRECT TYPE OF PRONOUN

In some sentences, the wrong type of pronoun is used. For example, a reflexive pronoun might be used when a personal pronoun is needed.

SAMPLE ITEM

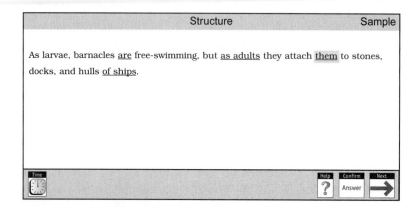

The reflexive pronoun is required because the subject and object are the same entity: *they attach themselves.*

D) INCORRECT INCLUSION OF PRONOUNS

Some errors involve the unnecessary use of pronouns. Often, this type of error occurs when a personal pronoun is used as a subject in a sentence that already has a noun subject.

SAMPLE ITEM

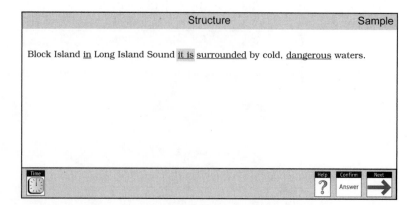

The subject of the sentence is *Block Island;* the personal pronoun *it* is an unnecessary repetition of the subject.

EXERCISE 23.1

Focus: Error Identification problems involving pronoun agreement.

Directions: If the underlined form is correct, mark the sentence *C*. If the underlined form is incorrect, mark the sentence *X* and write a correction for the underlined form in the blank below the sentence.

_____ 1. Unlike other marsupial animals, the opossum does not transport <u>their</u> babies in a pouch.

_____

_____ 2. A talus is an accumulation of rock fragments found at the base of a cliff or on a slope beneath <u>them.</u>

_____

_____ 3. Investment banking is concerned with the sale of government bonds and <u>he</u> also deals with corporate stocks and bonds.

_____

_____ 4. Compared to the fossil record of animals, <u>that</u> of plants is relatively skimpy.

_____

_____ 5. The emerald gets <u>their</u> beautiful green color from titanium and chromium impurities in the stone.

_____

_____ 6. The viola is larger and heavier than the violin, and <u>she</u> has a darker, somewhat nasal tone.

_____

_____ 7. Storms on the planet Jupiter may be larger than the planet Earth <u>itself</u>.

_____

_____ 8. The molecules of a liquid are held together tighter than <u>that</u> of a gas.

_____

_____ 9. Ducks make nests out of leaves and <u>its</u> own feathers.

_____

_____ 10. The clipper ship *Flying Cloud* was one of the fastest ships of <u>their</u> kind.

_____

_____ 11. When babies reach the age of one, <u>her</u> growth begins to slow down.

_____

_____ 12. The arrangement of keys on the keyboard of a personal computer is almost the same as <u>those</u> on a standard typewriter.

_____

EXERCISE 23.2

Focus: Written Expression problems involving incorrect types and forms of pronouns.

Directions: If the underlined form is correct, mark the sentence *C*. If the underlined form is incorrect, mark the sentence *X* and write a correction for the underlined form in the blank below the sentence.

_____ 1. Artist Margaret Leng Tan combines dance and piano playing in <u>hers</u> performances.

    _____

_____ 2. Years of breeding domestic rabbits has given <u>their</u> softer, finer fur than wild rabbits.

    _____

_____ 3. New England poet Edwin A. Robinson moved to New York City in 1896 and devoted <u>himself</u> to his writing.

    _____

_____ 4. There are between 100 and 400 billion stars in <u>ours</u> galaxy, the Milky Way.

    _____

_____ 5. The atoms of a crystal always arrange <u>them</u> into a specific array called a lattice.

    _____

_____ 6. Fred Astaire and Gene Kelly were basically tap dancers, but <u>they</u> both added some ballet movements to their dance steps.

    _____

_____ 7. Attorney Clarence Darrow was known for <u>him</u> defense of unpopular persons and causes.

    _____

_____ 8. Savannah, Georgia has preserved to a remarkable degree <u>it</u> historic houses and famous gardens.

    _____

_____ 9. Ice fishermen sometimes build small, moveable huts to protect <u>them</u> from the cold winds.

    _____

_____ 10. People with myopia, or nearsightedness, have trouble focusing on distant objects, but <u>their</u> can see nearby objects clearly.

    _____

EXERCISE 23.3

Focus: Identifying errors involving pronoun problems. (Note: One or two items in this exercise do NOT focus on pronoun errors. These are marked in the answer key with an asterisk.)

Directions: Decide which of the four underlined words or phrases would not be considered correct and put an X under that expression.

1. <u>A beaver</u> uses its strong front <u>teeth</u> to cut down trees and <u>peel off</u> <u>its</u> bark.

2. "Sprung" wood floors, used in <u>top quality</u> basketball courts <u>and</u> dance studios, <u>they are</u> the safest surfaces for indoor <u>exercise</u>.

3. Ants cannot see red light, so <u>it is</u> possible to observe <u>themselves</u> in an artificial nest <u>without</u> disturbing <u>their</u> activities.

4. The glaciers in Olympia National Park are <u>unusual</u> because <u>they</u> are found at altitudes lower than <u>these</u> at <u>which</u> glaciers are usually found.

5. In <u>his</u> novels, Sinclair Lewis <u>drew</u> critical portraits of Americans <u>who</u> thought of <u>them</u> as model citizens.

6. Elizabeth Peabody, <u>founder</u> of the first American kindergarten, <u>she helped</u> gain <u>acceptance</u> of that institution <u>as a</u> regular part of public education.

7. <u>Almost</u> bacteria <u>have</u> strong cell walls <u>much</u> like <u>those</u> of plants.

8. Bees <u>collect</u> pollen, <u>which</u> <u>furnishes</u> protein for <u>its</u> diet.

9. A small business often limits <u>their</u> operations <u>to</u> a single <u>neighborhood</u> or a group of neighboring <u>communities</u>.

10. A caricature is a picture <u>in which</u> the subject's <u>distinctive</u> features <u>they are</u> deliberately <u>exaggerated</u>.

11. The <u>principles</u> used in air conditioning are <u>basically</u> the same as <u>those</u> used by the human body to cool <u>himself</u>.

12. In <u>that</u> age of computers, <u>it is</u> difficult to imagine how tedious <u>the work of</u> bookkeepers and clerks must <u>have been</u> in the past.

13. <u>If</u> the vegetation on a tundra <u>is walked</u> on, <u>it</u> may take years <u>recover</u>.

14. The naturalist Edwin Way Teal <u>illustrated</u> <u>his</u> books with <u>photographers</u> <u>he</u> had taken <u>himself</u>.

15. <u>The first</u> great <u>public library</u> in the United States <u>it was</u> founded in Boston <u>in the</u> 1830s.

LESSON 24: Singular and Plural Nouns

Singular and plural nouns are tested only in Error Identification items.

A) PLURAL NOUNS IN PLACE OF SINGULAR NOUNS AND SINGULAR NOUNS IN PLACE OF PLURAL NOUNS

Underlined nouns in the Error Identification section may be incorrect because they are plural but should be singular, or because they are singular but should be plural.

Sometimes it is clear that a singular subject is incorrectly used because the verb is plural, or that a plural noun is used incorrectly because the verb is singular. In this type of item, the verb will NOT be underlined because this is not a verb error.

Sometimes it is obvious that a plural or a singular noun is needed because of the determiners that precede the noun. Certain determiners are used only before singular nouns while other determiners are used only before plural nouns.

Determiners Used with Singular Nouns	Determiners Used with Plural Nouns
a/an	two, three, four, etc.
one	dozens of, hundreds of, thousands of, etc.
a single	a few (of)
each	many (of)
every	a number of
this	the number
that	a couple (of)
	several (of)
	every one of
	each one of
	each of
	one of
	these

Each *contestant* won a prize.
Each of the *contestants* won a prize.
This *flower* is a yellow rose.
These *flowers* are yellow roses.
I attended only one *game* this season.
It was one of the most exciting *games* that I've ever attended.

SAMPLE ITEMS

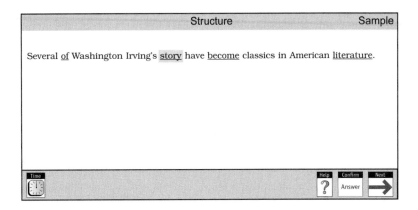

Structure	Sample

Several <u>of</u> Washington Irving's story have <u>become</u> classics in American <u>literature</u>.

Time ⏰   Help **?**   Confirm Answer   Next ➡️

In this item, both the determiner before the noun (*Several of*) and the plural verb (*have*) indicate that a plural noun (*stories*) should be used.

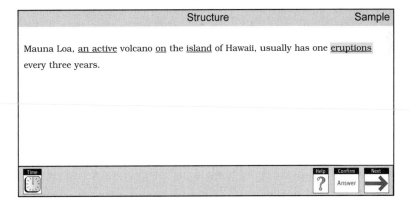

Structure	Sample

Mauna Loa, <u>an active</u> volcano <u>on</u> the <u>island</u> of Hawaii, usually has one eruptions every three years.

Time ⏰   Help **?**   Confirm Answer   Next ➡️

A singular noun must be used after the determiner *one*.

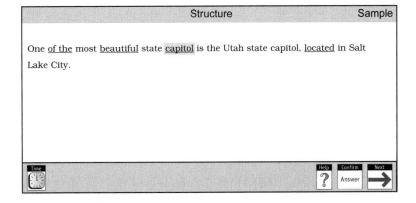

Structure	Sample

One <u>of the</u> most <u>beautiful</u> state capitol is the Utah state capitol, <u>located</u> in Salt Lake City.

Time ⏰   Help **?**   Confirm Answer   Next ➡️

The correct pattern is *one of the* + superlative adjective + plural noun. The plural noun *capitols* must therefore be used.

B) ERRORS INVOLVING IRREGULAR PLURALS

Most plural nouns in English end in -s, but a few are irregular. Only the most common irregular plurals are tested on the TOEFL® test. (Irregular plurals that come to English from other languages, such as Latin or Greek—*data, cacti, alumnae,* or *phenomena,* for example—will NOT be tested.

Common Irregular Plural Nouns	
child	children
man	men
woman	women
foot	feet
mouse	mice
fish	fish
sheep	sheep
series	series

SAMPLE ITEM

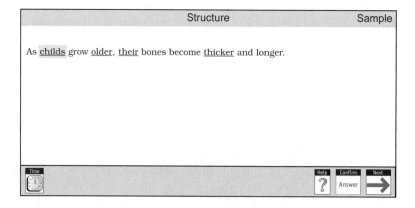

The correct plural form of *child* is *children.*

C) ERRORS WITH PLURAL FORMS OF NON-COUNT NOUNS

In some items a non-count noun (such as *information, silver, art, luggage, bread,* and so on) is incorrectly given as a plural noun.

SAMPLE ITEM

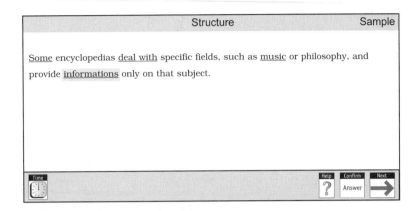

Information is an uncountable noun and cannot be pluralized.

D) ERRORS WITH PLURAL COMPOUND NOUN

Compound nouns consist of two nouns used together to express a single idea: *grocery store, travel agent, dinner party*, and *house cat*, for example. Only the second noun of compound nouns is pluralized: *grocery stores, travel agents, dinner parties*, and *house cats*. (There are rare exceptions to this rule—*sports cars* and *women doctors*, for example—but these won't be tested.)

SAMPLE ITEM

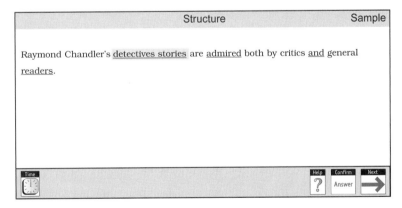

The correct plural form of this compound noun is *detective stories*.

E) ERRORS INVOLVING PLURAL FORMS OF NUMBERS AND MEASUREMENT

Some errors involve numbers + measurements:

They went for a *six-mile* walk.
They walked *six miles*.

In the first sentence, the number + measurement is used as an adjective, and the measurement is singular. In the second, the measurement is a noun and is therefore plural.

Numbers like *hundred*, *thousand*, and *million* may be pluralized when they are used indefinitely—in other words, when they do not follow other numbers.

seven thousand	thousands
five million dollars	millions of dollars

SAMPLE ITEMS

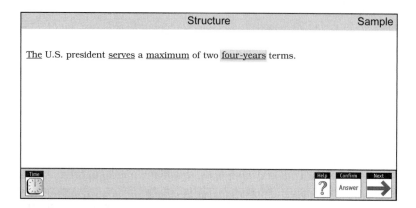

When used before a noun, a number + measurement is singular.

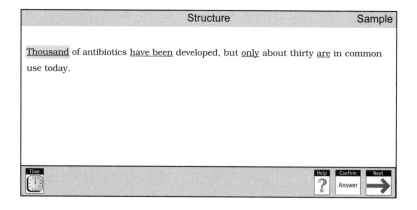

The plural form *thousands* should be used.

EXERCISE 24

Focus: Error Identification problems involving singular and plural nouns. (Note: Several items in this exercise do NOT focus on word-form errors. These are marked in the answer key with an asterisk.)

Directions: Decide which of the four underlined words or phrases would not be considered correct, and put an X under that expression.

1. The <u>male</u> mandril is <u>one</u> of the <u>most</u> colorful of all <u>mammal</u>.

2. Zoonoses are <u>diseases</u> that can <u>be transmitted</u> to <u>humans</u> beings by <u>animals</u>.

3. <u>Many</u> championship <u>automobiles</u> and <u>motorcycle</u> <u>races</u> take place in Daytona Beach, Florida.

4. The Newbery Award is granted every <u>years</u> to the <u>authors</u> of outstanding <u>books</u> for <u>children</u>.

5. <u>The</u> major <u>source</u> of <u>air</u> pollution vary from <u>city</u> to city.

6. <u>Around</u> seventy-five <u>percents</u> of the <u>Earth's surface</u> is covered by <u>water</u>.

7. <u>All college</u> and universities get their <u>funds</u> from a <u>variety</u> of <u>sources</u>.

8. Russell Cave <u>in</u> northeastern Alabama was the <u>home</u> of cliff-dwelling Indians <u>thousand</u> of <u>years</u> ago.

9. The Federalist Papers are a <u>500-pages</u> collection <u>of</u> eighteenth century <u>newspaper</u> articles written <u>to support</u> the Constitution.

10. The mathematician and <u>astronomer</u> David Rittenhouse <u>was</u> one of the first <u>man</u> of <u>science</u> in the American colonies.

11. Insurance <u>underwriter</u> insure <u>people</u> against many <u>types</u> of <u>risks</u>.

12. The electric <u>toaster</u> was one of the <u>earliest</u> <u>appliance</u> to be developed for the <u>kitchen</u>.

13. Tornadoes can pick up <u>objects</u> as heavy as <u>automobiles</u> and carry them for <u>hundreds</u> of <u>foot</u>.

14. Many <u>kinds</u> of <u>vegetables</u> are <u>growth</u> in California's Imperial Valley.

15. In typical <u>pioneer</u> settlements, <u>men</u>, women, and <u>children</u> worked from morning until night at <u>farms</u> and household tasks.

16. Few of the <u>doctors</u> practicing in the thirteen North American <u>colonies</u> had formal training in the field of <u>medicines</u>.

17. The <u>pine</u> tree is probably the <u>more</u> important lumber <u>tree</u> in <u>the world</u>.

18. In 1821 Emma Willard <u>founded</u> Troy Female Seminary, <u>the first institution</u> of higher <u>education</u> for <u>woman</u> in the United States.

19. <u>Adult</u> humans have more than a <u>trillions</u> <u>cells</u> in their <u>bodies</u>.

20. Phytoplankton is <u>found</u> only in the upper <u>layers</u> of the <u>ocean</u>, where <u>sunlights</u> can reach.

LESSON 25: Prepositions

Prepositions are used in the following ways:

- ◼ In adverbial phrases that show time, place, and other relationships

  in the morning   on Pacific Avenue   to the park

  before dinner   by a student

- ◼ After certain nouns

  a cause of   a reason for   a solution to

- ◼ After certain adjectives and participles

  different from   enough of   disappointed in

- ◼ After certain verbs

  combine with   rely on   refer to

- ◼ In phrasal prepositions (two- or three-word prepositions)

  according to   together with   on account of

- ◼ In certain set expressions

  by far   in general   on occasion   at last

A **prepositional phrase** consists of a preposition (*in, at, with, for, until,* and so on) followed by a noun phrase or pronoun, which is called the **prepositional object.**

In the autumn maple leaves turn red.

Beacon Hill is one of the most famous neighborhoods *in Boston.*

With luck, there won't be any more problems.

This house was built *by John's grandfather.*

Often prepositional phrases come at the beginning or the end of sentences, but they may appear in other parts of the sentence as well.

Sentence Completion

This type of item is generally missing a preposition, its object, or the entire prepositional phrase.

You may see prepositions in distractors, especially before the subject of a sentence. Remember, the subject of a sentence cannot be the object of a preposition.

*In the autumn is my favorite season.   (INCORRECT)

**Without a notebook* is no way to go to class.   (INCORRECT)

SAMPLE ITEMS

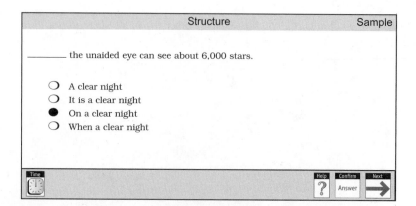

The first choice is incorrect because there is no word to connect the noun phrase *A clear night* to the rest of the sentence. The second choice consists of an independent clause, but there is no connector to join it to the other clause. The last choice seems to form a subordinate clause, but the clause lacks a verb. The best choice is the third one.

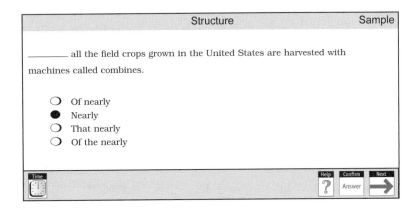

The first and last choices are incorrect because the subject of a sentence (*all the field crops*) cannot be the object of a preposition (*of*). The third choice creates a noun clause, but the noun clause lacks a verb. The best answer is the second choice.

Error Identification

Errors with prepositions are among the most difficult errors to catch.

There are two main types of preposition errors that you may see in the Written Expression part of the test:

A) ERRORS IN PREPOSITION CHOICE

The wrong preposition is used for the context of the sentence.

Some of the rules for choosing the correct prepositions are given in the Mini-Lessons (pages 309–317) but you will never be able to memorize all the rules for preposition use in English. The more you practice, though, the more you will develop a "feel" for determining which preposition is correct in any given situation.

There are two particular situations involving preposition choice that are often tested in Error Identification:

■ **Errors with *from . . . to* and *between . . . and***

Both these expressions are used to give the starting time and ending time. They can also be used to show relationships of place and various other relationships.

He lived in Seattle *from* 1992 *to* 1997.

He lived in Seattle *between* 1992 *and* 1997.

Route 66 ran *from* Chicago *to* Santa Monica, California.

Route 66 ran *between* Chicago *and* Santa Monica, California.

Errors usually involve an incorrect pairing of those words, or the incorrect use of other prepositions:

*between A *to* B (INCORRECT)   *from X *and* Y (INCORRECT)
*between A *with* B (INCORRECT)

■   **Errors with *since, for,* and *in***

Since is used before a point in time with the present perfect tense—but never with the past tense. *For* is used before a period of time with the present perfect and other tenses. *In* is used before certain points in time (years, centuries, decades) with the past tense and other tenses—but never with the present perfect tense.

He's lived here *since* 1998.   (CORRECT)

He's lived here *for* several years.   (CORRECT)

He moved here *in* 1998.   (CORRECT)

Errors involve the use of one of these prepositions for another:

*He's lived here *in* 1998.   (INCORRECT)

*He's lived here *since* several years.   (INCORRECT)

*He moved here *since* 1998.   (INCORRECT)

SAMPLE ITEMS

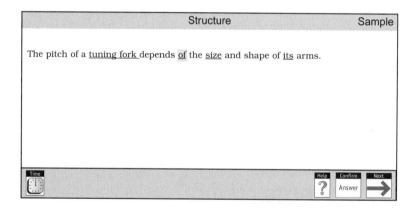

The correct preposition after the verb *depend* is *on,* not *of.*

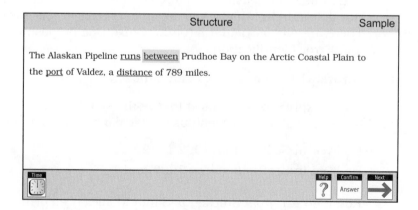

The correct pattern is *from . . . to.*

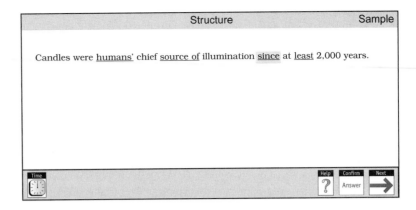

Before a period of time (*at least 2,000 years*) the preposition *for* should be used.

B) INCORRECT INCLUSION OR OMISSION OF PREPOSITIONS

A preposition is used when one is not needed, or not used when one is needed.

SAMPLE ITEMS

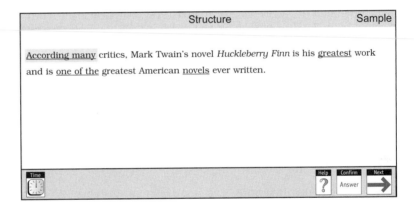

The preposition *to* has been omitted from the phrase *according to.*

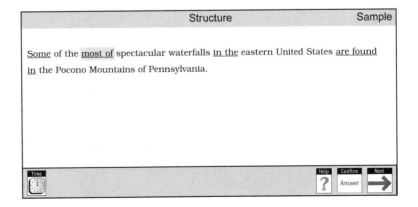

The best answer is the second underlined expression. The preposition *of* should not be used. (When *most* means "majority," it can be used with *of*: "Most of the people agree . . . ," for example. However, in this sentence, *most* is part of the superlative form of the adjective *spectacular*, and so cannot be used with *of*.)

EXERCISE 25.1

Focus: Choosing correct prepositions based on context.

Directions: Underline the prepositions that correctly complete the sentences below.

1. Wage rates depend (in/on) part (from/on) the general prosperity (of/for) the economy.

2. (For/To) an injection to be effective (on/against) tetanus, it must be administered (by/within) seventy-two hours (of/for) the injury.

3. The invention (of/for) the hand-cranked freezer opened the door (by/to) commercial ice cream production, and (for/since) then, the industry has grown (in/into) a four billion dollar a year industry.

4. (At/On) the time (of/in) the Revolutionary War, the North American colonies were merely a long string (with/of) settlements (along/among) the Atlantic Coast (between/from) Maine and Georgia.

5. The probability (of/for) two people (in/on) a group (of/for) ten people having birthdays (in/on) the same day is about one (in/of) twenty.

6. Showboats were floating theaters that tied up (at/to) towns (in/on) the Ohio and Mississippi Rivers to bring entertainment and culture (to/at) the people (of/in) the frontier.

7. Scrimshaw, the practice (of/for) carving ornate designs (in/on) ivory, was first practiced (by/of) sailors working (by/with) sail needles while (in/on) long sea voyages.

8. Assateague Island, (off/of) the coast (off/of) Maryland, is famous (for/to) its herds (of/with) wild ponies.

9. (In/On) order (for/to) an object to be visible, light must travel (from/for) that object (at/to) a person's eyes.

10. (In/On) the 1930s and 1940s, when train travel was (on/at) its peak, passengers could look forward (for/to) wonderful meals (on/at) trains.

11. (In/Since) the 1960s, op art, which was based (in/on) scientific theories (of/for) optics, employed patterns (of/in) lines and colors that seemed to change shape as the viewer looked (on/at) them.

12. The first national convention devoted (for/to) the issue (of/with) women's rights, organized partly (of/by) Elizabeth Cady Stanton, was held (in/on) her hometown (in/of) Seneca Falls, New York (in/on) 1848.

13. (In/Since) 1716 a party (of/for) explorers led (by/with) Lieutenant Governor Spotswood (of/in) Virginia tried (in/on) vain to find a route (through/of) the Appalachian Mountains.

14. Dolphins rely (in/on) echolocation, a form (of/for) navigation similar (with/to) the sonar systems used (on/at) submarines.

15. Analytical geometry, (in/on) which algebraic ideas are used (for/to) the description (of/for) geometric objects, has been (in/on) use (for/since) the seventeenth century.

EXERCISE 25.2

Focus: Identifying errors involving the inclusion or omission of prepositions.

Directions: If there is a preposition unnecessarily included in a sentence, mark that sentence *I* and underline the preposition. If there is a preposition incorrectly omitted from a sentence, mark that sentence *O*, underline the word before and after the missing preposition, and write the correct preposition on the line at the end of the sentence. If the sentence is correctly written, mark that sentence *C*. The first one is done as an example.

_O_   1. According polls taken throughout the twentieth century, Lincoln and Washington are the pre-eminent American presidents   *to*

____   2. Today, many varieties of fruit are available year round, thanks improved storage and shipping techniques. _____

____   3. The origin of the Moon remains a mystery. _____

____   4. Traffic jams can cause of pollution, delays, and short tempers. _____

____   5. The Sun's rays heat the Earth's surface, on which then radiates the heat into the air. _____

____   6. A warm-blooded animal is one that keeps the same body temperature regardless the air temperature. _____

____   7. Charlie Parker, considered by many the greatest improvisor in the history of jazz, influenced many other jazz musicians. _____

____   8. Most people are aware the need to visit their dentist regularly. _____

____   9. Muscle fibers are attached bones by tendons. _____

____   10. In his essay "Self Reliance," Ralph Waldo Emerson told to his readers why they should not depend on the ideas of others. _____

____   11. The crayfish is a freshwater crustacean related the lobster. _____

____   12. Charles Goren was an expert the game of bridge. _____

____   13. Stomata are the tiny openings in the leaves of plants through which oxygen and carbon dioxide pass. _____

____   14. Ducks have small oil glands by which keep their feathers oily and repel water. _____

____   15. The tail of a comet always points away the Sun. _____

____ 16. Lichens grow in extreme environments in where no other plant can exist.

_____

____ 17. Not all of waterfalls are formed in the same way. _____

____ 18. The pulmonary artery carries blood from the right side the heart to the lungs.

_____

____ 19. In addition to the 12 constellations of the zodiac, 30 other constellations were

familiar people of ancient times. _____

____ 20. The American singer Marian Anderson trained both in the United States and in

abroad. _____

EXERCISE 25.3

Focus: Structure problems involving prepositions. (Note: Several items in this exercise do NOT focus on prepositions. These are marked in the answer key with asterisks.)

Directions: For Sentence Completion items, mark the oval next to the answer choice that correctly completes the sentence. For Error Identification items, put an *X* under the underlined portion of the sentence that would not be considered correct.

1. _____ seed of a flowering plant is covered by a dense protective coat.

   ○ On each

   ○ Each

   ○ Each of

   ○ That each

2. Dynamite is ordinarily detonated _____ called a blasting cap.

   ○ a device is used

   ○ that a device

   ○ with a device

   ○ the use of a device

3. Water polo is a game <u>in which</u> is played <u>in the water</u> <u>by two</u> teams, each <u>with</u> seven players.

4. _____ 1900 there were some 300 bicycle factories in the United States which produced over a million bicycles.

   ○ In

   ○ Because in

   ○ It was in

   ○ That in

5. A thick layer of fat called blubber keeps whales warm even _____ coldest water.
   - ○ though the
   - ○ in the
   - ○ the
   - ○ of the

6. <u>Many of</u> radio stations <u>began</u> <u>broadcasting</u> baseball games <u>during</u> the 1920s.

7. _____ the United States, the general movement of air masses is from west to east.
   - ○ Across
   - ○ To cross
   - ○ They cross
   - ○ It's across

8. The <u>economy of</u> Maine is based <u>to a</u> great extent <u>in its</u> forests, which cover eighty <u>percent</u> of its surface area.

9. The removal <u>of</u> waste <u>materials</u> is <u>essential to</u> all <u>live</u>.

10. The bark of a tree thickens _____.
    - ○ with age
    - ○ it gets older
    - ○ as older
    - ○ by age

11. John Diefenbaker, prime minister of Canada <u>during</u> 1957 to 1963, <u>is given</u> <u>much of</u> the credit <u>for the adoption</u> of the Canadian Bill of Rights.

12. A substance that is harmless to a person who has no allergies can cause mild to serious reactions in a person _____ allergies.
    - ○ has
    - ○ which having
    - ○ can have
    - ○ with

13. The first stage <u>on</u> the manufacturing <u>of all</u> <u>types of</u> clothing is the <u>cutting of</u> the material.

14. <u>All of</u> the wheat grown <u>throughout</u> the world <u>belongs one</u> <u>of fourteen</u> species.

15. In 1886 a number of national unions formed the American Federation of Labor _____.
    - ○ Samuel Gompers was its leader
    - ○ under the leadership of Samuel Gompers
    - ○ which, under Samuel Gompers' leadership
    - ○ Samuel Gompers led it

16. Harmonicas and autoharps _____ folk instruments.

   ○ are examples
   ○ for example
   ○ are examples of
   ○ as examples of

17. There are <u>approximately</u> 600 <u>different</u> species <u>of</u> trees <u>native of</u> the continental United States.

18. _____ industries, such as banking and travel, in which computers are not a convenience but a necessity.

   ○ Where some
   ○ In some
   ○ Some
   ○ There are some

19. Waterwheels, <u>which</u> appeared <u>on</u> the fourth century B.C., were probably <u>the first</u> machines not powered <u>by</u> humans or animals.

20. <u>Since</u> centuries, Native American tribes in the Southwest have <u>valued</u> turquoise and have <u>used</u> it <u>in jewelry</u>.

21. One of the oldest large suspension bridges still _____ today is the George Washington Bridge between New York City and Fort Lee, New Jersey.

   ○ using
   ○ is used
   ○ the use of
   ○ in use

22. Loggerhead turtles lay <u>thousands eggs</u> <u>at a single</u> time, but only a <u>few</u> survive <u>to adulthood</u>.

23. <u>In nowadays</u>, commercial bakeries use complex, automated machines, but the basic principles <u>of baking</u> have changed <u>little</u> <u>for thousands</u> of years.

24. <u>In</u> the mid-1900s, an <u>increasing</u> number <u>of jobs</u> in the United States have involved the <u>handling of</u> information.

25. At Louisville, Kentucky, the Ohio River is a little more than a mile _____.

   ○ width
   ○ in wide
   ○ widely
   ○ in width

LESSON 26: Articles

Articles are specifically tested only in Error Identification items.

Like errors with prepositions, errors with articles are sometimes hard to catch. This is partly because of the complexity of the article system in English, and partly because articles, like prepositions, are "small words" and your eye tends to skip over errors involving these words.

The basic uses of articles are explained in the chart:

Indefinite Articles *a* and *an*	Definite Article *the*	No Article (∅)

A or *an* is used before singular nouns when one does not have a specific person, place, thing, or concept in mind:
 	
  an orange
  a chair
	The is used before singular, plural, and non-count nouns when one has a specific person, place, thing, or concept in mind:
	
	  the orange
	  the oranges
	  the fruit
	  the chair
	  the chairs
	  the furniture
		No article is used before noncount nouns or plural nouns when one does not have specific persons, places, concepts, or things in mind:
		
		  ∅ oranges
		  ∅ fruit
		  ∅ chairs
		  ∅ furniture

The indefinite article *a* is used before words that begin with a consonant sound (*a chair, a book*); *an* is used before words that begin with a vowel sound (*an orange, an ocean liner*). Before words that begin with the letters *h-* and *u-*, either *a* or *an* can be used, depending on the pronunciation of the words.

Vowel Sounds	Consonant Sounds
an honor	a hat
an umbrella	a university

There are also some specific rules for using (or not using) articles that you should be aware of.

■   An indefinite article can be used to mean "one." It is also used to mean "per."

    a half, a quarter, a third, a tenth

    a mile a minute (one mile per minute)

    an apple a day (one apple per day)

■   A definite article is used when there is only one example of the thing or person, or when the identity of the thing or person is clear.

    The Moon went behind some clouds. (There's only one Moon.)

    Please open the *door*. (You know which door I mean.)

■ A definite article is usually used before these expressions of time and position:

the morning	the front	the beginning
the afternoon	the back	the end
the evening*	the middle	
	the top	
the past	the bottom	
the present		
the future		

*No article is used in the expression "at night."

■ A definite article comes before a singular noun that is used as a representative of an entire class of things. This is especially common with the names of animals, trees, inventions, musical instruments, and parts of the body.

The tiger is the largest cat.

My favorite tree is *the oak.*

The Wright Brothers invented *the airplane.*

The oboe is a woodwind instrument.

The heart pumps blood.

■ A definite article is used before expressions with an ordinal number. No article is used before expressions with cardinal numbers.

the first	one
the fourth chapter	Chapter Four
the seventh volume	Volume Seven

■ A definite article is used before decades and centuries.

the 1930s	the 1800s
the fifties	the twenty-first century

■ A definite article is usually used before superlative forms of adjectives.

the widest river   the most important decision

■ A definite article is used in quantity expressions in this pattern: quantifier + *of* + *the* + noun.

many of the textbooks	not much of the paper
some of the water	most of the students
all of the people	a few of the photographs

These expressions can also be used without the phrase *of the.*

many textbooks	not much paper
some water	most students
all people	a few photographs

■ A definite article is used before the name of a group of people or a nationality. No article is used before the name of a language.

The Swedish are proud of their ancestors, *the Vikings.*

She learned to speak *Swedish* when she lived in Stockholm.

- When an adjective is used without a noun to mean "people who are . . . ," a definite article is used.

    Both *the young* and *the old* will enjoy this movie.

    The poor have many problems.

- A definite article is usually used before a noncount noun or a plural noun when they are followed by a modifier. No article is used when these nouns appear alone and have a general meaning.

    The rice that I bought today is in that bag.

    Rice is a staple in many countries.

    Trees provide shade.

    The trees in this park are mostly evergreens.

- A definite article is used before the name of a field of study followed by an *of* phrase. If a field is used alone or is preceded by an adjective, no article is used.

    the literature of the twentieth century   literature

    the history of the United States   American history

    A definite article is also used before plural fields.

    the fine arts

- Definite articles are used before the "formal" names of nations, states, and cities. (These usually contain *of* phrases.) No articles are used before the common names of nations, states, provinces, and cities. (There are a few exceptions to this rule, such as Great Britain, the Phillippines, and The Hague.)

    the United States of America   America

    the state of Kansas   Kansas

    the province of Manitoba   Manitoba

    the city of Philadelphia   Philadelphia

- Definite articles are used before most plural geographic names: the names of groups of lakes, mountains, and islands. No article is used before the names of individual lakes, mountains, and islands.

    the Great Lakes   Lake Powell

    the Rocky Mountains   Mount Washington

    the Aleutian Islands   Long Island

Error Identification

In Error Identification items, there are three main types of errors involving articles:

A) INCORRECT ARTICLE CHOICE

The most common error is the use of *a* in place of *an* or vice versa. Fortunately, this is also the easiest type of error to detect. Another error is *a* or *an* used in place of *the*, or *the* in place of *a* or *an*.

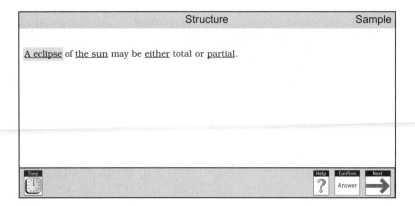

Structure	Sample

A eclipse of the sun may be either total or partial.

Time   Help ?   Confirm Answer   Next →

An must be used before a noun beginning with a vowel sound such as *eclipse*.

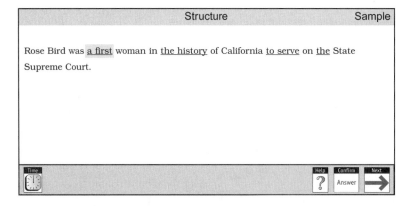

Structure	Sample

Rose Bird was a first woman in the history of California to serve on the State Supreme Court.

Time   Help ?   Confirm Answer   Next →

A first is incorrect. In a phrase with an ordinal number (such as *first*), the definite article *the* must be used.

B) INCORRECT OMISSION OR INCLUSION OF AN ARTICLE

Sometimes an article is used when none is needed, or one is omitted when one is required.

SAMPLE ITEMS

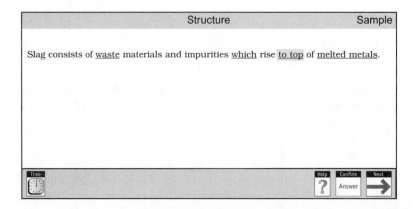

Structure	Sample

Slag consists of waste materials and impurities which rise to top of melted metals.

Time   Help ?   Confirm Answer   Next →

The definite article *the* should not be omitted from the phrase *the top of.*

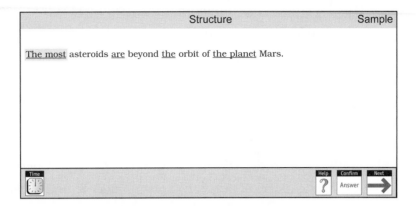

Definite articles are only used before quantity expressions that contain *of* phrases. (*Most asteroids* or *Most of the asteroids* would both be correct in this sentence.)

C) USE OF A DEFINITE ARTICLE IN PLACE OF A POSSESSIVE

A definite article may be incorrectly used in place of a possessive word—*its*, *his*, *her*, or *their*.

SAMPLE ITEM

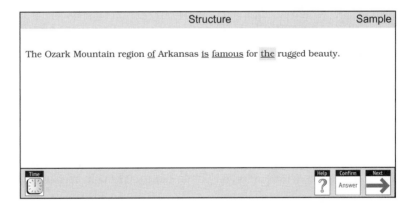

The should correctly read *its* because the sentence refers to the beauty belonging to the Ozark Mountain region.

EXERCISE 26.1

Focus: Identifying the correct and incorrect use of articles.

Directions: Underline the forms that correctly complete the sentence.

1. Only about (the one/one) percent of (the water/water) on Earth is (the fresh/fresh) water.

2. (The mineral/Mineral) phosphate is (the most/most) common ingredient of all types of (the fertilizers/fertilizers).

3. (The/A) process of refining minerals requires (a/an) huge amount of (an electrical/electrical) energy.

4. (A humor/Humor) runs through (the American/American) literature from (the earliest/earliest) times until (the present/present).

5. (The ozone/Ozone) layer acts as (a/an) umbrella against (the most/most) of (the Sun's/Sun's) dangerous rays.

6. In (the early/early) 1800s, Sequoia, (a Cherokee/Cherokee) leader, created (the/a) first written form of (a North/North) American Indian language.

7. (The Goddard/Goddard) family of (the New/New) England produced some of (the/a) finest furniture made in (the United/United) States in (the eighteenth/eighteenth) century.

8. (The popcorn/Popcorn) has (a/the) same food value as any other kind of (a corn/corn).

9. One of (the most/most) important tools for (a research/research) in (the social/social) sciences is (a well/well) written questionnaire.

10. Native to (the American/American) West, (the/a) coyote came east early in (the twentieth/twentieth) century after (its/the) chief natural competitor (the/a) wolf died out over (a hundred/hundred) years ago.

11. (The nineteenth/Nineteenth) century astronomer Alvan G. Clark built hundreds (of/of the) refracting telescopes during (the/his) lifetime.

12. (The Hawaiian/Hawaiian) Islands are among (the most/most) geographically isolated islands in (the world/world).

EXERCISE 26.2

Focus: Identifying errors with articles. (Note: One or two items in this exercise do NOT focus on article errors. These are marked in the answer key with an asterisk.)

Directions: Decide which of the four underlined words or phrases would not be considered correct and put an X under that expression.

1. The most butterfly eggs are coated with a sticky substance that holds them to plants.

2. A number of large insurance companies have the headquarters in Hartford, Connecticut.

3. To be effective, an advertisement must first attract an attention.

4. Virgin Islands National Park features a underwater preserve with coral reefs and colorful tropical fish.

5. Arthritis, <u>a painful</u> swelling of <u>the</u> joints, is often associated <u>with old</u> people, but can afflict <u>young</u> as well.

6. Wilmington is <u>an only</u> large <u>city</u> in <u>the state</u> <u>of</u> Delaware.

7. About <u>the third</u> of <u>the Earth's</u> <u>land</u> surface is covered by relatively <u>flat plains</u>.

8. In <u>the 1920s</u> <u>gasoline</u> companies began giving away <u>free</u> road maps to <u>the customers</u>.

9. <u>The tropic</u> of Cancer <u>is imaginary</u> line that marks <u>the northern</u> boundary of <u>the Earth's</u> tropical zone.

10. <u>Hereford cows</u> are one of <u>the most common</u> breeds of <u>cattle</u> raised for <u>the beef</u>.

11. American soprano Kathleen Battle taught <u>music</u> in elementary school before <u>beginning</u> <u>the career</u> as <u>a professional</u> singer.

12. In 1891 <u>first</u> state law to help <u>local</u> communities pay for <u>highways</u> was passed <u>in</u> New Jersey.

13. Phi Beta Kappa is <u>a honor</u> society that encourages <u>scholarship</u> in <u>science</u> and <u>the arts</u>.

14. Grandfather Mountain, <u>a highest</u> mountain in <u>the</u> Blue Ridge <u>mountain range</u>, is <u>in</u> North Carolina.

15. <u>The eardrum</u> is <u>the only</u> organ in <u>a human</u> body that is capable of detecting changes <u>in air</u> pressure.

16. It was <u>around</u> 1925 that <u>an accurate</u>, convenient system for <u>record</u> the choreography <u>of ballet</u> was developed.

17. <u>At beginning</u> of <u>the Civil War</u>, Matthew Brady was authorized to accompany <u>the Union Army</u> and take <u>photographs</u>.

18. Richard Byrd was <u>the first</u> person in <u>the history</u> to fly <u>over</u> <u>the</u> North Pole.

19. In 1878 <u>in San Francisco</u>, Kate Wiggin <u>open</u> <u>the first</u> free kindergarten on <u>the West Coast</u>.

20. <u>The willow tree</u> is one of <u>the first trees</u> to get its leaves <u>in the spring</u> and one of the last to <u>lose it</u> in the autumn.

LESSON 27: Word Order

Word order is tested in both types of Structure items.

Sentence Completion

All of the answer choices for a Sentence Completion item involving word order contain more or less the same words, but they are arranged in four different orders. The word order is "scrambled" in three choices; in one it is correct. Most items involve three or four words.

- ● X Y Z
- ○ Y X Z
- ○ Z Y X
- ○ X Z Y

Word order problems are easy to identify because the answer choices are exactly—or almost exactly—the same length, so the answer choices form a rectangle.

- ● so far away from
- ○ away so far from
- ○ from so far away
- ○ away from so far

Many different types of structures are used in word order problems. One of the most common is a phrase with a superlative adjective or adverb.

Word order items are the only Sentence Correction items in which the distractors may be ungrammatical. In other types of Sentence Correction problems, distractors are always correct in some context. However, at least two of the choices may be grammatical. The correct choice depends on the context of the sentence. See the first Sample Item on page 265 for an example of this.

It is sometimes easy to eliminate distractors in word order items by making sure they "fit" with the rest of the sentence. If you are not sure which remaining answer is correct, use your ear. Say the sentence to yourself (silently) to see which sounds best. Sometimes in word order problems, the answer that looks best doesn't always sound best when put into the sentence.

A special type of word order problem involves **inversions.** This type of sentence uses question word order (auxiliary + subject + main verb) even though the sentence is not a question. When are inversions used?

■ When the negative words listed below are placed at the beginning of a clause for emphasis

not only	never
not until	seldom
nowhere	rarely
at no time	scarcely
by no means	no sooner

Seldom *have I heard* such beautiful music.

Not only *did the company* lose profits, but it also had to lay off workers.

■ When a clause begins with one of these expressions with the word *only,* an inversion is used in that clause.

only in (on, at, by, etc.)   only recently   only once

Only in an emergency *should you use* this exit.

Only recently *did she return* from abroad.

Only by asking questions *can you learn.*

■ When sentences begin with these expressions with the word *only*, the subject and verb of the second clause are inverted

> only if   only when
>
> only because   only after
>
> only until

> Only if you have a serious problem *should you* call Mr. Franklin at home.
>
> Only when you are satisfied *is the sale* considered final.

■ When clauses begin with the word *so* + an adjective or participle

> So rare *is this coin* that it belongs in a museum.
>
> So confusing *was the map* that we had to ask a police officer for directions.

■ When clauses begin with expressions of place or order, the subject and verb are inverted (but auxiliary verbs are not used as they would be in questions)

> In front of the museum *is a statue.*
>
> Off the coast of California *lie the Channel Islands.*
>
> First *came a police car,* then *came an ambulance.*

SAMPLE ITEMS

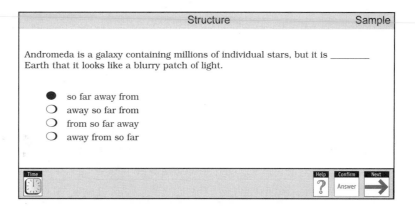

Only the first choice has the correct word order for this sentence. The word order in the second and fourth choices would be incorrect in any sentence. The third choice might be correct in certain sentences, but is not correct here.

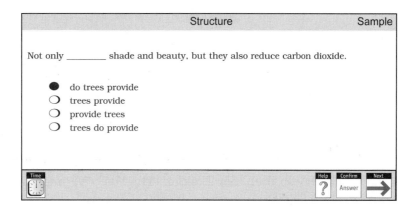

Only the first choice correctly uses question word order after *not only*. The second and third choices do not use an auxiliary verb, which is required here. The fourth choice does not follow the correct word order: auxiliary + subject + main verb.

Error Identification

Most word order errors in Written Expression consist of two words in reverse order. Some of the most common examples of this type of error are given below:

Error	Example	Correction
noun + adjective	drivers careful	careful drivers
noun + possessive	clothing women's	women's clothing
main verb + auxiliary	finished are	are finished
adjective + adverb	a basic extremely idea	an extremely basic idea
participle + adverb	baked freshly bread	freshly baked bread
adverb, adjective, participle, or quantifier + *almost*	totally almost late almost finished almost all almost	almost totally almost late almost finished almost all
verb + subject in an indirect question or other *wh-* clause	Someone asked me where is the post office. I spoke to Joan when was she here.	Someone asked me where the post office is. I spoke to Joan when she was here.
subject + verb in a direct question	Someone asked, "Where the post office is?"	Someone asked, "Where is the post office?"
enough + adjective*	enough good	good enough
too + *much* + adjective**	This issue is too much important to ignore.	This issue is much too important to ignore.

Enough can correctly be used before nouns: *enough money, enough time.*
**Too much* can correctly be used before non-count nouns: *too much homework, too much trouble.*

SAMPLE ITEM

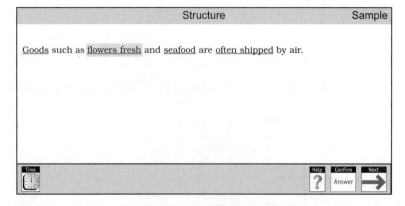

You should choose the second option. The adjective *fresh* must come before the noun *flowers*: *fresh flowers.*

EXERCISE 27.1

Focus: Identifying correct and incorrect word order in sentences.

Directions: If the word order of the underlined form is correct, mark the sentence *C*. If the word order is incorrect, mark the sentence *X* and write a correction in the blank below the sentence.

____ 1. The Douglas fir is the <u>source chief</u> of lumber in the state of Oregon.

_____

____ 2. The painted turtle is a <u>colored brightly</u>, smooth-shelled turtle.

_____

____ 3. Trained in Europe, John Sargent became <u>an extremely successful</u> portrait painter in the United States.

_____

____ 4. For thousands of years, humankind has asked the question, "How old <u>the Earth is</u>?"

_____

____ 5. For thousands of years, humankind has wondered how old <u>is the Earth</u>.

_____

____ 6. Ammonia, a compound of nitrogen and hydrogen, has many <u>industrial uses</u>.

_____

____ 7. The Atlantic coastline of the United States is about 400 <u>longer miles</u> than the Gulf coastline.

_____

____ 8. Identical colors may appear to be quite different when <u>are they</u> viewed against different backgrounds.

_____

____ 9. Zoos provide an opportunity to study a wide range of animals, often in their <u>habitats natural</u>.

_____

____ 10. The development of transistors made <u>possible it</u> to reduce the size of many electronic devices.

_____

____ 11. The air of the upper atmosphere is just <u>enough dense</u> to ignite meteors by friction.

_____

____ 12. Monterey, California has <u>long been</u> a center for artists and artisans.

_____

_____ 13. Cirrus clouds are composed <u>entirely almost</u> of ice crystals.

_____

_____ 14. Many sailboats are equipped with small engines for times when there is not <u>enough wind</u>.

_____

_____ 15. Prior to the 1940s, most runways were <u>too much</u> short for long distance airplanes to take off from, so many long distance aircraft were seaplanes.

_____

_____ 16. Margaret Wise Brown was a successful author of many <u>books children's</u>.

_____

_____ 17. <u>All of</u> the stringed instruments, the lute is probably the most difficult to play.

_____

_____ 18. "Information overload" occurs when an individual or an organization has <u>much too</u> information to process at one time.

_____

_____ 19. Twelve drawings usually have to be prepared for <u>second each</u> of animated film.

_____

_____ 20. <u>Of all</u> the members of the class of animals known as arachnids, such as spiders, scorpions, and ticks, have eight legs and bodies divided into two main parts.

_____

EXERCISE 27.2

Focus: Structure problems involving word order. (Note: Several items in this exercise do NOT focus on word order. These sentences are marked in the answer key with asterisks.)

Directions: For Sentence Completion items, mark the oval next to the answer choice that correctly completes the sentence. For Error Identification items, put an *X* under the underlined portion of the sentence that would not be considered correct.

1. Hills known as land islands, or salt domes, are _____ Louisiana's marshlands.

   ○ extremely interesting features of

   ○ of extremely interesting features

   ○ interesting extremely features of

   ○ extremely interesting of features

2. During <u>pioneer times</u>, <u>the</u> Allegheny Mountains were a <u>barrier major</u> <u>to transportation</u>.

3. An umbra is a <u>shadow's darkest</u> <u>central part</u> where <u>is light</u> <u>totally excluded</u>.

4. _____ of chamber music is the string quartet.
   - ⭘ The famous most form
   - ⭘ The most famous form
   - ⭘ The form most famous
   - ⭘ Most the form famous

5. In Philadelphia's Franklin Institute, <u>there is</u> a <u>working model</u> of a <u>human heart</u> <u>enough large</u> for visitors to walk through.

6. Not until the seventeenth century _____ to measure the speed of light.
   - ⭘ did anyone even attempt
   - ⭘ anyone did even attempt
   - ⭘ did anyone attempt even
   - ⭘ did even attempt anyone

7. Alfalfa is _____ for livestock.
   - ⭘ a primarily grown crop
   - ⭘ grown primarily a crop
   - ⭘ a crop grown primarily
   - ⭘ a grown crop primarily

8. The Franklin stove, which became common in the 1790s, burned wood _____ an open fireplace.
   - ⭘ efficiently much more than
   - ⭘ much more efficiently than
   - ⭘ much more than efficiently
   - ⭘ more efficiently much than

9. Mutualism is a <u>relationship between</u> <u>animal species</u> <u>in which</u> <u>benefit both</u>.

10. Reinforced concrete is concrete that is strengthened by metal bars _____ .
    - ⭘ in it that are embedded
    - ⭘ embedded that are in it
    - ⭘ are that it embedded in
    - ⭘ that are embedded in it

11. Most southern states had set up primary school systems by the late eighteenth century, but only in New England _____ and open to all students.
    - ⭘ primary schools were free
    - ⭘ were primary schools free
    - ⭘ free were primary schools
    - ⭘ were free primary schools

12. Sloths are <u>moving slow</u>, shaggy mammals that are <u>often seen</u> hanging <u>upside down</u> from <u>tree limbs</u>.

13. Geometry is useful _____ carpentry and navigation.
    - ○ as in such diverse occupations
    - ○ such as in diverse occupations
    - ○ in such diverse occupations as
    - ○ diverse occupations such as in

14. To grow well, a tree must be well-suited to the area where is it planted.

15. The minerals grains in basalt are much too small to be seen with the unaided eye.

16. Frank Lloyd Wright is known for his original highly methods of harmonizing buildings with their surroundings.

17. _____ of the early years of space exploration was the discovery of the Van Allen radiation belt in 1958.
    - ○ Perhaps the greatest triumph
    - ○ The triumph perhaps greatest
    - ○ The greatest perhaps triumph
    - ○ The triumph greatest perhaps

18. Some algae are microscopic and consist of one only cell, but others are large plants containing many cells.

19. A fully grown male mountain lion may be eight long feet.

20. Today _____ major new products without conducting elaborate market research.
    - ○ corporations hardly introduce ever
    - ○ hardly ever corporations introduce
    - ○ hardly ever introduce corporations
    - ○ corporations hardly ever introduce

21. Across the Chesapeake Bay from the rest of the state _____, whose farms produce beans, tomatoes, and other garden vegetables.
    - ○ there lies Maryland's Eastern Shore
    - ○ lies Maryland's Eastern Shore
    - ○ Maryland's Eastern Shore lies there
    - ○ Maryland's Eastern Shore lies

22. Stone fruits are fruits such as peaches and plums in which a hard pit surrounded is by soft pulp.

23. Acidophilus bacteria are _____ in an acid medium.
    - ○ those that grow best
    - ○ those grow best that
    - ○ that those grow best
    - ○ grow best those that

24. Job enrichment is a <u>technique used</u> to increase <u>satisfaction workers'</u> by <u>giving them</u> <u>more responsibilities</u>.

25. The first <u>permanent European</u> settlement in <u>what is now</u> Mississippi <u>was a</u> <u>center trading</u> in Biloxi.

26. _____ great apes, the gibbon is the smallest.
    - ◯ Four of the types of
    - ◯ The four types of
    - ◯ Four types of the
    - ◯ Of the four types of

27. Most <u>country music</u> songs are <u>deeply personal</u> and <u>deal with</u> themes of love, <u>lonely</u>, and separation.

28. It is difficult _____ through swamps because of tangled roots and shallow waterways.
    - ◯ to navigate even for small boats
    - ◯ for even small boats to navigate
    - ◯ even small boats for to navigate
    - ◯ even to navigate for small boats

29. Charleston, South Carolina has <u>many beautiful</u> homes, but <u>none almost</u> of them <u>were designed</u> by <u>professional architects</u>.

30. So complicated _____ that consumers who use a product are seldom aware of where all its components come from.
    - ◯ today trade is international
    - ◯ today international trade is
    - ◯ is international trade today
    - ◯ international trade is today

REVIEW TEST F: Structure

Directions: For Sentence Completion items, mark the oval next to the answer choice that correctly completes the sentence. For Error Identification items, put an *X* under the underlined portion of the sentence that would not be considered correct.

Commercial bakeries can make <u>thousands of</u> <u>loaves of</u> bread <u>on one time</u> by <u>using</u> automated equipment.

| Time | | Help ? | Confirm Answer | Next → |

_____ book *Jubilee*, which was based on the life of her great-grandmother, Margaret Walker was awarded the Pulitzer Prize.

- ◯ For her
- ◯ Her
- ◯ It was her
- ◯ That her

| Time | | Help ? | Confirm Answer | Next → |

North America is <u>a third</u> <u>largest</u> <u>of the</u> seven <u>continents</u>.

| Time | | Help ? | Confirm Answer | Next → |

Rarely _____ more than fifty miles from the coast.

- ◯ redwood trees grow
- ◯ redwood trees do grow
- ◯ grow redwood trees
- ◯ do redwood trees grow

| Time | | Help ? | Confirm Answer | Next → |

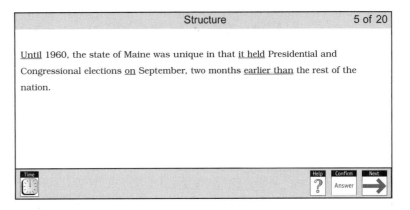

Until 1960, the state of Maine was unique in that it held Presidential and Congressional elections on September, two months earlier than the rest of the nation.

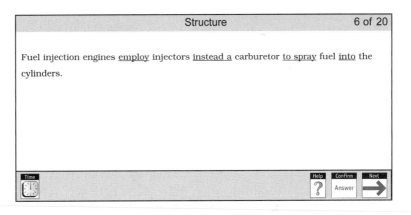

Fuel injection engines employ injectors instead a carburetor to spray fuel into the cylinders.

Nerve cells, or neurons, _____ in the human body.

- ○ the most complex cells are
- ○ are the most complex cells
- ○ most complex the cells are
- ○ most are the complex cells

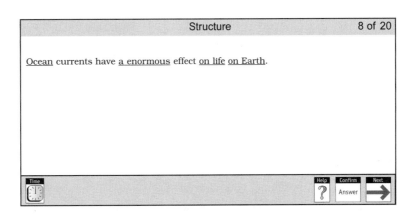

Ocean currents have a enormous effect on life on Earth.

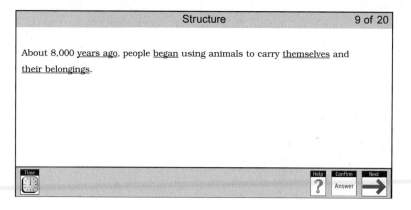

About 8,000 <u>years ago</u>, people <u>began</u> using animals to carry <u>themselves</u> and <u>their belongings</u>.

Time

Help ? Confirm Answer Next

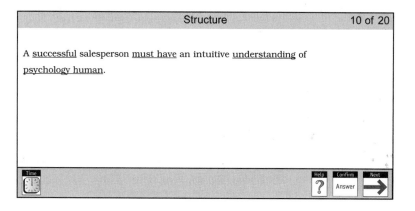

A <u>successful</u> salesperson <u>must have</u> an intuitive <u>understanding</u> of <u>psychology human</u>.

Time

Help ? Confirm Answer Next

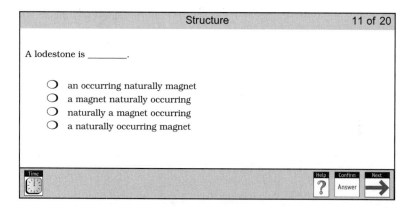

A lodestone is _____.

○ an occurring naturally magnet
○ a magnet naturally occurring
○ naturally a magnet occurring
○ a naturally occurring magnet

Time

Help ? Confirm Answer Next

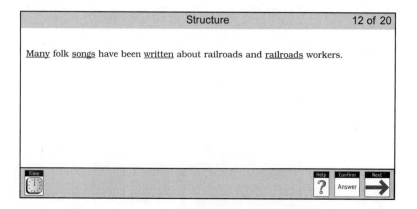

<u>Many</u> folk <u>songs</u> have been <u>written</u> about railroads and <u>railroads</u> workers.

Time

Help ? Confirm Answer Next

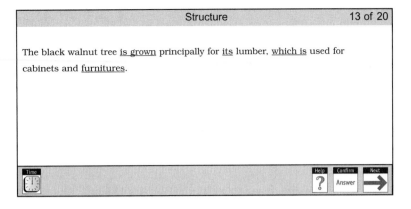

The black walnut tree <u>is grown</u> principally for <u>its</u> lumber, <u>which is</u> used for cabinets and <u>furnitures</u>.

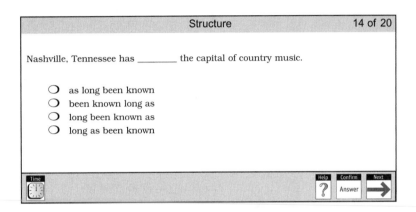

Nashville, Tennessee has _____ the capital of country music.

○ as long been known
○ been known long as
○ long been known as
○ long as been known

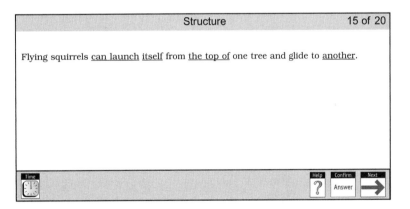

Flying squirrels <u>can launch</u> <u>itself</u> from <u>the top of</u> one tree and glide to <u>another</u>.

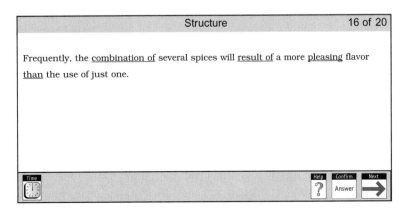

Frequently, the <u>combination of</u> several spices will <u>result of</u> a more <u>pleasing</u> flavor <u>than</u> the use of just one.

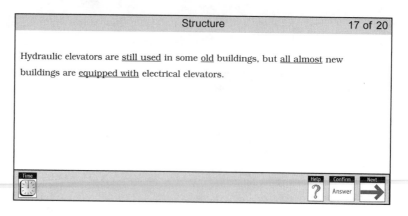

Hydraulic elevators are <u>still used</u> in some <u>old</u> buildings, but <u>all almost</u> new buildings are <u>equipped with</u> electrical elevators.

Time Help ? Confirm Answer Next

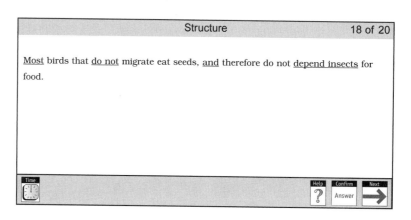

<u>Most</u> birds that <u>do not</u> migrate eat seeds, <u>and</u> therefore do not <u>depend insects</u> for food.

Time Help ? Confirm Answer Next

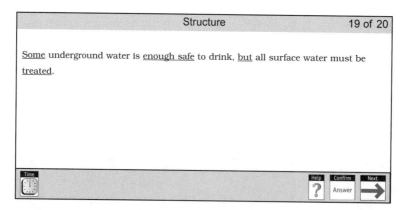

<u>Some</u> underground water is <u>enough safe</u> to drink, <u>but</u> all surface water must be <u>treated</u>.

Time Help ? Confirm Answer Next

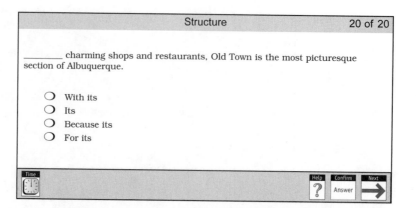

_____ charming shops and restaurants, Old Town is the most picturesque section of Albuquerque.

○ With its
○ Its
○ Because its
○ For its

Time Help ? Confirm Answer Next

LESSON 28: Conjunctions

Conjunctions are connecting words; they join parts of a sentence. In this lesson, we'll look at two main types of conjunctions.

Coordinate conjunctions are used to join equal sentence parts: single words, phrases, and independent clauses. When two full clauses are joined, they are usually separated by a comma. The coordinate conjunctions you will most often see in Structure problems are listed in the chart below:

Coordinate Conjunction	Use	Examples
and	addition	Hereford cows are brown *and* white. Matthew washed his car *and* cleaned up the garage.
or	choice, possibility, alternative	This plant can be grown in a house *or* in a garden. Her action was very brave *or* very foolish.
but	contrast, opposition	He brought his wallet *but* forgot his checkbook. The book discussed some interesting ideas *but* it wasn't very well written.
nor	negation	He's never taken a class in sociology, *nor* does he intend to. I didn't eat breakfast *nor* lunch.
so	effect	It was a bright day, *so* Laura put on her sunglasses.

(The conjunction *so* is used to join only clauses—not single words or phrases.)

Correlative conjunctions are two-part conjunctions. Like coordinate conjunctions, they are used to join words, phrases, and clauses.

Correlative Conjunction	Use	Example
both . . . and	addition	*Both* wolves *and* coyotes are members of the dog family.
not only . . . but also	addition	Dominic studied *not only* mathematics *but also* computer science.
either . . . or	choice, possibility	We need *either* a nail *or* a screw to hang up this picture.
neither . . . nor	negation (not A and not B)	*Neither* the television *nor* the stereo had been turned off.
whether . . . or	choice	Harriet couldn't decide *whether* to study *or* to go out.

Sentence Completion

In Sentence Completion items, either a coordinate conjunction is missing or one of the pair of correlative conjunctions is missing.

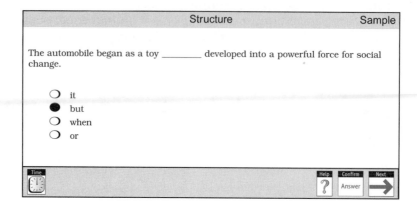

There is a contrast in this sentence; the role of the automobile as a toy in its early days is contrasted with its later role as a force for social change. The only word among the four choices that indicates contrast is the second choice, *but.*

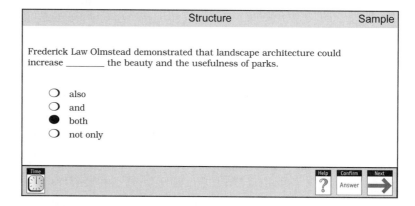

The correct structure for this sentence is *both . . . and.* The first three choices do not follow this pattern. (In the fourth choice, *not only* must be paired with *but also* to be correct.)

       Conjunctive adverbs (*moreover, therefore, however, nevertheless,* and so on) are also used to join clauses, but in Sentence Completion problems, these words are most often used as distractors—they seldom appear as correct answers.

Error Identification

There are two types of errors involving conjunctions:

A) ERRORS WITH CORRELATIVE CONJUNCTIONS

Errors usually involve an incorrect combination of the two parts, such as *neither . . . or* or *not only . . . and.* Anytime you see a sentence containing correlative conjunctions you should be on the lookout for this type of error. This is an easy error to spot!

       Another error is the use of *both . . . and* to join three elements.

SAMPLE ITEMS

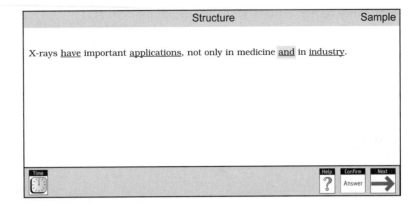

The correct pattern is *not only . . . but also.*

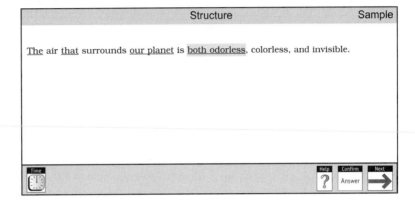

Because *both . . . and* can only be used to join two elements, the word *both* must be eliminated to correct the sentence.

B) ERRORS WITH COORDINATE CONJUNCTIONS

This type of item usually involves the confusion of *and, or,* or *but.*

SAMPLE ITEM

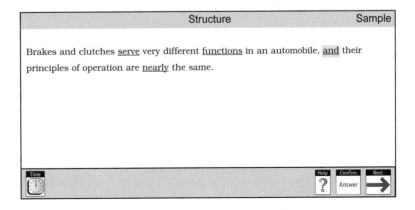

The first clause discusses how brakes and clutches are different; the second clause discusses how they are the same. Therefore, the conjunction joining them must show contrast. The third underlined expression should read *but*.

EXERCISE 28

Focus: Structure problems involving conjunctions. (Note: Several items in this exercise do NOT focus on conjunctions. These are marked in the answer key with asterisks.)

Directions: For Sentence Completion items, mark the oval next to the answer choice that correctly completes the sentence. For Error Identification items, put an *X* under the underlined portion of the sentence that would not be considered correct.

1. Model airplanes <u>can be</u> guided <u>both</u> by <u>control wires</u> or <u>by</u> radio transmitters.

2. Specialty stores, unlike department stores, handle only one line of merchandise _____ a limited number of closely related lines.
   - ○ either
   - ○ but
   - ○ instead
   - ○ or

3. Thomas Eakins studied not only painting _____ anatomy when he was training to become an artist.
   - ○ moreover
   - ○ but also
   - ○ as well
   - ○ and

4. <u>Information</u> in a computer can be lost <u>because</u> it is <u>not longer</u> stored <u>or</u> because it is stored <u>but</u> cannot be retrieved.

5. A mosaic is a <u>picture</u> <u>done</u> from small bits of <u>either</u> <u>colored</u> glass or tile.

6. Although topology is the youngest branch of geometry, _____ is considered the most sophisticated.
   - ○ but it
   - ○ so it
   - ○ it
   - ○ however it

7. John Lancaster Spaulding <u>was</u> not only a <u>religious</u> leader <u>and also</u> a social <u>reformer</u>.

8. In 1923 Jean Toomer wrote a book titled *Cane* which combined fiction _____ poetry to describe the experience of being black in the United States.
   - ○ and
   - ○ to
   - ○ also
   - ○ or

9. <u>Although</u> fish can hear, <u>they</u> have neither <u>external</u> ears <u>or</u> eardrums.

10. In <u>all</u> animals, whether simple <u>and</u> complex, enzymes aid in the <u>digestion</u> of <u>food</u>.

11. Endive can be used _____ as a salad green or as a cooking vegetable.

    ○ such
    ○ both
    ○ either
    ○ neither

12. <u>The two most</u> common methods florists <u>are used to</u> tint flowers are the spray method <u>and</u> the <u>absorption</u> method.

13. Beekeepers <u>can</u> sell <u>both</u> the honey and the beeswax that <u>their</u> bees <u>produces</u>.

14. Glucose does not have to be digested, _____ it can be put directly into the bloodstream.

    ○ so
    ○ while
    ○ and since
    ○ such

15. The human brain is <u>often</u> compared to a computer, <u>and</u> such <u>an analogy</u> can be <u>misleading</u>.

16. Not only <u>rust corrodes</u> the <u>surface</u> of metal, <u>but it also</u> weakens its internal <u>structure</u>.

17. Natural fiber comes from either animal _____ plant sources.

    ○ or
    ○ otherwise
    ○ and
    ○ nor

18. A work of science fiction <u>generally</u> uses scientific <u>discoveries</u> and advanced technology, either real <u>or</u> imaginary, as part of <u>their</u> plot.

19. Community theater not only provides <u>entertainment</u> for local audiences <u>as well as</u> furnishes a <u>creative</u> outlet <u>for</u> amateurs interested in drama.

20. Paint is _____ used to protect wood.

    ○ not only the substance
    ○ the substance which is not only
    ○ not only a substance which is
    ○ not the only substance

21. Designing fabrics <u>require</u> not only <u>artistic</u> talent <u>but also</u> a knowledge of fiber <u>and</u> of textile machinery.

22. When acoustic engineers design a factory, their goal is to suppress sound,

    _____ they design a concert hall, their goal is to transmit sound faithfully.

    ○ or when

    ○ and so

    ○ but when

    ○ when

23. The heron is a long-legged wading bird that preys on both frogs, fish, and eels.

24. Demographers believe most metropolitan areas will continue to grow in _____

    population and area in the future.

    ○ moreover

    ○ both

    ○ together

    ○ besides

25. Most crustaceans live in the sea, _____ some live in fresh water, and a few

    have ventured onto land.

    ○ both

    ○ also

    ○ but

    ○ and

LESSON 29: Comparisons

You may see sentences involving **comparisons** in both types of Structure items. Many of these involve the comparative or superlative forms of adjectives.

Most adjectives have three forms: the **absolute** (the basic adjective form), the **comparative**, and the **superlative**. Comparatives are used to show that one item has more of some quality than another does. The comparative adjective is often followed by the word *than*.

George is *taller than* his brother.

Superlatives are used to show that one item in a group of three or more has the greatest amount of some quality.

He was the *tallest* man in the room.

The chart explains how comparatives and superlatives are formed:

	Absolute	Comparative	Superlative
One-syllable adjectives	warm	warmer than	the warmest
Two-syllable adjectives ending with *-y*	funny	funnier than	the funniest
Other two-syllable adjectives	common	more common than	the most common
Adjectives with three or more syllables	important	more important than	the most important

Some two-syllable adjectives have two correct forms of both the comparative and the superlative:

simpler *or*	narrower *or*	cleverer *or*	politer *or*
more simple	more narrow	more clever	more polite
simplest *or*	narrowest *or*	cleverest *or*	politest *or*
most simple	most narrow	most clever	most polite

A "negative" comparison can be expressed with the words *less* and *least*. *Less* and *least* are used no matter how many syllables an adjective has.

less bright than	less expensive than
the least bright	the least expensive

The absolute form of a few adjectives ends in *-er* (*tender, bitter, slender, clever,* and so on). Don't confuse these with the comparative forms (both *more tender* and *tenderer* are considered correct forms of the comparative).

Many adverbs also have comparative and superlative forms. The comparative and superlative forms of all *-ly* adverbs are formed with *more* and *most*.

more brightly	more importantly
most brightly	most importantly

A few adjectives and adverbs have irregular comparative and superlative forms:

Irregular Comparatives and Superlatives		
good/well	better than	the best
bad/badly	worse than	the worst
far	farther than	the farthest
	further than	the furthest

(*Far* has two comparative and superlative forms, depending on how the word is used, but the distinction between these two forms will not be tested.)

Be sure that a sentence compares similar things or concepts.

> **The ears of African elephants are bigger than Indian elephants.*   (INCORRECT)
>
> *The ears of African elephants are bigger than those of Indian elephants.* (CORRECT)

The first sentence above is incorrect because it compares two dissimilar things: an African elephant's ears and an Indian elephant. In the second, the word *those* refers to ears, so the comparison is between similar things.

Another type of comparison involves the phrase *as . . . as*.

> The lab lasted *as long as* the class did.
>
> There weren't as *many people at the meeting as* I had thought there would be.

The words *like/alike* and *unlike/not alike* can be used to express similarity or difference. These words are usually used in these patterns:

Like A, B . . .	Unlike X, Y . . .
A, like B, . . .	X, unlike Y, . . .
A is like B.	X is unlike Y.
A and B are alike.	X and Y are not alike.

> *Like birds, mammals* are warm-blooded.
>
> *Birds, like mammals,* are warm-blooded.
>
> *Birds are like mammals* in that they are both warm-blooded.
>
> *Birds and mammals are alike* in that they are both warm-blooded.

The word *like* is sometimes confused with the word *as*. When *like* is used, it is followed by a noun or pronoun. *As* is used to introduce a clause containing a subject and a verb.

> I did my experiment just *as* Paul did his.
>
> My results were much *like* Paul's.

Other phrases can be used to show similarity and difference:

A is the same as B	X is different from Y
A and B are the same	X and Y are different
A is similar to B	X differs from Y

A special kind of comparison is called a **proportional statement.** A proportional statement follows this pattern: *The more A, the more B.*

> *The higher* the humidity, *the more uncomfortable* people feel.

Sentence Completion

The most common type of Sentence Completion item involves a missing comparative adjective phrase. The verb may also be missing from the sentence.

You may see sentences that involve the use of *like/alike* or *unlike* or other expressions that show similarity or difference. Still other sentences involve proportional statements.

SAMPLE ITEMS

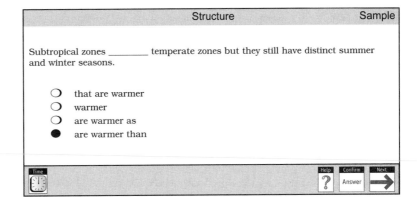

The first choice creates a relative clause, which is not appropriate in this sentence; also, the choice lacks the word *than*. The second choice lacks both a verb and the word *than*. The third choice incorrectly uses *as* in place of *than*.

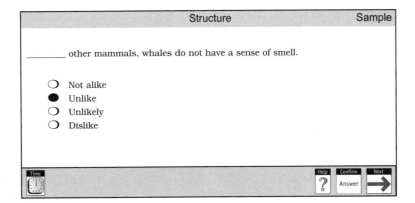

The first choice is used only in the pattern, "A and B are not alike." The third and fourth choices are not used in comparisons (*unlikely* is an adjective meaning "not probable;" *dislike* is a verb meaning "not enjoy, not admire"). The second choice is best.

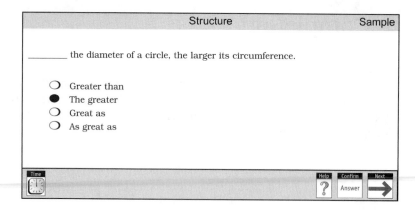

_____ the diameter of a circle, the larger its circumference.

- ○ Greater than
- ● The greater
- ○ Great as
- ○ As great as

The correct pattern for a proportional statement is *the more A, the more B*. Only the second choice follows this pattern.

Error Identification

There are three common types of errors involving comparisons:

A) INCORRECT CHOICE OF THE THREE ADJECTIVE FORMS

Any of the three forms—absolute, comparative, or superlative—may be incorrectly used in place of one of the other forms.

SAMPLE ITEMS

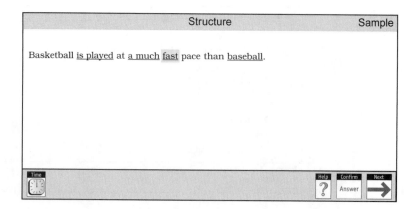

Basketball <u>is played</u> at <u>a much</u> <u>fast</u> pace than <u>baseball</u>.

The comparative form *faster* is needed because two concepts—the pace of basketball and the pace of baseball—are being compared.

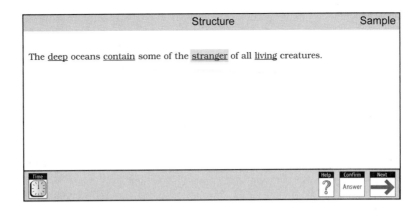

This sentence does not compare two groups; a superlative form (*strangest*) is required.

B) INCORRECT FORMS OF COMPARATIVES AND SUPERLATIVES

Forms such as *more bigger, most hot, beautifulest,* and so on may appear.

SAMPLE ITEM

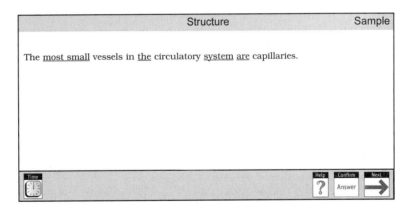

The correct form is <u>smallest</u> because <u>small</u> is a one-syllable adjective.

C) WRONG CHOICE OF *LIKE/ALIKE* AND *LIKE/AS*

The word *alike* is incorrectly used in patterns where *like* should be used or *like* is used in patterns where *alike* is correct.

The word *like* is also sometimes confused with the word *as*. Remember: for comparisons, *like* is followed by a noun or pronoun but *as* is followed by a clause. (The word *as* is also used after certain verbs: *classify as, serve as, identify as, regard as, use as, be known as,* and others.)

SAMPLE ITEMS

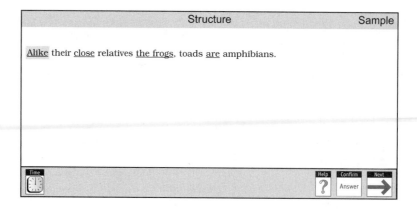

The first underlined choice doesn't follow the correct pattern: *Like A, B* . . .

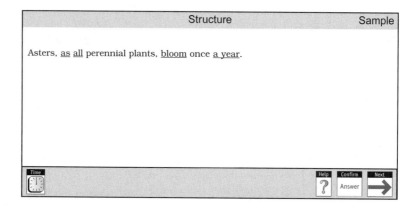

Before a noun phrase (*all perennial plants*), *like* should be used instead of *as*.

EXERCISE 29

Focus: Structure problems involving comparisons. (Note: Several items in this exercise do NOT focus on comparison. These are marked in the answer key with asterisks.)

Directions: For Sentence Completion items, mark the oval next to the answer choice that correctly completes the sentence. For Error Identification items, put an *X* under the underlined portion of the sentence that would not be considered correct.

1. The American and Canadian political <u>systems</u> are <u>like</u> in that <u>both</u> are <u>dominated</u> by two major parties.

2. Wild strawberries are _____ cultivated strawberries.
   - ○ not sweeter
   - ○ not as sweet as
   - ○ less sweeter than
   - ○ not sweet as

3. The period is probably the most easiest punctuation mark to use.

4. When metal replaced wood in the construction of ships' hulls, more strong ships could be built.

5. Sea bass _____ freshwater bass.
   - ○ are larger than
   - ○ the larger the
   - ○ are as large
   - ○ than are larger

6. Charcoal is the more commonly used cooking fuel in the world.

7. Automobiles, airplanes, and buses use more energy per passenger _____.
   - ○ as do trains
   - ○ than trains do
   - ○ trains do
   - ○ like trains

8. Few American politicians have spoken more eloquently as William Jennings Bryan.

9. The larger a drop of water, _____ freezing temperature.
   - ○ the higher its
   - ○ its higher
   - ○ higher than its
   - ○ the highest

10. _____ San Diego and San Francisco, Los Angeles has no natural harbor.
    - ○ Dissimilar
    - ○ Unlike
    - ○ Dislike
    - ○ Different

11. During a depression, economic conditions are far worst than they are during a recession.

12. The spinal column is alike the brain in that its main functions can be classified as either sensory or motor functions.

13. The water of the Great Salt Lake is _____ seawater.
    - ○ saltier than that of
    - ○ as salty as that of
    - ○ saltier than
    - ○ so salty as

14. Fungi are the most important decomposers of forest soil, just like bacteria are the most important decomposers of grassland soil.

15. A psychosis is a severe mental disorder, _____ a neurosis.

    ○ the most serious
    ○ as serious
    ○ more serious than
    ○ as though serious

16. The surfboards <u>used</u> thirty-five years <u>ago</u> were <u>more heavy</u> than <u>the ones</u> used by surfers today.

17. <u>The</u> horse chestnut has a <u>stronger</u>, <u>bitter</u> taste than <u>other</u> chestnuts.

18. The social system of bumblebees is not as complex _____.

    ○ than honeybees
    ○ as honeybees
    ○ that honeybees are
    ○ as that of honeybees

19. Chicago's Field Museum <u>is one</u> of <u>the largest</u> and <u>better known</u> natural history museums <u>in the</u> United States.

20. The administration of private colleges is nearly _____ that of public colleges.

    ○ same
    ○ just as
    ○ the same as
    ○ similar

21. <u>Of Canada's ten</u> provinces, Prince Edward Island <u>is</u> the <u>less</u> <u>populous</u>.

22. One of <u>the most basic</u> American <u>contribution</u> to technology <u>was</u> the <u>so-called</u> "American system" of interchangeable machine parts.

23. The cello <u>is</u> <u>shorter</u> and <u>slender</u> <u>than the</u> double bass.

24. <u>The</u> finback whale is <u>the fastest</u> of all whales, <u>and only</u> the blue whale is <u>largest</u>.

25. A butterfly _____ a moth in a number of ways.

    ○ is different
    ○ different from
    ○ the difference is
    ○ differs from

LESSON 30: Appositives

This point is only tested in Sentence Completion items.

An **appositive** is a noun phrase that explains or rephrases another noun phrase. It usually comes after the noun which it rephrases. It may also come before the subject of a sentence.

> Buffalo Bill, *a famous frontiersman,* operated his own Wild West Show. (appositive following a noun)

> *A famous frontiersman,* Buffalo Bill operated his own Wild West Show. (appositive before the subject)

Appositives are actually reduced adjective clauses that contain the verb *to be.* However, unlike adjective clauses, they do not contain a marker or a verb.

> Oak, *which is one of the most durable hardwoods,* is often used to make furniture. (adjective clause)

> Oak, *one of the most durable hardwoods,* is often used to make furniture. (appositive)

Appositives are usually separated from the rest of the sentence by commas, but short appositives (usually names) are not.

> Economist *Paul Samuelson* won a Nobel Prize in 1970.

In Structure items, all or part of an appositive phrase may be missing. In addition, the noun that the appositive refers to or other parts of the main clause may be missing.

SAMPLE ITEM

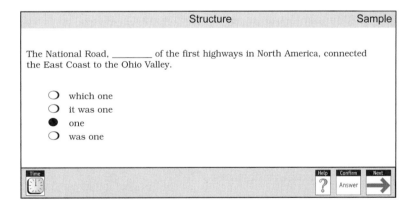

The first choice is incorrect; there is no verb in the relative clause. The second choice has no connecting word to join the clause to the rest of the sentence. The fourth choice is incorrect because a verb cannot be used in an appositive phrase. The third choice is best.
Note: *which was one* would also be a correct answer for this problem.

EXERCISE 30

Focus: Structure problems involving appositives. (Note: Several items in this exercise do NOT focus on appositives. These are marked in the answer key with asterisks.)

Directions: Choose the one option that correctly completes each sentence, then mark the appropriate oval.

1. The Democratic Party is older than the other major American political party,
    _____.

    ○   which the Republican party
    ○   the Republican party
    ○   it is the Republican party
    ○   the Republican party is

2. _____ relations with friends and acquaintances, play a major role in the
    social development of adolescents.

    ○   What are called peer group relations are
    ○   Peer group relations are
    ○   Peer group relations, the
    ○   By peer group relations, we mean

3. Joseph Henry, _____ director of the Smithsonian Institute, was President
    Lincoln's advisor on scientific matters.

    ○   the first
    ○   to be the first
    ○   was the first
    ○   as the first

4. The Wasatch Range, _____ extends from southeastern Idaho into northern
    Utah.

    ○   which is a part of the Rocky Mountains,
    ○   a part of the Rocky Mountains that
    ○   is a part of the Rocky Mountains
    ○   a part of the Rocky Mountains, it

5. _____ Ruth St. Denis turned to Asian dances to find inspiration for her
    choreography.

    ○   It was the dancer
    ○   The dancer
    ○   That the dancer
    ○   The dancer was

6. _____ a vast network of computers that connects many of the world's
    businesses, institutions, and individuals, primarily through modems and phone
    lines.

    ○   The Internet,
    ○   That the Internet, as
    ○   The Internet is
    ○   The Internet, which

7. In 1878 Frederick W. Taylor invented a concept called scientific management, _____ of obtaining as much efficiency from workers and machines as possible.

   ○ it is a method
   ○ a method which
   ○ a method
   ○ called a method

8. A group of Shakers, _____ settled around Pleasant Hill, Kentucky in 1805.

   ○ members of a strict religious sect who
   ○ whose members of a strict religious sect
   ○ members of a strict religious sect,
   ○ were members of a strict religious sect

9. In physics, _____ "plasma" refers to a gas which has a nearly equal number of positively and negatively charged particles.

   ○ the term
   ○ by the term
   ○ is termed
   ○ terming

10. Norbert Wiener, _____ mathematician and logician, had an important role in the development of the computer.

   ○ who, as a
   ○ was both a
   ○ whom a
   ○ a

11. Vanilla, _____ is grown chiefly for its seedpod, which yields a flavoring extract.

   ○ a tropical plant of the orchid family that
   ○ a tropical plant of the orchid family,
   ○ it is a tropical plant of the orchid family that
   ○ as a tropical plant of the orchid family

12. The organs of taste are the _____ which are mainly located on the tongue.

   ○ groups of cells, are taste buds
   ○ taste buds, are groups of cells
   ○ taste buds, these are groups of cells
   ○ taste buds, groups of cells

LESSON 31: Misplaced Modifiers

Misplaced modifiers are tested only in Sentence Completion items.

A **misplaced modifier** is a participial phrase or other modifier that comes before the subject, but does not refer to the subject. Look at this sentence:

> *Driving down the road, a herd of sheep suddenly blocked the road in front of Liza's car. (INCORRECT)

This sentence is incorrect because it seems to say that a herd of sheep—rather than Liza—was driving down the road. Sheep, of course, don't have driver's licenses. The participial phrase is misplaced. The sentence could be corrected this way:

> As Liza was driving down the road, a herd of sheep suddenly blocked the road in front of her.   (CORRECT)

This sentence now correctly has Liza in the driver's seat instead of the sheep. The following sentence structures are often misplaced:

Misplaced Structure	Example	Correction
present participle	Walking along the beach, the whale was spotted by the men.	Walking along the beach, the men spotted the whale.
past participle	Believed to be over 9,000 years old, archaeologists recently found the oldest known piece of cloth.	Archaeologists recently found the oldest known piece of cloth, believed to be over 9,000 years old.
appositive	A resort city in Arkansas, the population of Hot Springs is about 35,000.	A resort city in Arkansas, Hot Springs has a population of about 35,000.
reduced adverb clause	While peeling onions, the chef's eyes began to water.	While he was peeling onions, the chef's eyes began to water.
adjective phrases	Warm and mild, everyone enjoys the climate of the Virgin Islands.	Everyone enjoys the warm, mild climate of the Virgin Islands.
expressions with *like* or *unlike*	Like most cities, parking is a problem in San Francisco.	Like most cities, San Francisco has a parking problem.

Structure items with misplaced modifiers are usually easy to spot. They typically consist of a modifying element at the beginning of the sentence followed by a comma, with the rest or most of the rest of the sentence missing. The answer choices tend to be long. To find the answer, you must decide which subject the modifier correctly refers to.

SAMPLE ITEM

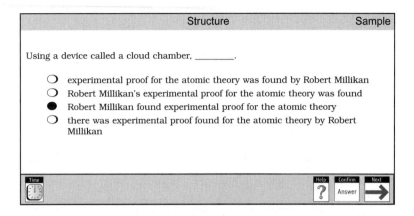

Structure	Sample

Using a device called a cloud chamber, _____.

○ experimental proof for the atomic theory was found by Robert Millikan
○ Robert Millikan's experimental proof for the atomic theory was found
● Robert Millikan found experimental proof for the atomic theory
○ there was experimental proof found for the atomic theory by Robert Millikan

The first and second choices are incorrect because the modifier (*Using a device called a cloud chamber . . .*) could not logically refer to the subjects (*experimental proof* and *Robert Millikan's experimental proof*). The fourth choice is incorrect because a modifier can never properly refer to the introductory words *there* or *it.*

EXERCISE 31

Focus: Structure problems involving misplaced modifiers. (Note: ALL the items in this exercise focus on misplaced modifiers.)

Directions: Choose the one option that correctly completes the sentences, then mark the appropriate oval.

1. Fearing economic hardship, _____.

   ○ many New Englanders emigrated to the Midwest in the 1820s

   ○ emigration from New England to the Midwest took place in the 1820s

   ○ it was in the 1820s that many New Englanders emigrated to the Midwest

   ○ an emigration took place in the 1820s from New England to the Midwest

2. Rich and distinctive in flavor, _____.

   ○ there is in the southern United States a very important nut crop, the pecan

   ○ the most important nut crop in the southern United States, the pecan

   ○ farmers in the southern United States raise pecans, a very important nut crop

   ○ pecans are the most important nut crop in the southern United States

3. Orbiting from 2.7 to 3.6 billion miles from the Sun, _____.

   ○ the astronomer Clyde Tombaugh discovered Pluto in 1930

   ○ Pluto was discovered by the astronomer Clyde Tombaugh in 1930

   ○ it was in 1930 that the astronomer Clyde Tombaugh discovered Pluto

   ○ the discovery of Pluto was made by Clyde Tombaugh in 1930

4. A popular instrument, _____.

   ○ only a limited role has been available to the accordion in classical music

   ○ there is only a limited role for the accordion in classical music

   ○ classical music provides only a limited role for the accordion

   ○ the accordion has played only a limited role in classical music

5. Unlike most birds, _____.

   ○ the heads and necks of vultures lack feathers

   ○ feathers are not found on the heads and necks of vultures

   ○ vultures do not have feathers on their heads and necks

   ○ there are no feathers on vultures' heads and necks

6. Widely reproduced in magazines and books, _____.

   ○ Ansel Adams depicted the Western wilderness in his photographs

   ○ the Western wilderness was depicted in the photographs of Ansel Adams

   ○ Ansel Adams' photographs depicted the Western wilderness

   ○ it was through his photographs that Ansel Adams depicted the Western wilderness

7. Smaller and flatter than an orange, _____.

   ○ a tangerine is easy to peel and its sections separate readily

   ○ the peel of a tangerine is easily removed and its sections are readily separated

   ○ it's easy to peel a tangerine and to separate its sections

   ○ to peel a tangerine is easy, and its sections can be readily separated

8. Like the federal government, _____.

   ○ taxation provides most of the funds for state and local governments as well

   ○ state and local governments obtain most of their funds through taxation

   ○ through taxation is how state and local governments obtain most of their funds

   ○ funds are provided from taxation for state and local governments

9. Originally settled by Polynesians around 700 AD, _____.

   ○ Hawaii received its first European visitor in 1778, when Captain James Cook landed there

   ○ Hawaii's first European visitor, Captain James Cook, landed there in 1778

   ○ in 1778 the first European, Captain James Cook, visited Hawaii

   ○ the first European to visit Hawaii was Captain James Cook, landing there in 1778

10. Unlike most modernist poets, _____ based on ordinary speech.

    ○ Robert Frost's poems were

    ○ the works of Robert Frost were

    ○ Robert Frost wrote poems that were

    ○ the poetry written by Robert Frost was

11. Named for its founder, _____ in Ithaca, New York.

   ○ in 1865 Ezra Cornell established Cornell University

   ○ Cornell University was established in 1865 by Ezra Cornell

   ○ it was in 1865 that Cornell University was established by Ezra Cornell

   ○ Ezra Cornell established Cornell University in 1865

12. While living in New Orleans, _____ the Creole people of Louisiana.

   ○ a book of folklore, *Bayou Folk,* was written by Kate Chopin about

   ○ *Bayou Folk,* a book of folklore, was written by Kate Chopin about

   ○ the subject of Kate Chopin's book *Bayou Folk* was the folklore of

   ○ Kate Chopin wrote *Bayou Folk,* a book about the folklore of

LESSON 32: Negatives

Problems with negative words are seen in both types of Structure items.

The following **negative words** are commonly seen in answer choices in this type of problem:

Negative Word	Use	Meaning	Example
no	adjective	not any	There was *no* milk in the refrigerator.
none	pronoun	not one	They took a lot of pictures, but almost *none* of them turned out.
nothing	pronoun	not anything	There was *nothing* in Mr. Lamonde's briefcase.
no one	pronoun	not anyone	*No one* arrived at the meeting on time.
nor	conjunction	and . . . not	He's never been fishing, *nor* does he plan to go.
without	preposition	not having	Sue likes her coffee *without* milk or sugar.
never	adverb	at no time	I've *never* been to Alaska.

The negative word *not* is used to make almost any kind of word or phrase negative: verbs, prepositional phrases, infinitives, adjectives, and so on.

Both *no* and *not* can be used before nouns, depending on meaning.

> There is *no* coffee in the pot. (It's empty.)
>
> This is *not* coffee. (It's tea.)

The adjective *no* is also used before the word *longer* to mean "not anymore."

> I *no longer* read the afternoon paper.

Sentence Correction

The four answer choices in this type of item are usually all negative words.

SAMPLE ITEM

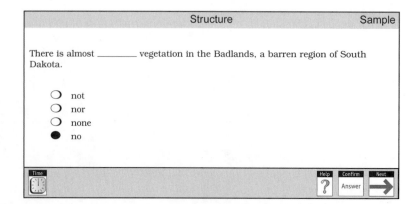

The first, second, and third choices cannot be used before nouns as adjectives.

Error Identification

The most common type of Error Identification item involving negatives is the incorrect use of *no* for *not* or *not* for *no*.

SAMPLE ITEM

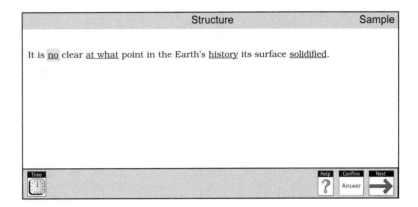

The word *not* should be used before an adjective.

EXERCISE 32

Focus: Structure problems involving negative words. (Note: Several items in this exercise do NOT focus on negative words. These are marked in the answer key with asterisks.)

Directions: For Sentence Completion items, mark the oval next to the answer choice that correctly completes the sentence. For Error Identification items, put an X under the underlined portion of the sentence that would not be considered correct.

1. Early carpenters, having _____ nails, had to use wooden pegs to secure their constructions.

    ○ no

    ○ not

    ○ without

    ○ neither

2. Old Faithful is the most famous but _____ the most powerful geyser in Yellowstone National Park.

    ○ none of

    ○ no

    ○ nothing

    ○ not

3. Joseph Priestly, the <u>discoverer</u> of oxygen, had little or <u>not</u> interest in <u>science</u> until he <u>met</u> Benjamin Franklin in Paris.

4. Mobile homes were _____ counted as permanent houses until the 1960 census.

   ○ not

   ○ nor

   ○ no

   ○ none

5. Most solo musicians play _____ sheet music in front of them.

   ○ without

   ○ not having

   ○ lacking

   ○ none of

6. Desertification is the creation of deserts where _____ had existed before.

   ○ never

   ○ no one

   ○ none

   ○ not one

7. A peanut is <u>not</u> actually a nut <u>but</u> a legume <u>alike</u> peas <u>and</u> beans.

8. Glass snakes are actually legless lizards, _____ snakes.

   ○ no

   ○ not

   ○ nor

   ○ none

9. Twenty-four carat gold is <u>no</u> one hundred <u>percent</u> gold because <u>pure gold</u> is <u>too soft</u> to be used in jewelry.

10. There is _____ truth to the old expression, "Lightning never strikes the same place twice."

    ○ without

    ○ none

    ○ no

    ○ not

11. _____ single person can be said to have invented the computer.

    ○ There was not a

    ○ Never a

    ○ Not one of

    ○ No

12. A serious study of physics is impossible _____ a knowledge of mathematics.

   ○ not with
   ○ no
   ○ not having
   ○ without

13. Not two fingerprints have ever been found to be exactly the same.

14. One of the few stands of forest on the East Coast of the United States that has _____ been harvested is Hutcheson Forest in New Jersey.

   ○ no
   ○ never
   ○ none
   ○ nothing

15. Until the 1960s, customers could open small savings accounts at U.S. post offices, but that service is _____ offered.

   ○ no longer
   ○ not longer
   ○ no long
   ○ not along

REVIEW TEST G: Structure

Directions: For Sentence Completion items, mark the oval next to the answer choice that correctly completes the sentence. For Error Identification items, put an *X* under the underlined portion of the sentence that would not be considered correct.

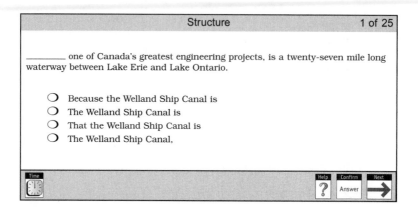

_____ one of Canada's greatest engineering projects, is a twenty-seven mile long waterway between Lake Erie and Lake Ontario.

- ○ Because the Welland Ship Canal is
- ○ The Welland Ship Canal is
- ○ That the Welland Ship Canal is
- ○ The Welland Ship Canal,

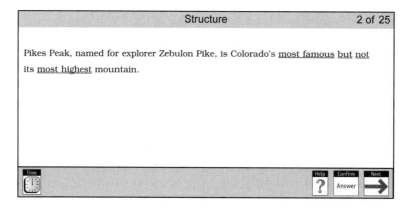

Pikes Peak, named for explorer Zebulon Pike, is Colorado's <u>most famous</u> <u>but</u> <u>not</u> its <u>most highest</u> mountain.

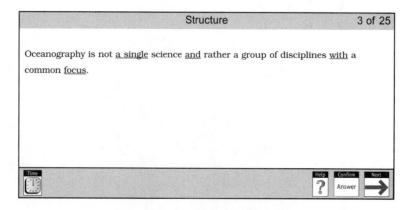

Oceanography is not <u>a single</u> science <u>and</u> rather a group of disciplines <u>with</u> a common <u>focus</u>.

The art of landscape architecture is _____ that of architecture itself.

- ○ almost as old as
- ○ as almost old
- ○ almost as old than
- ○ old as almost

The term *forgetting* refers <u>to</u> the loss, whether temporary <u>and</u> long-term, of material <u>that</u> has previously been <u>learned</u>.

Early astronomers believed that the fainter a star, _____.

- ○ it was farther away
- ○ the farther away was it
- ○ that it was farther away
- ○ the farther away it was

Released in 1915, _____.

- ○ D. W. Griffith made an epic film about the Civil War, *Birth of a Nation*
- ○ the Civil War was the subject of D. W. Griffith's epic film, *Birth of a Nation*
- ○ D. W. Griffith's epic film *Birth of a Nation* was about the Civil War
- ○ the subject of D. W. Griffith's epic film *Birth of a Nation* was the Civil War

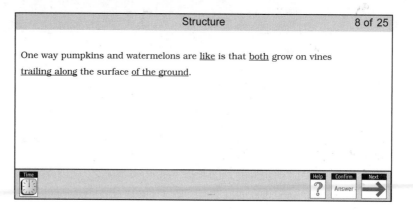

One way pumpkins and watermelons are <u>like</u> is that <u>both</u> grow on vines <u>trailing along</u> the surface <u>of the ground</u>.

Time   Help ?   Confirm Answer   Next →

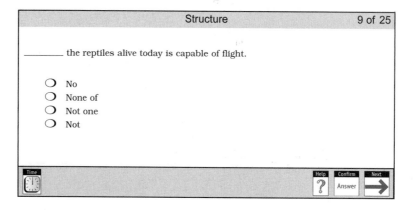

_____ the reptiles alive today is capable of flight.

- ○ No
- ○ None of
- ○ Not one
- ○ Not

Time   Help ?   Confirm Answer   Next →

<u>When</u> the female oriole is <u>absent from</u> the nest, <u>the male</u> oriole serves <u>like</u> a sentinel.

Time   Help ?   Confirm Answer   Next →

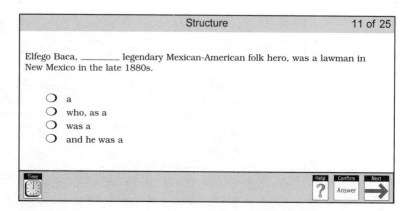

Elfego Baca, _____ legendary Mexican-American folk hero, was a lawman in New Mexico in the late 1880s.

- ○ a
- ○ who, as a
- ○ was a
- ○ and he was a

Time   Help ?   Confirm Answer   Next →

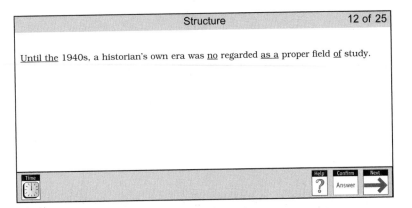

<u>Until the</u> 1940s, a historian's own era was <u>no</u> regarded <u>as a</u> proper field <u>of</u> study.

Time   Help ?   Confirm Answer   Next →

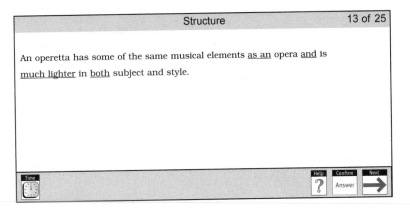

An operetta has some of the same musical elements <u>as an</u> opera <u>and</u> is <u>much lighter</u> in <u>both</u> subject and style.

Time   Help ?   Confirm Answer   Next →

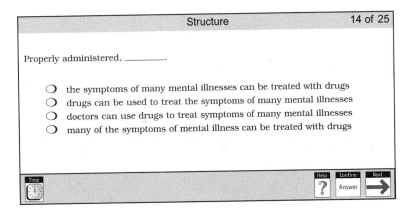

Properly administered, _____.

- ○ the symptoms of many mental illnesses can be treated with drugs
- ○ drugs can be used to treat the symptoms of many mental illnesses
- ○ doctors can use drugs to treat symptoms of many mental illnesses
- ○ many of the symptoms of mental illness can be treated with drugs

Time   Help ?   Confirm Answer   Next →

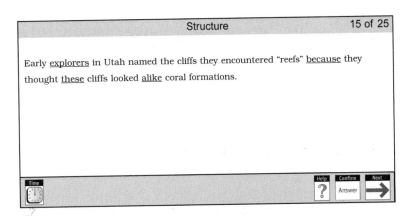

Early <u>explorers</u> in Utah named the cliffs they encountered "reefs" <u>because</u> they thought <u>these</u> cliffs looked <u>alike</u> coral formations.

Time   Help ?   Confirm Answer   Next →

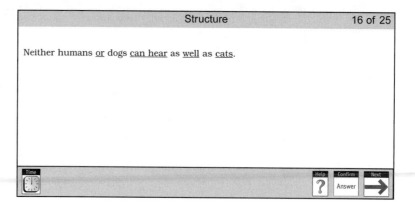

Neither humans <u>or</u> dogs <u>can hear</u> as <u>well</u> as <u>cats</u>.

Time

Help ? Confirm Answer Next →

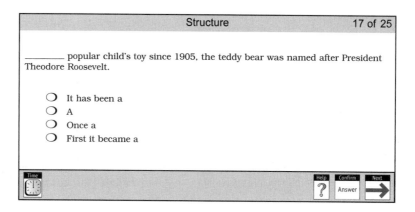

_____ popular child's toy since 1905, the teddy bear was named after President Theodore Roosevelt.

○ It has been a
○ A
○ Once a
○ First it became a

Time

Help ? Confirm Answer Next →

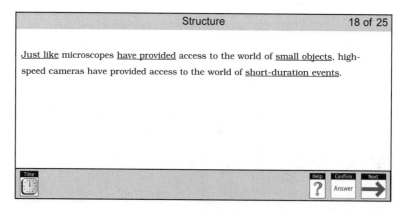

<u>Just like</u> microscopes <u>have provided</u> access to the world of <u>small objects</u>, high-speed cameras have provided access to the world of <u>short-duration events</u>.

Time

Help ? Confirm Answer Next →

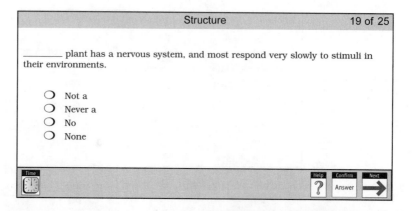

_____ plant has a nervous system, and most respond very slowly to stimuli in their environments.

○ Not a
○ Never a
○ No
○ None

Time

Help ? Confirm Answer Next →

Gold topaz is <u>much rare</u> <u>than</u> <u>either</u> white or <u>blue</u> topaz.

Vermont is the only state in New England _____ an Atlantic coastline.

- ○ without
- ○ not with
- ○ which not having
- ○ doesn't have

The Colorado beetle is a beautiful insect, _____ it causes a great deal of damage to food crops.

- ○ but
- ○ what
- ○ or
- ○ which

Jupiter's moons can be easily seen through _____ binoculars or a small telescope.

- ○ either
- ○ if
- ○ whether
- ○ or

The Kennedy-Nixon race <u>of 1960</u> was the <u>most closest</u> U.S. <u>presidential</u> election of <u>the</u> twentieth century.

Time | Help ? | Confirm Answer | Next →

_____ a river on land, an ocean current does not flow in a straight line.

○ Alike
○ Likewise
○ Like
○ Likely

Time | Help ? | Confirm Answer | Next →

MINI-LESSONS FOR SECTION 2:
Preposition Use

It is important for the Structure section that you know the correct usage of prepositions.

Adjective/Participle + Prepositions

acceptable to	divided into	opposed to
accustomed to	disappointed in/with	opposite of
acquainted with	eligible for	perfect for
adequate for	equal to	pleased with
afraid of	equipped with	possible for
associated with	essential to/for	preferable to
aware of	expert at	related to
based on	familiar with	relevant to
capable of	famous for	responsible for
characteristic of	free of	rich in
close to	independent of/from	safe from
composed of	inferior to	satisfied with
concerned with	married to	suitable for
contrary to	native to	suprised at/by
dependent on	necessary for	typical of
different from	next to	

Noun + Prepositions

approach to	example of	origin of
attention to	exception to	price of
basis for	experience with	probability of
cause of	expert on	problem with
combination of	form of	process of
component of	group of	quality of
concept of	idea for	reason for
contribution to	improvement in	reference to
cure for	increase in	reliance on
danger of	influence on	result of
decrease in	interest in	solution to
demand for	native of	supply of
effect of/on*	need for	variety of

*effect + of + cause
effect + on + thing or person affected
(The effect of heat on rocks . . .)

Verb + Prepositions

account for	attribute to	compete with
adjust to	begin with	concentrate on
agree with/on*	believe in	consist of
approve of	belong to	contribute to
attach to	combine with	cooperate with

deal with	insist on	rely on
decide on	interfere with	replace with
depend on	participate in	result in
detach from	plan on	search for
devote to	react to	substitute for
emerge from	refer to	withdraw from
engage in		

*agree with is usually used with people
agree on is usually used with an issue, plan, etc.
(I agreed with Maria.
The committee agreed on a plan of action.)

Phrasal Prepositions

according to	in addition to	instead of
ahead of	in case of	on account of
along with	in contrast to	prior to
because of	in favor of	regardless of
due to	in regards to	thanks to
except for	in spite of	together with
for the sake of	in the process of	

In, On, and At

Expressions of time

in
- \+ century (*in the eighteenth century*)
- \+ decade (*in the 1960s*)
- \+ year (*in 2001*)
- \+ season (*in the summer*)
- \+ month (*in July*)
- \+ parts of the day (*in the morning, in the evening, in the afternoon*)

on
- \+ days of the week (*on Wednesday*)
- \+ dates (*on October 7*)

at
- \+ time of day (*at 6 P.M.; at noon*)
- \+ night

Expressions of place

in
- \+ continent (*in Africa*)
- \+ country (*in Mexico*)
- \+ state (*in Pennsylvania*)
- \+ city (*in Los Angeles*)
- \+ building (*in the bank*)
- \+ room (*in the auditorium*)
- \+ *the world*

on
- \+ street (*on Maxwell Street*)
- \+ floor of a building (*on the fourth floor*)
- \+ *Earth*

at   +   address (*at 123 Commonwealth Avenue*)

The prepositions *in, on,* and *at* are also used in a number of set expressions:

in a book/magazine/newspaper	on a bus/train/etc.	at best/worst
in charge (of)	on fire	at first/last
in common (with)	on the other hand	at least/most
in danger (of)	on purpose	at the moment
in detail	on radio/television	at once
in existence	on the whole	at the peak (of)
in the front/middle/back		at present
in general		at birth
in other words		at death
in the past/future		at random
in practice		
in a row		
in style		
in theory		
in use		

Other prepositions

- *By* is often used with forms of communication and transportation:

  by car, by plane, by phone, by express mail

  (Note: if the noun is plural or is preceded by a determiner, the prepositions *in* or *on* must be used: *in cars, on a boat, on the telephone, in a taxi*)

- *By* is also used with gerunds to show how an action happened:

  How did you get an appointment with Dr. Bloom?

  By calling his secretary.

- *With* is used to indicate the idea of accompaniment or possession:

  Melanie came to the party *with her friend*.

  He wanted a house *with a garage*.

  Without indicates the opposite relationship:

  Melanie came to the party *without her friend*.

  He bought a house *without a garage*.

- *With* also indicates that an instrument was used to perform an action:

  He opened the door *with a key*.

  Without indicates the opposite relationship:

  He opened the door *without a key*.

- *By* and *for* are also used in the following expressions:

by chance	for example
by far	for free
by hand	for now

- *For* is sometimes used to show purpose:

  She went to the store *for toothpaste and shampoo.*

MINI-LESSON 2.1
Adjectives/Participles + Prepositions, Part A

Directions: Fill in the blanks in the sentences below with the correct prepositions.

1. I was disappointed _____ the grade I received on my last essay.

2. The Medical Center is close _____ campus.

3. Since she graduated, Anne has not been dependent _____ her parents for financial support.

4. Catherine became accustomed _____ spicy foods when she was traveling.

5. Table salt is composed _____ two highly poisonous elements, sodium and chlorine, but it is necessary _____ human health.

6. Is your bicycle equipped _____ a light?

7. This computer isn't capable _____ running this software.

8. Bluegrass music is somewhat different _____ other types of country music.

9. Idaho is famous _____ its potatoes.

10. Was your choice of research topic acceptable _____ your instructor?

11. People who are afraid _____ heights are called acrophobes.

12. Water is essential _____ all life.

13. Were you aware _____ the regulation against smoking in this area?

14. Although tepees are sometimes associated _____ all Native Americans, they are actually characteristic only _____ the tribes of the Great Plains.

15. Will this office be adequate _____ your needs?

16. I'm not familiar _____ that song.

17. One meter is approximately equal _____ a yard.

18. There is a persistent belief that all types of fruit are rich _____ vitamin C, but some types, such as apples, bananas, and pineapples, have very low levels of C.

19. This summer, Ms. Depuy will be eligible _____ a three-week vacation.

20. What Milton said is contrary _____ common sense.

MINI-LESSON 2.2
Adjectives/Participles + Prepositions, Part B

Directions: Fill in the blanks in the sentences below with the correct prepositions.

1. The art museum is located next _____ the Museum of Natural History.

2. Many vegetables, including tomatoes, potatoes, and corn, are native _____ the New World.

3. All the world's fur seals can be divided _____ two distinct but closely related families.

4. This apartment would be too crowded for two people, but it's perfect _____ one.

5. A purchasing agent is responsible _____ buying equipment and supplies for his or her firm.

6. Were you surprised _____ the grade you received?

7. House cats are distantly related _____ lions and tigers.

8. Is this type of soil suitable _____ growing tomatoes?

9. The point that Murray brought up wasn't really relevant _____ the discussion.

10. Organically raised crops are free _____ chemical pesticides and herbicides.

11. A grade of A− is preferable _____ one of B+.

12. If you're not satisfied _____ your essay, then I suggest that you rewrite it.

13. Abolitionists were people who were opposed _____ the practice of slavery in the years before the Civil War.

14. The United States became independent _____ England in 1776.

15. President James Madison was married _____ one of the most famous of all first ladies, Dolley Madison.

MINI-LESSON 2.3
Nouns + Prepositions

Directions: Fill in the blanks in the sentences below with the correct prepositions.

1. A decrease _____ the supply _____ a good usually results in an increase _____ the price _____ that good.

2. Once scientists fully understand the cause _____ a disease, it becomes easier for them to find a cure _____ it.

3. Professor Lyle noticed a distinct improvement _____ the quality _____ her students' work.

4. It is believed that sunspots have an influence _____ Earth's weather patterns.

5. Have you had much experience _____ computers?

6. There are thirty known meteor craters on Earth, and many other formations that are believed to be the result _____ meteor impacts.

7. The Dorothy Chandler Pavilion is part _____ the Los Angeles Music Center.

8. Linguists have many theories about the origin _____ language.

9. This is an exception _____ the general rule.

10. What approach should I take _____ this problem?

11. Anthropologists say that no group _____ people completely lack the concept _____ family.

12. There is no basis _____ the existence of the week in the movement of the Sun, Moon, and Earth as there is _____ that of the day, month, and year.

13. Only a native _____ the United States can serve as President.

14. Economists don't agree on the effect government spending has _____ the economy.

15. Margaret Knight designed some of the components _____ the rotary engine.

MINI-LESSON 2.4
Verbs + Prepositions

Directions: Fill in the blanks in the sentences below with the correct prepositions.

1. Cytology is the branch of biology that deals _____ the structure, form, and life of cells.

2. Maybe you should begin your speech _____ some jokes.

3. Let's concentrate _____ solving this problem before we discuss the others.

4. People want friends they can rely _____ .

5. Most essays consist _____ an introduction, a body, and a conclusion.

6. Many types of animals react _____ a solar eclipse as they do _____ the coming of night.

7. If you are engaged _____ any extracurricular activities, you should mention that fact on your résumé.

8. Iron combines _____ oxygen to form rust.

9. Do you agree _____ Paula?

10. The accident resulted _____ several minor injuries.

11. Storms on the Sun can interfere _____ radio broadcasts on the earth.

12. By the late 1940s, television had begun to seriously compete _____ radio for audience and advertisers.

13. James didn't have any trouble adjusting _____ the climate in Atlanta because he'd grown up in the South.

14. William insists _____ getting up early, even on weekends.

15. What does this symbol refer _____?

16. Occupational physicians search _____ the causes of injury and sickness at the workplace.

17. Many companies participated _____ the trade fair.

18. How do you account _____ this discrepancy?

19. Do you believe _____ any superstitions?

20. Workaholics devote too much of their time _____ their jobs.

MINI-LESSON 2.5
Phrasal Prepositions

Directions: Fill in the blanks in the sentences below with the correct prepositions.

1. Work on the new highway will be finished ahead _____ schedule.

2. _____ spite _____ the warnings, Phil dove off the cliff.

3. Freelan O. Stanley, along _____ his identical twin brother Francis E. Stanley, invented the steam-powered automobile.

4. Prior _____ her wedding, Nicole's last name was Brooks.

5. Are you _____ favor _____ that amendment or against it?

6. _____ account _____ a lack of funds, the university library will now close at nine instead _____ at eleven.

7. The water in an artificial lake, _____ contrast _____ that of a natural lake, usually lies well above the level of the lake's lowest outlet so that it can be released as needed.

8. Due _____ a computer error, $100,000 was transferred into Judy's checking account.

9. Regardless _____ the final score, I'm sure this will be an exciting game.

10. Glider pilots can actually increase their altitude _____ means _____ hot air currents called thermals.

11. Thanks _____ the financial aid he received, he was able to attend the university.

12. _____ case _____ an emergency, dial 911.

MINI-LESSON 2.6
In, On, and *At,* Part A

Directions: Fill in the blanks in the sentences below with the prepositions *in, on,* or *at.*

1. John F. Kennedy was the first President of the United States to be born _____ the twentieth century.

2. Most fruit trees bloom _____ March or April.

3. Gettysburg, the greatest battle ever fought _____ North America, took place _____ July 1863.

4. I like to shower _____ the morning, but my roommate likes to shower _____ night.

5. The President lives _____ the White House, which is located _____ 1600 Pennsylvania Avenue _____ Washington, D.C.

6. Many advertising agencies are located _____ Madison Avenue _____ New York City.

7. Jazz was so popular _____ the 1920s that the decade is sometimes called the Jazz Age.

8. Leaves turn red and gold _____ the autumn.

9. Most college football games are played _____ Saturdays.

10. Both Washington and Lincoln were born _____ February. Washington was born _____ February 22, Lincoln _____ February 12.

11. About 90% of all the people _____ New Jersey live _____ cities.

12. The New Year is celebrated _____ midnight _____ January 1.

13. Dean Hughes' office is _____ the Administration Building _____ the third floor.

14. Quebec is the largest province _____ Canada.

15. The First World War ended _____ 5 A.M. _____ the eleventh day _____ the eleventh month _____ 1918.

MINI-LESSON 2.7
In, *On*, and *At*, Part B

Directions: Fill in the blanks in the sentences below with the prepositions *in*, *on*, or *at*.

1. Did you hear that news _____ television or read it _____ the newspaper?

2. The members of a jury are chosen _____ random from a list of voters.

3. Video phones are not practical _____ present, but they may be _____ the near future.

4. Mr. Lee is _____ charge of the marketing department.

5. Please come here _____ once.

6. I'm sure he didn't break the plate _____ purpose.

7. Airfares are usually highest _____ the summer when travel is _____ its peak.

8. _____ the whole, I enjoyed the movie.

9. Do you and your roommates have much _____ common?

10. Claudia has gotten so many speeding tickets that she's _____ danger of losing her driver's license.

11. The story _____ the magazine described the incident _____ great detail.

12. There must be _____ least one vowel in virtually every English word.

13. Five oak trees were planted _____ a row _____ front of the school.

14. This type of music is no longer _____ style.

15. _____ general, I found zoology to be an easier subject than botany.

16. The American Constitution has been _____ existence for over two hundred years.

17. Like many other baby birds, ducklings are blind _____ birth.

18. This book is based _____ part on fact.

19. The ship was _____ fire.

20. _____ theory, this idea is quite difficult to understand; _____ the other hand, it is quite simple _____ practice.

MINI-LESSON 2.8
In, *On*, and *At*, Part C and Other Prepositions

Directions: Fill in the blanks in the sentences below with the correct prepositions.

1. Magnetic compasses are not very useful on ships _____ steel hulls.

2. Penicillin was discovered more or less _____ chance.

3. Legal aid organizations provide legal advice for poor people for small fees or _____ free.

4. Alaska is _____ far the largest state.

5. Amoebas are so small that they can't be seen _____ a microscope; they can't be seen _____ the naked eye.

6. Fruits, vegetables, and other agricultural products are generally shipped _____ truck.

7. Semaphore operators communicate _____ using flags.

8. Until the mid-nineteenth century, shoes were made _____ hand, and most of them were "straight;" _____ other words, they could be worn _____ either foot.

9. Ice hockey is played _____ a hard rubber disk called a puck.

10. No gasoline-powered vehicles are permitted _____ Mackinac Island _____ Lake Huron. Most people there travel _____ foot, _____ horse-drawn taxis, or _____ bicycles.

11. Prefabricated housing has been _____ use since _____ least the 1820s when a number of partly assembled houses were sent _____ ship from New England _____ Hawaii.

12. They stopped at the café _____ a cup of coffee.

Guide to Reading

University of Montana.

About Reading

This part of the exam tests your ability to read and answer items about passages in formal written English. It contains four or five passages. After each passage there are 10 to 14 items about that passage for a total of 50 to 60 questions in this part. The passages vary in length from about 250 to about 350 words.

This section tests your ability to find main ideas, supporting ideas, and details, to use context clues to understand the meaning of vocabulary, to draw inferences, to recognize coherence, to figure out the organization of the passage, and to perform other basic reading skills.

This part of the test is **linear**—it is NOT computer adaptive. You can skip items and come back to them later, or change answers at a later time. The items you are given are not chosen according to your previous answers. Because this section is linear, the tactics you use will be somewhat different from those in the first two parts of the test.

Some item types are "computer unique"—they did not appear on the paper-based test. There are also item types that have changed somewhat to take advantage of the computer's capabilities.

The Passages

The passages cover a wide range of topics, but in general can be classified as follows:

1. **Science and technology** Includes astronomy, geology, chemistry, physics, mathematics, zoology, botany, medicine, engineering, and mechanics
2. **North American history, government, geography, and culture**
3. **Art** Includes literature, painting, sculpture, architecture, dance, and drama
4. **Social science** Includes anthropology, economics, psychology, urban studies, and sociology
5. **Biography**

Some passages may be classified in more than one way. For example, a biography might be about the life of a historical figure, an artist, or a scientist.

If there is a national context for any of the passages, it is American or occasionally Canadian. Therefore, if a passage is about history, it will be about the history of the United States or Canada.

Although the passages deal with various topics, the style in which they are written is similar, and they usually follow fairly simple patterns of organization.

The vocabulary used in the Reading portion is sophisticated but not unrealistically complex. However, there will almost certainly be words that you do not recognize. Sometimes you can guess the meaning of these words by context. It is not necessary to understand all the vocabulary in the passages in order to answer the items.

The Items

According to the way they are answered, there are three types of items on the test.

A) STANDARD MULTIPLE-CHOICE ITEMS

These are very similar to the items found on the paper-based test. Most multiple-choice items can be categorized as one of the following seven types of items:

Standard Multiple-Choice Items

Type of Items	Explanation	Example
Overview Items	These ask you to identify an answer choice that correctly summarizes the author's main idea, the subject of the whole passage, or the author's reason for writing the passage. Other overview items ask you about the author's attitude or about the organization of the passage.	What is the main idea of the passage? What is the passage primarily about? Why did the author write the passage? What tone does the author take in the passage? Which of the following best describes the organization of the passage?
Detail Items	These ask you to locate and identify answers to items about specific information and details in the passage. For a few of these, you will click on pictures rather than on verbal answers.	According to the passage, where did . . . ? According to the author, why did . . . ? Which of the following is true, according to the passage? Which of the following is the best illustration of . . . ?
Negative Items	These ask which of the answer choices is NOT discussed in the passage.	Which of the following is NOT true about . . . ? All of the following are true EXCEPT . . . ?
Inference Items	These ask you to draw conclusions based on information in the passage.	The author implies that which of the following is true? Which of the following can be inferred from the passage?
Purpose Items	These ask you to explain why the author of the passage uses a certain word, sentence, or example, or what the purpose of a sentence or example is.	Why does the author mention . . . in paragraph 2? What is the purpose of the following sentence in paragraph 2?
Vocabulary-in-Context Items	These ask you to identify the meaning of a word or phrase as used in the passage.	Look at the word _____ in the passage. Which of the following is closest in meaning to _____ ?
Reference Items*	These ask you to identify the noun to which a pronoun or other expression refers.	"The word it in line 15 refers to . . . " "In line 20, the word there refers to which of the following?"

* Most reference items are "click on" items, but a few are multiple choice.

About half the multiple-choice items have **closed stems;** they begin with direct questions. The others have **open stems;** they begin with incomplete sentences.

Closed Stem

Which of the following is the main topic of the passage?

Open Stem

The main topic of the passage is

B) CLICK ON THE PASSAGE ITEMS

These types of items are not followed by a list of four possible answers with ovals by them. Instead, you must click on some part of the passage. For most of these items, you can only click on the part of the passage that is in **bold** or in a paragraph that is marked with an arrow. For a few items, you can click anywhere in the passage.

Click on the Passage Items		
Type of Item	**Explanation**	**Example**
Scanning Items	These ask you to find a word, phrase, or paragraph in the passage that plays a specific logical or organizational role in the passage.	Click on the paragraph in the passage that outlines . . . Click on the sentence in paragraph 2 that explains . . .
Synonym/Antonym Items	These ask you to find a word or phrase in a marked part of the passage that has the same meaning (synonym) or the opposite meaning (antonym) as a highlighted word.	Look at the word ___ in the passage. Click on the word or phrase in the **bold** text that is closest in meaning to ___ . Look at the word ___ in the passage. Click on the word or phrase in the **bold** text that is most nearly opposite ___ in meaning.
Reference Items	These ask you to find in a marked portion of a passage the noun to which a highlighted pronoun or other word refers to.	Look at the word them in the passage. Click on the word or phrase in the **bold** text it refers to.

C) SENTENCE ADDITION ITEMS

This type of item provides you with a sentence that can be inserted into a passage. You must decide where this sentence belongs. When you see a sentence addition item, small black squares will appear between the sentences in part of the passage—usually one or two paragraphs long. You have to click on the squares between the two sentences where you think the sentence should be inserted.

What is the best way to attack the passages?

First, read the article at a comfortable speed. After you have read the first screen, scroll through the rest of the passage at a steady pace.

Word-by-word reading slows you down and interferes with your comprehension. Try to read in units of thought, grouping words into related phrases.

During your first reading, don't worry about understanding or remembering details. You can come back and look for that information later. Try to get a general idea of what each of the paragraphs is about and what the passage as a whole is about.

What is the best way to answer the items?

It's important to remember that your goal is not to understand the passages perfectly but to answer as many items correctly as you can. You need to focus on the items, not the passage.

Although you CAN skip items in this section, this is not a good idea. You should answer each item as it comes up even if you have to guess. However, if you have any doubts, you should write down the number of that item on your notepaper. (You will be given six sheets of notepaper after the break between Section 2 and 3; it is actually for the Writing section, but you can use it during the Reading section as well to keep track of difficult items.)

Are there any "secrets" for finding answers in the passage quickly?

Yes! When you are answering some types of items—mainly detail items and inference items—the most important factor is simply to locate the information quickly. Here are some pointers that will help:

1) The items—except for the first and maybe the last item in each set—strictly follow the order of the passage. In other words, the answers for the first few items will be near the top of the passage. To find information for the last few items, you will have to scroll down to the last part of the passage.

2) Reference items and vocabulary items can help you pinpoint the information you need to answer other types of items. Let's say that Item 2 is a synonym item. The computer will highlight a word. Let's say Item 3 is a detail item and Item 4 is an inference item. Then let's say Item 5 is a reference item. Again the computer will highlight a word. This tells us that the information needed to answer Items 3 and 4 is somewhere between the two words that were highlighted.

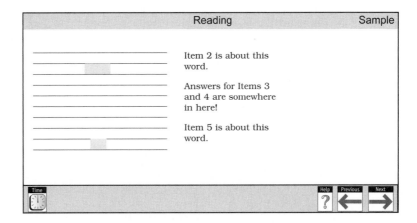

What are some important factors in scoring high in this section?

Timing is important. Most test-takers find this section the hardest to complete because reading the passages takes up so much time. You will have 70 to 90 minutes to complete this section—an average of about fifteen minutes to read each passage and answer the items about it. Use the clock on the screen to pace yourself.

What should you do if, near the end of the test, you realize that you don't have enough time to finish? Don't panic! Let's say that you have one more passage to complete and there are only about four or five minutes remaining. You should skim over the passage to get the main idea. Answer the first item about the passage (which will probably be a main idea item). Then answer all of the vocabulary items and reference items because these require less time. (You'll need to click on the Next icon to locate these). Then go back and answer any remaining items (clicking on the Prev icon). Refer to the passage as little as possible. If you can't find the information needed to answer the item in about ten seconds, just pick the choice that seems most logical. Then, in the last few seconds, answer any remaining items by clicking on your "guess answer."

On the other hand, if you *do* finish the test before time is called, go back and work on items that you had trouble with the first time. Don't exit this section until all the time is up.

Concentration is another important factor. This is the longest section of the test. For some people, it's the most difficult. You may find it hard to concentrate on a computer screen for so long. Your eyes may get tired. You may find it more difficult to maneuver through passages on a screen than in a book.

Practice can help. Besides working through the lessons and tests on the accompanying CD-ROM, read as much material on computer as possible. Visit sites on the Internet that interest you or work with CD-ROM encyclopedias.

Computer Skills for the Reading Section

When you return from your break, you will begin the Reading section. As in all sections, the directions will appear on the screen. You should immediately click the Dismiss Directions icon.

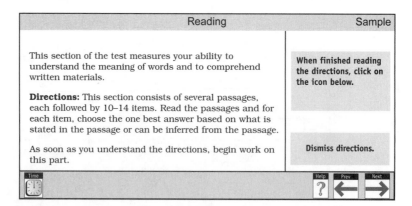

The first reading will then appear, and at the bottom left of that screen, so will an icon labeled Proceed. Say that you want to see the first item before you start to read, so you click on Proceed. What happens?

Absolutely nothing! That's because the program makes you read through the passage—or at least scroll to the bottom of the passage—before it will let you see any items.

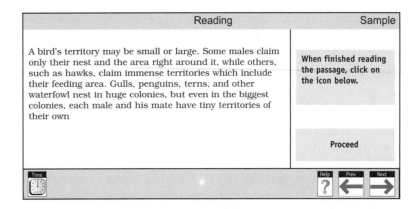

Since the first item will probably be a main topic item, it is a good idea to quickly scroll to the bottom of the passage, then click the Proceed icon, look at the item, and then do your first reading of the passage.

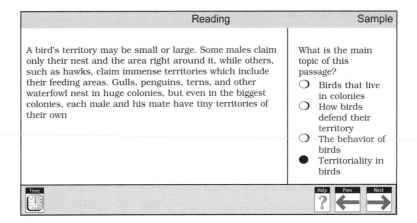

Navigating through the Passage

Because the actual passages are too long to fit on the screen at one time, you will have to scroll through the passages to read them, and then scroll backwards and forwards to find the information that you need to answer the items. There are a number of ways to scroll through a passage:

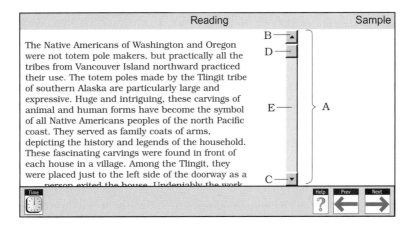

First, look at the scroll bar, which separates the passage from the items. It is labeled (A).

1) You can click **once** on the up arrow (B) or down arrow (C) at the top and bottom of the scroll bar. This moves the text up or down one line on the screen. This may be the most comfortable way for you to scroll when you are doing your first reading or when you are looking for specific information to answer detail or inference items.

2) You can click on the up or down arrow on the scroll bar and hold it down. As long as you hold down the arrow, the text will scroll rapidly up or down. This is a good way to move quickly through the passage.

3) Using your mouse, you can position the pointer on the slider (D) and move through the passage as quickly or as slowly as you like by "pushing" the slider up or down with the pointer.

4) To go very quickly from the end of the passage to the beginning or from the beginning to end, just click on the "empty space," (E), above or below the slider and the text will instantly scroll to the top or bottom of the passage. You can use this method when you have finished your first reading and want to return to the top of the passage to begin answering the items, or if you want to be able to click on the Precede button immediately.

5) When you are at the top of the passage, the word Beginning will appear over the scroll bar. When you are at the bottom of the passage, you will see the word Finish. When you are anywhere else in the passage, the phrase More Available will appear.

Navigating through the Section

You may have noticed that the icons at the bottom of the Reading screens are somewhat different from those in the two previous sections. That is because Reading is not computer adaptive. There is no Answer Confirm icon; instead there is an icon marked Prev (meaning "Previous item") and one marked Next. When you finish answering an item, you simply click Next. If you decide to return to the item you just finished, click Prev. You can use these two buttons to move as far forward or backward as you want, from item to item, and from passage to passage. Until time runs out, you can move anywhere you like within the Reading section just by clicking on these two arrows.

Choosing Answers

Answering the multiple choice items is easy—just click on the oval or anywhere in the first line of the answer. The oval will darken. To change your answer, just click on another answer. Then click Next and the next item will appear.

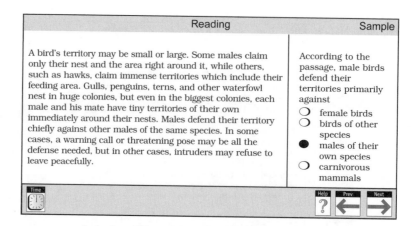

For a few items, you may have to click on a picture rather than on words.

To answer Click on the Passage items, you simply click on the word, phrase, or sentence in the marked section that you think is correct. Parts of a paragraph are marked with **bold;** whole paragraphs are marked with an arrow (→). The program will not allow you to click on anything outside the marked sections. The word, phrase, or sentence that you choose will be highlighted. To change your answer, click on another word, phrase, or sentence.

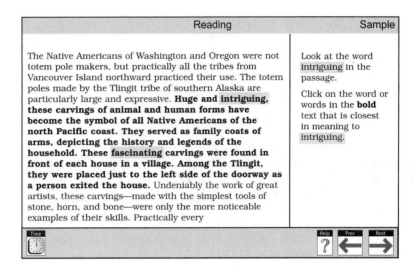

To answer Sentence Addition items, you must click on the black rectangle between the sentences where you think the sentence should be inserted. The sentence that you chose will then appear in that position. To change your answer, click on another square.

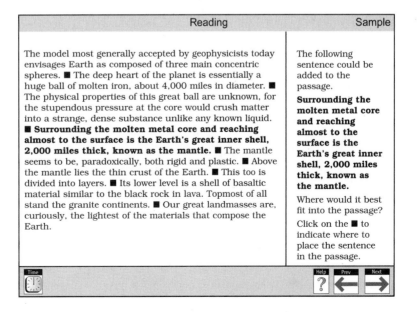

- As with the other sections, be familiar with the directions. When the directions appear, click on the Dismiss Directions icon right away.

- Quickly scroll to the bottom of the passage, then click on the Proceed icon to make the first item appear. Read the first item.

- Read the passage at a comfortable speed.

- Answer the items, referring to the passage when necessary.

- Eliminate answer choices that are clearly wrong or do not answer the questions. If more than one option remains, guess.

- Answer each item as it appears, but write down the number of difficult or time-consuming items on the notepaper you have been given so that you can come back to these items later if you have time.

- Don't spend too much time on any one item or passage.

- If you haven't finished when only a few minutes remain, don't start guessing blindly. Skim the remaining passage or passages quickly, then answer the first item in each set. Next, answer any vocabulary or reference items. After that, read the remaining items, and if you can't find the answer quickly, choose the one that seems most logical to you.

- When there are only a few seconds left, use the Next button to quickly go through the remaining items and guess at the answers. Don't leave any items unanswered.

- Even if you answer the last item, don't stop working until time runs out. Go back and check the items that you marked as difficult and if you finish those, check the rest of your work.

Time: 90 minutes

This section of the test measures your ability to understand the meaning of words and to comprehend written materials.

Directions: This section consists of several passages, each followed by 10–14 questions. Read the passages and for each question, choose the one best answer based on what is stated in or can be inferred from the passage.

As soon as you understand the directions, begin work on this part.

Passage 1

The technology of the North American colonies did not differ strikingly from that of Europe, but in one respect, the colonists enjoyed a great advantage. Especially by comparison with Britain, Americans had a wonderfully plentiful supply of wood.

The first colonists did not, as many people imagine, find an entire continent covered by a climax forest. Even along the Atlantic seaboard, the forest was broken at many points. Nevertheless, there was an abundant supply of fine trees of all types, and through the early colonial period, those who pushed westward encountered new forests. By the end of the colonial era, the price of wood had risen slightly in eastern cities, but wood was still readily available.

The availability of wood brought advantages that have seldom been appreciated. Wood was a foundation of the economy. Houses and all manner of buildings were made of wood to a degree unknown in Britain. Secondly, wood was used as a fuel for heating and cooking. Thirdly, it was used as the source of important industrial compounds, such as potash, an industrial alkali; charcoal, a component of gunpowder; and tannic acid, used for tanning leather.

The supply of wood conferred advantages, but had some negative aspects as well. Iron at that time was produced by heating iron ore with charcoal. Because Britain was so stripped of trees, she was unable to exploit her rich iron mines. But the American colonies had both iron ore and wood; iron production was encouraged and became successful. Britain had to abandon the charcoal method and went on to develop coke smelting. The colonies did not follow suit because they had plenty of wood and besides, charcoal iron was stronger than coke iron. Coke smelting led to technological innovations and was linked to the emergence of the Industrial Revolution. The former colonies lagged behind Britain in industrial development because their supply of wood led them to cling to charcoal iron.

1. What does the passage mainly discuss?

   ○ The advantages of using wood in the colonies

   ○ The effects of an abundance of wood on the colonies

   ○ The roots of the Industrial Revolution

   ○ The difference between charcoal iron and coke iron

2. The word strikingly in the first paragraph is closest in meaning to

   ○ realistically

   ○ dramatically

   ○ completely

   ○ immediately

3. Which of the following is a common assumption about the forests of North America during the colonial period?

   ○ They contained only a few types of trees.

   ○ They existed only along the Atlantic seaboard.

   ○ They had little or no economic value.

   ○ They covered the entire continent.

4. Look at the word plentiful in the **bold** text below.

> **Especially by comparison with Britain, Americans had a wonderfully plentiful supply of wood.**
>
> **The first colonists did not, as many people imagine, find an entire continent covered by a climax forest. Even along the Atlantic seaboard, the forest was broken at many points. Nevertheless, there was an abundant supply of fine trees of all types, and through the early colonial period, those who pushed westward encountered new forests.**

Underline the word or phrase in the **bold** text that has the same meaning as plentiful.

5. According to the passage, by the end of the colonial period, the price of wood in eastern cities

   ○ rose quickly because wood was becoming scarce

   ○ was much higher than it was in Britain

   ○ was slightly higher than in previous years

   ○ decreased rapidly because of lower demand for wood

6. What can be inferred about houses in Britain during the period written about in the passage?

   ○ They were more expensive than American houses.

   ○ They were generally built with imported materials.

   ○ They were typically smaller than homes in North America.

   ○ They were usually built from materials other than wood.

7. Why does the author mention gunpowder in paragraph 3?

   ○ To illustrate the negative aspects of some industrial processes

   ○ To give an example of a product made from wood compounds

   ○ To remind readers that the colonial era ended in warfare

   ○ To suggest that wood was not the only important product of the colonies

8. The phrase follow suit in paragraph 4 means
   - ○ do the same thing
   - ○ make an attempt
   - ○ have the opportunity
   - ○ take a risk

9. According to the passage, why was the use of coke smelting advantageous?
   - ○ It led to advances in technology.
   - ○ It was less expensive than wood smelting.
   - ○ It produced a stronger type of iron than wood smelting.
   - ○ It stimulated the demand for wood.

10. Look at the phrase cling to in the bold text below.

    Britain had to abandon the charcoal method and went on to develop coke smelting. The colonies did not follow suit because they had plenty of wood and besides, charcoal iron was stronger than coke iron. Coke smelting led to technological innovations and was linked to the emergence of the Industrial Revolution. The former colonies lagged behind Britain in industrial development because their supply of wood led them to cling to charcoal iron.

    Underline the word or phrase in the **bold** text that is most nearly OPPOSITE in meaning to the phrase cling to.

11. Put an X next to the paragraph that outlines the main disadvantage of an abundance of wood.

Passage 2

The Peales were a distinguished family of American artists. Charles Willson Peale is best remembered for his portraits of the leading figures of the American Revolution. He painted portraits of Franklin and Jefferson, and over a dozen of George Washington. His life-size portrait of his sons Raphaelle and Titian was so realistic that George Washington reportedly once tipped his hat to the figures in the painting.

Charles Willson Peale gave up painting in his middle age and devoted his life to the Peale Museum, which he founded in Philadelphia. The world's first popular museum of art and natural science, it featured paintings by Peale and his family as well as displays of animals in their natural settings. Peale found the animals himself and devised a method of taxidermy to make the exhibits more lifelike. The museum's most popular display was the skeleton of a mastodon—a huge, extinct elephant—which Peale unearthed on a New York farm in 1801.

Three of Peale's seventeen children were also famous artists. Raphaelle Peale often painted still lifes of flowers, fruit, and cheese. His works show the same luminosity and attention to detail that the works of the Dutch masters show. In the late eighteenth century, however, still lifes were not the fashion. Portraiture was the rage, and so Raphaelle Peale found few buyers at that time. His brother Rembrandt studied under his father and painted portraits of many noted people, including one of George Washington. Another brother, Reubens Peale, painted mostly landscapes and portraits.

James Peale, the brother of Charles Willson Peale, specialized in miniatures. His daughter Sarah Miriam Peale was probably the first professional female portrait painter in America.

12. What is the main topic of the passage?
   - ○ The life of Charles Willson Peale
   - ○ Portraiture in the eighteenth century
   - ○ The Peale Museum
   - ○ A family of artists

13. Look at the word He in the **bold** text below.

   The Peales were a distinguished family of American artists. Charles Willson Peale is best remembered for his portraits of leading figures of the American Revolution. He painted portraits of Franklin and Jefferson, and over a dozen of George Washington.

   Underline the word or phrase in the **bold** text that the word He refers to.

14. The author probably mentions in the first paragraph that Washington tipped his hat to the figures in the painting to indicate that
   - ○ Charles Willson Peale's painting was very lifelike
   - ○ Washington respected Charles Willson Peale's work
   - ○ Washington was friendly with Raphaelle and Titian Peale
   - ○ the painting of the two brothers was extremely large

15. Look at the word displays in the **bold** text.

   The world's first popular museum of art and natural science, it featured paintings by Peale and his family as well as displays of animals in their natural settings. Peale found the animals himself and devised a method of taxidermy to make the exhibits more lifelike.

   Underline the word or phrase in the **bold** text that has the same meaning as displays.

16. For which of the following terms does the author give a definition in the second paragraph?
   - ○ Natural science
   - ○ Skeleton
   - ○ Taxidermy
   - ○ Mastodon

17. Which of the following questions about the Peale Museum does the passage NOT supply enough information to answer?

  ○ Who found and prepared its animal exhibits?

  ○ In what city was it located?

  ○ Where did its most popular exhibit come from?

  ○ In what year was it founded?

18. The word unearthed in paragraph 2 is closest in meaning to

  ○ showed

  ○ dug up

  ○ located

  ○ looked over

19. Look at the word rage in the bold text below.

  His works show the same luminosity and attention to detail that the works of the Dutch masters show. In the late eighteenth century, however, still lifes were not the fashion. Portraiture was the rage, and so Raphaelle Peale found few buyers at that time.

  Underline the word or phrase in the **bold** text that has the same meaning as rage.

20. According to the passage, Rembrandt Peale and his father both painted

  ○ miniatures

  ○ portraits of George Washington

  ○ paintings of flowers, fruit, and cheese

  ○ pictures of animals

21. Underline the sentence in paragraph 3 in which the author compares the paintings of one of the Peale family with those of other artists.

22. Which of the following is NOT one of the children of Charles Willson Peale?

  ○ Titian Peale

  ○ Reubens Peale

  ○ Raphaelle Peale

  ○ Sarah Miriam Peale

23. The author's attitude toward the Peales is generally

  ○ envious

  ○ puzzled

  ○ admiring

  ○ disappointed

Passage 3

According to the best evidence gathered by space probes and astronomers, Mars is an inhospitable planet, more similar to Earth's Moon than to Earth itself—a dry, stark, seemingly lifeless world. Mars' air pressure is equal to

Earth's at an altitude of 100,000 feet. The air there is 95% carbon dioxide. Mars has no ozone layer to screen out the Sun's lethal radiation. Daytime temperatures may reach above freezing, but because the planet is blanketed by the mere wisp of an atmosphere, the heat radiates back into space. Even at the equator, the temperature drops to –50°C (–60°F) at night. Today there is no liquid water, although valleys and channels on the surface show evidence of having been carved by running water. The polar ice caps are made of frozen water and carbon dioxide, and water may be frozen in the ground as permafrost.

Despite these difficult conditions, certain scientists believe that there is a possibility of transforming Mars into a more earth-like planet. Nuclear reactors might be used to melt frozen gases and eventually build up the atmosphere. This in turn could create a "greenhouse effect" that would stop heat from radiating back into space. Frozen water could be thawed to form a polar ocean. Once enough ice has melted, suitable plants could be introduced to build up the level of oxygen in the atmosphere so that, in time, the planet would support animal life from Earth and even permanent human colonies. "Not many years ago, no one would have considered this a viable plan," said Christopher McKay, a research scientist at the National Aeronautics and Space Administration. "But now it's starting to look feasible. We could begin work in four or five decades."

The idea of "terra-forming" Mars, as enthusiasts call it, has its roots in science fiction. But as researchers develop a more profound understanding of how Earth's ecology supports life, they have begun to see how it may be possible to create similar conditions on Mars. Don't plan on homesteading on Mars any time soon, though. The process could take hundreds of years to complete and the cost would be staggering.

24. With which of the following is the passage primarily concerned?
   ○ The possibility of changing the Martian environment
   ○ The challenge of interplanetary travel
   ○ The advantages of establishing colonies on Mars
   ○ The need to study the Martian ecology

25. The word stark in the first paragraph is closest in meaning to
   ○ harsh
   ○ unknown
   ○ dark
   ○ distant

26. The word there in the first paragraph refers to
   ○ a point 100 miles above the Earth
   ○ the Earth's Moon
   ○ Mars
   ○ outer space

27. According to the passage, the Martian atmosphere today consists mainly of

   ○ carbon dioxide

   ○ oxygen

   ○ ozone

   ○ water vapor

28. Underline the sentence in the first paragraph that explains why Mars is so cold at night.

29. Which of the following does the author NOT list as a characteristic of the planet Mars that would make colonization difficult?

   ○ There is little liquid water.

   ○ Daytime temperatures are dangerously high.

   ○ The Sun's rays are deadly.

   ○ There is little air surrounding the planet.

30. It can be inferred from the passage that the greenhouse effect mentioned in paragraph 2 is

   ○ the direct result of nuclear reactions

   ○ the cause of low temperatures on Mars

   ○ the result of the introduction of green plants

   ○ a possible means of warming Mars

31. Look at the word thawed in the **bold** text below.

Frozen water could be thawed to form a polar ocean. Once enough ice has melted, suitable plants could be introduced to build up the level of oxygen in the atmosphere so that, in time, the planet would support animal life from Earth and even permanent human colonies.

Underline the word or phrase in the **bold** text that has the same meaning as thawed.

32. Look at the word feasible in the **bold** text.

"Not many years ago, no one would have considered this a viable plan," said Christopher McKay, a research scientist at the National Aeronautics and Space Administration. "But now it's starting to look feasible. We could begin work in four or five decades."

Underline the word or phrase in the **bold** text that has the same meaning as feasible.

33. According to Christopher McKay, the possibility of transforming Mars

   ○ could occur only in science fiction stories

   ○ cannot begin for hundreds, even thousands of years

   ○ is completely impractical

   ○ could be started in 40 to 50 years

34. According to the passage, the knowledge needed to transform Mars comes from

- ○ the science of astronomy
- ○ a knowledge of Earth's ecology
- ○ data from space probes
- ○ science fiction stories

35. Look at the word they in the **bold** text.

The idea of "terra-forming" Mars, as enthusiasts call it, has its roots in science fiction. But as researchers develop a more profound understanding of how Earth's ecology supports life, they have begun to see how it may be possible to create similar conditions on Mars.

Underline the word or phrase in the **bold** text that the word they refers to.

36. The word staggering in paragraph 3 is closest in meaning to

- ○ astonishing
- ○ restrictive
- ○ increasing
- ○ unpredictable

Passage 4

Another critical factor that plays a part in susceptibility to colds is age. A study done by the University of Michigan School of Public Health revealed particulars that seem to hold true for the general population. Infants are the most cold-ridden group, averaging more than six colds in their first year. Boys have more colds than girls up to age three. After the age of three, girls are more susceptible than boys, and teenage girls average three colds a year to boys' two.

The general incidence of colds continues to decline into maturity. Elderly people who are in good health have as few as one or two colds annually. One exception is found among people in their twenties, especially women. The rate at which they are infected with colds rises because people in this age group are most likely to have young children. Adults who delay having children until their thirties and forties experience the same sudden increase in cold infections.

The study also found that economics plays an important role. As income increases, the frequency at which colds are reported in the family decreases. Families with the lowest income suffer a third more colds than families at the highest end. Lower income generally forces people to live in more cramped quarters than those typically occupied by wealthier people, and crowded conditions increase the opportunities for the cold virus to travel from person to person. The degree to which deficient nutrition affects susceptibility to colds is not yet clearly established. However, an inadequate diet is suspected of lowering resistance generally.

37. The paragraph that precedes this one most probably deals with
    ○ minor diseases other than colds
    ○ the recommended treatment of colds
    ○ another factor that affects susceptibility to colds
    ○ methods of preventing colds among elderly people

38. Which of the following is closest in meaning to the word particulars?
    ○ Minor errors
    ○ Specific facts
    ○ Small distinctions
    ○ Individual people

39. What does the author claim about the study discussed in the passage?
    ○ It contains many inconsistencies.
    ○ It specializes in children.
    ○ It contradicts the results of earlier studies in the field.
    ○ Its results apparently are relevant to the population as a whole.

40. According to the passage, which of the following groups is most likely to catch colds?
    ○ Infant boys
    ○ Young girls
    ○ Teenage boys
    ○ Elderly women

41. Look at the word incidence in the **bold** text.

    The general incidence of colds continues to decline into maturity. Elderly people who are in good health have as few as one or two colds annually. One exception is found among people in their twenties, especially women. The rate at which they are infected with colds rises because people in this age group are most likely to have young children.

    Underline the word or phrase in the **bold** text that has the same meaning as incidence.

42. Information in paragraph 2 supports which of the following conclusions?
    ○ Men are more susceptible to colds than women.
    ○ Children infect their parents with colds.
    ○ People who live in cold climates have more colds than those in warm ones.
    ○ People who don't have children are more susceptible to colds than those who do.

43. Look at the phrase people in this age group in the **bold** text.

    Elderly people who are in good health have as few as one or two colds annually. One exception is found among people in their twenties, especially women. The rate at which they are infected with colds rises because people in this age group are most likely to have young children. Adults who delay having children until their thirties and forties experience the same sudden increase in cold infections.

Underline the word or phrase in the **bold** text that the phrase people in this age group refers to.

44. The author's main purpose in writing the last paragraph of the passage was to

  ○ present one way in which cold viruses are transmitted

  ○ prove that a poor diet causes colds

  ○ discuss the relationship between income and frequency of colds

  ○ explain the distribution of income among the people in the study

45. Look at the word cramped in the **bold** text.

  Families with the lowest income suffer a third more colds than families at the highest end. Lower income generally forces people to live in more cramped quarters than those typically occupied by wealthier people, and crowded conditions increase the opportunities for the cold virus to travel from person to person.

  Underline the word or phrase in the **bold** text that has the same meaning as cramped.

46. The following sentence can be added to paragraph three.

  Low income may also have an adverse effect on diet.

  Where would it best fit in the paragraph?

  The study also found that economics plays an important role. ■ As income increases, the frequency at which colds are reported in the family decreases. ■ Families with the lowest income suffer a third more colds than families at the highest end. ■ Lower income generally forces people to live in more cramped quarters than those typically occupied by wealthier people, and crowded conditions increase the opportunities for the cold virus to travel from person to person. ■ The degree to which deficient nutrition affects susceptibility to colds is not yet clearly established. ■ However, an inadequate diet is suspected of lowering resistance generally.

  Circle the black square (■) that indicates the best position for the sentence.

47. Look at the word deficient in the **bold** text.

  Lower income generally forces people to live in more cramped quarters than those typically occupied by wealthier people, and crowded conditions increase the opportunities for the cold virus to travel from person to person. The degree to which deficient nutrition affects susceptibility to colds is not yet clearly established. However, an inadequate diet is suspected of lowering resistance generally.

  Underline the word or phrase in the **bold** text that has the same meaning as deficient.

48. The author's tone in this passage could best be described as

○ neutral and objective
○ humorous
○ tentative but interested
○ highly critical

Passage 5

The roots of plants have such a pronounced ability to synthesize complicated organic compounds that, about sixty years ago, scientists began to wonder if roots could grow independent of the rest of the plant. Indeed they could. Plant physiologists were able to grow roots by themselves in solutions in laboratory flasks.

The scientists found that the nutrition of isolated roots is quite simple. They require sugar (for carbon and an energy source), the usual minerals, and a few vitamins such as B₁ and niacin. These roots can get along fine on mineral inorganic nitrogen. Roots are capable of making their own proteins for new cell growth and other organic compounds such as nucleic acids. As far as organic nitrogen compounds are concerned, then, roots can thrive without leaves. All these activities by roots require energy, of course. This comes from sugar. The process of respiration in the cells of the root uses sugar to make the high energy compound ATP (adenosine triphosphate) which drives the biochemical reactions. Respiration also requires oxygen, for the same reasons it does in all plants and animals.

The study of isolated roots has provided an understanding of the relationship between shoots and roots in intact plants. The leaves of the shoot provide the roots with sugar and vitamins while the roots provide the shoot with water and minerals. In addition, the roots can also provide the shoot with organic nitrogen compounds. This comes in handy for the growth of buds in the early spring when leaves are not yet functioning. Once leaves begin photosynthesizing, they produce protein, but only mature leaves can "export" protein to the rest of the plant in the form of amino acids.

The plant is a wonderful chemical factory. It is the link between the minerals of the soil and the nutrition of animals.

49. What is the main topic of the passage?

○ The relationship between a plant's roots and its shoot
○ What can be learned by growing roots in isolation
○ How plants can be grown without roots
○ What elements are necessary for the growth of plants

50. The word pronounced in the first paragraph is closest in meaning to

○ obvious
○ spoken
○ minor
○ unknown

51. Which of these pictures best illustrates the experiment conducted by the plant physiologists mentioned in the first paragraph?

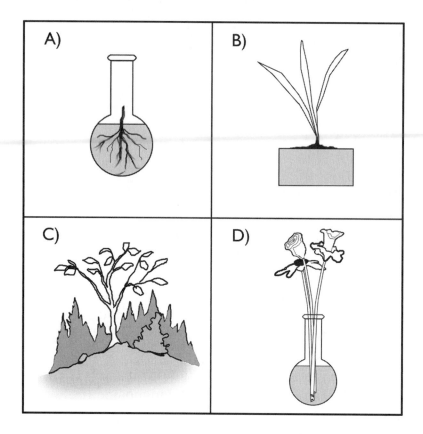

52. Look at the word themselves in the **bold** text.

Plant physiologists were able to grow roots by themselves in solutions in laboratory flasks.

Underline the word or phrase in the **bold** text that the word themselves refers to.

53. The following sentence could be added to paragraph 2.

However, they do not require organic nitrogen compounds.

Where would it best fit into the paragraph?

The scientists found that the nutrition of isolated roots is quite simple. ■ They require sugar (for carbon and an energy source), the usual minerals, and a few vitamins such as B_1 and niacin. ■ These roots can get along fine on mineral inorganic nitrogen. ■ Roots are capable of making their own proteins for new cell growth and other organic compounds such as nucleic acids. ■ As far as organic nitrogen compounds are concerned, then, roots can thrive without leaves. ■ All these activities by roots require energy, of course. ■ This comes from sugar. ■ The process of respiration in the cells of the root uses sugar to make the high energy compound ATP (adenosine triphosphate) which drives the biochemical reactions. ■ Respiration also requires oxygen, for the same reasons it does in all plants and animals.

Circle the black square (■) that indicates the best position for the sentence.

54. Look at the word thrive in the **bold** text.

   These roots can get along fine on mineral inorganic nitrogen. Roots are capable of making their own proteins for new cell growth and other organic compounds such as nucleic acids. As far as organic nitrogen compounds are concerned, then, roots can thrive without leaves.

   Underline the word or phrase in the **bold** text that has the same meaning as thrive .

55. Look at the word this in the **bold** text.

   Roots are capable of making their own proteins for new cell growth and other organic compounds such as nucleic acids. As far as organic nitrogen compounds are concerned, then, roots can thrive without leaves. All these activities by roots require energy, of course. This comes from sugar.

   Underline the word or phrase in the **bold** text that this refers to.

56. It can be inferred from paragraph 2 that ATP is

   ◯ an organic chemical

   ◯ the tip of a root

   ◯ a biochemical process

   ◯ an inorganic mineral

57. The word intact in paragraph 3 is closest in meaning to

   ◯ mature

   ◯ wild

   ◯ whole

   ◯ tiny

58. The phrase come in handy in paragraph 3 indicates that the process is

   ◯ useful

   ◯ predictable

   ◯ necessary

   ◯ successful

59. It can be inferred from the passage that, in the early spring, the buds of plants

   ◯ "export" protein in the form of amino acids

   ◯ do not require water

   ◯ have begun photosynthesizing

   ◯ obtain organic compounds from the roots

60. Which of the following best describes the organization of the passage?

   ◯ The results of two experiments are compared.

   ◯ A generalization is made and several examples of it are given.

   ◯ The findings of an experiment are explained.

   ◯ A hypothesis is presented, and several means of proving it are suggested.

**This is the end of Preview Test 3: Reading.
You may go back and check your answers until time is up.**

LESSON 33: Overview Items

A) MAIN IDEA, MAIN TOPIC, AND MAIN PURPOSE ITEMS

After almost every passage, the first item is an **overview item** about the main idea, main topic, or main purpose of a passage. **Main idea items** ask you to identify the most important thought in the passage. Answer choices for main idea items are usually complete sentences.

SAMPLE QUESTIONS

- What is the main idea of the passage?
- The primary idea of the passage is . . .
- Which of the following best summarizes the author's main idea?

When there is not a single, readily-identified main idea, you may see **main topic items**. These ask you what the passage is generally "about." Answer choices for main topic items are phrases.

SAMPLE QUESTIONS

- The main topic of the passage is . . .
- What does the passage mainly discuss?
- The passage is primarily concerned with . . .

Main purpose items require you to understand *why* an author wrote a passage. Answer choices for main purpose items usually begin with infinitives.

SAMPLE QUESTIONS

- The author's purpose in writing is to . . .
- What is the author's main purpose in the passage?
- The main point of this passage is to . . .
- Why did the author write the passage?

SAMPLE ANSWER CHOICES

- To define . . .
- To discuss . . .
- To illustrate . . .
- To distinguish between . . . and . . .
- To relate . . .
- To propose . . .
- To support the idea that . . .
- To compare . . . and . . .

The correct answers for main idea, main topic, and main purpose items correctly summarize the main points of the passage; they must be more general than any of the supporting ideas or details, but not so general that they include ideas outside the scope of the passages.

Distractors for this type of item have one of these characteristics:

- They are too specific.
- They are too general.

- They are incorrect according to the passage.
- They are irrelevant (unrelated) to the main idea of the passage.

If you're not sure of the answer for one of these items, go back and quickly scan the passage. You can usually infer the main idea, main topic, or main purpose of the entire passage from an understanding of the main ideas of the paragraphs that make up the passage and the relationship between them.

SAMPLE ITEM

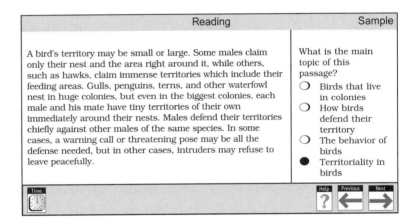

The first choice deals with particular types of birds—gulls, penguins, and others—but the passage concerns all birds. The second choice deals only with the concept of defending a territory. This is the topic of the last two sentences, but not of the passage as a whole. The third choice is too general; there are many types of bird behavior that this passage does not examine. The fourth choice is best, because the entire passage deals with various aspects of birds' territories.

B) OTHER OVERVIEW ITEMS

A number of other items test your overall understanding of the passage. These are often the last item in a set of items.

Tone items ask you to determine the author's feelings about the topic by the language that he or she uses in writing the passage. Look for vocabulary that indicates if the author's feelings are positive, negative, or neutral.

SAMPLE QUESTIONS

- What tone does the author take in writing this passage?
- The tone of this passage could best be described as . . .

SAMPLE ANSWER CHOICES

- Positive
- Favorable
- Optimistic
- Amused

- Negative
- Critical
- Unfavorable
- Angry

- Neutral
- Objective
- Impersonal

- Pleased
- Respectful
- Humorous
- Defiant
- Worried
- Outraged

Most Reading passages have a neutral tone, but sometimes an author may take a position for or against some point. However, answer choices that indicate strong emotion—*angry, outraged, sad*, and so forth—will seldom be correct. The answer choice *humorous* will probably never be correct.

Attitude items are very similar to tone items. Again, you must understand the author's opinion. The language that the author uses will tell you what his or her position is.

SAMPLE QUESTIONS

- What is the author's attitude toward . . . ?
- The author's opinion of ____ is best described as . . .
- The author's attitude toward ____ could best be described as one of . . .
- How would the author probably feel about . . . ?

Another type of attitude item presents four statements and asks how the author would feel about them.

- Which of the following recommendations would the author most likely support?
- The author would be LEAST likely to agree with which of the following statements?
- The author of the passage would most likely be in favor of which of the following policies?

Organization items ask about the overall structure of a passage.

SAMPLE QUESTIONS

- Which of the following best describes the organization of the passage?

SAMPLE ANSWER CHOICES

- A general concept is defined and examples are given.
- Several generalizations are presented, from which a conclusion is drawn.
- The author presents the advantages and disadvantages of ____.
- The author presents a system of classification for ____.
- Persuasive language is used to argue against ____.
- The author describes ____.
- The author presents a brief account of ____.
- The author compares ____ and ____.

Items about previous or following paragraphs ask you to assume that the passage is part of a longer work: what would be the topic of the hypothetical paragraph that precedes or follows the passage? To find the topic of the previous paragraph, look for clues in the first line or two of the passage; for the topic of the following passage, look in the last few lines. Sometimes incorrect answer choices mention topics that have already been discussed in the passage.

SAMPLE QUESTIONS

- With what topic would the following/preceding paragraph most likely deal?
- The paragraph prior to/after the passage most probably discusses . . .
- It can be inferred from the passage that the previous/next paragraph concerns . . .
- What most likely precedes/follows the passage?

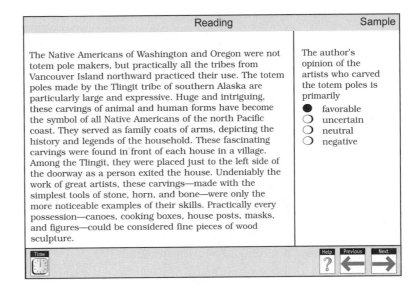

The author says the carvings are the work "of great artists" and that their other works "could be considered fine pieces of wood sculpture." His feelings towards the artists are clearly favorable.

EXERCISE 33.1

Focus: Identifying correct answers and recognizing distractors in main idea/main topic/main purpose items.

Directions: Read the passages. Then mark each answer choice according to the following system:

    S   Too specific
    G   Too general
    X   Incorrect
    I   Irrelevant
    C   Correct

The first one is done as an example.

Passage 1

There are two main types of cell division. Most cells are produced by a process called mitosis. In mitosis, a cell divides and forms two identical daughter cells, each with the same number of chromosomes. Most one-celled creatures reproduce by this method, as do most of the cells in multicelled plants and animals. Sex cells, however, are formed in a special type of cell division called meiosis. This process reduces the number of chromosomes in a sex cell to half the number found in other kinds of cells. Then, when sex cells unite, they produce a single cell with the original number of chromosomes.

1. What is the main topic of this passage?

    _S_ (A) The method by which one-celled organisms reproduce

    _C_ (B) A comparison between mitosis and meiosis

    _X_ (C) Meiosis, the process by which identical cells are produced

Passage 2

The last gold rush belongs as much to Canadian history as it does to American. The discovery of gold along the Klondike River, which flows from Canada's Yukon Territory into Alaska, drew some 30,000 prospectors to the north seeking their fortune—though only a tiny fraction of these "sourdoughs" would get rich. The Yukon became a territory and its capital of the time, Dawson, would not have existed without the gold rush. The gold strike furnished material for a dozen of Jack London's novels; it inspired Robert Service to write "The Shooting of Dan McGrew" and other poems; and it provided the background for the wonderful Charlie Chaplin movie, *The Gold Rush*. It also marked the beginnings of modern Alaska.

2. This author's main purpose in writing is to

    ____ (A) discuss the significance of mining in Canada and the United States

    ____ (B) show the influence of the Klondike gold strike on the creative arts

    ____ (C) point out the significance of the Klondike gold strike

Passage 3

Until the nineteenth century, when steamships and transcontinental trains made long-distance travel possible for large numbers of people, only a few adventurers, mainly sailors and traders, ever traveled out of their own countries. "Abroad" was a truly foreign place about which the vast majority of people knew very little indeed. Early map makers therefore had little fear of being accused of mistakes, even though they were often wildly inaccurate. When they compiled maps, imagination was as important as geographic reality. Nowhere is this more evident than in old maps illustrated with mythical creatures and strange humans.

3. Which of the following best expresses the main idea of the passage?

    ____ (A) Despite their unusual illustrations, maps made before the nineteenth century were remarkably accurate.

    ____ (B) Old maps often included pictures of imaginary animals.

    ____ (C) Map-makers could draw imaginative maps before the nineteenth century because so few people had traveled.

Passage 4

Circumstantial evidence is evidence not drawn from the direct observation of a fact. If, for example, there is evidence that a piece of rock embedded in a wrapped chocolate bar is the same type of rock found in the vicinity of the candy factory, and that rock of this type is found in few other places, then there is circumstantial evidence that the stone found its way into the candy during manufacture and suggests that the candy-maker was negligent even though there is no eyewitness evidence that this is true. Despite a popular notion to look down on the quality of circumstantial evidence, it is of great usefulness if there is enough of it and if it is properly interpreted. Each circumstance, taken singly, may mean little, but a whole chain of circumstances can be as conclusive as direct evidence.

4. What is the main idea of the passage?

____ (A) A manufacturer's negligence can be shown by direct evidence only.

____ (B) Enough circumstantial evidence is as persuasive as direct evidence.

____ (C) Circumstantial evidence can be very useful in science.

Passage 5

The Northwest Ordinance was passed by Congress in 1787. It set up the government structure of the region north of the Ohio River and west of Pennsylvania, then called the Northwest Territory. It established the conditions under which parts of the territory could become states having equality with the older states. But the ordinance was more than just a plan for government. The law also guaranteed freedom of religion and trial by jury in the Territory. It organized the territory into townships of 36 square miles and ordered a school to be built for each township. It also abolished slavery in the Territory. The terms were so attractive that thousands of pioneers poured into the Territory. Eventually, the Northwest Territory became the states of Ohio, Indiana, Illinois, Michigan, and Wisconsin.

5. What is the main topic of this passage?

____ (A) The structure of government

____ (B) The provisions of an important law

____ (C) The establishment of schools in the Northwest Territory

Passage 6

The story of the motel business from 1920 to the start of World War II in 1941 is one of uninterrupted growth. Motels (the term comes from a combination of the words *motor* and *hotels*) spread from the West and the Midwest all the way to Maine and Florida. They clustered along transcontinental highways such as U.S. Routes 40 and 66 and along the north-south routes running up and down both the east and west coasts. There were 16,000 motels by 1930 and 24,000 by 1940. The motel industry was one of the few industries that was not hurt by the Depression of the 1930s. In fact, their cheap rates attracted travelers who had very little money.

6. What does the passage mainly discuss?

____ (A) How the Depression hurt U.S. motels

____ (B) The origin of the word *motels*

____ (C) Two decades of growth for the motel industry

Passage 7

An old but still useful proverb states, "Beware of oak, it draws the stroke." This saying is particularly handy during thunderstorm season. In general, trees with deep roots that tap into groundwater attract more lightning than do trees with shallow, drier roots. Oaks are around 50 times more likely to be struck than beeches. Spruces are nearly as safe as beeches. Pines are not as safe as these two, but are still much safer than oaks.

7. What is the author's main point?

_____ (A) Old proverbs often contain important truths.

_____ (B) Trees with shallow roots are more likely to avoid lightning than those with deep roots.

_____ (C) The deeper a tree's roots, the safer it is during a thunderstorm.

Passage 8

Alternative history is generally classified as a type of science fiction, but it also bears some relation to historical fiction. This type of writing describes an imaginary world that is identical to ours up to a certain point in time, but at that point, the two worlds diverge; some important historical event takes place in one world but not in the other, and the worlds follow different directions. Alternative histories might describe worlds in which the Roman Empire had never fallen, in which the Spanish Armada had been victorious, or in which the South had won the Civil War. Or they may suppose that some technology had been introduced earlier in the world's history than actually happened. For example: What if computers had been invented in Victorian times? Many readers find these stories interesting because of the way they stimulate the imagination and get people thinking about the phenomenon of cause and effect in history.

8. What is the main idea of this passage?

_____ (A) Alternative histories describe worlds in which history has taken another course.

_____ (B) Alternative histories are a type of historical novel.

_____ (C) Science fiction writers have accurately predicted certain actual scientific developments.

Passage 9

Until the late 1700s, metal could not be turned on a lathe to make it uniformly smooth and round because the operator could not guide the cutting tool evenly by hand against the turning piece. This problem was solved by David Wilkinson of Pawtucket, Rhode Island. In 1798 he invented a machine in which the cutter was clamped into a moveable slide that could be advanced precisely, by hand crank, parallel to the work. The slide rest, as it came to be called, has many uses. It permits the manufacture of parts so uniform that they can be interchanged. Without it, mass production would not have been possible. As it turns out, the great English machinist Henry Maudslay developed nearly the same mechanism a few years before, but this was unknown to Wilkinson and does not diminish his accomplishment.

9. Why did the author write this passage?

_____ (A) To prove that Wilkinson's invention was based on Maudslay's.

_____ (B) To demonstrate the importance of mass production to American society.

_____ (C) To show the usefulness of Wilkinson's invention.

Passage 10

Almost every form of transportation has given someone the idea for a new type of toy. After the Montgolfier brothers flew the first balloon, toy balloons became popular playthings. In the nineteenth century, soon after railroads and steamships were developed, every child had to have model trains and steamboats. The same held true for automobiles and airplanes in the early twentieth century. Toy rockets and missiles became popular at the beginning of the space age, and by the 1980s, there were many different versions of space shuttle toys.

10. The main idea of this passage is that

_____ (A) inventors have been inspired by toys to build new forms of transportation

_____ (B) toy automobiles and airplanes were very popular in the early 1900s

_____ (C) toy design has often followed developments in transportation

READING EXERCISE 33.2

Focus: Answering a variety of overview items about short passages.

Directions: Read the passages and mark the best answer choice.

Passage 1

American folk music originated with ordinary people at a time when the rural population was isolated and music was not yet spread by radio, tapes, CDs, or music videos. It was transmitted by oral tradition and is noted for its energy, humor, and emotional impact. The major source of early American folk songs was music from the British Isles, but songs from Africa as well as songs of the Native Americans had a significant part in its heritage. Later settlers from other countries also contributed songs. In the nineteenth century, composer Steven Foster wrote some of the most enduringly popular of all American songs, which soon became part of the folk tradition. Beginning in the 1930s, Woody Guthrie gained great popularity by adapting traditional melodies and lyrics and supplying new ones as well. In the 1950s and 1960s, singer-composers such as Pete Seeger, Bob Dylan, and Joan Baez continued this tradition by creating "urban" folk music. Many of these songs dealt with the important social issues of the time, such as racial integration and the war in Vietnam. Later in the 1960s, musical groups such as the Byrds and the Turtles combined folk music and rock and roll to create a hybrid form known as *folk-rock*.

1. The primary purpose of this passage is to

   ○ trace the development of American folk music

   ○ explain the oral tradition

   ○ compare the styles of two folk-rock groups

   ○ outline the influence of Steven Foster

Passage 2

Every scientific discipline tends to develop its own special language because it finds ordinary words inadequate, and psychology is no different. The purpose of this special jargon is not to mystify non-psychologists; rather, it allows psychologists to accurately describe the phenomena they are discussing and to communicate with each other effectively. Of course, psychological terminology consists in part of everyday words such as *emotion, intelligence,* and *motivation,* but psychologists use these words somewhat differently. For example, a non-psychologist may use the term *anxiety* to mean nervousness or fear, but most psychologists reserve the term to describe a condition produced when one fears events over which one has no control.

2. The main topic of this passage is

   ○ effective communication

   ○ the special language of psychology

   ○ two definitions of the word "anxiety"

   ○ the jargon of science

Passage 3

Gifford Pinchot was the first professionally trained forester in the United States. After he graduated from Yale University in 1889, he studied forestry in Europe. In the 1890s he managed the forest on the Biltmore estate in North Carolina (now Pisgah National Forest) and became the first person to practice scientific forestry. Perhaps his most important contribution to conservation was persuading President Theodore Roosevelt to set aside millions of acres in the West as forest reserves. These lands now make up much of the national parks and national forests of the United States. Pinchot became the Chief Forester of the U.S. Forest Service in 1905. Although he held that post for only five years, he established guidelines that set forest policy for decades to come.

3. The passage primarily deals with

   ○ Gifford Pinchot's work on the Biltmore estate

   ○ the practice and theory of scientific forestry

   ○ the origin of national parks and national forests in the United States

   ○ the contributions Gifford Pinchot made to American forestry

Passage 4

Off-Broadway theater developed in New York City in about 1950 as a result of dissatisfaction with conditions on Broadway. Its founders believed that

Broadway theater was overly concerned with producing safe, commercially-successful hit plays rather than drama with artistic quality. Off-Broadway producers tried to assist playwrights, directors, and performers who could not find work on Broadway. Off-Broadway theaters were poorly equipped, had limited seating, and provided few conveniences for audiences. But the originality of the scripts, the creativity of the performers, and the low cost of tickets made up for these disadvantages, and off-Broadway theater prospered. However, by the 1960s, costs began to rise and by the 1970s off-Broadway theater was encountering many of the difficulties of Broadway and had lost much of its vitality. With its decline, an experimental movement sometimes called *off-off-Broadway theater* developed.

4. What is the main idea of this passage?

   ○ After initial success, off-Broadway theater began to decline.

   ○ Off-Broadway theaters produced many hit commercial plays.

   ○ Theaters on Broadway were not well equipped.

   ○ Tickets for off-Broadway plays were relatively cheap.

5. The paragraph that follows this passage most likely deals with

   ○ the help that off-Broadway producers provided directors, playwrights, and performers

   ○ methods off-Broadway theaters used to cope with rising prices

   ○ the development of off-off-Broadway theater

   ○ the decline of Broadway theater

Passage 5

At the time of the first European contact, there were 500 to 700 languages spoken by Native Americans. These were divided into some 60 language families, with no demonstrable linguistic relationship among them. Some of these language families spread across several of the seven cultural areas. The Algonquin family, for instance, contained dozens of languages and occupied a vast territory. Speakers of Algonquin languages included the Algonquins of the Eastern Woodland, the Blackfeet of the Great Plains, and the Wiyots and Yuroks of California. Other language families, like the Zuni family of the Southwest, occupied only a few square miles of area and contained only a single tribal language.

6. What is the main idea of this passage?

   ○ Each of the cultural areas was dominated by one of the language families.

   ○ The Zuni language is closely related to the Algonquin language.

   ○ There is considerable diversity in the size and the number of languages in the language families of Native Americans.

   ○ Contact with Europeans had an extraordinary effect on the languages of the Native Americans of North America.

Passage 6

Further changes in journalism occurred around this time. In 1846 Richard Hoe invented the steam cylinder rotary press, making it possible to print newspapers faster and cheaper. The development of the telegraph made possible much speedier collection and distribution of news. Also in 1846, the first wire service was organized. A new type of newspaper appeared around this time, one that was more attuned to the spirit and needs of the new America. Although newspapers continued to cover politics, they came to report more human interest stories and to record the most recent news, which they could not have done before the telegraph. New York papers, and those of other northern cities, maintained corps of correspondents to go into all parts of the country to cover newsworthy events.

7. The main purpose of the passage is to
   - ○ present a brief history of American journalism
   - ○ outline certain developments in mid-nineteenth century journalism
   - ○ explain why 1846 was such an important year in U.S. history
   - ○ present some biographical information about Richard Hoe

8. What is the most probable topic of the paragraph preceding this one?
   - ○ Other types of rotary presses
   - ○ Alternatives to using wire services
   - ○ Newspapers that concentrated on politics
   - ○ Other developments in journalism

9. The tone of the passage could best be described as
   - ○ objective
   - ○ optimistic
   - ○ angry
   - ○ humorous

Passage 7

In the western third of North America, the convoluted folds of the Earth's surface and its fractured geologic structure tend to absorb the seismic energy of an earthquake. Even if an earthquake measuring 8.5 on the Richter scale struck Los Angeles, its force would fade by the time it reached San Francisco, some 400 miles away. But in the eastern two-thirds of the continent the same energy travels more easily. The earthquake that struck New Madrid, Missouri in 1811, estimated at 8 on the Richter scale, shook Washington, D.C., about 800 miles away, and was felt as far as Boston and Toronto.

10. Which of the following best expresses the main idea of this passage?
   - ○ If a major earthquake strikes Los Angeles, it will probably damage San Francisco as well.
   - ○ The New Madrid earthquake of 1811 was felt in Boston and Toronto.
   - ○ The geology of the western United States is much more complex than that of the eastern United States.
   - ○ Earthquakes travel farther in the East than in the West.

Passage 8

There has never been an adult scientist who has been half as curious as any child between the ages of four months and four years. Adults sometimes mistake this superb curiosity about everything as a lack of ability to concentrate. The truth is that children begin to learn at birth, and by the time they begin formal schooling at the age of five or six, they have already absorbed a fantastic amount of information, perhaps more, fact for fact, than they will learn for the rest of their lives. Adults can multiply by many times the knowledge children absorb if they appreciate this curiosity while simultaneously encouraging children to learn.

11. What is the main idea of this passage?

   ○ Children lack the ability to concentrate.

   ○ Young children with a healthy sense of curiosity may become scientists as adults.

   ○ The first few years of school are the most important ones for most children.

   ○ Adults can utilize children's intense curiosity to help children learn more.

Passage 9

Settlement houses were institutions established to improve living conditions in poor city neighborhoods in the late 1800s and early 1900s. Settlement houses, also known as neighborhood centers, offered health, educational, recreational, and cultural activities. In addition to direct services, they contributed to efforts to promote better housing, cleaner streets, and laws to regulate child labor. They offered courses in English language and U.S. government to immigrants. The first to open in the United States was University Settlement in New York City. It was established by the social reformer Stanton Coit in 1886. The most famous example was Hull House, established by the well-known reformer Jane Addams in Chicago in 1890. Settlement houses were usually staffed by idealistic young college graduates who were eager to improve the conditions of the poor.

12. The passage mainly discusses

   ○ the curriculum of English language and U.S. government classes

   ○ the idealism of college graduates

   ○ the function and history of settlement houses

   ○ the life of several American social reformers

Passage 10

Isadora Duncan was a daring, dynamic innovator in dance. While she was not very successful in teaching her highly personal style of dance to others, she taught a generation of dancers to trust their own forms of expression. She rebelled against the rigid, formal style of classical ballet. Inspired by the art of Greece, she usually danced barefoot in a loose, flowing Greek tunic. She found further inspiration in nature and used dance movements to mirror the waves of the sea and passing clouds.

Isadora Duncan was born in San Francisco in 1877. She gave her first performance in 1899. Early failures gave way to triumphant performances in Budapest, Berlin, London, and finally, in 1908, back in the United States. She lived in Europe most of her life, establishing dancing schools for children there. She died in 1927 near Nice, France in a freak accident, her long scarf being caught in the wheel of an open sports car in which she was riding.

13. The author's attitude toward Isadora Duncan could best be described as one of

   ○ displeasure

   ○ admiration

   ○ compassion

   ○ amazement

14. Which of the following best describes the organization of the passage?

   ○ The author first discusses Isadora Duncan's style of dance and then her life history.

   ○ The first paragraph deals with Isadora Duncan's role as a teacher, the second with her role as a performer.

   ○ The author first discusses Isadora Duncan's shortcomings and then her positive points.

   ○ First there is an analysis of Isadora Duncan's influences and then of her lasting contributions to dance.

Passage 11

Through the centuries, the dream of medieval alchemists was to discover how to turn lead and other "base" metals into gold. Some alchemists were fakes, but many were learned men with philosophical goals. Their quest was based on the ancient idea that all matter consists of different proportions of just four substances—earth, water, fire, and air. They believed that it was possible to adjust the proportions of the elements that made up lead by chemical means so that it turned into gold, a process called transmutation. Their experiments were concerned with finding the substance—which they called the *philosopher's stone*—that, when added to lead, would cause this astonishing change to take place. Alchemists also searched for the *elixir of life,* a substance that could cure diseases and prolong life. They failed on both counts. However, their techniques for preparing and studying chemicals helped lay the foundation for the modern science of chemistry.

15. Which of the following statements best summarizes the author's attitude toward medieval alchemists?

   ○ Although they were all fakes, they made important contributions to science.

   ○ Their discovery of the philosopher's stone was more important than the achievements of modern chemists.

   ○ Although their theories were sound, they lacked the equipment needed to accomplish their goals.

   ○ They were unable to realize their goals, but they helped prepare the way for modern chemistry.

EXERCISE 33.3

Focus: Understanding the meaning of multi-paragraph passages by identifying the main point of each paragraph.

Directions: Read the following passages and the questions about them. Decide which of the choices best answers the item, and mark the answer.

Passage 1

In most of Europe, farmers' homes and outbuildings are generally located within a village. Every morning, the farmers and farm laborers leave their villages to work their land or tend their animals in distant fields, and return to their villages at the end of the day. Social life is thus centripetal; that is, it is focused around the community center, the village. Only in certain parts of Quebec has this pattern been preserved in North America.

Throughout most of North America, a different pattern was established. It was borrowed from northern Europe, but was pushed even further in the New World where land was cheap or even free. It is a centrifugal system of social life, with large isolated farms whose residents go to the village only to buy goods and procure services. The independence associated with American farmers stems from this pattern of farm settlement. The American farmer is as free of the intimacy of the village as is the urbanite.

1. The main topic of the first paragraph is
   - ○ European farm products
   - ○ social life in Quebec
   - ○ the European pattern of rural settlement

2. The main topic of the second paragraph is
   - ○ the relative isolation of North American farm families
   - ○ the relationship between farmers and urbanites in North America
   - ○ the low cost of farmland in North America

3. The main topic of the entire passage is
   - ○ a comparison of farming in northern and southern Europe
   - ○ the difference between farming in Quebec and the rest of North America
   - ○ European influence on American agriculture
   - ○ a contrast between a centripetal system of rural life and a centrifugal system

Passage 2

While fats have lately acquired a bad image, one should not forget how essential they are. Fats provide the body's best means of storing energy, a far more efficient energy source than either carbohydrates or proteins. They act as insulation against cold, as cushioning for the internal organs, and as lubricants. Without fats, there would be no way to utilize fat soluble vitamins. Furthermore, some fats contain fatty acids that provide necessary growth factors, strengthen the immune system, and help with the digestion of other foods.

An important consideration of fat intake is the ratio of saturated fats to unsaturated fats. Saturated fats, which are derived from dairy products, animal fats, and tropical oils, increase the amount of cholesterol in the blood. Cholesterol may lead to coronary heart disease by building up in the arteries of the heart. However, unsaturated fats, derived from vegetable oils, tend to lower serum cholesterol if taken in a proportion twice that of saturated fats.

The consumption of a variety of fats is necessary, but the intake of too much fat may lead to a variety of health problems. Excessive intake of fats, like all nutritional excesses, is to be avoided.

4. The main idea of the first paragraph is that fats

    ○ deserve their bad image

    ○ serve important functions in the body

    ○ store energy more efficiently than proteins or carbohydrates

5. What is the main idea of the second paragraph?

    ○ Unsaturated fats may reduce cholesterol levels.

    ○ The consumption of any type of fat leads to heart disease.

    ○ It is important to eat the proper proportion of saturated fats and unsaturated fats.

6. The main idea of the third paragraph is that

    ○ people are eating less and less fat today

    ○ fats should be gradually eliminated from the diet

    ○ excessive consumption of fats may be dangerous to one's health

7. With which of the following is the whole passage primarily concerned?

    ○ The role of fats in human health

    ○ The dangers of cholesterol

    ○ The benefits of fats in the diet

    ○ The importance of good nutrition

Passage 3

The term *weathering* refers to all the ways in which rock can be broken down. It takes place because minerals formed in a particular way (say at high temperatures, in the case of igneous rocks) are often unstable when exposed to various conditions. Weathering involves the interaction of the lithosphere (the Earth's crust) with the atmosphere and hydrosphere (air and water). It occurs at different rates and in different ways, depending on the climactic and environmental conditions. But all kinds of weathering ultimately produce broken minerals and rock fragments and other products of the decomposition of stone.

Soil is the most obvious and, from the human point of view, the most important result of the weathering process. Soil is the weathered part of the Earth's crust that is capable of sustaining plant life. Its character depends on the nature of the rock from which it is formed. It also depends on the climate and on the relative "age" of the soil. Immature soils are little more than broken rock fragments. Over time, immature soil develops into mature soil, which contains quantities of humus, formed from decayed plant matter. Mature soil is darker, richer in microscopic life, and more conducive to plant growth.

8. The first paragraph primarily describes

   ○ the process by which rocks are broken down

   ○ the weathering of igneous rocks

   ○ gradual changes in the Earth's weather patterns

9. The main topic of the second paragraph is

   ○ a description of immature soil

   ○ the growth of plants

   ○ the evolution of soil

10. The main idea of the entire passage is that

   ○ weathering breaks down rocks and leads to the development of soil

   ○ soils may be classified as mature or immature

   ○ the process of soil development is more important to humans than is that of weathering

   ○ the Earth's crust is constantly changing

Passage 4

The first Dutch outpost in New Netherland was made at Fort Orange (now Albany) in 1624; it became a depot of the fur trade. But the most important settlement was at the southern tip of Manhattan, commanding the great harbor at the mouth of the Hudson River. Peter Minuit, first governor-general of New Netherland, "purchased" title to the island from the Canarsie Indians for the equivalent of twenty-four dollars worth of trinkets. However, the Canarsie Indians might be described as tourists from Brooklyn; Minuit had to make a later payment to the group that was actually resident there.

In 1626 engineers from Holland arrived in Manhattan to construct Fort Amsterdam. Within its rectangular walls, permanent houses were built, replacing the thatched dwellings of the original Manhattanites. The fort became the nucleus of the town of New Amsterdam. Soon Manhattan had its first skyline: the solid outline of the fort, the flagstaff, the silhouette of a giant windmill, and the masts of trading ships.

The Dutch West India Company established dairy farms in the vicinity of New Amsterdam. Each morning, the cattle were driven to the "Bouwerie" (now the Bowery), a large open common in the city. Just southwest of the Bouwerie was the Bowling Green, a level area where the burghers played ninepins, the ancestor of modern bowling. The Bowling Green became the site of a cattle fair where livestock were marketed; beer and sausage was available from booths; cheese, lace, and linen were sold by farmers' wives; and Native American women sold baskets and other handicrafts. These colorful gatherings, and other aspects of everyday life in New Amsterdam, are described in Washington Irving's rollicking book, *History of New York by Diedrich Knickerbocker*.

The last and most powerful governor-general of New Netherland was Peter Stuyvesant, famous for his temper and his wooden leg. He annexed the Swedish colony of Delaware and ordered the streets of New Amsterdam laid out in an orderly manner and numbered. He did his best to obtain military and financial aid from Holland against the British. When the British sent emissaries demanding the surrender of the colony, he wanted to fight.

Four British warships, commanded by Colonel Richard Nicolls, sailed into the harbor in 1664. The fort was long out of repair and there was a shortage of ammunition. Stuyvesant had no choice but to surrender. New Netherlands became the British colony of New York, and New Amsterdam became New York City.

11. What is the main topic of the first paragraph?

    ○ The first Dutch settlement in New Netherland

    ○ Peter Minuit's acquisition of Manhattan

    ○ Tourism in Manhattan

12. The second paragraph deals primarily with

    ○ the establishment of Fort Amsterdam

    ○ the skyline of Manhattan

    ○ the thatched houses of the Native Americans

13. The third paragraph mainly describes

    ○ aspects of everyday life in New Amsterdam

    ○ the origin of the game of modern bowling

    ○ Washington Irving's book about New Amsterdam

14. What does the fourth paragraph mainly discuss?

    ○ The annexation of the Swedish colony of Delaware

    ○ The ordering of the streets in New Amsterdam

    ○ A description of Peter Stuyvesant and his accomplishments

15. What does the fifth paragraph mainly discuss?

    ○ The fall of New Amsterdam

    ○ The tactics of seventeenth century naval warfare

    ○ The life of Colonel Nicolls

16. What is the primary topic of the entire passage?

    ○ A history of the British colony of New York

    ○ The origin and importance of the cattle fair

    ○ European colonization in the New World

    ○ Forty years of Dutch rule in New Amsterdam

LESSON 34: Detail, Negative, and Scanning Items

A) DETAIL ITEMS

Detail items ask about explicit facts and details given in the passage. They often contain one of the *wh-* item words: *who, what, when, where, why, how much,* and so on.

Detail items often begin with the phrases "According to the passage, . . ." or "According to the author . . . ." When you see these phrases, you know that the information needed for an answer is directly stated somewhere in the passage (unlike answers for inference items).

To answer detail items, you have to locate and identify the information that the item asks about. If you are not sure from your first reading where to look for specific answers, use the following techniques.

- Focus on one or two key words as you read the stem of each item. These are usually names, dates, or other nouns—something that will be easy to find as you scan. Lock these words in your mind.

- Scan the passage as you scroll down looking for these words or their synonyms. Look only for these words. Do NOT try to read every word of the passage.

- Remember that items follow the order of the passage. Therefore, you should always scroll DOWN from the last item you answered, never up.

- Sometimes you can use reference items and vocabulary items to help you pinpoint the location of the information you need. (See page 322 in the introduction to this section for more information about this technique.)

- When you find the key words in the passage, carefully read the sentence in which they occur. You may have to read the sentence preceding or following that sentence as well.

- Compare the information you read with answer choices.

Correct answers for detail items are seldom the same, word for word, as information in the passage; they often contain synonyms and use different grammatical structures.

There are generally more detail items in the Reading section than any other type except vocabulary items.

SAMPLE ITEM

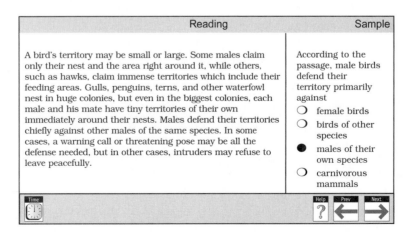

The passage states that male birds "defend their territory chiefly against other males of the same species." There is no mention in the passage of any of the other options.

B) NEGATIVE ITEMS

These items ask you to determine which of the four choices is not given in the passage. These items contain the words NOT, EXCEPT, or LEAST (which are always capitalized).

- According to the passage, all of the following are true EXCEPT
- Which of the following is NOT mentioned in the passage?
- Which of the following is the LEAST likely?

Scan the passage to find the answers that ARE correct or ARE mentioned in the passage. Sometimes the three distractors are clustered in one or two sentences; sometimes they are scattered throughout the passage. The correct answer, of course, is the one that does not appear.

Negative items often take more time than other items. Therefore, you may want to guess and come back to these items later if you have time. Remember to keep track of the items that you guessed at on the notepaper you were given.

SAMPLE ITEMS

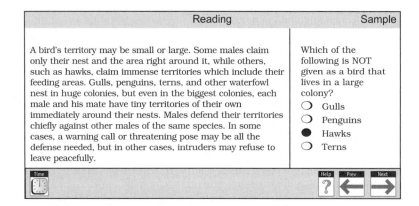

Gulls and penguins are given as examples of birds that live in huge colonies, and who have only small territories. Hawks are given as examples of birds that have large territories.

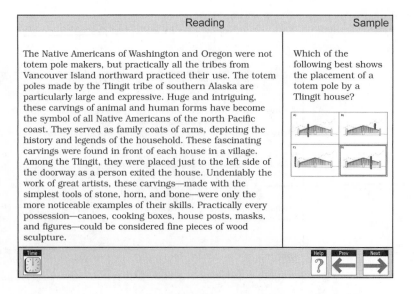

The passage says that, among the Tlingit, the poles were placed just to the left side of the doorway as a person exited the house—as shown in Figure D.

C) SCANNING ITEMS

These items ask you to find a sentence (or sometimes a paragraph) in the passage that plays a certain role in the organization of a paragraph or passage. When you find the sentence or paragraph, you can click anywhere on it and it will be highlighted. Use the same techniques for scanning that are given in Part A for detail items.

SAMPLE ITEMS

- ■ Click on the sentence in Paragraph 1 that explains . . .
- ■ Click on the sentence in Paragraph 3 that discusses . . .
- ■ Click on the sentence in Paragraph 4 that stresses . . .
- ■ Click on the paragraph in the passage that outlines . . .

To answer items that require you to click on a paragraph, you will have to scroll through the whole passage.

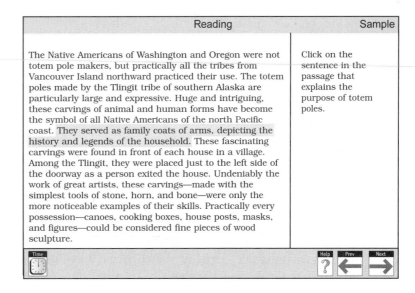

The highlighted sentence above tells what function the totem poles served in the culture of the tribes.

EXERCISE 34.1

Focus: Reading passages to locate answers for scanning items.

Directions: For each item, locate the sentences in the paragraphs that the items ask about and underline them.

Passage 1

Antlers grow from permanent knoblike bones on a deer's skull. Deer use their antlers chiefly to fight for mates or for leadership of a herd. Among most species of deer, only the males have antlers, but both male and female caribou and reindeer (which are domesticated caribou) have antlers. Musk deer and Chinese water deer do not have antlers at all.

Deer that live in mild or cold climates lose their antlers each winter. New ones begin to grow the next spring. Deer that live in tropical climates may lose their antlers and grow new ones at other times of year. New antlers are soft and tender. Thin skin grows over them as they develop. Short, fine hair on the skin makes it look like velvet. Full-grown antlers are hard and strong. The velvety skin dries up and the deer rubs the skin off by scraping its antlers against trees. The antlers fall off several months later.

The size and shape of a deer's antlers depend on the animal's age and health. The first set grows when the deer is from one to two years old. On most deer, the first antlers are short and straight. As deer mature, their antlers grow larger and form intricate branches.

1. Find the sentence in paragraph 1 that explains how deer primarily use their antlers.

2. Find the sentence in paragraph 2 that explains how deer remove the skin from their antlers.

3. Find the sentence in paragraph 3 that describes the antlers of young deer.

Passage 2

Not until the 1830s was there any serious attempt to record the songs and stories of the Native Americans. Henry Schoolcraft collected a great deal of authentic folklore from the Ojibwa tribe and from several other groups. But Schoolcraft lived in a romantic age. There seems to be little doubt that he not only changed but also invented some of the material, and that he mixed the traditions of several tribes. In spite of his failings, he did succeed in bringing the traditions of Native Americans to the attention of the American public.

Schoolcraft's work contrasted sharply with that of the ethnographers who worked in the last decade of the nineteenth century and the first decade of the twentieth. Their aim was to achieve complete accuracy in creating a record of Native American life. They tended to take notes in the original language. With the development of the phonograph, it became possible to preserve not just words but also the tone and emphasis of oral delivery.

4. Find the sentence in paragraph 1 that indicates how Schoolcraft's work had a positive influence.

5. Find the sentence in paragraph 2 that explains what the primary goal of the ethnographers was.

Passage 3

Because of exposure to salt spray and fog, coastal and ocean structures such as bridges, pipelines, ships, and oil rigs require more corrosion protection than structures located inland. One study found that anti-corrosion coatings with a 25 year lifespan inland were good for only five years in coastal areas. Seeking to reduce maintenance coasts for gantries and other structures at the Kennedy Space Center on Florida's Atlantic Coast, NASA (the National Aeronautic and Space Administration) conducted research aimed at developing a superior coating.

This coating had to resist salt corrosion as well as protect launch structures from hot rocket exhaust. The successful research resulted in a new type of inorganic coating that has many commercial applications.

6. Find the sentence in the passage that outlines the qualities for the coating that were required by NASA.

Passage 4

In 1903 the Wright brothers made the first powered flight in history at Kitty Hawk, North Carolina. This site was chosen because of its winds, which would lift the plane like a kite. The first attempt lasted only twelve seconds and covered a distance of less than the wing span of the largest airplanes of modern aircraft. Soon the Wrights and other inventors and pilots were busy improving the airplane. They made much longer flights and even put it to some practical uses. In 1909 the Wrights delivered the first military plane to the United States Army. As early as 1914 a plane had begun to carry passengers on daily flights, and in 1918 regular air-mail service was started between Washington and New York.

7. Find a sentence that offers a description of the first airplane flight.

Passage 5

Today's supermarket is a large departmentalized retail store. It sells mostly food items, but also health and beauty aids, housewares, magazines, and much more. The dominant features of supermarkets are large in-store inventories on self-service aisles and centralized checkout lines.

The inclusion of non-food items on supermarket shelves was once considered novel. This practice is sometimes called "scrambled marketing." It permits the supermarket, as well as other types of retail stores, to sell items that carry a higher margin than most food items. In general, however, supermarket profits are slim—only about one to three percent. Owners rely on high levels of inventory turnover to reach their profit goals.

Supermarkets were among the first retailers to stress discount strategies. Using these strategies, supermarkets sell a variety of high-turnover goods at low prices. To keep prices down, of course, supermarkets must keep their costs down. Other than the cost of the goods they sell, supermarkets' primary costs involve personnel. By not offering delivery and by hiring cashiers and stockers rather than true sales personnel, supermarkets are able to keep prices at a relatively low level.

8. Find the sentence in paragraph 1 that gives the most important characteristics of supermarkets.
9. Find the sentence in paragraph 2 that explains the advantage of "scrambled marketing."
10. Find the sentence in paragraph 3 that explains how supermarkets are able to sell goods cheaply.

Passage 6

There have been many significant innovations in the energy efficiency of windows. One of the most recent is filling the gap between two panes of glass with argon instead of air. Argon is a naturally occuring inert gas that is as transparent as air. Since argon is extremely dense, there is less movement of the gas between the glass panes and therefore, less heat is lost. Adding argon instead of air can improve the insulation value of windows by 30 percent. Argon also deadens outdoor noise.

11. Find the sentence that explains how the use of argon improves insulation.

Passage 7

Washington Irving, born in New York City in 1783, was the first American to win international recognition as a literary figure. In 1809 he published his first important work, *History of New York by Dietrich Knickerbocker,* with its amusing caricatures of Dutch colonists. When his family business failed, Irving was forced to become a full-time writer. In 1819 he published *The Sketch Book.* Utilizing a pleasing style and quiet humor, he combined English, Dutch, and American themes. This collection included the immortal "Rip Van Winkle" and "Legend of Sleepy Hollow." Later turning to Spanish locales and biographies, Irving did much to interpret America to Europe and Europe to America.

12. Find the sentence that explains why Washington Irving became a professional writer.

Passage 8

The concepts of analogy and homology are probably easier to exemplify than to define. When different species are structurally compared, certain features can be described as either analogous or homologous. For example, flight requires certain rigid aeronautical principles of design, yet birds, bats, and insects have all conquered the air. The wings of these three types of animals derive from different embryological structures but perform the same functions. In this case, the flight organs of these creatures can be said to be analogous.

In contrast, features that arise from the same structures in the embryo but are used in different functions are said to be homologous. The pectoral fins of a fish, the wings of a bird, and the forelimbs of a mammal are all homologous structures. They are genetically related in the sense that both the forelimb and the wing evolved from the fin.

13. Find the sentence in paragraph 1 that explains how analogous structures are both similar to and different from one another.

14. Find the sentence in paragraph 2 that provides examples of homologous structures.

EXERCISE 34.2

Focus: Answering detail, negative, and scanning items about reading passages.

Directions: Read the following passages and the questions about them. Decide which of the choices best answers the item, and mark the answer.

Passage 1

Mesa Verde is the center of the prehistoric Anasazi culture. It is located in the high plateau lands near Four Corners, where Colorado, Utah, New Mexico, and Arizona come together. This high ground is majestic but not forbidding. The climate is dry but tiny streams trickle at the bottom of deeply cut canyons, where seeps and springs provided water for the Anasazi to irrigate their crops. Rich red soil provided fertile ground for their crops of corn, beans, squash, tobacco, and cotton. The Anasazi domesticated the wild turkey and hunted deer, rabbits, and mountain sheep.

For a thousand years the Anasazi lived around Mesa Verde. Although the Anasazi are not related to the Navajos, no one knows what these Indians called themselves, and so they are commonly referred to by their Navajo name, Anasazi, which means "ancient ones" in the Navajo language.

Around 550 A.D., early Anasazi—then a nomadic people archaeologists call the Basketmakers—began constructing permanent homes on mesa tops. In the next 300 years, the Anasazi made rapid technological advancements, including the refinement of not only basket-making but also pottery making and weaving. This phase of development is referred to as the Early Pueblo Culture.

By the Great Pueblo Period (1100–1300 A.D.), the Anasazi population swelled to over 5,000 and the architecturally ambitious cliff dwellings came into being. The Anasazi moved from the mesa tops onto ledges on the steep canyon walls, creating two and three story dwellings. They used sandstone blocks and mud mortar. There were no doors on the first floors and people used ladders to get into the building. All the villages had underground chambers called *kivas*. Men held tribal councils there and also used them for secret religious ceremonies and clan meetings. Winding paths, ladders, and steps cut into the stone led from the valleys below to the ledges on which the villages stood. The largest settlement contained 217 rooms. One might surmise that these dwellings were built for protection, but the Anasazi had no known enemies, and there is no sign of conflict.

But a bigger mystery is why the Anasazi occupied these structures for such a short time. By 1300 Mesa Verde was deserted. It is conjectured that the Anasazi abandoned their settlements because of drought, overpopulation, crop failure, or some combination of these. They probably moved southward and were incorporated into the pueblo villages that the Spanish explorers encountered two hundred years later. Their descendants may still live in the Southwest.

1. The passage does NOT mention that the Anasazi hunted
   - ○ sheep
   - ○ turkeys
   - ○ deer
   - ○ rabbits

2. The name that the Anasazi used for themselves
   - ○ means "Basketmakers" in the Navajo language
   - ○ is unknown today
   - ○ was given to them by archaeologists
   - ○ means "ancient ones" in the Anasazi language

3. How long did the Early Pueblo Culture last?

   ○ 200 years

   ○ 300 years

   ○ 550 years

   ○ 1000 years

4. Where did the Anasazi move during the Great Pueblo Period?

   ○ To settlements on ledges of canyon walls

   ○ To pueblos in the south

   ○ Onto the tops of the mesas

   ○ Onto the floors of the canyons

5. According to the passage, the Anasazi dwellings were made primarily of

   ○ grass

   ○ wood

   ○ sandstone

   ○ animal skins

6. According to the passage, the Anasazi entered their buildings

   ○ by means of ladders

   ○ from underground chambers

   ○ by means of stone stairways

   ○ through doors on the first floor

7. According to the passage, *kivas* were used for all of the following purposes EXCEPT

   ○ clan meetings

   ○ food preparation

   ○ religious ceremonies

   ○ tribal councils

8. According to the passage, the LEAST likely reason that the Anasazi abandoned Mesa Verde was

   ○ drought

   ○ overpopulation

   ○ war

   ○ crop failure

9. Put an X next to the paragraph that presents theories about why the Anasazi left their settlements.

Passage 2

Dulcimers are musical instruments that basically consist of wooden boxes with strings stretched over them. In one form or another, they have been around since ancient times, probably originating with the Persian santir. Today there are two varieties: the hammered dulcimer and the Appalachian, or mountain, dulcimer. The former is shaped like a trapezoid, has two or more strings, and is played with wooden mallets. It is the same instrument played in a number of Old World countries. The Appalachian dulcimer is classified by musicologists as a box zither. It is a descendant of the Pennsylvania Dutch *scheitholt* and the French *epinette*. Appalachian dulcimers are painstakingly fashioned by artisans in the mountains of West Virginia, Kentucky, Tennessee, and Virginia. These instruments have three or four strings and are plucked with quills or the fingers. They are shaped like teardrops or hourglasses. Heart-shaped holes in the sounding board are traditional. Most performers play the instruments while seated with the instruments in their laps, but others wear them around their necks like guitars or place them on tables in front of them. Originally used to play dance music, Appalachian dulcimers were popularized by performers such as John Jacob Niles and Jean Ritchie during the folk music revival of the 1960s.

10. According to the passage, which of the following is NOT an ancestor of the Appalachian dulcimer?

   O   The box zither

   O   The santir

   O   The scheitholt

   O   The epinette

11. According to the passage, how many strings does the Appalachian dulcimer have?

   O   One or two

   O   Three or four

   O   Four or five

   O   Six or more

12. According to the passage, the holes in the sounding board of an Appalachian dulcimer generally look like which of the following?

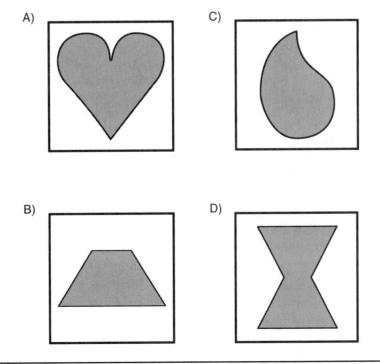

A)

C)

B)

D)

13. According to the author, most performers play the Appalachian dulcimer

   ○ while sitting down

   ○ with the instrument strapped around their neck

   ○ while standing at a table

   ○ with wooden hammers

14. According to the author, what are John Jacob Niles and Jean Ritchie known for?

   ○ Playing dance music on Appalachian dulcimers

   ○ Designing Appalachian dulcimers

   ○ Helping to bring Appalachian dulcimers to the public's attention

   ○ Beginning the folk music revival of the 1960s

15. Underline the sentence in the passage that tells where Appalachian dulcimers are usually made.

Passage 3

Humanitarian Dorothea Dix was born in Hampden, Maine in 1802. At the age of 19, she established a school for girls, the Dix Mansion School, in Boston, but had to close it in 1836 due to her poor health. She wrote and published the first of many books for children in 1824. In 1841 Dix accepted an invitation from the state legislature to teach classes at a prison in East Cambridge, Massachusetts. She was deeply disturbed by the sight of mentally ill persons thrown in the jail and treated like criminals. For the next 18 months, she toured Massachusetts institutions where other mental patients were confined, and reported the shocking conditions she found to the legislature. When improvements followed in Massachusetts, she turned her attention to the neighboring states and then to the West and South.

During the Civil War, Dix served as superintendent of women nurses for the Army. Afterwards she saw special hospitals for the mentally ill built in some 15 states. Although her plan to obtain public land for her cause failed, she aroused concern for the problem of mental illness all over the United States as well as in Canada and Europe. Dix's success was due to her independent and thorough research, her gentle but persistent manner, and her ability to secure the help of powerful and wealthy supporters.

16. In what year was the Dix Mansion School closed?

   ○ 1821

   ○ 1824

   ○ 1836

   ○ 1841

17. Underline the sentence in the first paragraph that explains why Dorothea Dix first went to a prison.

18. Where was Dorothea Dix first able to bring about reforms in the treatment of the mentally ill?

   ○ Canada

   ○ Massachusetts

   ○ The West and South

   ○ Maine

19. Dorothea Dix was NOT successful in her attempt to

  ○ become superintendent of nurses

  ○ publish books for children

  ○ arouse concern for the mentally ill

  ○ obtain public lands

20. Underline the sentence in paragraph 2 in which the author gives specific reasons why Dix was successful.

Passage 4

Ambient divers, unlike divers who go underwater in submersible vehicles or pressure resistant suits, are exposed to the pressure and temperature of the surrounding (ambient) water. Of all types of diving, the oldest and simplest is free diving. Free divers may use no equipment at all, but most use a face mask, foot fins, and a snorkel. Under the surface, free divers must hold their breath. Most free divers can only descend 30 to 40 feet, but some skilled divers can go as deep as 100 feet.

SCUBA diving provides greater range than free diving. The word SCUBA stands for Self-Contained Underwater Breathing Apparatus. SCUBA divers wear metal tanks with compressed air or other breathing gases. When using open-circuit equipment, a SCUBA diver simply breathes air from the tank through a hose and releases the exhaled air into the water. A closed-circuit breathing device, also called a rebreather, filters out carbon dioxide and other harmful gases and automatically adds oxygen. This enables the diver to breathe the same air over and over.

In surface-supplied diving, divers wear helmets and waterproof canvas suits. Today, sophisticated plastic helmets have replaced the heavy copper helmets used in the past. These divers get their air from a hose connected to compressors on a boat. Surface-supplied divers can go deeper than any other type of ambient diver.

21. Ambient divers are ones who

  ○ can descend to extreme depths

  ○ use submersible vehicles

  ○ use no equipment

  ○ are exposed to the surrounding water

22. According to the passage, a free diver may use any of the following EXCEPT

  ○ a rebreather

  ○ a snorkel

  ○ foot fins

  ○ a mask

23. According to the passage, the maximum depth for expert free divers is around

  ○ 30 feet

  ○ 40 feet

  ○ 100 feet

  ○ 400 feet

24. When using closed-circuit devices, divers

  ○ exhale air into the water

  ○ hold their breath

  ○ breathe the same air again and again

  ○ receive air from the surface

25. According to the passage, surface-supplied divers today use helmets made from

  ○ glass

  ○ copper

  ○ plastic

  ○ canvas

26. Underline the sentence in paragraph 3 that explains how surface-supplied divers are able to breathe.

Passage 5

In 1862, during the Civil War, President Lincoln signed the Morrill Act. The measure was named for its sponsor, Congressman (later Senator) Justin S. Morrill of Vermont. Popularly called the Land Grant Act, it provided each state with 30,000 acres of public land for each senator and each representative it had in Congress. It required that the land be sold, the proceeds invested, and the income used to create and maintain colleges to teach agriculture and engineering.

Although not all states used the money as planned in the act, some thirty states did establish new institutions. Purdue University, the University of Illinois, Texas A & M, Michigan State, and the University of California all trace their roots to the Morrill Act. Eighteen states gave the money to existing state universities to finance new agricultural and engineering departments. A few gave their money to private colleges. For example, Massachusetts used much of its funds to endow the Massachusetts Institute of Technology. One state changed its mind. Yale University, a private institute, was chosen to be funded in Connecticut but farmers protested, and the legislature moved the assets to the University of Connecticut.

Most students chose to study engineering. Agriculture was not even considered a science until it had been dignified by the work of research stations. These were established at land grant institutions in 1887 by the Hatch Act. Gradually, universities broke away from the narrow functions Congress had assigned them. Eventually they came to provide a full range of academic offerings, from anthropology to zoology.

Today there are some 69 land grant institutions in all 50 states, the District of Columbia, and Puerto Rico. About one in five college students in the United States attends land grant schools.

27. According to the passage, when the Morrill Act was signed, its sponsor was

  ○ a senator

  ○ a general

  ○ a congressman

  ○ an engineer

28. According to the passage, what did the bill say about the land that was given to the states?

   ○ It had to be used by farmers.

   ○ Universities had to be built on it.

   ○ It had to be sold.

   ○ The states could decide what to do with it.

29. According to the passage, the greatest number of states spent the money they received from the Morrill Act on

   ○ endowing public universities

   ○ creating departments of agriculture and engineering

   ○ establishing new universities

   ○ rebuilding schools that had been damaged in the Civil War

30. Which of these states funded a private college?

   ○ Connecticut

   ○ Massachusetts

   ○ Illinois

   ○ California

31. Who objected to the way the Connecticut legislature initially decided to spend its funds?

   ○ Farmers

   ○ Students

   ○ Senators

   ○ Engineers

32. What was one effect of the Hatch Act of 1887?

   ○ To establish agricultural research stations

   ○ To force land grant institutes to offer different types of courses

   ○ To strengthen engineering programs

   ○ To give universities more academic independence

33. Underline the sentence in paragraph 3 that explains how the types of courses offered at land grant institutes changed over the years.

34. How many land grant institutions are in operation at present?

   ○ 5

   ○ 50

   ○ 69

   ○ 100

35. Put an X by the paragraph in which the author lists the main provisions of the Morrill Act.

LESSON 35: Inference and Purpose Items

A) INFERENCE ITEMS

As in the Listening section, there are items in the Reading section that require you to make **inferences.** The answers to these questions are not directly provided in the passage—you must "read between the lines." In other words, you must make conclusions based indirectly on information in the passage. Many test-takers find these the most difficult items in the Reading section.

Inference items may be phrased in a number of ways. Many of these items contain some form of the words *infer* or *imply.*

- Which of the following can be inferred from the passage?
- It can be inferred from the passage that . . .
- The author implies that . . .
- Which of the following does the passage imply?
- Which of the following would be the most reasonable guess about _____?
- The author suggests that . . .
- It is probable that . . .

SAMPLE ITEM

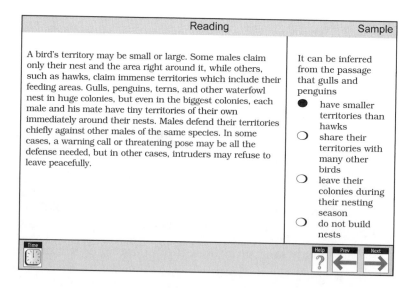

The passage says that birds such as hawks which claim their feeding areas have large territories compared to those which do not, so the first choice is correct. Birds living in colonies have "tiny territories . . . immediately around their nests," indicating that their feeding areas would not be part of their territories. The second choice contradicts the passage, which states that "each male and his mate have tiny territories of their own." The third choice is unlikely because the passage indicates that these birds' nests are part of large colonies; they would not leave during nesting season. The fourth choice is incorrect because the passage states that these birds' nests are part of their territories, therefore, the birds must build nests.

B) PURPOSE ITEMS

These questions ask why the author of a passage mentions a specific piece of information, includes a certain quote from a person or a study, or uses some particular word or phrase.

SAMPLE QUESTIONS

- ■ Why does the author mention ————— ?
- ■ Why does the author give an example of ————— ?
- ■ The author refers to ————— to indicate that . . .
- ■ The author quotes ————— in order to show . . .
- ■ The phrase ————— in line ————— is mentioned to illustrate the effect of . . .

SAMPLE ITEM

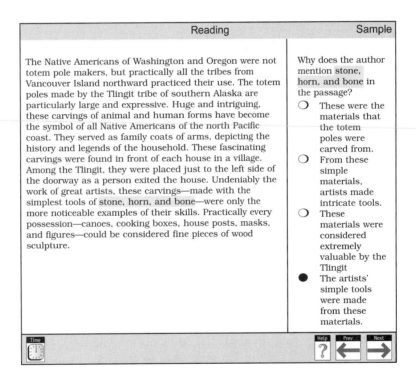

The fourth choice is correct. The passage states "these carvings [were] made with the simplest tools of stone, horn, and bone." The first choice is incorrect since the passage does not mention what totem poles were made from. The second choice is incorrect because the passage refers to the tools as "the simplest," not intricate. The third choice cannot be right because the passage does not supply information about what the Tlingit considered valuable.

EXERCISE 35.1

Focus: Identifying valid inferences based on sentences.

Directions: Read each sentence and mark the one answer choice—(A), (B), or (C)—that is a valid inference based on that sentence.

1. A metalworker of 3,000 years ago would recognize virtually every step of the lost-wax process used to cast titanium for jet engines.

   ____ (A) Titanium has been forged for thousands of years.

   ____ (B) The lost-wax method of casting is very old.

   ____ (C) Metalworking has changed very little in 3,000 years.

2. When apple growers talk about new varieties of apples, they don't mean something developed last month, last year, or even in the last decade.

   ____ (A) Apple growers haven't developed any new varieties in recent decades.

   ____ (B) Some varieties of apples can be developed in a short time, but others take a long time.

   ____ (C) New varieties of apples take many years to develop.

3. High cholesterol used to be thought of as only a problem for adults.

   ____ (A) High cholesterol is no longer a problem for adults.

   ____ (B) Only children have a problem with high cholesterol.

   ____ (C) High cholesterol affects both adults and children.

4. Alpha Centauri, one of the closest stars to Earth, is just 4.3 light years away. It can be seen only from the Southern Hemisphere. However, the closest star, other than our own Sun of course, is a tiny red star, Proxima Centauri, that is not visible without a telescope.

   ____ (A) Proxima Centauri is the closest star to the Earth.

   ____ (B) Alpha Centauri is invisible from Earth without a telescope.

   ____ (C) Proxima Centauri is closer than 4.3 light years from the Earth.

5. Compared with the rest of its brain, the visual area of a turtle's brain is comparatively small since turtles, like all other reptiles, depend mainly on senses other than sight.

   ____ (A) No reptile uses sight as its primary sense.

   ____ (B) Animals that depend on sight all have larger visual areas in their brain than turtles do.

   ____ (C) The visual areas of other reptiles are comparatively smaller than those of turtles.

6. Contrary to popular belief, there is no validity to the stories one hears of initials carved in a tree by a young boy becoming elevated high above his head when he visits the tree as an old man.

   ____ (A) Trees don't grow the way many people think they do.

   ____ (B) If a child carves initials in a tree, it won't grow.

   ____ (C) Over time, initials that are carved into a tree will be elevated.

7. Illegible handwriting does not indicate weakness of character as even a quick glance at the penmanship of George Washington, Franklin D. Roosevelt, or John F. Kennedy reveals.

   ____ (A) Washington, Roosevelt, and Kennedy all had handwriting that was difficult to read.

   ____ (B) A person's handwriting reveals a lot about that person.

   ____ (C) The author believes that Washington, Roosevelt, and Kennedy had weak characters.

8. William Faulkner set many of his novels in and around an imaginary town, Jefferson, Mississippi, which he closely patterned after his hometown of Oxford, Mississippi.

____ (A) William Faulkner wrote many of his novels while living in Jefferson, Mississippi.

____ (B) The town of Oxford, Mississippi exists only in Faulkner's novels.

____ (C) Faulkner actually wrote about his hometown but did not use its real name.

9. Most fish take on the coloration of their natural surroundings to a certain degree, so it is not surprising that the fish inhabiting warm, shallow waters around tropical reefs are colored all the brilliant tints of the rainbow.

____ (A) Tropical fish are unlike other fish because they take on the coloration of their environment.

____ (B) Tropical fish are brightly colored because they inhabit warm waters.

____ (C) Tropical reefs are brightly colored environments.

10. Although sheepherding is an older and more beloved occupation, shepherds never caught the attention of American film makers the way cowboys did.

____ (A) There have been more American films about cowboys than about shepherds.

____ (B) Films about shepherds are older and more beloved than films about cowboys.

____ (C) Cowboys are generally younger than shepherds.

11. The Okefenokee Swamp is a fascinating realm that both confirms and contradicts popular notions of a swamp, because along with huge cypresses, dangerous quagmires, and dim waterways, the Okefenokee has sandy pine islands, sunlit prairies, and clear lakes.

____ (A) Although most swamps are not very interesting, the Okefenokee is an exception.

____ (B) The Okefenokee has features that are not commonly associated with swamps.

____ (C) Unlike most swamps, the Okefenokee does not have huge cypresses, dangerous quagmires, or dim waterways.

12. As an architect, Thomas Jefferson preferred the Roman style, as seen in the buildings of the University of Virginia, to the English style of architecture favored by Charles Bullfinch.

____ (A) The architecture of the University of Virginia was influenced by the Roman style.

____ (B) Bullfinch was an English architect.

____ (C) Jefferson preferred to build in the English style of architecture.

13. In all cultures, gestures are used as a form of communication, but the same gestures may have very different meanings in different cultures.

____ (A) No two cultures use the same gestures.

____ (B) A person from one culture may misunderstand the gestures used by a person from another culture.

____ (C) One gesture almost never has the same meaning in two cultures.

14. Even spiders that do not build webs from silk use it for a variety of purposes, such as constructing egg sacs and nursery tents.

   ____ (A) All spiders build webs.

   ____ (B) Spiders that build webs don't build egg sacs or nursery tents.

   ____ (C) Silk is used by all spiders.

15. In theory, a good screwdriver should last a lifetime, but it seldom does, generally because it is used as a substitute for other tools.

   ____ (A) All screwdrivers, if they are really good, last a lifetime.

   ____ (B) If you want a screwdriver to last a lifetime, use other tools to substitute for it.

   ____ (C) Using a screwdriver for purposes it was not intended can shorten its life.

EXERCISE 35.2

Focus: Answering inference and purpose questions.

Directions: Read the following passages and the questions about them. Decide which of the choices best answers the question, and mark the answer.

Passage 1

Pigeons have been taught to recognize human facial expressions, upsetting long-held beliefs that only humans have evolved the sophisticated nervous systems to perform such a feat. In recent experiments at the University of Iowa, eight trained pigeons were shown photographs of people displaying emotions of happiness, anger, surprise, and disgust. The birds learned to distinguish between these expressions. Not only that, but they were able to correctly identify the same expressions on photographs of unfamiliar faces. Their achievement does not suggest, of course, that the pigeons had any idea what the human expressions meant.

Some psychologists have theorized that, because of the importance of facial expression to human communication, humans have developed special nervous systems capable of recognizing subtle expressions. The pigeons cast doubt on that idea, however.

In fact, the ability to recognize facial expressions of emotion is not necessarily innate even in human babies, but may have to be learned in much the same way as pigeons learn. In experiments conducted several years ago at the University of Iowa, it was found that pigeons organize images of things into the same logical categories that humans do.

None of this work would come as any surprise to Charles Darwin, who long ago wrote about the continuity of mental development from animals to humans.

1. From the passage, which of the following can be inferred about pigeons?

   ○ They can show the same emotions that humans can.
   ○ They can understand human emotions.
   ○ They can identify only the expressions of people they are familiar with.
   ○ They have more sophisticated nervous systems than was once thought.

2. The passage implies that, at birth, human babies

- ⭕ have nervous systems capable of recognizing subtle expressions
- ⭕ can learn from pigeons
- ⭕ are not able to recognize familiar faces
- ⭕ may not be able to identify basic emotions through facial expressions

3. Why does the author mention the experiments conducted several years ago at the University of Iowa?

- ⭕ They proved that pigeons were not the only kind of animal with the ability to recognize facial expressions.
- ⭕ They were contradicted by more recent experiments.
- ⭕ They proved that the ability to recognize human expressions was not innate in human babies.
- ⭕ They showed the similarities between the mental organization of pigeons and that of humans.

4. If Charles Darwin could have seen the results of this experiment, his most probable response would have been one of

- ⭕ rejection
- ⭕ surprise
- ⭕ agreement
- ⭕ amusement

Passage 2

The spectacular and famous eruptions of Old Faithful geyser in Yellowstone National Park do not occur like clockwork. Before the earthquake of 1959, eruptions came every 60 to 65 minutes; today they are as little as 30 minutes or as much as 90 minutes apart. Changes in weather and in atmospheric pressure can influence the regularity of the eruptions and the height of the column. The geyser usually gives a warning: a short burst of steam. Then a graceful jet of water and steam rises up to 150 feet in the air, unfurling in the sunlight with the colors of the rainbow playing across it.

The eruption is only the visible part of the spectacle. In order for a geyser to erupt, there are three necessary ingredients: a heat source, a water supply, and a plumbing system. In the geyser fields of Yellowstone, a steady supply of heat is provided by hot spots of molten rock as little as two miles below the surface. The water supply of Old Faithful comes from groundwater and rainfall, but other geysers in Yellowstone are located on river banks. Geysers have various types of plumbing systems. Geologists studying Old Faithful theorized that it had a relatively simple one consisting of an underground reservoir connected to the surface by a long, narrow tube. In 1992 a probe equipped with a video camera and heat sensors was lowered into the geyser and confirmed the existence of a deep, narrow shaft and of a cavern, about the size of a large automobile, about 45 feet beneath the surface.

As water seeps into Old Faithful's underground system, it is heated at the bottom like water in a teakettle. But while water in a kettle rises because of convection, the narrow tube of the plumbing system prevents free circulation.

Thus, the water in the upper tube is far cooler than the water at the bottom. The weight of the water puts pressure on the column, and this raises the boiling point of the water near the bottom. Finally, the confined, superheated water rises, and the water in the upper part of the column warms and expands, some of it welling out of the mouth of the geyser. This abruptly decreases the pressure on the superheated water, and sudden, violent boiling occurs throughout much of the length of the tube, producing a tremendous amount of steam and forcing the water out of the vent in a superheated mass. This is the eruption, and it continues until the water reservoir is emptied or the steam runs out.

There are two main types of geysers. A fountain geyser shoots water out in various directions through a pool. A columnar geyser such as Old Faithful shoots water in a fairly narrow jet from a conical formation at the mouth of the geyser that looks like a miniature volcano.

5. It can be inferred from the passage that the earthquake of 1959 made Old Faithful geyser erupt

   ○ more frequently

   ○ less regularly

   ○ more suddenly

   ○ less spectacularly

6. Why does the author mention a rainbow in paragraph 1?

   ○ The column of water forms an arc in the shape of a rainbow.

   ○ In the sunlight, the column of water may produce the colors of the rainbow.

   ○ Rainbows can be seen quite frequently in Yellowstone National Park.

   ○ The rainbow, like the geyser, is an example of the beauty of nature.

7. It can be inferred from the passage that which of the following would be LEAST likely to cause any change in Old Faithful's eruptions?

   ○ A drop in atmospheric pressure

   ○ An earthquake

   ○ A rise in the water level of a nearby river

   ○ A period of unusually heavy rainfall

8. The passage implies that Old Faithful would probably not erupt at all if

   ○ the climate suddenly changed

   ○ the tubes of its plumbing system were much wider

   ○ there had not been an earthquake in 1959

   ○ its underground tubes were much longer

9. The author implies that, compared to Old Faithful, many other geysers

   ○ are more famous

   ○ have a more complex plumbing system

   ○ shoot water much higher into the air

   ○ have far larger reservoirs

10. The author mentions the probe that was lowered into Old Faithful in 1992 to indicate that

○ it is very difficult to investigate geysers

○ the geologists' original theory about Old Faithful was correct

○ Old Faithful's structure was more intricate than had been believed

○ some very surprising discoveries were made

11. The author probably compares the formation at the mouth of Old Faithful with a volcano because of the formation's

○ age

○ power

○ size

○ shape

Passage 3

In 1881 a new type of weed began spreading across the northern Great Plains. Unlike other weeds, the tumbleweed did not spend its life rooted to the soil; instead it tumbled and rolled across fields in the wind. The weed had sharp, spiny leaves that could lacerate the flesh of ranchers and horses alike. It exploited the vast area of the plains, thriving in regions too barren to support other plants. With its ability to generate and disseminate numerous seeds quickly, it soon became the scourge of the prairies.

To present-day Americans, the tumbleweed symbolizes the Old West. They read the Zane Grey novels in which tumbleweeds drift across stark western landscapes and remember classic western movies in which tumbleweeds share scenes with cowboys and covered wagons. Yet just over a century ago, the tumbleweed was a newcomer. The first sign of the invasion occurred in North and South Dakota in the late 1870s.

Farmers had noticed the sudden appearance of the new, unusual weed. One group of immigrants, however, did not find the weed at all unfamiliar. The tumbleweed, it turns out, was a native of southern Russia, where it was known as the Tartar thistle. It was imported to the United States by unknown means.

Frontier settlers gave the plant various names: saltwort, Russian cactus, and wind witch. But botanists at the U.S. Department of Agriculture preferred the designation *Russian thistle* as the plant's common name. However, these botanists had a much harder time agreeing on the plant's scientific name. Generally botanists compare a plant to published accounts of similar plants or to samples kept as specimens. Unfortunately, no book described the weed and no samples existed in herbaria in the United States.

12. Which of the following can be inferred about tumbleweeds?

○ They have strong, deep roots.

○ They require a lot of care.

○ They reproduce efficiently.

○ They provide food for ranchers and animals.

13. The passage suggests that most present-day Americans
    ○ consider the tumbleweed beneficial
    ○ don't know when tumbleweeds came to North America
    ○ have never heard of tumbleweeds
    ○ believe tumbleweeds are newcomers to the United States

14. The author mentions the novels of Zane Grey and classic western movies in paragraph 2 because they
    ○ tell the story of the invasion of tumbleweeds
    ○ are sources of popular information about tumbleweeds
    ○ present unbelievable descriptions of tumbleweeds
    ○ were written long before tumbleweeds were present in the United States

15. It is probable that the "group of immigrants" mentioned in paragraph 3
    ○ was from southern Russia
    ○ had lived in North and South Dakota for many years
    ○ imported tumbleweeds into the United States
    ○ wrote a number of accounts about tumbleweeds

16. From the passage it can be inferred that the botanists at the U.S. Department of Agriculture
    ○ could not find any tumbleweeds on the plains
    ○ gave the names saltwort, Russian cactus, and wind witch to the tumbleweed
    ○ could not decide on a common designation for the tumbleweed
    ○ found it difficult to classify the plant scientifically

Passage 4

For most modern airports, the major design problem is scale—how to allow adequate space on the ground for maneuvering wide-body jets while permitting convenient and rapid movement of passengers departing, arriving, or transferring from one flight to another.

Most designs for airport terminals take one of four approaches. In the linear plan, the building may be straight or curved. The passengers board aircraft parked next to the terminal. This plan works well for small airports that need to provide boarding areas for only a few aircraft at a time.

In the pier plan, narrow corridors or piers extend from a central building. This plan allows many aircraft to park next to the building. However, it creates long walking distances for passengers.

In the satellite plan, passengers board aircraft from small terminals that are separated from the main terminals. Passengers reach the satellites by way of overhead shuttle trains or underground passageways that have shuttle trains or moving sidewalks.

In the transporter plan, some system of transport is used to move passengers from the terminal building to the aircraft. If buses are used, the passengers must climb a flight of stairs to board the aircraft. If mobile lounges are used, they can link up directly with the aircraft and protect passengers from the weather.

17. It can be inferred that scale would not pose a major design problem at airports if

○ airports were larger

○ aircraft did not need so much space to maneuver on the ground

○ other forms of transportation were more efficient

○ airplanes could fly faster

18. The linear plan would probably be best at

○ a busy airport

○ an airport used by many small aircraft

○ an airport with only a few arrivals or departures

○ an airport that serves a large city

19. The passage implies that the term "satellite plan" is used because

○ satellites are launched and tracked from these sites

○ small terminals encircle the main terminal like satellites around a planet

○ the plan makes use of the most modern, high-technology equipment

○ airports that make use of this plan utilize data from satellites

20. The passage suggests that shuttle trains transfer passengers to satellite terminals from

○ airplanes

○ the main terminal

○ downtown

○ other satellite terminals

21. It can be inferred that mobile lounges would be more desirable than buses when

○ passengers are in a hurry

○ flights have been delayed

○ the weather is bad

○ passengers need to save money

Passage 5

The sea has been rising relative to the land for at least 100 years, geologists say. During that same period, the Atlantic coast has eroded an average of two to three feet per year, the Gulf coast even faster. Many engineers maintain that sea walls and replenished beaches are necessary to protect the nation's shoreline. Too many people live or vacation in Miami Beach, Atlantic City, or Martha's Vineyard to allow their roads and buildings to simply fall into the sea.

The problem with sea walls is that they simply don't work. One study has shown that, in fact, sea walls accelerate the erosion of beaches.

Faced with the loss of their beaches, other communities have tried a simple but expensive solution: replace the lost sand. These replenishment programs, however, are costly and of dubious value. Another study has shown that only ten percent of replenished beaches lasted more than five years.

22. It can be inferred from the passage that the author

   ○ opposes the use of both sea walls and beach replenishment

   ○ believes beach replenishment would be more effective than sea walls

   ○ opposes any actions to protect the shoreline

   ○ denies that beach erosion is a problem

23. Why does the author mention Miami Beach, Atlantic City, and Martha's Vinyard?

   ○ These are communities with sea walls.

   ○ These are communities that have implemented replenishment programs.

   ○ These are communities in danger of beach erosion.

   ○ These are communities which have lost roads and buildings to erosion.

24. The author cites the two studies in the passage in order to

   ○ suggest that the sea is not rising as fast as was originally believed

   ○ strengthen the engineers' contention that sea walls and replenished beaches are necessary

   ○ propose two new solutions to beach erosion

   ○ support his own position

LESSON 36: Vocabulary Items

Vocabulary items ask about the meaning of words or phrases in the Reading passages. You can often use other words in the same sentence or in nearby sentences to get an idea of the meaning of the word or phrase that you are being asked about. These surrounding words are called the **context.**

You will generally see more Vocabulary items in the Reading section than any other type of item.

Most items ask about single words (usually nouns, verbs, or adjectives). Some ask about phrases involving several words.

In any kind of reading, there are often clues that can help you determine the meaning of words you do not know:

■ **Synonyms**

The first state to institute compulsory education was Massachusetts, which made it mandatory for students to attend school 12 weeks a year.

The word *mandatory* is a synonym for the word compulsory.

■ **Examples**

Many gardeners use some kind of mulch, such as chopped leaves, peat moss, grass clippings, pine needles, or wood chips, in order to stop the growth of weeds and hold in moisture.

From the examples given, it is clear that mulch is a kind of plant matter.

■ **Contrast**

In the 1820s, the Southern states supported improvements in the national transportation system, but the Northern states balked.

Since the Southern states supported improvements and since a word signaling contrast (*but*) is used, it is clear that the Northern states disagreed with this idea, and that the word *balked* must mean something like *refused.*

■ **Word analysis**

A tiger standing in tall grass is almost invisible because of its striped markings.

The prefix in- means *not.* The root -vis- means *see.* The suffix -ible means *able to.* Even if you are not familiar with this word, you could probably guess that it means *not able to be seen* by an analysis of its parts.

■ **General context**

In a desert, vegetation is so scanty that it is incapable of supporting any large human population.

As is generally known, deserts contain little vegetation, so clearly the word scanty must mean *scarce* or *barely sufficient.*

When answering Vocabulary items, you will most often use general context to help you choose the correct answer.

There are two types of vocabulary items on the computer-based test: Multiple-Choice and Click on the Passage.

Multiple-Choice Vocabulary Items

In Multiple-Choice items, you must determine which of four words or phrases listed below the stem can best substitute for a word or words in the passage.

You should follow these steps to answer Multiple-Choice Vocabulary items:

1. Look at the word being asked about and the four answer choices. If you are familiar with the word, guess which answer is correct, but don't click on the answer yet.

2. Read the sentence in which the word appears. (The word will be highlighted in the passage and the paragraph marked with an arrow, so it will be easy to find.) See if context clues in the sentence or in the sentences before or after help you guess the meaning.

3. If you are not sure which answer is correct, read the sentence with each of the four answer choices in place. Does one seem more logical, given the context of the sentence, than the other three? If not, do any seem illogical? (Those you can eliminate.)

4. If you're still not sure, make the best guess you can and go on. If you have time, come back to this item later.

SAMPLE ITEM

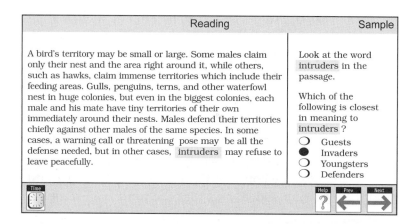

If you plug these four answer choices into the passage, only the second choice is logical. A bird would not have to defend its territory against a *guest*. There is no reason to think that the other male bird is a *youngster*. A bird would not defend its own territory against a *defender*. Only the second choice makes sense.

Click on the Passage Vocabulary Items

In this type of item, a word or phrase in the passage is highlighted. The context of the passage—the sentence in which it appears, and perhaps one or two sentences before or after that—appear in **bold.**

Most of these items ask you to find **synonyms.** You have to click on the word or phrase in the bold text that is closest in meaning to the highlighted word.

To answer synonym items, follow these steps:

1. Look at the word being asked about. If you are familiar with the word, look for words in the bold text that have the same meaning.

2. If you are not familiar with the word, read the bold text looking for context clues.

3. If you can't find a synonym, identify possible answers. The word you are looking for will almost always be the same part of speech—verb, noun, or adjective—as the highlighted word. If the highlighted word is an adjective, try to find all the other adjectives in the bold text.

4. Now read the sentence to yourself with the possible answers in place of the highlighted word. Does one make more sense, given the context of the sentence, than the other three? Do any seem illogical? (Those you can eliminate.)

5. If you're still not sure, make the best guess you can and go on. If you have time, come back to this item later.

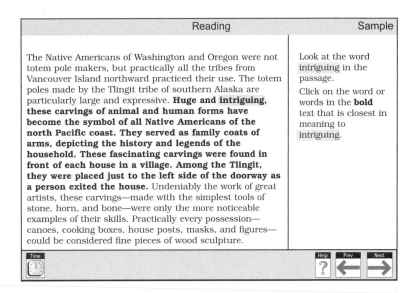

Reading	Sample
The Native Americans of Washington and Oregon were not totem pole makers, but practically all the tribes from Vancouver Island northward practiced their use. The totem poles made by the Tlingit tribe of southern Alaska are particularly large and expressive. **Huge and intriguing, these carvings of animal and human forms have become the symbol of all Native Americans of the north Pacific coast. They served as family coats of arms, depicting the history and legends of the household. These fascinating carvings were found in front of each house in a village. Among the Tlingit, they were placed just to the left side of the doorway as a person exited the house.** Undeniably the work of great artists, these carvings—made with the simplest tools of stone, horn, and bone—were only the more noticeable examples of their skills. Practically every possession—canoes, cooking boxes, house posts, masks, and figures—could be considered fine pieces of wood sculpture.	Look at the word intriguing in the passage. Click on the word or words in the **bold** text that is closest in meaning to intriguing.

The words intriguing and *fascinating* are both used to describe totem poles and they have the same meaning. If you were not sure which answer was correct, you could identify possible answers. Since intriguing describes a noun, it must be an adjective. The other adjectives besides *fascinating* in the bold text are *huge, massive,* and *left. Huge* can be eliminated because it is used in the same phrase as intriguing—two words with the same meaning are not used to describe one noun in the same phrase. The adjective *left* does not make any sense if we substitute it for the word intriguing in the sentence.

A few items ask you to find **antonyms.** For these items, you have to find the word or phrase in the bold text that is most nearly **opposite** in meaning to the highlighted word.

Here are the steps you should follow to answer antonym items:

1. Look at the word being asked about. If you are familiar with the word, look for words in the bold text that have the opposite meaning.

2. If you are not familiar with the highlighted word, read the bold text looking for context clues.

3. If you can't find an antonym, identify possible answers. As with synonyms, the word you are looking for will almost always be the same part of speech as the highlighted word. Try to find words with opposite meanings from among the possible answers.

4. Look for contrast words such as *but, however, although, while,* and *despite* that signal a contrast with the highlighted word.

> A is _____ but it is certainly not _____.
>
> Although B may often _____, it can never _____.

5. If you're still not sure, make the best guess you can and go on. If you have time, come back to this item later.

SAMPLE ITEM

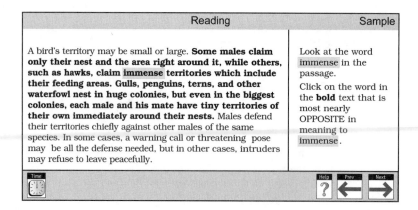

Reading	Sample
A bird's territory may be small or large. **Some males claim only their nest and the area right around it, while others, such as hawks, claim** immense **territories which include their feeding areas. Gulls, penguins, terns, and other waterfowl nest in huge colonies, but even in the biggest colonies, each male and his mate have tiny territories of their own immediately around their nests.** Males defend their territories chiefly against other males of the same species. In some cases, a warning call or threatening pose may be all the defense needed, but in other cases, intruders may refuse to leave peacefully.	Look at the word immense in the passage. Click on the word in the **bold** text that is most nearly OPPOSITE in meaning to immense.

The word immense (meaning *very large*) is used to describe the territories of hawks. This is contrasted with the territories of gulls, penguins, and terns, which are described as *tiny*. Therefore you should click on *tiny*.

EXERCISE 36.1

Focus: Using context clues to answer "click on" vocabulary items.

Directions: Write the word from the passage that is the closest in meaning (or most nearly opposite in meaning) in the blanks.

Passage 1

Everyday life in the British colonies of North America may now seem glamorous, especially as reflected in antique shops. But judged by modern standards, it was quite a drab existence. For most people, the labor was heavy and constant from daybreak to nightfall.

Basic comforts now taken for granted were lacking. Public buildings were often not heated at all. Drafty homes were heated only by inefficient fireplaces. There was no running water or indoor plumbing. The flickering light of candles and whale oil lamps provided inadequate illumination. There was no sanitation service to dispose of garbage; instead, long-snouted hogs were allowed to roam the streets, consuming refuse.

1. Find the word or phrase in paragraph 1 that is most nearly OPPOSITE in meaning to the word glamorous. _____

2. Find the word or phrase in paragraph 2 that is closest in meaning to the word refuse. _____

Passage 2

Blood is a complex fluid composed of several types of cells suspended in plasma, the liquid portion of the blood. Red blood cells make up the vast majority of blood cells. Hemoglobin in the red blood cells picks up oxygen in the blood and delivers it to the tissues of the body. Then these cells carry carbon dioxide from the body's cells to the lungs.

Think of it as a railroad that hauls freight. The cargo (oxygen) is loaded into a railroad car (hemoglobin). Then the locomotive (a red blood cell) carries the cars where they are needed. After unloading, the train returns with a different cargo (carbon dioxide) and the process starts over.

Hemoglobin is the part of the cell that traps oxygen and carbon dioxide. It contains a compound called porphyrin that consists of a carbon-based ring with four nitrogen atoms facing a central hole. The nitrogen bonds to an iron atom, and the iron then captures one molecule of oxygen or carbon dioxide.

3. Find the word or phrase in paragraph 2 that is closest in meaning to the word hauls . ⎯⎯⎯⎯⎯⎯⎯⎯⎯⎯

4. Find the word or phrase in paragraph 2 that is closest in meaning to the word cargo . ⎯⎯⎯⎯⎯⎯⎯⎯⎯⎯

5. Find the word or phrase in paragraph 3 that is closest in meaning to the word traps . ⎯⎯⎯⎯⎯⎯⎯⎯⎯⎯

Passage 3

Taking over as president of Harvard in 1869, Charles W. Eliot pioneered a break with the traditional curriculum. The usual course of studies at U.S. universities at the time emphasized classical languages, mathematics, rhetoric, and ethics. Eliot initiated a system under which most required courses were dropped in favor of elective courses. The university increased its offerings and stressed physical and social sciences, the fine arts, and modern languages. Soon other universities all over the United States were following Harvard's lead.

6. Find the word or phrase in the passage that is closest in meaning to the word pioneered . ⎯⎯⎯⎯⎯⎯⎯⎯⎯⎯

7. Find the word or phrase in the passage that is closest in meaning to the word curriculum . ⎯⎯⎯⎯⎯⎯⎯⎯⎯⎯

8. Find the word or phrase in the passage that is closest in meaning to the word emphasized . ⎯⎯⎯⎯⎯⎯⎯⎯⎯⎯

9. Find the word or phrase in the passage that is most nearly OPPOSITE in meaning to the word required . ⎯⎯⎯⎯⎯⎯⎯⎯⎯⎯

Passage 4

The Pleiades, named after the seven sisters of Greek mythology, is a star cluster that can be seen with the naked eye. It appears as a dipper-shaped group of stars high overhead on autumn evenings. It is so young (only a few million years old) that many of its stars appear to be surrounded by a luminous blue mist . This haze is actually starlight reflecting off debris left behind after the stars were formed. Our own Sun's stellar neighborhood probably looked much like this just after its formation.

10. Find the word or phrase in the passage that is closest in meaning to the word cluster . _____

11. Find the word or phrase in the passage that is closest in meaning to the word mist . _____

Passage 5

Interior designers may claim that a solitary goldfish displayed in a glass bowl makes a striking minimalist fashion statement, but according to a team of British researchers, goldfish learn from each other and are better off in groups than alone. In one experiment, two groups of goldfish were released into a large aquarium separated by a transparent plastic panel. On one side, food was hidden in various locations. The fish on that side foraged for the food while the fish on the other side of the clear panel watched. When released into the feeding area, these observant fish hunted for the food exactly in the proper locations. Other experiments showed that fish raised in a group are less fearful of attack than fish raised alone. And not only are they less skittish , they are also better at avoiding enemies in the event of actual danger.

12. Find the word or phrase in the passage that is closest in meaning to the word solitary . _____

13. Find the word or phrase in the passage that is closest in meaning to the word transparent . _____

14. Find the word or phrase in the passage that is closest in meaning to the word foraged . _____

15. Find the word or phrase in the passage that is closest in meaning to the word skittish . _____

Passage 6

Although business partnerships enjoy certain advantages over sole proprietorships, there are drawbacks as well. One problem that may afflict partnerships is the fact that each general partner is liable for the debts incurred by any other partner. Moreover, he or she is responsible for lawsuits resulting from any partner's malpractice. Interpersonal conflicts may also plague partnerships. All partnerships, from law firms to rock groups, face the problem of personal disagreements. Another problem is the difficulty of dissolving partnerships. It is much easier to dissolve a sole proprietorship than it is to terminate a partnership. Generally, a partner who wants to leave must find someone—either an existing partner or an outsider acceptable to the remaining partners—to buy his or her interest in the firm.

16. Find the word or phrase in the passage that is most nearly OPPOSITE in meaning to the word drawbacks . _____

17. Find the word or phrase in the passage that is closest in meaning to the word liable . _____

18. Find the word or phrase in the passage that is closest in meaning to the word conflicts . _____

19. Find the word or phrase in the passage that is closest in meaning to the word plague . _____

20. Find the word or phrase in the passage that is closest in meaning to the word dissolve . _____

Passage 7

Some 2,400 years ago, the Greek philosophers Democritus and Leucippus suggested that if you slice an item, such as a loaf of bread, in half, and then in half again and again until you could cut it no longer, you would reach the ultimate building block. They called it an atom.

The atom is infinitesimal . To grasp the scale of the atom, look at the dot over an *i* on this page. Magnify this dot by a million times through an electron microscope, and you will see an array of a million ink molecules. If you could somehow blow up this image a million times, you would see the fuzzy image of the largest atoms. And as minute as atoms are, they are composed of still tinier subatomic particles.

21. Find the word or phrase in paragraph 1 that is closest in meaning to the word slice . _____

22. Find the word or phrase in paragraph 2 that is closest in meaning to the word infinitesimal . _____

23. Find the word or phrase in paragraph 2 that is closest in meaning to the phrase blow up . _____

EXERCISE 36.2

Focus: Answering both types of vocabulary items about words or phrases in reading passages.

Directions: Answer the items about the vocabulary in the passages. Mark the proper oval for multiple-choice items and underline the appropriate word or phrase in the bold text to answer "click on" items.

Passage 1

The Civil War created feverish manufacturing activity to supply critical material, especially in the North. When the fighting stopped, the stage was set for dramatic economic growth. Wartime taxes on production had vanished and the few taxes that remained leaned heavily on real estate , not on business. The population flow from farm to city increased and the labor force it provided was buttressed by millions of recent immigrants. These newcomers were willing to work for low wages in the mills of the North and on the railroad crews of the Midwest and West.

The federal government's position towards economic expansion was nothing if not accommodating . The government established tariff barriers, provided loans and grants to build a transcontinental railroad, and assumed a studied stance of nonintervention in private enterprise. The Social Darwinism of British philosopher Herbert Spencer and American economist William Graham Summer prevailed . The theory was that business, if left to its own devices , would eliminate the weak and nurture the strong. But as business expanded, the rivalry heated up. In the 1880s, five railroads operating between New York and Chicago vied for traffic, and two more were under construction. As a result of the battle, the fare between the cities decreased to one dollar. Petroleum companies likewise competed savagely and, in the 1880s, many of them failed.

1. The word feverish in paragraph 1 is closest in meaning to

   ○ extremely rapid

   ○ sickly and slow

   ○ very dangerous

   ○ understandable

2. Which of the following is closest in meaning to the word critical in paragraph 1?

   ○ Industrial

   ○ Serious

   ○ Crucial

   ○ Impressive

3. The phrase the stage was set in paragraph 1 is closest in meaning to which of the following?

   ○ The game was over.

   ○ The progress continued.

   ○ The foundation was laid.

   ○ The direction was clear.

4. Look at the word newcomers in the **bold** text.

   The population flow from farm to city increased, and the labor force it provided was buttressed by millions of recent immigrants. These

---

newcomers were willing to work for low wages in the mills of the North and on the railroad crews of the Midwest and West.

Underline the word or phrase in the **bold** text that is closest in meaning to the word newcomers.

5. The phrase real estate in paragraph 1 refers to

◯ tools and machines

◯ personal income

◯ new enterprises

◯ land and buildings

6. The word buttressed in paragraph 1 is closest in meaning to

◯ concerned

◯ supplemented

◯ restructured

◯ enlightened

7. The word accommodating in paragraph 2 is closest in meaning to

◯ persistent

◯ indifferent

◯ balanced

◯ helpful

8. Look at the word stance in the **bold** text.

The federal government's position towards economic expansion was nothing if not accommodating. It established tariff barriers, provided loans and grants to build a transcontinental railroad, and assumed a studied stance of nonintervention in private enterprise.

Underline the word or phrase in the **bold** text that is closest in meaning to the word stance.

9. The word prevailed in paragraph 2 is closest in meaning to

◯ influenced

◯ predominated

◯ premiered

◯ evolved

10. The phrase left to its own devices in paragraph 2 means

◯ forced to do additional work

◯ allowed to do as it pleased

◯ made to change its plans

◯ encouraged to produce more goods

11. Look at the word vied in the **bold** text.

In the 1880s, five railroads operating between New York and Chicago vied for traffic, and two more were under construction. As a result of the battle, the fare between the cities decreased to one dollar. Petroleum companies likewise competed savagely and, in the 1880s, many of them failed.

Underline the word or phrase in the **bold** text that is closest in meaning to the word vied .

12. The word savagely in paragraph 2 is closest in meaning to

- ○ fiercely
- ○ suddenly
- ○ surprisingly
- ○ genuinely

Passage 2

All birds have feathers, and feathers are unique to birds. No other major group of animals is so easy to categorize . All birds have wings, too, but wings are not peculiar to birds.

Many adaptations are found in both feathers and wings. Feathers form the soft down of geese and ducks, the long showy plumes of ostriches and egrets, and the strong flight feathers of eagles and condors. Wings vary from the short, broad ones of chickens, who seldom fly, to the long, slim ones of albatrosses, who spend almost all their lives soaring on air currents. In penguins, wings have been modified into flippers and feathers into a waterproof covering. In kiwis, the wings are almost impossible to detect .

Yet diversity among birds is not so striking as it is among mammals. The difference between a hummingbird and a penguin is immense, but hardly as startling as that between a bat and a whale. It is variations in details rather than in fundamental patterns that has been important in the adaptation of birds to many kinds of ecosystems.

13. Look at the words peculiar to in the **bold** text.

All birds have feathers, and feathers are unique to birds. No other major group of animals is so easy to categorize. All birds have wings, too, but wings are not peculiar to birds.

Underline the word or phrase in the **bold** text closest in meaning to the words peculiar to .

14. The word categorize in paragraph 1 is closest in meaning to

- ○ appreciate
- ○ comprehend
- ○ classify
- ○ visualize

15. The word showy in paragraph 2 is closest in meaning to which of the following?
    ○ Ornamental
    ○ Graceful
    ○ Colorless
    ○ Powerful

16. Look at the word slim in the **bold** text below:

    Feathers form the soft down of geese and ducks, the long showy plumes of ostriches and egrets, and the strong flight feathers of eagles and condors. Wings vary from the short, broad ones of chickens, who seldom fly, to the long, slim ones of albatrosses, who spend almost all their lives soaring on air currents.

    Underline the word or phrase in the **bold** text most nearly OPPOSITE in meaning to the word slim .

17. The word detect in paragraph 2 is closest in meaning to
    ○ utilize
    ○ extend
    ○ observe
    ○ describe

18. Which of the following is closest in meaning to the word diversity in paragraph 3?
    ○ Function
    ○ Heredity
    ○ Specialty
    ○ Variety

19. Look at the word striking in the **bold** text below:

    Yet diversity among birds is not so striking as it is among mammals. The difference between a hummingbird and a penguin is immense, but hardly as startling as that between a bat and a whale.

    Underline the word or phrase in the **bold** text closest in meaning to the word striking .

20. The word hardly in paragraph 3 is closest in meaning to
    ○ definitely
    ○ not nearly
    ○ possibly
    ○ not softly

21. The word fundamental in paragraph 3 is closest in meaning to
    ○ basic
    ○ shifting
    ○ predictable
    ○ complicated

Passage 3

Manufactured in the tranquil New England town of Concord, New Hampshire, the famous Concord Coach came to symbolize the Wild West. Its rugged body and a suspension system of leather straps could handle the hard jolts from rough roads. A journalist describing a railroad shipment of 30 coaches bound for Wells, Fargo and Company wrote, "They are splendidly decorated . . . the bodies red and the running parts yellow. Each door is superbly painted, mostly with landscapes, and no two coaches are exactly alike."

Wells, Fargo and Company was founded in 1852 to provide mail and banking services for the gold camps of California and later won a monopoly on express services west of the Mississippi. A Wells, Fargo Concord Coach carried nine to fourteen passengers plus baggage and mail. The accommodations were by no means plush. However, while conditions may have been primitive and service not always prompt, the stagecoach was still the swiftest method of travel through much of the Far West.

22. The word tranquil in paragraph 1 is closest in meaning to
   ○ peaceful
   ○ busy
   ○ industrial
   ○ tiny

23. The word symbolize in paragraph 1 is closest in meaning to
   ○ recollect
   ○ fulfill
   ○ deny
   ○ represent

24. Which of the following could best substitute for the word rugged in paragraph 1?
   ○ Streamlined
   ○ Roomy
   ○ Sturdy
   ○ Primitive

25. Which of the following is closest in meaning to the word jolts in paragraph 1?
   ○ Signs
   ○ Shocks
   ○ Sights
   ○ Shots

26. The phrase bound for in paragraph 1 is closest in meaning to
   ○ belonged to
   ○ headed for
   ○ built by
   ○ connected with

27. Look at the word splendidly in the **bold** text below:

"**They are splendidly decorated . . . the bodies red and the running parts yellow. Each door is superbly painted, mostly with landscapes, and no two coaches are exactly alike.**"

Underline the word or phrase in the **bold** text closest in meaning to the word splendidly .

28. Look at the word plush in the **bold** text below:

The accommodations were by no means plush . However, while conditions may have been primitive and service not always prompt, the stagecoach was still the swiftest method of travel through much of the Far West.

Underline the word or phrase in the **bold** text most nearly OPPOSITE in meaning to the word plush .

29. Which of the following is closest in meaning to the word swiftest in paragraph 2?

   O Most comfortable
   O Cheapest
   O Most direct
   O Fastest

Passage 4

The Hopi people of Arizona stress the institutions of family and religion. They emphasize a harmonious existence which makes the self-sacrificing individual the ideal. The Hopi individual is trained to feel his or her responsibility to and for the Peaceful People—the Hopi's own term for themselves. Fighting, bullying, and attempting to surpass others bring automatic rebuke from the community.

Implicit in the Hopi view is an original and integrated theory of the universe. With this they organize their society in such a way as to obtain a measure of security from a harsh and hazardous environment made up of human foes , famine, and plagues. They conceive of the universe—humans, animals, plants, and supernatural spirits—as an ordered system functioning under rules known to them alone. These rules govern their behavior, emotions, and thoughts in a prescribed way.

30. Look at the word stress in the **bold** text below.

The Hopi people of Arizona stress the institutions of family and religion. They emphasize a harmonious existence which makes the self-sacrificing

individual the ideal. The Hopi individual is trained to feel his or her responsibility to and for the *Peaceful People*—the Hopi's own term for themselves.

Underline the word or phrase in the **bold** text closest in meaning to the word stress .

31. Which of the following could best substitute for the word harmonious in paragraph 1?

    ○ Cooperative

    ○ Dangerous

    ○ Philosophical

    ○ Exclusive

32. The word term in paragraph 1 is closest in meaning to

    ○ era

    ○ name

    ○ area

    ○ law

33. The word bullying in paragraph 1 is closest in meaning to

    ○ lying

    ○ organizing

    ○ entertaining

    ○ tormenting

34. Which of the following can replace the word rebuke in paragraph 1 with the least change in meaning?

    ○ Prestige

    ○ Criticism

    ○ Reaction

    ○ Acknowledgment

35. Which of the following could best be substituted for the word hazardous in paragraph 2?

    ○ Dangerous

    ○ Random

    ○ Familiar

    ○ Changing

36. The word foes in paragraph 2 is closest in meaning to

    ○ fears

    ○ needs

    ○ enemies

    ○ failures

37. Look at the word prescribed in the **bold** text below.

> **They conceive of the universe—humans, animals, plants, and supernatural spirits—as an ordered system functioning under rules known to them alone. These rules govern their behavior, emotions, and thoughts in a prescribed way.**

Underline the word or phrase in the **bold** text closest in meaning to the word prescribed .

Passage 5

Canadian researchers have discovered a set of genes that determine the lifespan of the common nematode, a type of worm. This finding sheds new light on the aging process that may allow them to delay the inexorable process of aging and death.

By manipulating the newly discovered genes, the team at McGill University in Montreal was able to increase the lifespan of the nematode fivefold. Altering the genes apparently slowed the metabolism of the worms to a more leisurely pace. This caused the DNA effects thought to bring about aging to accumulate more slowly. The causes of aging in humans are undoubtedly more involved than those in nematodes. However, researchers are confident that these discoveries will provide invaluable clues about this hitherto mysterious process.

38. The word determine in paragraph 1 is closest in meaning to
   ○ control
   ○ modify
   ○ maintain
   ○ shorten

39. Which of the following is closest in meaning to the phrase sheds new light on in paragraph 1?
   ○ Contradicts what is known about
   ○ Gives new meaning to
   ○ Provides more information about
   ○ Calls further attention to

40. The word inexorable in paragraph 1 is closest in meaning to
   ○ cruel
   ○ essential
   ○ unstoppable
   ○ incomprehensible

41. Look at the word manipulating in the **bold** text below.

> **By manipulating the newly discovered genes, the team at McGill University**

in Montreal was able to increase the lifespan of the nematode fivefold. Altering the genes apparently slowed the metabolism of the worms to a more leisurely pace.

Underline the word or phrase in the **bold** text closest in meaning to the word manipulating .

42. Look at the phrase more leisurely in the **bold** text below.

Altering the genes apparently slowed the metabolism of the worms to a more leisurely pace. This caused the DNA effects thought to bring about aging to accumulate more slowly. The causes of aging in humans is undoubtedly more involved than those in nematodes.

Underline the word or phrase in the **bold** text closest in meaning to the phrase more leisurely .

43. The word involved in paragraph 2 is closest in meaning to
   ○ committed
   ○ serious
   ○ apparent
   ○ complicated

44. Which of the following is closest in meaning to the word clues in paragraph 2?
   ○ Plans
   ○ Secrets
   ○ Discoveries
   ○ Hints

45. The word hitherto in paragraph 2 is closest in meaning to
   ○ universally
   ○ almost
   ○ previously
   ○ somewhat

LESSON 37: Reference Items

Reference items ask you to find the noun (called the **referent**) that a pronoun or other word refers to.

Two things to remember:

1) The referent almost always comes before the reference word in the passage.

2) The referent is NOT always the noun that is closest to the reference word in the sentence.

On the computer-based test, most reference items are Click on the Passage items but a few are Multiple-Choice items.

A) CLICK ON REFERENCE ITEMS

When you see this type of item, a section of the passage—usually one or two sentences—appears in **bold** text, just as in Vocabulary items. A pronoun or other reference word will be highlighted. You have to find the referent in the bold text that the highlighted word or phrase refers to.

You can identify "possible answers" in the bold text according to the type of reference word that is highlighted. For example, if the pronoun he is being asked about, you would only look for nouns that name a singular male person. Here's a list of common reference words and the kinds of nouns they refer to:

Reference Words	Possible Referents
she her hers herself	A singular female
he his him himself	A singular male
it its itself	A singular thing, place, animal, action, idea
they their them themselves	Plural persons, things, places, animals, actions, ideas
who whose	Person(s)
which	Thing(s), place(s), animal(s), action(s), idea(s)
that (relative pronoun)	Person(s), thing(s), place(s), animal(s), action(s), idea(s)
then	Time
there	Place
this that (demonstrative)	Singular thing, action, idea
these those	Plural things, actions, ideas

This, that, these, and *those* can also be used with nouns: *this person, that time, those animals, these places.*

After you have identified possible answers, you should read the sentence with the answers in place of the reference. Which one is the most logical substitute? If you are not sure, you can at least eliminate unlikely choices and guess.

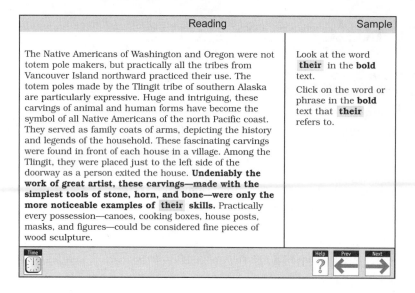

In the bold text, there are a number of plural nouns that their might refer to: artists, carvings, tools, and examples. However, if you substitute the words *carvings, tools,* or *examples* for their, the sentences are not very logical. Only people can possess skills. You should click on the word *artists*.

B) MULTIPLE-CHOICE REFERENCE ITEMS

A few reference items will ask you to choose which one of four nouns a pronoun or other word refers to. Again, you should read the sentence with each of the four choices in place of the highlighted word to decide which of the four answers is the most logical.

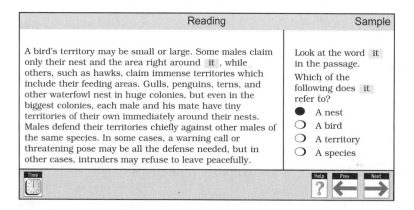

Of these four choices, only *a nest* is a logical substitute for it in the sentence. In general, reference items tend to be the easiest type of Reading item.

EXERCISE 37.1

Focus: Identifying the referents for pronouns and other expressions in sentences and very short passages.

Directions: Read the items. Decide which word or phrase in the items is the correct referent for the highlighted word or phrase and underline it or (for Multiple-Choice items) mark the correct answer. If there are two highlighted words or phrases, underline the first reference and double underline the second.

---

1. X-rays allow art historians to examine paintings internally without damaging them .

2. The poisonous, plantlike anemone lives in a coral reef. When a small fish ventures near this creature , it is stung and eaten. For some reason, the anemone makes an exception of the clown fish. When the clown fish is endangered by another fish, it dashes among the anemone's tentacles. It even builds its nest where the anemone can protect it .

3. Florists often refrigerate cut flowers to protect their fresh appearance.

   ○ florists

   ○ flowers

4. Unlike a box kite, a flat kite needs a tail to supply drag and to keep it pointed toward the sky. A simple one consists of cloth strips tied end to end.

5. Water is an exception to many of nature's rules because of its unusual properties.

6. Ropes are cords at least .15 inches in diameter made of three or more strands which are themselves formed of twisted yarns.

   ○ yarns

   ○ ropes

   ○ strands

   ○ cords

7. Grocers slice sides, quarters, and what are called primal cuts of beef into smaller pieces. These pieces are then packaged and sold.

8. Leaves are found on all deciduous trees, but they differ greatly in size and shape.

9. Yasuo Kuniyashi was born in Japan in 1883 and studied art at the Los Angeles School of Art and Design. He also studied art in New York City, where he gave his first one-man show. In 1925 Kuniyashi moved from there to Paris where he was influenced by the works of Chagall and other artists.

   ○ Japan

   ○ Paris

   ○ Los Angeles

   ○ New York City

10. In the past, biologists considered mushrooms and other fungi a type of non-green plant. Today, however, they are most commonly regarded as a separate kingdom of living things.

11. William Dean Howells, a contemporary and friend of Mark Twain, wrote a number of books that realistically portrayed life on farms in Midwestern America. One of his followers, Hamlin Garland, was even more bitter in his criticism of rural America than his mentor .

12. The Wisconsin Dells is a region where the Wisconsin River cuts through soft sandstone. The strange formations that have been carved out of the rocks there are a delight to tourists. They have names such as Devil's Elbow, Grand Piano, and Fat Man's Misery.

13. After electron microscopes were invented, scientists found many new viruses. Some of them were round, some oval, and some corkscrew-shaped.

  ○ electron microscopes
  ○ viruses
  ○ scientists

14. The detailed information in maps is now produced almost entirely from satellite photography rather than by ground surveying because this method is faster, cheaper, and more accurate.

15. An elephant is bigger than a mouse because it has trillions more cells, not because its cells are any bigger.

EXERCISE 37.2

Focus: Answering reference items based on longer passages.

Directions: Read the following passages and the items about them. Mark the proper oval for Multiple-Choice items and underline the correct referents for "Click on" items.

Passage 1

In addition to the various types of deep mining, several types of surface mining may be used when minerals lie relatively close to the surface of the earth. One type is open pit mining. The first step is to remove the overburden, the layers of rock and earth lying above the ore, with giant scrapers. The ore is broken up by a series of blasting operations. Power shovels pick up the pieces and load them into trucks. These carry it up ramps to ground level. Soft ores are removed by drilling screws, called augers.

Another type is called placer mining. Sometimes heavy metals such as gold are found in soil deposited by streams and rivers. The soil is picked up by a power shovel and transferred to a long trough. Water is run through the soil in the trough. This carries soil particles away with it. The metal particles are heavier than the soil and sink to the bottom where they can be recovered.

The finishing-off process of mining is called mineral concentration. In this process, the desired substances are removed from the waste in various ways. One technique is to bubble air through a liquid in which mineral particles are suspended. Chemicals are added that make them cling to the air bubbles. The bubbles rise to the surface with the ore particles attached, and they can be skimmed off and saved.

1. Look at the word them in the **bold** text below.

   The ore is broken up in a series of blasting operations. Power shovels pick up the pieces and load them into trucks.

   Underline the word or phrase in the **bold** text that them refers to.

2. Look at the word These in the **bold** text on the following page.

Power shovels pick up the pieces and load them into trucks. These carry it up ramps to ground level. Soft ores are removed by drilling screws, called augers.

Underline the word or phrase in the **bold** text that These refers to.

3. The phrase Another type in paragraph 2 is a reference to another type of
   ○ deep mining
   ○ ore
   ○ metal
   ○ surface mining

4. Look at the word it in the **bold** text below.

   The soil is picked up by a power shovel and transferred to a long trough. Water is run through the soil in the trough. This carries soil particles away with it .

   Underline the word or phrase in the **bold** text that it refers to.

5. Look at the word they in the **bold** text below.

   This carries soil particles away with it. The metal particles are heavier than the soil and sink to the bottom where they can be recovered.

   Underline the word or phrase in the **bold** text that they refers to.

6. In paragraph 3, the phrase this process refers to
   ○ surface mining
   ○ the depositing of soil
   ○ mineral concentration
   ○ placer mining

7. Look at the word they in the **bold** text below.

   Chemicals are added that make them cling to the air bubbles. The bubbles rise to the surface with the ore particles attached, and they can be skimmed off and saved.

   Underline the word or phrase in the **bold** text that they refers to.

Passage 2

Mount Rainier, the heart of Mt. Rainier National Park, is the highest mountain in the state of Washington and in the Cascade Range. The mountain's summit is broad and rounded. It is 14,410 feet above sea level and has an area of about one square mile. Numerous steam and gas jets occur around the crater, but the volcano has been sleeping for many centuries.

Mount Rainier has a permanent ice cap and extensive snow fields, which give rise to over forty glaciers. These feed swift streams and tumbling waterfalls that race through the glacial valleys. Forests extend to 4,500 feet. There are alpine meadows between the glaciers and the forests which contain beautiful wildflowers. The Nisqually Glacier is probably the ice region that is most often explored by visitors. Paradise Valley, where hotel accommodations are available, perches on the mountain's slope at 2,700 feet. The Wonderland Trail encircles the mountain. Its 90 mile length can be covered in about a week's time.

8. Look at the word It in the **bold** text below.

   Mount Rainier, the heart of Mt. Rainier National Park, is the highest mountain in the state of Washington and in the Cascade Range. The mountain's summit is broad and rounded. It is 14,410 feet above sea level and has an area of about one square mile.

   Underline the word or phrase in the **bold** text that It refers to.

9. Look at the word These in the **bold** text below.

   Mount Rainier has a permanent ice cap and extensive snow fields, which give rise to over forty glaciers. These feed swift streams and tumbling waterfalls that race through the glacial valleys.

   Underline the word or phrase in the **bold** text that These refers to.

10. The word which in paragraph 2 refers to
    ○ forests
    ○ wildflowers
    ○ alpine meadows
    ○ glacial valleys

11. Look at the word Its in the **bold** text below.

    Paradise Valley, where hotel accommodations are available, perches on the mountain's slope at 2,700 feet. The Wonderland Trail encircles the mountain. Its 90 mile length can be covered in about a week's time.

    Underline the word or phrase in the **bold** text that Its refers to.

Passage 3

Some people associate migration mainly with birds. Birds do travel vast distances, but mammals also migrate. Caribou graze on the grassy slopes of northern Canada. When the weather turns cold, these animals travel south until spring. Their tracks are so well-worn that they are clearly visible from the air. Another example is the Alaska fur seal. These seals breed only in the Pribilof Islands in the Bering Sea. The young are born in June, and by September are strong enough to go with their mothers on a journey of over 3,000 miles. Together they swim down the Pacific coast of North America. The females and young travel as far as southern California. The males do not journey so far. They swim only to the Gulf of Alaska. In the spring, males and females all return to the islands, and there the cycle begins again. Whales are among the greatest migrators of all. The humpback, fin, and blue whales migrate thousands of miles each year from the polar seas to the tropics. Whales eat huge quantities of tiny plants and animals. These are most abundant in cold polar waters. In winter, the whales move to warm waters to breed and give birth to their young.

12. Look at the word they in the **bold** text below.

   Caribou graze on the grassy slopes of northern Canada. When the weather turns cold, these animals travel south until spring. Their tracks are so well-worn that they are clearly visible from the air.

   Underline the word or phrase in the **bold** text that they refers to.

13. The phrase Another example in the passage refers to an example of a
   ○ migratory mammal
   ○ place where animals migrate
   ○ bird
   ○ person who associates migration with birds

14. Look at the word They in the **bold** text below.

   The females and young travel as far as southern California. The males do not journey so far. They swim only to the Gulf of Alaska. In the spring, males and females all return to the islands, and there the cycle begins again.

   Underline the word or phrase in the **bold** text that They refers to.

15. In the passage, the word there refers to
   ○ the Gulf of Alaska
   ○ the Pribilof Islands
   ○ southern California
   ○ the Pacific coast of North America

16. Look at the word These in the **bold** text below.

   Whales eat huge quantities of tiny plants and animals. These are most abundant in cold polar waters. In winter, the whales move to warm waters to breed and give birth to their young.

   Underline the word or phrase in the **bold** text that These refers to.

Passage 4

Design is the arrangement of materials to produce certain effects. It plays a role in visual arts and also in the creation of commercial products. Designers are concerned with the direction of lines, the size of shapes, and the shading of colors. They arrange these patterns in ways that are satisfying to viewers. There are various elements involved in creating a pleasing design.

Harmony, or *balance,* can be obtained in a number of ways. It may be either symmetrical (in balance) or asymmetrical (out of balance, but still pleasing to the eye). Or a small area may balance a large area if it has an importance to the eye (because of color or treatment) equaling that of the larger area.

Contrast is the opposite of harmony. The colors red and orange harmonize, since orange contains red. A circle and an oval harmonize, as they are both made up of curved lines. But a triangle does not harmonize with a circle. Because of its straight lines and angles, it is in contrast.

Unity occurs when all the elements in a design combine to form a consistent whole. Unity resembles balance. A design has balance if its masses are balanced, or if its tones and colors harmonize. But unity differs from balance because it implies that balanced elements work together to form harmony in the design as a whole.

17. Look at the word They in the **bold** text below.

   Designers are concerned with the direction of lines, the size of shapes, and the shading of colors. They arrange these patterns in ways that are satisfying to viewers.

   Underline the word or phrase in the **bold** text that They refers to.

18. Look at the word that in the **bold** text below.

   Or a small area may balance a large area if it has an importance to the eye (because of color or treatment) equaling that of the larger area.

   Underline the word or phrase in the **bold** text that that refers to.

19. Look at the word they in the **bold** text below.

   The colors red and orange harmonize, since orange contains red. A circle and an oval harmonize, as they are both made up of curved lines.

   Underline the word or phrase in the **bold** text that they refers to.

20. Look at the word it in the **bold** text below.

   A circle and an oval harmonize, as they are both made up of curved lines. But a triangle does not harmonize with a circle. Because of its straight lines and angles, it is in contrast.

   Underline the word or phrase in the **bold** text that it refers to.

21. In paragraph 4, the word it refers to

   ○ unity

   ○ balance

   ○ a design

   ○ a consistent whole

Passage 5

In most of the earliest books for children, illustrations were an afterthought. But in the Caldecott "toy books," they were almost as important as the lines of copy, and occupied far more space. One can almost read the nursery rhymes from the dramatic action in the pictures.

Since then, thousands of successful picture books have been published in the United States and in many countries around the world. In the best , the text and illustrations seem to complement each other perfectly. Often a single person is both author and illustrator—for example, Robert McCloskey *(Make Way for Ducklings)* and Arnold Lobel *(Frog and Toad Together)*. Many others have been produced by an author-artist team, as in *The Happy Lion*, written by Louise Fatio and illustrated by Roger Duvoisin, and *King Bidgood's in the Bathtub*, written by Audrey Wood and illustrated by her husband Don Wood.

Wordless picture books have also become popular. With a little help, three- or four-year olds can follow the sequence of events and they can understand the stories suggested in them. One of the most delightful examples of a wordless book is Jan Ormerod's *Sunshine.*

American publishers have also drawn on artists from other countries whose original, imaginative works have brought their different visions to American children's book illustration. Among them are Leo Lionni from Italy, Feodor Rojankovsky from Russia, and Taro Yashima from Japan.

22. Look at the word they in the **bold** text below.

   In most of the earliest books for children, illustrations were an afterthought. But in the Caldecott "toy books," they were almost as important as the lines of copy, and occupied far more space.

   Underline the word or phrase in the **bold** text that they refers to.

23. The phrase the best in paragraph 2 refers to the best
   - ◯ picture books
   - ◯ illustrations
   - ◯ authors
   - ◯ nursery rhymes

24. Look at the word they in the **bold** text below.

   Wordless picture books have also become popular. With a little help, three- or four-year olds can follow the sequence of events and they can understand the stories suggested in them.

   Underline the word or phrase in the **bold** text that they refers to.

LESSON 38: Sentence Addition Items

This type of item provides you with a sentence that can be added to a passage. You have to decide where to place this sentence. Black squares will appear between the sentences of one of the paragraphs of the passage. You have to click on the square where you think the sentence belongs. There will probably be from four to ten possible sites where you can insert the sentence.

You will generally see two to five Sentence Addition items per test.

Sentence Addition problems test your knowledge of paragraph organization and **coherence**. You can think of coherence as the "glue" that holds the sentences of a paragraph together.

There are some devices that writers use to achieve cohesion. You can use these as clues to help you find the best place to put the missing sentences. These devices may occur in either the missing sentence or the passage.

1. **Signal words**

   Scientists have many theories about why the Ice Ages took place. *However*, none of these theories can fully explain why ice sheets form at certain periods and not at others.

   Stone tools are more durable than bones. *Therefore*, the tools of early humans are found more frequently than the bones of their makers.

   If we watch a cell divide under a microscope, what do we see? *First*, the nucleus of the cell begins to look different. The dense material thins out in the middle, forming two parts. *Then* these two parts separate, and there are two nuclei instead of one. *Finally*, a new cell wall forms between the new nuclei. The cell has divided.

2. **Personal pronouns**

   Blood travels first through the great arteries. *It* then passes into smaller arteries until reaching the capillaries. *They* join to form veins, which carry the blood back to the heart.

3. **Demonstratives**

   There were a number of methods of improving worker motivation and performance introduced in the 1970s. One of *these* was called Management by Objectives (M.O.). *This technique* was designed to improve morale by having workers set their own goals.

4. **Synonyms**

   The earliest remains of ancient animals are those of soft bodied jellyfish-like animals, worms, and proto-insects. *The fossils* of these creatures show us that, while some animals remained simple, others were becoming increasingly complex.

5. **Repetition of words**

   Hydrilla is an invasive plant impoted to Florida from Sri Lanka forty years ago for use in aquariums. *Hydrilla* has overgrown more than 40 percent of the state's rivers and lakes, making life miserable for boaters and often impossible for native wildlife.

In addition to these language clues, you can also use content clues. The missing sentence might be in contrast to one of the sentences in the passage, or one of the sentences in the paragraph might be in contrast to the missing sentence. The missing sentence might give an example of something mentioned in the passage, or might represent a missing step from a process or a chronology described in the passage.

In order for anyone to answer this type of item correctly, there must be some clues in either the missing sentence or the passage. There must be something—an idea or a word or a phrase—that links the missing sentence either to the sentence that comes before it or to the one that comes after it. It's up to you to find the clues!

You should follow these steps when you answer a sentence addition problem:

1. Read the missing sentence carefully and read over the sentences marked with squares.

2. Look for signal words, personal pronouns, demonstratives, synonyms, and repetition of words, first in the sentence and then in the passage. Do any of these devices link the missing sentence to any other sentence in the passage?

3. Look for places in the passage where the focus seems to shift from one topic to another abruptly, with no transition.

4. If the answer is not clear, look for content clues that tie the sentence either to the sentence that comes before it or to the sentence that comes after it.

5. You may be able to eliminate certain squares between two sentences because those sentences are closely joined and could not logically be separated.

6. If you still cannot find the answer, guess and go on.

Sentence Addition items are generally quite difficult and take up a lot of your time—and you don't get any extra credit for answering these questions correctly! Don't spend too much time on these items on your first time through the test. If possible, come back to them later if you have extra time.

Here is an example of a Sentence Adition item:

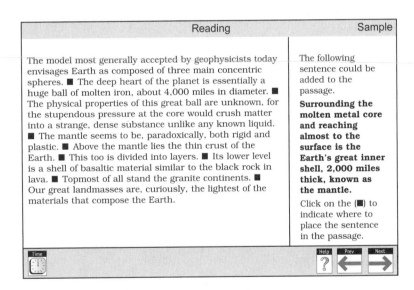

Your first choice may be to click on the second square. However, those two sentences are linked by the phrase *this great ball*, which refers to the core of the Earth, so they shouldn't be separated. The best answer is the third square. The repetition of the phrase *the mantle* in the missing sentence and in the sentence that follows the third square links those two sentences, and logically a sentence about the mantle—which separates the core from the crust—belongs in this position.

EXERCISE 38

Focus: Understanding paragraph organization and cohesion and answering sentence addition questions.

Directions: Circle the square to mark the place where the sentence best fits into the passage.

Passage 1

When a mammal is young, it looks much like a smaller form of an adult. ■ However, animals that undergo metamorphosis develop quite differently from mammals. ■ The young of these animals, which are called larvae, look very little like the mature forms and have a very different way of life. ■ Take the example of butterflies and caterpillars, which are the larval form of butterflies. ■ Caterpillars, on the other hand, are wingless and have more than six legs. They move by crawling and feed on leaves. ■ To become adults, the larvae must radically change their forms. ■

To accomplish this change, a larva must go through the process of metamorphosis. ■ It does this in the second stage of life, called the pupa stage. ■ When they are ready to pupate, caterpillars settle in sheltered positions. ■ Some spin a cocoon around themselves. ■ The caterpillar then sheds its old skin and grows a protective pupal skin. ■ Inside this skin, the body of the caterpillar gradually transforms itself. ■ The wingbuds, which were under the caterpillar's skin, grow into wings. ■ When the change is complete the pupal skin splits open and the butterfly emerges. ■ But soon it dries out, its wings unfurl, and it flies off. ■ Now it is ready to mate and to lay eggs that will develop into larvae. ■

1. The following sentence can be added to paragraph 1.

   Butterflies have two pairs of wings and six legs and feed on the nectar of flowers.

   Circle the correct square (■) to show where it would best fit into the paragraph.

2. The following sentence can be added to paragraph 2.

   At first it is damp and its wings are curled up.

   Circle the correct square (■) to show where it would best fit into the paragraph.

Passage 2

The process of miniaturization began in earnest with the transistor, which was invented in 1947. ■ It was much smaller than the smallest vacuum tube it was meant to replace and, not needing a filament, it consumed far less power and generated virtually no waste heat. ■ There was almost no limit to how small the transistor could be once engineers had learned how to etch electronic circuits onto a substrate of silicon. ■ In the 1950s the standard radio had five vacuum tubes and dozens of resistors and capacitors, all hand-wired and soldered onto a chassis about the size of a hardbound book. ■ In fact, the limiting factor in making appliances smaller is not the size of the electronic components but the human interface. ■ There is no point in reducing the size of a palm-held computer much further unless humans can evolve smaller fingers. ■

3. The following sentence can be added to the passage.

   Today all that circuitry and much more can fit into a microprocessor smaller than a postage stamp.

   Circle the correct square (■) to show where it would best fit into the passage.

Passage 3

It is believed that the first Americans were hunters who arrived by way of the only link between the hemispheres, the Siberian-Alaskan land bridge. ■ This strip of land remained above water until about 10,000 years ago. ■ These migrants unquestionably brought with them the skills to make weapons, fur clothing, and shelters against the bitter cold. ■ It seems safe to assume that they also brought myths and folktales from the Old World. ■ But which myths and which folktales? ■

Among myths, the most impressive candidate for Old World origin is the story of the Earth Diver. ■ This is the story of a group of water creatures who take turns diving for a piece of solid land. ■ The duck, the muskrat, the turtle, the crawfish, or some other animal succeeds but has to dive so deep that by the time it returns to the surface, it is half-drowned or dead. ■ The animals magically enlarge this tiny piece of solid land until it becomes the Earth. ■ Not every Native American tribe has a myth about the creation of the world, but of those that do, the Earth Diver myth is the most common. ■ It is found in all regions of North America except the Southwestern United States and the Arctic regions, and is also found in many locations in Asia and the Pacific Islands. ■

Another common myth is that of the Theft of Fire. ■ In this story, a creature sets out to steal fire from a distant source, obtains it, often through trickery, and carries it home. ■ The best known version of this story is the Greek myth of Prometheus. ■ Other Old World versions of this story are told in Central Asia, India, and Africa. ■ In some New World locations it is replaced by Theft of the Sun, Theft of Daylight, or Theft of Heat stories. ■

4. The following sentence can be added to paragraph 1.

    More recent arrivals no doubt took the same route, crossing on winter ice.

    Circle the correct square (■) to show where it would best fit into the paragraph.

5. The following sentence can be added to paragraph 2.

    But in its claws, the other animals find a bit of mud.

    Circle the correct square (■) to show where it would best fit into the paragraph.

6. The following sentence can be added to paragraph 3.

    In the New World, it appears among many Native American tribes west of the Rocky Mountains and in the American Southeast.

    Circle the correct square (■) to show where it would best fit into the paragraph.

Passage 4

When drawing human figures, children often make the head too large for the rest of the body. ■ A recent study offers some insight into this common disproportion in children's illustrations. ■ As part of the study, researchers asked children between four and seven years old to make several drawings of adults. ■ When they drew frontal views of these subjects, the size of the heads was markedly enlarged. ■ The researchers suggest that children draw bigger heads when they know they must leave room for facial details. ■ Therefore, the distorted head size in children's illustrations is a form of planning ahead and not an indication of a poor sense of scale. ■

7. The following sentence can be added to the passage.

   However, when the children drew rear views of the adults, the size of the heads was not nearly so exaggerated.

   Circle the correct square (■) to show where it would best fit into the passage.

Passage 5

It has been observed that periods of maximum rainfall occur in both the northern and southern hemispheres at about the same time. ■ This phenomenon cannot be adequately explained on a climatological basis, but meteors may offer a plausible explanation. ■ When the Earth encounters a swarm of meteors, each meteor striking the upper reaches of the atmosphere is vaporized by frictional heat. ■ The resulting debris is a fine smoke or powder. ■ This "stardust" then floats down into the lower atmosphere, where such dust might readily serve as nuclei upon which ice crystals or raindrops could form. ■ The delay of a month allows time for the dust to fall through the upper atmosphere. ■ Occasionally, large meteors leave visible traces of dust. ■ In a few witnessed cases, dust has remained visible for over an hour. ■ In one extreme instance—the great meteor that broke up in the sky over Siberia in 1908—the dust cloud traveled all over the world before disappearing. ■

8. The following sentence can be added to the passage.

   Confirmation that this phenomenon actually happens is found in the observed fact that increases in world rainfall come about a month after meteor systems are encountered in space.

   Circle the correct square (■) to show where it would best fit into the passage.

Passage 6

Lawn tennis is a comparatively modern modification of the ancient game of court tennis. ■ Major Walter C. Wingfield thought that something like court tennis might be played outdoors on the grass and in 1873 he introduced his new game under the name *Sphairistikè* at a lawn party in Wales. ■ Players and spectators soon began to call the new game "lawn tennis." ■ In 1874 a woman named Mary Outerbridge returned to New York with the basic equipment of the game, which she had obtained from a British Army store in Bermuda. ■ The first game of lawn tennis in the United States was played on the grounds of the Staten Island Cricket and Baseball Club in 1874. ■

The game went on in a haphazard fashion for a number of years. ■ A year later, the U.S. Lawn Tennis Association was formed. ■ International matches for the Davis Cup began in 1900. ■ They were played at Chestnut Hill, Massachusetts between British and American players. ■ The home team won this first championship match. ■

9. The following sentence can be added to paragraph 1.

   It was an immediate success and spread rapidly, but the original name quickly disappeared.

   Circle the correct square (■) to show where it would best fit into the paragraph.

10. The following sentence can be added to paragraph 2.

    Then in 1879, standard equipment, rules, and measurements for the court were instituted.

    Circle the correct square (■) to show where it would best fit into the paragraph.

Passage 7

Photosynthesis is the process by which plants capture the Sun's energy to convert water and carbon dioxide into sugars to fuel their growth. ■ In fact, chlorophyll is so essential to the life of plants that it forms almost instantly in seedlings as they come in contact with sunlight. ■ A green pigment, chlorophyll is responsible for the green coloring of plants. ■ But what turns the leaves of deciduous plants brilliant red and orange and gold in the autumn? ■

Trees do not manufacture new pigments for fall. ■ Orange, red, yellow, and other colored pigments are present in the leaves throughout the spring and summer. ■ However, these are masked by the far greater quantity of chlorophyll. ■ When the days grow shorter and temperatures fall, leaves sense the onset of fall. ■ They form an "abscission layer." ■ This layer is a barrier of tissue at the base of each leaf stalk. ■ Thus, sugar builds up in the leaf, causing the chlorophyll to break down. ■ The greens of summer then begin to fade. ■ The orange, red, yellow, and brown pigments now predominate, giving the leaves their vibrant autumn colors. ■

11. The following sentence can be added to paragraph 1.

    This process cannot take place without chlorophyll.

    Circle the correct square (■) to show where it would best fit into the paragraph.

12. The following sentence can be added to paragraph 2.

    It prevents nourishment from reaching the leaf and, conversely, prevents sugar created in the leaf from reaching the rest of the tree.

    Circle the correct square (■) to show where it would best fit into the paragraph.

Passage 8

Prairie dogs are among the most sociable wild animals of North America. ■ They are members of the squirrel family. ■ Why they are called "dogs" is a mystery. ■ At one time, they thrived nearly everywhere on the semi-arid prairie lands of the Great Plains. ■ Native Americans even used prairie dog colonies as landmarks on the relatively featureless plains. ■ Today, though, their range is greatly reduced. ■ They survive in large numbers mainly in protected areas such as Devil's Tower National Monument, Wind Cave National Park, and Theodore Roosevelt National Park. ■

Prairie dogs live in densely populated areas called towns. ■ Large towns are divided into wards, which are separated by topographic features such as hills, roads, streams, or belts of trees. ■ Wards, in turn, are divided into coteries. ■ The typical coterie contains one adult male, three to four adult females, and several juveniles. ■ If two or more adult males reside in the same coterie, one is dominant. ■ The residents of each coterie protect their territory from invaders, including prairie dogs from other coteries. ■

13. The following sentence can be added to paragraph 1.

They bear no resemblance to dogs, except that their call sounds a little like the bark of a small dog.

Circle the correct square (■) to show where it would best fit into the paragraph.

14. The following sentence can be added to paragraph 2.

However, coterie size can vary anywhere from two to about forty individuals.

Circle the correct square (■) to show where it would best fit into the paragraph.

Passage 9

In the early nineteenth century, the United States was still an overwhelmingly rural nation. ■ Shrewd showmen saw that there was a fortune to be made in taking shows to the people. ■ By 1820 there were some 30 small "mud show" circuses (so named because of the treacherous muddy roads and fields over which their wagons had to travel). ■ This innovation enabled circuses to perform in rain or shine. ■ Like circuses today, early nineteenth century circuses featured wild animal acts, bareback riders, acrobats, trapeze and high wire artists, circus bands, and, of course, clowns. ■ It was not until after the Civil War, however, that circuses became huge, three-ring spectacles involving hundreds of performers. ■

15. The following sentence can be added to the passage:

The number of shows increased rapidly after the first "Big Top" circus tent was introduced in 1826.

Circle the correct square (■) to show where it would best fit into the passage.

Time: 75 minutes
This review test measures your ability to understand the meaning of words and to comprehend written materials.

Directions: This test consists of several passages, each followed by 10–15 questions. Read the passages and, for each question, choose the one best answer based on what is stated in the passage or can be inferred from the passage. As soon as you understand the directions, begin work.

Passage 1

Humans have struggled against weeds since the beginnings of agriculture. Marring our gardens is among the milder effects of weeds—any plants that thrive where they are unwanted. They destroy wildlife habitats and impede farming. Their spread eliminates grazing areas and accounts for one-third of all crop loss. They compete for sunlight, nutrients, and water with useful plants. They may also hamper harvesting.

The global need for weed control has been answered mainly by the chemical industry. Its herbicides are effective and sometimes necessary, but some pose serious problems, particularly if they are misused. Toxic compounds may injure animals, especially birds and fish. They threaten the public health when they accumulate in food plants, ground water, and drinking water. They also directly harm workers who apply them.

In recent years, the chemical industry has introduced several herbicides that are more ecologically sound than those of the past. Yet new chemicals alone cannot solve the world's weed problems. Hence, an increasing number of scientists are exploring biological alternatives that harness the innate weed-killing powers of living organisms, primarily insects and microorganisms.

The biological agents now used to control weeds are environmentally benign and offer the benefit of specificity. They can be chosen for their ability to attack selected targets and leave crops and other plants untouched, including plants that might be related to the target weeds. They spare only those that are naturally resistant or those that have been genetically modified for resistance. Furthermore, a number of biological agents can be administered only once, after which no added applications are needed. Chemicals typically must be used several times per growing season.

Biological approaches may never supplant standard herbicides altogether, but they should sharply limit the use of dangerous chemicals and reduce the associated risks. They might also make it possible to conquer weeds that defy management by conventional means.

1. With what topic does this passage primarily deal?

   ○ The importance of the chemical industry

   ○ The dangers of toxic chemicals

   ○ Advantages of biological agents over chemical ones

   ○ A proposal to ban the use of all herbicides

2. The word marring in paragraph 1 is closest in meaning to

   ○ spoiling

   ○ dividing

   ○ replacing

   ○ planting

3. Look at the word hamper in the **bold** text below.

   They destroy wildlife habitats and impede farming. Their spread eliminates grazing areas and accounts for one-third of all crop loss. They compete for sunlight, nutrients, and water with useful plants. They may also hamper harvesting.

   Click on the word or phrase in the **bold** text that is closest in meaning to the word hamper .

4. Which of the following terms does the author define in paragraph 1?

   ○ Nutrients

   ○ Grazing areas

   ○ Weeds

   ○ Wildlife habitats

5. Look at the word harm in the **bold** text below.

   Its herbicides are effective and sometimes necessary, but some pose serious problems, particularly if they are misused. Toxic compounds may injure animals, especially birds and fish. They threaten the public health when they accumulate in food plants, ground water, and drinking water. They also directly harm workers who apply them.

   Click on the word or phrase in the **bold** text that is closest in meaning to the word harm .

6. With which of the following statements about the use of chemical agents as herbicides would the author most likely agree?

   ○ It should be increased.

   ○ It has become more dangerous recently.

   ○ It is safe but inefficient.

   ○ It is occasionally required.

7. Which of the following is NOT given as an advantage of using biological agents over chemical herbicides?

   ○ They are less likely to destroy desirable plants.

   ○ They are safer for workers.

   ○ They are more easily available.

   ○ They do not have to be used as often.

8. According to the passage, biological agents consist of

   ○ insects and microorganisms

   ○ useful plants

   ○ weeds

   ○ herbicides

9. The following sentence can be added to the paragraph below:

   In contrast, some of the most effective chemicals kill virtually all the plants they come in contact with.

   Where would it best fit in the paragraph?

   The biological agents now used to control weeds are environmentally benign and offer the benefit of specificity. ■ They can be chosen for their ability to attack selected targets and leave crops and other plants untouched, including plants that might be related to the target weeds. ■ They spare only those that are naturally resistant or those that have been genetically modified for resistance. ■ Furthermore, a number of biological agents can be administered only once, after which no added applications are needed. ■ Chemicals typically must be used several times per growing season. ■

   Circle the black square (■) that indicates the best position for the sentence.

10. The word applications in paragraph 4 could best be replaced by which of the following?

    ○ Requests

    ○ Special purposes

    ○ Treatments

    ○ Qualifications

11. Look at the word they in the **bold** text below.

    Biological approaches may never supplant standard herbicides altogether, but they should sharply limit the use of dangerous chemicals and reduce the associated risks.

    Underline the word or phrase in the **bold** text that the word they refers to.

12. Look at the word standard in the **bold** text on the following page.

Biological approaches may never supplant standard herbicides altogether, but they should sharply limit the use of dangerous chemicals and reduce the associated risks. They might also make it possible to conquer weeds that defy management by conventional means.

Underline the word or phrase in the **bold** text that is closest in meaning to the word standard .

13. Which of the following best describes the organization of the passage?

○ A general idea is introduced and several specific examples are given.

○ A recommendation is analyzed and rejected.

○ A problem is described and possible solutions are compared.

○ Two possible causes for a phenomenon are compared.

Passage 2

West Side Story is a musical tragedy based on William Shakespeare's timeless love story, *Romeo and Juliet.* It is set in the early 1950s, when gang warfare in big cities led to injuries and even death. *West Side Story* transformed the Montagues and Capulets of Shakespeare's play into rival street gangs, the Jets and the Sharks. The Sharks were newly arrived Puerto Ricans, the Jets native-born New Yorkers. The plot tells the story of Maria, a Puerto Rican whose brother Bernardo is the leader of the Sharks, and of Tony, a member of the Jets. As the opposing gangs battle in the streets of New York, these two fall in love. While attempting to stop a street fight, Tony inadvertently kills Maria's brother Bernardo and is ultimately killed himself.

West Side Story featured the talents of a trio of theatrical legends. Leonard Bernstein, who composed the brilliant score , was a classical composer and the conductor of the New York Philharmonic. Stephen Sondheim, making his Broadway debut, revealed a remarkable talent for writing lyrics. Among the hit songs of the play are "Tonight," "Maria," "America," "Gee Officer Krupke," and "I Feel Pretty." Jerome Robbins' electrifying choreography broke new ground for musical theater in the 1950s. Before *West Side Story,* no one thought that dance could be as integral to a narrative as the music and the lyrics. But the dances in *West Side Story* are among the most thrilling elements of the play.

The play opened on September 26, 1957. It ran for 734 performances, toured for 10 months, and then returned to New York for an additional 246 performances. The classic motion picture staring Natalie Wood was released in 1961. It garnered ten Academy Awards, including ones for Best Picture and Best Director. The play was successfully revived in New York in 1980 and then again in 1995, almost forty years after its premier performance.

14. The author's attitude toward the play is generally

○ favorable

○ critical

○ emotional

○ regretful

15. According to the passage, when does the action of the play *West Side Story* take place?

○ In Shakespeare's time

○ In the early 1950s

○ In 1957

○ In 1980

16. It can be inferred from the passage that the Capulets and Montagues

○ were families in Shakespeare's play

○ were 1950s street gangs

○ fought against the Jets and Sharks

○ were groups of actors, dancers, and singers

17. Look at the word rival in the **bold** text below.

West Side Story transformed the Montagues and Capulets of Shakespeare's play into rival street gangs, the Jets and the Sharks. The Sharks were newly arrived Puerto Ricans, the Jets native-born New Yorkers. The plot tells the story of Maria, a Puerto Rican whose brother Bernardo is the leader of the Sharks, and of Tony, a member of the Jets. As the opposing gangs battle in the streets of New York, these two fall in love.

Underline the word or phrase in the **bold** text that is closest in meaning to the word rival .

18. Underline the sentence in paragraph 1 that introduces the main characters in *West Side Story.*

19. According to the article, the words to the songs of *West Side Story* were written by

○ Jerome Robbins

○ Leonard Bernstein

○ William Shakespeare

○ Stephen Sondheim

20. The word score in paragraph 2 could best be replaced by which of the following?

○ Talent

○ Music

○ Performance

○ Dialogue

21. Look at the word electrifying in the **bold** text below:

Jerome Robbins' electrifying choreography broke new ground for musical theater in the 1950s. Before West Side Story, no one thought that dance could be as integral to a narrative as the music and the lyrics. But the dances in West Side Story are among the most thrilling elements of the play.

Underline the word or phrase in the **bold** text that is closest in meaning to the word electrifying.

22. Look at the word ones in the **bold** text below.

The play opened on September 26, 1957. It ran for 734 performances, toured for 10 months, and then returned to New York for an additional 246 performances. The classic motion picture starring Natalie Wood was released in 1961. It garnered ten Academy Awards, including ones for Best Picture and Best Director.

Underline the word or phrase in the **bold** text that the word ones refers to.

23. What can be inferred from the passage about musical plays produced before *West Side Story*?

    ○   They involved fewer songs.

    ○   Dance was not such an important feature in them.

    ○   They depended on dance and song more than on plot.

    ○   Legendary talents did not help create them.

24. During its initial appearance in New York, how many times was *West Side Story* performed?

    ○   10

    ○   26

    ○   246

    ○   734

Passage 3

The National Automobile Show in New York has been one of the top auto shows in the United States since 1900. On November 3 of that year about 8,000 people looked over the "horseless carriages." It was opening day, and the first opportunity for the automobile industry to show off its wares to a large crowd; however, the black-tie audience treated the occasion more as a social affair than as a sales extravaganza. It was also on the first day of this show that William McKinley became the first U.S. president to ride in a car.

The automobile was not invented in the United States. That distinction belongs to Germany. Nikolaus Otto built the first practical internal-combustion engine there in 1876. Then German engineer Karl Benz built what are regarded as the first modern automobiles in the mid-1880s. But the United States pioneered the merchandising of the automobile. The auto show proved to be an effective means of getting the public excited about automotive products.

By happenstance, the number of people at the first New York show equaled the entire car population of the United States at that time. In 1900 ten million bicycles and an unknown number of horse-drawn carriages provided the prime means of personal transportation. Only about 4,000 cars were assembled in the United States in 1900, and only a quarter of those were gasoline powered. The rest ran on steam or electricity.

After viewing the cars made by 40 car makers, the show's audience favored electric cars because they were quiet. The risk of a boiler explosion turned people away from steamers, and the gasoline powered cars produced smelly fumes. The Duryea Motor Wagon Company, which launched the American auto industry in 1895, offered a fragrant additive designed to mask the smells of the naphtha that it burned. Many of the 1900 models were cumbersome —the Gasmobile, the Franklin, and the Orient, for example, steered with a tiller like a boat instead of with a steering wheel. None of them was equipped with an automatic starter.

These early model cars were practically handmade and were not very dependable. They were basically toys of the well-to-do. In fact, Woodrow Wilson, then a professor at Princeton University and later President of the United States, predicted that automobiles would cause conflict between the wealthy and the poor. However, among the exhibitors at the 1900 show was a young engineer named Henry Ford. But before the end of the decade, he would revolutionize the automobile industry with his Model T Ford. The Model T, first produced in 1909, featured a standardized design and a streamlined method of production—the assembly line. Its lower costs made it available to the mass market.

Cars at the 1900 show ranged in price from $1,000 to $1,500, or roughly $14,000 to $21,000 in today's prices. By 1913, the Model T was selling for less than $300, and soon the price would drop even further. "I will build cars for the multitudes," Ford said, and he kept his promise.

25. The passage implies that the audience viewed the 1900 National Automobile Show primarily as

  ○ a formal social occasion

  ○ a chance to buy automobiles at low prices

  ○ an opportunity to learn how to drive

  ○ a chance to invest in one of thirty-two automobile manufacturers

26. According to the passage, who developed the first modern car?

  ○ Karl Benz

  ○ Nikolaus Otto

  ○ William McKinley

  ○ Henry Ford

27. Underline the sentence in paragraph 2 that explains the U.S. contribution to the early development of automobiles.

28. Approximately how many cars were there in the United States in 1900?

  ○ 4,000

  ○ 8,000

  ○ 10 million

  ○ An unknown number

29. Which of the following is closest in meaning to the phrase by happenstance as used in paragraph 3?

○ Generally

○ For example

○ Coincidentally

○ By design

30. Approximately how many of the cars assembled in the year 1900 were gasoline powered?

○ 32

○ 1,000

○ 2,000

○ 4,000

31. According to the passage, people at the 1900 National Automobile Show favored cars powered by

○ electricity

○ naphtha

○ gasoline

○ steam

32. Look at the word fragrant in the **bold** text below.

The risk of a boiler explosion turned people away from steamers, and the gasoline powered cars produced smelly fumes. The Duryea Motor Wagon Company, which launched the American auto industry in 1895, offered a fragrant additive designed to mask the smells of the naphtha that it burned. Many of the 1900 models were cumbersome—the Gasmobile, the Franklin, and the Orient, for example, steered with a tiller like a boat instead of with a steering wheel.

Underline the word or phrase in the **bold** text that is most nearly OPPOSITE in meaning to the word fragrant .

33. The purpose of the additive mentioned in paragraph 4 was to

○ increase the speed of cars

○ make engines run more efficiently

○ hide strong smells

○ make cars look better

34. The word cumbersome in paragraph 4 is closest in meaning to

○ clumsy

○ unshapely

○ fragile

○ inconvenient

35. Which of the following is NOT mentioned in the passage as steering with a tiller rather than with a steering wheel?

○ A Franklin

○ A Duryea

○ An Orient

○ A Gasmobile

36. Look at the phrase well-to-do in the **bold** text below.

These early model cars were practically handmade and were not very dependable. They were basically toys of the well-to-do. In fact, Woodrow Wilson, then a professor at Princeton University and later President of the United States, predicted that automobiles would cause conflict between the wealthy and the poor.

Underline the word or words in the **bold** text that is closest in meaning to the phrase well-to-do .

37. The following sentence can be added to paragraph 3.

The cars he exhibited at the 1900 show apparently attracted no special notice.

Where would it best fit in the paragraph?

These early model cars were practically handmade and were not very dependable. ■ They were basically toys of the well-to-do. ■ In fact, Woodrow Wilson, then a professor at Princeton University and later President of the United States, predicted that automobiles would cause conflict between the wealthy and the poor. ■ However, among the exhibitors at the 1900 show was a young engineer named Henry Ford. ■ But before the end of the decade, he would revolutionize the automobile industry with his Model T Ford. ■ The Model T, first produced in 1909, featured a standardized design and a streamlined method of production—the assembly line. ■ Its lower costs made it available to the mass market.

Circle the black square (■) that indicates the best position for the sentence.

38. What was the highest price asked for a car at the 1900 National Automobile Show in the dollars of that time?

○ $300

○ $1,500

○ $14,000

○ $21,000

Passage 4

Georgia O'Keeffe was born in Sun Prairie, Wisconsin in 1887. She studied at the Art Institute of Chicago (1905) and the Art Students League in New York

City (1907–1908). Beginning as an advertising illustrator, she supported herself until 1918 by teaching art in public schools and colleges in Texas. Her paintings were first exhibited in 1919 at "291," an experimental art gallery in New York City owned by the photographer Alfred Stieglitz, which was frequented by some of the most influential artists of the time. O'Keeffe married Stieglitz in 1924.

Early in her career, O'Keeffe developed a personal, highly refined style. Her early paintings were mostly abstract designs. In the 1920s she produced enigmatic depictions of flowers and precise cityscapes of New York City. Whether painting mysterious flowers or austere buildings, she captured their beauty by intuitively magnifying their shapes and simplifying their details.

O'Keeffe's style changed dramatically in 1929 during a visit to New Mexico. She was enchanted by the bright Southwestern sun, the dramatic landscapes, the ancient Spanish architecture, the strange vegetation, and the blanched bones of cattle. She then adopted her characteristic style. Thereafter, she most often painted desert landscapes, frequently with the whitened skull of a longhorn in the foreground. She used vivid hues that, as one critic put it, "shock the senses."

O'Keeffe permanently moved to a small adobe house in New Mexico the year after the death of her husband in 1946. Her paintings continued to be exhibited annually at several New York galleries, and they hang in the permanent collections of most major American museums. In her later years, she became the dean of Southwestern painters and one of the best known of American artists. She continued to paint until a week or so before her death in 1986.

39. The author's main purpose in writing this passage was to
   ○ criticize Georgia O'Keeffe's style of painting
   ○ discuss the early career of an important American artist
   ○ compare abstract art and landscape art
   ○ give the highlights of Georgia O'Keeffe's artistic career

40. According to the passage, where did Georgia O'Keeffe receive her formal art training?
   ○ Sun Prairie, Wisconsin
   ○ Chicago and New York City
   ○ Texas
   ○ New Mexico

41. The word frequented in paragraph 1 is closest in meaning to
   ○ visited
   ○ supported
   ○ founded
   ○ favored

42. The following sentence can be added to the paragraph below.

    After that date, she devoted herself entirely to painting.

    Where would it best fit in the paragraph?

Georgia O'Keeffe was born in Sun Prairie, Wisconsin in 1887. ■ She studied at the Art Institute of Chicago (1905) and the Art Students League in New York City (1907–1908). ■ Beginning as an advertising illustrator, she supported herself until 1918 by teaching art in public schools and colleges in Texas. ■ Her paintings were first exhibited in 1919 at "291," an experimental art gallery in New York City owned by the photographer Alfred Stieglitz, which was frequented by some of the most influential artists of the time. ■ O'Keeffe married Stieglitz in 1924.

    Circle the black square (■) that indicates the best position for the sentence.

43. Look at the word enigmatic in the **bold** text below.

    O'Keefe's early paintings were mostly abstract designs. In the 1920s she produced enigmatic depictions of flowers and precise cityscapes of New York City. Whether painting mysterious flowers or austere buildings, she captured their beauty by intuitively magnifying their shapes and simplifying their details.

    Underline the word or words in the **bold** text that is closest in meaning to the word enigmatic.

44. Which of the following scenes would probably most interest Georgia O'Keeffe as the subject of a painting after 1929?

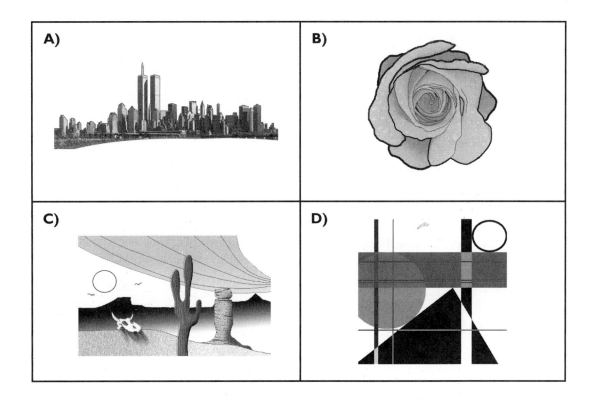

A)

B)

C)

D)

45. Which of the following had the greatest influence on changing O'Keeffe's style of painting?

   ○ A trip to the Southwest

   ○ Alfred Stieglitz's photographs

   ○ Her job as an advertising illustrator

   ○ Meeting influential artists

46. Look at the word blanched in the **bold** text below.

   She was enchanted by the bright Southwestern sun, the dramatic landscapes, the ancient Spanish architecture, the strange vegetation, and the blanched bones of cattle. She then adopted her characteristic style. Thereafter, she most often painted desert landscapes, often with the whitened skull of a longhorn in the foreground.

   Underline the word or phrase in the **bold** text that is closest in meaning to the word blanched .

47. The word hues in paragraph 3 is closest in meaning to

   ○ designs

   ○ subjects

   ○ styles

   ○ colors

48. Look at the word they in the **bold** text below.

   Her paintings continued to be exhibited annually at several New York galleries, and they hang in the permanent collections of most major American museums. In her later years, she became the dean of Southwestern painters and one of the best known of American artists.

   Underline the word in the **bold** text that they refers to.

49. Georgia O'Keeffe permanently moved to New Mexico in

   ○ 1929

   ○ 1946

   ○ 1947

   ○ 1986

50. It can be inferred from the passage that, in her later years, O'Keeffe

   ○ continued to be successful

   ○ returned to Wisconsin

   ○ could not match the successes of her early career

   ○ took up photography

This is the end of Review Test H: Reading.

You may go back and check your answers

until time is up.

MINI-LESSONS FOR SECTION 3: Vocabulary Building

These Mini-Lessons consist of lists of over 500 words and their synonyms as well as practice exercises. Although vocabulary is no longer tested in discrete items in Section 3, there are two types of vocabulary-in-context questions in the Reading section. These exercises will improve your ability to use context to choose the word that best fits into a sentence.

MINI-LESSON 3.1

abandon *v.* desert, leave behind

able *adj.* capable, qualified, fit

abolish *v.* end, eliminate

abrupt *adj.* sudden, hasty, unexpected

acclaim *v.* applaud, praise, honor; *n.* praise, applause, honor

acrid *adj.* bitter, sharp, biting

adapt *v.* adjust, modify

adept *adj.* skillful, expert

adhere *v.* stick, cling

admonish *v.* warn, caution, advise

adorn *v.* decorate, ornament

advent *n.* coming, arrival

adverse *adj.* hostile, negative, contrary

affluent *adj.* rich, wealthy, prosperous, well-to-do

aggravate *v.* (1) annoy, irritate (2) intensify, worsen

aggregate *adj.* entire, total, combined

agile *adj.* graceful, nimble, lively

ailment *n.* sickness, illness, disease

allot *v.* divide, distribute

amazing *adj.* astonishing, astounding, surprising, startling

amiable *adj.* agreeable, congenial, pleasant

anticipate *v.* foresee, expect, predict

anxious *adj.* (1) worried, nervous, apprehensive (2) eager, avid

appraise *v.* evaluate, estimate, assess

apt *adj.* (1) appropriate, suitable, correct, relevant, proper (2) likely, prone

arduous *adj.* difficult, strenuous, exhausting

arid *adj.* dry, barren

aroma *n.* fragrance, smell, odor, scent

artificial *adj.* synthetic, imitation, manmade

astonishing *adj.* surprising, amazing, astounding

astute *adj.* intelligent, clever, perceptive

attain *v.* accomplish, achieve

augment *v.* supplement, increase, strengthen, expand

austere *adj.* strict, harsh, severe, stern

authentic *adj.* genuine, true

aversion *n.* dislike, hostility, fear

awkward *adj.* clumsy

Directions: Complete the following sentences by filling in the blanks with vocabulary items (A), (B), or (C) according to the context of the sentences. The first one is done as an example.

1. Penicillin can have an ___(A)___ effect on a person who is allergic to it.

    (A) adverse   (B) anxious   (C) awkward

2. Burning rubber produces an _____ smoke.

    (A) adept   (B) arid   (C) acrid

3. Rationing is a system for _____ scarce resources.

    (A) allotting   (B) adapting   (C) appraising

4. Anthrax is generally an _____ of sheep and cattle, but may also be transmitted to humans.

    (A) ailment   (B) aroma   (C) aversion

5. Lawrence Gilman is admired for his _____, scholarly musical criticism.

    (A) austere   (B) astute   (C) abrupt

6. Mountain climbing is an _____ sport.

    (A) austere   (B) arduous   (C) anxious

7. Turtles _____ their eggs after they lay them and never see their young.

    (A) abandon   (B) appraise   (C) adorn

8. Scholarships allow some students from less _____ families to attend college.

    (A) artificial   (B) affluent   (C) amiable

9. Jewelers are sometimes asked to _____ jewelry for insurance purposes.

    (A) attain   (B) abandon   (C) appraise

10. Acrobats must be extremely _____.

    (A) awkward   (B) affluent   (C) agile

11. Southern Arizona has an _____ climate.

    (A) arid   (B) astute   (C) acrid

12. A person suffering from claustrophobia has an _____ to confined spaces.

    (A) ailment   (B) aversion   (C) acclaim

13. Perhaps the most _____ evolutionary development in penguins is a gland that can remove salt from seawater.

    (A) arid   (B) astonishing   (C) amiable

14. Readers in the eighteenth century found Thomas Paine's pamphlet *Common Sense* extremely persuasive, in part because it was written in an interesting style and contained many _____ quotations.

    (A) apt   (B) anxious   (C) awkward

15. In a domed stadium, natural grass cannot be grown, so _____ turf must be used on the playing field.

    (A) acrid   (B) aggregate   (C) artificial

MINI-LESSON 3.2

baffle *v.* confuse, puzzle, mystify

balmy *adj.* mild, warm

ban *v.* prohibit, forbid

bar *v.* prevent, obstruct, block

barren *adj.* sterile, unproductive, bleak, lifeless

barter *v.* trade, exchange

beckon *v.* summon, call, signal

belligerent *adj.* hostile, aggressive

beneficial *adj.* helpful, useful, advantageous

benevolent *adj.* benign, kind, compassionate

bias *n.* prejudice

blanched *adj.* whitened, bleached, pale

bland *adj.* mild, tasteless, dull

blatant *adj.* flagrant, obvious, overt

blend *v.* mix, mingle, combine; *n.* mixture, combination

bloom *v.* blossom, flower, flourish

blunder *v.* make a mistake; *n.* error, mistake

blunt *adj.* (1) unsharpened, dull (2) rude, abrupt, curt

blurry *adj.* unfocused, unclear, indistinct

bold *adj.* brave, courageous

bolster *v.* support, sustain, boost, buttress

bond *v.* join, connect; *n.* tie, link, connection

boom *v.* expand, prosper; *n.* expansion, prosperity, growth

brace *v.* support, reinforce

brilliant *adj.* (1) bright, shiny, radiant, dazzling (2) talented, gifted, intelligent

brisk *adj.* (1) lively, quick, vigorous (2) cool, chilly, invigorating

brittle *adj.* fragile, breakable, weak

bulky *adj.* huge, large, clumsy

buttress *v.* support, bolster, boost

Directions: Complete the following sentences by filling in the blanks with vocabulary items (A), (B), or (C) according to the context of the sentences.

1. Many flowers _____ in the spring.
   (A) blend   (B) brace   (C) bloom

2. The Virgin Islands, located in the Caribbean, have a _____ climate.
   (A) blurry   (B) brittle   (C) balmy

3. Before currency came into use, people used the _____ system.
   (A) barter   (B) blunder   (C) bias

4. The airline _____. It sent me to Atlanta but my luggage to Montreal.
   (A) buttressed   (B) baffled   (C) blundered

5. People with ulcers should eat _____ foods.
   (A) bold   (B) bland   (C) bulky

6. Steel is not as _____ as cast iron; it doesn't break as easily.
   (A) brisk   (B) brittle   (C) brilliant

7. At one time, the city of Boston _____ Walt Whitman's poetry because it was considered immoral.
   (A) banned   (B) boomed   (C) braced

8. Many people think of deserts as _____ regions, but many species of plants and animals have adapted to life there.
   (A) bland   (B) barren   (C) balmy

9. An autocratic ruler who serves his people well is sometimes called a _____ dictator.
   (A) blatant   (B) belligerent   (C) benevolent

10. Robert Goddard was a _____ pioneer in the field of rocketry.
   (A) brilliant   (B) balmy   (C) brisk

11. I enjoy taking walks on _____ autumn mornings.
   (A) barren   (B) brisk   (C) blurry

12. The victim was apparently struck by a club or some other _____ object.

   (A) bland (B) brittle (C) blunt

13. Some geese are _____, attacking anyone who comes near them.

   (A) beneficial (B) biased (C) belligerent

14. The glass factories of Toledo, Ohio _____ after Michael Owens invented a process that could turn out bottles by the thousands.

   (A) barred (B) bolstered (C) boomed

MINI-LESSON 3.3

calamity *n.* disaster, catastrophe

candid *adj.* honest, truthful, realistic

capable *adj.* competent, able, efficient, skillful

carve *v.* cut, sculpt, slice

casual *adj.* (1) informal, relaxed (2) accidental, chance

caustic *adj.* biting, harsh, sarcastic

cautious *adj.* careful, alert, prudent

celebrated *adj.* distinguished, famous, prominent

charming *adj.* delightful, lovely, attractive

cherish *v.* appreciate, esteem, treasure

choice *n.* selection, option; *adj.* exceptional, superior

cite *v.* quote, mention, refer to, list

clash *v.* argue, dispute, quarrel; *n.* argument, conflict, dispute

classify *v.* categorize

clever *adj.* smart, sharp, witty, bright

cling *v.* stick, adhere, hold

clog *v.* block, obstruct

clumsy *adj.* awkward, inept

coax *v.* persuade, urge

colossal *adj.* huge, enormous, gigantic

commence *v.* begin, initiate, start

commerce *n.* trade, business

commodity *n.* product, good, merchandise

compel *v.* force, require, coerce

competent *adj.* adept, skillful, capable, able

Directions: Complete the following sentences by filling in the blanks with vocabulary items (A), (B), or (C) according to the context of the sentences.

1. The Red Cross and the Red Crescent provide relief in case of _____ such as floods, earthquakes, and hurricanes.

   (A) clashes (B) commodities (C) calamities

2. Spoken language is generally more _____ than written language.

   (A) casual (B) capable (C) cautious

3. When writing research papers, writers must _____ the sources they use.

   (A) coax (B) cite (C) clog

4. Monkeys are _____ as primates.

   (A) compelled (B) classified (C) cherished

5. _____ remarks can offend people.

   (A) Charming (B) Caustic (C) Clever

6. Sculptors use hammers and chisels to _____ statues from stone.

   (A) cherish (B) compel (C) carve

7. The Space Age _____ in October, 1957 when Sputnik, the first artificial satellite, was launched by the Soviet Union.

(A) commenced   (B) coaxed   (C) cited

8. Workers must be very _____ when dealing with toxic substances.

(A) caustic   (B) clumsy   (C) cautious

9. Microorganisms on the surface of separate particles of soil _____ together, making the particles themselves cohere.

(A) cling   (B) clash   (C) compel

10. With the growth of international _____, the economies of the world have become more interdependent.

(A) commodity   (B) commerce   (C) choice

11. The Lincoln Memorial in Washington, D.C. features a _____ statue of the sixteenth president created by Daniel Chester French.

(A) colossal   (B) caustic   (C) casual

12. Corn, cotton, sugar, and many other goods are bought and sold in _____ markets.

(A) choice   (B) commerce   (C) commodity

13. Artists of the so-called "Ashcan School" of American art portrayed their subjects in a _____ fashion that concealed none of their flaws.

(A) candid   (B) choice   (C) charming

14. Water hyacinths grow so profusely that they may _____ waterways.

(A) clog   (B) cling   (C) carve

MINI-LESSON 3.4

complement *v.* supplement, complete; *n.* supplement, addition

compliment *v.* praise, flatter, commend; *n.* praise, flattery

comprehensive *adj.* complete, thorough, exhaustive

compulsory *adj.* necessary, obligatory, mandatory

concede *v.* admit, acknowledge, recognize

concise *adj.* brief, short, abbreviated

concrete *adj.* tangible, specific, real

congregate *v.* assemble, gather

conspicuous *adj.* noticeable, obvious, prominent

contemplate *v.* think about, ponder, speculate

controversial *adj.* disputable, debatable

convenient *adj.* accessible, available, handy

conventional *adj.* standard, ordinary, normal

cope with *v.* deal with, manage, handle

copious *adj.* abundant, ample, plentiful

cordial *adj.* congenial, warm, friendly

courteous *adj.* polite, refined, gracious

covert *adj.* secret, hidden

cozy *adj.* (1) comfortable, warm (2) friendly, intimate, close

crave *v.* desire, long for, hope for

crooked *adj.* (1) curved, twisted, zigzag (2) dishonest, corrupt

crucial *adj.* critical, decisive, key

crude *adj.* (1) rude, impolite,

vulgar (2) unprocessed,
raw, unrefined

cruel *adj.* brutal, vicious,
ruthless

cryptic *adj.* secret, hidden,
mysterious

curb *v.* restrict, limit,
control

curious *adj.* (1) inquisitive
(2) odd, strange, unusual

curt *adj.* abrupt, blunt,
impolite

Directions: Complete the following sentences by filling in the blanks with vocabulary items (A), (B), or (C) according to the context of the sentences.

1. The use of seat belts is _____ in many states; failure to wear them may result in fines.

    (A) covert   (B) cruel   (C) compulsory

2. Every summer, black bears from all over southern Alaska _____ along the McNeil River to fish for salmon.

    (A) crave   (B) curb   (C) congregate

3. An abstract is a _____ form of an academic article. Many journals publish abstracts so readers can decide if it is worthwhile to read the full version of the article.

    (A) concise   (B) comprehensive   (C) concrete

4. Before 1754, Britain and the North American colonies had a _____ relationship, but after that, their relationship became strained.

    (A) conspicuous   (B) cozy   (C) curt

5. Automated teller machines provide a _____ means of banking twenty-four hours a day.

    (A) cordial   (B) crooked   (C) convenient

6. Lombard Street in San Francisco, which zigzags up Nob Hill, is known as the world's most _____ street.

    (A) controversial   (B) crooked   (C) cryptic

7. A good writer supports his or her generalizations with _____ examples.

    (A) concrete   (B) curious   (C) crude

8. Many hunters wear orange and other bright colors in order to be as _____ as possible, and therefore avoid being shot by other hunters by mistake.

    (A) covert   (B) crucial   (C) conspicuous

9. Movie directors use music to _____ the action on the screen.

    (A) contemplate   (B) complement   (C) compliment

10. Workers in the service sector should be trained to act as _____ as possible.

    (A) crudely   (B) courteously   (C) curtly

11. Trouble-shooting is the process of identifying and _____ problems.

    (A) conceding   (B) coping with   (C) craving

---

12. A _____ banjo has five strings.

    (A) conventional   (B) copious   (C) cryptic

MINI-LESSON 3.5

damp *adj.* moist, wet, humid

daring *adj.* bold, courageous, brave

dazzling *adj.* shining, sparkling, blinding, bright

declare *v.* announce, proclaim

defective *adj.* flawed, faulty, broken, malfunctioning

defiant *adj.* rebellious, insubordinate

delicate *adj.* exquisite, fragile

delightful *adj.* charming, attractive, enchanting

delusion *n.* illusion, dream, fantasy

demolish *v.* tear down, destroy, wreck

dense *adj.* thick, solid, packed

desist *v.* stop, cease, discontinue

device *n.* instrument, tool, mechanism

devise *v.* invent, plan, figure out

dim *adj.* unclear, faint, indistinct

din *n.* noise, clamor, commotion

dire *adj.* desperate, grievous, serious

discard *v.* abandon, leave behind

dismal *adj.* gloomy, depressing, dreary

disperse *v.* scatter, distribute, spread

dispute *n.* argument, quarrel, debate, clash, feud

distinct *adj.* discrete, separate, different

distinguished *adj.* celebrated, notable, famous, well-known

divulge *v.* reveal, admit, disclose

dogged *adj.* stubborn, determined, persistent

dominate *v.* rule, control, govern

dot *v.* are located in, are scattered around; *n.* spot, point

downfall *n.* collapse, ruin, destruction

doze *v.* sleep, nap

draw *v.* (1) sketch, make a picture; (2) pull, attract

drawback *n.* disadvantage, weakness, flaw

dreary *adj.* dismal, gloomy, bleak

drench *v.* wet, soak

drowsy *adj.* sleepy, tired

dubious *adj.* doubtful, skeptical, uncertain

durable *adj.* lasting, enduring, resistant

dwell *v.* live, reside, inhabit

dwelling *n.* house, home, residence

dwindle *v.* decrease, diminish

dynamic *adj.* energetic, forceful, active, vibrant

Directions: Complete the following sentences by filling in the blanks with vocabulary items (A), (B), or (C) according to the context of the sentences.

1. The snow on the mountaintop was _____ in the bright morning sun.

    (A) dazzling   (B) dogged   (C) dim

2. A person who has been accused of a crime cannot be forced to _____ any information that is self-incriminating.

    (A) divulge   (B) desist   (C) disperse

3. Roses have a _____ beauty.

    (A) dense   (B) delicate   (C) dire

4. An odometer is a _____ for measuring distance.

    (A) device   (B) delusion   (C) dwelling

5. The amount of open space has _____ as more and more land is developed.

    (A) dominated   (B) dwindled   (C) dispersed

6. Hermit crabs live in shells that have been _____ by other animals.

   (A) declared (B) divulged (C) discarded

7. Richard Byrd and his pilot Floyd Bennett undertook a _____ flight to the North Pole in May of 1926.

   (A) daring (B) defiant (C) distinct

8. Steep, round hills called knobs _____ southern Indiana.

   (A) demolish (B) dot (C) dwell

9. Artists Nathaniel Currier and James Merritt Ives produced some _____ prints of nineteenth century New England scenes which collectors prize for their charm.

   (A) dreary (B) dim (C) delightful

10. Economists define _____ goods as ones intended to last more than four months.

    (A) durable (B) dense (C) delicate

11. One cause of the American Revolution was a _____ over taxation.

    (A) drawback (B) din (C) dispute

12. Florida has a humid climate. Summers there are particularly hot and _____.

    (A) dynamic (B) damp (C) dogged

13. All bookkeeping systems have certain advantages and certain _____.

    (A) drawbacks (B) delusions (C) downfalls

14. A person suffering from hypothermia, the extreme loss of body heat, may first feel _____.

    (A) dogged (B) distinguished (C) drowsy

15. Handwriting experts try to compare a _____ signature against at least three genuine specimens before judging its authenticity.

    (A) dubious (B) dismal (C) dim

16. Bats help _____ seeds in tropical forests.

    (A) devise (B) disperse (C) drench

17. A carburetor _____ air into an engine and mixes it with fuel.

    (A) desists (B) draws (C) dots

MINI-LESSON 3.6

eerie *adj.* strange, odd, unusual, frightening

elderly *adj.* old, aged

electrify *v.* excite, thrill, exhilarate

elegant *adj.* sophisticated, polished

eligible *adj.* suitable, qualified, acceptable

eminent *adj.* celebrated, distinguished, famous

emit *v.* send out, discharge

enchanting *adj.* delightful, charming, captivating

encounter *v.* meet, find, come across; *n.* meeting, confrontation

endeavor *n.* attempt, venture

endorse *v.* authorize, approve, support

enhance *v.* intensify, amplify, strengthen

ensue *v.* follow, result

entice *v.* lure, attract, tempt

era *n.* period, age, stage

essential *adj.* critical, vital, crucial, key

esteem *v.* cherish, honor, admire

evade *v.* escape, avoid, elude

exhaustive *adj.* thorough, complete, comprehensive

exhilarating *adj.* exciting, thrilling, stimulating, electrifying

extravagant *adj.* excessive, lavish

fable *n.* story, tale

fabled *adj.* legendary, mythical, famous

facet *n.* aspect, point, feature

faint *adj.* dim, pale, faded, indistinct

falter *v.* hesitate, waver

fancy *adj.* decorative, ornate, elaborate

fasten *v.* attach, secure

fatal *adj.* mortal, lethal, deadly

fatigue *v.* tire, exhaust; *n.* exhaustion, weariness

faulty *adj.* flawed, inferior

feasible *adj.* possible

fee *n.* payment, fare

feeble *adj.* weak, fragile, frail

ferocious *adj.* fierce, savage, violent

fiery *adj.* (1) blazing, burning (2) passionate, fervent

fitting *adj.* suitable, proper, apt, appropriate

flagrant *adj.* blatant, obvious

flaw *n.* defect, imperfection, fault

flee *v.* escape, go away, elude

flimsy *adj.* fragile, frail, weak, feeble

forego *v.* abandon, give up

foremost *adj.* chief, principal, leading

fragment *n.* particle, piece, bit

fragrant *adj.* aromatic, scented

fraudulent *adj.* false, deceptive, deceitful

fundamental *adj.* basic, integral, elemental

fuse *v.* join, combine, unite

fusion *n.* blend, merger, union

futile *adj.* useless, pointless, vain

Directions: Complete the following sentences by filling in the blanks with vocabulary items (A), (B), or (C) according to the context of the sentences.

1. In 1906 much of San Francisco was destroyed by an earthquake and the fires that _____.

   (A) evaded   (B) ensued   (C) encountered

2. The writer H. P. Lovecraft wrote many _____ stories about the supernatural.

   (A) essential   (B) eerie   (C) extravagant

3. A new _____ of aviation began in 1947 when Chuck Yeager became the first pilot to fly faster than the speed of sound.

   (A) fable   (B) endeavor   (C) era

4. Vance Packard's book *The Hidden Persuaders* deals with the tactics advertisers use to _____ consumers.

   (A) endorse   (B) entice   (C) enhance

5. Riding a roller coaster is _____ experience.

   (A) an exhilarating   (B) a fancy   (C) a feeble

6. Riveting is a means of _____ metal plates together with hot metal bolts.

   (A) enhancing   (B) fleeing   (C) fastening

7. In the United States, citizens are _____ to vote at the age of eighteen.

   (A) fitting   (B) elderly   (C) eligible

8. Barracudas are _____ predators, sometimes called the "tigers" of tropical waters.

   (A) faulty   (B) futile   (C) ferocious

9. Certain gases such as neon _____ light when exposed to an electrical current.

   (A) emit   (B) evade   (C) esteem

10. People make more mistakes when they are _____ than when they are fresh.

    (A) exhaustive   (B) eminent   (C) fatigued

11. A _____ in a jewel makes it less valuable.

    (A) fragment   (B) facet   (C) flaw

12. Honeysuckle is a plant that has _____ white or yellowish blossoms.

    (A) elderly   (B) fragrant   (C) fiery

13. Some insects can detect the ultrasonic pulses that bats use to detect their prey and can therefore _____ the bats.

    (A) evade   (B) forego   (C) electrify

14. The snowy egret builds _____ nest from a few twigs and pieces of grass.

    (A) a faint   (B) an extravagant   (C) a flimsy

15. When lightening strikes sand, the intense heat sometimes _____ the grains of sand into thin glass tubes called fulgurites.

    (A) falters   (B) fastens   (C) fuses

16. A common carrier is a company that provides public transportation for a _____.

    (A) fee   (B) fable   (C) flaw

MINI-LESSON 3.7

gala *adj.* festive, happy, joyous

gap *n.* break, breach, opening

garrulous *adj.* talkative

gaudy *adj.* showy, flashy, conspicuous

genial *adj.* pleasant, cordial, agreeable

gentle *adj.* mild, kind, considerate

genuine *adj.* authentic, real, valid

glitter *v.* sparkle, shine, glisten

glory *n.* grandeur, majesty, fame

gorgeous *adj.* attractive, beautiful

grade *n.* quality, value, worth

graphic *adj.* clear, explicit, vivid

grasp *v.* (1) grab, seize, grip (2) understand

grave *adj.* serious, grievous

gregarious *adj.* sociable, friendly

grim *adj.* severe, dreary, bleak, somber

grip *v.* hold, grasp, seize; *n.* hold, grasp, possession

grueling *adj.* exhausting, difficult, arduous

gullible *adj.* innocent, naive, trusting, credulous

hamper *v.* delay, obstruct, hinder, block

haphazard *adj.* random, chance, aimless, unplanned

hardship *n.* difficulty, trouble

harm *v.* injure, damage

harmony *n.* accord, agreement, peace

harness *v.* control, utilize

harsh *adj.* severe, rough, strict

hasty *adj.* quick, rushed, hurried

hazardous *adj.* dangerous, risky

heed *v.* obey, listen to, mind, follow

hinder *v.* block, obstruct, hamper

hoist *v.* lift, raise, pick up

hue *n.* color, tint, shade

huge *adj.* enormous, giant, colossal, immense

hurl *v.* pitch, throw, fling

Directions: Complete the following sentences by filling in the blanks with vocabulary items (A), (B), or (C) according to the context of the sentences.

1. During the construction of skyscrapers, cranes are used to _____ building materials to the upper floors.

    (A) hurl   (B) harness   (C) hoist

2. The 26 mile long Boston Marathon is a _____ foot race.

    (A) gorgeous   (B) grueling   (C) hasty

3. Dams can _____ the power of rivers, but they may also destroy their beauty.

    (A) heed   (B) harness   (C) hurl

4. The more facets a diamond has, the more it _____.

    (A) glitters   (B) harms   (C) hinders

5. Many people celebrate the New Year with _____ parties.

    (A) gala   (B) grueling   (C) haphazard

6. Think it over for a while; don't make a _____ decision.

    (A) genuine   (B) gullible   (C) hasty

7. Bad weather _____ the rescue crews trying to locate the life rafts.

    (A) hampered   (B) grasped   (C) harnessed

8. Gorillas look ferocious but are actually quite _____ creatures.

    (A) gaudy   (B) gentle   (C) gorgeous

9. Con artists are criminals who take advantage of _____ people by tricking them and taking their money.

    (A) garrulous   (B) grim   (C) gullible

10. A recent study showed that agriculture is the most _____ occupation.

    (A) hazardous   (B) genial   (C) haphazard

11. At Harper's Ferry, West Virginia, the Potomac River has cut a picturesque _____ through the Blue Ridge Mountains.

    (A) grip   (B) glory   (C) gap

12. Wool from different sheep, or even wool from different parts of the same sheep, is not all of the same _____.

    (A) harmony   (B) grade   (C) hardship

13. The interior of Alaska has brief summers and long, _____ winters.

    (A) grave   (B) harsh   (C) huge

14. Animals that live in herds or packs are considered _____.

    (A) hasty   (B) gregarious   (C) gullible

MINI-LESSON 3.8

idea *n.* concept, notion, thought

ideal *n.* model, standard; *adj.* perfect, model, standard

idle *adj.* (1) inactive, unused, inert (2) lazy

illusion *n.* (1) fantasy, delusion (2) an erroneous perception or concept

illustration *n.* picture, drawing, description

imaginary *adj.* unreal, fantastic, fictitious

imaginative *adj.* creative, original, clever

immense *adj.* huge, enormous, massive, colossal

impair *v.* damage, injure, spoil

impartial *adj.* fair, unbiased, neutral

implement *v.* realize, achieve, put into practice, execute; *n.* tool, utensil, instrument

incessant *adj.* constant, ceaseless, continuous

increment *n.* increase, amount

indifferent *adj.* uncaring, apathetic, unconcerned

indigenous *adj.* native

indispensable *adj.* necessary, essential, vital, critical

indistinct *adj.* unclear, blurry, hazy

induce *v.* persuade, convince, coax

inept *adj.* incompetent, awkward, clumsy

inexorable *adj.* unstoppable

infamous *adj.* notorious, shocking

infinite *adj.* limitless, endless, boundless

infinitesimal *adj.* tiny, minute, minuscule

ingenious *adj.* brilliant, imaginative, clever, inventive

ingenuous *adj.* naive, trusting, gullible

inhabit *v.* live, dwell, reside, populate

inhibit *v.* control, limit, restrain

initial *adj.* original, first, beginning, introductory

innate *adj.* natural, inborn

innocuous *adj.* harmless, inoffensive

intense *adj.* powerful, heightened, concentrated

intricate *adj.* complicated, complex, involved

irate *adj.* angry, furious, upset

jagged *adj.* rough, rugged, uneven, irregular

jeopardy *n.* danger, hazard, risk, threat

jolly *adj.* joyful, happy, cheerful, jovial

jolt *v.* shock, jar, shake up, surprise; *n.* blow, surprise, shock

keen *adj.* (1) sharp (2) shrewd, clever, bright (3) eager, enthusiastic

key *adj.* principle, crucial, important

knack *n.* skill, ability, aptitude, talent

Directions: Complete the following sentences by filling in the blanks with vocabulary items (A), (B), or (C) according to the context of the sentences.

1. Many people feel that Hawaii has an almost _____ climate.

    (A) idle   (B) impartial   (C) ideal

2. A plow is a farm _____ used to break up soil and prepare the land for planting.

    (A) increment   (B) knack   (C) implement

3. A laser uses a synthetic ruby to concentrate light into an extremely _____ high-energy beam.

    (A) intense   (B) indistinct   (C) incessant

4. Jesse James was an _____ outlaw, well known as a bank robber and gun fighter.

   (A) inept   (B) ingenuous   (C) infamous

5. Antibiotics _____ the growth of bacteria.

   (A) inhabit   (B) jolt   (C) inhibit

6. Line A-B appears to be longer than line C-D, but this is an optical _____.

   (A) illusion   (B) ideal   (C) illustration

7. Stockholders may be too _____ to vote in corporate elections, so they let management vote for them by proxy.

   (A) infamous   (B) indifferent   (C) ingenious

8. The heavily populated states of California, Texas, New York, and Florida are _____ states for any candidate in a presidential election.

   (A) initial   (B) impartial   (C) key

9. A virus is so _____ that it can be seen only with an electron microscope.

   (A) infinite   (B) intricate   (C) infinitesimal

10. The _____ character Falstaff is one of Shakespeare's finest comic creations.

   (A) keen   (B) jolly   (C) irate

11. Anyone can learn basic cooking skills; you don't need a special _____.

   (A) knack   (B) idea   (C) implement

12. Alcohol _____ one's ability to drive.

   (A) jolts   (B) impairs   (C) induces

13. The _____ people of Australia were called aborigines by the European settlers.

   (A) indigenous   (B) ingenuous   (C) innate

14. The rhinoceros has a poor sense of sight but _____ sense of smell.

   (A) an immense   (B) an inept   (C) a keen

15. The equator is _____ line running around the center of the Earth.

   (A) an imaginative   (B) a jagged   (C) an imaginary

16. A glacier's progress is slow but _____.

   (A) indispensable   (B) inexorable   (C) intricate

17. The _____ garter snake, often spotted in yards, parks, and gardens, is sometimes mistaken for a venomous snake.

   (A) irate   (B) ingenuous   (C) innocuous

lack *v.* need, require, not have; *n.* shortage, absence, scarcity

lag *v.* fall behind, go slowly

lavish *adj.* luxurious, plentiful, abundant

lax *adj.* careless, negligent, loose

legendary *adj.* mythical, fabled, famous

legitimate *adj.* proper, authentic, valid

lethargic *adj.* slow, listless, sluggish, lazy

likely *adj.* probable, plausible, credible

linger *v.* remain, stay

link *v.* join, connect, fasten, bind; *n.* connection, tie

long *v.* desire, wish for

lucid *adj.* clear, plain, understandable

lucrative *adj.* profitable, money-making

lull *v.* soothe, calm, quiet; *n.* pause, break

lure *v.* attract, tempt, entice

lurid *adj.* shocking, sensational, graphic

lurk *v.* prowl, sneak, hide

luster *n.* shine, radiance, brightness

luxurious *adj.* lavish, elegant, plush

magnificent *adj.* majestic, impressive, splendid

magnitude *n.* size, extent, amount

mandatory *adj.* necessary, obligatory, compulsory

mar *v.* damage, ruin, deface, spoil

massive *adj.* huge, giant, colossal, immense

memorable *adj.* unforgettable, impressive, striking

mend *v.* fix, repair

mild *adj.* gentle, moderate, calm, temperate

mingle *v.* blend, combine, mix

minute *adj.* tiny, minuscule, infinitesimal

monitor *v.* observe, watch

moral *adj.* honorable, ethical

morale *n.* spirit, confidence, attitude

murky *adj.* unclear, cloudy, foggy, dark

mysterious *adj.* puzzling, strange

mythical *adj.* legendary, imaginary, fictional

Directions: Complete the following sentences by filling in the blanks with vocabulary items (A), (B), or (C) according to the context of the sentences.

1. Medieval books called bestiaries contained pictures and descriptions of _____ creatures such as unicorns and dragons.

   (A) mandatory   (B) lax   (C) mythical

2. In colonial times, cod fishing off the coast of New England was a _____ occupation.

   (A) luxurious   (B) lethargic   (C) lucrative

3. Parents often sing to children to _____ them to sleep.

   (A) lurk   (B) lure   (C) lull

4. Julius Caesar is known not only for his military and political skills but also for his _____, informative writing.

   (A) lucid   (B) lurid   (C) lavish

5. A cobbler _____ damaged shoes.

   (A) mars   (B) mends   (C) lacks

6. One of the _____ exhibits of Impressionist art is found at the Art Institute of Chicago.

   (A) mildest   (B) most memorable   (C) most lucid

---

7. Quarks are _____ particles that are believed to be the fundamental unit of matter.

   (A) massive   (B) minute   (C) mythical

8. Paperback novels in the 1940s and 1950s often had _____ covers to attract readers' attention.

   (A) lurid   (B) murky   (C) legitimate

9. One problem caused by a rising crime rate is a _____ of space in prisons.

   (A) lag   (B) lack   (C) link

10. The _____ lumberjack Paul Bunyan and his giant blue ox Babe are two of the most famous figures in American folklore.

    (A) legendary   (B) moral   (C) likely

11. The transcontinental railroad, _____ the East Coast with the West Coast, was completed at Promontory Point, Utah in 1869.

    (A) linking   (B) monitoring   (C) mingling

MINI-LESSON 3.10

negligible *adj.* unimportant, trivial

nimble *adj.* graceful, agile

notable *adj.* remarkable, conspicuous, striking

notify *v.* inform, tell

notion *n.* idea, concept, thought

notorious *adj.* infamous, disreputable

novel *adj.* new, innovative

objective *adj.* fair, impartial, unbiased, neutral; *n.* goal, purpose, aim

oblong *adj.* oval

obscure *adj.* unfamiliar, ambiguous, little-known

obsolete *adj.* antiquated, out of date, outmoded

odd *adj.* strange, unusual, peculiar, curious

offspring *n.* young, children, descendants

ominous *adj.* threatening, menacing, dangerous

opulent *adj.* luxurious, plush, affluent

ornamental *adj.* ornate, decorative, elaborate

outgoing *adj.* (1) open, friendly (2) departing, leaving

outlook *n.* (1) opinion, view (2) prospect, forecast

outstanding *adj.* excellent, exceptional, notable, well-known

overall *adj.* general, comprehensive

overcast *adj.* cloudy, gloomy

overcome *v.* subdue, defeat, overwhelm

overlook *v.* ignore, disregard, neglect

oversee *v.* supervise, manage, direct

oversight *n.* error, mistake, omission

overt *adj.* open, obvious, conspicuous

overtake *v.* catch up with, reach

overwhelm *v.* (1) astonish, astound, shock (2) inundate, engulf (3) conquer, defeat, overcome

Directions: Complete the following sentences by filling in the blanks with vocabulary items (A), (B), or (C) according to the context of the sentences.

1. The black clouds of a gathering thunderstorm look quite _____.

   (A) ominous   (B) negligible   (C) overcast

2. Pulitzer Prizes are awarded to _____ journalists, novelists, poets, and other writers.

   (A) objective   (B) outstanding   (C) notorious

3. An _____ plant is cultivated chiefly for its beauty.

  (A) opulent   (B) obscure   (C) ornamental

4. Franklin D. Roosevelt was able to _____ his physical handicaps; he didn't permit them to interfere with his living a vigorous life.

  (A) oversee   (B) overcome   (C) overtake

5. The poetry of Ezra Pound is sometimes difficult to understand because it contains so many _____ references.

  (A) notable   (B) obscure   (C) objective

6. The Bessemer process was once the most common method of making steel, but today this process is considered _____.

  (A) odd   (B) novel   (C) obsolete

7. Dolley Payne Madison, the wife of President James Madison, impressed the city of Washington with her stylish clothes and warm, _____ manner.

  (A) nimble   (B) ominous   (C) outgoing

8. The town planning commission said that their financial _____ for the next fiscal year was optimistic; they expect increased tax revenues.

  (A) outlook   (B) oversight   (C) notion

9. The new play was so successful that the demand for tickets was _____.

  (A) odd   (B) overwhelming   (C) negligible

10. A book's table of contents provides readers with an _____ idea of what the book is about.

  (A) outgoing   (B) overt   (C) overall

11. Because ultraviolet light from the Sun can penetrate clouds, it is possible to get a sunburn on an _____ day.

  (A) obscure   (B) overcast   (C) overt

12. Although the accident appeared serious, only a _____ amount of damage was done.

  (A) novel   (B) notable   (C) negligible

MINI-LESSON 3.11

pace *n.* rate, speed

painstaking *adj.* careful, conscientious, thorough

pale *adj.* white, colorless, faded

paltry *adj.* unimportant, minor, trivial

particle *n.* piece, bit, fragment

path *n.* trail, track, way, route

peculiar *adj.* (1) strange, odd, puzzling (2) distinctive, characteristic, unique, special

penetrate *v.* enter, go through, pierce, puncture

perceive *v.* observe, sense, notice

peril *n.* danger, hazard, risk, threat

perpetual *adj.* constant, endless, eternal

perplexing *adj.* puzzling, mystifying, confusing

pierce *v.* penetrate, puncture, stab

pivotal *adj.* important, key, crucial

plausible *adj.* likely, credible, believable

plead *v.* appeal, beg

plush *adj.* luxurious, opulent, rich, elegant

ponder *v.* consider, think about, reflect on

portion *n.* share, part, section, segment

postpone *v.* delay, put off, defer

potent *adj.* strong, powerful, effective

pounce *v.* jump, leap, spring

precious *adj.* expensive, costly, rare

precise *adj.* accurate, exact, definite

premier *adj.* (1) first, opening, earliest, initial (2) chief, leading, foremost

pressing *adj.* urgent, crucial, compelling

pretext *n.* excuse, pretense, justification

prevail *v.* succeed, win, triumph

prevalent *adj.* common, widespread, popular

prior *adj.* earlier, preceding, former

probe *v.* investigate, inquire into

procure *v.* obtain, acquire, secure

profound *adj.* important, significant, deep

profuse *adj.* plentiful, abundant, copious

prompt *adj.* punctual, timely

prosper *v.* flourish, thrive, succeed

provoke *v.* (1) irritate, anger, annoy (2) cause, trigger

prudent *adj.* careful, sensible, cautious

pulverize *v.* crush, grind, powder

pungent *adj.* bitter, harsh, biting, sharp

pursue *v.* chase, follow, seek

puzzling *adj.* mystifying, confusing, baffling

Directions: Complete the following sentences by filling in the blanks with vocabulary items (A), (B), or (C) according to the context of the sentences.

1. Turquoise is not valuable enough to be classified as a _____ stone.

    (A) perpetual   (B) pale   (C) precious

2. The invention of the lever was of _____ importance.

    (A) potent   (B) profound   (C) premier

3. Hospitals define *urgent care* as medical care given to somewhat less _____ medical problems than emergency care.

    (A) perplexing   (B) pressing   (C) prudent

4. Tool makers must have the ability to work very _____ in order to meet exact specifications.

    (A) precisely   (B) profoundly   (C) plausibly

5. _____ of dust in the air may trigger allergies in some people.

    (A) Portions   (B) Pretexts   (C) Particles

6. When a tiger spots its prey, it crouches down and then _____.

    (A) pleads   (B) ponders   (C) pounces

7. X-rays cannot _____ lead.

    (A) provoke   (B) penetrate   (C) pursue

8. Sherlock Holmes, a fictional detective, solved many _____ crimes.

    (A) puzzling   (B) prevalent   (C) prompt

9. Mallows are plants that grow _____ in prairies, woods, and marshes.

(A) profusely   (B) profoundly   (C) preciously

10. Certain spices give foods a _____ taste.

(A) painstaking   (B) pungent   (C) pale

11. Trade with Britain and the West Indies allowed colonial seaports such as Boston to _____ .

(A) postpone   (B) provoke   (C) prosper

12. A _____ investor never takes unnecessary financial risks.

(A) perplexing   (B) prudent   (C) premier

13. To make cement, limestone is first _____, and the resulting power is then mixed with clay and water at high temperatures.

(A) probed   (B) pulverized   (C) pierced

14. Outbreaks of cholera and other diseases were _____ in mining camps during the California gold rush because of the crowded, unsanitary conditions.

(A) peculiar   (B) plausible   (C) prevalent

15. Only a small _____ of Carlsbad Cavern in New Mexico has been lighted and opened to visitors.

(A) peril   (B) portion   (C) pace

16. Acting teacher Stella Adler played a _____ role in the development of the Method school of acting.

(A) pivotal   (B) precious   (C) plush

MINI-LESSON 3.12

quaint *adj.* charming, picturesque, curious

quake *v.* shiver, shake, tremble

quandary *n.* problem, dilemma, predicament

quarrel *n.* argument, dispute, disagreement

quest *n.* search, journey, venture

radiant *adj.* bright, shiny, glowing

ragged *adj.* torn, tattered, worn

range *v.* (1) extend, vary, fluctuate (2) roam, wander; *n.* scope, extent, spectrum

rash *adj.* thoughtless, careless, reckless

raw *adj.* (1) uncooked (2) unprocessed, unrefined, crude

raze *v.* demolish, level, knock down

recede *v.* retreat, go back, subside, withdraw

reckless *adj.* careless, rash

recollect *v.* recall, remember

recount *v.* narrate, tell

refine *v.* improve, process, purify

refuge *n.* shelter, haven, retreat

rehearse *v.* practice, train, go over

reliable *adj.* dependable, trustworthy

relish *v.* enjoy, savor, like

remedy *n.* treatment, cure

remnant *n.* remainder, balance, fragment

remote *adj.* isolated, distant

renowned *adj.* famous, celebrated, notable

resent *v.* dislike, take offense at

retract *v.* withdraw, pull back

riddle *n.* puzzle, mystery

rigid *adj.* (1) stiff, unbending (2) harsh, severe, strict

rip *v.* tear, cut, slash

ripe *adj.* mature, developed

risky *adj.* dangerous, hazardous, treacherous

roam *v.* travel, wander, range

rough *adj.* (1) uneven, jagged, rugged (2) difficult (3) impolite

route *n.* way, course, path, road

rudimentary *adj.* elementary, fundamental, primitive

rugged *adj.* (1) jagged, rough, uneven (2) strong, sturdy

rumor *adj.* gossip, story

rural *adj.* agricultural

ruthless *adj.* cruel, brutal, vicious

Directions: Complete the following sentences by filling in the blanks with vocabulary items (A), (B), or (C) according to the context of the sentences.

1. Motorists can be fined for driving _____.

   (A) recklessly   (B) reliably   (C) rigidly

2. Musicians have to _____ before performing.

   (A) rehearse   (B) resent   (C) recollect

3. At the end of the Ice Ages, glaciers began to _____.

   (A) quake   (B) raze   (C) recede

4. Big Sur, a wild section of California's coastline, is known for its _____ beauty.

   (A) ragged   (B) rash   (C) rugged

5. Wetlands provide _____ for many species of birds, reptiles, mammals, and amphibians.

   (A) riddles   (B) refuge   (C) rumors

6. Wrecking balls are used to _____ buildings.

   (A) rip   (B) quake   (C) raze

7. The northernmost section of the Rocky Mountains, the Brooks Range, is located in a _____ section of Alaska.

   (A) remote   (B) ruthless   (C) radiant

8. Dogs can hear a greater _____ of sounds than humans.

   (A) remnant   (B) quandary   (C) range

9. Visitors to Vermont delight in the beautiful scenery and picturesque villages and enjoy staying in some of the _____ country inns there.

   (A) rough   (B) ragged   (C) quaint

10. _____ materials have less economic value than processed materials.

    (A) Raw   (B) Rash   (C) Renowned

11. Many medieval stories dealt with _____, such as the story of the search for the Holy Grail.

    (A) quarrels   (B) quandaries   (C) quests

12. The Tennessee Valley Authority helped bring cheap electricity to farmers in the _____ South.

   (A) reliable   (B) rural   (C) rugged

13. Bobsledding is a fast, _____ sport.

   (A) risky   (B) quaint   (C) ripe

14. Quite logically, early roads in North America tended to follow the _____ of rivers.

   (A) remedies   (B) routes   (C) quandaries

15. Alex Haley's novel *Roots* _____ the history of an American family beginning in the mid-1700s in Africa.

   (A) recounts   (B) refines   (C) relishes

MINI-LESSON 3.13

salvage *v.* save, rescue, recover, retrieve

scale *v.* climb; *n.* (1) range, spectrum (2) proportion

scarce *adj.* rare, sparse

scatter *v.* disperse, spread

scent *n.* aroma, fragrance, odor, smell

scrap *v.* abandon, get rid of; *n.* piece, fragment

seasoned *adj.* experienced, veteran

secluded *adj.* hidden, isolated, secret

sensational *adj.* thrilling, exciting, shocking

serene *adj.* quiet, peaceful, calm, tranquil

sever *v.* cut, slice off

severe *adj.* (1) harsh, strict, austere (2) undecorated, plain

shatter *v.* break, smash, fragment

sheer *adj.* (1) steep, sharp, abrupt (2) transparent, thin, filmy

shimmer *v.* shine, glow, glisten, gleam

shred *v.* rip up, tear up

shrewd *adj.* clever, sly

shrill *adj.* piercing, high-pitched

shun *v.* avoid, stay away from

shy *adj.* timid, reserved

significant *adj.* important, vital, major

signify *v.* symbolize, stand for, indicate

simulate *v.* imitate, reproduce

sketch *v.* draw; *n.* drawing, picture, diagram

slender *adj.* thin, slim, slight

sluggish *adj.* slow, listless, lazy, lethargic

sly *adj.* cunning, clever, shrewd

soak *v.* wet, drench, saturate

solace *n.* comfort, consolation, relief

somber *adj.* serious, grave, solemn

sort *v.* classify, categorize; *n.* type, kind, variety

sound *adj.* safe, solid, secure; *n.* noise

Directions: Complete the following sentences by filling in the blanks with vocabulary items (A), (B), or (C) according to the context of the sentences.

1. One of the most popular peaks for mountain climbers to _____ is El Capitan in Yosemite National Park.

   (A) scale   (B) soak   (C) shun

2. Grey foxes are not particularly rare animals, but they are seldom seen because they are so _____.

   (A) sluggish   (B) somber   (C) shy

3. _____ workers are more valuable to employers than beginners.

   (A) Shrill   (B) Seasoned   (C) Sluggish

4. The Shakers were a strict religious group that _____ worldly pleasure.

(A) scrapped   (B) shunned   (C) sketched

5. The city of Denver's plan to build a subway system was _____ in the 1970s.

(A) scattered   (B) sorted   (C) scrapped

6. Even after a ship has sunk, its cargo can often be _____ .

(A) severed   (B) shattered   (C) salvaged

7. Some economists believe that the best way to get a _____ economy moving again is to cut taxes.

(A) sensational   (B) sluggish   (C) shrewd

8. Government bonds and blue-chip stocks are _____ investments.

(A) sound   (B) shy   (C) scarce

9. If a person's spinal cord is _____, paralysis results.

(A) soaked   (B) severed   (C) salvaged

10. Silk is a _____ fabric.

(A) sheer   (B) shrewd   (C) slender

11. A green flag _____ the beginning of an automobile race.

(A) scatters   (B) simulates   (C) signifies

12. The raw materials of paper—wood pulp, rags, or old paper—must be _____ and cleaned before the paper-making process begins.

(A) severed   (B) shredded   (C) sketched

13. A home aquarium should _____ a fish's natural habitat as closely as possible.

(A) soak   (B) simulate   (C) salvage

14. Foxfire is an eerie, _____ blue light, often seen in swamps, that is caused by the natural burning of methane from decaying plants.

(A) serene   (B) somber   (C) shimmering

MINI-LESSON 3.14

sow *v.* plant

span *v.* extend, bridge, connect; *n.* length, extent, range

spawn *v.* generate, create, produce; *n.* offspring, descendants

specific *adj.* definite, particular, exact

specimen *n.* example, sample

spectacular *adj.* dramatic, sensational, impressive

spell *n.* interval, period, time

spirited *adj.* lively, energetic, vigorous

splendid *adj.* excellent, superb, wonderful

spoil *v.* (1) ruin, mar (2) decay, deteriorate, decompose, rot

spot *v.* locate, find, see; *n.* (1) location, site (2) mark, stain, speck

spur *v.* stimulate, impel, encourage, provoke; *n.* inducement, stimulus

stable *adj.* steady, secure, stationary, fixed

stage *v.* present, put on; *n.* grade, step, level, phase

stain *v.* color, tint, discolor, dye; *n.* spot, mark, blemish

stale *adj.* (1) old, dry (2) dull, trite, uninteresting

stall *v.* halt, delay, put off

stately *adj.* dignified, grand, magnificent, elegant

steep *adj.* sheer, perpendicular

stern *adj.* firm, severe, strict, harsh

strenuous *adj.* difficult, arduous

strife *n.* conflict, dispute, struggle

strive *v.* attempt, try

struggle *v.* fight, argue, dispute; *n.* conflict, strife, battle, effort

stubborn *adj.* rigid, uncompromising, obstinate

sturdy *adj.* strong, rugged, well-built

subsequent *adj.* later, succeeding, following, ensuing

subtle *adj.* indirect, suggestive, implied

suitable *adj.* appropriate, correct, apt

summit *n.* peak, apex, zenith

sundry *adj.* miscellaneous, diverse, various

superb *adj.* excellent, splendid

supplant *v.* replace, substitute for

supple *adj.* pliable, flexible, bendable

sway *v.* (1) wave, rock, swing, bend (2) persuade, influence

sweeping *adj.* complete, exhaustive, general, comprehensive

swift *adj.* fast, quick, rapid

swivel *v.* rotate, spin, turn

Directions: Complete the following sentences by filling in the blanks with vocabulary items (A), (B), or (C) according to the context of the sentences.

1. High pressure cells may bring brief warm _____ even in the middle of winter.

   (A) struggles   (B) spells   (C) spans

2. The _____ cliffs of the Na Pali coast on the Hawaiian island of Kauai rise over 4,000 feet from the sea.

   (A) swift   (B) steep   (C) subtle

3. The process of refining oil involves a number of _____.

   (A) specimens   (B) spots   (C) stages

4. In high winds, skyscrapers will _____ slightly.

   (A) swivel   (B) sway   (C) stall

5. Severe thunderstorms may _____ tornadoes.

   (A) spoil   (B) strive   (C) spawn

6. The snow-covered _____ of Mount Hood is the highest point in the state of Oregon.

   (A) spur   (B) summit   (C) span

7. D. W. Griffith was the first director of _____ films. These were movies made on a colossal scale.

   (A) stately   (B) suitable   (C) spectacular

8. Cheetahs are the _____ of all land mammals, with top speeds of up to 70 miles per hour.

   (A) stalest   (B) subtlest   (C) swiftest

9. Salt can be used to keep meat from _____ .

   (A) struggling   (B) spoiling   (C) stalling

10. Because they must be able to break a path through icebound waters, icebreakers have to be very _____ boats.

(A) stately   (B) sturdy   (C) supple

11. According to studies, most people who divorce _____ remarry.

(A) specifically   (B) subsequently   (C) stubbornly

12. A roadbed supplies a _____ base for a highway.

(A) stable   (B) sundry   (C) sweeping

13. Every year, the Folger Shakespeare Library in Washington, D.C. _____ a number of plays.

(A) stalls   (B) stages   (C) spans

14. Farmers sometimes _____ crops such as timothy or clover and then plow them under the soil to increase its fertility.

(A) supplant   (B) spur   (C) sow

15. The geographical center of the North American continent is a _____ near Drake, North Dakota.

(A) spot   (B) stage   (C) summit

16. Many medical tests require a blood _____ .

(A) spell   (B) specimen   (C) stain

17. Because of their protective coloration, ghost crabs are hard to _____ .

(A) spur   (B) spawn   (C) spot

18. The Virginia reel is a _____ dance mainly performed by children.

(A) stale   (B) spirited   (C) supple

MINI-LESSON 3.15

tact *n.* diplomacy, discretion, poise

tale *n.* story

tame *v.* domesticate, master; *adj.* docile, domesticated, gentle

tamper (with) *v.* interfere (with)

tangle *v.* knot, twist; *n.* knot

tart *adj.* sour, tangy, piquant

taunt *v.* insult, mock, torment

tedious *adj.* boring, dull, tiresome

telling *adj.* effective, convincing, forceful

temperate *adj.* mild, moderate

tempting *adj.* alluring, attractive, enticing

tender *adj.* (1) delicate, soft (2) gentle, loving (3) sore, painful

thaw *v.* melt, warm up

thorough *adj.* complete, comprehensive

thoroughfare *n.* avenue, street

thrifty *adj.* economical, inexpensive

thrilling *adj.* exciting, stimulating, stirring, electrifying

thrive *v.* prosper, flourish

thwart *v.* prevent, impede, obstruct

tidings *n.* news, message

tilt *v.* incline, slope

timid *adj.* fearful, shy, retiring

tint *n.* color, hue, shade, tone; *v.* color, stain, dye

tiresome *adj.* tedious, dull, boring

toil *v.* labor, work; *n.* exertion, labor, work

tolerant *adj.* patient, impartial, open-minded

torment *v.* taunt, abuse, bully

torrent *n.* flood, deluge

tough *adj.* durable, strong

tow *v.* haul, draw, pull, drag

toxic *adj.* poisonous, noxious

trait *n.* characteristic, feature, quality

treacherous *adj.* dangerous, hazardous

trickle *n.* drip, leak

triumph *n.* victory, success, achievement; *v.* win, succeed, prevail

trivial *adj.* unimportant, minor

trying *adj.* demanding, difficult, troublesome

tug *v.* pull, draw; *n.* pull

Directions: Complete the following sentences by filling in the blanks with vocabulary items (A), (B), or (C) according to the context of the sentences.

1. Citric acid gives lemons and limes their _____ taste.

   (A) temperate   (B) toxic   (C) tart

2. The use of robots has eliminated certain _____ factory jobs.

   (A) tedious   (B) thrilling   (C) timid

3. One should never buy food or medicine if the packaging has obviously been _____ .

   (A) tangled   (B) thwarted   (C) tampered with

4. Alfred Hitchcock directed a number of _____ psychological dramas; among the most exciting were *Psycho* and *North by Northwest*.

   (A) timid   (B) trivial   (C) thrilling

5. Tides are caused by the _____ of the Moon's gravity.

   (A) tangle   (B) torrent   (C) tug

6. Many people find chocolate _____ .

   (A) tempting   (B) tender   (C) telling

7. Peachtree Street is the main _____ in Atlanta.

   (A) triumph   (B) thoroughfare   (C) tale

8. In her book *Silent Spring*, Rachel Carson wrote about insecticides and their _____ effects on animal life.

   (A) tiresome   (B) tender   (C) toxic

9. In the desert, dry creek beds may turn into raging _____ after heavy rainstorms.

   (A) trickles   (B) torrents   (C) toils

10. Colonial coral _____ mainly in warm, tropical waters.

    (A) thrives   (B) tames   (C) tows

11. _____ such as hair color and eye color are inherited genetically from one's parents.

    (A) Traits   (B) Tangles   (C) Tints

12. Washington Irving collected and interpreted many famous old _____, including the legends of Rip Van Winkle and the Headless Horseman.

    (A) tales   (B) tidings   (C) traits

---

13. Wild rabbits are _____ creatures that mainly rely on their keen senses of hearing and smell to evade danger.

(A) tiresome   (B) timid   (C) treacherous

14. The dura mater is a _____ protective membrane that covers the spinal cord and brain.

(A) tender   (B) tough   (C) temperate

MINI-LESSON 3.16

ultimate *adj.* (1) conclusive, definite, final (2) maximum, highest

unbearable *adj.* intolerable, agonizing

uncouth *adj.* impolite, rude, vulgar

underlying *adj.* fundamental, basic

undertake *v.* try, attempt

ungainly *adj.* awkward, unskillful

uniform *adj.* consistent, regular

unique *adj.* singular, one of a kind, special

unravel *v.* solve, explain

unruly *adj.* unmanageable, disorganized, disorderly

unsound *adj.* defective, faulty, unsafe

uphold *v.* support, sustain

upkeep *n.* maintenance

uproar *n.* disorder, disturbance, commotion

urge *v.* encourage, advise, implore

urgent *adj.* pressing, compelling

utensil *n.* tool, implement, device

utter *v.* say, speak; *adj.* total, absolute, complete

vacant *adj.* empty, unoccupied

vague *adj.* unclear, uncertain, ambiguous

vain *adj.* (1) useless, pointless, unsuccessful (2) conceited, proud

valid *adj.* genuine, authentic, legitimate

vanish *v.* disappear, go away

variable *adj.* changeable, shifting

vast *adj.* huge, enormous, extensive, immense

venomous *adj.* poisonous

verbose *adj.* talkative, wordy

verge *n.* brink, edge, threshold

vessel *n.* (1) container, bottle (2) ship

vex *v.* irritate, anger, annoy

viable *adj.* (1) alive, living (2) feasible, practical, possible

vicinity *n.* area, proximity, zone

vigorous *adj.* dynamic, energetic, spirited

vital *adj.* critical, crucial, key, essential

vivid *adj.* clear, distinct, graphic

vow *v.* promise, pledge, swear; *n.* oath, promise, pledge

Directions: Complete the following sentences by filling in the blanks with vocabulary items (A), (B), or (C) according to the context of the sentences.

1. To be fair, laws must be _____ applied to all persons.

(A) urgently   (B) vaguely   (C) uniformly

2. Rattlesnakes are the most common _____ snakes in the United States.

(A) ungainly   (B) venomous   (C) variable

3. The League of Women Voters _____ all citizens to vote.

(A) urges   (B) vexes   (C) upholds

4. In his novel *The Red Badge of Courage*, Steven Crane _____ describes a Civil War battle.

(A) vividly   (B) uniformly   (C) vitally

5. An Erlenmeyer flask is a glass _____ used in chemistry labs.

   (A) vessel   (B) vow   (C) verge

6. Aerobics is _____ form of exercise.

   (A) a viable   (B) an uncouth   (C) a vigorous

7. A metropolitan area consists of a central city and any suburban areas in its

   _____ .

   (A) vicinity   (B) vessel   (C) upkeep

8. Medical scientists still do not fully understand the _____ causes of migraine headaches.

   (A) unruly   (B) underlying   (C) viable

9. The kidneys play a _____ role in maintaining health by removing impurities from the bloodstream.

   (A) valid   (B) viable   (C) vital

10. The myth of Narcissus tells the story of a handsome but _____ young man who stares at his reflection in a pool of water for so long that he turns into a flower.

    (A) vain   (B) unbearable   (C) verbose

11. The fork has been used as an eating _____ at least since the twelfth century.

    (A) vessel   (B) utensil   (C) urge

12. The Great Plains cover _____ area.

    (A) a vast   (B) a viable   (C) an ultimate

13. A city's park and recreation budget must include funds for the _____ on buildings and grounds.

    (A) uproar   (B) verge   (C) upkeep

14. Mary Munsfeldt _____ some of the puzzles involving insects and the pollination of plants.

    (A) undertook   (B) upheld   (C) unraveled

15. Linguists say that hundreds of the world's languages may _____ in the next few decades because the number of speakers of these languages is dwindling rapidly.

    (A) vanish   (B) utter   (C) urge

16. A lack of parking spaces is a _____ problem in most cities.

    (A) unique   (B) vacant   (C) vexing

MINI-LESSON 3.17

wage *n.* salary, pay, earnings

wander *v.* roam, travel, range

wane *v.* shrink, decrease, decline

ware *n.* good, merchandise

warn *v.* alert, caution, advise

warning *n.* alarm, alert

warp *v.* deform, bend, twist

wary *adj.* careful, cautious, alert

weary *adj.* tired, exhausted, fatigued

well-to-do *adj.* rich, wealthy, affluent

wholesome *adj.* healthy, nutritious, beneficial

wicked *adj.* evil, corrupt, immoral

widespread *adj.* extensive, prevalent, sweeping

wily *adj.* crafty, cunning, shrewd

wise *adj.* astute, prudent, intelligent

withdraw *v.* retreat, pull out, remove

wither *v.* dry, shrivel, wilt

withhold *v.* reserve, retain, hold back

witty *adj.* comic, clever, amusing

woe *n.* trouble, distress, sorrow

wonder *v.* think about, speculate, ponder *n.* marvel, miracle

wound *v.* injure, hurt; *n.* injury

yearn *v.* desire, crave, want

yield *v.* (1) give up, surrender (2) produce, supply *n.* production, output, crop

zealous *adj.* enthusiastic, eager

zenith *n.* peak, tip, apex, summit

zone *n.* area, vicinity, region

Directions: Complete the following sentences by filling in the blanks with vocabulary items (A), (B), or (C) according to the context of the sentences.

1. If boards become wet, they may _____ .

   (A) wither   (B) yield   (C) warp

2. Whole grains and fresh fruit and vegetables are _____ foods.

   (A) wicked   (B) wholesome   (C) well-to-do

3. You must be _____ when buying a used car; be sure the engine is in good condition.

   (A) weary   (B) zealous   (C) wary

4. In the past, many salesmen tried to sell their _____ door-to-door.

   (A) wares   (B) woes   (C) wages

5. Humorist Will Rogers wrote many _____ newspaper columns.

   (A) wily   (B) weary   (C) witty

6. Congress sets the minimum _____, which is the lowest amount of money workers may be paid per hour.

   (A) wage   (B) yield   (C) zone

7. Intelligent policies are needed so that public funds are used _____ .

   (A) wholesomely   (B) zealously   (C) wisely

8. The green revolution was a system of farming which depended on new varieties of seeds and the increased use of irrigation and fertilizers. It greatly increased farmers' _____ .

   (A) wonders   (B) yields   (C) woes

9. Some superstitions are familiar to many cultures. For example, there is a _____ belief that black cats bring bad luck.

(A) widespread   (B) wily   (C) wicked

10. A green belt is a parklike _____ around a city in which development is not permitted.

(A) zenith   (B) wound   (C) zone

11. George Ropes painted portraits of sea captains, prosperous merchants, and other _____ citizens of eighteenth century Massachusetts.

(A) zealous   (B) well-to-do   (C) wicked

12. In his 1961 book *Night Comes to the Cumberlands*, Harry M. Caudil painted a grim picture of the _____ of the Appalachian region.

(A) woes   (B) wares   (C) yields

Guide to Essay Writing

Arkansas State University

About Essay Writing

On the computer-based test, the Essay Writing section is a MANDATORY (required) section of every test. This section (previously called the Test of Written English, or the TWE) is given after the three multiple-choice sections of the test. The Writing section differs from the rest of the TOEFL® test in that it is **productive.** Instead of choosing one of four answer choices, you have thirty minutes in which to write your own short essay. You may either write your answer with pencil and paper or word-process (type) it on the computer. If you choose to write the essay by hand, someone at the center will give you a special test form on which to write it.

The Prompts

The Essay Writing section consists of a single essay topic, called a **prompt.** There is no choice of topic; you must write on the prompt that is given. All of the prompts are very general. They do not require any special knowledge, and they are not about any controversial issues.

Some common contexts for essay writing prompts are: education, business, the future, technology, travel, family, friendship, sports and games, entertainment, communication, and transportation.

There are three common types of prompts:

1) **Defend an opinion**

This type of prompt presents two points of view and asks you to choose one side to support. These prompts usually follow this pattern: "Some people believe A, but other people believe B. Which do you believe?"

SAMPLE ITEM

> Some people believe that money spent on space research benefits all of humanity. Other people take the opposite view and say that money spent on this type of research is wasted. Tell which point of view you agree with and explain why, using specific details and reasons.

2) **Agree or disagree with a statement**

This type of prompt presents a general statement and asks whether you agree or disagree with it.

SAMPLE ITEM

> Do you agree or disagree with this statement?
>
> It is much easier to learn in a small class than in a large one.
>
> Use specific examples and reasons to support your answer.

3) Explain the importance of a development, invention, or phenomenon

This type of prompt essentially says, "There have been many important X's in the world, such as _____. Choose another example of X, and explain why it is important."

SAMPLE ITEM

> Developments in transportation such as the automobile have had an enormous impact on modern society. Choose another development in transportation that you think is of great importance. Use specific examples and reasons for your choice.

ETS now publishes a list of all the prompts that will appear on the test in any given year. You can find this list in the *Bulletin* and on the TOEFL® web site. Of the 110 topics listed, you will see one on the day that you test. (If only you knew which one!) It's a good idea to look over this list and think about how you would respond to each topic.

The Writing Process

You have only thirty minutes to write the essay, so you will be under a certain amount of time pressure. You should divide your time more or less like this:

Pre-Writing 　Reading the prompt 　Thinking about the prompt 　Brainstorming and note taking 　Making an informal outline	About 5 minutes

Writing the Essay	About 20 minutes

Checking the Essay 　Looking for and correcting structural, 　mechanical, and grammatical problems	About 5 minutes

The Essay

To get a top score in this section, your essay should be around 200–300 words in length. Typically, this type of essay is organized into four or five paragraphs.

$$\boxed{\text{Introductory Paragraph}}$$

$$\boxed{\text{Body Paragraph \# 1}}$$

$$\boxed{\text{Body Paragraph \# 2}}$$

$$\boxed{\text{Concluding Paragraph}}$$

Some essays may have a third or even fourth body paragraph.

Specific hints for organizing each paragraph are provided in Lesson 40, "Writing the Essay."

COMPUTER OR HANDWRITTEN?

You have the choice of writing the essay by hand or word-processing it. Which method should you choose?

You should probably handwrite the essay if you . . .

- have little or no experience typing
- cannot type more than about 10–15 words a minute in English
- have seldom or never used a keyboard with English characters

Otherwise, you should definitely write the essay on the computer. In fact, word-processing is such an important skill to have—especially if you plan to attend a university in an English-speaking country—that you may want to consider learning how to type before you take the test. There are computer programs that can teach you the basics or you can practice on your own.

Here are some advantages of writing the essay on computer:

- The finished product is much neater and will be easier for the readers to read.
- There are certain functions—especially cut and paste—that you can do only on a computer.
- If you are somewhat experienced at word-processing, you can work much more quickly on the computer than with a pencil.
- You can make corrections more quickly and more neatly.

- Finally—and this may be the most important advantage—if you word-process your essay, you will get your final grade in about two weeks, but if you handwrite your essay, it will take about five weeks.

Scoring the Essay

At ETS, your essay is read by two readers who score it **holistically.** In other words, the essay is not judged according to individual mistakes you might make but by the overall effectiveness of your writing.

These are some of the points that scorers look for:

- **Topic**

   Does the writer write on the topic that is given in the prompt? Does the essay respond to the entire prompt or just to part of it?

- **Organization**

   Is the essay clearly divided into an introduction, a body, and a conclusion? Does the writer seem to follow an overall plan or does he or she move from point to point for no particular reason?

- **Development**

   Does the writer use specific reasons, examples, and details to support his or her ideas?

- **Clarity**

   Are the writer's ideas expressed clearly? Can a reader move from the beginning of the essay to the end without being confused?

- **Unity**

   Are all the paragraphs directly related to the main idea of the essay? Are all the sentences in each paragraph clearly related?

- **Coherence**

   Do the paragraphs and the sentences follow each other in an orderly way? Are transitions used to connect paragraphs and sentences?

- **Sentence variety**

   Does the writer use sentences involving different structures and of different lengths?

- **Vocabulary**

   Does the writer use sophisticated language?

- **Grammar**

   Are there frequent grammatical mistakes? Do the mistakes make it difficult to understand the writer's thoughts?

- **Spelling**

   Are there many misspelled words? Is it sometimes difficult to understand which word the writer intended?

- **Mechanics**

   Are there frequent mistakes in capitalization and punctuation? Are the paragraphs indented?

The score is based on a scale of 1 to 6; half point scores (5.5, 4.5, and so on) are also given. The scoring system ETS uses is similar to the following one:

Score	Explanation of Score
6	Strongly indicates the ability to write a well-organized, well-developed, and logical essay. Specific examples and details support the main ideas. All the elements of the essay are unified and cohesive. A variety of sentence structures are used successfully and sophisticated vocabulary is employed. Grammatical and mechanical errors are infrequent but a few minor mistakes may occur.
5	Indicates the ability to write an organized, developed, and logical essay. The main ideas are adequately supported by examples and details. Sentence structure may be less varied than that of a level 6 essay, and vocabulary less sophisticated. Some grammatical and mechanical errors will appear.
4	Indicates some ability in writing an acceptable essay, but involves weaknesses in organization and development. Sentence structure and vocabulary may lack sophistication and there may be frequent grammatical and mechanical errors.
3	Indicates a moderate ability to write an acceptable essay. Although main ideas may be adequately supported, serious weaknesses in organization and development are apparent. Sentence structure and vocabulary problems occur frequently. Grammatical errors are frequent and may make the writer's ideas difficult to comprehend.
2	Indicates the inability to write an acceptable essay. Organization and development are very weak or nonexistent. May lack unity and cohesion. Few specific details are given in support of the writer's ideas. If details are given, they may seem inappropriate. Significant and frequent errors in grammar occur throughout the essay, making it difficult to understand the writer's ideas. Writer may not have fully understood the essay prompt.
1	Strongly indicates the inability to write an acceptable essay. No apparent development or organization. Sentences may be brief and fragmentary and unrelated to each other. Very significant grammatical and mechanical errors occur throughout the essay and make it very difficult to understand any of the author's ideas. Writer may have completely misunderstood the essay prompt.
0	Did not write an essay, did not write on the topic, or wrote in a language other than English.

Following are six essays, each illustrating one of the six scores. They are written on the following topic:

Some people believe that money spent on space research benefits all of humanity. Other people take the opposite view and say that money spent on this type of research is wasted. Tell which point of view you agree with and explain why, using specific details and reasons.

Essay 1

Score: 6

It has become quite a common proverb that "there is no free lunch." Another way to say this is that spending money always has it's "opportunity cost." In other words, money spent on some venture could have been used for financing some other alternative venture. Some people believe that money spent on space research has a benefit for all people. Other people believe that there are better opportunities for spending this fund.

The first group of people say that space research has helped all peoples' lives very much. They point out that research on space has informed us about many environmental damages which we have caused to our planet. Similarly, they say that today's modern satelite system is due to the research done in the past on space. There are also many new materials and inventions that can be traced directly to space research. These people want to spend more money on research, visit all the planets, and build space colonies.

In the other hand, there are people who think that money spent on space is a complete wastage because it does not have enough direct benefit to all of the humanity. For example, billions of US$ were spent on the Project Apollo and they only brought back a bag of rocks. In the meanwhile, there is a sizeable portion of the humanity that does not have any access to food, education, sanitation, health care, and especially peace.

Personally, I find that I cannot allign myself completely with either group. I have some reservation about both positions. No one can deny that weather satelites and communication satelites are a good investment. But I think that "unrealistic" research like exploring Mars or Venus does not have any good bearing on most of humans' development at the present time. Some scientists may be interested in the composition of those planets, but the opportunity cost is too much. In my opinion, it is like the poor man who wants to buy diamond jewlry when his family does not have enough food to eat or clothes to wear.

Essay 2

Score: 5

Some people do really believe that space reseaches benefit all of humanity. And it's quite understandable because all the history of humanity development is connected with the space discovers. From the beginning people have been looking the sky and observing the star's movement and its influence. For example, everyone knows about astrology and how ancient people try to predict the future using knowledge of the stars.

The present space discovery started in 1957, when the sputnik was launched. The first person flew in the space in 1961, and after several years first Americans landed on moon.

Nowdays space researches can solve a lot of problems, For example, reseaches with new materials and technologies. Such materials can be used in medicine, chemistry, and etc. With the help of space satellites we can observe the atmosphere around the Earth and that's why we can try to predict storms and so on. Through such observation we can save people's lifes and decrease destructions, also we can solve problems with the different kinds of pollutions of ocean and atmosphere.

However, it is quite understandable the position of those who say that space researches are wasted. There are to many places where the main problem of life is to survive. My native country once was part of Soviet Union, where the big first steps in space were taken. I see people there who works hard and doesn't receive enough or any salary. I wonder if they approve the space reseaches?

But I'm sure that if we concentrate only on the question of how to survive, the humanity will lose the reason for development. If we refuse from space researches, or any kind of the scientific researches, we will stop moving forward. And the absence of moving forward means the death of the humanity's spirit. That's why I agree with the statement.

Essay 3

Score: 4

One of history's greatest event caught us here in the 21st century. An international space station members have decoded some of the mysterious sounds recorded lately. It seems human being from other planet are going to meet us as their lost brothers. Psychologists say, that the emotions and style of thinking of these message senders as compared with Earth population is very close to twins! These messages are spread out throughout the space only once in hundred year. These message senders can teach us things that will take thousand of years to learn by ourselves.

Almost this is as great as the discovery ten years ago, when the big meteor going to hit the Earth was seen by a satellite and could be exploded before it could make any damage.

Could you imagine the perspective if we were stopped space research as some scientists and other peoples had requested at the beginning of the 21st century.

(Article of the World Tribune, 28 December 2049)

Essay 4

Score: 3

Well, about the topic, I think that there others subjects much more importants to be researching. One of them, and to me the most important, is the health. The cancer cure is not totally developed yet. The AIDs' victims increasing at an incredibly way. So, although I find in "space" a very fascinating and misterious subject, I should agree with the opposite view that the money spend on it wasted when are so many of people dying around the world as a result of unknowns diseases or not having answers or cures for the ones we already known, or because is not enough money for purification of the water or vaccines for the diseases. More money for the education is also very important.

I believe cientifics should focus "health" in the first place and then to extend the researches in other field.

Essay 5

Score: 2

At the first the research in any thing is very useful for people because without research we will not development our life, so that I believe that the money spent in space research benefit the humanity.

Maybe the other side people thing that the money which paid for these research is so much and if we paid it for poor people it well be help him in they life and help him for many thing like food or healthy or any way of they life.

But the people which agrees with have a lot of point for example: one of this is the life must be development. Other point, the rule materials become less and we must find a new one and must find new resource of power, so that they agree with a research in space.

Essay 6

Score: 1

The peoples take the opposive view because we don't buy something one time and we don't see another things. That is a save way.

the money is important things. for this reason to spent money the peoples need to be very cerfully I have two opinion for spent money. The money important to spent all humanity, because this point is very important. I'm not agree money wested. in the futurre very important

Computer Skills for the Essay Writing Section

This is the only part of the test in which you will primarily use the keyboard rather than the mouse.

If you decide to take this section on the computer, you will see a tutorial that explains how to take this section of the test.

You will first see a screen with the directions. You should immediately click on the Dismiss directions icon and go on.

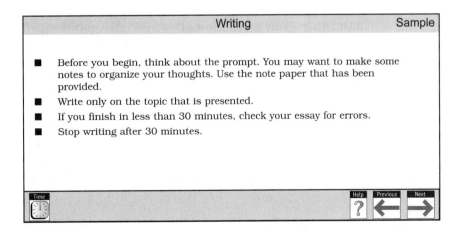

After you have dismissed the directions, you will see a screen that presents the prompt:

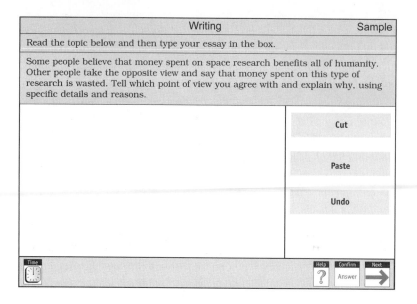

<table>
<tr><td colspan="2">Writing   Sample</td></tr>
</table>

Writing	Sample

Read the topic below and then type your essay in the box.

Some people believe that money spent on space research benefits all of humanity. Other people take the opposite view and say that money spent on this type of research is wasted. Tell which point of view you agree with and explain why, using specific details and reasons.

Cut

Paste

Undo

Time

Help ?   Confirm Answer   Next →

To begin, read the prompt carefully, think it over, and make notes. Then begin typing. To indent the first paragraph—and all paragraphs—you will have to hit the space bar five times. (For some reason, the tab key does not work in this program.)

Space Bar

The program for typing the essay is a simplified version of a standard word processing program. For the most part, all you need to do is type in the essay. Unfortunately, there are no "spell check" or "grammar check" tools! There are, however, a few simple commands you can put to use. You activate these commands by using your mouse and the three icons labeled **Cut, Paste,** and **Undo** on the right side of your screen.

■ CUT AND PASTE

You can use these two commands to move part of your essay to another place in the essay. To use these two commands, you must first **highlight text** (select something that you have written). To do this, use the mouse to position the blinking cursor to the beginning of the text that you want to select and click once. Then, holding down the left-click button on the mouse, slowly move the cursor over the text that you want to select. This highlights the text. In other words, it will appear in white letters on a black background.

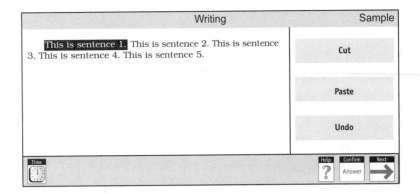

Now, click Cut. What happens? The highlighted text disappears.

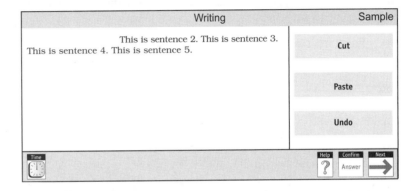

You can stop here if you just want to get rid of Sentence 1. But if you want to move it, use the mouse to position the blinking cursor where you want the text to go, and then click Paste. The text now magically reappears!

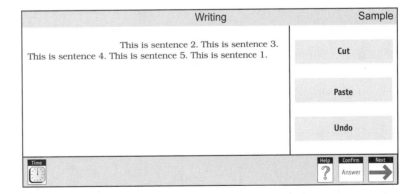

To summarize: In order to cut and paste . . .

- Position the cursor just before the material you want to move and click the mouse
- Highlight the material by dragging the cursor over it while holding down the left-click button on the mouse
- Click Cut and the text will disappear
- Position the cursor where you want the text to go
- Click Paste and the text reappears

■ UNDO

The Undo command will reverse any commands or typing you have just done. For example, if you cut and paste a sentence from one paragraph to another and then decide you want the sentence back where you first had it, click on Undo and the sentence will go back where it was before you did the cut and paste. You can also undo the last sentence that you typed.

If you decide that using the Undo command was a mistake, just click Undo again.

MOVING AROUND THE ESSAY

There are a number of commands you can use to move the cursor from one part of your essay to another.

- You can use the four arrow keys to move the cursor up, down, left, or right.
- You can move to the end of the line that you are working on by hitting the **End** key, or to the beginning of the line by hitting the **Home** key.

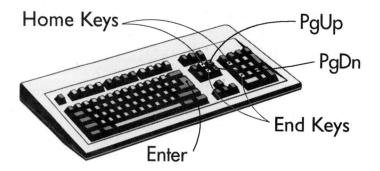

- You can move up and down through the essay quickly (one screen at a time) by hitting the **PgUp** or **PgDn** key.
- You can move to a new line (where you have not typed) by hitting the **Enter** key.

DELETING TEXT

There are a number of ways you can delete (erase) text.

- You can delete a letter to the left by hitting the **Backspace** key.
- You can delete one character to the right by hitting the **Del** (delete) key.
- You can delete a large piece of text by highlighting it and clicking on the **Cut** icon. It will disappear.
- If you decide you didn't really want to delete something, you can click on the **Undo** icon.

WARNING!

At the bottom of the screen in this section—just as in sections 1 and 2—are icons labeled **Next** and **Confirm Answer.** Do NOT click on these unless you have finished your essay ahead of time. Clicking on Next will NOT get you another topic—it will simply end the Essay Writing section.

Tactics for Essay Writing

- Decide before the test whether you are going to word process the essay or write it in longhand.
- As with all parts of the TOEFL® Test, be familiar with the directions for Essay Writing so that you don't have to waste time reading them.
- Use the clock on the screen to pace yourself. You have only a half hour in which to complete your work. Give yourself 5 minutes to read the prompt and plan the essay, 20 minutes to write it, and 5 minutes to check it.
- Don't exit the essay early. Keep working until time is up.
- Read the prompt carefully. You must write on the topic exactly as it is given.
- Before you begin to write, spend a minute or two "brainstorming." Think about the topic and the best way to approach it.
- Take notes and plan your essay before you begin.
- Follow a clear, logical organization. Most essays consist of three basic parts: an introduction, a body of two or three paragraphs, and a conclusion.
- Use concrete examples and specific reasons. Whenever you make a general statement, support it with specific examples. If you state an opinion, give reasons.
- Use signal words to indicate transitions. Signal words can be used to join paragraph to paragraph and sentence to sentence.
- If you choose to handwrite your essay, be sure your handwriting is as clear and legible as possible. Your handwriting should not be too big or too small.

If you intend to word process the essay, you should practice taking this preview test on the computer by using any word processing program. You can use the cut, paste, and undo functions, but don't use the spell-check, grammar-check, or thesaurus functions.

PREVIEW TEST 4: Essay Writing

■   Before you begin, think about the prompt. You may want to make some notes to organize your thoughts. Use the space for notes that has been provided.

■   Write only on the topic that is presented.

■   If you finish in less than 30 minutes, check your essay for errors.

■   Stop writing after 30 minutes.

ESSAY PROMPT

Good, affordable housing is one of the factors that makes a community a desirable place to live. Choose one other factor that you think is important. Give specific details and reasons for your choice.

NOTES

Use this space for essay notes only. Write the final version of your essay on the next two pages.

Name: _____

Write your essay here.

_____
_____
_____
_____
_____
_____
_____
_____
_____
_____
_____
_____
_____
_____
_____
_____
_____
_____
_____
_____
_____
_____
_____
_____
_____
_____
_____
_____
_____
_____
_____
_____
_____
_____

LESSON 39: Pre-Writing

You should spend about five minutes "pre-writing" the essay. What should you do during this time? You will have three main tasks:

1) Read the essay prompt (topic) carefully.

2) Brainstorm (think about) the topic.

3) Plan your essay.

During the second and third tasks, you should take notes to use as an outline when you write the essay.

You should spend only five minutes on pre-writing—but it's a very important time!

A) READING THE PROMPT

In some ways, this is the most important step of the entire process. If you don't understand the prompt, you can't properly respond to it. If you write an essay that does not fully respond to the prompt, you will receive a lower score, no matter how well you have written the essay.

The essay prompts tend to be written in very simple English. If any of the vocabulary is "difficult," it is usually explained.

Not only do you need to read the prompt carefully, you also need to understand what it is asking you to do. You need to analyze the prompt—to **paraphrase** it (put it into your own words) and to explain to yourself what it asks you to do. (You don't need to do this analysis in writing, only mentally.)

Read these analyses of the sample prompts given in the introduction:

> Some people believe that money spent on space research benefits all of humanity. Other people take the opposite view and say that money spent on this type of research is wasted. Tell which point of view you agree with and explain why, using specific details and reasons.

Analysis

This prompt says that there are two opinions about space research. Some people think that money spent on space research (for satellites, space shuttles, probes to other planets, and so on) is generally a good thing, helping all people. Other people think it is a waste of money. They think this money could be used for better things. To respond to this prompt, I have to decide which of these positions I want to support. I could give some good reasons why I think space research benefits everyone. On the other hand, if I choose to defend the opposite side of this argument, I have to explain why I think money for space research should be spent on something else.

> Do you agree or disagree with this statement?
>
> It is much easier to learn in a small class than in a large one.
>
> Use specific examples and reasons to support your answer.

Analysis

This prompt asks about my opinion of class size, and whether I think it has an effect on learning. I can choose one of two positions. One position is that small class size DOES make it easier to learn, and I'll need to give examples of ways in which it does. If I choose the other side, I have to say that size is NOT an important factor. I could say that a good teacher can make sure students learn in even a large class, and give examples of ways in which he or she could do that.

> Developments in transportation such as the automobile have had an enormous impact on modern society. Choose another development in transportation that you think is of great importance. Use specific examples and reasons for your choice.

Analysis

For this prompt, I have to choose some development in transportation that I think is important or almost as important as the development of the automobile. I can't choose the automobile because the prompt says to choose *another* development. I could, for example, choose the development of the railroad and talk about how this had an impact on the world in general or on one country in particular.

B) BRAINSTORMING

The process of brainstorming involves generating ideas on the topic. Just sit back for a moment and think about the topic and write down any ideas that come to you. These may be things you have read in newspapers and magazines, things you've heard in classes or on television, or personal experiences. These ideas may turn out to be useful or not—just write them all down.

Let's say that you are assigned the first prompt. You would try to think about anything—positive or negative—that you have read about or heard about in connection with space exploration, and quickly write these ideas down. For the second topic, you would probably use your own experiences. Can you remember any positive experience with either a large class or a small one? Any negative ones? Write them down.

Someone brainstorming the first topic might jot down these ideas:

many benefits for people on Earth—weather satellites, etc.

consumer products—PCs, freeze-dried foods, etc.

people think astronauts are heros

people need a challenge like space

but very expensive—money could be used in many other ways—schools, housing etc

C) PLANNING THE ESSAY

This stage of pre-writing actually blurs with Step B; while you are brainstorming, you are beginning to plan your essay.

The first step in planning is to choose your basic **thesis.** A thesis is the central or controlling idea of an essay. For the first two types of prompts—defending an opinion and agreeing/disagreeing with a statement—choosing a thesis simply means choosing which side of the argument you are going to support. For example, for the first prompt your thesis might be, "In my opinion, research in space benefits humanity." For the second, your thesis might be, "With the right teacher, large class size has little effect on learning." For the third prompt, you have to choose what development you are going to discuss. "I believe that the development of jet airliners was extremely important."

Remember, when you choose a thesis, there is no right or wrong answer. The readers at ETS don't care whether you are in favor of space research or against it, whether you like small classes or big ones, or whether you think the development of rockets, railroads, or roller skates was most important. In fact, you should choose whatever side of the argument is easiest to support. It's possible, for example, that you have had generally good experience in large classes, but that you can think of more reasons why small classes are better.

It is not necessary to fully support either point of view. Sample essay 1 (page 471) is an example of an essay that partially supports both points of view.

Once you have chosen a thesis, you need to think of ways to support it. Look at the notes you took while brainstorming. Are there any concrete details or compelling reasons that support the thesis you have chosen? If not, think of some now.

Next, you need to write a simple outline. You don't have to write a formal outline with Roman numerals and letters, just a basic plan for your four or five paragraphs.

You may be tempted to skip this step to save time, but writing an outline is very important. Following a simple outline is the best way to keep an essay organized, and good organization is one of the most important things readers look for in scoring your essay.

For the "opinion" prompts (types 1 and 2), there are two basic ways to organize your essay. One is to write two or more paragraphs, each providing a reason why your opinion is the "correct" one.

Introduction
Here is my opinion.

Body Paragraph 1
My opinion is right because . . .

Body Paragraph 2
My opinion is also right because . . .

Conclusion
As you can see, my opinion IS right.

Another approach is to restate both sides of the argument—A and B—in your introduction. The introduction does not say which side of the argument is "correct." Then, in one paragraph of the body, you provide several reasons to support the side that you do NOT agree with—opinion A. This tactic is sometimes called **admitting the opposition.** Then, in the next paragraph of the body, you give even stronger reasons why the other point of view, opinion B, is the better or more logical one. The conclusion restates the idea that opinion B is the right one.

Introduction
There are two possible opinions
on this topic, opinions A and B.
Which is better ?

Body Paragraph 1
Here are some reasons to believe opinion A is right.

Body Paragraph 2
Here are some even better reasons to believe opinion
B is right.

Conclusion
As you can see, opinion B IS right.

Simple outlines for the three prompts given in this lesson may look like this:

Prompt A

Notes

<u>Intro</u>: Space research for + 50 years: expensive—$ well spent or wasted?

−*ideas*	+*ideas*
costs billions; also human resources; no real benefits	*consumer products; e.g., PCs, freeze-dried foods, pacemakers*
e.g., trip to Moon only brought back rocks	*weather & communication satellites*
many important uses for this $ on Earth:	
e.g., education environment housing	*scientific knowledge about planets, Moon, even Earth*

<u>*Conclu*</u>: *As shown, many benefits—also, human race needs challenge just as individuals do—therefore, space research is worth all the money spent*

Prompt B

Notes

Intro: Sometimes it's necessary to have big classes. Good teacher can make big classes as good a learning environ as small ones

Introductory classes, lecture the same no matter what size
   Sometimes lecturers more dynamic in large cl

Some people think not as much interaction in big classes
But . . . teacher can break cl into small grps for
   discussion, projects, etc.
   teacher can use teaching asst. to lead discussion groups

Conclu . . . many people think small is best, but big classes can be good places to learn too

Prompt C

Notes

Intro: One of most important develop is internatl jet transport—since '60s—because of speed & low costs, has changed way people think abt travel

Speed: 100 yrs ago, took weeks to cross ocean: today, few hrs—this has changed people's concept of space

Low costs: In past, only wealthy could travel comfortably; poor people had to save for years—today, more and more people can travel
   businesspeople
   students
   tourists

Conclusion: countries no longer so isolated; people think of world as own hometowns

EXERCISE 39.1

Focus: Reading and analyzing Essay Writing prompts.

Directions: Read the six prompts given below. Then choose three prompts—one of each type—and write an analysis for each one similar to the analyses on pages 481–482.

Type A
Prompt 1

Some people believe that schools should primarily teach students how to best compete with others. Other people believe that schools should primarily teach students how to cooperate with others. Which of these approaches do you favor? Use specific reasons and examples to support your answer.

Prompt 2

Some university students prefer living in campus housing such as dormitories. Other students prefer living in off-campus housing, such as apartments. If you were faced with this decision, which of these two options would you choose? Use specific reasons and details to explain your choice.

Type B
Prompt 3

Do you agree or disagree with the following statement?

Professional athletes such as football stars and entertainers such as singers and actors are paid too much money for the work that they do.

Use specific details and examples to support your answer.

Prompt 4

Do you agree or disagree with the following statement?

It is better for university students to first get a general education, taking classes in many fields, than it is for them to take classes only in their own field of study.

Use specific details and examples to support your answer.

Type C
Prompt 5

Imagine that you can talk for one hour with any person who has lived at any time in history. Which person would you choose to meet? Use specific details and examples to explain your choice.

Prompt 6

Your hometown has just received a grant from an international organization to fund one single improvement project. Which of the following would you recommend to receive the funding?

the city airport
the local schools
the fire department
the public transportation system

the police department
the city parks
the streets and roads
the local hospitals
the art museum

Give specific examples and reasons to support your recommendation.

ANALYSIS 1

ANALYSIS 2

_____

_____

ANALYSIS 3

_____

_____

_____

_____

_____

_____

_____

EXERCISE 39.2

Focus: Brainstorming and taking notes on Essay Writing prompts.

Directions: Brainstorm the three prompts that you chose in Exercise 39.1 and take notes on any ideas that occur to you. Don't spend more than 1 or 2 minutes per prompt.

NOTES 1

NOTES 2

NOTES 3

EXERCISE 39.3

Focus: Writing informal outlines for essays.

Directions: Using the three prompts you chose in Exercise 39.1, write short, informal outlines for essays. Do not spend more than 3 or 4 minutes per outline.

OUTLINE 1

OUTLINE 2

OUTLINE 3

LESSON 40: Writing the Essay

After spending about five minutes on pre-writing, you are now ready to get down to the real task: writing the essay.

You have only about twenty minutes in which to write it, and you need to produce a 200–300 word essay. That's about 10–15 words a minute. You can do this if you concentrate and keep working.

ETS says that quality is more important than quantity in the essay, but typically only longer essays get top scores. A long essay does not guarantee a good score on this section, but a short essay almost guarantees a low one.

This lesson will discuss writing all three parts of the typical essay.

A) WRITING THE INTRODUCTION

There are a number of functions that a good introduction can serve (but no introduction will serve all these functions).

- To get the readers' attention
- To restate the ideas of the prompt
- To present some general background information about the topic
- To preview the main points that will appear in the essay
- To present a clear statement of the main idea of the essay. (This is called the **thesis statement**; it typically is the last sentence of the introduction, but sometimes it appears in the conclusion.)

Here are three introductory paragraphs, written in response to the three prompts presented in Lesson 39, page 471–472.

INTRODUCTION 1

For around fifty years, a number of nations have been involved in the exploration of outer space. This research has been very costly, of course. Has this money been well-spent or wasted?

This introduction makes a couple of very general statements about space research to provide background, and then asks if research is worth the cost. Notice that this question is NOT answered in the introduction. The answer to that question—which is really the thesis statement of the essay—will appear in the conclusion.

INTRODUCTION 2

Many students believe that small classes offer much better educational opportunities than large ones. However, in my experience, that is not necessarily true. I believe that, with a good teacher, a large class can provide as good a learning opportunity as a small one.

In the introduction, the writer paraphrases the prompt in the first sentence. However, in the second sentence the writer disagrees with the idea stated in the prompt. In the last sentence of the introduction, the writer gives the thesis statement: that learning depends on good teaching, not class size.

INTRODUCTION 3

I believe that one of the most important developments in transportation has been the development of international jet transport. Jet airliners first appeared in the early 1960s. Since then, planes have gotten bigger and faster and capable of flying longer distances. Jet transport has had some revolutionary effects. Because of the high speeds and the relatively low costs of this type of travel, it has changed the way people look at the world.

In the first sentence of the paragraph, the writer answers the question brought up in the prompt. The writer then goes on to provide a little background information about this development, and then provides a preview of the main points that the body of the essay will discuss: speed and low costs and how these have changed people's view of the world.

B) WRITING THE BODY OF THE ESSAY

It is in the body of the essay that the writer develops the thesis (main idea).

A typical paragraph in the body begins with a **topic sentence** which contains the main idea of that paragraph (just as the thesis statement contains the main idea of the essay). It also contains several sentences that support this main idea. The writer should provide specific details, reasons, examples, and/or personal experiences to support these sentences.

> **Topic sentence**
> **Supporting sentence**
>> Detail
>> Detail
> **Supporting sentence**
>> Detail
>> Detail

Remember that the supporting sentences and the details must be directly relevant to the main idea of the paragraph; do not include irrelevant material.

Look at these paragraphs from the body of essays written in response to the prompts on pages 471–472.

BODY 1

Some people believe that all or most space research should be eliminated because of its incredible expense, not only in terms of money, but also in terms of scientific and human resources. These people point out the fact that it cost billions of dollars to send astronauts to the Moon, but all they brought back were some worthless rocks. These people say that the money and effort now being wasted in outer space could be spent on more important projects right here on Earth, such as providing housing for homeless people, improving the educational system, saving the environment, and finding cures for diseases.

However, other people believe that space research has provided many benefits to humankind. They point out that hundreds of useful products, from personal computers to heart pacemakers to freeze-dried foods, are the direct or indirect results of space research. They say that weather and communication satellites, which are also products of space research, have benefitted people all over the globe. In addition to these practical benefits, supporters of the space program point to the scientific knowledge that has been acquired about the Sun, the Moon, the planets, and even our own Earth as a result of space research.

In the first paragraph, the writer "admits the opposition," giving reasons why opinion A (money spent on space is wasted) is correct. This is clearly stated in the topic sentence of the first paragraph. The writer then provides reasons to support this idea: there have been no great rewards for spending all this money (just "worthless rocks") and lists more important ways to spend this money, such as on housing and education.

In the second paragraph, the writer presents the opposite point of view, that money spent on space has benefitted everyone. Specific benefits are listed: useful products, weather and communications satellites, and scientific knowledge.

BODY 2

When I was an undergraduate student, most of the large classes I took were introductory classes for first- and second-year students. For example, I took classes in world history and economics that had over 100 students and met in large lecture halls. I think these classes were as good as some of the small classes I took later. At the basic level, the lectures that a professor gives are basically the same no matter what size the class is. Moreover, the professors who taught these classes seemed more enthusiastic and energetic than the teachers I had in smaller classes. Personally, I think they enjoyed having a large audience!

One supposed advantage of small classes is that there is usually a lot more interaction among students and between the teacher and the students than in large ones. However, in the large classes I took, there were discussion sessions held every week with a graduate teaching assistant in which there was a lot of interaction. Besides, the teachers for these classes had long office hours, and they were always willing to answer questions and talk over problems.

The writer uses personal experiences with large and small classes in both paragraphs to support the thesis statement. In the first paragraph, the writer says that in introductory classes the teachers' lectures are basically the same no matter how many students there are. In fact, in the writer's experience, teachers were more dynamic in larger classes.

The second paragraph says that people think there is more interaction in small classes than in large ones, but that, in fact, the writer found there was a lot of interaction in the weekly discussion sessions held in conjunction with the large classes. The writer also says that the teachers held long office hours in which to answer questions.

BODY 3

The most obviously important characteristic of jet travel is the high speed involved. A hundred years ago, it took weeks to cross the Atlantic or Pacific oceans by ship. However, today, those same trips can be completed in a matter of hours. One can attend a meeting in Paris and have dinner in New York on the same day. These amazing speeds have changed people's concepts of space. Today the world is much smaller than it was in the past.

Another important aspect of jet travel is its relatively low cost. An international journey one hundred years ago was extremely expensive. Only wealthy people could afford to travel comfortably, in first class. Poor people had to save for years to purchase a ticket, and the conditions in which they traveled were often miserable. Today it is possible for more and more people in every country to travel in comfort. Thus it is possible for business people to do business all over the world, for students to attend universities in other countries, and for tourists to take vacations anywhere in the world.

In its topic sentence, the first paragraph gives the first reason why jet transport is an important development: its speed. It goes on to compare the speed of jets with those of ships one hundred years ago, gives an example of the speed of jets (meeting in Paris, dinner in New York), and shows the effect of this speed on the way people view the world.

The second paragraph begins by stating another important aspect of jet travel, its relatively low cost. The writer again compares travel today with travel in the past and shows how more and more people travel comfortably. The writer gives examples of specific types of people who have been affected by this: business people, students, and tourists.

C) WRITING THE CONCLUSION

The final paragraph of an essay should give the reader the feeling of completion, NOT a feeling that the writer has simply run out of ideas or out of time.

Here are some of the functions a conclusion can serve:

- To present the thesis statement (if this is NOT presented in the introduction)
- To restate the thesis statement (if this IS given in the introduction)
- To summarize the main points presented in the body
- To show the significance of the points made in the body
- To present one last compelling reason why the writer's opinion is the correct one

Look at these examples of concluding paragraphs:

CONCLUSION 1

I agree with those people who support space research and want it to continue. Space research, as shown, has already brought many benefits to humanity. Perhaps it will bring more benefits in the future, ones that we can't even imagine now. Moreover, just as individual people need challenges to make their lives more interesting, I believe the human race itself needs a challenge, and I think that the peaceful exploration of outer space provides just such a challenge.

This conclusion begins with the thesis statement for the essay—that the writer agrees with those that support space research. The writer also presents two more reasons why the reader should agree with this idea: because there may be more benefits in the future, and because space exploration provides a challenge for the human race.

CONCLUSION 2

In conclusion, I don't think that the size of a class is very important. I think that learning depends more on the quality of the teaching than on the number of students in the class.

This is a very simple conclusion that restates the thesis statement from the introduction and summarizes the main point of the body paragraphs.

CONCLUSION 3

To summarize, the speed and low cost of international jet travel have
changed the world. Individual nations are not as isolated as they were
in the past, and people now think of the whole planet as they once
thought of their own hometowns.

This conclusion summarizes points made in the body paragraphs and shows the
significance of these points.

EXERCISE 40.1

Focus: Writing introductions for essays.

Directions: Write introductory paragraphs for the three prompts you wrote notes for
in Lesson 39. If possible, write your introduction on a computer.

EXERCISE 40.2

Focus: Writing body paragraphs for essays.

Directions: Write body paragraphs for the three introductions you wrote in Exercise
40.1. If possible, write your paragraphs on a computer.

EXERCISE 40.3

Focus: Writing conclusions for essays.

Directions: Write conclusions for the three essays you wrote in Exercises 40.1 and
40.2. If possible, write your conclusions on a computer.

LESSON 41: Improving Your Essay

There are several techniques you can use to write more interesting, more sophisticated, and clearer essays.

A) VARYING SENTENCE LENGTH

Good writing in English consists of a more or less equal balance between short, simple sentences having only one clause and longer sentences containing two or more clauses. Make an effort to use sentences of various lengths.

Here are some of the most common ways to combine simple (one-clause) sentences:

1. With adjective clause markers (relative pronouns)

    There are many reasons to agree with this statement. I will discuss three of them in this essay.

    There are many reasons to agree with this statement, three of which I will discuss in this essay.

2. With adverb clause markers (subordinate conjunctions)

    The invention of the automobile is undoubtedly one of humankind's greatest inventions. Not everybody can enjoy the benefits of owning a car.

    Although the invention of the automobile is undoubtedly one of humankind's greatest inventions, not everybody can enjoy the benefits of owning a car.

3. With coordinate conjunctions (*but, and, or, so,* and so on)

    The invention of the automobile is undoubtedly one of humankind's greatest inventions. Not everybody can enjoy the benefits of owning a car.

    The invention of the automobile is undoubtedly one of humankind's greatest inventions, but not everybody can enjoy the benefits of owning a car.

Look back at the paragraphs you wrote for Exercises 40.1, 40.2, and 40.3. If most of the sentences you wrote were simple one-clause sentences, you should be combining some of these sentences using these and other techniques. On the other hand, if all of the sentences you wrote are complicated and contain two or more clauses, you should write some of these as shorter, simpler sentences.

B) VARYING THE ORDER OF SENTENCE PARTS

You should also vary the order of parts of a sentence. Begin some sentences with prepositional phrases or subordinate clauses.

Instead of

    I disagree with this idea for several reasons.

Try

    For several reasons, I disagree with this idea.

Instead of

    I support Idea A even though Idea B has some positive attributes.

Try

    Even though Idea B has some positive attributes, I support Idea A.

C) USING SIGNAL WORDS

Signal words can be used to join paragraph to paragraph and sentence to sentence. These words make your essay clearer and easier to follow. Some of these expressions and their meanings are given below.

1) Expressions used to list points, examples, or reasons

First example or reason

First,

For example,

The first reason for this is that . . .

Additional examples or reasons

Second, (Third, Fourth,)

A second (third, fourth) example is . . .

Another example is . . .

Another reason is that . . .

In addition,

Furthermore,

Moreover,

Final example or reason

Finally,

To give individual examples

For example,

For instance,

To give a specific example,

X is an example of Y.

To show contrast

However,

On the other hand,

Nevertheless,

To show a conclusion

Therefore,

Consequently,

Thus,

To show similarity

Likewise,

Similarly,

To begin a concluding paragraph

In conclusion,

In summary,

To express an opinion

In my opinion,

Personally,

2) Examples of the use of signal words

I agree with the idea of stricter gun control for a number of reasons. *First,* statistics show that guns are not very effective in preventing crime. *Second,* accidents involving guns frequently occur. *Finally,* guns can be stolen and later used in crimes.

I believe that a good salary is an important consideration when looking for a career. *However,* the nature of the work is more important to me. *Thus,* I would not accept a job that I did not find rewarding.

For me, the reasons for living in an urban area are stronger than the reasons for living in a rural community. *Therefore,* I agree with those people who believe it is an advantage to live in a big city.

Don't overuse signal words. Generally, don't use more than one or two per paragraph.

EXERCISE 41.1

Focus: Joining simple, one-clause sentences into more complicated sentences.

Directions: Using the words listed below, join the sentences into a single sentence. Don't change the order in which the clauses are given. In some cases, there may be more than one way to join the sentences.

so	but	who	or	even though
which	although	and	since	because

1. One of the most important holidays in my country is Independence Day. It is celebrated on September 16th.

   _____

   _____

2. Young children have a special talent for language learning. Children should be taught other languages at an early age.

   _____

   _____

3. My brother began studying at the university. He has taken several large classes.

   _____

   _____

4. Some forms of advertising serve a useful purpose. Many forms of advertising do not.

   _____

   _____

5. A friend is an acquaintance. He or she will help you whenever possible.

   _____

   _____

6. I believe corporations should do more to recycle materials. I believe they should do more to reduce air pollution.

   _____

   _____

7. Small classes are the best environment for learning. Sometimes universities must have large classes.

   _____

   _____

8. We must develop alternative sources of energy. Air pollution will get worse and worse.

_____

_____

EXERCISE 41.2

Focus: Varying the order of adverb clauses and prepositional phrases.

Directions: You wrote four sentences in the previous exercise using adverb clause markers (*because, since, although,* and *even though*). Rewrite these four sentences in the first four spaces below, changing the order of the main clause and the adverb clause.

Then rewrite the next four sentences, changing the position of prepositional phrases or other sentence parts.

1. _____

   _____

2. _____

   _____

3. _____

   _____

4. _____

   _____

5. Students get more personal attention in small classes.

   _____

   _____

6. I would use e-mail if I needed to get in touch with a business associate.

   _____

   _____

7. I have asked myself that question again and again.

   _____

   _____

8. My favorite place in the world to visit is Greece because of its long and fascinating history.

   _____

   _____

EXERCISE 41.3

Focus: Recognizing signal words and understanding their use.

Directions: A number of signal words are used in the sample introductions, bodies, and conclusions presented in Lesson 40. Look back at these samples and underline all the signal words that you can find. In each case, try to understand why the writer used those words.

EXERCISE 41.4

Focus: Using signal words to link sentences.

Directions: Use the signal words listed to link the sentences below. In some cases, there may be more than one correct answer. Not all the signal words will be used.

| likewise | however | furthermore | in conclusion |
| therefore | on the other hand | for example | personally |

1. I believe that women should have the right to serve in the military. _____, I don't believe that they should be assigned to combat roles.

2. Many actors, rock musicians, and sports stars receive huge amounts of money for the work that they do. _____, a baseball player was recently offered a contract worth over twelve million dollars. _____, I feel that this is far too much to pay a person who simply provides entertainment.

3. The development of the automobile has had a great impact on people everywhere. _____, the development of high-speed trains has had an impact on people in many countries, including my home country of France.

4. I used to work in a restaurant when I was in college. I realize what a difficult job restaurant work is. _____, whenever I go out to eat, I try to leave a good tip for my waiter or waitress.

5. Many people would agree with the idea that the best use for the open space in our community is to build a shopping center in this community. _____, there are other people who feel we should turn this open space into a park.

6. The use of computer technology has had a major impact on the way many people work. _____, it has also changed the way many people spend their leisure time.

EXERCISE 41.5

Focus: Using sentence variety to improve the quality of writing in an essay.

Directions: The following essay contains short, simple sentences consisting of only one clause. Rewrite the essay. Combine sentences, vary the order of sentence parts, use signal words, and make whatever other changes you think are necessary to create a more interesting essay.

Remember, don't eliminate all single-clause sentences. Good writing consists of a mixture of short, simple sentences and longer, more complicated ones.

This essay was written in response to the following prompt.

> Some people like to go to the same place for their vacations. Other people like to take their vacations in different places. Which of these two choices do you prefer? Give specific reasons for your choice.

There are certain people. They always like to take their vacations in the same place. They return from a vacation. They ask themselves, "When can I go back there again?" There are other people. They like to go many places. They like to do many different things on their vacations. They return from a vacation. They ask themselves, "Where can I go next?"

My parents are perfect examples of the first kind of people. They always like to go to a lake in the mountains. They went there on their honeymoon. They bought a vacation cabin there. They bought it several years after they were married. They have gone there two or three times a year for over twenty-five years. My parents have made friends. They have made friends with the people who also own cabins there. They enjoy getting together with them. Both my parents enjoy sailing and swimming. My father likes to go fishing. My parents enjoy variety. They say they can get variety by going to their cabin at different times of the year. They particularly like to go there in the autumn. The leaves are beautiful then.

I am an example of a person. I like to go to different places for her vacation. I was a child. I went to my parents' cabin. I got older. I wanted to travel to many different places. I spent a lot of time and money learning how to ski. I wanted to travel to places where I could ski. I could ski in Switzerland. I was interested in visiting historic places. I went to Angkor Wat in Cambodia. It was difficult to get there. I would like to go to Egypt. I want to see the pyramids there. I would like to go to Rome. I want to see the Coliseum there.

I enjoy going to familiar places. I find that going to strange places is more exciting. The world is so huge and exciting. I don't want to go to the same place twice. I also understand my parents' point of view. They believe that you can never get to know a place too well.

EXERCISE 41.6

Focus: Using sentence variety to improve the quality of your own writing.

Directions: Look back at the three introductions, bodies, and conclusions you wrote for Exercises 40.1, 40.2, and 40.3. Can these essays be improved by varying the length of the sentences (either combining short sentences or breaking longer ones into two sentences), by varying the order of sentence parts, or by using signal words appropriately? Make any changes in these paragraphs that you think will make them clearer and more interesting.

LESSON 42: Checking and Editing Your Essay

You should spend the last five minutes of the thirty minute period **checking** your essay (looking for errors) and **editing** it (correcting the errors). There are three types of checking and editing you should do. Of course, you can do any editing more easily and more neatly if you write the essay on computer.

A) CHECKING FOR AND EDITING ORGANIZATIONAL PROBLEMS

You will not have time to make any major changes in the organization of the essay. However, you should ask yourself these questions:

■ Is there a thesis statement that summarizes the main idea of the essay? (If not, add it.)

■ Do all the sentences in the essay support this main idea? (If not, delete them.)

B) CHECKING FOR AND EDITING GRAMMATICAL ERRORS

There are many types of grammatical errors that you can check for. Some of the more common ones are listed here:

1) **Verb errors**
    Verb errors are so common that you should carefully check all the verbs in the essay. Be sure that the verb agrees with the subject, that the verb is in the right tense, and that you are using active forms and passive forms appropriately.

                           is
    Each of these theories ~~are~~ very important.

        moved
    I ~~have moved~~ to my present apartment three months ago.

        agree
    I ~~am agree~~ with this statement.

2) **Pronoun error**
    The most common pronoun error involves pronoun agreement (using a singular pronoun to refer to a plural noun or using a plural pronoun to refer to a singular noun).

    The only way this problem can be solved is with the help of the
                   It
    government. ~~They~~ must spend more money on schools and teachers' salaries in order to improve the educational system.

3) **Sentence fragments and run-on sentences**
    A **sentence fragment** is an incomplete sentence; the sentence is missing an essential element, such as the subject or verb. A **run-on sentence** is a sentence that goes on "too long." It usually consists of two or more clauses that are not properly connected.

                                      such as
    My country imports several agricultural products. ~~For example,~~ wheat and beef.

I believe the most important subject I have ever studied is

. Psychology
economics, ~~psychology~~ is another important subject.

4) **Singular and plural words**

Check nouns to make sure a singular form is used when needed and a plural form is used when needed. Also remember that there is no plural adjective form in English as there is in some languages.

research
In my opinion, medical ~~researches~~ should receive more funding.

scientific
Many ~~scientifics~~ experiments still need to be performed.

5) **Word forms**

Be sure you are using the correct form (adjective, adverb, noun, or verb) of the word.

institution
To me, the most important ~~institutional~~ in any country is the legal

system.

There are, of course, many other types of grammatical errors. If you have ever taken a writing class, look at the corrections the teacher made on your papers to see what kinds of mistakes you commonly made, and look for those mistakes when you check your essay.

C) CHECKING AND EDITING MECHANICAL ERRORS

1) **Spelling errors**

Look for words that you may have misspelled. Look especially for words that are similar in your language and English but have different spellings. However, don't spend too much time looking for spelling mistakes—the scorers will not subtract much for misspellings unless they are especially frequent and make it difficult to understand your essay.

2) **Punctuation errors**

The most important thing to check is that each sentence ends with a period or, in the case of questions, with a question mark. Also check for commas after initial adverb clauses, between cities and states or cities and countries, and between dates and years.

I come from the West African country of Togo. My country became an independent republic on April 27, 1960.

When I first came to the United States, I lived in Cambridge, Massachusetts.

3) **Capitalization errors**

Be sure that you have capitalized the first word of every sentence, the names of people and places, and the word *I*.

EXERCISE 42.1

Focus: Correcting grammatical and mechanical errors in essay paragraphs.

Directions: Each of the following paragraphs contain a number of mistakes. Find the mistakes, cross them out, and when necessary, write the correction above the error.

PARAGRAPH 1

There is many species of animals in the world threatened with extinction. One threatened animal is tiger. I believe that is very important that governments protect tiger. In Indonesia tigers protected by the government. Many of them is killed every year.

PARAGRAPH 2

The technology has had major impact in many field. Nowadays we can't even suppose business, communication, or traveling without computers. I want to discuss about the impact of computers on the education. The modern technology has made live easy for students and professors. If a student want to contact with a professor, you haven't problem. It is enough only to send professor's an e-mail and you haven't to go to office. More over, many university created special network for students in order to make the studying process easy for its students. For such kind net you could enter only by using your pass word and identification number. There are many categories you can chose to enter, such as "student tools" or "assignment box" where you can know about your homeworks. Also is possible to access to the university library to make researches. Computers also give students opportunity to gather informations about various topic from the internet. It is one of most easiest ways of making research for student. One other way that computers can help students, especially those from another countries, to stay touch with their freinds and family at their home, personally I could not study in usa if not contact with my family, because I am both student as well as work as a manager in my families business so I must stay in touch with my assistents.

PARAGRAPH 3

One of the most interesting book I am reading recently was a biography of winston churchill. he was prime minister of the great britain during the world war II. of course many peopel know what a great leadership he was during the war. but I found his life before and after the war were also very interesting.

PARAGRAPH 4

Some people are believing that is impossible falling in love with someone "at first sight." In the other hand, there are others people who are believing that you recognition a person that you love immediately. I know its possible falling in love at first sight. Because this happened to my wife and I.

PARAGRAPH 5

If you are ever in thailand in month of may I suggest you to go to the Rocket Festival. It held every year in a small town called yasothon about 300 mile from bangkok. bangkok has many beautiful temples, including the temple of the dawn. This festival is well known and famous in thailand. People from all over the country join the local people in celebrate. The local farmers launch hundred of colorful rockets for gaining the favor of spirits who they believe will bring rain to their rice crops. However, if you go, you need being careful. Both farmers or tourists sometime injure or even kill by rockets that goes out of control.

PARAGRAPH 6

When I was child I live in the town of Sendai, the biggest city in the north part of japan. My grandmother live in Tokyo. Which is in the center part of Japan. While I was live in Sendai, I often went to see my grandmother, but it takes five hours to get to tokyo by local train. Since 1983, the high speed express train called the "Shinkansen" built, and connected between Sendai and Tokyo. For me personally, this was most importent development in transportation. It now take only a hour and half to travel to Tokyo from Sendai. The trip become very easy. It also was a great impact on sendai. Economics development there increased. In the negative side, prices for housing and other things went up. In the whole, however, this development was very big benefit for the city.

PARAGRAPH 7

I'm from Korea. Once, Koreans had large families. They lived three times families altogether (grandparents-parents-children). They were almost farmers, so they preferred large numbers of families. In present, Korea has develop and society change from agriculture to industrial. Many people has moved from rural areas to urban ones. Because their job in the city. For example my husband went to Seoul in 1994 for his college. He leaved his parents and lived alone. After his graduation, he got a job at Seoul. At that time we worked together. After we marraied, we lived at Seoul. Of course his parents want us to live together them as Koreans traditional do, but we have no jobs in parents area. For me personal, I think this changes of society are natural and reasonable.

PARAGRAPH 8

When I first come to the united states I was only 17 years old and have never been away from home. I come here for one year. I lived with a family american in suburban of new orleans louisiana. I went to high school there. Imagine how difficult is it for me on a first day of school. I didn't know where should I go or what should I do. I spoken only little english. However, I was very fortunate. The daughter of my host families neighbors recognizing me, and she did everything for helping me. Not only she helped me talk with the principal of the school and she introduced me my teacher for the first class. She even eat lunch with me. I am still remembering her great kindness!

EXERCISE 42.2

Focus: Checking and editing your own writing.

Directions: Look back at the three introductions, bodies, and conclusions you wrote for Exercises 40.1, 40.2, and 40.3. Look for organizational, grammatical, and mechanical errors and make corrections. Don't spend more than five minutes per essay.

If you intend to word-process the essay, you should practice taking this Review Test on the computer by using any word processing program. You can use the cut, paste, and undo functions, but don't use the spell-check, grammar-check, or thesaurus functions.

REVIEW TEST I: Essay Writing

- ■ Before you begin, think about the prompt. You may want to make some notes to organize your thoughts. Use the space for notes that has been provided.

- ■ Write only on the topic that is presented.

- ■ If you finish in less than 30 minutes, check your essay for errors.

- ■ Stop writing after 30 minutes.

ESSAY PROMPT

Do you agree or disagree with this statement?

The most important knowledge does not come from books.

Use specific reasons and examples to explain your choice.

Notes

Use this space for essay notes only. Write the final version of your essay on the next two pages.

Name: _____

Write your essay here.

_____
_____
_____
_____
_____
_____
_____
_____
_____
_____
_____
_____
_____
_____
_____
_____
_____
_____
_____
_____
_____
_____
_____
_____
_____
_____
_____

MINI-LESSONS FOR SECTION 4:
More Writing Practice

The best way to get ready for the Essay Writing section is to practice, practice, practice. Use as many of the following prompts as you can to plan, write, and check your essays. Give yourself thirty minutes per essay. If you want other prompts for even more practice, look at the current TOEFL® *Bulletin* or go to the TOEFL® web site.

Foods can tell a lot about the country where they are prepared and eaten. What have you learned about a country by eating its foods? Use specific details and examples to explain your response.

Many young people spend a lot of their time playing computer games. Discuss the advantages and disadvantages of this. Use specific reasons and examples in your answer.

Think of the best teacher that you have ever had. What qualities made him or her a good teacher? Use specific details and examples to support your response.

Do you agree or disagree with the following statement?

The most important feature of a university is its library.

Use specific examples and details in your answer.

Imagine that you have received a loan from a bank to open a business. What type of business would you open? Use specific details and reasons in your answer.

Imagine that you have won an airline ticket to anywhere in the world that you want to visit. Where would you go? Give specific reasons for your choice.

Some people prefer to attend university in their hometown. Others would rather attend a university in some other city. If you were faced with this choice, what would you do? Give specific examples and reasons in your answer.

The government has decided to provide more funds to help develop one sector of the economy. Which of the following sectors would you recommend receive these additional funds?

heavy industry (such as steel or chemical factories)
light industry (such as textile factories)
high tech (such as computer companies)
financial (such as banks)
service (such as hotels)

Give specific examples and reasons for your recommendation.

If you needed to communicate with a business associate in another city, what method would you choose? Give specific details and reasons for your choice.

Read and think abut the following statement:

Many people behave differently when they are traveling than when they are at home.

Do you agree or disagree with the statement? Use specific reasons and details to support your choice.

An acquaintance is thinking about studying your language. How would you persuade him or her that this would be a good decision? Use specific reasons and details in your response.

Education is constantly changing. In what ways do you think it will change in the next ten years? Use specific details and examples in your answer.

Which section of a newspaper do you enjoy reading the most? Give specific reasons for your choice.

A roommate is a person with whom you share a dormitory room, an apartment, or a house. If you were looking for a roommate, which of these qualities would you consider the most important?

| sense of humor | reliability | intelligence |
| friendliness | cleanliness | open-mindedness |

Use specific details and reasons in your response.

Some people prefer to work for a company and receive a salary. Other people prefer to own their own business. Which of these do you prefer? Give specific reasons and details in your answer.

Two Complete
Practice Tests

University of San Francisco

About Taking the Practice Tests

One of the best ways to prepare for the TOEFL® test is to take realistic practice tests. The tests included with this program are up-to-date versions of the latest computer-based tests and include all the new item-types found on the computer-based test. As closely as possible, they duplicate the actual test in terms of format, content, and level of difficulty. Of course, it is not possible to completely duplicate the computer-testing environment in a book, but if you can do well on these versions of the test, you should do well on the computer-based test when you actually take it.

There are certain guidelines you should follow for each section when you take these tests in the book:

■ **Listening**

To take the Listening Section, you will have to use the audio tapes or CDs. The items in this part are timed as the items were on the paper-and-pencil version of the TOEFL® test—in other words, they are 12 seconds apart. However, if you are taking this test alone, you can stop the tape or use the fast forward to give yourself more time or less time. If possible, listen to the taped material through headphones.

While the dialogues and talks are being read, you should look only at the photos. While the questions are being read, look only at the questions. Don't look at the four answer choices until you have heard the questions. Don't skip items and don't go back to any items after you have finished.

■ **Structure**

Use a watch to time yourself for this section. Do not skip any items and don't go back to any items after you have answered them.

■ **Reading**

Use a watch to time yourself. When working on this section, you CAN skip items and go back to them after you have marked the answers.

■ **Essay Writing**

Time yourself carefully. If possible, write your essay on a computer.

Scoring the Practice Tests

You can use the charts on the next pages to calculate a range of scores for the tests in this book. After completing each test, obtain a raw score by counting the number of correct answers in the three sections. Then look at the conversion chart to determine the range of scaled scores for each section. Add the three low scores from the range of scores for each section, then the three high scores. Your "actual" score on the TOEFL® test will lie somewhere in that range of numbers. You will then have to estimate your score for the Essay Writing section and add that number to your Structure score before you arrive at a final score. You can use the chart on the next page to estimate your Essay Writing score.

Suppose that, on Practice Test 1, you had 28 correct answers in Listening Comprehension, 21 in Structure and Written Expression, and 40 in Reading Comprehension. And suppose that your estimated score on Essay Writing is 4. Your adjusted structure scores are now 24–25. Your score on the practice test would lie between 230 and 240.

	Raw Score (number correct)	Range of Scaled Scores (from Conversion Chart, page 506)
Section 1	28	21-22
Section 2	21	13-14
Section 3	40	24-26
Estimated score on Section 4	4	Add 11 to both Section 2 scores

SCORE CONVERSION CHART: PRACTICE TEST 1

Section 1		Section 2		Section 3	
Raw Scores	Range of Scaled Scores	Raw Scores	Range of Scaled Scores	Raw Scores	Range of Scaled Scores
36–38	28–30	24–25	14–15	48–50	28–30
33–35	25–26	21–23	13–14	45–47	27–29
30–32	23–24	18–20	12–13	43–44	26–28
27–29	21–22	15–17	11–12	41–42	25–27
24–26	19–20	12–14	10–11	39–40	24–26
21–23	17–18	9–11	8–10	37–38	23–25
18–20	15–16	6–8	7–9	35–36	22–24
15–17	13–14	3–5	6–8	33–34	21–23
12–14	11–12	0–2	4–6	31–32	20–22
9–11	9–10			29–30	19–21
6–8	7–9			27–28	18–20
3–5	5–6			25–26	17–19
0–2	3–4			23–24	16–18
				21–22	15–17
				19–20	14–16
				17–18	13–15
				15–16	12–14
				13–14	11–13
				11–12	9–12
				9–10	8–10
				7–8	7–9
				5–6	6–8
				3–4	5–7
				0–2	4–6

If your estimated score on the Essay Writing Section is __6__, add __15__ points to your Structure Score.

        __5.5__, add __14__

        __5__, add __13__

        __4.5__, add __12__

        __4__, add __11__

        __3.5__, add __10__

        __3__, add __9__

        __2.5__, add __7__

        __2__, add __6__

        __1.5__, add __5__

        __1__, add __3__

PERSONAL SCORE RECORD

Use the blanks below to chart your progress as you take the Practice Tests.

PRACTICE TEST 1

Section 1	Section 2	Section 3	Section 4 (Estimated)	Total Score

PRACTICE TEST 2

Section 1	Section 2	Section 3	Section 4 (Estimated)	Total Score

Section 1: Listening

This section tests your ability to comprehend spoken English. It is divided into two parts, each with its own directions. There are 38 questions. The material that you hear and the questions about the material are presented only once.

PART A: DIRECTIONS

Each item in this part consists of a brief dialogue involving two speakers. Following each conversation, a third voice asks a question. When you have heard each dialogue and question, read the four answer choices and select the <u>one</u> that best answers the question based on what is directly stated or on what can be inferred.

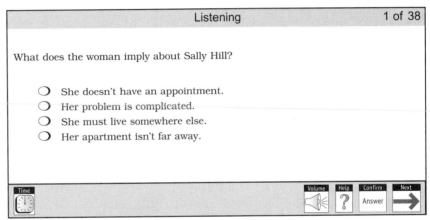

Listening   1 of 38

What does the woman imply about Sally Hill?

○ She doesn't have an appointment.
○ Her problem is complicated.
○ She must live somewhere else.
○ Her apartment isn't far away.

Time | Volume | Help | Confirm Answer | Next →

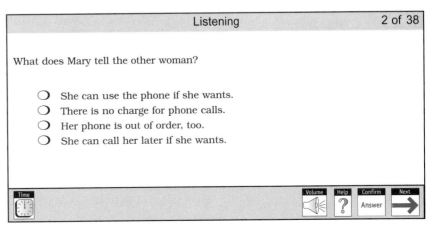

Listening   2 of 38

What does Mary tell the other woman?

○ She can use the phone if she wants.
○ There is no charge for phone calls.
○ Her phone is out of order, too.
○ She can call her later if she wants.

Time | Volume | Help | Confirm Answer | Next →

What did Lillian's parents do?

○ Disapproved of Lillian's plan.
○ Watered Lillian's plants.
○ Traveled overseas.
○ Caught colds.

Time Volume Help Confirm Next
                    ?   Answer

What does the woman say her roommate did last night?

○ She cleaned up after cooking.
○ She forgot to put the pots and pans away.
○ She went out in a terrible storm.
○ She put some plants in the kitchen.

Time Volume Help Confirm Next
                    ?   Answer

How did the woman mainly learn about trees?

○ She studied forestry in college.
○ She once worked in a forest.
○ She read a lot of books about them.
○ Her father taught her.

Time Volume Help Confirm Next
                    ?   Answer

What does Tom ask Brenda?

- ◯ How many pages he must write.
- ◯ What Professor Barclay discussed.
- ◯ How long the class lasted.
- ◯ When the paper is due.

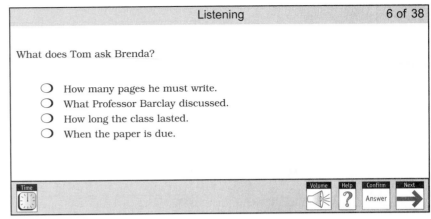

What does the woman imply about Julie?

- ◯ She doesn't like any music except classical.
- ◯ There is some classical music she doesn't like.
- ◯ She likes classical music but she can't play it.
- ◯ Classical music doesn't interest her at all.

What does the man say about the history test?

- ◯ He was too busy to study for it.
- ◯ He did quite well on it.
- ◯ He left some questions unanswered on it.
- ◯ He took it two times.

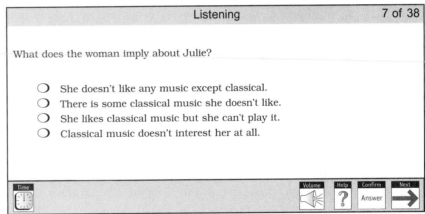

What does the woman say about the desk?

○ It was too expensive.
○ She bought it at the shop next door.
○ It was given to her as a gift.
○ She paid very little for it.

Time | Volume | Help ? | Confirm Answer | Next →

What can be inferred from the conversation?

○ The weather is going to change soon.
○ Emma's last two classes have been canceled.
○ The weather hasn't been pleasant until today.
○ Emma's classes will be held outside today.

Time | Volume | Help ? | Confirm Answer | Next →

What does the woman mean?

○ Gary thanked her for the tape player.
○ She wants her tape player back.
○ She's glad Gary is finally here.
○ Gary can keep her tape player.

Time | Volume | Help ? | Confirm Answer | Next →

What does the woman mean?

- ○ She originally supported Margaret Ling.
- ○ She can no longer support Ed Miller.
- ○ Ed Miller is no longer running in the race.
- ○ Margaret Ling is no longer a student.

Time   Volume   Help   Confirm   Next
Answer

What does the man suggest the woman do?

- ○ Borrow Stephanie's computer.
- ○ Get her own computer.
- ○ Save some money.
- ○ Stay home and complete her assignment.

Time   Volume   Help   Confirm   Next
Answer

What does the man say about Shelly?

- ○ She seems to be feeling better.
- ○ She has quite an imagination.
- ○ She takes beautiful pictures.
- ○ She's too sick to go out.

Time   Volume   Help   Confirm   Next
Answer

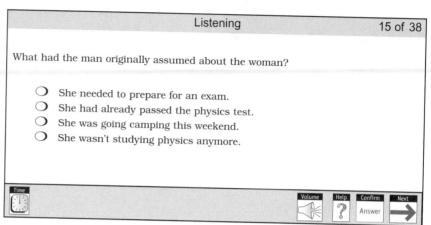

What had the man originally assumed about the woman?

○ She needed to prepare for an exam.
○ She had already passed the physics test.
○ She was going camping this weekend.
○ She wasn't studying physics anymore.

Time   Volume   Help   Confirm   Next
Answer

PART B: DIRECTIONS

Part B involves longer talks. After each of these talks, there are a number of questions. You will hear each talk only once. When you have read and heard the questions, read the answer choices and select the best answer or answers based on what is directly stated or on what can be inferred.

Don't forget: During actual exams, taking notes during the Listening Section is not permitted.

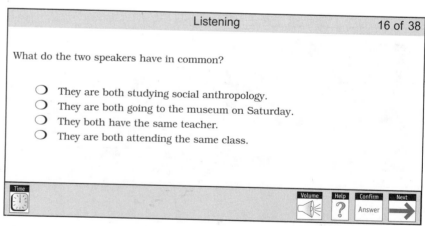

What do the two speakers have in common?

○ They are both studying social anthropology.
○ They are both going to the museum on Saturday.
○ They both have the same teacher.
○ They are both attending the same class.

Time   Volume   Help   Confirm   Next
Answer

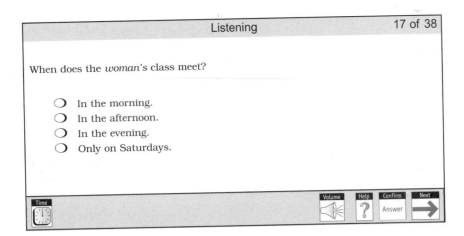

When does the *woman's* class meet?

○ In the morning.
○ In the afternoon.
○ In the evening.
○ Only on Saturdays.

Time | Volume | Help ? | Confirm Answer | Next →

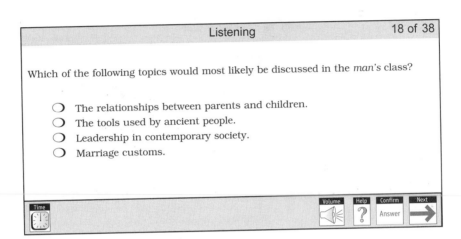

Which of the following topics would most likely be discussed in the *man's* class?

○ The relationships between parents and children.
○ The tools used by ancient people.
○ Leadership in contemporary society.
○ Marriage customs.

Time | Volume | Help ? | Confirm Answer | Next →

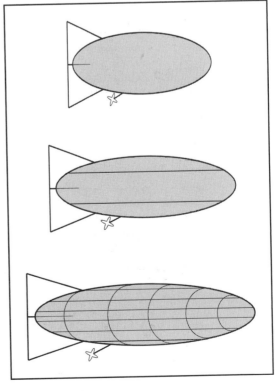

What is the main subject of the lecture?

○ An outcome of a football game.
○ The development of jet engines.
○ The results of the *Hindenburg* disaster.
○ Airships of the past, present, and future.

Time | Volume | Help ? | Confirm Answer | Next →

Match the type of airship with the category in which it belongs

Place the letter of the choice in the proper box. Use each choice only once.

(A) The Italian airship *Norge*.

(B) The blimp *Columbia*.

(C) The German zeppelin *Hindenburg*.

[ ]

[ ]

[ ]

Rigid airship

Semi-rigid airship

Non-rigid airship

Time | Volume | Help ? | Confirm Answer | Next →

What does the speaker say about the Italian airship *Norge*?

○ It flew over the North Pole.
○ It was involved in military operations in World War I.
○ It had a very unusual design.
○ It carried many paying passengers across the Atlantic.

Time | Volume | Help ? | Confirm Answer | Next →

What event in the history of airships took place in Lakehurst, New Jersey in 1937?

○ The age of large airships ended in disaster there.
○ It was there that the first blimp was designed.
○ The first zeppelin to cross the Atlantic landed there.
○ It was there that the last zeppelin was built.

Time | Volume | Help ? | Confirm Answer | Next →

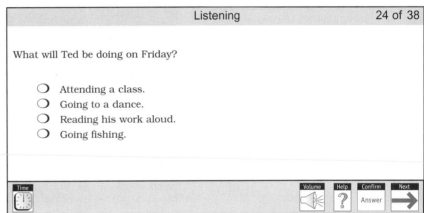

What can be inferred about airships of the future?

Choose two.

☐ They would be safer than the rigid airships of the past.
☐ They would be much larger than the airships of the past.
☐ They would fly faster than modern jet airliners.
☐ They would use less fuel than modern jet airliners.

Time | Volume Help Confirm Next
Answer

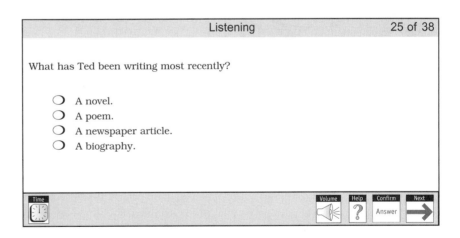

What will Ted be doing on Friday?

○ Attending a class.
○ Going to a dance.
○ Reading his work aloud.
○ Going fishing.

Time | Volume Help Confirm Next
Answer

What has Ted been writing most recently?

○ A novel.
○ A poem.
○ A newspaper article.
○ A biography.

Time | Volume Help Confirm Next
Answer

What is the subject of Ted's most recent writing?

○   Childhood memories.
○   The lives of his college classmates.
○   The experiences of commercial fishers.
○   A trip to Alaska.

Time | Volume | Help | Confirm | Next
| | ? | Answer |

The speaker mentions three types of materials that make up glaciers. Give the order in which these materials appear.

Place the letter of the choice in the proper box. Use each choice only once. One choice will NOT be used.

(A) Firn.   (C) Rock ice.
(B) Glacial ice.   (D) Ordinary snow.

1.
2.
3.

Time | Volume | Help | Confirm | Next
| | ? | Answer |

Where can continental glaciers be found today?

Choose two.

☐ Greenland.
☐ West Virginia.
☐ Iceland.
☐ Antarctica.

Time | Volume | Help | Confirm | Next
| | ? | Answer |

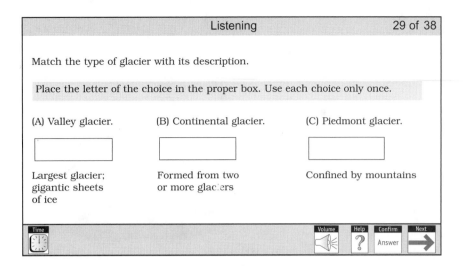

Match the type of glacier with its description.

Place the letter of the choice in the proper box. Use each choice only once.

(A) Valley glacier.　　　　(B) Continental glacier.　　　　(C) Piedmont glacier.

Largest glacier;
gigantic sheets
of ice

Formed from two
or more glaciers

Confined by mountains

Time　　　　　　　　　　　　　　　Volume　Help　Confirm　Next
　　　　　　　　　　　　　　　　　　　　　？　Answer

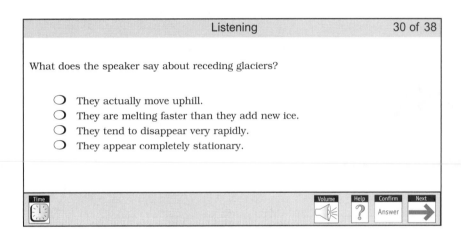

What does the speaker say about receding glaciers?

- ○　They actually move uphill.
- ○　They are melting faster than they add new ice.
- ○　They tend to disappear very rapidly.
- ○　They appear completely stationary.

Time　　　　　　　　　　　　　　　Volume　Help　Confirm　Next
　　　　　　　　　　　　　　　　　　　　　？　Answer

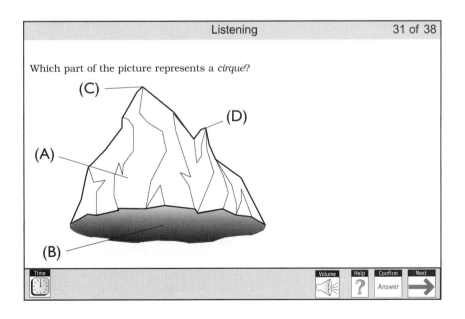

Which part of the picture represents a *cirque*?

(C)

(D)

(A)

(B)

Time　　　　　　　　　　　　　　　Volume　Help　Confirm　Next
　　　　　　　　　　　　　　　　　　　　　？　Answer

Which part of the picture represents a *horn*?

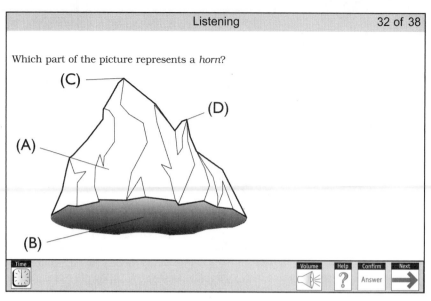

What is the main topic of this discussion?

○ The Uniform Time Act.
○ The role of daylight saving time in wartime.
○ Ways to save energy.
○ The history of daylight saving time.

When are clocks in the United States set *back*?

○ In the spring.
○ In the summer.
○ In the fall.
○ In the winter.

According to the professor, how would most people probably have characterized Benjamin Franklin's plan for daylight saving time when it was first proposed?

○ As confusing.
○ As innovative.
○ As ridiculous.
○ As wasteful.

When was daylight saving time first actually put into effect?

○ In the 1790s.
○ During the Civil War.
○ During World War I.
○ During World War II.

Time · Volume · Help ? · Confirm Answer · Next →

Which of these groups opposed daylight saving time?

Choose two.

☐ Military leaders.
☐ Farmers.
☐ Writers.
☐ Parents of small children.

Time · Volume · Help ? · Confirm Answer · Next →

What was the effect of the Uniform Time Act of 1966?

○ To help standardize daylight saving time.
○ To establish year round daylight savings time.
○ To abolish daylight saving time.
○ To shorten daylight saving time.

Time · Volume · Help ? · Confirm Answer · Next →

This is the end of Section 1. Go on to Section 2.

Section 2: Structure

Time: 20 minutes

This section tests your ability to recognize both correct and incorrect English structures.

Directions: There are two types of items in this section. One type involves a sentence that is missing a word or phrase. Four words or phrases appear below the sentence. You must choose the one that best completes the sentence.

_____ large natural lakes are found in the state of South Carolina.

○ There are no
○ Not the
○ It is not
● No

This sentence should properly read, "No large natural lakes are found in the state of South Carolina." You should select the fourth choice, _No._

The other type of item involves a sentence in which four words or phrases have been underlined. You must identify the one underlined word or phrase that must be changed for the sentence to be considered correct.

<u>When</u> painting a fresco, an artist <u>is applied</u>

paint <u>directly</u> to the damp plaster <u>of a wall.</u>

This sentence should read, "When painting a fresco, an artist applies paint directly to the damp plaster of a wall." You should therefore select the second underlined answer, _is applied._

As soon as you understand the directions, begin work on this section.

There are 25 questions.

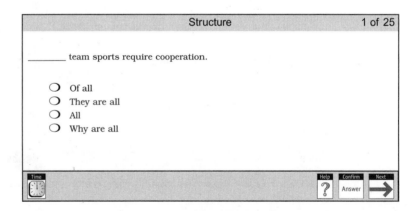

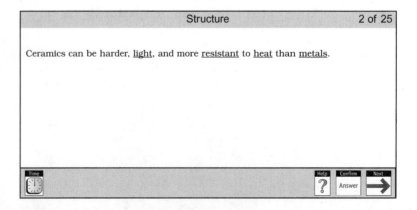

Not everyone realizes that the most largest organ of the human body is the skin.

Clifford Holland, _____ civil engineer, was in charge of the construction of the first tunnel under the Hudson River.

○ He was a
○ a
○ being a
○ who was, as a

Mold is extremely destruction to books in a library.

A tapestry consists of a foundation weave, called the warp, which across are passed different colored threads, called the weft, forming decorative patterns.

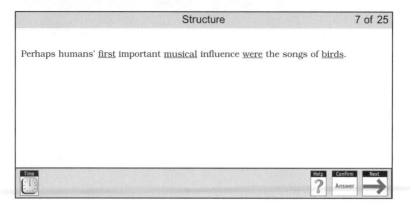

Perhaps humans' <u>first</u> important <u>musical</u> influence <u>were</u> the songs of <u>birds</u>.

Time | Help ? | Confirm Answer | Next →

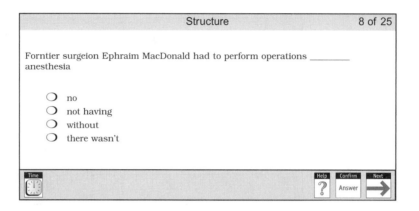

Forntier surgeion Ephraim MacDonald had to perform operations _____ anesthesia

- ○ no
- ○ not having
- ○ without
- ○ there wasn't

Time | Help ? | Confirm Answer | Next →

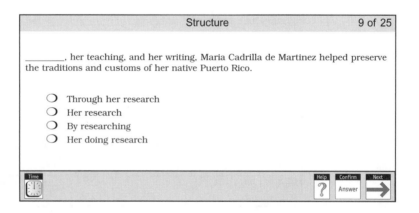

_____, her teaching, and her writing, Maria Cadrilla de Martinez helped preserve the traditions and customs of her native Puerto Rico.

- ○ Through her research
- ○ Her research
- ○ By researching
- ○ Her doing research

Time | Help ? | Confirm Answer | Next →

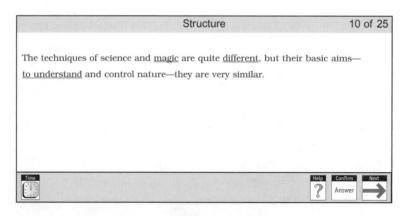

The techniques of science and <u>magic</u> are quite <u>different</u>, but their basic aims—
<u>to understand</u> and control nature—they are very similar.

Time | Help ? | Confirm Answer | Next →

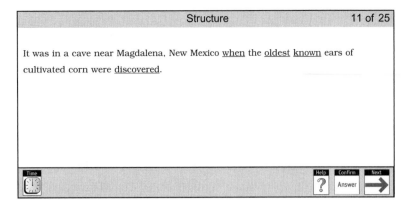

It was in a cave near Magdalena, New Mexico <u>when</u> the <u>oldest</u> <u>known</u> ears of cultivated corn were <u>discovered</u>.

Time | Help ? | Confirm Answer | Next →

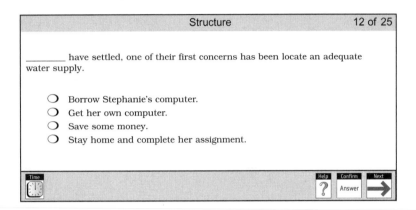

_____ have settled, one of their first concerns has been locate an adequate water supply.

- ○ Borrow Stephanie's computer.
- ○ Get her own computer.
- ○ Save some money.
- ○ Stay home and complete her assignment.

Time | Help ? | Confirm Answer | Next →

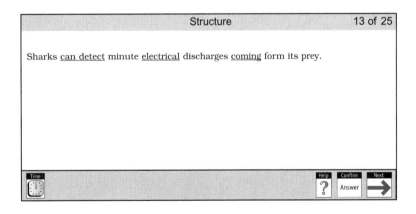

Sharks <u>can detect</u> minute <u>electrical</u> discharges <u>coming</u> form its prey.

Time | Help ? | Confirm Answer | Next →

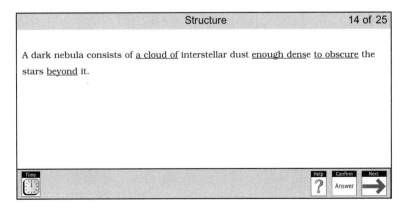

A dark nebula consists of <u>a cloud of</u> interstellar dust <u>enough dense</u> <u>to obscure</u> the stars <u>beyond</u> it.

Time | Help ? | Confirm Answer | Next →

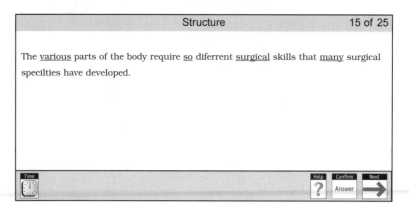

The <u>various</u> parts of the body require <u>so</u> diferrent <u>surgical</u> skills that <u>many</u> surgical specilties have developed.

Time   Help ?   Confirm Answer   Next →

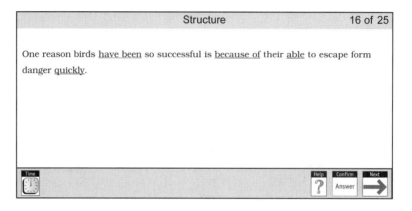

One reason birds <u>have been</u> so successful is <u>because of</u> their <u>able</u> to escape form danger <u>quickly</u>.

Time   Help ?   Confirm Answer   Next →

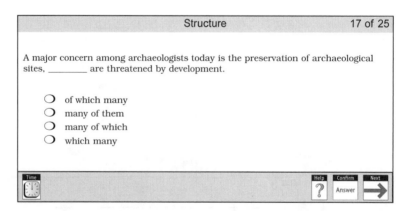

A major concern among archaeologists today is the preservation of archaeological sites, _____ are threatened by development.

- ○ of which many
- ○ many of them
- ○ many of which
- ○ which many

Time   Help ?   Confirm Answer   Next →

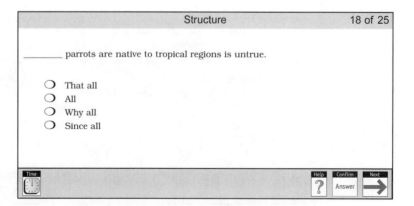

_____ parrots are native to tropical regions is untrue.

- ○ That all
- ○ All
- ○ Why all
- ○ Since all

Time   Help ?   Confirm Answer   Next →

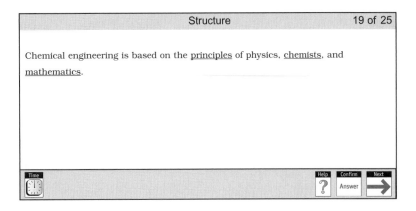

Chemical engineering is based on the <u>principles</u> of physics, <u>chemists</u>, and <u>mathematics</u>.

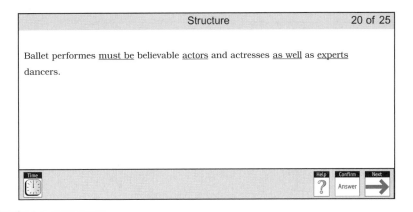

Ballet performes <u>must be</u> believable <u>actors</u> and actresses <u>as well</u> as <u>experts</u> dancers.

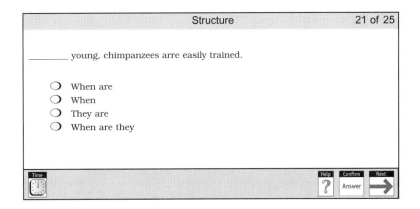

_____ young, chimpanzees arre easily trained.

○ When are
○ When
○ They are
○ When are they

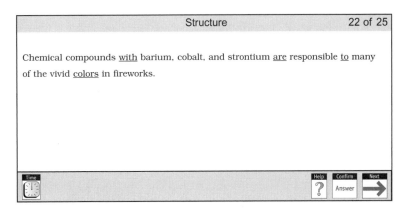

Chemical compounds <u>with</u> barium, cobalt, and strontium <u>are</u> responsible <u>to</u> many of the vivid <u>colors</u> in fireworks.

Rarely _____ seen far from water.

○ spotted turtles
○ spotted turtles are
○ have spotted turtles
○ are spotted turtles

The higher the temperature of a molecule, _____

○ the more energy it has
○ than it has more energy
○ more energy has it
○ it has more energy

The <u>work</u> of the early American woodcarvers had <u>many</u> artistic qualities, but these craftsmen probably <u>did not</u> think of <u>them</u> as artists.

This is the end of Section 2. Go on to Section 3.

Section 3: Reading

Time: 80 minutes

This section of the test measures your ability to understand the meaning of words and to comprehend written materials.

Directions: This section consists of several passages, each followed by 10–14 questions. Read the passages and, for each question, choose the one best answer based on what is stated in or can be inferred from the passage.

As soon as you understand the directions, begin work on this part.

Passage 1

The Sun today is a yellow dwarf star. It has existed in its present state for about 4 billion, 600 million years and is thousands of times larger than the Earth. The Sun is fueled by thermonuclear reactions near its center that convert hydrogen to helium. They release so much energy that the Sun can shine for about 10 billion years with little change in its size or brightness. This balance of forces keeps the gases of the Sun from pulling any closer together.

By studying other stars, astronomers can predict what the rest of the Sun's life will be like. About 5 billion years from now, the core of the Sun will shrink and become hotter. The temperature at the surface will fall. The higher temperature of the interior will increase the rate of thermonuclear reactions. The outer regions of the Sun will expand approximately 35 million miles, about the distance to Mercury, which is the closest planet to the Sun. The Sun will then be a red giant star. Temperatures on the Earth will become too hot for life to exist.

Once the Sun has used up its thermonuclear energy as a red giant, it will begin to shrink. After it shrinks to about the size of the Earth, it will become a white dwarf star. The Sun may throw off huge amounts of gases in violent eruptions called nova explosions as it changes from a red giant to a white dwarf.

After billions of years as a white dwarf, the Sun will have used up all its fuel and will have lost its heat. Such a star is called a black dwarf. After the Sun has become a black dwarf, the Earth will be dark and cold. If any atmosphere remains there, it will have frozen onto the Earth's surface.

1. What is the primary purpose of this passage?
   - ○ To alert people to the dangers posed by the Sun
   - ○ To discuss conditions on Earth in the far future
   - ○ To present a theory about red giant stars
   - ○ To describe changes that the Sun will go through

2. The word fueled in paragraph 1 is closest in meaning to
   - ○ powered
   - ○ bombarded
   - ○ created
   - ○ propelled

3. Look at the word They in the **bold** text below.

It has existed in its present state for about 4 billion, 600 million years and is thousands of times larger than the Earth. The Sun is fueled by thermonuclear reactions near its center that convert hydrogen to helium. They release so much energy that the Sun can shine for about 10 billion years with little change in its size or brightness.

Underline the word or phrase in the **bold** text that the word They refers to.

4. The following sentence can be added to paragraph 1.

It maintains its size because the heat deep inside the Sun produces pressure that offsets the force of gravity.

Where would it best fit in the paragraph?

The Sun today is a yellow dwarf star. ■ It has existed in its present state for about 4 billion, 600 million years and is thousands of times larger than the Earth. ■ The Sun is fueled by thermonuclear reactions near its center that convert hydrogen to helium. ■ They release so much energy that the Sun can shine for about 10 billion years with little change in its size or brightness. ■ This balance of forces keeps the gases of the Sun from pulling any closer together.

Circle the black square (■) that indicates the best position for the sentence.

5. It can be inferred from the passage that the Sun

   ○ is approximately halfway through its life as a yellow dwarf

   ○ has been in existence for 10 billion years

   ○ is rapidly changing in size and brightness

   ○ will continue as a yellow dwarf for another 10 billion years

6. Look at the word core in the **bold** text below.

About 5 billion years from now, the core of the Sun will shrink and become hotter. The temperature at the surface will fall. The higher temperature of the interior will increase the rate of thermonuclear reactions.

Underline the word or phrase in the **bold** text that is most nearly OPPOSITE in meaning to the word core.

7. What will probably be the first stage of change as the Sun becomes a red giant?

   ○ The core will cool off and use less fuel.

   ○ The surface will become hotter and shrink.

   ○ The Sun will throw off huge amounts of gases.

   ○ The core will grow smaller and hotter.

8. When the Sun becomes a red giant, what will conditions be like on Earth?

   ○ Its atmosphere will freeze and become solid.

   ○ It will be enveloped in the expanding surface of the Sun.

   ○ It will become too hot for life to exist.

   ○ It will be destroyed in nova explosions.

9. As a white dwarf, the Sun will be

   ○ the same size as the planet Mercury

   ○ thousands of times smaller than it is today

   ○ around 35 million miles in diameter

   ○ cold and dark

10. According to the passage, which of the following best describes the sequence of stages that the Sun will probably pass through?

   ○ Yellow dwarf, white dwarf, red giant, black giant

   ○ Red giant, white dwarf, black dwarf, nova explosion

   ○ Yellow dwarf, red giant, white dwarf, black dwarf

   ○ White giant, red giant, black dwarf, yellow dwarf

11. The phrase throw off in paragraph 3 is closest in meaning to

   ○ eject

   ○ burn up

   ○ convert

   ○ let in

12. Look at the word there in the **bold** text below.

   After billions of years as a white dwarf, the Sun will have used up all its fuel and will have lost its heat. Such a star is called a black dwarf. After the Sun has become a black dwarf, the Earth will be dark and cold. If any atmosphere remains there, it will have frozen onto the Earth's surface.

   Underline the word or phrase in the **bold** text that the word there refers to.

13. Which of the following best describes the tone of the passage?

   ○ Alarmed

   ○ Pessimistic

   ○ Comic

   ○ Objective

Passage 2

It is said that George Washington was one of the first to realize how important the building of canals would be to the nation's development. In fact, before he became President, he headed the first company in the United States to build a canal which was to connect the Ohio and Potomac rivers. It was never completed, but it showed the nation the feasibility of canals. As the country expanded westward, settlers in western New York, Pennsylvania, and Ohio needed a means to ship goods. Canals linking natural waterways seemed to supply an effective method.

In 1791 engineers commissioned by the state of New York investigated the possibility of a canal between Albany on the Hudson River and Buffalo on Lake Erie to link the Great Lakes area with the Atlantic seacoast. It would avoid the mountains that served as a barrier to canals from the Delaware and Potomac rivers.

The first attempt to dig the canal, to be called the Erie Canal, was made by private companies but only a comparatively small portion was built before the project was halted for lack of funds. The cost of the project was an estimated five million dollars, an enormous amount for those days. There was some on-again-off-again federal funding, but this time the War of 1812 put an end to construction. In 1817 DeWitt Clinton was elected Governor of New York and persuaded the state to finance and build the canal. It was completed in 1825, costing two million dollars more than expected.

The canal rapidly lived up to its sponsors' faith, quickly paying for itself through tolls . It was far more economical than any other form of transportation at the time. It permitted trade between the Great Lake region and the East coast, robbing the Mississippi River of much of its traffic. It allowed New York to supplant Boston, Philadelphia, and other eastern cities as the chief center of both domestic and foreign commerce. Cities sprang up along the canal. It also contributed in a number of ways to the North's victory over the South in the Civil War.

An expansion of the canal was planned in 1849. Increased traffic would undoubtedly have warranted its construction had it not been for the development of the railroads.

14. Why does the author most likely mention George Washington in the first paragraph?
     ○ He was President at the time the Erie Canal was built.
     ○ He was involved in pioneering efforts to build canals.
     ○ He successfully opened the first canal in the United States.
     ○ He commissioned engineers to study the possibility of building the Erie Canal.

15. The word feasibility in paragraph 1 is closest in meaning to

     ○ profitability
     ○ difficulty
     ○ possibility
     ○ capability

16. Look at the word means in the **bold** text below:

It was never completed, but it showed the nation the feasibility of canals. As the country expanded westward, settlers in western New York, Pennsylvania,

and Ohio needed a means **to ship goods. Canals linking natural waterways seemed to supply an effective method.**

Underline the word or phrase in the **bold** text that is closest in meaning to the word means.

17. According to the passage, the Erie Canal connected the

    ○ Potomac and Ohio rivers

    ○ Hudson River and Lake Erie

    ○ Delaware and Potomac rivers

    ○ Atlantic Ocean and the Hudson River

18. Look at the word halted in the **bold** text below:

    The first attempt to dig the canal, to be called the Erie Canal, was made by private companies but only a comparatively small portion was built before the project was halted **for lack of funds. The cost of the project was an estimated five million dollars, an enormous amount for those days. There was some on-again-off-again federal funding, but this time the War of 1812 put an end to construction.**

    Underline the word or phrase in the **bold** text that is closest in meaning to the word halted .

19. The phrase on-again-off-again in paragraph 3 could be replaced by which of the following with the least change in meaning?

    ○ Intermittent

    ○ Unsolicited

    ○ Ineffectual

    ○ Gradual

20. The completion of the Erie Canal was financed by

    ○ the state of New York

    ○ private companies

    ○ the federal government

    ○ DeWitt Clinton

21. The actual cost of building the Erie Canal was

    ○ five million dollars

    ○ less than had been estimated

    ○ seven million dollars

    ○ more than could be repaid

22. The word tolls in paragraph 4 is closest in meaning to which of the following?

    ○ Jobs

    ○ Grants

    ○ Links

    ○ Fees

23. Which of the following is NOT given as an effect of the building of the Erie Canal in paragraph 4?

○ It allowed the East coast to trade with the Great Lakes area.

○ It took water traffic away from the Mississippi River.

○ It helped determine the outcome of the Civil War.

○ It established Boston and Philadelphia as the most important centers of trade.

24. What can be inferred about railroads in 1849 from the information in the last paragraph?

○ They were being planned but had not yet been built.

○ They were seriously underdeveloped.

○ They had begun to compete with the Erie Canal for traffic.

○ They were weakened by the expansion of the canal.

25. The word warranted in paragraph 5 is closest in meaning to

○ guaranteed

○ justified

○ hastened

○ prevented

Passage 3

It's a sound you will probably never hear, a sickened tree sending out a distress signal. However, a team of scientists at the U.S. Department of Agriculture's Forest Service has recently heard the cries, and they think some insects also hear the trees and are drawn to them like vultures attracted to a dying animal.

Researchers hypothesized that these sounds—actually vibrations produced by the surface of plants—were caused by a severe lack of moisture. They fastened electronic sensors to the bark of drought-stricken trees and clearly heard distress calls. According to one of the scientists, most parched trees transmit their plight in the 50- to 500-kilohertz range. (The unaided human ear can detect no more than 20 kilohertz.) They experimented on red oak, maple, white pine, aspen, and birch and found that all make slightly different sounds. With practice, scientists could identify the species of tree by its characteristic sound signature.

The scientists surmise that the vibrations are created when the water columns inside tubes that run the length of the trees are cracked as a result of too little water flowing through them. These fractured columns send out distinctive vibration patterns. Because some insects communicate at ultrasonic frequencies, they may pick up the trees' vibrations and attack the weakened trees. Researchers are now running tests with potted trees that have been deprived of water to see if the sound is what attracts the insects. "Water-stressed trees also have a different smell from other trees, and they experience thermal changes, so insects could be responding to something other than sound," one scientist said.

26. Which of the following is the main topic of the passage?
    ○ The vibrations produced by insects
    ○ The mission of the U.S. Forest Service
    ○ The effect of insects on trees
    ○ The sounds made by trees

27. The word them in paragraph 1 refers to
    ○ trees
    ○ scientists
    ○ insects
    ○ vultures

28. Look at the word drawn in the **bold** text below:

    It's a sound you will probably never hear, a sickened tree sending out a distress signal. However, a team of scientists with the U.S. Department of Agriculture's Forest Service has recently heard the cries, and they think some insects also hear the trees and are drawn to them like vultures attracted to a dying animal.

    Underline the word or phrase in the **bold** text that is closest in meaning to the word drawn.

29. Look at the word parched in the **bold** text below:

    Researchers hypothesized that these sounds—actually vibrations produced by the surface of plants—were caused by a severe lack of moisture. They fastened electronic sensors to the bark of drought-stricken trees and clearly heard distress calls. According to one of the scientists, most parched trees transmit their plight in the 50- to 500-kilohertz range. (The unaided human ear can detect no more than 20 kilohertz.)

    Underline the word or phrase in the **bold** text that is closest in meaning to the word parched .

30. The word plight in paragraph 2 is closest in meaning to
    ○ cry
    ○ condition
    ○ need
    ○ presence

31. Underline the sentence in the second paragraph that explains how the researchers conducted their experiment.

32. It can be inferred from the passage that the sounds produced by the trees
    ○ serve as a form of communication among trees
    ○ are the same no matter what type of tree produces them
    ○ cannot be heard by the unaided human ear
    ○ fall into the 1–20 kilohertz range

33. Look at the word fractured in the **bold** text below:

The scientists surmise that the vibrations are created when the water columns inside tubes that run the length of the trees are cracked as a result of too little water flowing through them. These fractured columns send out distinctive vibration patterns.

Underline the word or phrase in the **bold** text that is closest in meaning to the word fractured .

34. Which of the following is believed to be a cause of the trees' distress signals?

○ Torn roots

○ Attacks by insects

○ Experiments by scientists

○ Lack of water

35. Look at the word they in the **bold** text below:

These fractured columns send out distinctive vibration patterns. Because some insects communicate at ultrasonic frequencies, they may pick up the trees' vibrations and attack the weakened trees.

Underline the word or phrase in the **bold** text that the word they refers to.

36. In paragraph 3, the phrase pick up could best be replaced by which of the following?

○ Perceive

○ Lift

○ Transmit

○ Attack

37. All of the following are mentioned as possible factors in drawing insects to weakened trees EXCEPT

○ thermal changes

○ smells

○ sounds

○ changes in color

38. It can be inferred from the passage that, at the time the passage was written, research concerning the distress signals of trees

○ had been conducted many years previously

○ had been unproductive up until then

○ was continuing

○ was no longer sponsored by the government

Passage 4

Probably the most famous film commenting on twentieth century technology is *Modern Times*, made in 1936. Charlie Chaplin was motivated to make the film by a reporter who, while interviewing him, happened to describe working conditions in industrial Detroit. Chaplin was told that healthy young farm boys were lured to the city to work on automotive assembly lines. Within four or five years, these young men's health was destroyed by the stress of work in the factories.

The film opens with a shot of a mass of sheep jammed into pens. Abruptly the scene shifts to a scene of factory workers packed into a narrow entranceway, jostling one another on their way to a factory. This biting tone of criticism, however, is not sustained throughout the film. It is replaced by a gentle note of satire. Chaplin preferred to entertain rather than lecture to the audience.

Scenes of factory interiors account for only about one-third of the footage of *Modern Times,* but they contain some of the most pointed social commentary as well as the funniest comic situations. No one who has seen the film can ever forget Chaplin vainly trying to keep pace with the fast-moving conveyor belt, almost losing his mind in the process. Another popular scene features an automatic feeding machine brought to the assembly line so that workers need not interrupt their labor to eat. It hurls food at Chaplin, who is strapped into his position on the assembly line and cannot escape. This serves to illustrate people's utter helplessness in the face of machines that are meant to serve their basic needs.

Clearly, *Modern Times* has its faults, but despite its flaws, it remains the best film treating technology within a social context. It does not offer a radical social message, but it does accurately reflect the sentiments of many who feel they are victims of an over-mechanized world.

39. The author's main purpose in writing this passage is to

  ○ criticize the factory system of the 1930s

  ○ analyze an important film

  ○ explain Chaplin's style of acting

  ○ discuss how film reveals the benefits of technology

40. According to the passage, Chaplin got the idea for the film *Modern Times* from

  ○ a newspaper article

  ○ a scene in a movie

  ○ a job he had once held

  ○ a conversation with a reporter

41. Look at the word jammed in the **bold** text below:

Within four or five years, these young men's health was destroyed by the stress of work in the factories.

The film opens with a shot of a mass of sheep jammed into pens. Abruptly the scene shifts to a scene of factory workers packed into a narrow entranceway, jostling one another on their way to a factory.

Underline the word or phrase in the **bold** text that is closest in meaning to the word jammed .

42. It can be inferred from the passage that two-thirds of the film *Modern Times*

○ is extremely unforgettable

○ takes place outside a factory

○ is more critical than the other third

○ entertains the audience more than the other third

43. Look at the word biting in the **bold** text below:

This biting tone of criticism, however, is not sustained throughout the film. It is replaced by a gentle note of satire. Chaplin preferred to entertain rather than lecture to the audience.

Underline the word or phrase in the **bold** text that is most nearly OPPOSITE in meaning to the word biting .

44. Which of the following could best replace the phrase losing his mind in paragraph 3?

○ Getting fired

○ Doing his job

○ Going insane

○ Falling behind

45. The following sentence can be added to paragraph 3.

All at once, this feeding device begins to malfunction.

Where would it best fit in the paragraph below?

Scenes of factory interiors account for only about one-third of the footage of *Modern Times*, but they contain some of the most pointed social commentary as well as the funniest comic situations. ■ No one who has seen the film can ever forget Chaplin vainly trying to keep pace with the fast-moving conveyor belt, almost losing his mind in the process. ■ Another popular scene features an automatic feeding machine brought to the assembly line so that workers need not interrupt their labor to eat. ■ It hurls food at Chaplin, who is strapped into his position on the assembly line and cannot escape. ■ This serves to illustrate people's utter helplessness in the face of machines that are meant to serve their basic needs. ■

Circle the black square (■) that indicates the best position for the sentence.

46. Look at the word their in the **bold** text below:

It hurls food at Chaplin, who is strapped into his position on the assembly line and cannot escape. This serves to illustrate people's utter helplessness in the face of machines that are meant to serve their basic needs.

Underline the word or phrase in the **bold** text that the word their refers to.

47. According to the passage, the purpose of the scene involving the feeding machine is to show people's

- ○ ingenuity
- ○ adaptability
- ○ helplessness
- ○ independence

48. The word utter in paragraph 3 is closest in meaning to which of the following?

- ○ Notable
- ○ Complete
- ○ Regrettable
- ○ Necessary

49. Look at the word faults in the **bold** text below:

Clearly, *Modern Times* has its faults, but despite its flaws, it remains the best film treating technology within a social context. It does not offer a radical social message, but it does accurately reflect the sentiments of many who feel they are victims of an over-mechanized world.

Underline the word or phrase in the **bold** text that is closest in meaning to the word faults .

50. The author would probably use all of the following words to describe the film *Modern Times* EXCEPT

- ○ revolutionary
- ○ entertaining
- ○ memorable
- ○ satirical

**This is the end of Section 3.
You may go back and check your answers in
Section 3 until time is up for this section.
Then go on to Section 4.**

Section 4: Essay Writing

- Before you begin, think about the prompt. You may want to make some notes to organize your thoughts. Use the space for notes that has been provided.
- Write only on the topic that is presented.
- If you finish in less than 30 minutes, check your essay for errors.
- Stop writing after 30 minutes.

ESSAY PROMPT

There are many different types of movies, including action movies, science fiction movies, and comedies. Which type of movie do you enjoy most? Why is this type your favorite? Use specific details and examples in your response.

Notes

Use this space for essay notes only. Write the final version of your essay on the next two pages.

Name: _____

Write your essay here.

_____

_____

_____

_____

_____

_____

_____

_____

_____

_____

_____

_____

_____

_____

_____

_____

_____

_____

_____

_____

_____

_____

_____

_____

_____

_____

_____

Name: _____

Section 1: Listening

This section tests your ability to comprehend spoken English. It is divided into two parts, each with its own directions. There are 36 questions. The material that you hear and the questions about the material are presented only once.

PART A: Directions

Each item in this part consists of a brief dialogue involving two speakers. Following each conversation, a third voice asks a question about the dialogue. When you have heard each dialogue and question, read the four answer choices and select the one that best answers the question based on what is directly stated or on what can be inferred.

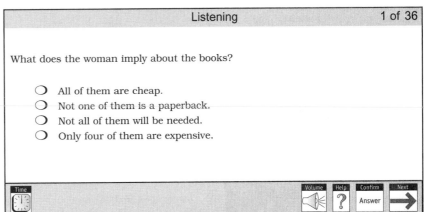

Listening   1 of 36

What does the woman imply about the books?

○   All of them are cheap.
○   Not one of them is a paperback.
○   Not all of them will be needed.
○   Only four of them are expensive.

Time   Volume   Help   Confirm   Next
               ?   Answer

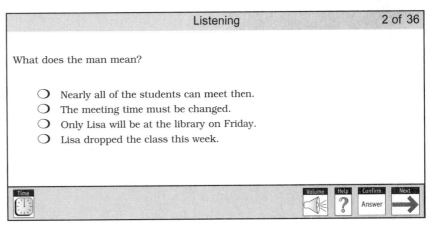

Listening   2 of 36

What does the man mean?

○   Nearly all of the students can meet then.
○   The meeting time must be changed.
○   Only Lisa will be at the library on Friday.
○   Lisa dropped the class this week.

Time   Volume   Help   Confirm   Next
               ?   Answer

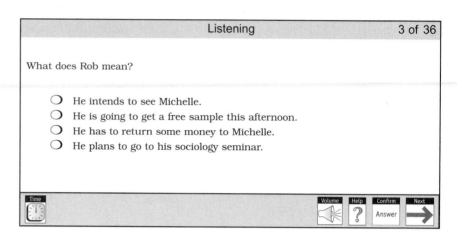

What does Rob mean?

○ He intends to see Michelle.
○ He is going to get a free sample this afternoon.
○ He has to return some money to Michelle.
○ He plans to go to his sociology seminar.

Time   Volume   Help   Confirm Answer   Next →

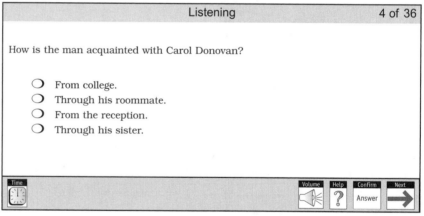

How is the man acquainted with Carol Donovan?

○ From college.
○ Through his roommate.
○ From the reception.
○ Through his sister.

Time   Volume   Help   Confirm Answer   Next →

What does the woman mean?

○ Housing near campus is getting cheaper and cheaper.
○ She doesn't need to live close to campus.
○ It's not easy to find inexpensive housing near campus.
○ The man could find housing if he looked carefully.

Time   Volume   Help   Confirm Answer   Next →

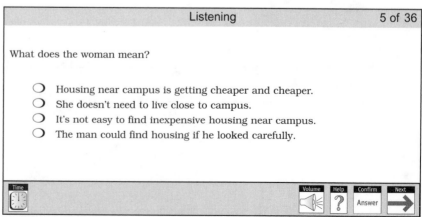

What does Rick mean?

○ He's studying only history this term.
○ This is his final term.
○ He's not taking as many classes this term.
○ This term, he's added one more class.

Time   Volume Help Confirm Next
                 ?   Answer

What was the woman's opinion of David's comments?

○ They were kind.
○ They were confusing.
○ They were impolite.
○ She doesn't want to say.

Time   Volume Help Confirm Next
                 ?   Answer

What does the woman tell the man?

○ He doesn't have to complete the form.
○ He shouldn't waste time.
○ He should take a form.
○ He doesn't have to hurry.

Time   Volume Help Confirm Next
                 ?   Answer

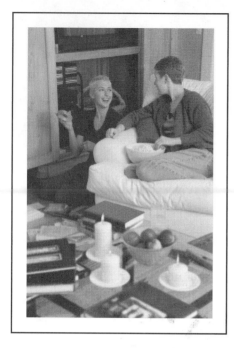

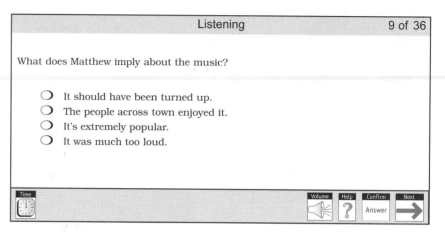

What does Matthew imply about the music?

○ It should have been turned up.
○ The people across town enjoyed it.
○ It's extremely popular.
○ It was much too loud.

Time   Volume   Help   Confirm   Next
                  ?   Answer

What does the man imply about the weekend?

○ It was quite relaxing.
○ The weather wasn't very good.
○ It was unexpectedly busy.
○ It was perfectly planned.

Time   Volume   Help   Confirm   Next
                  ?   Answer

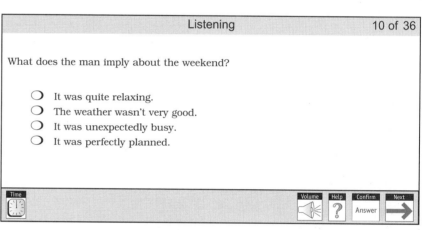

What can be inferred from this conversation?

○ The lab is generally locked on Saturdays.
○ The man doesn't have a key to the lab.
○ Something strange happened in the lab on Saturday.
○ The lab should never be locked.

Time   Volume   Help   Confirm   Next
                  ?   Answer

What does the man say about Morgan?

○ She's an art student.
○ She's afraid of flying.
○ She did well on the test.
○ She just got her pilot's license.

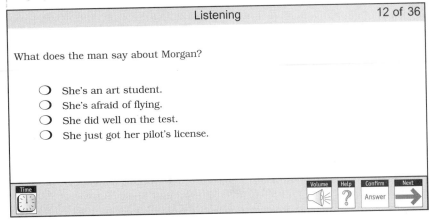

What can be inferred about these two speakers?

○ They must go to an orientation session.
○ They are not new students.
○ They won't be allowed to register.
○ They were given the wrong schedule.

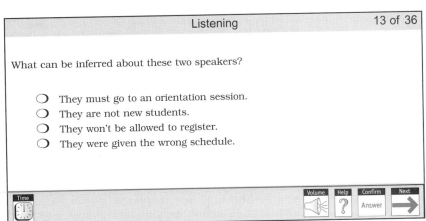

What had Larry *originally* assumed?

○ He hadn't been smiling.
○ His picture hadn't been taken.
○ It wasn't a good picture.
○ The woman wouldn't show him the picture.

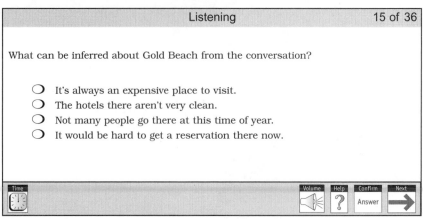

What can be inferred about Gold Beach from the conversation?

- ○ It's always an expensive place to visit.
- ○ The hotels there aren't very clean.
- ○ Not many people go there at this time of year.
- ○ It would be hard to get a reservation there now.

Time	Volume	Help	Confirm	Next
		?	Answer	→

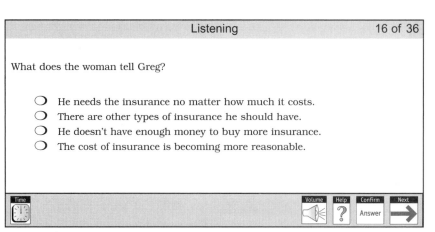

What does the woman tell Greg?

- ○ He needs the insurance no matter how much it costs.
- ○ There are other types of insurance he should have.
- ○ He doesn't have enough money to buy more insurance.
- ○ The cost of insurance is becoming more reasonable.

Time	Volume	Help	Confirm	Next
		?	Answer	→

PART B: Directions

Part B involves longer talks. After each of these talks, there are a number of questions.

You will hear each talk only once.

When you have read and heard the questions, read the answer choices and select the best answer or answers based on what is directly stated or on what can be inferred.

Don't forget: During actual exams, taking notes during the Listening Section is not permitted.

Which of the following is Cecilia trying to find?

○ A two-bedroom apartment.
○ A sofa.
○ A chair.
○ A roommate.

Time Volume Help Confirm Next
Answer

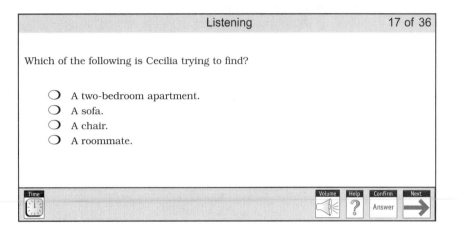

Which of the following does Cecilia *initially* forget to tell the man?

○ Her phone number.
○ The location of the apartment.
○ The best time to call her.
○ Her first name.

Time Volume Help Confirm Next
Answer

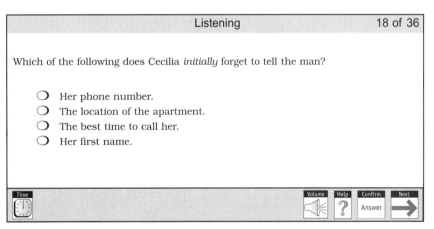

What is the total amount that the two advertisements will cost for one week?

○ $5.
○ $15.
○ $30.
○ $250.

Time Volume Help Confirm Next
Answer

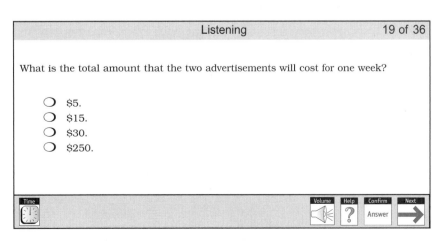

AUDREY FLACK   DUANE HANSON

Which of the following did Audrey Flack use to paint *Farb Family Portrait?*

Choose two.

☐   A video camera.

☐   A slide projector.

☐   Acrylic paints.

☐   Watercolors.

Time | Volume | Help | Confirm | Next
| | ? | Answer | →

Which of the following illustrations would most likely be classified as a work of photo realism?

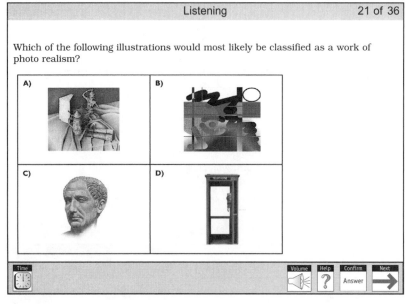

A)   B)   C)   D)

Time | Volume | Help | Confirm | Next
| | ? | Answer | →

According to the speaker, why are the works of sculptor Duane Hanson so remarkable?

○   They are very valuable.
○   They are quite large.
○   They are highly abstract.
○   They are extremely lifelike.

Time | Volume | Help | Confirm | Next
| | ? | Answer | →

What does the teacher ask the class to do over the weekend?

○ Write down their reactions to the slides.
○ Take some photographs.
○ Attend an exhibit at an art museum.
○ Study for a test.

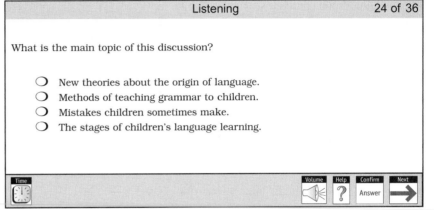

What is the main topic of this discussion?

○ New theories about the origin of language.
○ Methods of teaching grammar to children.
○ Mistakes children sometimes make.
○ The stages of children's language learning.

The professor discusses sounds, words, and phrases that children use at certain ages. Match the sound or phrase with the age at which a typical child would first begin to use it.

Place the letter of the choice in the proper box. Use each choice only once.

(A) "Na-na."   (B) "Koo, koo."   (C) "More milk."

[   ]   [   ]   [   ]

2–4 months   4–6 months   1 year–18 months

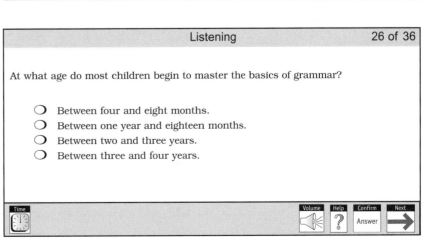

At what age do most children begin to master the basics of grammar?

○ Between four and eight months.
○ Between one year and eighteen months.
○ Between two and three years.
○ Between three and four years.

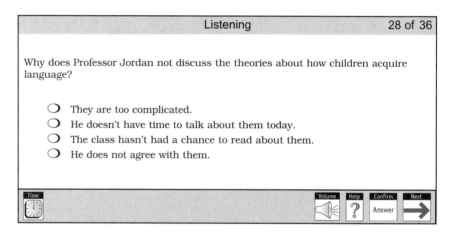

What does Professor Jordan say about the grammatical mistakes that two- and three-year-olds make?

- ⚪ They are the same in all languages.
- ⚪ They are often misinterpreted.
- ⚪ They are learned by imitation.
- ⚪ They are quite logical.

Time Volume Help ? Confirm Answer Next →

Why does Professor Jordan not discuss the theories about how children acquire language?

- ⚪ They are too complicated.
- ⚪ He doesn't have time to talk about them today.
- ⚪ The class hasn't had a chance to read about them.
- ⚪ He does not agree with them.

Time Volume Help ? Confirm Answer Next →

Who won the Outstanding Faculty Award *last* year?

- ⚪ Professor Kim.
- ⚪ Professor Callahan.
- ⚪ Chancellor Davis.
- ⚪ Professor Woods.

Time Volume Help ? Confirm Answer Next →

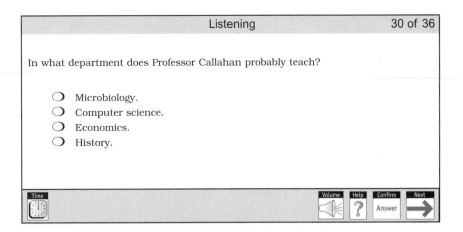

In what department does Professor Callahan probably teach?

○   Microbiology.
○   Computer science.
○   Economics.
○   History.

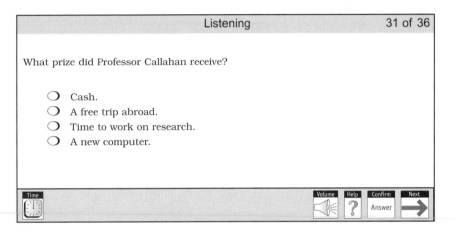

What prize did Professor Callahan receive?

○   Cash.
○   A free trip abroad.
○   Time to work on research.
○   A new computer.

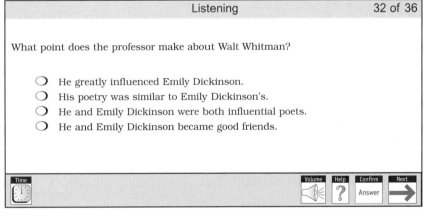

What point does the professor make about Walt Whitman?

○   He greatly influenced Emily Dickinson.
○   His poetry was similar to Emily Dickinson's.
○   He and Emily Dickinson were both influential poets.
○   He and Emily Dickinson became good friends.

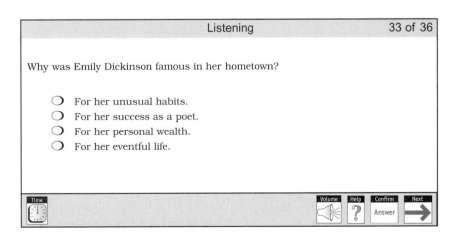

Why was Emily Dickinson famous in her hometown?

○   For her unusual habits.
○   For her success as a poet.
○   For her personal wealth.
○   For her eventful life.

What does the professor say that he particularly admires about the poems of
Emily Dickinson?

- ○ Their titles.
- ○ Their economy.
- ○ Their range of subject matter.
- ○ Their great length.

The professor mentions several events in the history of the publication of Emily
Dickinson's poetry. Put these events in the proper order.

Place the letter of the choice in the proper box. Use each choice only once.

(A)   Harvard University buys manuscripts.

(B)   Family discovers poems.

(C)   Collection of 30 poems is published.

(D)   Several poems appear in newspapers and magazines.

1.
2.   .
3.
4.

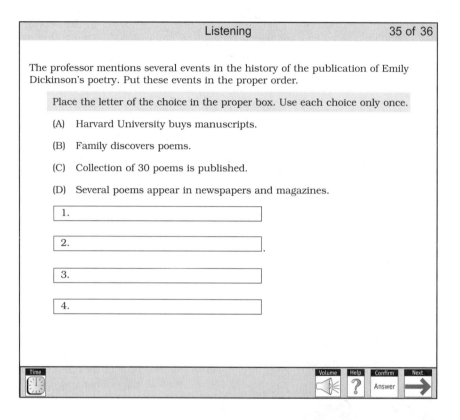

About how many of Emily Dickinson's poems were probably included in the
collection published by Harvard University?

- ○ 10.
- ○ 30.
- ○ 200.
- ○ 1,700.

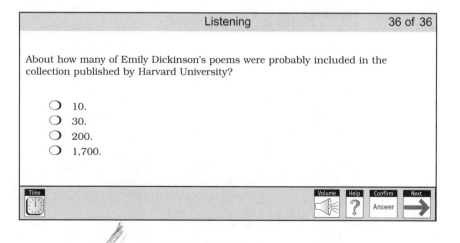

This is the end of Section 1. Go on to Section 2.

Section 2: Structure

Time: 20 minutes

This section tests your ability to recognize both correct and incorrect English structures.

Directions: There are two types of items in this section. One type involves a sentence that is missing a word or phrase. Four words or phrases appear below the sentence. You must choose the one that best completes the sentence.

_____ large natural lakes are found in the state of South Carolina.

- ◯ There are no
- ◯ Not the
- ◯ It is not
- ● No

This sentence should properly read, "No large natural lakes are found in the state of South Carolina." You should select the fourth choice, *No*.

The other type of item involves a sentence in which four words or phrases have been underlined. You must identify the one underlined word or phrase that must be changed for the sentence to be considered correct.

<u>When</u> painting a fresco, an artist <u>is applied</u> paint <u>directly</u> to the damp plaster <u>of a wall</u>.

This sentence should read, "When painting a fresco, an artist applies paint directly to the damp plaster of a wall." You should therefore select the second underlined answer, *is applied*.

As soon as you understand the directions, begin work on this section.

There are 25 questions.

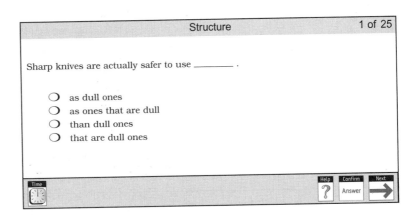

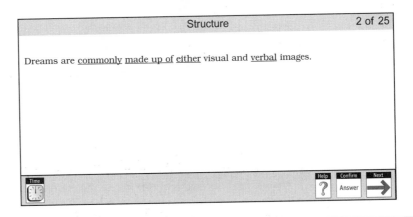

The Yale *Daily News* is <u>oldest than</u> any <u>other</u> college newspaper <u>still</u> <u>in operation</u> in the United States.

Daniel Webster, Thaddeus Stevens, and many others _____ prominent in public life began their careers by teaching school.

- ○ they became
- ○ once they became
- ○ became
- ○ who became

Mary Rinehart was <u>a pioneer</u> in the <u>field</u> of <u>journalist</u> <u>in the early</u> twentieth century.

A mastery of calculus depends on _____ of algebra.

- ○ an understanding
- ○ is understood
- ○ to understand
- ○ understand

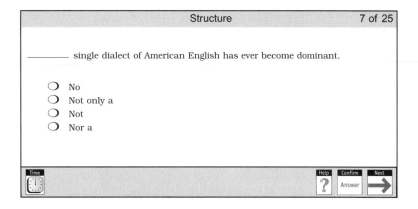

_____ single dialect of American English has ever become dominant.

○ No
○ Not only a
○ Not
○ Nor a

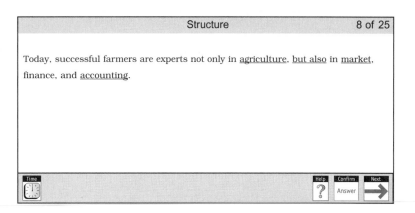

Today, successful farmers are experts not only in <u>agriculture</u>, <u>but also</u> in <u>market</u>, finance, and <u>accounting</u>.

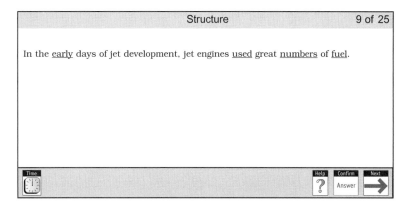

In the <u>early</u> days of jet development, jet engines <u>used</u> great <u>numbers</u> of <u>fuel</u>.

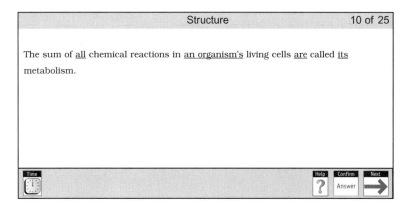

The sum of <u>all</u> chemical reactions in <u>an organism's</u> living cells <u>are</u> called <u>its</u> metabolism.

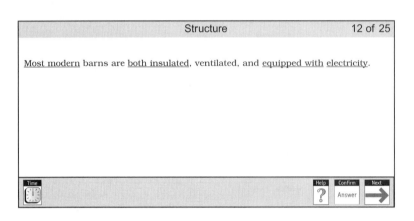

_____ not a musician himself, Laurens Hammond developed an electronic keyboard instrument called the Hammond organ.

○ Although
○ That
○ Despite
○ For

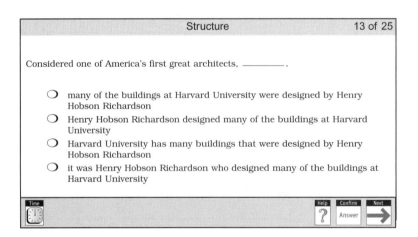

Most modern barns are both insulated, ventilated, and equipped with electricity.

Considered one of America's first great architects, _____ .

○ many of the buildings at Harvard University were designed by Henry Hobson Richardson
○ Henry Hobson Richardson designed many of the buildings at Harvard University
○ Harvard University has many buildings that were designed by Henry Hobson Richardson
○ it was Henry Hobson Richardson who designed many of the buildings at Harvard University

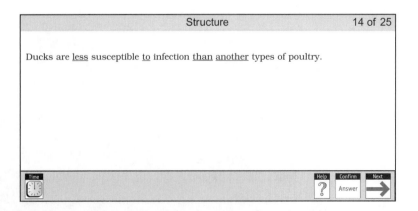

Ducks are less susceptible to infection than another types of poultry.

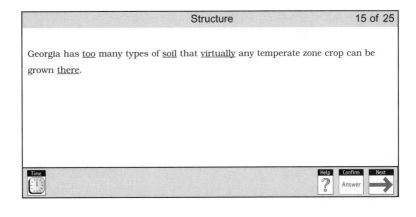

Georgia has <u>too</u> many types of <u>soil</u> that <u>virtually</u> any temperate zone crop can be grown <u>there</u>.

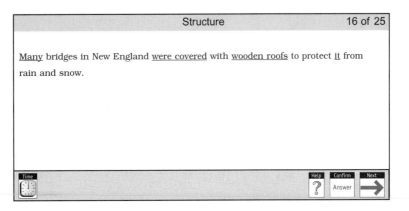

<u>Many</u> bridges in New England <u>were covered</u> with <u>wooden roofs</u> to protect <u>it</u> from rain and snow.

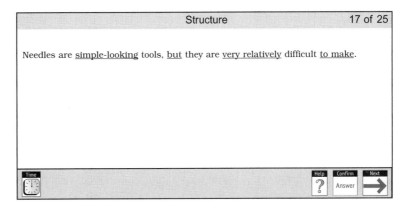

Needles are <u>simple-looking</u> tools, <u>but</u> they are <u>very relatively</u> difficult <u>to make</u>.

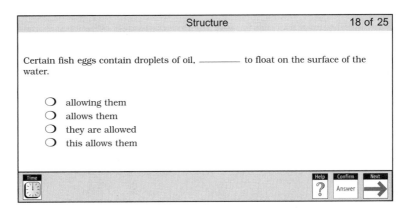

Certain fish eggs contain droplets of oil, _____ to float on the surface of the water.

    ○   allowing them
    ○   allows them
    ○   they are allowed
    ○   this allows them

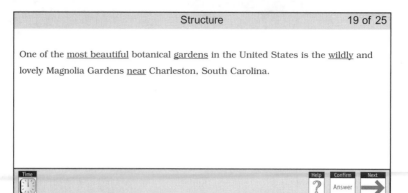

One of the <u>most beautiful</u> botanical <u>gardens</u> in the United States is the <u>wildly</u> and lovely Magnolia Gardens <u>near</u> Charleston, South Carolina.

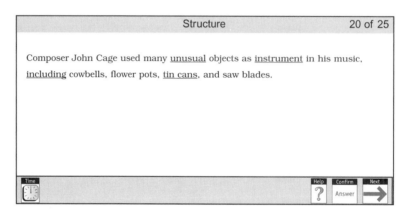

Composer John Cage used many <u>unusual</u> objects as <u>instrument</u> in his music, <u>including</u> cowbells, flower pots, <u>tin cans</u>, and saw blades.

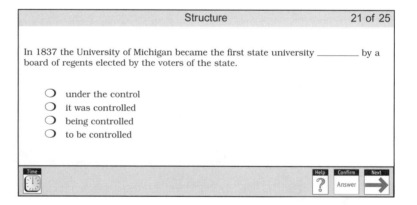

In 1837 the University of Michigan became the first state university _____ by a board of regents elected by the voters of the state.

- ○ under the control
- ○ it was controlled
- ○ being controlled
- ○ to be controlled

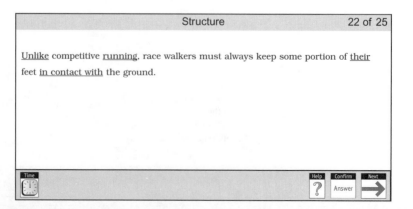

<u>Unlike</u> competitive <u>running</u>, race walkers must always keep some portion of <u>their</u> feet <u>in contact with</u> the ground.

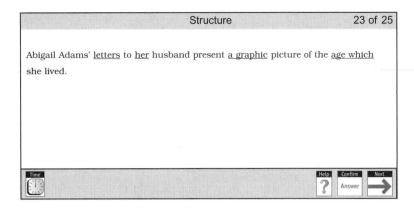

Abigail Adams' <u>letters</u> to <u>her</u> husband present <u>a graphic</u> picture of the <u>age which</u> she lived.

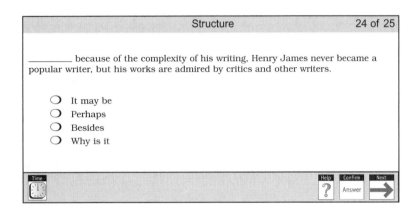

_____ because of the complexity of his writing, Henry James never became a popular writer, but his works are admired by critics and other writers.

- ○ It may be
- ○ Perhaps
- ○ Besides
- ○ Why is it

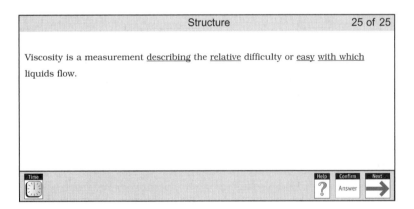

Viscosity is a measurement <u>describing</u> the <u>relative</u> difficulty or <u>easy with which</u> liquids flow.

This is the end of Section 2. Go on to Section 3.

Section 3: Reading

Time: 90 minutes

This section of the test measures your ability to understand the meaning of words and to comprehend written materials.

Directions: This section consists of several passages, each followed by 10–14 questions. Read the passages and, for each question, choose the one best answer based on what is stated in or can be inferred from the passage.

As soon as you understand the directions, begin work on this part.

Passage 1

The time when humans crossed the Arctic land bridge from Siberia to Alaska seems remote to us today, but actually represents a comparatively recent stage in the prehistory of humans, an era when polished stone implements and bows and arrows were already being used, and dogs had already been domesticated.

When these early migrants arrived in North America, they found the woods and plains dominated by three types of American mammoths, along with their distant and rather primitive cousins, the mastodons. The woolly mammoth reigned in the north, the Columbian mammoth in middle North America, and the imperial mammoth in the south. These elephants were distinguished from today's elephants mainly by their thick, shaggy coats, by their huge, upward-and-outward curving tusks, and by a prominent hump on their backs. They had arrived on the continent hundreds of thousands of years before their human followers. Here, as in the Old World, there is evidence that humans hunted these elephants, as shown by the numerous spear points found with mammoth remains .

Then, at the end of the Ice Age, when the last glaciers had retreated to their present Arctic limits, there was a relatively sudden and widespread extinction of elephants. In the New World, both mammoths and mastodons vanished. In the Old World, only Indian and African elephants survived.

How were these gigantic, seemingly successful mammoths wiped out? Was it human activity that doomed them? Perhaps, but at that time, although they were cunning hunters, humans were still widely scattered and not very numerous. It is difficult to see how they could have prevailed over the mammoth to such an extent as to cause their sudden and complete extinction.

1. With which of the following is the passage primarily concerned?

    ○ Migration from Siberia to Alaska

    ○ Techniques used to hunt mammoths

    ○ The prehistory of humans

    ○ Humans and mammoths in the New World

2. Look at the word remote in the **bold** text below:

The time when humans crossed the Arctic land bridge from Siberia to Alaska seems remote to us today, but actually represents a comparatively recent stage in the prehistory of humans, an era when polished stone implements and bows and arrows were already being used, and dogs had already been domesticated.

Underline the word or phrase in the **bold** text that is most nearly OPPOSITE in meaning to the word remote .

3. The word implements in paragraph 1 is closest in meaning to

- ○ tools
- ○ ornaments
- ○ houses
- ○ carvings

4. The phrase these early migrants in paragraph 2 refers to

- ○ mammoths
- ○ humans
- ○ dogs
- ○ mastodons

5. Look at the word reigned in the **bold** text below:

When these early migrants arrived in North America, they found the woods and plains dominated by three types of American mammoths, along with their distant and rather primitive cousins, the mastodons. The woolly mammoth reigned in the north, the Columbian mammoth in middle North America, and the imperial mammoth in the south.

Underline the word or phrase in the **bold** text that is closest in meaning to the word reigned .

6. Where did the imperial mammoths live?

- ○ In Alaska
- ○ In the central portion of North America
- ○ In the southern part of North America
- ○ In South America

7. It can be inferred that when humans crossed into the New World, they

- ○ had previously hunted mammoths in Siberia
- ○ had never seen mammoths before
- ○ brought mammoths with them from the Old World
- ○ soon learned to use dogs to hunt mammoths

8. Which of the following illustrations best depicts the tusks of a mammoth?

9. Which of the following could best substitute for the word remains in paragraph 2?
    ○ Bones
    ○ Drawings
    ○ Footprints
    ○ Spears

10. Look at the phrase wiped out in the **bold** text below:

    In the Old World, only Indian and African elephants survived.

    How were these huge, seemingly successful mammoths wiped out ? Was it human activity that doomed them? Perhaps, but at that time, although they were cunning hunters, humans were still widely scattered and not very numerous.

    Underline the word or phrase in the **bold** text that is closest in meaning to the phrase wiped out .

11. The passage supports which of the following conclusions about mammoths?

   ○ Humans hunted them to extinction.

   ○ The freezing temperatures of the Ice Age destroyed their food supply.

   ○ The cause of their extinction is unknown.

   ○ Competition with mastodons caused them to become extinct.

12. The word cunning in paragraph 4 is closest in meaning to

   ○ clever

   ○ determined

   ○ efficient

   ○ cautious

13. Which of the following is NOT true about prehistoric humans at the time of the mammoths' extinction?

   ○ They were relatively few in number.

   ○ They knew how to use bows and arrows.

   ○ They were concentrated in a small area.

   ○ They were skilled hunters.

Passage 2

Just before and during World War I, a number of white musicians came to Chicago from New Orleans playing in an idiom they had learned from blacks in that city. Five of them formed what eventually became known as the Original Dixieland Jazz Band under the leadership of Nick LaRocca. The band moved to New York in 1917 and won fame there. That year they recorded the first phonograph record in the style that became known as jazz.

The first important jazz recording by black musicians was made in Chicago in 1923 by "King" Oliver's Creole Jazz Band, a group that featured some of the foremost jazz musicians of the time, including trumpet player Louis Armstrong. Armstrong's dynamic trumpet style became famous worldwide. Other band members had previously played in Fate Marable's band, which traveled up and down the Mississippi River entertaining passengers on riverboats. Many white groups, among them the New Orleans Rhythm Kings and the Wolverines, adopted the style of the Creole Jazz Band.

The characteristics of this early type of jazz, known as Dixieland jazz, included a complex interweaving of melodic lines among the coronet or trumpet, clarinet, and trombone, and a steady chomp-chomp beat provided by the rhythm section, which included the piano, bass, and drums. Most bands used no written notations, preferring "head" arrangements agreed on verbally. Improvisation was an indispensable element. Even bandleaders such as Duke Ellington, who provided his musicians with written arrangements, permitted them plenty of freedom to improvise when playing solos.

All during the 1920s, jazz gained in popularity. In fact, the period itself became known as "the jazz era." All sections of the country were caught up in the music and the dances associated with it. The two most important performance and recording centers were Chicago and New York. The most influential jazz artists in Chicago were members of small bands such as the Wolverines, usually consisting of only four or five musicians. These bands usually contained two trumpets, one or two trombones, three or four reeds, and a five or six musician rhythm section. They played in revues, large dance halls, and theaters. Bands would become larger still during the next age of jazz, the Swing era.

14. What is the main topic of this passage?
  - ○ The early history of jazz
  - ○ The music of World War I
  - ○ The relationship of melody and rhythm in jazz
  - ○ The New York recording industry in the 1920s

15. Look at the word idiom in the **bold** text below:

   Just before and during World War I, a number of white musicians came to Chicago from New Orleans playing in an idiom they had learned from blacks in that city. Five of them formed what eventually became known as the Original Dixieland Jazz Band under the leadership of Nick LaRocca. The band moved to New York in 1917 and won fame there. That year they recorded the first phonograph record in the style that became known as jazz.

   Underline the word or phrase in the **bold** text that is closest in meaning to the word idiom .

16. The musicians who made the earliest jazz recordings were originally from
  - ○ New Orleans
  - ○ Chicago
  - ○ New York
  - ○ Mississippi

17. When was the first important recording by black jazz musicians made?
  - ○ In 1917
  - ○ In 1923
  - ○ In the late 1920s
  - ○ In the early 1930s

18. According to the passage, Louis Armstrong was a member of which of the following?
  - ○ The Original Dixieland Jazz Band
  - ○ Fate Marable's riverboat bands
  - ○ "King" Oliver's Creole Jazz Band
  - ○ The New Orleans Rhythm Kings

19. According to the passage, which of the following instruments helped provide the beat for Dixieland jazz?
  - ○ The coronet
  - ○ The piano
  - ○ The trombone
  - ○ The clarinet

20. Look at the word them in the **bold** text below:

Even bandleaders such as Duke Ellington, who provided his musicians with written arrangements, permitted them plenty of freedom to improvise when playing solos.

Underline the word or phrase in the **bold** text that the word them refers to.

21. Duke Ellington is given as an example of a bandleader who
    - ○ could not read music
    - ○ did not value improvisation
    - ○ discouraged solo performances
    - ○ used written arrangements

22. Which of the following phrases would be LEAST likely to be applied to Dixieland jazz?
    - ○ Relatively complex
    - ○ Highly improvisational
    - ○ Rhythmic and melodic
    - ○ Rigidly planned

23. The following sentence can be added to paragraph 4.

In New York City, on the other hand, the trend was toward larger groups.

Where would it best fit in the paragraph?

All during the 1920s, jazz gained in popularity. ■ In fact, the period itself became known as "the jazz era." All sections of the country were caught up in the music and the dances associated with it. ■ The two most important performance and recording centers were Chicago and New York. ■ The most influential jazz artists in Chicago were members of small bands such as the Wolverines, usually consisting of only four or five musicians. ■ These bands usually contained two trumpets, one or two trombones, three or four reeds, and a five or six musician rhythm section. ■ They played in revues, large dance halls, and theaters. ■ Bands would become larger still during the next age of jazz, the Swing era.

Circle the black square (■) that indicates the best position for the sentence.

24. According to the passage, who were the Wolverines?
    - ○ A band that played in large dance halls
    - ○ A New York City group
    - ○ A group of Swing musicians
    - ○ A small jazz band

25. Put an *X* by the paragraph in which the author provides the most detailed description of early jazz music.

26. The paragraph following this one most likely deals with
    - ○ the music of small bands
    - ○ the Swing era
    - ○ music that influenced Dixieland music
    - ○ other forms of music popular in the 1920s

A pioneering study by Donald Appleyard made the astounding discovery that a sudden increase in the volume of traffic through an area affects people in the same way that a sudden increase in crime does. Appleyard made this startling observation by studying three blocks of houses in San Francisco that looked much alike and had the same kind of middle-class and working-class residents, with approximately the same ethnic mix. The difference was that only 2,000 cars a day ran down Octavia Street (LIGHT street, in Appleyard's terminology) while Gough Street (MEDIUM street) was used by 8,000 cars daily, and Franklin Street (HEAVY street) had around 16,000 cars a day. Franklin Street often had as many cars in an hour as Octavia Street had in a day.

Heavy traffic brought with it danger, noise, fumes, and soot, directly, and trash secondarily. That is, the cars didn't bring in much trash, but when trash accumulated, residents seldom picked it up. The cars, Appleyard determined, reduced the amount of territory residents felt responsible for. Franklin Street residents hardly ever interacted with their neighbors and went out on the street only when they had some compelling reason to do so. Many covered their doors and windows and spent most of their time in the rear of their houses. Most families with children had already moved elsewhere.

Conditions on Octavia Street were much different. Residents picked up trash. They sat on their front steps and chatted with neighbors. They had three times as many friends and twice as many acquaintances as the people on Franklin.

On Gough Street, residents said that the old feeling of community was disappearing as traffic increased. People were becoming more and more preoccupied with their own concerns. A number of families had recently moved and more were considering it. Those who were staying expressed deep regret at the destruction of their community.

27. Look at the word astounding in the **bold** text below:

> **A pioneering study by Donald Appleyard made the astounding discovery that a sudden increase in the volume of traffic through an area affects people in the same way that a sudden increase in crime does. Appleyard made this startling observation by studying three blocks of houses in San Francisco that looked much alike and had the same kind of middle-class and working-class residents, with approximately the same ethnic mix.**

Underline the word in the **bold** text that is closest in meaning to the word astounding.

28. The three streets mentioned in this passage are different in that

- ⃝ they are in different cities
- ⃝ the residents are of different ethnic backgrounds
- ⃝ they have varying amounts of traffic
- ⃝ the income levels of the residents vary considerably

29. Approximately how many cars use Franklin Street daily?

  ○ 2,000

  ○ 8,000

  ○ 16,000

  ○ 20,000

30. All of the following are direct results of heavy traffic EXCEPT

  ○ increased amounts of trash

  ○ greater danger to residents

  ○ more pollution

  ○ more noise

31. Look at the phrase hardly ever in the **bold** text below:

That is, the cars didn't bring in much trash, but when trash accumulated, residents seldom picked it up. The cars, Appleyard determined, reduced the amount of territory residents felt responsible for. Franklin Street residents hardy ever interacted with their neighbors and went out on the street only when they had some compelling reason to do so.

Underline the word or phrase in the **bold** text that is closest in meaning to the phrase hardly ever .

32. Look at the word Many in the **bold** text below:

Franklin Street residents hardly ever interacted with their neighbors and went out on the street only when they had some compelling reason to do so. Many covered their doors and windows and spent most of their time in the rear of their houses. Most families with children had already moved elsewhere.

Underline the word or phrase in the **bold** text that the word Many refers to.

33. The following sentence could be added to paragraph 2.

Even so, traffic noise was a constant intrusion into their lives.

Where would it best fit in the paragraph?

Heavy traffic brought with it danger, noise, fumes, and soot, directly, and trash secondarily. ■ That is, the cars didn't bring in much trash, but when trash accumulated, residents seldom picked it up. ■ The cars, Appleyard determined, reduced the amount of territory residents felt responsible for. ■ Franklin Street residents hardly ever interacted with their neighbors and went out on the street only when they had some compelling reason to do so. ■ Many covered their doors and windows and spent most of their time in the rear of their houses. ■ Most families with children had already moved elsewhere.

Circle the black square (■) that indicates the best position for the sentence.

34. On which street is there the most social interaction?

   ○ Octavia Street

   ○ Gough Street

   ○ Franklin Street

   ○ There is no significant social interaction on any of the three streets.

35. The word chatted in paragraph 3 is closest in meaning to

   ○ joked

   ○ talked

   ○ argued

   ○ walked

36. Which of the following is NOT a statement you would expect from a resident of Gough Street?

   ○ "People here are unhappy because the neighborhood is deteriorating."

   ○ "People on this street think mostly of themselves."

   ○ "People who live here have more and more space for which they feel responsible."

   ○ "A number of people here are preparing to leave."

37. In what order does the author present detailed discussions of the three streets?

   ○ LIGHT, MEDIUM, HEAVY

   ○ HEAVY, MEDIUM, LIGHT

   ○ HEAVY, LIGHT, MEDIUM

   ○ LIGHT, HEAVY, MEDIUM

Passage 4

Rachel Carson was born in 1907 in Springdale, Pennsylvania. She studied biology at the Pennsylvania College for Women, and zoology at Johns Hopkins University, where she received her master's degree in 1932. She taught biology at the University of Maryland from 1933 to 1936. In 1936 she was hired as an aquatic biologist by the U.S. Fish and Wildlife Service, where she worked most of her life.

Carson's first book, *Under the Sea-Wind*, was published in 1941. This book received excellent reviews, but sales were poor until its reissue in 1952. In that year she published *The Sea Around Us*, for which she won the National Book Award for nonfiction. It provided a fascinating look beneath the ocean's surface, emphasizing human history as well as geology and marine biology. She was praised for her intriguing imagery and language, which had an almost poetic quality, as well as for her scientific accuracy. To write this book, Carson consulted no less than 1,000 printed sources. She had voluminous correspondence and frequent discussions with experts in the field. However, she always realized the limitations of her non-technical readers. In 1955 Carson published *The Edge of the Sea*, a look at the mysterious border between the land and the ocean.

In 1962 Carson published *Silent Spring*, which sparked considerable controversy regarding the use of pesticides and which basically led to the formation of the worldwide environmental movement. It proved how much harm was done by the uncontrolled, reckless use of insecticides such as DDT. She detailed how they poison the food supply of animals, kill birds and fish, and contaminate human food. At the time, spokesmen for the chemical industry mounted personal attacks against Carson and issued propaganda to prove that her findings were flawed. However, her work was vindicated by a 1963 report of the President's Science Advisory Committee.

38. The passage mainly discusses Rachel Carson's work as

    ○ a research biologist

    ○ a teacher

    ○ an administrator

    ○ a writer

39. According to the passage, what did Carson primarily study at Johns Hopkins University?

    ○ Oceanography

    ○ History

    ○ Literature

    ○ Zoology

40. For which of these books did Carson receive an award?

    ○ *Under the Sea-Wind*

    ○ *The Sea Around Us*

    ○ *The Edge of the Sea*

    ○ *Silent Spring*

41. It can be inferred from the passage that in 1952, Carson's book *Under the Sea-Wind*

    ○ was outdated

    ○ became more popular than her other books

    ○ was praised by critics

    ○ sold many copies

42. Look at the word intriguing in the **bold** text below:

    In that year she published *The Sea Around Us*, for which she won the National Book Award for nonfiction. It provided a fascinating look beneath the ocean's surface, emphasizing human history as well as geology and marine biology. She was praised for her intriguing imagery and language, which had an almost poetic quality, as well as for her scientific accuracy.

    Underline the word or phrase in the **bold** text that is closest in meaning to the word intriguing .

43. Which of the following was NOT mentioned in the passage as a source of information for *The Sea Around Us?*

   ◯ Printed matter

   ◯ Talks with experts

   ◯ A research expedition

   ◯ Letters from scientists

44. Which of the following words or phrases is LEAST accurate in describing *The Sea Around Us?*

   ◯ Highly technical

   ◯ Poetic

   ◯ Interesting

   ◯ Well researched

45. Look at the word It in the **bold** text below:

   In 1962 Carson published *Silent Spring*, which sparked considerable controversy regarding the use of pesticides and which basically led to the formation of the worldwide environmental movement. It proved how much harm was done by the uncontrolled, reckless use of insecticides such as DDT.

   Underline the word or phrase in the **bold** text that the word It refers to.

46. The word reckless in paragraph 3 is closest in meaning to

   ◯ unnecessary

   ◯ limited

   ◯ continuous

   ◯ irresponsible

47. According to the passage, *Silent Spring* is primarily

   ◯ an attack on the use of chemical preservatives in food

   ◯ a discussion of the hazards insects pose to the food supply

   ◯ a warning about the dangers of misusing insecticides

   ◯ a history of the environmental movement

48. Underline the sentence in paragraph 3 that explains two consequences of the publishing of *Silent Spring.*

49. Why does the author of the passage mention the report of the President's Science Advisory Committee (paragraph 3)?

   ◯ To provide an example of government propaganda

   ◯ To support the ideas in *Silent Spring*

   ◯ To indicate a growing government concern with the environment

   ◯ To validate the chemical industry's claims

What is meant by the term *economic resources?* In general, these are all the natural, synthetic, and human resources that go into the production of goods and services. This obviously covers a lot of ground : factories and farms; the tools and machines used in production; transportation and communication facilities; innumerable types of labor; land and mineral resources. Economic resources can be broken down into two general categories: property resources—land and capital—and human resources—labor and entrepreneurial skills.

What do economists mean by *land?* Much more than the non-economist. Land refers to all natural resources that are usable in the production process: arable land, forests, mineral and oil deposits, water resources, and so on. What about *capital?* Capital goods, or investment goods, are all the synthetic aids to producing, storing, transporting, and distributing goods and services. Capital goods, or tools, differ from consumer goods in that the latter satisfy wants directly, while the former do so indirectly by facilitating the production of consumer goods. It should be noted that *capital* as defined here does not refer to money. Money alone produces nothing.

The term *labor* refers to the physical and mental talents of humans used to produce goods or services (with the exception of a certain set of human talents, entrepreneurial skills, which will be considered a separate category because of their special significance). Thus the services of a factory worker or an office worker, a ballet dancer or an astronaut all fall under the heading of labor.

All economic resources have one fundamental characteristic in common: they are limited in supply. Certainly the economy of a nation may possess vast amounts of natural resources, capital goods, and labor. However, the supply of these resources is not infinite. A lack of semiskilled and skilled workers, for example, may present a major obstacle to the production process. The same can be said for a shortage of the other factors of production.

50. What is the author's main purpose in writing this passage?

  - ◯ To explain the concept of labor

  - ◯ To criticize certain uses of capital

  - ◯ To contrast capital goods and consumer goods

  - ◯ To define economic resources

51. In paragraph 1, the author uses the expression This obviously covers a lot of ground to indicate that

  - ◯ the factories and farms discussed in the passage are very large

  - ◯ economic resources are discussed in great depth

  - ◯ the topic of economic resources is a broad one

  - ◯ land is an important concept in economics

52. When non-economists use the term *land*, its definition

   ○ is much more general than when economists use it

   ○ is much more restrictive than when economists use it

   ○ changes from place to place

   ○ includes all types of natural resources

53. The word arable in paragraph 2 is closest in meaning to

   ○ dry

   ○ fertile

   ○ developed

   ○ open

54. Look at the phrase the latter in the **bold** text below:

   Capital goods, or investment goods, are all the synthetic aids to producing, storing, transporting, and distributing goods and services. Capital goods, or tools, differ from consumer goods in that the latter satisfy wants directly, while the former do so indirectly by facilitating the production of consumer goods.

   Underline the word or phrase in the **bold** text that the phrase the latter refers to.

55. Which of the following would be considered a capital good as defined in the passage?

   ○ A railroad

   ○ Money

   ○ A deposit of coal

   ○ Human skills

56. The author does NOT offer a definition for which of the following terms in the passage?

   ○ Land

   ○ Production

   ○ Labor

   ○ Capital

57. Look at the word heading in the **bold** text below:

   The term *labor* refers to the physical and mental talents of humans used to produce goods or services (with the exception of a certain set of human talents, entrepreneurial skills, which will be considered a separate category because of their special significance). Thus the services of a factory worker or an office worker, a ballet dancer or an astronaut all fall under the heading of labor.

Underline the word or phrase in the **bold** text that is closest in meaning to the word heading .

58. The skills of all the following could be considered examples of labor, as defined in the passage, EXCEPT

⭕ artists and scientists

⭕ workers who produce services, not goods

⭕ office workers

⭕ entrepreneurs

59. Look at the word infinite in the **bold** text below:

All economic resources have one fundamental characteristic in common: they are limited in supply. Certainly the economy of a nation may possess vast amounts of natural resources, capital goods, and labor. However, the supply of these resources is not infinite .

Underline the word or phrase in the **bold** text that is most nearly OPPOSITE in meaning to the word infinite .

60. Look at the word lack in the **bold** text below:

A lack of semiskilled and skilled workers, for example, may present a major obstacle to the production process. The same can be said for a shortage of the other factors of production.

Underline the word or phrase in the **bold** text that is closest in meaning to the word lack .

**This is the end of Section 3.
You may go back and check your answers in
Section 3 until time is up for this section.
Then go on to Section 4.**

Section 4: Essay Writing

- Before you begin, think about the prompt. You may want to make some notes to organize your thoughts. Use the space for notes that has been provided.

- Write only on the topic that is presented.

- If you finish in less than 30 minutes, check your essay for errors.

- Stop writing after 30 minutes.

ESSAY PROMPT

Some people feel that facilities such as museums, zoos, and parks should be subsidized by the government. Other people feel that only the people who use these facilities should have to pay for them. What position do you agree with? Use specific reasons and details to support your response.

Notes

Use this space for essay notes only. Write the final version of your essay on the next two pages.

Name: _____

Write your essay here.

_____
_____
_____
_____
_____
_____
_____
_____
_____
_____
_____
_____
_____
_____
_____
_____
_____
_____
_____
_____
_____
_____
_____
_____
_____
_____
_____
_____
_____
_____
_____

Name: _____

Preview Test 1: Listening
Answer Sheet

1. (A) (B) (C) (D)		21. (A) (B) (C) (D)
2. (A) (B) (C) (D)		22. (A) (B) (C) (D)
3. (A) (B) (C) (D)		23. (A) (B) (C) (D)
4. (A) (B) (C) (D)		24. (A) (B) (C) (D)
5. (A) (B) (C) (D)		25. (A) (B) (C) (D)
6. (A) (B) (C) (D)		26. (A) (B) (C) (D)
7. (A) (B) (C) (D)		27. (A) (B) (C) (D)
8. (A) (B) (C) (D)		28. (A) (B) (C) (D)
9. (A) (B) (C) (D)		29. (A) (B) (C) (D)
10. (A) (B) (C) (D)		30. (A) (B) (C) (D)
11. (A) (B) (C) (D)		31. (A) (B) (C) (D)
12. (A) (B) (C) (D)		32. (A) (B) (C) (D)
13. (A) (B) (C) (D)		33. (A) (B) (C) (D)
14. (A) (B) (C) (D)		34. (A) (B) (C) (D)
15. (A) (B) (C) (D)		35. (A) (B) (C) (D)
16. (A) (B) (C) (D)		36. (A) (B) (C) (D)
17. (A) (B) (C) (D)		37. (A) (B) (C) (D)
18. (A) (B) (C) (D)		38. (A) (B) (C) (D)
19. (A) (B) (C) (D)		39. (A) (B) (C) (D)
20. (A) (B) (C) (D)		40. (A) (B) (C) (D)

Preview Test 2: Structure
Answer Sheet

1. (A) (B) (C) (D)		14. (A) (B) (C) (D)
2. (A) (B) (C) (D)		15. (A) (B) (C) (D)
3. (A) (B) (C) (D)		16. (A) (B) (C) (D)
4. (A) (B) (C) (D)		17. (A) (B) (C) (D)
5. (A) (B) (C) (D)		18. (A) (B) (C) (D)
6. (A) (B) (C) (D)		19. (A) (B) (C) (D)
7. (A) (B) (C) (D)		20. (A) (B) (C) (D)
8. (A) (B) (C) (D)		21. (A) (B) (C) (D)
9. (A) (B) (C) (D)		22. (A) (B) (C) (D)
10. (A) (B) (C) (D)		23. (A) (B) (C) (D)
11. (A) (B) (C) (D)		24. (A) (B) (C) (D)
12. (A) (B) (C) (D)		25. (A) (B) (C) (D)
13. (A) (B) (C) (D)		

Preview Test 3: Reading
Answer Sheet

1. Ⓐ Ⓑ Ⓒ Ⓓ	31. Ⓐ Ⓑ Ⓒ Ⓓ
2. Ⓐ Ⓑ Ⓒ Ⓓ	32. Ⓐ Ⓑ Ⓒ Ⓓ
3. Ⓐ Ⓑ Ⓒ Ⓓ	33. Ⓐ Ⓑ Ⓒ Ⓓ
4. Ⓐ Ⓑ Ⓒ Ⓓ	34. Ⓐ Ⓑ Ⓒ Ⓓ
5. Ⓐ Ⓑ Ⓒ Ⓓ	35. Ⓐ Ⓑ Ⓒ Ⓓ
6. Ⓐ Ⓑ Ⓒ Ⓓ	36. Ⓐ Ⓑ Ⓒ Ⓓ
7. Ⓐ Ⓑ Ⓒ Ⓓ	37. Ⓐ Ⓑ Ⓒ Ⓓ
8. Ⓐ Ⓑ Ⓒ Ⓓ	38. Ⓐ Ⓑ Ⓒ Ⓓ
9. Ⓐ Ⓑ Ⓒ Ⓓ	39. Ⓐ Ⓑ Ⓒ Ⓓ
10. Ⓐ Ⓑ Ⓒ Ⓓ	40. Ⓐ Ⓑ Ⓒ Ⓓ
11. Ⓐ Ⓑ Ⓒ Ⓓ	41. Ⓐ Ⓑ Ⓒ Ⓓ
12. Ⓐ Ⓑ Ⓒ Ⓓ	42. Ⓐ Ⓑ Ⓒ Ⓓ
13. Ⓐ Ⓑ Ⓒ Ⓓ	43. Ⓐ Ⓑ Ⓒ Ⓓ
14. Ⓐ Ⓑ Ⓒ Ⓓ	44. Ⓐ Ⓑ Ⓒ Ⓓ
15. Ⓐ Ⓑ Ⓒ Ⓓ	45. Ⓐ Ⓑ Ⓒ Ⓓ
16. Ⓐ Ⓑ Ⓒ Ⓓ	46. Ⓐ Ⓑ Ⓒ Ⓓ
17. Ⓐ Ⓑ Ⓒ Ⓓ	47. Ⓐ Ⓑ Ⓒ Ⓓ
18. Ⓐ Ⓑ Ⓒ Ⓓ	48. Ⓐ Ⓑ Ⓒ Ⓓ
19. Ⓐ Ⓑ Ⓒ Ⓓ	49. Ⓐ Ⓑ Ⓒ Ⓓ
20. Ⓐ Ⓑ Ⓒ Ⓓ	50. Ⓐ Ⓑ Ⓒ Ⓓ
21. Ⓐ Ⓑ Ⓒ Ⓓ	51. Ⓐ Ⓑ Ⓒ Ⓓ
22. Ⓐ Ⓑ Ⓒ Ⓓ	52. Ⓐ Ⓑ Ⓒ Ⓓ
23. Ⓐ Ⓑ Ⓒ Ⓓ	53. Ⓐ Ⓑ Ⓒ Ⓓ
24. Ⓐ Ⓑ Ⓒ Ⓓ	54. Ⓐ Ⓑ Ⓒ Ⓓ
25. Ⓐ Ⓑ Ⓒ Ⓓ	55. Ⓐ Ⓑ Ⓒ Ⓓ
26. Ⓐ Ⓑ Ⓒ Ⓓ	56. Ⓐ Ⓑ Ⓒ Ⓓ
27. Ⓐ Ⓑ Ⓒ Ⓓ	57. Ⓐ Ⓑ Ⓒ Ⓓ
28. Ⓐ Ⓑ Ⓒ Ⓓ	58. Ⓐ Ⓑ Ⓒ Ⓓ
29. Ⓐ Ⓑ Ⓒ Ⓓ	59. Ⓐ Ⓑ Ⓒ Ⓓ
30. Ⓐ Ⓑ Ⓒ Ⓓ	60. Ⓐ Ⓑ Ⓒ Ⓓ

Practice Test 1: Answer Sheet

SECTION 1	SECTION 2	SECTION 3

SECTION 1

1. (A) (B) (C) (D)
2. (A) (B) (C) (D)
3. (A) (B) (C) (D)
4. (A) (B) (C) (D)
5. (A) (B) (C) (D)
6. (A) (B) (C) (D)
7. (A) (B) (C) (D)
8. (A) (B) (C) (D)
9. (A) (B) (C) (D)
10. (A) (B) (C) (D)
11. (A) (B) (C) (D)
12. (A) (B) (C) (D)
13. (A) (B) (C) (D)
14. (A) (B) (C) (D)
15. (A) (B) (C) (D)
16. (A) (B) (C) (D)
17. (A) (B) (C) (D)
18. (A) (B) (C) (D)
19. (A) (B) (C) (D)
20. (A) (B) (C) (D)
21. (A) (B) (C) (D)
22. (A) (B) (C) (D)
23. (A) (B) (C) (D)
24. (A) (B) (C) (D)
25. (A) (B) (C) (D)
26. (A) (B) (C) (D)
27. (A) (B) (C) (D)
28. (A) (B) (C) (D)
29. (A) (B) (C) (D)
30. (A) (B) (C) (D)
31. (A) (B) (C) (D)
32. (A) (B) (C) (D)
33. (A) (B) (C) (D)
34. (A) (B) (C) (D)
35. (A) (B) (C) (D)
36. (A) (B) (C) (D)
37. (A) (B) (C) (D)
38. (A) (B) (C) (D)

SECTION 2

1. (A) (B) (C) (D)
2. (A) (B) (C) (D)
3. (A) (B) (C) (D)
4. (A) (B) (C) (D)
5. (A) (B) (C) (D)
6. (A) (B) (C) (D)
7. (A) (B) (C) (D)
8. (A) (B) (C) (D)
9. (A) (B) (C) (D)
10. (A) (B) (C) (D)
11. (A) (B) (C) (D)
12. (A) (B) (C) (D)
13. (A) (B) (C) (D)
14. (A) (B) (C) (D)
15. (A) (B) (C) (D)
16. (A) (B) (C) (D)
17. (A) (B) (C) (D)
18. (A) (B) (C) (D)
19. (A) (B) (C) (D)
20. (A) (B) (C) (D)
21. (A) (B) (C) (D)
22. (A) (B) (C) (D)
23. (A) (B) (C) (D)
24. (A) (B) (C) (D)
25. (A) (B) (C) (D)

SECTION 3

1. (A) (B) (C) (D)
2. (A) (B) (C) (D)
3. (A) (B) (C) (D)
4. (A) (B) (C) (D)
5. (A) (B) (C) (D)
6. (A) (B) (C) (D)
7. (A) (B) (C) (D)
8. (A) (B) (C) (D)
9. (A) (B) (C) (D)
10. (A) (B) (C) (D)
11. (A) (B) (C) (D)
12. (A) (B) (C) (D)
13. (A) (B) (C) (D)
14. (A) (B) (C) (D)
15. (A) (B) (C) (D)
16. (A) (B) (C) (D)
17. (A) (B) (C) (D)
18. (A) (B) (C) (D)
19. (A) (B) (C) (D)
20. (A) (B) (C) (D)
21. (A) (B) (C) (D)
22. (A) (B) (C) (D)
23. (A) (B) (C) (D)
24. (A) (B) (C) (D)
25. (A) (B) (C) (D)
26. (A) (B) (C) (D)
27. (A) (B) (C) (D)
28. (A) (B) (C) (D)
29. (A) (B) (C) (D)
30. (A) (B) (C) (D)
31. (A) (B) (C) (D)
32. (A) (B) (C) (D)
33. (A) (B) (C) (D)
34. (A) (B) (C) (D)
35. (A) (B) (C) (D)
36. (A) (B) (C) (D)
37. (A) (B) (C) (D)
38. (A) (B) (C) (D)
39. (A) (B) (C) (D)
40. (A) (B) (C) (D)
41. (A) (B) (C) (D)
42. (A) (B) (C) (D)
43. (A) (B) (C) (D)
44. (A) (B) (C) (D)
45. (A) (B) (C) (D)
46. (A) (B) (C) (D)
47. (A) (B) (C) (D)
48. (A) (B) (C) (D)
49. (A) (B) (C) (D)
50. (A) (B) (C) (D)

Practice Test 2: Answer Sheet

SECTION 1

1. Ⓐ Ⓑ Ⓒ Ⓓ
2. Ⓐ Ⓑ Ⓒ Ⓓ
3. Ⓐ Ⓑ Ⓒ Ⓓ
4. Ⓐ Ⓑ Ⓒ Ⓓ
5. Ⓐ Ⓑ Ⓒ Ⓓ
6. Ⓐ Ⓑ Ⓒ Ⓓ
7. Ⓐ Ⓑ Ⓒ Ⓓ
8. Ⓐ Ⓑ Ⓒ Ⓓ
9. Ⓐ Ⓑ Ⓒ Ⓓ
10. Ⓐ Ⓑ Ⓒ Ⓓ
11. Ⓐ Ⓑ Ⓒ Ⓓ
12. Ⓐ Ⓑ Ⓒ Ⓓ
13. Ⓐ Ⓑ Ⓒ Ⓓ
14. Ⓐ Ⓑ Ⓒ Ⓓ
15. Ⓐ Ⓑ Ⓒ Ⓓ
16. Ⓐ Ⓑ Ⓒ Ⓓ
17. Ⓐ Ⓑ Ⓒ Ⓓ
18. Ⓐ Ⓑ Ⓒ Ⓓ
19. Ⓐ Ⓑ Ⓒ Ⓓ
20. Ⓐ Ⓑ Ⓒ Ⓓ
21. Ⓐ Ⓑ Ⓒ Ⓓ
22. Ⓐ Ⓑ Ⓒ Ⓓ
23. Ⓐ Ⓑ Ⓒ Ⓓ
24. Ⓐ Ⓑ Ⓒ Ⓓ
25. Ⓐ Ⓑ Ⓒ Ⓓ
26. Ⓐ Ⓑ Ⓒ Ⓓ
27. Ⓐ Ⓑ Ⓒ Ⓓ
28. Ⓐ Ⓑ Ⓒ Ⓓ
29. Ⓐ Ⓑ Ⓒ Ⓓ
30. Ⓐ Ⓑ Ⓒ Ⓓ
31. Ⓐ Ⓑ Ⓒ Ⓓ
32. Ⓐ Ⓑ Ⓒ Ⓓ
33. Ⓐ Ⓑ Ⓒ Ⓓ
34. Ⓐ Ⓑ Ⓒ Ⓓ
35. Ⓐ Ⓑ Ⓒ Ⓓ
36. Ⓐ Ⓑ Ⓒ Ⓓ

SECTION 2

1. Ⓐ Ⓑ Ⓒ Ⓓ
2. Ⓐ Ⓑ Ⓒ Ⓓ
3. Ⓐ Ⓑ Ⓒ Ⓓ
4. Ⓐ Ⓑ Ⓒ Ⓓ
5. Ⓐ Ⓑ Ⓒ Ⓓ
6. Ⓐ Ⓑ Ⓒ Ⓓ
7. Ⓐ Ⓑ Ⓒ Ⓓ
8. Ⓐ Ⓑ Ⓒ Ⓓ
9. Ⓐ Ⓑ Ⓒ Ⓓ
10. Ⓐ Ⓑ Ⓒ Ⓓ
11. Ⓐ Ⓑ Ⓒ Ⓓ
12. Ⓐ Ⓑ Ⓒ Ⓓ
13. Ⓐ Ⓑ Ⓒ Ⓓ
14. Ⓐ Ⓑ Ⓒ Ⓓ
15. Ⓐ Ⓑ Ⓒ Ⓓ
16. Ⓐ Ⓑ Ⓒ Ⓓ
17. Ⓐ Ⓑ Ⓒ Ⓓ
18. Ⓐ Ⓑ Ⓒ Ⓓ
19. Ⓐ Ⓑ Ⓒ Ⓓ
20. Ⓐ Ⓑ Ⓒ Ⓓ
21. Ⓐ Ⓑ Ⓒ Ⓓ
22. Ⓐ Ⓑ Ⓒ Ⓓ
23. Ⓐ Ⓑ Ⓒ Ⓓ
24. Ⓐ Ⓑ Ⓒ Ⓓ
25. Ⓐ Ⓑ Ⓒ Ⓓ

SECTION 3

1. Ⓐ Ⓑ Ⓒ Ⓓ
2. Ⓐ Ⓑ Ⓒ Ⓓ
3. Ⓐ Ⓑ Ⓒ Ⓓ
4. Ⓐ Ⓑ Ⓒ Ⓓ
5. Ⓐ Ⓑ Ⓒ Ⓓ
6. Ⓐ Ⓑ Ⓒ Ⓓ
7. Ⓐ Ⓑ Ⓒ Ⓓ
8. Ⓐ Ⓑ Ⓒ Ⓓ
9. Ⓐ Ⓑ Ⓒ Ⓓ
10. Ⓐ Ⓑ Ⓒ Ⓓ

SECTION 3

11. Ⓐ Ⓑ Ⓒ Ⓓ
12. Ⓐ Ⓑ Ⓒ Ⓓ
13. Ⓐ Ⓑ Ⓒ Ⓓ
14. Ⓐ Ⓑ Ⓒ Ⓓ
15. Ⓐ Ⓑ Ⓒ Ⓓ
16. Ⓐ Ⓑ Ⓒ Ⓓ
17. Ⓐ Ⓑ Ⓒ Ⓓ
18. Ⓐ Ⓑ Ⓒ Ⓓ
19. Ⓐ Ⓑ Ⓒ Ⓓ
20. Ⓐ Ⓑ Ⓒ Ⓓ
21. Ⓐ Ⓑ Ⓒ Ⓓ
22. Ⓐ Ⓑ Ⓒ Ⓓ
23. Ⓐ Ⓑ Ⓒ Ⓓ
24. Ⓐ Ⓑ Ⓒ Ⓓ
25. Ⓐ Ⓑ Ⓒ Ⓓ
26. Ⓐ Ⓑ Ⓒ Ⓓ
27. Ⓐ Ⓑ Ⓒ Ⓓ
28. Ⓐ Ⓑ Ⓒ Ⓓ
29. Ⓐ Ⓑ Ⓒ Ⓓ
30. Ⓐ Ⓑ Ⓒ Ⓓ
31. Ⓐ Ⓑ Ⓒ Ⓓ
32. Ⓐ Ⓑ Ⓒ Ⓓ
33. Ⓐ Ⓑ Ⓒ Ⓓ
34. Ⓐ Ⓑ Ⓒ Ⓓ
35. Ⓐ Ⓑ Ⓒ Ⓓ
36. Ⓐ Ⓑ Ⓒ Ⓓ
37. Ⓐ Ⓑ Ⓒ Ⓓ
38. Ⓐ Ⓑ Ⓒ Ⓓ
39. Ⓐ Ⓑ Ⓒ Ⓓ
40. Ⓐ Ⓑ Ⓒ Ⓓ
41. Ⓐ Ⓑ Ⓒ Ⓓ
42. Ⓐ Ⓑ Ⓒ Ⓓ
43. Ⓐ Ⓑ Ⓒ Ⓓ
44. Ⓐ Ⓑ Ⓒ Ⓓ
45. Ⓐ Ⓑ Ⓒ Ⓓ
46. Ⓐ Ⓑ Ⓒ Ⓓ
47. Ⓐ Ⓑ Ⓒ Ⓓ
48. Ⓐ Ⓑ Ⓒ Ⓓ
49. Ⓐ Ⓑ Ⓒ Ⓓ
50. Ⓐ Ⓑ Ⓒ Ⓓ
51. Ⓐ Ⓑ Ⓒ Ⓓ
52. Ⓐ Ⓑ Ⓒ Ⓓ
53. Ⓐ Ⓑ Ⓒ Ⓓ
54. Ⓐ Ⓑ Ⓒ Ⓓ
55. Ⓐ Ⓑ Ⓒ Ⓓ
56. Ⓐ Ⓑ Ⓒ Ⓓ
57. Ⓐ Ⓑ Ⓒ Ⓓ
58. Ⓐ Ⓑ Ⓒ Ⓓ
59. Ⓐ Ⓑ Ⓒ Ⓓ
60. Ⓐ Ⓑ Ⓒ Ⓓ

SINGLE USER INSTALLATION

1. Insert the CD-ROM. From Program Manager, choose **Run** from the **File** menu. *Windows 95 users, click the* **Start** *button and choose* **Run.**

2. In the Command Line box, type **d:\install.exe** where *d* is the letter of your CD-ROM drive. Press **Enter** or **OK.**

   NOTE: *TOEFL Mastery*™, *CBT Edition Installation Disk* is required for the installation process. The Disk may be used *one* time for *one* installation. To move *TOEFL Mastery*™, *CBT Edition CD-ROM* to another computer, you must first run the program **Remove.exe,** or the Installation Disk will not work.

3. Follow the instructions on your screen. After successful installation, click on Close, exit Windows, and reboot your computer. The CD must be in the CD drive to run the program.

10-USER NETWORK INSTALLATION

1. From **My Computer,** click on the drive that the software will be resident on the file server.

2. Create a folder, name it TOEFL_TM.

3. Insert the TOEFL Mastery CD ROM in the CD ROM drive, and click on the CD ROM drive letter from **My Computer.**

4. Copy the complete contents of the CD ROM and paste it to the TOEFL_TM directory on the file server that was created in Step 2.

5. To install the TOEFL Mastery for the CBT on each of the 10 workstations where it is to run, insert the install disk in the floppy drive. Click on **Start** and choose **Run.** In the **Open** box, type **H:\TOEFL_TM\install.exe** where H:\TOEFL_TM is the directory containing all the files copied from the CD, then press Enter.

6. Follow the instructions on your screen.

SYSTEM REQUIREMENTS: 8 MB RAM; 8MB on the local Hard Drive; Windows 3.1 or higher; 165 MB on the file server Hard Drive if copying CD to the file server; CD-ROM drive; 3.5″ floppy drive; Sound-Blaster compatible sound card; 486 PC or higher; SVGA display; 16-bit color.